W9-BTP-890

An Introduction to

PHILOSOPHICAL
ANALYSIS

PRENTICE-HALL PHILOSOPHY SERIES
ARTHUR E. MURPHY, PH.D., EDITOR

JOHN HOSPERS

Professor of Philosophy
Brooklyn College, City University of New York

An Introduction to
PHILOSOPHICAL
ANALYSIS

PRENTICE-HALL, INC.

Englewood Cliffs, N. J.

First printing . . . . September, 1953

Second printing . . . . June, 1954

Third printing . . . . . . December, 1954

Fourth printing . . . . . . February, 1957

Fifth printing . . . . July, 1958

Sixth printing . . . . December, 1958

Seventh printing . . . . July, 1959

Eighth printing . . . . August, 1960

Ninth printing . . . . December, 1961

Tenth printing . . . . June, 1963

Eleventh printing . . . . June, 1964

Twelfth printing . . . . . December, 1964

PRINTED IN THE UNITED STATES OF AMERICA

49167—C

Preface

Those who approach philosophy for the first time do so from a variety of motives. Some are drawn into philosophy from their interest in the sciences, some from the arts, some from religion; others come to philosophy without any academic background, motivated by an uneasiness about "the meaning of things" or "what the world is all about"; still others have no motivation more specific than that of wanting to know what kind of thing people are talking about when they use the word "philosophy." Accordingly, the demands which different people make of philosophy, the questions they expect it to answer, are as diverse as the motives leading them to it; and as a result, the books which are written to satisfy these demands are similarly diverse. Often two books professing to introduce readers to philosophy contain little or none of the same material. For these reasons it is impossible to write a book that will satisfy all, or even (perhaps) a majority of, readers.

One might try to overcome this difficulty by writing a book so comprehensive that all the problems which anyone considered philosophical would be treated in it, and the reader would have only to select those portions in which he was most interested. This, however, is hardly possible in practice: a book of a thousand pages would not begin to suffice for the purpose. Nor would it be feasible to devote just a few pages to each problem: this would leave only outline-summaries of the various issues which would mean very little to the reader; he might learn the meanings of some terms and absorb a few "general trends" from such a presentation, but he would not have been given enough material to make the problems come alive for him. The capsule method is even less successful in philosophy than it is elsewhere. The only apparent solution, then, would be to include not all, but only some, of the problems in the field. This method has its drawbacks, for no matter which problems are included and which are excluded, many readers are bound to object to both some of the inclusions and some of the exclusions. Yet this is the policy that has been followed in this book, as the one with the fewest all-round disadvantages. Among the problems to which (though in some cases touched upon briefly) no separate sections have been devoted are: the problem of universals, theories about time and space, the foundations of mathematics, the philosophical implications of twentieth century physics, primary and secondary qualities of matter, and general theory of value. Sections on these have been omitted regretfully, in some cases after they had been written. To keep the book from reaching unmanageable lengths, an attempt has been made not to duplicate material that is found in most introductory books on logic and scientific method. Thus, for example, hypotheses and evidence are discussed, but chiefly as an occasion for airing the philosophical controversy about the status of unobservable entities.

There are innumerable terms and distinctions which would have to be introduced if the treatment were to be complete or even entirely accurate, which nevertheless have not been included here. In some cases the terms that have been introduced have been given a clarity and unambiguousness which they do not always possess in philosophical writing and discussion: terms such as "analytic" and "a priori" have been presented as if the issues raised by them were somewhat simpler than they actually are. The only excuse for this is that without some definite pegs to hang his thoughts on, the reader who is new to philosophy would be lost. There should be very little, however, which is learned here which will have to be unlearned at a later stage.

The author wishes to express his gratitude to the following publishers for permission to quote: Harcourt, Brace & Co., from *The Mind and Its Place in Nature* by C. D. Broad and *Language in Action* by S. I. Hayakawa; Houghton Mifflin Co., from *Invitation to Philosophy* by Durant Drake; University of California Press, from *The Rise of Scientific Philosophy* by Hans Reichenbach and *University of California Publications in Philosophy;* Harper & Bros., from *A Philosophy of Science* by W. H. Werkmeister; Methuen & Co., from *Perception* by H. H. Price; Longmans, Green & Co., from *Selected Papers on Philosophy* by William James; Cambridge University Press, from *Principia Ethica* by G. E. Moore; The Macmillan Company and St. Martin's Press Incorporated, from *The*

Critique of Pure Reason by Immanuel Kant (translated by Norman Kemp Smith) ; The Macmillan Company, from *Foundations of Empirical Knowledge* by A. J. Ayer; University of North Carolina Press, from the author's *Meaning and Truth in the Arts;* and the editors of *Mind* and *Aristotelian Society Proceedings,* excerpts from essays by C. L. Stevenson, C. E. M. Joad, C. D. Broad, and T. E. Jessop. Thanks are also due to Professors Monroe C. Beardsley, Herbert Feigl, Wilfrid Sellars, Martin Lean, Michael Scriven, and May Brodbeck for their valuable suggestions in the preparation of this book.

J. H.
Minneapolis

Contents

Introduction

Where shall we begin in our study of philosophy? Should we not begin by defining our subject—by stating what philosophy is?

In most subjects we can do this rather easily, but in the case of philosophy we cannot. (1) For one thing, we would be prejudicing our treatment at the outset, for different writers have set forth very different conceptions of what philosophy is. This is not the case in mathematics or medicine or the natural sciences, but it is true in philosophy. (2) Moreover, if we attempted to state a definition now —if we said that philosophy is the systematic interpretation of all of experience, or an analysis of propositions, or the subject-matter dealing with the most ultimate issues that arise in the minds of human beings, or in any of a number of ways that are far more technical than these—we might be uttering impressive and high-sounding phrases, but we would not find them very helpful. Most of the terms occurring in such attempted definitions are misleading in one way or another and would have to be clarified. Many of them, in fact, stand just as much in need of explanation as does the word "philosophy" itself. And to show what these terms mean would take us into the midst of the very subject-matter, philosophy, which we were setting out to explain. (3) In Chapter 1 we shall consider many problems which have to do with defining words in general, and at the end of that chapter we shall take up once again the problem of defining the word "philosophy" in particular. Accordingly, we shall say no more now about the general nature of philosophy.

A few preliminary cautions, however, may be in order here:

1. Philosophy will try to interrelate, connect, synthesize if you will, the various other branches of learning—including most of the subjects included in a liberal arts education. Consequently, the more you know about these subjects—mathematics, the natural sciences, the social sciences, literature, the arts—the better off you will be in undertaking the study of philosophy, and the more you will be able to grasp the significance of what philosophy tries to do.

Studying philosophy should enable you to correlate all the other subjects you have studied so that you can "see them together" and view them as a whole.

2. We shall not *primarily* be asking the questions that laymen usually think of when they hear the word "philosophy," namely "philosophy of life." These questions are raised, but we shall come upon them gradually and in the context of discussions (sometimes about other things) that can shed light on them. One must first develop the tools for dealing with them. By the time you come to consider these questions in a more mature fashion, you may wish to recast the questions themselves so as to make them much clearer than you are now capable of doing. Now you may feel only a vague, inchoate unrest; then you will be able to express it more articulately, and thus to deal with it more adequately.

Where, then, shall we begin? Different persons may prefer to start at different places; but it will be most economical of effort in the long run if we begin with a study of language: not a study of the history of words, or the derivation of words, or the structural similarities of words, or for that matter anything about words which is peculiar to specific languages, but rather the nature and function of language in general—especially the relation of words to what words stand for. This often goes by the name "semantics"; or, we might alliteratively call it, the study of Words and the World.

Why is a study of semantics necessary to a study of philosophy? It is, indeed, helpful in a study of any subject matter whatever. But it is especially useful in the case of philosophy. Philosophy is an abstract subject matter full of pitfalls for the unwary: it is not like mathematics, in which the answer is either right or wrong and you can usually tell rather quickly where you have gone astray; nor is it like the natural sciences, in which experiments can be conducted to decide who is right and who is wrong. Moreover, philosophy (at least in some of its aspects) appeals strongly to our emotions—and this appeal carries with it an almost fatal tendency to indulge in metaphorical expressions and unclear modes of speaking, so that it is often difficult, especially in the midst of a lengthy discussion, to be clear about exactly what we are saying or even exactly what the question is which we are asking. Philosophy is difficult enough without leaving unnecessary obstacles in our way. A careful study of Chapter 1 should help to remove the most important and the most recurrent of these obstacles.

1

Words and the World

I. THE RELATION OF WORDS TO THINGS

Signs and symbols. Every day of our lives we encounter situations in which one thing stands for, or means, another. A red light at a traffic intersection means that we are required to stop; a red flag means that danger is nearby; a wailing siren means that an ambulance is approaching; one kind of bell means that someone is at the door; another, that class is over. The second member of each of these pairs is the thing in which we are really interested; but the first is more convenient or accessible, so we use it to stand for the second.

In all of these cases, human beings have decided that the first member of each pair shall be made to stand for the second. But not all cases of one thing standing for another are like this. Some things stand for others regardless of what human beings decide. Clouds of a certain kind stand for rain—that is, they indicate that rain can be expected; a twister in the sky means that a tornado is approaching; a sudden drop in the barometric pressure means that a storm is on the way; and so on. We have not invented or devised these relationships; they are already there—we merely find them and record them. They are the same for all people and in all languages.

Sometimes these are known as *natural symbols,* as opposed to the first kind, which are known as *arbitrary symbols.* But more often things of the second kind are called *signs*—thus nimbus clouds are signs, not symbols, of rain—while things of the first kind are called simply *symbols.* This is the usage which we shall employ here. We shall use the word "symbol" to refer only to those cases of standing-for in which one thing has been *made* to stand for another, by a decision of some human being or group of human beings.

1

Such symbols are called arbitrary because it is simply a matter of choice which item in experience is chosen to stand for the thing in question. We could have used something other than a red light as a stop signal at an intersection; there is no *natural* relationship, or relationship in nature, between the light and what it stands for as there is between clouds and what they stand for. Nor is there any reason why people had to make three dots and a dash stand for the letter *V* in the Morse code. All such things are the result of human decisions.

These symbols are also called *conventional* because after one person or group decided to use this to stand for that, other people decided to do the same thing, and the practice spread: that is, these symbols were adopted by common *convention,* and thus were made into conventional symbols. (A symbol that you alone decided upon, such as a white chalk-mark on a fencepost that you want to replace next spring, would be arbitrary—arbitrarily selected by you—but not conventional.) If people did not agree to use the same symbol for the same thing, communication would be vastly more difficult than it is. Thus, to avoid confusion, people in many nations use the red light to mean "stop," the red flag to stand for danger, the white flag to indicate peace overtures, and so on.

Sometimes symbols are used in complicated groups, or systems. Musical notation is an example. There are symbols standing for quarter tones and whole tones, sharps and flats, repeats, and so on. So precise is this system of symbols at its most complete, when it includes metronomic readings, changes of tempo, and variations in dynamics, that from reading what is on a page of music we can pretty well gather what the composer intended the music to sound like, leaving aside certain elements of musical interpretation that are dependent on technique and which are virtually impossible to indicate on paper.

The most complicated of all systems of symbols is *language.* It is because of language that we are discussing symbols here. Words are symbols, and every language (English, French, Sanskrit, and so forth) is a system of symbols. Every symbol in these systems stands for something because human beings have made them do so. Human beings have devised noises and made them into symbols. Unless people had taken and made them stand for things in the world, they would be *merely* noises, not words. Different noises are made to stand for different things, and a large body of people comes to use these noises in the same way. In this way, the words, begun as arbitrary symbols, become conventional symbols. When they are thus given meanings, the noises *become* words; the noise is, as it were, baptized into a word.

Words stand for things. When we say that words stand for things, we do not mean that all words stand for physical things such as tables, trees, and automobiles; we are using the word "thing" in a very broad sense, such as when we say, "A funny thing happened yesterday" or "I'll tell him a thing or two." Some words stand for psychological states: "fear," "drowsiness," and so on. Other words stand for abstractions—things which (in the opinion of most people) would not exist unless there were concrete things for them to belong to: "whiteness," "intelligence." Thus far, all our examples have been nouns; but there are also the noun-substitutes, or pronouns—"you," "he," "that," and so forth—whose meaning in a particular case depends on the time, place, and other circumstances in which they are uttered. Some words stand for actions—"run," "eat," "think"; these are the verbs. Adjectives usually stand for qualities: "white," "heavy," "virtuous," "superior." Adverbs usually stand for manners of doing things: "slowly," "fastidiously." Prepositions stand for relations: "in," "above," "between," and the like.

Even so, not all words stand for things, at least not in the same way that the above kinds of words do. (1) There are *connective* words—the conjunctions—such as "and," "or," "because," "therefore." If this were a book on logic we would have to give a detailed account of the functions of such words. Here it is enough to point out that, while they do not stand for things themselves, they serve to connect words and combinations of words that do. They make a great deal of difference to the total meaning of sentences: thus, "She is going *and* I am going" is quite different in meaning from "She is going *or* I am going." (2) There are *emotive* words: words which do not stand for things but serve to release certain feelings in the speaker and/or evoke certain feelings in the listener. The whole subject of the emotive effects of language can be most fruitfully discussed in connection with a study of sentences, later in this chapter, rather than of individual words, with which we are concerned here. The purest emotive words are the interjections: "hurrah," "phooey," "whoopee," and so on. Most emotive words are also used to stand for things, and therefore are impure examples of emotive words: "nasty," "beautiful," "contemptible." The problem of finding out what such words stand for, and of disentangling their emotive effects from the things they stand for, will concern us in more detail in Chapters 7 and 8. Meanwhile we should be careful to distinguish *emotive* words from *emotion* words: thus, "sadness" is an emotion word because it names an emotion, while "alas" is an emotive word because the use of it tends to express and evoke an emotion.

The meanings of words are given, not discovered. A woman once remarked, "I don't see how the astronomers found the names of all those stars." The error is obvious: astronomers have discovered many things about the stars, but not their names, for these names were not discovered but *given*. The words naming the stars are noises which, by arbitrary choice and then by convention, came to be used to stand for the various stars. The names are not related to the objects named in the way that twisters in the sky are related to tornadoes. People *discovered* that twisters are connected with tornadoes, but they *assigned* the meanings to noises which made them words. Here is a man-made relationship: human beings, by stipulating meanings for noises, caused this relationship to exist; they did not discover it already existing.

But don't you and I discover the meanings of words? Didn't we discover, for example, what the names of different stars are? *We* didn't name this one "Arcturus"; we learned, or discovered, its name. Again the answer should be obvious: we, you and I, did not name this star "Arcturus"; we discovered it; but what we discovered was simply the fact that other human beings already used this noise to stand for this star—and we simply fell in with this same usage. People used this noise to stand for this star long before we were born; these people, in turn, learned it from others before them—and so on back until we arrive at the individual or group of individuals who did not discover or learn the name, but *gave* it. In the case of most words, these individuals are now unknown or forgotten.

No right and wrong words for things. Whoever started using one of the noises that now constitute the English language to stand for some thing, was not using the right or the wrong noise with which to do it: he was merely selecting one of an infinite multitude of possible noises and arbitrarily making it stand for that thing. His choice might be inconvenient, for example, if he selected a noise fifteen syllables long to stand for something he wanted to talk about a hundred times a day. Even so, it would not be the *wrong* noise. There are no right or wrong words for things.

But aren't certain words wrong? Suppose the name "Finns" has been used to stand for a certain people; then isn't the land they live in rightly called "Finland" and wrongly called anything else?

It would not be wrong to call it something else: some other noise might have been given instead, and it would not have been the wrong noise. But *once some names have already been given*, it is often most *convenient* to be guided in the rest of the name-giving process by those names which are already there. If the name "Finns" has already been given to a certain people, and the word "land" means what it does now, what is more convenient than to call the land "Finland," "land of the Finns"? Although it is easiest to remember that way, there are many cases where this has not been done, but other entirely unrelated names have been given, and these names are not wrong. The word "Finland" is still not a *natural* symbol for that country: the "natural" relation here is not one of resemblance between the word and the country, but between the word "Finland" and the other words "Finn" and "land."

But surely it is wrong to call some things by certain names? If I called the thing on which I am sitting a lamp instead of a chair, surely that would be wrong, wouldn't it?

Yes, it would be wrong *if* we meant by the noise "lamp" what people who speak English *already mean* by it, something that (among other things) serves to give light. You are surely not sitting on a thing that gives light, and to say that you did would be wrong: more precisely, it would be false. But of course you *could* use the noise "lamp" to stand for it if you wanted to; to do so would only be extremely confusing to other people because they already use the word "lamp" to stand for something different. We would then have *two* meanings for the noise "lamp," the one you just gave it and the conventional one which those who speak English have used for generations. In order not to mislead them, you would (if you wanted to stick to your new usage) have to tell them in advance that you were not using the noise "lamp" to mean the same thing that they were. Even so, the situation would be greatly complicated by your new usage: every time you used the noise "lamp" they would have to remember that you were using it to mean something different from the thing *they* had used the word to mean for many years. Moreover, such complication would be needless: it would serve no purpose; there would be nothing to be said for it and everything to be said against it. Nevertheless it would not be wrong: if you used the noise in this queer way it would only be unnecessarily confusing. It would only be wrong (false) if you said "I'm sitting on a lamp" and used the word "lamp" in this sentence in the conventional sense you had just rejected. The error in it would be that of using a noise to stand for a thing which by convention had been referred to by a *different* noise, and then turning right around and using this noise (perhaps unconsciously) in its conventional sense. You would be stipulating one meaning for a noise and actually using it with a different meaning.

The moral of this is that if you want to avoid unnecessary confusion in the use of language, you had better refer to a thing by the same noise that other people already use in referring to it.

Freedom of stipulation. Still, you don't have to; no law forces you to. If you want to be different and use a different noise for the same thing that others use the noise "lamp" to refer to, you are welcome to do so. "Anybody can use any noise he wants to refer to anything he wants, as long as he makes clear what he is using the noise to refer to." This is the rule of freedom of stipulation. Its results, as we have seen, would be confusing if you made use of this freedom anywhere but on an island of which you were the sole inhabitant; for wherever there are people, there are already certain noises made to stand for certain things. If you lived alone all your life, or if there were no other people in the world, there would be no objection whatever; but in such a situation you would not need any language at all. However, your freedom to stipulate is always there; the only question is whether it is practical or useful in any way to avail yourself of it.

The rule of common usage. Because of the unnecessary confusion and inconvenience that would be brought about if you tried to inflict a set of symbols of your own invention upon society and everyone else did the same, the rule that is usually suggested for your employment of words is that you *follow common usage*. This is what we ordinarily do without being told to do it, simply because it would be pointless to invent a new noise to stand for a thing when another noise is already being used by everyone around us. We find it easier simply to fall in line with a usage which is already established. When we *do* employ a word in a way contrary to common usage, we should inform our hearers of what we *are* using it to mean. Conversely, when we do not inform our hearers of what we are using our words to mean, they have a right to take for granted that we are using them in their conventional sense—in other words, that we are following common usage.

We do not ordinarily act as perversely and capriciously as in the above example of the word "lamp." Nevertheless, the rule of common usage can be of considerable practical importance, as the following example will illustrate:

In scientific or pseudo-scientific circles it is sometimes said that "nothing is really solid." Even the table, which looks so solid, is really not solid at all: if we could look at it through ultra-microscopic eyes, we should find that it is a hurly-burly of atoms and electrons separated by distances which are enormous compared with their own sizes; thus the table consists mostly of empty space. No sample of matter that we would ever encounter on the earth, then, is "really solid."

But in common usage, things like tables, trees, boards, and sidewalks are spoken of as "solid," while puddles of water, melted butter, and hydrogen gas are not. Are all our statements about the solidity of tables then mistaken? No, for when we say that a table is solid we mean that if we put our hands on it they will not go through the surface, as they would through the surface of a vessel of water, and perhaps also that it retains its shape unless subjected to heat or pressure. If something fulfills these requirements, we call it solid; that is what "solid" means in ordinary usage. The scientist's account of the table is undoubtedly correct (at any rate this is not the place to discuss it), but if the scientist or anyone else says that the table is not really solid at all, his assertion is misleading unless he specifies how he is using the word. In daily life if someone said, "Be careful up there; the board is solid enough, but the plaster isn't," he would be easily understood, and the hearer would avoid stepping on the plaster for fear that it would give way if he did. But if, the board being no different from what it was before, the speaker said, "Neither the board nor the plaster is solid," this would be misleading because the hearer would probably conclude that the board was as insecure as the plaster and therefore he would not venture up on the rafters at all.

Exceptions to the rule of common usage. Should one *always* stick to common usage of a word? There are several qualifications we might wish to add to the rule of common usage:

1. There may not be a word for what you want to talk about. In this case, you cannot stick to common usage of a word because there is no word to stick to. Perhaps then you undertake to make one up: that is, to take a noise and use it to refer to something that has not been given a name in your language before. This, then, will be a new arbitrary symbol. If your usage catches on and other people adopt it, your noise will have become a conventional symbol; it will then have attained common usage. When the mathematician Kasner found that he wanted to refer frequently to the tenth power of ten, he asked his little grandson, "What would *you* call it?" "Googol," was the immediate response. And so the noise (now a word) "googol" has attained common usage in writings on popular mathematics.

2. Sometimes there is a common usage for a word, but you want to depart from it because the thing that the word stands for already has another word standing for it. For example, some persons now tend to use the word "God" to refer simply to nature as a whole. The word "God" already has a common usage, to refer to a supernatural Being. The word "nature" also has a common usage, to refer to the totality of things, events, and processes in the universe. Even though the word "God" were very commonly used in this new sense, you might want to resist this tendency; you would want to depart from this increasingly common usage because its results would be confusing. Word 1 stands for Thing 1; Word 2 stands for Thing 2; why complicate the matter by trying to make Word 1 also stand for Thing 2? Sometimes common usage may tend to do this, and when it does, it may well be in the interest of clarity to resist such usage.

More often, however, when a word or phrase is used in violation of common usage this is not done in the interest of clarity, but in the interest of beguiling you into accepting an unwarranted conclusion. Thus, if someone said, "There are no democracies left in the world," you might be misled by his assertion, until you discovered that he was using the word "democracy" to apply only to governments in which every citizen is a voting member of a national legislature (instead of voting for representatives to do this). You and he may argue at cross-purposes until you realize that he is using the word in this rather unusual sense. Similarly, if someone said to you, "There aren't really any material objects in the world— there are only spirits," you might be surprised at this "information," then skeptical, then inclined to deny it vehemently. But your surprise would vanish if you found that he was using the word "spirits" in such a broad way as to include trees, houses, planets, and so on—the very things to which common usage already assigns the phrase "material objects." Often people, perhaps without knowing what they are doing, will flaunt one of their assertions as a new discovery about the universe, whereas in reality they are merely manipulating words and employing them in violation of common usage without informing their hearers of the fact.

3. Sometimes, and this is perhaps the most important case of all, a word does stand for something in common usage, but is employed with such haziness and indefiniteness that you are not satisfied in following common usage by continuing to use the word. The word "good," for example, is considered (by some people) so indefinite in its reference as to make its continued use confusing and unprofitable. They feel that the word as now used is simply a blanket term covering a nest of confusions, and they want to avoid this situation in the interest of clarity, even at the expense of ignoring common usage.

When it seems to you that you would only be perpetuating confusion by continuing to follow common usage of a word, you can do either of two things: (1) you can drop the word altogether, and try to say what you want to say more precisely by using different words; or (2) you can keep on using the same word but try to purify it by using it in some special and more precise sense—generally by restricting it rather arbitrarily to some specific portion of the hazy area of reference which it now has. (If you were going to use it to mean something entirely different, there would be no point in continuing to use the same word at all: thus, there would be no point in using the word "good" to mean "two or more feet high.")

Common usage is a guide to meaning, not to truth. With the above qualifications, common usage is a guide for determining what you shall use your words to mean. But it does not determine whether a statement in which you use these words is true or false. Common usage is recommended, with qualifications, as the most useful and convenient guide in your use of language. It does not guarantee that the statements you make are true. (Thus, "Two plus two make five" is false, although each word in this sentence is being employed in its usual sense.) Still less does the rule of common usage recommend that you follow common usage in the quite different sense of following tribal or national customs, or that you hold to beliefs which are commonly held. Neither, of course, does it deny it; it is simply irrelevant either way.

Words that stand for other words. When we talk about cats, we use the word "cats" without quotation marks; but when we want to talk about the *word* "cats," what do we do? A *word* can be what a certain word stands for just as well as a table or a tree or Arcturus can. Sometimes we want to talk about cats, and so we need a word for them; but sometimes (less frequently) we may want to talk about the word which we use to stand for cats—and we want a word for that too.

It would be possible for us to use one word to stand for the *things*, cats, and a quite different word to stand for the *word*, "cats." But this would be very inconvenient and cumbersome, especially if we did the same thing with every word in the language. If we had 100,000 words for things, we would then need 100,000 more words to stand for those words. Then, if we wanted to talk about these words in turn, we would need 100,000 more—and so on *ad infinitum*. Instead, we adopt the policy, when we want to talk about the *word* "cats," of using the same word over again, only *in quotation marks*. Thus:

> Cats have tails.
> "Cats" has four letters.

This is the policy that is adopted in most philosophical writing and throughout this book—including this paragraph. And if we want to go further and talk about the word that we have just used to name the word "cats," we use the same word once more and place still another pair of quotation marks around it. Thus:

> " 'Cats' " is a word which stands for the word "cats," which stands for cats.

The meanings of the word "meaning." Words which stand for things have meaning—in one sense of the word "meaning." But there are other senses of the word "meaning," in which not only words but things other than words can be said to have meanings. Much confusion may result if we do not keep this fact in mind. Here are not all, but a few of the most important senses of the word "meaning":

1. *Sign.* Nimbus clouds mean rain—that is, they are signs of rain. The relation between the two, as we have seen, was not devised by human beings. (It is not the *word* "clouds" that stands for rain. The word "clouds" stands for the thing, clouds; and the thing, clouds, stands for [is a sign of] the thing, rain.)

2. *Cause.* Here are footprints in the sand; they look strange; what is their meaning? The question being asked here is, What is their cause? a bear? a strange monster?

3. *Effect.* In countless cases in which the word "meaning" is used, effect is meant. President Roosevelt's pronouncement after Pearl Harbor, "This means war," surely could be translated, "The effect of this will be war."

It is in this sense that emotive words have meaning. They do not stand for things, as we have seen, but they do cause certain definite feelings in those who hear the words. Their meaning, in this sense, is their effect on those who hear them. Thus, being told that her dress is gorgeous causes the lady to "feel good all over," though it is by no means clear what the word "gorgeous" stands for; in all likelihood the speaker is not using it to stand for anything, but merely to have the desired effect upon the lady.

4. *Explanation.* The notion of explanation is closely connected with cause, as we shall see. Often when we ask for the meaning of some event, we are asking for an explanation of why it occurred.

5. *Intention.* "I meant to wash the dishes" means the same as "I intended to wash the dishes." "My meaning in saying this was . . ." equals "My intent in saying this was . . ."

6. *Purpose.* Sometimes this is the same as intention: "My intent in going to the country was . . .," "My purpose in going to the country was . . ." But we also attribute purposes to inanimate things to which we do not mean to attribute an intention. Thus we ask, "What is the meaning of the universe?" and some persons at any rate take this to mean the same as "What is the purpose of the

universe?" But the word "purpose" has more than one meaning, as we shall see in Chapter 3.

"What is the meaning of . . . ?" questions. It is not always clear which of the meanings of the word "meaning" we mean (intend) when we ask a meaning-question. In particular, we should be extremely careful whether we are asking about the meaning of a *word* (i.e., what thing the word stands for) or about the meaning of the *thing* symbolized by the word in one of the above senses of "meaning" which apply to things. Here are a few examples:

1. "What is the meaning of euthanasia?" Should the word "euthanasia" have quotation marks around it here? It should, if it is intended as an inquiry into what the *word* "euthanasia" stands for; and, in nine cases out of ten, this is probably what the person is asking. If the questioner already knew the meaning of the word, he would not be likely to ask the question; if he asked the question even after he knew what the word meant, doubtless he would be inquiring about the thing, euthanasia; and in asking about the meaning of the thing, euthanasia, he would probably be asking something (perhaps not knowing himself exactly what) about what it causes.

2. "You don't appreciate what war means." Here it is unlikely that the inquirer is ignorant of what the *word* "war" stands for; he already knows that it has to do with armed conflict. In uttering the sentence, then, he is saying something about the thing, war. In all probability he is saying something about what conditions war causes or brings about—devastation, broken homes, poverty, and the like.

3. "What is the meaning of life?" Here again it is almost surely not the word "life" about which the person is inquiring. He knows what the *word* means, and he is probably asking something (again, he may not clearly realize what) about an explanation of the thing, life. He knows that living things grow, reproduce, and so on, but wants to know, in some sense of "explain" (see Chapter 3), how these remarkable characteristics are to be explained. Or he may have in mind another sense of "life," so that his question could be translated "What is the meaning of existence?" What this question means is not nearly so clear, but perhaps it could be translated, "What is the *purpose* of existence?" but here again, questions about purpose can mean different things. At any rate, the question is not about the word, but about the thing named by the word, although

what it is that he wants to know about the thing may not be clear even to himself. Before it is possible to answer a question, one must first know exactly what the question is which is to be answered.

"**What is . . . ?" questions.** The same difficulties pervade a closely related group of questions, beginning with the words "what is." What is syzygy? What is matter? What is time? What is man? What is philosophy? Sometimes, in asking these questions, we want to know what thing a *word* is used to stand for: for example, "What is syzygy?" could be translated "What does the word 'syzygy' mean?" When the reply is given, "The point on the moon's orbit at which it is in direct line with the sun and the earth," our question has been answered. But if we ask, "What is time?" we are probably not asking what the *word* "time" means; we already know that (though we may not be able to define it, as we shall see later in this chapter). We may not be at all clear about *what* information about the thing, time, we are requesting. In very general questions like this the difficulty often lies with the unclarity of a question and not with the impossibility of an answer: once again, to have a clear answer we must first have a clear question. At any rate, it seems as if we are asking something about the *thing* rather than about the *word*.

Much confusion can result if we fail to keep this distinction in mind. Two persons may be arguing about the question "What is lightning?" One may say, "For hundreds of years, until the discoveries of Benjamin Franklin and others showing that lightning was a form of electricity, nobody knew what lightning was." Another person may reply, "But people have known for thousands of years what lightning is. What they didn't know until less than 200 years ago is what the *explanation* of lightning is. But the ancients knew lightning when they saw it—you surely can't deny that." The two persons, of course, are not really disagreeing at all; they are arguing at cross purposes, since they are not discussing the same question. The one is talking about the word, the other about the thing. In one sense, people have always known what lightning is—they have known what the *word* "lightning" (or synonymous words in other languages) means or stands for. After all, words have no meanings except those that people give them, and knowing what a word means is simply knowing what meaning the users of a language have given to a certain noise. People who speak the English language usually know very well what the word "lightning" means. Perhaps they are not always able to give a strict definition of the word,[1] but they do know how to apply the word "lightning" to the world, what phenomena the word names and what it does not name, and in this sense they know what they mean by the word. What people have not always known is how the thing, lightning, can be explained, and in this sense, people living 200 years ago as well as some people today do not know what lightning is.

Recapitulation. The main point of this section, which we should fix firmly in mind before proceeding further, can be put in this way: words are no more than the *labels* of things. We want to talk about things, so we attach labels to them. The world is like a vast array of bottles, many of which we want to label; and the words are the labels.

Words merely label things—they have no closer a relationship to the things than labels on bottles do to bottles. Any label will do, so long as we agree upon it and use it consistently. The bottle would still contain the same stuff even if a different label were pasted on it; and the thing would still be the same thing even if a different word were used to stand for it. "A rose by any other name would smell as sweet."

II. CLASS WORDS AND CLASSIFICATIONS

There is something wrong here, something important that has been omitted so far. Can we say simply that words name things— in the broad sense of "thing" explained on page 3—and let it go at that? Aren't there millions of things in the world for which human beings have names? Yet we clearly do not have millions of words in the English language or any other language. Let us examine the situation:

1. We are all confronted by a world full of things of all sorts which are different from each other in many respects and also resemble one another in many respects.

2. If you were the only person in the world, you would not need words to stand for these things in order to communicate with others. But there are other people in the world, and you want to talk about

---

[1] See the next section, especially the paragraph entitled "Can we know what X is without knowing the definition of 'X'?" below, pp. 62–63.

these things in your experience, even when the things themselves
are not there. So you devise words for them.

3. But if you tried to have a word for each individual thing
(whether a physical object, a mental process, a quality, or an
action), you would quickly get into difficulty. There are just too
many things in the world. You would have to supply too many
words. Moreover, when you became aware of some things you
hadn't known about before, or when you got into a new environment, you would have to have words for them in order to talk
about them. The new things might be very much like many of the
things you had already named, but no matter how much like them
they might be, you would have to devise different words because
these things would be different. Clearly, nothing of this sort actually
happens.

What is the way out? By now the answer should be obvious: you
use one word to stand for lots of different things.

There are some words which you use to stand for one thing only.
You call your daughter "Margaret," your parrot "Polly," your dog
"Rover." You may even call your house "Sunny Gables." These are
called *proper names*, because they are used to label one particular
thing only. But most of the words in any language are *class words*,
because they do not label just one individual thing but a whole
class of different things. Thus, corresponding to proper names, we
have the common names, or class words, "daughter," "parrot,"
"dog," "house." Each of these words is used to stand for many,
many particular things.[2] Such words are an absolute necessity if we
are to have a manageable language.

Having class words is an enormous advantage from the point of

[2] It often happens that there are some proper names shared by more than
one particular thing. More than one town has been named "Knoxville"; more
than one person has been called "Robert Smith." But, as our ensuing discussion
will make clearer, these words are still proper names because there is no *common characteristic* which underlies membership in the class. If you used the
noise "Cerlifs" to stand for everybody named "Robert Smith," then "Cerlif"
would be a class word: it would stand for the characteristic of having been
named "Robert Smith," just as the class word "bird" now stands for the
characteristics of being feathered and being vertebrate. Some words that were
once used only as proper names have come to be used as class words as well:
thus, "He is at Dunkirk," but "Let's not make this a Dunkirk." The test is
always this: if a word is a class word, there must be some *basis for membership in the class*. Otherwise, a phenomenon such as two people getting the
same name is just a "linguistic accident."

view of economy of language. We can still talk about anything we want to with a language of a few thousand words that does not unduly tax our memory. But it introduces a complication into our account of the relation of words to things—the fact that one word is made to do double duty, triple duty, million-fold duty, in standing for a vast multitude of particular things. It is extremely important that we examine this complication further, for most of our troubles in using language stem from it.

One word is made to stand for perhaps a million particular things. But how are we to know which particular things a word is to stand for? Must we say that the phrase "human being" stands for Robert Smith, Eugene Robinson, Abraham Lincoln . . . and then enumerate every individual in the human race, concluding, "The phrase 'human being' stands for all of these"? If this were so, the use of class words would not be an economy. We would still have to have a proper name for each individual in the class in order to say what the class word stood for; or else we would have to roam all over the world pointing to particular creatures, saying for example, "By the phrase 'human being' I mean this creature, that creature, that one over there . . ." concluding, "By 'human being' I mean all of those individuals." Actually, we never do anything like this, and could not even if we tried. In fact, don't we often know what a class word means without knowing how many particular things the word or phrase stands for, or whether there are individuals corresponding to the word at all?

The solution to the difficulty is this: We have a basis for grouping together many different particular things (or particulars) and putting the same label (word) on them all. This basis is always some *resemblance* among these different particulars, some characteristic or group of characteristics *which they all have in common,* by virtue of which we apply the same word to all of them. Thus, in explaining the meaning of the word "cow" we do not have to mention Farmer Jones' cows Dewdrop, Buttercup, and the rest, and then give names to all hitherto unnamed cows so as to get a complete list; nor do we have to point them all out in explaining what we mean by the word "cow." We need only explain what characteristics something has to have before we will use the word "cow" to apply to it. (This is not always as easy as it may seem, as we shall shortly discover.) We say, in effect, "Before I (and other users of the English language) call a thing an X—that is, before we use the word 'X' to apply to it—the thing must have characteristics A, B, C. . . . If it has characteristics A, B, C . . ., the word 'X' is used to refer to it; otherwise not." Thus we distinguish cows from horses on the basis of certain characteristics which cows have but horses do not, and vice versa. In doing this we need not know how many cows and horses there are in the world, nor even whether there are any at all. All we need to say is, "To anything that has characteristics A, B, C, . . the word 'X' is applicable (in our language). If it should turn out that there is nothing that has this particular combination of characteristics, the only result is that there is nothing for the word 'X' to apply to."

Advantage and disadvantage of class words. When we employ class words, then, we group many things together under one heading (we attach the same printed label to many bottles) on the basis of characteristics which these things have in common. In using the same word to refer to many things, we are (at least for the moment) treating these individuals as if they were all alike, and ignoring their differences. In this fact lie both the advantage and the disadvantage of class words.

Advantage: Different though things may be from each other, they do have common characteristics, and class words serve to remind us of them. The Boston aristocrat and the African Hottentot differ from each other in many respects, but they share certain basic characteristics which entitle them both to the label "human being." The word "above" applies not only to the relation which the chandelier in my dining room bears to the dining room table, but also to the relation which your upstairs bedroom bears to your kitchen. Suppose that there were no class words, and that Smith built himself a house and gave it a proper name which we shall call "N"; then Jones built himself a house and gave it a proper name, "O"; then Black did the same and called it "P." Now you come along. You cannot say that you are going to build a *house,* because there are no class words. You have no way of indicating in words the similarity between what you are going to build and what the others have already built. Yet you may want a word which covers them all and thus points up the similarity among them. Thus we get class words. As people became aware of resemblances among objects, they differentiated between groups of things by giving them different class names. The fact that various languages often do not have equivalent class names shows in how many ways people can verbalize their experiences. For example, some languages have words for strawberries, gooseberries, and the like, but no general word for berries. The ancient Greeks were the first to name, and hence presumably to think of, the widest class of all—that of Being.

Disadvantage: Class words tend to obliterate the differences among things and overemphasize their similarities. Two things may be referred to by the same word, while they may be much more different than alike. One should not assume that two things with the same class word are identical; yet having the same word for both of them tends to make one assume this unconsciously. "Oh, another banker," says the shopgirl as she goes out on a new date. But bankers, like all other creatures, differ in many ways from each other. "One star differeth from another in glory," says the psalmist. We should guard against the tendency to make the inference, "Identical names, therefore identical things." Even the same thing is different at different times. Class words may tend to *fossilize* our conception of the ever-changing, infinitely various world of things to make us conceive the world as being composed of static *types* rather than of different things, some of which are similar enough to each other to be given the same name.

> Light passes through a solid crystal. This many persons deem a standing miracle. What we see excites no surprise. The passage through solid crystal is the marvel. We know the difficulty which would attend the passage of our hand through the crystal, and we deem the passage of the light identical with the passage of the hand. Nothing is more fallacious than thus to construe the word "passage" in these different uses of it. The two operations possess the requisite analogy to make the word "passage" applicable to both, but its meaning in each application is what our senses reveal, and not what the identity of the word implies.[3]

Classification. Probably no two things in the universe are exactly alike in all respects. Consequently, no matter how much alike two things may be, we may still use the characteristics in which they differ as a basis for putting them in different classes. Thus, even if two icicles were exactly alike in shape, size, and chemical structure

[3] Alexander B. Johnson, *A Treatise on Language* (Berkeley: University of California Press, 1947), p. 85. (First published 1836.)

(even when examined under a very powerful microscope)—though doubtless this would never happen—we could call one, say, a "flep" and the other a "flup" because one was hanging from the north side of the house and the other from the west side. (We would be using "flep" to refer to any icicle of that very specific shape, size, and composition, hanging on the north side of such-and-such kinds of dwellings.) Or, if the two exactly similar icicles hung an inch apart, we could make the fact that the one was west of the other the basis for putting them into different classes and using different class words for them. We *could* make the criteria for membership in a class so detailed and specific that in the entire universe there would exist no more than one member of each class. In practice we do not do this, for language then would be just as unmanageable as it would be if all words were proper names. What we do is to use rather inclusive class words, such as "cow," and then, if the need arises, we can make differences within this class the basis for further distinctions, such as "Guernsey cow," "brindle cow," and so on, marking out as many sub-classes as we find convenient within the main class. (Every profession carries this process of subdivision further than laymen do. We talk vaguely about bones, nerves, and muscles, but medical men must speak of pituitary glands, ganglia, medulla oblongata, and the like.)

In the same way, there are probably no two things in the universe so different from one another that they do not have some characteristics in common which can be made the basis for membership in the same class. For example, a thought and a sandpile are vastly different, but both are "temporal entities," i.e., they occur in time. Triangles, trees, the square root of −1, running, and the relation of being above, though they belong in utterly different categories, have in common at least the fact that they have all been thought of by me in the last ten minutes! In practice this fact would hardly justify us in devising a class word to include all of them, but it could be done: we could use a noise, say "biltrus," and say that a biltrus is anything thought of by me. Often we do in fact build up wider and more inclusive classifications, such as "Guernsey," "cow," "mammal," "animal," "organism," "physical thing," "existing thing," each successive word applying to more and more particular things because the requirements for membership in the class are progressively fewer and less restrictive.

Are there natural classes of things? The common characteristics which we take as criteria for the use of a class word are a matter of convenience. Our classifications depend on our interests and our need for recognizing both the similarities and the differences among things. Many overlapping classifications can be equally valid. Animals are classified in one way by the zoologist, in another way by the fur industry, in still another way by the leather industry. Houses are classified in one way by the architect, in another way by the gas inspector, and in still another by the tax collector. Moreover, as we have seen, there are many things in the world which we could group into classes if we wished, but since there is no need for it, we do not bother. Doubtless there are tables in the world that have been painted twice, then taken upstairs after twenty-one years' use, then brought down again and sold as antiques. But we have not bothered to devise a class word for tables that possess in common this rather peculiar set of characteristics.

There are as many possible classes in the world as there are common characteristics or combinations thereof which can be made the basis of classification. Those to which we may be most accustomed we often tend to think of as the "natural," the inevitable, the only correct classifications. This, of course, is a mistake. If we were more interested in the colors of creatures than in their shapes, or if animals always bred true to color but offspring of the same parents had a chaotic variety of shapes, sizes, number of legs, and so on, then, doubtless, we would consider classification by color more "natural" or more "right" than classification by any other means. If their being poisonous or non-poisonous, or their being capable or incapable of becoming domesticated, depended consistently upon their colors, then doubtless we would classify them according to their colors.

Nature guides us, but does not dictate to us, in the selection of classes. Nature guides us in the sense that we often find in nature certain *regularly recurring combinations of characteristics,* so that it seems useful to assign them a name. Thus, let us suppose (though this is an oversimplification) that we use the word "dog" for anything that is a mammal, barks, has long ears, has a long nose, and wags its tail when it is pleased or excited. The class of dogs is a natural class in the sense that these characteristics pretty regularly occur together (not with perfect regularity, however: there are "monsters" or freaks of nature). For example, we find that creatures having the other "doggish" characteristics also usually bark and do not meow or hiss. It is easy and convenient, then, to lump all these individuals together under one class word, "dog." A different but overlapping combination of characteristics is employed for the use of the word "cat." Let us say that anything having characteristics A, B, C, and D is called "dog," and anything having A, E, F, and G is called "cat." We could, if we liked, devise another word and use it to refer to anything having characteristics B, E, H, and J—for example, any five-footed mammal, green in color, which has a long slender nose and purrs. But as far as we know there are no such creatures, so it is simply not useful to us to devise such a classification.

Are classes in nature or are they man-made? As so often happens, the answer depends on the meaning of the question. Classes are in nature in the sense that the *common characteristics* can be found in nature, waiting (as it were) to be made the basis for a classification. On the other hand, classes are man-made in the sense that the *act of classifying* is the work of human beings, depending on their interests and needs. We could quite validly have made classifications quite different from those we did make by selecting from the infinite reservoir of nature *different* groups of common characteristics (as bases for classification) from those we did select.

Extending a classification. When we want to give a name to a class of things which is like but not exactly like a class for which we already have a name, we are faced by a choice: shall we extend the old name to include the different but related things, or shall we keep the old name as it is and devise a new name for the new class? Shall we call the new anti-tank weapons "guns" (with a qualifying adjective in front) on the basis of their similarity to the things we already call "guns," or shall we call them by a new name, "bazookas," on the basis of their differences from the things we call "guns"? Shall we call communism a religion, because of certain qualities of devotion, fanatical loyalty, and submergence of the self in a common cause, which it shares with ways of life and thought we already refer to as religions, or shall we deny the term "religion" to it because it professes no belief in a supernatural Being? What of a chemical element possessing every characteristic usually associated with the name, except its weight? Shall we put it into a different class and distinguish it with a new name, or shall we retain the old name and say that they all belong in the same class, perhaps distinguishing this group from the rest of the class by means of the word "isotope"?

If we use the old name, we shall be putting less of a tax on the memory by not asking others to learn a new word. More important, by using the same word for both, we shall be calling attention to the similarity between the new class and the old. But at the same time we shall be obscuring the differences between the new things and the old, tending to make others believe that the new thing is like the old because it has the same name. On the other hand, if we use a new word we shall make the differences quite clear, but we may also tend to keep others from being aware of genuine similarities between the two.

Which procedure we adopt in any particular case will depend largely on whether it is the likenesses or the differences that strike us as the more important. On the basis of that, we shall either recommend or reject a new name. Sometimes we are able to compromise by devising a new name made out of old ones; for example, when a creature was born whose mother was a tiger and whose father was a lion, a new class word was devised for labeling all such creatures: "tigon."

The fact that often passes unheeded in these disputes is that it is simply a matter of using words, of applying labels to things. There is no one right or wrong way of classifying things, just as we saw in the last section that there are no right or wrong words naming things. It is not a question of "Is it really a lion? is it really a tiger? is it really a new species? Is this really a religion or is it something else?" To argue the matter in this way would betray a fundamental ignorance of the relation of words to things. It is rather a question of (1) what characteristics does this have? and (2) now that this has been determined, shall we call it by a new name or an old one? The problem is one of deciding what noises to use to stand for what combination of characteristics, not one of discovering in some mysterious way "what the thing really is."

Ambiguity. If all words were proper names and if there were no duplication of words, there would be one word for every thing and one thing for every word. This, as we saw, would make language unmanageable. Instead, a word is made to stand for a class of things. There is still a further step: many words stand for more than one class of things; they are *ambiguous*.

Ambiguity is one of the most pervasive features of language, and it can be very misleading. In most cases it is not, because we can tell from the *context* (other words in the same sentence, or other sentences) which meaning of the ambiguous word or phrase is meant. Thus, no one would confuse the class of acts named by the verb "bolt" with the class of tools named by the noun "bolt." The context, "Don't bolt your food," or "Help me fasten this bolt," indicates clearly which meaning is intended. Ambiguities such as this give us no trouble, and probably most of us do not realize how ambiguous most of the words we use in daily life actually are. "I believe in you" means the same as "I have confidence in you," while "I don't believe in ghosts" means the same as "I don't believe that ghosts exist." Yet we may never have been conscious of the fact that the phrase "believe in" is ambiguous. (Sometimes, in fact, the very word "ambiguity" is restricted so as to mean only *misleading* ambiguity, where the context does not indicate which meaning is being employed.)

Ambiguity can, however, be misleading, and we shall find many examples of this in our study of philosophy. When someone says, "They went to look at the construction," he may mean that they went to look at (1) the process of constructing something or (2) that which was constructed. This is an example of *process-product* ambiguity: the same word stands for the process and the product of that process. Ambiguous words which are closely related in their meanings are most apt to be misleading, for we may shift from one meaning of the word to another without knowing it. Thus the word "meaning" discussed above is misleadingly ambiguous. Ordinarily the word "sound" is not misleading, but when someone asks, "If a tree falls in a forest and nobody is there to hear it, is there a sound?" it is misleading, for the answer depends on which sense of the word "sound" is being used: in the sense of sound-waves (alternating rarefactions and condensations of the air) there is, but in the sense of auditory sensation there is not.

Whenever you use an ambiguous word and there is a possibility that its use may be misleading, you should, of course, clearly specify which sense of the word you are using. This rule about ambiguity is similar to the rule of common usage discussed in the previous section, except that in ambiguity we are confronted with *several* common usages of a word.

Figurative language. One of the most common kinds of ambiguity occurs when we take some word or phrase and use it in a figurative, or metaphorical, sense; the metaphorical sense is related to the literal one but is not the same. Thus one person may call another a rat, a cat, a snake, a bull, a weasel, a fox, a buffalo, a pigeon, and so forth; yet the person addressed is not being told that he or she literally is one of these animals. Calling the person by one of these names is a picturesque way of saying that he possesses some qualities which the animal has or is traditionally supposed to have. There is always some relation between the literal and the figurative use of the word and the ambiguity is never a "linguistic accident." Thus we speak of a kernel of grain, a grain of truth; a sharp knife, a sharp student; your shadow, a shadow of your former self; a cool evening, a cool reception; a heavy weight, a heavy heart; a house on fire, on fire with anger; a warm temperature, a warm color.

Usually this kind of ambiguity is not misleading. But figurative language *can* be dangerous. It becomes so when we no longer know what we mean by the figurative expression we are using. Using it is like writing a check; there must be cash in the bank (literal meaning) to back it up. Usually this is not difficult to supply. "He was consumed with rage" is a picturesque way of saying that he was very angry; "sharp tongued" means disposed to cavil, utter sarcastic comments, and the like; "She is a walking shadow" means that she is very thin, fragile-looking, perhaps pale and anemic. But what would it mean to say that the entire world is but a shadow? Perhaps the person who says it can specify what he means, but until he does so the expression is not clear.

Limits of ambiguity. As a glance through the dictionary will show, the majority of the words in the English language are ambiguous in one way or another. Yet we should be careful not to "detect" ambiguities when they are not there:

1. A word is not ambiguous simply because it stands for many particular things. The word "see" is not ambiguous because you can see a horse and then see a tree. Both are instances of seeing, and a word is not ambiguous just because there are different instances of its application. The word "see" means the same in both cases, though of course the things seen are different. The word "see" can

be used ambiguously: when we say, "Do you see what I'm driving at?" we make no reference to vision. It is this last use and not the existence of many *instances* of seeing (in the visual sense) that makes the word ambiguous.

2. A word is not ambiguous because we can break up the class of things it refers to into smaller classes or sub-classes. We can break up the class of colors into the class of reds, the class of yellows, etc. But the word "color" is not made ambiguous by the fact that red, yellow, etc. are colors. They are colors in exactly the same sense of the word "color." (A different sense of the word is being used, however, when we say "Her personality has so much color.") The fact that there are kinds of X does not make the word "X" ambiguous; it is ambiguous when it is used in two or more senses, that is, when it is used to stand for two or more classes of things.

III. DEFINING CHARACTERISTICS AND DEFINITIONS

Denotation and designation. By convention, words stand for things (Section I), and unless they are proper names they stand for classes of things. But we have also talked as if words stood rather for *characteristics*. Which of these is correct?

Both of them: words stand for both, but not in the same way. Words *denote*, and they also *designate*. The word "cow" denotes Bossy, Dewdrop, and all the particular things to which the word "cow" is applicable; and the entire class of these particular things is called its *denotation*. But it *designates* a set of characteristics, namely, those characteristics which a thing must have in order for the word "cow" to be applicable to it.

Of the two, designation is by far the more important, for the characteristics which a word designates will determine what the particular things are which the word denotes. If we know what a word designates, we know the *conditions of applicability* of the word; we know under what conditions we can apply the word to a given particular thing in the world and under what conditions we cannot. "When a thing has characteristics A, B, and C, then the word 'X' (in our language) is applicable to it; otherwise, it is not."

Knowing only the denotation of a word is not enough. If we had never heard the word "city," but were told that New York is a city, Chicago is a city, Paris is a city, and so on, we might suspect that being a center of population and containing a large number of people had something to do with a thing's being called a city, since Coyote Canyon and Buzzard Gulch were never listed as cities. Even if we had before us the *total denotation* of the word—a complete list of all the cities in the world—we would still want some *criterion* which would enable us to tack the label "city" on some things and not others. In other words, even if we had a complete list of cities, we would still want to know why, *by virtue of what characteristics,* these were included on the list and others excluded. It would become especially urgent to know this if we wanted to talk about some center of population in the distant future, or one of your imagination, with *possible* and not merely *actual* ones. What would entitle them to be called cities? Here the list of actual cities will not help; we must know the criterion for the use of the word "city": "What are the characteristics whose presence *would* entitle something to the word 'city,' whether that something actually exists or not?" In short, we must know not merely what things the word denotes, but what characteristics it designates. When we state all the characteristics it designates, we are giving its *definition.*

Defining and accompanying characteristics. Usually a definition comprises several *defining characteristics.* Everything in the world has an indefinitely large (some would say an infinitely large) number of characteristics; but those characteristics *without* which the thing would not be labeled by a certain word are the characteristics which *define* that word—its defining characteristics. A sentence which lists the complete set of defining characteristics is the *definition* of the word. Those characteristics of a thing without which the word would still apply to it are its *accompanying* characteristics.[4]

For example, triangles have many characteristics. Some are large, some small. Some are scalene, some isosceles, some equilateral. But there is something by virtue of which they are all triangles, and without which they would not be triangles; these characteristics are the defining ones, which together constitute the definition of "tri-

---

[4] Sometimes the defining characteristics are called *essential,* and the accompanying ones *accidental,* characteristics.

Sometimes a thing's characteristics are called its *properties.* This is a usage often employed in philosophy, but unfortunately the word "properties" is ambiguous: it is also used to mean (1) *only* those characteristics which are defining, and (2) *only* those characteristics which a thing would have in isolation from other things (its intrinsic as opposed to its relational characteristics—a distinction to be discussed shortly).

angle." Having three sides is a defining characteristic, for anything that did not have this would not be called a triangle. Being a plane figure is another, being a closed figure another, being bounded by straight lines still another. But being at least two inches high is not, for something could still be a triangle without being at least two inches high.

The test of whether a certain characteristic is defining is always this: would the same word still apply if the thing lacked the characteristic? If the answer is no, the characteristic is defining; if the answer is yes, it is merely accompanying. Can a triangle have unequal sides and still be a triangle? Yes. Then having equal sides is not a defining characteristic of triangles. Can a triangle have unequal sides and still be an equilateral triangle? No. Then having equal sides is defining of equilateral triangles. A defining characteristic is a *sine qua non* (literally "without which not"). Would this thing still be an X if it didn't have characteristic A? If it would not, then having A is a *sine qua non* of its being an X—it is defining.

This is not the same question as "Would it still have A if it weren't an X?" The answer to this last question might well be yes even if the answer to the first one was no. Would it still be a triangle if it weren't a plane figure? No. Would it still be a plane figure if it weren't a triangle? It very well might: it could be a square, a parallelogram, a pentagon, etc. Having A is essential to its being an X, but being an X is not essential to its having A. Y and Z may also have A. In other words, there are many classes of things in the world that have *some* defining characteristics in common. The characteristic of being solid is defining of many things—chairs, trees, ice, etc.

Clearly this does not mean (imply) that all these words have the same definition. A definition states *all* the defining characteristics, and two words would not have the same definition unless *all* the defining characteristics were the same. The words "asteroid" and "planetoid" have the same definition and therefore designate the same total set of characteristics. But there are not many words like this; it would obviously be a pointless duplication of language. One word may be defined by characteristics A, B, and C, and another word by characteristics A, B, and D; but two words will not often have the same total set of defining characteristics, and hence the same definition.

Scope of definitions. When you try to formulate a definition for a word in common use, or evaluate a definition suggested by someone else, there are three important things to keep in mind:

1. The denotation should not be too broad. If you defined "telephone" simply as "instrument for communication," your definition would be so broad as to include many things that no one would call telephones. You have to narrow or restrict the definition by *adding* one or more defining characteristics: you must say what kind of instrument for communication a telephone is, as distinguished from other such instruments.

2. The denotation of the word should not be too narrow. If you defined "tree" as "plant with green leaves, at least 50 feet tall, growing vertically from the ground," your definition would be so narrow as to exclude many things that we now call trees. Many trees—that is, many things we call trees—are not so tall, some do not have green leaves nor any leaves at all, and so forth. You have to broaden this definition by *subtracting* defining characteristics, so that all the things we call trees can still be denoted by the word "tree" on your definition.

Sometimes a suggested definition is too broad and too narrow at the same time. Defining "telephone" as "instrument of long-distance communication" is too narrow, for the things we call telephones are often used for short-distance communication; at the same time it is too broad, for without this unsatisfactory restricting condition it covers many things which are not called telephones at all. The problem is to get all the defining characteristics into the definition, but none that are not defining.

3. Even if the denotation of the word is neither too broad nor too narrow, the definition may be unsatisfactory. Two terms may have exactly the same denotation and still designate quite different characteristics. Suppose that four characteristics, A, B, C, and D, *always* occurred together, so that there was nothing in the universe that had A without also having the other three, and vice versa. Suppose further that one person uses a word, "X," to designate characteristics A, B, and C; and that another person uses a word, "Y," to designate characteristics A, B, and D. The denotations of the two words will be exactly the same: everything having A, B, and C will also have

D, and everything having A, B, and D will also have C. The two words will, for all practical purposes, mean the same thing: for they will denote the same things, though they do not designate the same characteristics.

Suppose that a definition of the word "elephant" is suggested: "an animal that draws water up its trunk and squirts it into its mouth." Let us assume for the sake of simplicity that every elephant does this, and that everything that does this is an elephant (that is, nothing *but* elephants do this). The definition is thus neither too broad nor too narrow as far as its denotation is concerned. But now let us ask: "Couldn't a creature do this and still not be an elephant? Some creature, perhaps, on another planet or a new creature yet to develop; or a zebra on which had been grafted a trunk which could be used in this way? Couldn't a thing *fail* to do this and still be an elephant? Perhaps one that had his trunk-mechanism stopped up, or one that eschews the use of water?" If we are to use the word "elephant" in any ordinary sense, the answer is surely yes. Such creatures may not actually exist; but that does not matter: a zebra who fulfilled the requirements of the definition would still not be an elephant, and an elephant who couldn't use his trunk would still be an elephant, and we can know this *without* knowing whether either of these creatures actually exists. It is enough to know that *if* the first existed it would not be an elephant, and if the second existed it would—just as we can know that *if* I had eaten a pound of arsenic I wouldn't be writing at this moment, even though I did not actually eat a pound of arsenic.

In other words, a definition must be adequate to the *possible* as well as the actual cases. We want to know what are the characteristics, the presence of which would entitle something to be called an elephant and the absence of which would keep it from being called one. To know this, we must go beyond the actual denotation of the word. "The practical test in fact, when we wish to know whether any proposed definition is a true one or not, is to try whether by conceivable variation of circumstances we can cause it to break down, by its exclusion of what we are resolved to retain or its inclusion of what we are resolved to reject." [5] If every round thing was red and every red thing was round, the words "red" and "round" would have the same denotation: everything on a complete

[5] J. Venn, *Empirical Logic* (New York: Macmillan, 1889), p. 304.

list of red things would also be on a complete list of round things, and vice versa; nor could anyone ever point to a red thing that was not also a round thing, and vice versa. And yet the words "red" and "round" would not mean the same: "red" would still be a color-word and "round" a shape-word. No sameness of denotation could ever give them the same designation.

When we are distinguishing defining from accompanying characteristics, then, we should be particularly careful about the *universally accompanying* characteristics: when D *always* accompanies A, B, and C, we may think that it belongs in the definition. But let us then ask ourselves, "Even though D always accompanies A, B, and C, *if* sometime D did *not* accompany A, B, and C, would the thing in question still be called an X?" If the answer is yes, the characteristic is still accompanying and not defining. (Even if all right acts produced happiness and all acts producing happiness were right, it would not follow that "being right" and "producing happiness" mean the same: for the producing of happiness may be only a universal accompaniment of being right.)

Shifts in defining characteristics. The tendency, however, is for a universally accompanying characteristic to become defining. This does not mean that one characteristic is both defining and accompanying at the same time; it means only that the designation of the word sometimes shifts gradually in the history of a language, so that the word does not designate the same characteristics at all times. The most usual direction of this shift is for universally accompanying characteristics to become incorporated (perhaps unconsciously) into the definition. Let us suppose that the word "whale" was once used to apply to anything that had characteristics A, B, and C. But then it was discovered that the creatures that had A, B, and C, also had another characteristic, D—they were mammals. This came to be added to the list of defining characteristics, for today nothing that was non-mammalian would be called a whale. (Let no one say that in discovering that whales were mammals we *found* the correct definition of the word "whale." We *could* have kept on using the word "whale" in the old way, so that if a creature having A, B, and C turned up without D, we would have called it a whale in spite of its non-mammalian character. But much zoological classification had already taken place on the basis of whether the creatures were mammalian or not, and it was most convenient simply to shift this definition a bit to accommodate the existing classification.)

Verbal disputes. Often, when we use a word, we do not have clearly in mind what characteristics the word is being used to designate, and as a result we get into unnecessary confusions and disputes.

Example 1. Here is a table. Would it still be a table if I painted it a different color? Yes—nobody would use color (in the case of tables) as a defining characteristic. Would it still be a table if I used it for a different purpose? Yes. Would it still be a table if I somehow petrified the wood into stone? Yes—what it is made of is not a defining characteristic. Would it still be a table if I took off one of its legs? Yes, probably we would still call it a table. Suppose I took off all four legs? Then it would not be called a table but a table-top. (Thus, having legs—at least one—is a defining characteristic of "table"; without legs it is not a table; that it is, we would not use the *word* "table" to apply to it.) Suppose I chopped it to pieces; would it still be a table? No, it would be pieces of wood that had been a table but were so no longer. We so use the word "table" that the general form or shape of the thing is essential to its being called a table, but not its material composition; we use the one characteristic as defining, the other not. Of course we *could* have chosen the defining characteristics differently: we simply found this one the most convenient, for we needed a class name to talk about objects of a certain general shape, regardless of what they were made of. Had our interests been different, we would have made the word designate a different set of characteristics.

The issue, "When is it a table and when isn't it?" is a *verbal* issue —one which involves only the meanings of words, in this case the word "table." There is no dispute about the *facts*—whether the object can be painted, chopped to pieces, etc. Different people might witness the whole series of operations and yet disagree on "when it stopped being a table." Nor is the dispute clarified by assertions that "we are here searching for the *essence* of a table (or tablehood)" or that "we are trying to find *the real nature of* a table." One can use this language if he likes, provided he realizes that all we are doing is trying to bring to light what the characteristics are which we take as defining of the word, and get them all together into a definition, so that we shall know exactly when to apply the

word and when not to do so. Once it is made clear what characteristics are being used as defining, the whole controversy dissolves.
Example 2. William James records the following incident: [6]

> Some years ago, being with a camping party in the mountains, I re-
> turned from a solitary ramble to find everyone engaged in a ferocious
> metaphysical dispute. The *corpus* of the dispute was a squirrel—a live
> squirrel supposed to be clinging to one side of a tree trunk; while over
> against the tree's opposite side a human being was imagined to stand,
> This human witness tries to get sight of the squirrel by moving rapidly
> round the tree, but no matter how fast he goes, the squirrel moves as
> fast in the opposite direction, and always keeps the tree between him-
> self and the man, so that never a glimpse of him is caught. The re-
> sultant metaphysical problem now is this: *Does the man go round the
> squirrel or not?* He goes round the tree, sure enough, and the squirrel
> is on the tree; but does he go round the squirrel? In the unlimited
> leisure of the wilderness discussion had been worn threadbare. Every-
> one had taken sides and was obstinate; and the numbers on both sides
> were even. Each side, when I appeared, therefore appealed to me to
> make it a majority. Mindful of the scholastic adage that whenever you
> meet a contradiction you must make a distinction, I immediately
> sought and found one, as follows: "Which party is right," I said, "de-
> pends on what you *practically mean* by 'going round' the squirrel. If
> you mean passing from the north of him to the east, then to the south,
> then to the west, and then to the north of him again, obviously the
> man does go round him, for he occupies these successive positions. But
> if on the contrary you mean being first in front of him, then on the
> right of him, then behind him, then on his left, and finally in front
> again, it is quite obvious that the man fails to go round him for by
> compensating movements the squirrel makes, he keeps his belly turned
> towards the man all the time, and his back turned away. Make the
> distinction, and there is no occasion for any further dispute. You are
> both right and both wrong, according as you conceive the verb 'to go
> round' in one practical fashion or the other."
>   Although one or two of the hotter disputants called my speech a
> shuffling evasion, saying they wanted no quibbling or scholastic hair-
> splitting, but meant just plain English "round," the majority seemed
> to think that the distinction had assuaged the dispute.

The question, of course, is whether being right of, front of, left of,
back of the squirrel is taken as a defining characteristic of "going
round," or whether being north, west, south, and east of the squirrel
is so taken; in the first case the answer to "Is the man going round

[6] William James, *Pragmatism* (New York: Longmans, Green & Company),
pp. 43–45.

the squirrel?" is yes, in the second case, no. It all depends on how we define the preposition "round." This difficulty may never have faced us before because usually everything that goes round something else in the first sense also does so in the second, such as a planet going round the sun. But now, when the one occurs without the other, we have to decide which one we are going to take as defining.

Example 3. When can you be said to be in the same train as the one you were in last week? "This is the Twentieth Century Limited." "Oh, that's the same train I took to New York last week." But is it necessarily the same set of cars? Apparently not; for you might take the Twentieth Century Limited from Chicago yesterday and I might take it from Chicago today, although we are certainly not in the same set of cars, for the set of cars you took yesterday is today in New York.

Rather than argue, "It *is* the same train!" "It isn't!" let us ask what we mean by the phrase "same train"—in other words, what are the characteristics which define it. Do we call two sets of cars the same train if they have the same labels or signs (such as "Twentieth Century Limited") attached to them?

But this too does not seem to be our criterion. If someone went out on the sly and switched labels on every car of the Twentieth Century Limited, would it cease to be the Twentieth Century Limited at the moment when the signs were removed? Of course not; we would say that the *labels* are now the wrong ones. (Or suppose there were no labels on the cars at all; then it would still be the Twentieth Century Limited—it would just be ever so much harder to discover that it was.) Similarly, this would still be Spamm Street even though a prankster relabeled it "Spasm Street" or took the signs off entirely.

What, then, makes this the Twentieth Century Limited and not another train? Surely the fact that the official in charge of naming and scheduling gave it that name; if the person in charge, in his official capacity, were to change the name, then it would no longer be the Twentieth Century Limited but, say, the Droit de Seigneur.

Once it is realized that the issue is a verbal one, we shall not argue the question as if it were an insoluble one (where "no one will ever know the right answer") or some deep mystery in the nature of things. There are many factual questions which are difficult enough to answer, for it is difficult and sometimes impossible to know what the facts are, particularly if they are facts outside the sphere of observation. But many questions that pose as factual questions are really *verbal* questions, such as the ones in these examples. These questions we can answer by clearing up the meanings of our words. There are enough difficult problems which are not verbal without unnecessarily adding the verbal ones to the list.

Just as many disputes can be resolved by clearing up words, so can *questions*. It is not always clear from the wording of a question whether it is information about *things* or about *words* that would answer it. The "what is" and "what is the meaning of" questions in Section 1 are examples. Questions beginning with "What *is the nature of* . . ." are usually (whether the questioners are aware of it or not) requests for defining characteristics. Sometimes, when we ask, "What is the nature of cats?" or "What is the nature of water?" we are asking for accompanying characteristics as well as defining ones: we want to know what some of the most usual or important characteristics of cats or water are, whether defining or not. But more often when we want to know about the nature of X, we want to know the defining characteristics of X, those characteristics in the absence of which we would not call the thing an X. The same holds for "essence-questions." "What *is the essence of* X?" is usually a disguised request for the definition, or at least some of the defining characteristics, of X. Those characteristics without which something would not be an X are the characteristics which constitute "the essence" of X.

Importance of the distinction between defining and accompanying characteristics. In many cases when we attribute a characteristic to a thing, we do not make clear whether or not the characteristic we are mentioning is one we consider to be defining. Yet it is often of the utmost importance that we do this: for whether, and in what manner, our statement will be disputed depends entirely on which kind of characteristic it is. To state a defining characteristic is to state a part of the meaning (definition) of a term; but to state an accompanying characteristic is to state some fact, not about the term itself (for the accompanying characteristic is no part of its meaning), but something about the thing named by the term. Thus:

> Steel is an alloy of iron.
> Steel is used for purposes of construction.

The first sentence states a defining characteristic, for if something were not an alloy of iron it would not be steel (that is, the word "steel" would not apply to it); but the second sentence states an accompanying characteristic, for if steel were no longer used for purposes of construction it would still be steel. The first sentence, then, states part of the meaning of the *word*, "steel"; on the other hand, the second sentence asserts a fact about the *thing*, steel. Often it is virtually impossible to tell from a sentence whether the speaker is stating the meaning of a *word* or stating a fact about the *thing* named by the word. "The good student is the one who gets the highest grades," someone says. Is he stating all or a part of what he *means* by the phrase "good student"? Is he defining the term, or is he taking for granted that we know what the phrase "good student" means and asserting that all good students *also* get the highest grades? Often the speaker himself is not clear about this. Yet if we want to dispute the statement, we shall have to know which it is, for in the first case we shall be disputing a *verbal usage*, and in the second case we shall be disputing an alleged *fact*. In the first case we might say, "You may use the phrase 'good student' to mean that, but most people would probably define the phrase differently." In the second case we might say, "But it isn't true that all good students get high grades; here is one that doesn't." The issue is verbal in the first case, factual in the second.

The situation is made still worse if the speaker shifts his ground during the course of the argument. For example:

> A: All swans are white.
> B: In Australia there are black swans.
> A: But those creatures are black—so they can't be swans!

Ordinarily A's first assertion would be taken as a factual statement (whether true or false) about swans, in other words, as a statement of an accompanying characteristic; being white is not considered a defining characteristic of swans. As a factual statement, however, A's assertion can be disputed, and is in fact disputed by B. So A makes his first statement invulnerable to disproof by any facts whatsoever; he does so by turning it from a factual statement into a statement about the *word* "swan," making whiteness defining of being a swan. Clearly, if that is what he had been stating in the first place, B would not have challenged the statement in the way he did; he would simply have commented on the unusual manner in which A was using the word "swan." B naturally took A's statement as a statement about the creatures, swans, not about the word. A then promptly switched the meaning of his first assertion from that of a factual statement into a definition.

Needless to say, A has not eliminated any black swans from the world by this verbal sleight of hand. Those creatures remain quite undisturbed by A's maneuver. He may succeed in preventing B from *calling* them by the *name* "swans," but swans by any other name are just as black. True, B may be puzzled and not know how to answer A. "After all," he may think, "I can't say there are black swans if being white is a part of the very meaning of the word." Yet he will remain convinced that the black swans still exist. The puzzlement, of course, is needless: there would have been no trouble to begin with if A and B had been clear about defining and accompanying characteristics. (A may do the same thing, with better effect, in a more abstract controversy: "The good students are those who get the highest grades." "Here is a good student who just doesn't get high grades." "He doesn't? Well, then, he can't be a good student.")

Definition and existence. When you have stated the defining characteristics of X, you have proved nothing one way or the other about whether an X exists. In other words, if you know what the term "X" *designates*, you still know nothing about what the term "X" *denotes*. The word "horse" denotes many things, and the word "centaur" (a creature half man and half horse) denotes no things whatever, for there are no centaurs.[7] But the meaning of the two words is equally clear; we know what characteristics something has to have to be labeled "centaur" just as well as we know what characteristics something has to have to be labeled "horse." When you are able to define a word in terms of characteristics A, B, and C, you have still not shown that there *exists* anything in the universe that has characteristics A, B, and C. You cannot legislate centaurs

---

[7] Let us not say that there are centaurs because we can imagine them or draw pictures of them. What we can draw are centaur-pictures and what we imagine are centaur-images; but centaur-pictures and centaur-images are not centaurs, and there still are no centaurs. The term "centaur-pictures" has denotation as there are many things denoted by this term (on vases and the like); however, the term "centaur" has no denotation at all, at least not on the earth.

into existence by defining a word, any more than you can legislate black swans out of existence by redefining the word "swan." From defining "X," you can draw no conclusions whatever about whether there are any X's in the world; that is not a matter for definition but for scientific investigation.

It is interesting to observe in this connection that if the word "meaning" referred to denotation only, words such as "centaur," "brownie," "elf," "dragon," and "gremlin" (since they have no denotation) would all mean the same, namely, nothing. But of course they do mean something, and they all have different meanings, that is, different designations. Each term designates a different set of characteristics, although nothing that has these characteristics happens to exist.

Attempts to make all characteristics defining. Another kind of difficulty in which people sometimes find themselves can be avoided if they keep clearly in mind the distinction between those characteristics which are defining and those which are not.

"How," we are sometimes asked, "can something be the same thing as before, and yet be subject to many changes? How can a human being change from a boy to a man and still remain the same human being? Isn't everything in the universe constantly changing? Heracleitus (500 B. C.) said that you can't step into the same river twice, because the water you stepped into the time before has already gone downstream. Similarly, scientists tell us that there is not a single cell in your body that was there seven years ago. But how then can I say I am the same person that I was then? Can't I say I am not responsible for a debt I contracted then because I'm not the same person any longer? Indeed, everything in the universe is in constant flux. Even things that seem still, such as the table on which I am now writing, are congeries of atoms and electrons, and are not in the same state for two split-seconds together. How then am I entitled to speak of it as the same table for two split-seconds together? But if I cannot speak of the same object existing for two moments running, how can words be applicable to the world? How can language, which consists of a comparatively static group of words, name items in the shifting, ever-changing flux which is the world if the names don't even apply from one moment to the next?"

It should not be difficult now to allay these fears, not by denying the statements which scientists assert, but by remembering the principles we have thus far learned. Doubtless changes are going on in the table every moment, even though our eyes cannot detect them; the same is true of changes in you and me. But the table does not on that account cease to be the same object it was before; nor do I cease to be the same person. Nor, for that matter, is it a different river at this moment although no drop of water in it is any longer in the same place it was before. It is not a *defining* characteristic of rivers that they always contain the same drops of water, much less that these drops of water be at the same place from moment to moment; and as long as this characteristic is not defining, it can keep on being the same river even though the water in it is always changing. The table can undergo any number of changes and still be a table, and indeed the same table it was before as long as it does not cease to have those characteristics which *make* it a table, in other words its defining characteristics.[8] You are the same person as you were ten years ago (does not the use of the word "you" imply this?) even though many things have happened to you in the interim, such as the replacement of every cell in your body by other cells. In general: many characteristics of a thing can change or disappear and be replaced by others, and the thing in question will still be that kind of thing as long as the defining characteristics continue to be present. Thus, tadpoles change into frogs (they lose the defining characteristics of tadpoles), but frogs, although they undergo changes also, always remain frogs (they do not lose the defining characteristics of frogs). It is only if we foolishly take *every* characteristic that a thing has as defining that we reach the conclusion that a thing never persists even through the space of a second, for during the space of a second it always loses *some* characteristic or other, such as the characteristic of having some particular molecule in its body in some particular place. This conclusion can be avoided if we take (as we normally do) a *few* of the characteristics as defining and the rest of them as accompanying; the absence of a characteristic of the latter class in no way prevents it from being "the same river," "the same table," "the same person."

---

[8] The defining characteristics of "same table," "same river," are not the same as those of "table," "river." If a fairy princess could change a round oak table into a square iron table by waving a magic wand, it would still be a table but not *the same* table.

Intrinsic vs. relational characteristics. Any characteristic of a thing can be a defining one. Often, for reasons of convenience, it is the *intrinsic* characteristics, or the characteristics of a thing that do not depend on the existence of other things, which are made defining. Thus, in the case of chemical compounds it is the elements of which the thing is composed that are defining: "salt (ordinary table salt) is whatever is composed of one part sodium and one part chlorine." In the case of organisms it is usually the form or shape of the thing that is defining: thus horses and cows have much the same chemical composition but differ in shape and contour, and this is the distinguishing mark between them. In the case of inorganic objects, such as tables, again it is the shape that is defining: a wooden table would still be a table (that is, it would still be called "table") when petrified into stone, but it would no longer be a table if chopped up into kindling, even though the pile of kindling contained all the matter that was in the table.

But in the case of many words, it is not the intrinsic but the *relational* characteristics that are defining: in other words, characteristics which the thing has only in relation to other things. Thus what distinguishes the class of brothers from all other classes is not only an intrinsic characteristic, their sex, but their relation to other individuals, namely their having the same parents. Hundreds of words are defined in terms of relational, not intrinsic, characteristics: "brother," "husband," "friend," "physician," "general," "superior," "younger," "larger," and so on. One kind of relational characteristic which is sometimes defining is the object's *use*. Thus, words like "chair," "axe," "pen" are sometimes defined in terms of the object's use for sitting, chopping, and writing, rather than in terms of its appearance. Either way of defining these words would have some basis in common usage of them; and, once again, there is no "right" or "wrong" way of defining them. One should not say that there is only *one* right way of defining "axe," and that is in terms of the thing's use or function. (Ask yourself at this point: "How do *I* use the word 'axe'? Would I use the word 'axe' to label something used for chopping but which didn't look like the axes I've seen? Would I use the word 'axe' to label something which I'd call an axe on the basis of its appearance but which was neither designed nor used for chopping?")

Why the relation of words to the world is not precise. Thus far, we

have talked as if all we had to do was to separate out clearly the
defining from the accompanying characteristics, so that we could
mark out exactly the area of the world to which each word applied.
This is, indeed, extremely important, for the reasons we have discussed. But often in practice it is unfortunately impossible to do
this with precision. Why is this so? What are the difficulties in the
way?

The fact that words are ambiguous can hardly be listed as one of
them. If this were our only difficulty, we would have only to state
that word X in one sense designates characteristics A, B, and C,
word X in another sense designates characteristics A, D, and E,
and so on. Each word would still mark out a precise area of the
world, so long as we distinguished one sense of the word from another.

1. There is, however, one very pervasive difficulty, namely *vagueness*. In a general sense, all the difficulties we shall consider can be
said to belong under the heading of vagueness; but the term "vagueness" in philosophy and semantics is more often restricted, so that
words are said to be vague only when there are *continua* (plural of
"continuum") in the world. There is a continuum of colors: red
shades into orange, orange into yellow. By gradations the difficult
becomes the easy, the hot becomes the cold, the fast becomes the
slow. No sharp boundary line can conveniently be drawn for the
use of the word. You cannot say that the word is applicable to
everything in this area and inapplicable to everything outside it;
there is a penumbra or twilight-zone in which it is not clear whether
the word applies or not.

A   C   B
• ——————————— • ———————————— •
                          . D
                          . E
                          . F

Going from A to B in a straight line, you would cross C; C without doubt would be said to be *between* A and B. But would D be
between A and B? We might feel more hesitation here. "Well, not
directly between. But close enough. Let's say it is between." Ordinarily, for example, we would say that Cleveland is between New

York and Chicago, even though it is not on a straight line connecting them. (In that strict sense, *no* city would be between New York and Chicago, for a straight line between them would pass through the interior of the earth. Even if you choose some other strict sense of "between," such as "on the arc of a great circle connecting them," probably there is no city right on the line traced by this arc.)

Suppose our answer then is yes; now what of E? Is it between A and B? Well, if D is, you can hardly say that E is not—after all it is so close to D, it would be a bit arbitrary to say that D is but E is not. Then what of F? The same principle would apply again: E is between A and B, and F is right next to E, so F must be too . . . and so on until we have a point ten thousand miles away still between A and B!

Well, *that* point—call it X—isn't between A and B, surely. Yet E is, by our own admission. What can we make of this? Drawing the line between E and F seems unjustified: E would be between and F wouldn't, and they are so close together. But so is the line between F and G, between G and H, and so forth. There is *no* place where it is satisfactory to draw a boundary line. This is the "difficulty of the slippery slope": you want to go down from the top (you want to admit more than just C as being between A and B); but once you start down the slope, you can't seem to stop short of the bottom; yet you don't want to land *there* either. Set the boundary line anywhere you like, but you will fly in the face of common usage of the word.

You might say that this particular source of difficulty is nature's fault and not ours. We cannot draw a boundary line, except very arbitrarily, for the area of application of a word, simply because nature has presented us with a continuum which makes it impossible to do it satisfactorily.

Sometimes, for one special purpose or another, we have to do it, even though we feel uncomfortable about it. We have to draw the line between passing grades and failing grades, say, at 60, even though there is not much difference between a grade of 59 and a grade of 61—certainly far less than there is between the two passing grades of 61 and 100! But we are forced to draw it somewhere. Ordinarily we do not distinguish sharply between the area of application of the word "city" and that of the word "town," but for statistical purposes the Bureau of the Census has to draw it somewhere, so it draws the line at 2,500. In a town of 2,499 a child is born, and lo, we have a city. In common usage, however, we do not draw such a sharp line, for we can see no justification for it. Thus in common usage these terms remain vague. And vague words do not mark off precisely certain areas in the world: we can show some things to which they definitely do apply, and some others to which they definitely do not, but in between there is a hazy area in which we do not know whether to apply the word to the thing or whether not to do so.

2. Consider an ordinary word like "gold," the name of a chemical element, a metal. What are its characteristics? It is yellow, it has a certain definite melting-point, it has certain characteristic spectral lines, it combines chemically with such-and-such other elements in such-and-such combinations, it has a certain atomic weight, it is used chiefly in coins and jewelry. Now which of these characteristics are defining?

Some are fairly easy to exclude, for instance the use in coins and jewelry; clearly if gold were used for something else it would still be gold. (That is, it would still be *called* "gold," because we, in common usage, have not *made* its use a defining characteristic. Let us never forget that while the characteristics are there, it is we who make them defining. We could have used the noise in another way, to designate a different set of characteristics.) But of some characteristics we are not so certain. Does gold *have* to be yellow? Is this a defining characteristic? Before we reply yes, let us ask not whether all gold *is* yellow but whether it *has* to be—whether we would refuse to call any non-yellow thing gold, even if it had *all the other* characteristics associated with the word "gold." Suppose we came across something that had the required weight, melting point, ductility, and chemical properties, but was not yellow. Would it be gold? are we so sure that being yellow is defining?

Suppose we decide then that it is not really necessary, that being yellow is perhaps a universally accompanying characteristic, but not really a defining one. Now we might lean over to the other extreme: practically every characteristic that gold has is accompanying. We might say: "All that is required is that it have a certain atomic weight. This is the only characteristic that really belongs in the definition; all the rest are merely accompanying. The chemist identifies and defines gold by whether it has this particular weight.

That is all that really matters—that is what keeps gold where it is in the table of the elements. If it has this atomic weight it's gold, and if it doesn't it isn't. Things like color don't matter at all."

But is this any more satisfactory? Suppose that the chemist came across an element that had the required weight, but was purple in color, liquid at ordinary temperatures, had a whole new group of spectral lines, and so forth. Surely he would be reluctant, and so would you, to call it by the name "gold." Or suppose he came across something that was yellow, had the required melting-point, the usual spectral lines, and so forth, but did *not* have the required weight. Wouldn't it still be gold? Wouldn't he feel more inclined to call it gold than the thing that had only the required weight and *none* of the other characteristics?

Suppose, then, he sat down to make a list of all the characteristics that were really necessary, really defining, and *only* these. (He is aware by now that chemistry books often do not distinguish between the two—they list the characteristics of gold but do not say which are accompanying and which are defining.) If he listed only the atomic weight (call this characteristic A), he would feel unsatisfied—the specter of something that had all the other characteristics and not A would haunt him. If he listed a number of properties but not A, however, he would feel even more unsatisfied; he would feel that A was *more* essential than they were. Suppose, then, he listed all of them: not only the weight but the color (B), the spectral lines (C), the melting-point (D), and so on perhaps half a dozen others, he would feel that he had included too much: "Surely not all *this* is necessary?" If he did include all these, then if a thing lacked even *one* of them, it would not be gold! And surely that wouldn't be so! If something had A, B, C, D, E, and F, wouldn't he call it gold even though it lacked G? Then G was not defining. But this wouldn't prove that the first six were defining and G not, for if it had A, B, C, D, E, and G, he would still want to call it "gold" even though it lacked F. So apparently F wasn't defining either. And in the same way he could run through the whole list of characteristics, with none of them being defining. But surely that is absurd! You can't have a thing, or class of things, with *no* defining characteristics whatever! That would mean that there was *no* rule for the word's use—no characteristics that the word designated!

There are many words like this, in which if we are asked what

characteristics are really defining, what characteristics the thing
has to have to be this kind of thing, there is *no* characteristic which
we can point to—there is no characteristic which we absolutely cannot do without. But this does not imply that there is no rule of
usage, *no* conditions to be fulfilled in order for the word to be applicable—what it implies is that *no single characteristic is essential,
as long as the other ones are there.*

Thus, if we take A, B, C, D, E, F, and G, we can say that no
single one of them is essential as long as the others are present—the
thing can receive the name "X" as long as the *majority* of the characteristics are present. It is like the membership in a legislative
body—a quorum must be present, but it doesn't matter which members are there to constitute the quorum. No member is indispensable; there is no member that the meeting can't go on without; but
a majority must be there for it to be held.

How big a majority? All but one? Over 50 per cent? Two-thirds?
There is no definite answer. If it had only A, we wouldn't call it
an X. If it had A, B, C, D, E, F, and G, we would. Would we, if it
had only A and B? or if it had A and B and C? How many of the
characteristics associated with the name "X" would it have to *lack*
in order for us *not* to use the word "X" any more to apply to it?

This question cannot be answered in general. For one thing, it is
not the same for every word—one would have to take every word
separately. For another thing, each of the factors would not necessarily have the same weight. It might be that A was much more
important to our calling it an X than B was, though neither of
them was absolutely essential. We could not say that it was twice
as important, or $4\frac{1}{4}$ times as important—only that when the thing
lacked A (the other characteristics meanwhile remaining the same)
we *felt much more hesitant* to call it "X" than if it lacked B. Possibly if it lacked B we would require *all* the other characteristics to
be present before we would call this thing an X; but if it lacked A,
we would still call it "X" even though two or three or more of the
others were also absent. The meaning of the word is not precise
enough to enable us to give definite weights to each factor A, B, C
. . . the sum of which would tip the scales and make the word applicable. In this case the fault is not nature's but ours: we have not
made clear to ourselves what characteristics we intend to designate
by the term.

We see now how messy the situation has become. We cannot simply say that certain characteristics are defining and others accompanying, and if it has the defining characteristics you can give the name "X" and otherwise not. The situation is not so simple in actual word-usage. There are words, like "triangle" and "seven," that can be treated in this way. But the majority of words we use in ordinary life are not as definite in their meaning. Instead of there being a definite set of criteria for using the word—a specific body of defining characteristics by which we can absolutely test whether the word applies to a given thing or not—there is a set of criteria *none of which alone* is essential, but *several* (though no specific several) of which are required. (The vague word "several" is used advisedly: it can mean two, or three, or a majority, or all but one.)

Under an analysis like this words display enormous ambiguity. You and I might think we had the same characteristics in mind in using the word "gold," since we never disagreed on the denotation of the word, but when it came down to it you might continue to call it gold even though it was not yellow (in the presence, say, of three of the other characteristics) and I might not. Would you call the thing you find somebody living in a house if it provided shelter from the rain? No, you might call it a tent or something else. If it had a rigid enough top part for you to call it a roof? Then you would be more likely to speak of it as a house. But if it had no doors or windows? Then you might be less inclined to call it a house—though the doors and windows wouldn't be absolutely essential if every other feature was there. And so on.

3. But all this suggests a further difficulty. We have just spoken of "every feature" being there; but is there always, in connection with each word, a *definite number* of features of which we can even speak of a majority or quorum being there? We have talked so far as if any several of the characteristics A, B, . . . G were enough to make the word applicable: an indefinite several, but several, something between one and all. But can we be even as definite as that? How many is the "all"? Is there always a definite number to choose from?

There is not. And this constitutes another complication, another monkey-wrench in the machinery of neat and tidy defining characteristics and definitions.

If we label someone as "neurotic," what set of characteristics are we attributing to him? Perhaps he is nervous, perhaps he has a tic, perhaps he bursts into a temper at the slightest provocation, perhaps he is unstable and can't be depended on even in the most ordinary situations, and so on. None of these things is a defining characteristic of his being neurotic; he could do without one or more of them and be neurotic in spite of it. So far it is like the "gold" example. But is there a definite set of characteristics which make him neurotic? Who could make such a list? And who could be sure that it was a complete list (of the criteria he himself implicitly employed) even if he did? Could he be sure that there were no other characteristics the addition of which would make us more likely to call a person neurotic—characteristics which, if added, would add some weight to tip the scales in favor of his being called "neurotic"? Many times there is no such definite number of characteristics on the list. To assign a definite number is to construct an artificially simple verbal situation, often not found in actual word-usage. Probably it is not even present in the "gold" example, though, as words go, "gold" is a clear and precise word. We acted there, for the sake of simplicity, as if there were seven characteristics in question; but this could very easily be disputed. Who can list how many there are in the group of characteristics the presence of which (or of a majority of which) make us call someone "intelligent"?

Why have we not been aware of more of these things before? Nature is kind to us, on the whole, in presenting a world of things in which characteristics occur in groups, together. This is not very true of psychological phenomena, perhaps, but more so of physical. When something has a certain atomic weight, it *also* as a rule presents to us the yellow color and the characteristic spectral lines. Conveniently, mercifully, A and B and C come together—when we find the one we find the others—so we do not have to ask whether we would still call it by the same name if A and B occurred without C, or A without B and C. So as a rule we never bother to ask ourselves the question. But once we ask it, we find that we attach different importances to different characteristics, and discover considerable designative disparity beneath the denotative unity.

But how did this whole unfortunate situation arise? Don't we know what we mean by our own words?

We do attach meanings to words—we give them meanings, otherwise they would be mere noises. But the meanings we give are not clear and definite, only enough so to suit our practical purposes, and sometimes hardly even that. We know roughly what characteristics we have in mind when we give a noise a designation, but we do not know as a rule *exactly* which ones we would consider essential and which we could do without. We use a word, and we have a rather indefinite group of characteristics in mind when we use it, and we let it go at that.

"Don't the words really *have* more precise meanings, even though we don't know them?" The answer should now be obvious. Words have meanings only because we have *given* them meanings, otherwise they would be noises or pen-marks. And they have only *as much* meaning as we give them, no more. If the meaning we give them suffers from the drawbacks outlined above, then the meaning they *have* suffers from those drawbacks, since this is their only source of income. We cannot speak of the meaning as being "really clear, if only we could discover it—what is gold *really?*" The moon has no more light than it reflects from the sun.

Sometimes scientists and other specialists, realizing how sloppy our linguistic habits are, will devise their own special usages of words. They will say, "By 'X' I shall mean A, B, and C." Others may catch on, the word may become a conventional symbol, and an exact usage will now be started within the group. But this situation will generally not last long. For one thing, the word is already ambiguous—it has ordinary usage (however unclear) and the scientist's usage. And some other scientist, feeling the inadequacy of the ordinary sense of the word for his purposes, and either not knowing or ignoring his colleague's verbal innovation, will decide to mean by "X" A, B, and D. And this usage may catch on in other circles, so there will be a third meaning and a threefold ambiguity. (At least three—common usage may be ambiguous too.) But often this is the very thing that happens. Actually the above example is flattering to the scientific situation, because even a scientist often does not think through *exactly* what he will mean by the symbol "X," as we saw in the "gold" example. He may *think* he means simply A and B by "X," but when an instance occurs without C he may decide that "it isn't gold after all." That is, what he says explicitly to his colleagues and himself that he will mean by the word is often changed or contradicted in his actual practice, whether he realizes it or not.

4. But now a new complication descends upon us, the most sweeping of them all. Suppose we define "dragon" as "fire-breathing serpent." This sounds clear enough: two defining characteristics, and that's the end of the matter. But not so: for the questions we asked of the term can now be asked of each term in the *definition*. What is it to be a serpent? could it be a serpent and have one leg? or thicker than it was long? and what must something be like exactly to merit the word "fire"? and suppose the process weren't breathing exactly, but something like it in certain ways, maybe "breathing" would do. . . . And then of each of these words in turn: what is it exactly to have a leg? what kind of protuberance exactly must it be? would this (drawing a picture) be a leg? . . . And so on.

You triumphantly define "murder" as "unjustified killing." But under what conditions exactly is something unjustified? And what is killing? if you leave your child to die of exposure, is that killing? if you drive your wife to suicide, is that killing? or running down a pedestrian in an automobile because you hadn't bothered (or hadn't had the money) to get your car serviced? To kill must you commit a physical act? must you have a certain state of mind or intention? or is it enough that the person be dead because of you, regardless of what you intended or overtly did? And if you decide on the last-mentioned, what is the criterion for "person being dead because of you"? And so on. If "X" is defined in terms of characteristics A and B (an ideally clear situation, as we have seen!), then we must ask what A and B are defined in terms of. A is defined in terms of F, G, H, and B in terms of I, J, K. Then what are F, G, H, I, J, and K defined in terms of? Well, F is defined in terms of M, N, O. . . . But we shall soon run out of letters of the alphabet, and the point is becoming painfully clear.

Thus, even if we have solved the difficulties about one term, "X," and think we have achieved a clear definition, with definite defining characteristics, the presence of which will entitle the thing to be called "X" and the absence of which will prohibit it, we still find the same indefiniteness we were trying so hard to get rid of infesting the words we used in the definition to state these defining characteristics; and the same for those words in turn; and so on. Thus, suppose you call it a house if it has a roof, four walls, and so on; but even if we can agree on a set of defining characteristics for "house," we find that the same questions that confronted us with the word occur all over again with the words used in defining it. What exactly is it to be a roof? Is there one set of characteristics defining *that?* Whatever definition we arrive at for it, the same difficulty will recur for the words in the definition. A definition is no stronger than the words in it, just as a chain is no stronger than its weakest link. Every time you think you have an airtight rule for "X," it can turn out that the very constituents of the rule are not airtight themselves; the plugs that have been put in to fill up the gaps have to be filled up themselves. This phenomenon is sometimes called *"open texture of language."*

This is just the way language is built. As long as words are built up on the basis of previous imprecise words, and those in turn on others, this phenomenon will continue. The mathematical words are, in general, the least subject to it. Second, perhaps, are the words devised for special purposes in the various sciences. (Even here, words in the definition present more difficulty than at first might appear.) The only way to avoid this difficulty would be to invent an artificial language and not use a "natural language" such as English at all. In an artificial language we would start with a few words, left undefined ("primitive terms"), and then would define others in terms of these, and still others in terms of these, being sure at each stage not to use any words which had not been defined in terms of the primitive terms or other words defined at a prior stage in the process.

Finding words to state what we mean. The rules for the application of words to the world are, as we have just seen, not clear-cut and precise; they are given to all the sources of imprecision we have been discussing. Even if words did have exact rules for their application to things, it would not necessarily be easy to state their definitions. People find the greatest difficulty with this, and it is not always because they have not been given clear-cut rules of usage of those words. Indeed, people are often utterly unable to state definitions of words they are using and yet they seem to get along in actually using those words. Who can fail to recognize a cat? and yet who can say in words what he means by "cat"? True, there are possible borderline cases in which we would be undecided as to what to call a given creature—but the point here is that we can and do correctly refer to cats all our lives despite the fact that we cannot usually put into words what the rule for our usage of the word "cat" is—i.e., what we mean by the word when we use it. There are several reasons for this:

1. Often we have a criterion for using the word, but it is *implicit*, not explicit—"in the back of our minds," so to speak. That we have something in mind, however implicitly, is evident from the fact that we refuse to call some things "X" and assent to call others "X" in a *systematic way* which we would not be able to do if we were not doing it in conformity with some principle. When someone says to us "That's not a swan, it isn't white," we say "No, it's still a swan," and we are surely implying that whiteness is not defining of being a swan. And when someone points to a bat and says "That's a bird, see how it flies," we say, "No, it's not a bird at all; it's a mammal," implying that we know at least enough about the defining characteristics of birds and mammals to know which word applies to each —that flying is not a defining characteristic of birds although something else is. We may not know exactly what the dictionary says about the matter, but we know more about the criterion for use of the word than our inability to verbalize about the matter would seem to indicate.

2. Sometimes there are no words to pin down what we want to say in the definition and hence we would not be able to do it even though we were experts at verbalizing. Most words for animals, for instance, are defined according to the general visual appearance of those animals. A cat looks one way, a dog another, a fox still another. Of course, no two dogs look quite alike either, but still they have certain basic similarities to each other which they do *not* have to cats; and if we did not recognize these similarities we could not say of some things "That's a dog" and of others "That's a cat." But, if an animal such as a dog is defined according to its shape, what words have we for such shapes? [9] Aside from a few shape-words such as "square," "circular," "elliptical," "octagonal," "cubical,"

---

[9] We cannot define "dog" as "anything that comes from a dog," since this would obviously be circular—we would have the word "dog" in the definition and would still have to ask what it means. Neither can we define "dog" as "anything that has pups," for "pup" means "little dog" and here we have the word "dog" again. Even the dictionary is not of much help—it generally gives us a combination of accompanying characteristics (where the creature lives, what its habits are, and the like) with the Latin zoological name of the class, which is of course only to exchange one word for another—like saying that "dear" means the same as "cher" but not saying what either of them means.

"spherical," and so on, we do not have words which will distinguish one class of shapes from another. Suppose two pieces of glass break into jagged shapes, what names are there for these two shapes which would distinguish the one from the other? A picture will tell you at once—"a picture is worth ten thousand words"—but there simply is no name for the vast variety of shapes in the world, including the shapes of dogs and cats, or for that matter the shapes of any segment of the outlines of dogs and cats. (The dictionaries themselves usually give diagrams to supplement their "definitions" of animal-words.) We have a "criterion-in-mind," approximately at least, but we cannot put it into words for the very good reason that there are no words into which to put it.

3. Some words are indefinable by means of other words. The reason generally given for this is that they designate something that is unanalyzable. This is a controversial matter which we shall soon discuss.

Stipulative and reportive definitions. When we define a word, we are indicating (presumably to someone else) what the word means. —But this phrase should now sound suspicious. A word, as we have repeatedly observed, doesn't just "mean" something. A word is an arbitrary symbol which is given meaning by human beings. What, then, are we doing when we "indicate what a word means"? We are doing one of two things: either (1) we are stating what *we* are going to mean by it, or (2) we are reporting what people in general, more specifically those who use the language we are speaking, or sometimes some segment of those who use that language, already mean by it. In the first case we are stipulating a meaning, and we have a *stipulative* definition. In the second case we are reporting the usage of others, and we have a *reportive*, or *lexical*, definition.

Usually when we state definitions we state lexical or reportive definitions—the kind we generally get from a dictionary, which reports what meanings are actually attached to different words by the users of a language. (Only rarely does a dictionary try to stipulate or legislate meanings.) We do not usually invent meanings, we report those which the words already have—that is, have been given by others. Thus when we say "A triangle is a closed plane figure bounded by three straight lines" we are saying that English-speaking people use the noise "triangle" to mean the same as "closed

plane figure bounded by three straight lines." We do not have to
stipulate this meaning, we simply report the meaning that is already
there and, presumably, follow this usage ourselves. When a word
has an established meaning in our language we do not feel the need
to stipulate one. As a rule we stipulate only when (1) a word is ambiguous, and we want to indicate which sense we mean—even here
we do not usually stipulate a new meaning, but only point out
which of the several meanings that are already attached to the word
we are using on this occasion; or (2) we feel that a word already
in existence has no clear meaning and we stipulate a clearer one
than it already has—such as when we stipulate a meaning for "democracy," not implying thereby that this correctly reports how most
people speaking English use the word, but only that it is a more
precise one than people generally employ; or (3) we find no word
in existence for some meaning we have in mind, so we invent one:
this is pure stipulation, not report at all because no one has used
this noise before to mean what we are now meaning (intending) by
it.

Can definitions be true or false? It is sometimes said that a definition can be neither true nor false, because when you define a word
you are simply putting into words a resolution as to how you are
going to use the word, and a resolution cannot be true or false. To
this it is sometimes responded, "But a definition *is* true or false. If
someone said a triangle was a four-sided figure, or a horse, or a five-
foot bookshelf, he would be wrong—those would be false definitions!"

You may be inclined to agree with both parties, and it should not
take you long to figure out that both parties are right: the only
difficulty is that the one is talking about stipulative definitions and
the other about reportive definitions. (1) A stipulation is, indeed, a
resolution amounting to this: "Let us (or let me) use the noise 'X'
to mean so-and-so." And a resolution is neither true nor false, any
more than "Let me get out of this room" is true or false. A stipulative definition does not assert that anything is or is not the case; it
simply suggests that a certain noise be used to designate a certain
set of characteristics. On the other hand, (2) a reportive definition
is indeed true or false. If someone defines "triangle" as a four-sided
figure, meaning by this that the word "triangle" is used in English
to stand for figures with four sides, this would be a false state-

ment—it would be a false report about how a word in the English language is used. Reportive definitions are reports of word-usage, and there can be true reports and false reports. In this sense, then, definitions not only can be, but are, true or false.

Do we give definitions or do we find them? In the case of stipulative definitions, clearly we give them. In the case of reportive definitions, we find them in the sense that we find what meanings *other human beings have given* to the words. No one ever found a definition that somebody before him had not given.

People do sometimes speak of trying to discover a definition when no definition has yet been found. One is tempted to ask, "if nobody ever *gave* a definition to a word (or to a noise, to make it a word), how did it ever *acquire* one? Words don't have definitions 'just naturally.' What definition could a word have other than what people give it? Once again, to state a definition is to state what characteristics a word designates—in other words, to state its meaning in one sense of 'meaning.' Surely no one can deny that a word has only as much meaning as its users give it? If no meaning has been given it, it is just a noise."

All this will be admitted; nevertheless, there is a school of thought which holds that it is not merely words, but *things,* that people define. "All you have said applies to defining words; but more important than defining words is defining things."

What kind of activity is defining things supposed to be? We know what it is like to define a word; but what is it like to define a thing? Surely, we might think, the word "definition" applies only to symbols. This, however, is a verbal matter: *we* may prefer to restrict the word "definition" to symbols, while someone else may prefer to extend the use of the word "definition" to cover things as well as symbols. And surely he can extend the use of the word if he so desires (freedom of stipulation). The question is not "Can he extend the use of the word 'definition'?" but rather, "What kind of activity is one engaging in when he claims to be giving definitions of things?" The person who claims to do this is said to be a believer in *real definitions.* In that case, what are real definitions?

1. "Real definitions give us the meanings of things." The word "meaning" can be used to apply to things as well as to words, as we saw on pages 10–12; we may discover the meaning of a thing in the sense of its cause, its explanation, its inner structure, and so

forth. But is it not misleading to speak of this as definition? It is
misleading enough to speak of it as meaning!

2. Real definitions tell us the essence of things, the true nature
of things. The words "essence" and "nature" have been discussed on
page 34. Usually when we ask for the essence of something we are
asking for its *most essential* characteristics—those in terms of which
the word naming it is defined. "What is the essence of X?" we are
asked; and we reply by stating some or all of the defining characteristics of X. In these cases, what is defined is always a word or a
phrase—a symbol. The language of "essence," however, may mislead us into thinking that we are defining things.

3. Sometimes it happens that the most important, the most fundamental (in some sense) of the characteristics of a thing or group
of things has not yet been discovered, and that once this characteristic is discovered, it is made defining. When this happens, it may
be said that "the real definition" of the thing has been found. For
example, a psychologist may say, "For years we have hunted for
the definition of schizophrenia, and now we have found it." What
has been found? For years trained observers have found certain
patterns of behavior recurring, not every one of them in every case,
but most of them: A, B, C, D. . . . Now another characteristic, M,
is found, and M is more important than the rest, since knowing that
M is present enables psychologists to explain *why* some or all of the
other characteristics are present—just as knowing the atomic structure of an element explains some of its chemical properties. M is so
important to this whole set of characteristics that the word "X" (in
this case "schizophrenia") is now defined partially in terms of M:
in other words, M is made a defining characteristic. Now, one might
describe this situation by saying that he had *found* the definition of
X. It would be less misleading, however, if he said merely that he
had found a new characteristic of X, the presence of which explained the presence of previously observed characteristics, and
therefore it became convenient to shift the definition a bit in order
to make M a defining characteristic.

Word-word definitions and word-thing definitions. In this book,
at any rate, we shall speak only of defining words, not the things
named by the words. There are, however, two kinds of definition of
words which we may give: (1) word-word definitions, in which we
say that a certain word means the same as a certain other word or

words; (2) word-thing definitions, in which we say what characteristics a thing must have in order to be labeled by the word.

It is word-thing definitions which we have been discussing so far,
for we have been discussing the relation of words to the world. In
word-thing definitions, we either stipulate that the word shall, or
report that the word does, designate the characteristics a thing must
have for the word to apply to it.

In word-word definitions we merely relate the word to other
words. For example, "dog" means the same as "chien." We could
know that this English word means the same as that French word
without knowing what *things* either of them applied to, or what
characteristics the word designates. Again—this example is taken
from within one language—to be told that "asteroid" means the
same as "planetoid" is not to be told what either one of them
means. Usually, of course, when we are told that this expression
means the same as that, we already know what the first one designates. But it is possible that someone might know about every word
in one language its equivalent in another language, without knowing what is designated by a single word in either. Such a person
would have a system of word-word definitions but would be quite
unable to relate these words to the world: he would have no word-
thing definitions.

Ways of relating words to the world. 1. The clearest and most precise way of relating a word to the world is to state its (word-thing)
definition—to state what characteristics it designates. This gives,
as we have seen, a criterion for the use of the word. In common
usage there is often no single clear criterion, and to make the application of the word precise we must often stipulate a definition
rather than report one already in use.

2. Sometimes it is difficult or even impossible to state exactly
what the word means, but we are able to take the whole sentence
in which it is embedded and state what *it* means. Thus, we say
what the word "brother" means if we say, "X is the brother of Y
means that X is a male having the same parents as Y." This is
known as a *contextual* definition of "brother," or sometimes as a
definition-in-use.

3. We can show what a word means by listing some of the things
denoted by it. Thus one might say, " 'Bird?' That means robins,
chickadees, sparrows, wrens, and so on." This method, of course,

does not give us a criterion for the application of the word to the world; it simply tells us what a few of its applications are. Moreover, it may be misleading: we might conclude from a list of things denoted by the word that flying is a defining characteristic of birds, and this conclusion would be false. Incomplete and misleading though it is, however, denotation is often employed as a method of showing how a word applies to the world.

4. Thus far all the methods have involved the use of words. *Ostensive definition*, however, does not employ words at all. (One might say that it is not definition at all. That is a terminological matter concerning how broadly we wish to use the word "definition." But whether we call it definition or not, it is a way of connecting words with the world.) Ostensive definition, as the name implies, *shows* you, *confronts* you with, an instance or instances of the word's denotation. Showing someone a beech tree would be giving him an ostensive definition of the term "beech tree." No words except "beech tree" (with an act of pointing) need be used. All the other ways of applying words to the world involve words: they are verbal.[10]

It would seem that the meanings of at least *some* of the words in a language have to be indicated ostensively. Suppose for a moment that we have only verbal definitions. Each word is defined, and in doing so, other words are used. This will help us only if we already know what these other words mean. How will we find out what they mean? By having their meaning explained by the use of still other words. And so on. But how can this process go on forever? Must we not eventually come to the point where we directly connect words with things, and not with other words, lest we be caught up forever in the circle of our own words? If we do not sooner or later come to a point where we directly connect a word with a thing— sometimes by pointing, sometimes by more complicated non-verbal means—then the realm of words would be forever separated from the realm of things. To connect words with the world, we need ostensive definition. How, otherwise, would we have *begun* to learn the meanings of words? When we learned our first word, we could not learn it by having other words thrown at us, for we would not have known what they meant. As a matter of fact we probably

---

[10] Not merely word-word definitions but word-thing definitions are verbal, for in explaining what the defining characteristics are you are using words.

learned most of the words of ordinary life ostensively, although now, being adults and having accumulated a considerable reservoir of *words*, we learn most of our new words by means of them.

How could we learn the meaning of a word ostensively? If Mother points to the table and says "Table," how can we know from this what "table" means? We can know that *this particular thing* is called "table," but what about that thing over there? Is it a table too? Now Mother has to go through another act of pointing and says "chair." Then what about this thing here? It looks more like the first thing she pointed to than the second. Yes, here too she says "Table." And that thing in the corner? It's sort of like the others. No, here she says "Desk." Well, the two things she called "table" were more alike than either of them were to the thing she called "chair."

Or perhaps you thought that Desk and Table No. 1 were more alike than Table No. 1 was to Table No. 2. That puzzled you. Then you had to sit down to think what it was about Desk that was different from either of the others. After all, Desk was brown, Table No. 1 was brown, Table No. 2 was white. So it couldn't be the color. Desk was square, Table No. 1 was square, Table No. 2 was round. So it couldn't be the shape. Maybe it was that in Desk there were some funny-looking things that extended almost all the way to the floor and that you could pull out, but not so with Table No. 1 or Table No. 2. Or maybe it was that Mother sat down with pen and paper at Desk. Thus, by a gradual process of abstraction (sifting out the characteristics that all the things with one name had but none of the others did), you got a fair idea of what Mother meant when she used these words.

This is not intended to be an accurate description of a process through which you went in learning words; especially at an early age, it could hardly have been as explicit as that. Yet something of the kind must have gone on, otherwise you would never have grown up to use these words in the same way your parents did, even in the case of words standing for objects that you had never seen before. You certainly didn't learn them verbally; few adults have ever asked themselves, "What is the definition of 'table'?"

The business of giving ostensive definitions, and of learning them, is much more detailed than just pointing to something and pronouncing a word. At the least, it consists of a series of successive pointings and pronouncings, so that you can reflect on what the things given the same name had in common which weren't shared by those not given the same name. Indeed, with just one act of pointing to a table you wouldn't know what was meant—the table itself, its color, its shape, its upright position, what it was made of, or some other characteristic.

> Let us say that we are playing golf and that we have hit the ball in a certain way with certain unfortunate results, so that our companion says to us, "That's a bad *slice*." He repeats this remark every time our ball fails to go straight. If we are reasonably bright, we learn in a very short time to say, when it happens again, "That's a bad slice." On one occasion, however, our friend says to us, "That's not a *slice* this time; that's a *hook*." In this case we wonder what has happened, and we wonder what is different about the last stroke from those previous. As soon as we make the distinction, we have added still another word to our vocabulary. The result is that after nine holes of golf, we can use both these words accurately—and perhaps several others as well, such as "divot," "number-five iron," "approach shot," *without ever having been told what they mean*. Indeed, we may play golf for years without ever being able to give a dictionary definition of "to slice": "To strike (the ball) so that the face of the club draws inward across the face of the ball, causing it to curve toward the right in flight (with a right-handed player)." [11]

Nor is it always pointing that will do the trick. You certainly can't point to thoughts, emotions, or acts of willing. You can't point to fear or anxiety—you can only point to manifestations of them. You can't indicate the meaning of these terms directly at all —you can't enter your son's mind when he is afraid and say "That's fear"; but you can watch him when he gives every indication of being afraid and say "When you act that way, you're afraid." In doing this we rely on the assumption that when one person feels fear he behaves pretty much like another does when he feels fear, at least enough so that it is safe to use the same word for both persons' states. Because you cannot always tell, you sometimes label something "fear" which closer inspection or observation makes you label "anxiety."

Even the meanings of abstract words, like "change" and "again," can be indicated ostensively—we certainly never learned *them* ver-

[11] S. I. Hayakawa, *Language in Action* (New York: Harcourt Brace & Co., 1941), p. 45. Reprinted by permission of the publisher.

bally. (Try to define them verbally!) When you saw the neighbor's
car parked every day in front of your house, and finally it parked
next door; Mother said "Now it's in a different place," but she may
also have said, "Well! that's a change." And lest you think that
"change" just meant "cars parking in a different place," she used
the same word the next day to label something quite different—the
turning of the weather, or the sudden increase in the price of eggs.
By a gradual process of abstraction you learned how to use the word
"change." Or, when the car had a blowout in front of your house,
and the next day it happened to another car there, Mother said,
"Why, it's happened *again*." But you learned that it had nothing to
do with cars having blowouts when she used the word after you
spilled soup on the table for the second time. And so on—by this
gradual process of repetition and abstraction you came to know
(though not in these words of course) that the word "again" has to
do not with any event or type of event, but with the general *repeti-
tiveness* of the events. And in every case, you learned the meanings
of the words ostensively—it was a long time before you could grasp
the meaning of a word verbally, without being confronted with an
instance of its application.

Are there words that can be defined only ostensively? "Are there
indefinable words?" it is sometimes asked. If this question employs
a broad definition of the word "define," so that to define a word is
to indicate *in some way or other* what it means, the answer is clearly
No. If there were no way of indicating to another person what you
meant by it, its meaning could not be communicated, and it could
never become a conventional symbol. It might be an item in your
private vocabulary, to be used in communing with yourself, but it
could never become a part of a public language.

But if, in asking the question, one means to ask whether there are
words whose defining characteristic cannot be explained (by using
other words)—that is, whether there are words whose meaning cannot be indicated verbally, but only ostensively—then the question
is a controversial one. The issue might be argued this way:

A. Some words, principally those standing for elementary sense-expe-
riences such as "red," "color," "shrill," "pungent," "bitter," "fear," "anger,"
"love," "thought," and so on, simply cannot be defined verbally. Who can
say in words what the word "fear" means? Fear is something with which
everyone is acquainted through personal experience, but who can define the

word "fear" verbally? You may be able to state scientifically the conditions under which people have this feeling, or what the state of the nervous system is when fear is experienced, or what things fear is a response to, or to give a psychoanalytic explanation of it, but all these after all are not definitions of the *word* "fear" but facts about the *thing*, fear, and an acquaintance with the meaning of the "word" fear is *presupposed* in all these descriptions. The same is true of many other words: how, for example, would one define the word "red"? It may seem that here the case for definability is much easier, because we can give a definition in terms of wavelengths of light. But this again is a confusion. What we want defined is the word naming the color that we see—and it is not the wave-lengths that we see. Waves of light (within the span 4000–7500 Angstrom units) are only *correlated* with the colors that we see, but are not themselves the colors. We can say that *when* I see red, light-waves of this kind are emanating from the object to my eye; when I see orange, . . . and so on. But the presence of light-waves of this length is only an *accompanying* characteristic. I want to know what the word "red" means, not what the color red is correlated with. And this is just what no words can give me; only direct first-person experience of red can give that to me. If you have been born blind, I can never, by any number of words, tell you what "red" means; I could only talk about accompanying characteristics like the waves of light. If you have seen red, words are unnecessary; and if you haven't, they are useless. In short, here is one of those ultimate words in terms of which other words can be defined, but which cannot itself be defined by means of other words. Here language comes into direct contact with the world, and using more language won't help; for terms like "red" are the rock-bottom of language. Like the ultimate particles of physics which are the building-blocks of the physical universe, they cannot be broken down into further constituents.

B. But *are* words like "red" indefinable verbally? Granted, we can't define "red" in terms of wave-lengths. But can't we define "red" verbally as *the one and only color invariably associated with this range of wavelengths?* or perhaps as the color occurring at a given place on the spectrum? This is not a crude identification of red with a wave-length, but a definition of "red" as that which alone is associated with that wave-length. Why isn't this satisfactory?

A. But please keep in mind the distinction between defining and accompanying characteristics. Your attempted definition makes the same mistake as the one we both reject, though not as crudely. We see the color red; very well. Now suppose that in the course of events we came to see this color even in the total absence of wave-lengths—as indeed we now do when we see red spots before our eyes or see red in our dreams. Even if we never did in fact see red under these unusual conditions, it is always conceivable that the conditions under which we regularly see various colors might change. Then we couldn't say that red was associated with this wave-length; after all, if red became associated with a different wave-length, it would still be red, so the wave-length can't be a part of the definition. Just as steel which is no longer used for purposes of construction would still be steel, so red which is no longer correlated with a certain wave-length would still be red, if it looks the way red now does. The same would hold if we no longer saw the colors in their present order on the spectrum. The fact is this: regardless of where we see it, or with what concomitants or correlations, or in what order or arrangement, it's still red we see!

B. Couldn't we say that the word "red" names the color which to the normal eye, or to the normal eye under normal conditions, is accompanied by light-waves of length 4000–7500 Angstrom units? Then we'd get around these exceptional cases.

A. But suppose that the structure of the eye changed or optical laws changed, and nobody any longer saw red when light-waves of this length impinged on the retina? Just as it is possible that people now and then see red in the absence of these physical conditions, so it is possible that people regularly would come to see red in the absence of them.

B. But all these changed laws and changed conditions are hypothetical—the fact is that we *do* see red regularly when light within a definite span of wave-length is present.

A. True, but—so what? *If* we saw red without these physical conditions being present, it would still be red we saw. As long as that is the case, the physical conditions cannot constitute a defining characteristic. *If* steel were no longer used in construction, it would still be steel. Steel doesn't have to stop being used in construction, in order for that statement to be true. Remember Venn's motto: "The practical test in fact, when we wish to know whether any proposed definition is a true one or not, is to try whether by conceivable variation of circumstances we can cause it to break down, by its exclusion of what we are resolved to retain or its inclusion of what we are resolved to reject." In the present case all the conditions suggested break down—by easily conceivable variation of circumstances. Which shows again that these are merely *accompanying* characteristics—the mere external trappings of the red, as it were, not the red itself.

B. Perhaps. But here is a consideration that may not have occurred to you. You say that the man born blind can never know what the word "red" means, since the word names a color and he can't see colors. But he may be able to use the word as correctly and as accurately as any of the rest of us. He may be infallible in his use of the word. He can always tell when something is red—perhaps by feeling with his fingers the indicator on a machine that records wave-lengths of light. How could he use the word "red" correctly so systematically if he didn't know the meaning of the word?

A. Here again we get involved in accompanying characteristics. Remember the red-round example? Let's suppose that the man who is supposed to find out what things are red is blind. But he has been told reliably that everything that's red is round, and everything that's round is red. Each always accompanies the other. He can easily tell whether to say "That's red" or "That's not red" by feeling the thing's shape. One could accept his word on which things are red just as well as the word of a man who can see. An outsider might not even know that he couldn't see red but was just taking the presence of roundness as a sure sign that there was redness too. Yes, he would use the word "red" correctly—*as long as redness and round-ness continued happily to go together.* The minute this perfect correlation stopped, he would be lost. Don't you see? The man doesn't know what "red" means; he doesn't know what a thing has to look like in order to be red. Surely not that it be round—and yet *that is all he has to go by!*

The word "red," then, designates a color-quality which is the very thing the blind man can have no experience of. The blind man can never know *what* it is that the man with sight means by the term. All he can know is that the word "red" stands for an X which is distinguished from Y's and Z's. He can make the distinction too if redness always goes along with *other* characteristics which he *can* detect; but he can never make the distinction on the basis of a thing's *redness.*

B. What about the man who can see? Can *he* state a criterion for the use of the term "red"?

A. He has a criterion, of course—otherwise he would not know when to use the word "red" and when not to. But the criterion is simply whether this particular shade of color is present to his consciousness. *He* knows how to distinguish it from other colors, but there is no way of stating in *words* how to do this, and therefore he cannot communicate the criterion to those who do not also see red. In short, he has a criterion for the use of the word "red," but he cannot state it in words; all that can be stated in words turn out to be accompanying characteristics. The defining characteristic of "red" cannot be stated so as to distinguish it from other colors. Thus, you see, "red" is *verbally* indefinable.

This by no means puts an end to the controversy, but we shall not try to deal with it further here. The whole issue of verbally inde-finable words is still a controversial one.

Can you know what X is if you don't know the definition of "X"? We are now in a position to answer a few questions involving defi-nition, which previously might have puzzled us. Can we know what a cat is if we don't know the definition of the word "cat"?

The question, of course, is ambiguous. Let us assume that "know-ing what a cat is" means the same as "knowing the meaning of the word 'cat.'" Now, is knowing the meaning of the word the same as knowing its definition?

There is still an ambiguity here—in the word "meaning." Most people are quite sure that they know what a cat is—what the word "cat" means—though they are quite unable to say that a cat is a domesticated carnivorous quadruped, a mammal of the genus *Felis libyca domestica,* and the like. They are quite able, however, to distinguish cats from non-cats, to use the word "cat" and communicate their meaning, to point to cats without ever making a mistake. Being able to do these things, do they know what "cat" means? That depends:

1. If knowing the meaning is being able to state a definition, most people are unable to do this and hence do not know the meaning of the word in that strict sense.

2. If knowing the meaning is having some criterion for the use of the word (though they may be unable to state it), most people do. They might be puzzled if borderline cases occurred—for example, if their cat swelled to 50 times its normal size and started to bark, they would not know whether to say it had turned into something else or was simply a very unusual cat—but on the whole they know more about the characteristics they would consider defining than their inability to voice them would indicate. For example, they know approximately what a thing would have to look like before they would call it a cat, although they have no words for describing precisely these complex visual shapes.

3. If knowing the meaning of "cat" is merely being able to indicate ostensively some instances of cats, or perhaps to name (rather than point to) some denotations of the word, very few people are unable to do this. When we *first* learned the meaning of the word—ostensively—this is all we were able to do. Only gradually did we develop a criterion for the use of the word, thus becoming more efficient in handling it. In this process we graduated from knowing the meaning in sense 3 to knowing it in sense 2.[12]

Can you know any facts about X without knowing what X is? Can you know anything *about* a cat without knowing what a cat is? Can you know anything about man without knowing what man is? Again, the question is ambiguous.

If "knowing what X is" means the same as "knowing what the *word* 'X' means," everything will again depend on the sense in which one "knows what 'X' means." You can surely know a great many facts about cats (accompanying characteristics) without being able to say what the defining characteristics are or to state

---

[12] The word "definition" is also ambiguous. Thus, if listing denotations and indicating instances ostensively are called "definition" (definition in the broad sense that includes *any* way, however incomplete, of indicating what a word means) then, of course, "knowing the meaning" and "knowing the definition" are the same, and you know the definition in all three of the above cases of knowing the meaning.

the definition. On the other hand, if you had *no* criterion in mind whatever for the use of the term, how could you identify the X that you were giving facts about? At the very least you would have to be able to pick out some items in the universe, the X's, and separate them from other items which were not X's. And how could you do this unless you knew in some sense what the word "X" meant? If people do not really know what a certain word means, in *any* sense, how can they know what they are talking about when they use it? This much at least would seem to be essential before you can state any facts which you know to be facts *about X*.

IV. SENTENCES AND PROPOSITIONS

Ordinarily we utter not just words and phrases, but *sentences*. We shall not attempt here an exact definition of the word "sentence"; linguists and philologists have an interesting time with such questions. It is enough to say that on any definition of "sentence," a sentence is not merely a string of words. Even if every word in a string has a definite and precise meaning, the sentence does not necessarily have meaning. "Triangle square parallelogram circle" is not a sentence. Sentences are (metaphorically speaking) a "second dimension" of meaning, just as planes in geometry are a second dimension of space.

Common usage of language does not distinguish sharply between the word "sentence" and the word "proposition," though it more frequently employs the first. But this is one of those cases in which a special subject-matter has found it necessary for the sake of clarity to make a distinction between them. The distinction can perhaps be brought out best in this way: Different sentences can state one and the same proposition. Here are two sentences: "New York is larger than San Francisco" and "San Francisco is smaller than New York." These sentences differ from each other in several ways: the first contains the letter "s" three times, the second contains it four times. The first contains the word "larger," the second does not. Yet they both state the same proposition; they both give the same information, they both assert the existence of the same state of affairs. When you understand the meaning of the first sentence, you are understanding the same thing as you are when you understand the meaning of the second sentence. If you have been told the first and understand it, the second does not come to you as a *second* piece of information; it is the same information that was already conveyed by the first. If the two sentences are in different languages, the same thing holds: the sentence "Brutus killed Caesar" states the same proposition as does the Latin sentence "Brutus Caesarem occidit."

It is the proposition, not the sentence, which is true or false. The sentence merely states (sometimes we use the word "expresses") the proposition. Instead of saying, "This sentence is true," we say "The proposition expressed by this sentence is true" (and the same proposition could be expressed by a different sentence). When we talk about grammar, word combinations, and language in general— those things having to do with how meanings are expressed—we are talking about sentences. When, however, we are concerned with the meanings themselves rather than the means of their expression, it is the propositions to which we are directing our attention.

What sentences mean. We have examined the meanings of words; now what about the meanings of sentences?

1. Just as words are labels of things, think of sentences as labels of situations or *states-of-affairs*. Just as the word "chair" labels a thing, so the sentence "I am sitting on a chair" labels a situation, for example, the situation in which I now find myself, but not the situation I was in last night when I slept.

2. But just as most words stand for many things, so most sentences stand for many states-of-affairs. The sentence "A book is on the table" correctly labels a situation now on my study table, on the dining room table or on some tables in your house. The sentence denotes all these situations, and it designates those characteristics which a situation or state-of-affairs must have in order for the sentence to be applicable to that situation.

3. A sentence need not stand merely for *actual* states-of-affairs. It can stand also for nonexistent but imaginable or conceivable states-of-affairs that never existed and probably never will exist, in other words, for *possible* states-of-affairs, in a very broad sense of "possible" (logically possible) to be discussed in the next chapter.

If we said that a sentence stands for *actual* states-of-affairs, there would be no accounting for sentences expressing *false* propositions. What of the propositions expressed by these sentences: "Human beings have established communication with inhabitants of Mars";

"She jumped out of the window but instead of going downwards she flew upwards for ten thousand miles"; and so on? They are false, to be sure, but the sentences stand for *something*. If sentences could stand only for actual states-of-affairs, these sentences would stand for nothing and, in the most important sense of "meaning," would mean nothing. Yet clearly they are far from meaningless. Don't know well enough what they mean? And isn't it because we do that we are able to say that the propositions are false? Sentences, then, stand for states-of-affairs, but these states-of-affairs need not be actual.

Truth. A proposition is true when the state-of-affairs expressed by the sentence asserting it is *actual,* and false when it is not actual. The proposition expressed by the sentence "Snow is white" is true if, and only if, the situation it alleges is actual, that is, if snow really *is* white. Thus, to say

"Snow is white" is true [13]

is to say the same as

Snow is white.

The mysterious-sounding question "What is truth?" asked by Pontius Pilate becomes the question "What are true propositions?" The answer is simply this: "A true proposition is one standing for a state-of-affairs which is actual." However, the interesting questions about truth—those which people have somewhat inchoately in mind when they ask "What is truth?"—have chiefly to do with how a proposition can be known to be true. There are different kinds of truths, that is, different kinds of true propositions, and the ways of discovering whether or not they are true are not always the same. What kinds of truths there are, and how we can know them to be true, is the subject of the next chapter.

Ambiguity of the word "proposition." Do sentences stand for propositions? We have said that they stand for states-of-affairs. But propositions are true or false, and states-of-affairs are not true or false, they just *are,* exactly as tables aren't true or false, but simply are. Yet a sentence cannot stand both for what is true or false and what is not true or false. There must be something wrong here.

Again, there is an ambiguity, this time in the word "proposition."

[13] I.e., the proposition expressed by the sentence "Snow is white" is true.

The word can stand for (1) that which is true or false—not the sentence "Rover is a dog" but what this sentence has in common with all other sentences having the same meaning. But it can also stand for (2) what the sentence means: either what states-of-affairs it denotes, or what characteristics of states-of-affairs it designates. We are using the word "proposition" only in the first sense: thus, a proposition is true or false, but the sentence expressing it stands for states-of-affairs which either exist or do not exist.

Would there still be propositions even if there were no human beings? In the second sense, yes; there would still be possible states-of-affairs, even if there were no world at all. In the first sense, the answer would be no; without people there would be no language and no sentences, because there would be nobody to utter them.

There are many puzzles of a technical nature which we could get into at this point in pursuing the relation between sentences, propositions, and states-of-affairs. Many months could be spent in considering these alone. The solution of these puzzles, however, is of no particular relevance to the later portions of this book. The important thing to keep in mind here is the distinction between the false and the meaningless. A false proposition asserts a possible state-of-affairs to be actual when it is not (for example, "It rains every day all over the world"); a meaningless sentence expresses no proposition whatever, for there is no state-of-affairs whose actuality is being asserted.[14]

Meaningless sentences. But *can* sentences be meaningless? That depends, of course, on how broadly we use the word "sentence" and the word "meaning." To call every group of words a sentence would seem a bit liberal; grammarians at any rate would hesitate to call something a sentence unless the words in it were arranged in accordance with certain grammatical rules, involving at least that it have a subject term and a verb. Thus:

1. "Snigledz busay rethmuck" would not only be meaningless, but would not be considered a sentence. It is composed not of words but of mere noises which have been *given* no meanings and hence are not words. (Needless to say, if someone in his own private vo-

---

[14] In spite of the fact that the word "statement" may sometimes obscure the distinction between sentences and propositions, in succeeding chapters we shall use the word "statement" instead of "proposition." It is less stilted and far more in accord with common usage.

cabulary had assigned a meaning to each of these noises, if he were using them to mean the same as "The moon has risen," for example, his assertion would be a sentence expressing a proposition, albeit a proposition expressed in a peculiar and unconventional way.)

If even one noise that has been assigned no meaning occurs in the group, the whole sentence becomes meaningless: for example, "The snispera fell down"—unless, again, "snispera" has been made into an arbitrary symbol by its user. As far as common usage of language is concerned, it is meaningless, because it has been given no meaning. Is the whole expression a sentence? That depends on how broadly we use the word "sentence": we might call it a sentence because it is in grammatical form but a meaningless one because of the one meaningless noise; on the other hand, we might on that account refuse to call it a sentence at all.

2. We may have an assemblage not of mere noises but of actual words, and still not have a meaningful sentence. "Chair below unsightly fast" consists of four words, but because they don't add up to anything and lack even the subject-verb combination, they remain four individual words and are not a sentence.

3. Often a sentence is meaningless, not because it fails to contain words, nor because rules of syntax have not been observed, but because one or more of the words have no meaning *in this context*. For example, here on the earth we can speak of a direction as being up or down, and of one thing as being above or below another. "Down" means toward the center of the earth, and "A is above B" means the same as "A is further from the center of the earth than is B" (usually it also involves being pretty nearly in the same vertical line). If we landed on Mars in a space ship we could still speak of up and down, above and below, only now it would have reference to the center of Mars, not of the earth. But suppose we were out in the midst of space and not within the gravitational field of any particular planet or star. What would we then mean by asking whether we were going up or down, or were above or below something else? The words "up" and "down" and "above" and "below" have meaning only with reference to some body, usually a body like the earth, large enough to exert a considerable gravitational attraction; apart from this context, they are just as meaningless as "snispera." Thus, it would be meaningless to say that an object was above the universe in general, or above space (because

"above" has meaning only *within* space), or above the number 2 (though not above the *numeral* "2" written on the blackboard, which *stands for* the number), or above time, or above a logical contradiction, or above goodness—except, of course, in some figurative sense of these phrases.

It is perhaps a natural human tendency to assume that because a noise has (been given) meaning in one context, it has it in all contexts. But as we have just seen, this is not so; outside a definite spatial context the word "above" (interpreted literally and not figuratively) is as meaningless as if it were a mere noise. This third kind of meaningless sentence, then, is far more apt to mislead us into thinking there is meaning when there is not than either of the others. We shall find numerous examples of it in subsequent pages.

Non-assertive sentences. There are many sentences which no one would deny to be meaningful, yet which assert nothing. (1) *Questions.* "What time is it?" asserts nothing, and hence is neither true nor false; yet we all know what it means well enough to know how to answer it. (2) *Imperatives.* "Shut the door!" is not true or false; it asserts nothing; rather it commands. ("I have just shut the door," however, is an assertion, and it must be either true or false.) Milder imperatives which are not commands but rather suggestions, such as "Let's leave the room," assert nothing and thus are neither true nor false. (3) *Exclamations.* "Oh!" and "What a day!" are not usually considered sentences at all; at any rate, they express no propositions. Some exclamatory sentences, however, in addition to exclaiming, *imply* propositions. When you exclaim, "What a sunny day it is!" you are implying a proposition, namely that it is a sunny day, and this, of course, is either true or false. Someone might reply, "Why, that's not true, it's not a sunny day at all," thus showing that he interpreted your sentence to assert something. In every case the test to apply is "Is the answer 'That's true' or 'That's false' appropriate?" One and the same sentence uttering an exclamation might be intended to assert, when uttered by one speaker, and intended merely to exclaim and not assert at all, when uttered by another speaker. "What a day!" may be intended merely to let off steam, or it may be intended not only to do this but to assert that it is day rather than night at the time the exclamation is uttered.

Thus far none of the non-assertive sentences have even been in the declarative form in which assertions are usually cast. By far the most misleading kind of sentence is the one which is in assertive or declarative form and thus gives every indication that it asserts something, *but*, as it turns out, it asserts nothing whatever: it serves merely to "let off steam" and to "get up steam" in somebody else. In one sense of "meaning," such sentences have no meaning; but in other senses, they have.

Emotive meaning. When someone says, "That dress is gorgeous," the sentence is in the form of an assertion, like "That dress is green." But it is difficult to say *what* the person who utters the sentence is asserting. Does the first sentence say that the dress possesses a characteristic, gorgeousness, as the second sentence says that it possesses the characteristic of greenness? But if so what is this characteristic? It is very difficult to pin down what the first sentence asserts, because it is not clear what sort of a characteristic is designated by the word "gorgeous." Yet the effect of the sentence on the lady to whom it is addressed is clear: its effect is, as we say, to "make her feel good." Moreover, it may express approval of the dress on the part of the speaker; in uttering the sentence he probably does not intend to *assert* that he likes or approves the dress, but his sentence expresses (evinces) his approval. Both these effects of the utterance of the sentence—on the listener and on the speaker —may be clear and manifest, without what is being *asserted* being clear at all. In other words, it is not clear what *cognitive* meaning the sentence has, or even whether it has any at all; but there is no question what its *emotive* meaning is.

In Chapters 7 and 8 we shall be concerned with sentences of this type; we shall see how important it is to disentangle their cognitive meaning (what they assert) from their emotive meaning (what feelings they cause). What makes the situation so difficult is that so many sentences have cognitive meaning and emotive meaning at the same time. Not only this, but the proportions of each may vary from occasion to occasion of the sentence's utterance: one and the same sentence may be primarily cognitive in its meaning at one time, and primarily emotive at another time.

Assuming that some particular sentence has emotive meaning only, should it be called a *meaningful* sentence at all? This of course depends on how narrowly we choose to use the word "meaning." As long as we distinguish the various functions of sentences from each other, it does not much matter whether we call them all by the name of "meaning." One could restrict the use of the word "meaning" to what we have called cognitive meaning, saying that "the rest isn't meaning, but just effects." In this sense, sentences having only what we called emotive meaning would be strictly meaningless. Or, one could include effects of sentences as meanings (as we did with things in Section I), and say that there are different senses of the word "meaning," for example, cognitive meaning and emotive meaning. We shall adopt the latter terminology in this book, speaking of the emotional effects of sentences as meaning, but, of course, as emotive meaning, not meaning in the sense of designation.

Sometimes the term "emotive meaning" is used to apply to sentences only when the sentences have a fairly *widespread, uniform* response, just as a noise is called a word only if there is a convention, a widespread use of an arbitrary symbol. If this added restriction is accepted, we could say that a sentence like "I think you're absolutely wonderful" has a definite emotive meaning—just as definite as "Triangles have three angles" has cognitive meaning —because everyone who understands English will react to the words in pretty much the same way; to be called wonderful would make a person feel flattered and elated, not depressed. On the other hand, a sentence such as "You're an eager beaver," while it has effects, would not in this sense have emotive meaning, because there is no *uniform* response to it: in some it arouses favorable responses, in some unfavorable. (In this example the cognitive meaning is clearer: It is approximately equivalent to "You are industrious.")

If we keep in mind the distinction between cognitive and emotive meaning, we shall avoid many possible confusions. Do the two sentences "I am going away" and "Alas, I am going away" have the same meaning? This depends on whether we are talking about cognitive meaning only. Cognitively, the two sentences have the same meaning; they assert the same state-of-affairs, and the word "alas" adds nothing to the assertion. But in emotive meaning the two are quite different: the word "alas" adds an emotive effect to the sentence which the sentence would not have without it. In general, interjections do not change cognitive meaning but they make a difference to emotive meaning; that is their function in language.

Persuasive definitions. Persuasive definitions are closely related to emotive meaning, for their distinctive characteristic is that they employ emotive meaning. When a word has favorable emotive meaning, people want to use it to stand for whatever they like or approve, whether it is what the word already stands for in common usage or not; when it has unfavorable emotive meaning they want to use it for whatever they dislike or disapprove. Thus, the word "bastard" means illegitimate offspring—this is its cognitive meaning; but since the emotive meaning, the aura of feeling that surrounds the word, is unfavorable, people use the word as an epithet of contempt for anyone they dislike, regardless of whether he is an illegitimate offspring or not.

Thus far we have emotive use of a word but not yet a persuasive definition, since the word has not yet been redefined in accordance with the emotive meaning. If "bastard" were now redefined as "any person who cheats at cards or speaks contemptuously of everyone or plays tricks on you that he knows you don't like," this would be a persuasive definition: the word "bastard" would now have a *new* cognitive meaning, and it would have received this meaning because of the unfavorable emotive meaning of "bastard" in the former sense. The person might then say, "Illegitimate children aren't necessarily bastards; the *real* bastards are those who doublecross you. . . ." All he has done, of course, is to give an old word a new meaning; but the reason for doing it is to take advantage of, to capitalize on, the *unfavorable emotive meaning* that the word in its former sense possessed.

Let us now take a case in which the emotive meaning is favorable: [15] Suppose the word "cultured" has come to mean "acquainted with the arts." This is a cognitive meaning. But suppose it is popular, and a mark of esteem, to be acquainted with the arts; then the word "cultured" acquires a favorable emotive meaning in addition to its cognitive meaning. Now someone comes along who does not like the arts; he makes an after-dinner speech in which he says, "*True* culture is not acquaintance with the arts, but with science and technology." Of course there is no such thing as the *true* meaning of a word, there are only common and uncommon meanings, exact and inexact meanings. His audience is not sensitive to these distinctions and he successfully uses the emotive meaning the word "culture" already possesses in order to make them respond favorably to science and technology, which he wants them to like. He has given a persuasive definition of "cultured." The emotive mean-

[15] C. L. Stevenson, "Persuasive Definitions," *Mind,* 1938.

ing has remained attached to the same word, but its cognitive meaning has shifted; it has been given a new definition, based on the emotively *persuasive* character of the word.

Many words, particularly in controversial subjects such as politics, religion, morals, and art, are used persuasively; we should watch out for them. We need not avoid using persuasive definitions, but we should recognize them for what they are—mere verbal pyrotechnics designed to play upon our feelings, but which do not inform us of any new facts. We would be the dupes of verbal trickery if, in the "cultured" example, we remarked after the speech, "Well, maybe that's what true culture is, after all."

Pictorial meaning. But sentences can have meaning in still another sense. Sometimes a sentence is not intended to work on people's emotions (or to express those of the speaker), nor yet is it cognitive in its meaning. The sentence *can* be read for its cognitive meaning, and if one does so he will say "It's false," or "There is little or no evidence that this silly statement is true," and then dismiss it. But the speaker was not intending his sentence to state a proposition at all. "There's a little fairy princess inside your watch, and that's what makes it run." One could open the watch, examine it closely with a microscope, and retort, "Don't be silly: there's no such thing there. Besides, it's the wheels and springs and so on that make it run." But this remark would be an appropriate reply to the speaker's sentence only if he intended his sentence cognitively, to express a true proposition about the watch. He may not have meant his sentence to convey any information at all; he may simply have wished to implant in his hearer's mind an interesting *picture*. Many fantasies, childhood stories, and more ambitious works of the imagination were not intended to be read for their cognitive meaning and tested on that basis. To reply to the sentences in these stories as if they were intended to give information would be as inappropriate as an eighteenth-century critic's remark about *Gulliver's Travels*, that he "could scarce believe a word of it." (*Gulliver's Travels* was, of course, intended to assert by implication many things about human nature and society, but *not* that a real historical character named Gulliver landed at Lilliput, and so on.)

Picture-thinking is the name given to the habit of letting mental pictures interfere with one's thinking. One can have as many and as fascinating mental pictures as he likes, provided that he does not allow them to get confused with the cognitive meaning of what he is saying or hearing. If he is interested only in the poetic effect of the lines, he may not have to worry about cognitive meaning; but if he is engaged in a cognitive enterprise such as science, he must not get the cognitive and the pictorial confused with one another.[16] The results of doing so will be further brought out when we deal with the propositions of science in Chapter 3.

The strong psychological effects of *argument from analogy*—a kind of argument we shall take up in Chapter 5—is chiefly the effect of picture-thinking. "How can the mind possibly affect the body?" someone asks; "the smoke can't affect the locomotive from which it issues." If a person has a "visual mind," he may be so dominated by the mental picture of the smoke issuing from the locomotive that he does not stop to realize that no argument whatever against the mind affecting the body has been given. Yet this simple mental picture can often carry more conviction than many arguments. To a person so dominated by "picture-thinking," no arguments may appeal; but perhaps another mental picture can be substituted for the present one: instead of likening the relation of mind to body to the relation of smoke to locomotive, one could liken it to the relation of pilot to vessel—guiding the vessel and affecting the vessel's course very much indeed. If we succeed in implanting this image into the person's mind, he may become as convinced (and just as illegitimately) that mind affects body as he was unconvinced before. Neither "argument," of course, proves anything. The person who is easily taken in by such arguments from analogy will do well to separate the cognitive from the pictorial meaning of sentences.

We mean, not sentences mean. In this book, and in the study of philosophy in general, we shall be concerned with cognitive meaning, and with the others only insofar as they may become confused with it and require separating. But it is useful, not only in philosophy but in everyday discourse as well, that we distinguish them clearly from each other. (It is not being suggested that there *are* just these three senses of "meaning" which apply to sentences;

[16] In poetry, cognitive meaning, emotive meaning, and pictorial meaning of sentences all play a considerable role, the proportions of each varying, of course, from poem to poem.

others might be suggested, but we have distinguished these three because of confusions which might result if we did not do so.)

It is not always clear at first glance whether or not a sentence has cognitive meaning or, if it has, what that meaning is. If someone says, "The moon is a satellite of the earth," there is no doubt about the meaning of his assertion; but what if he is an artist and says things like "Rocks express the hard, brittle structure of the world," or "Music is a matter of individual emotion," or "Music conveys to us the intimate geometry of nature"? Does the second one mean, for example, that everyone reacts to music somewhat differently? or that the emotions felt by the composer are not exactly duplicated by those of anyone else? or that the emotions expressed vary from time to time or listener to listener? (And what exactly does "express" mean here?) It would seem a bit rash to condemn all utterances of this kind as meaningless; yet it is difficult to say what they *do* mean. Do they have meaning or not, and if so, how do we find out what it is?

Once again let us remind ourselves of the fact that meaning is not inherent in words and sentences; it is *given* them by their human users. Strictly speaking, it is not *sentences* that mean at all; we speak as if this were so, but this way of speaking is an ellipsis; actually it is *we* who mean various things by our sentences. Thus, instead of asking, "What does this sentence mean?" we should ask, "What do *you*, who uttered the sentence, mean by it?" Different speakers can use one and the same sentence to mean different things. It is to the speaker, not the sentence, that we must ultimately go if we want to know its meaning.

We must now make one qualification of the above account. Does the meaning of one's sentence have to be what he has in mind or intends by it when he utters it? To say even this is to be incautious. We sometimes use the phrase "one's meaning" or "one's real meaning" and not mean by that what he *consciously intended* at all. Perhaps the speaker himself really didn't know what he meant, or not all that he meant. Perhaps other persons hearing his sentence can better divine his meaning than he can himself, as a teacher surely can, at times, that of a student. If someone says that he means by a word one thing, but he constantly uses that word in sentences in such a way as to indicate that he doesn't really mean that at all, does he mean it or not? Not if by "his meaning" we mean simply his conscious intent; but possibly yes, if by "his meaning" we mean what his conscious intent *would be* if he had thought the matter through and were more consistent in his word-usage, or what a careful examination of the context would lead us to believe that he is really talking about whether he knows it or not. "If you know what a person means by a word or sentence he uses," we sometimes say, "don't accept what he *says* he means (what he intends) by it; listen to him use the word for a while; see when he applies the word and when he doesn't; see what things he will admit as instances and which he won't; see what *criterion* he seems to be employing for the use of the word, whether this coincides with what he says he means or not; and then you'll have your best idea of what he really means when he uses it." In this modified sense, we often can and do speak of a person's meaning as something other than his conscious intent; it is rather his *criterion* (consciously employed or not) for his use of the expression. You infer this meaning from his verbal behavior, not from his explanations (however sincere) of what he is intending.

But meaning is still *given* to words and sentences, and a word has no more meaning, and no clearer meaning, than it has been given. The only complication now is that sometimes the user of language has put into a word or sentence a different meaning from what he may consciously think he has. Meaning is still given, but not every user of language is fully aware of the nature of his own gift.

What is philosophy? The matters that have been discussed in this chapter have been intended as an introduction to the field of philosophy. Let us see, however, in concluding this introduction, how they apply to the term "philosophy" itself.

Questions beginning with "What is . . ." are notoriously ambiguous (see page 13). Accordingly, let us ask ourselves what we mean by the question "What is philosophy?" We could mean any of a number of things, but in the present context we can best translate it, "What is the meaning of the word 'philosophy'?"

We could, of course, simply *stipulate* a definition for it, but this would leave unanswered the question we intended to ask. We want to know not what meanings we *can* give the noise "philosophy" (we can give any, for we have freedom of stipulation [see page 6]), but what meaning it already *has*—what meaning users of language have already given it; in other words, we want a reportive definition (see page 52). What, then, is the true reportive definition of the word?

Here at once we encounter a difficulty: there is no one reportive definition of it. Different persons, and different groups of persons, use the word to stand for very different (though sometimes overlapping) things. Nor is this the worst: if the word merely had different senses, it would simply be ambiguous, and we could point out the different senses of the ambiguous word. But the word is also extremely vague, so vague that it is often not at all clear even approximately where one sense of the word leaves off and another begins. To some people, for example, philosophy has to do with the mysterious, the occult, in short, everything that cannot be observed with the senses. To others, it has to do with questions "too deep" for any other subject-matter. To still others, it has to do with the clarification of one's discourse about anything whatsoever.

What are we to do in such a situation? Shall we go contrary to common usage and stipulate a meaning for the word, trying to remain in the general area of the unclear usage already current (see page 9)? Many writers have already done this, each giving special meanings of their own to the word "philosophy." In part this is a natural and inevitable result if one wishes to discourse with clarity and precision. But clarity is not its sole motivation, for here persuasive definitions (see pp. 71–73) come into play. Capitalizing on the favorable emotive meaning which the word "philosophy" carries, at least in some circles, different writers have used the word "philosophy" to cover whatever enterprise (in the general area covered by common usage) they themselves felt the most deeply about, or did the best work in, or simply approved the most strongly. Persuasive definitions are perhaps the principal reason why there is such a tangle of meanings attached to the word "philosophy." Everyone wants to refer to his own favorite enterprise in speculation as "true philosophy."

Instead of trying to make a list of various persuasive definitions of the word "philosophy," let us remind ourselves of a point well worth remembering at this juncture: that a word has meaning in two dimensions at once, denotation and designation (see page 25), and that whereas there may be a vast disparity among writers on the designation of a term, there may yet be considerable agreement on its denotation. Different historians and critics, for example, agree

fairly well on which composers, painters, and poets are Romantics
and which are not, but they disagree almost limitlessly on what the
characteristics are which entitle them to the name—in other words
they disagree on the definition of the term "Romantic." Similarly,
there is considerable agreement about which problems are philosophical problems, but much disagreement about what it is that
makes them philosophical. All the problems we shall be discussing
in this book would be called philosophical by most of those who
have studied them; but many different accounts would be given
about the characteristics that make them philosophical. Some would
say that it is simply their non-empirical character, the fact that observation of the world will not settle them; some, that they are
"analyses of basic concepts" too broad or inclusive for treatment by
any of the special sciences; others, that they are all attempts to
think straight about ultimate issues confronting mankind; and still
others, perhaps, that no other recognized field of study deals with
these problems, while they yet remain for investigation, so this
residue might as well be graced with a name.

Even to insist on denotative agreement might seem to be going
too far. Many readers, on paging through this book, may say "But
most of this isn't what I've ever meant by the word 'philosophy,'
lots of these things I've never even heard of before." This, of course,
may well be true. In the most common usage, such as would be discovered by a Gallup poll, many of the issues treated in this book
would not enter even as denotations of the word "philosophy." But
the reason for this is simply that most persons, not having investi-
gated these issues systematically, have no conception of what is
involved in the attempt to answer the questions they ask and the
problems they raise. In common usage of the word "philosophy,"
philosophy is chiefly concerned with such questions as "What is the
meaning of life?" and "Are men machines?" and "What is the purpose of things?" and "What is the good?" Now, if we are not to be
put off with mere evasions on the one hand or mere emotive utterances on the other, we are led into a vast array of problems and
distinctions which may never have occurred to us when we began
the investigation. We may even be led to recast these original questions and put them into more precise form. At the very least, we
shall be more aware of the broader implications of these questions
and aware that simple "solutions" are as vague as they are hard to

defend. Some of the problems we come across for the first time in this book may even come to seem more fundamental than the ones that originally impelled us to study philosophy. Once we are aware of these problems, we shall probably agree that the only reason we did not include them in our denotation of "philosophy" is that we were not aware that they existed.

In this book we shall try systematically to discuss problems which those who have studied them would call philosophical. During the reading of this book, many ideas may occur to you as to what makes them philosophical. But we shall spend no more much-needed time disputing on whether they are properly called philosophical and if so what makes them so; this time can be far more fruitfully spent in introducing ourselves to the problems themselves, which, whether we give them the label "philosophical" or not, should prove interesting enough for their own sake. If a rose by any other name would smell as sweet, an important problem by any other name would still be a problem waiting for discussion and clarification. It is to the problems themselves, then, that we shall now turn.

SELECTED READINGS FOR CHAPTER 1

Readings are usually listed in approximate order of difficulty, beginning with the easiest. Thus it will be advisable, in general, to read an item occurring near the top of the list before one near the bottom. However, this listing need not be followed too religiously, for a reading that is difficult for one person may be easy for another, while another reading, difficult for the second person, may be easily understood by the first. Moreover, when a reading reference is especially apt, clear, or well presented, it is placed earlier on the list in spite of the fact that it may be more difficult *at first reading* than one which comes later on the list.

Because articles from philosophical periodicals are not as easily available as books, they are listed only when they offer a considerably better treatment of an issue than any of the book references.

Monroe C. Beardsley. *Practical Logic*. New York: Prentice-Hall, 1950. Chapters 4–6.

Max Black. *Critical Thinking*. Second edition, New York: Prentice-Hall, 1952. Chapters 9–11.

Richard Robinson. *Definition*. London: Oxford University Press, 1950.

Charles L. Stevenson. "Persuasive Definitions," *Mind*, 47, 1937.

Virgil C. Aldrich. "Pictorial Meaning and Picture Thinking," *Kenyon Review*, 5, 1943.

John Stuart Mill. *A System of Logic.* London: Longmans, Green & Co., 1843. Book I. (Also in Ernest Nagel (ed.), *John Stuart Mill's Philosophy of Scientific Method.* New York: Hafner Library of Classics, 1950.)

Plato. *Laches; Euthyphro; Meno.* Many editions.

Alexander B. Johnson. *A Treatise on Language.* Berkeley: University of California Press, 1947.

EXERCISES

1. "Isn't the word 'cat' the *right* word for this pet of mine that meows and purrs? Surely it would be applying the wrong name to it if I called it a buffalo!" "Well, there aren't any right and wrong names for things, so it would be equally right if you called it a buffalo." Resolve the argument.

2. When a child learns the meanings of words, he doesn't *invent words* for talking about things. What then is the point of saying that human beings give names rather than discover them?

3. What exceptions are there to the rule of common usage? Explain each one, together with reasons.

4. Answer this objection: "Nothing can be determined by appealing to common usage of language. You can't decide on an issue by showing how people use words! *Common usage may be wrong.* Suppose we tried to settle the question whether the earth is round by this method. In the Middle Ages one might have used the rule to prove that the earth is flat. Yet, as we know, that wouldn't prove for a moment that the earth really is flat."

5. Place quotation marks where they belong in the following sentences:

   a. Chien is the French word which means the same as the English word dog.

   b. Chien is the French word referring to dogs.

   c. The word order is important in determining the meaning of a sentence: for example, Brutus killed Caesar does not mean the same as Caesar killed Brutus.

   d. The word order contains five letters.

   e. There are cars passing along University Avenue is a true statement.

   f. The word cat names cats; and the name for the word cat is cat.

6. Distinguish by example at least five senses which the word "meaning" can have, to apply to things other than words.

7. Which of the last words in the following sentences should have quotation marks around them? Explain why.

   a. What is the meaning of your behavior?

   b. What is the meaning of this piece of news?

   c. What is the meaning of scopophilia?

   d. You don't know the meaning of love.

   e. Nobody knows the true meaning of life.

   f. This is the true meaning of democracy.

8. Criticize 7e and 7f for the phrase "true meaning." In what sense can there be a true meaning of things? Can there be a true meaning of words? Explain. How would you interpret the phrase "the true meaning of the word 'democracy'"?

9. Analyze the following "what is" questions and assertions.

a. Nobody knows what electricity is (we know only what it does).

b. Nobody knows what a cold is (we know only what its symptoms are).

c. What is telekinesis?

d. What is democracy, really?

e. Nobody in this group knows what this animal is.

f. What is truth?

10. "Many people are named 'Mary Smith,' so the name 'Mary Smith' isn't a proper name." What is wrong with this assertion? Explain.

11. What is the principal advantage, and the principal disadvantage, of using class words?

12. What alternatives are open in extending a classification? What are the consequences of each?

13. Are classifications arbitrary? Are there "natural classes" of things? Can classifications ever be wrong?

14. Would classes of things exist even if there were no human beings to classify them? Discuss.

15. "I want to find out what matter is (what religion is, what gold is, what man is) in its inner essence." What sort of things might the questioner be asking for? Do you think his request is legitimate, and why?

16. List at least 25 words or phrases that are used in both a literal and a figurative sense, using examples of both senses of each word in sentences.

17. Try to translate the following sentences containing figurative expressions into sentences not containing these expressions. (Try not to substitute one figurative expression for another.)

a. She was burned up with jealousy.

b. That's a high note (on the piano).

c. She has higher moral standards than he.

d. I'm above all that.

e. I want to have the matter firmly fixed in my mind.

f. It didn't really happen; it's all in your mind.

g. His mind is cluttered with all kinds of silly details.

h. He dived into a sea of troubles.

i. She was a shadow of her former self.

j. Life's but a walking shadow, a poor player. . . .

k. "All the world's a stage."

l. Life is but a dream.

m. "Architecture is frozen music."

n. "Life, like a dome of many-colored glass,
Stains the white radiance of eternity."

o. Her personality radiated warmth; she positively glowed.

p. When a man's Super-ego starts beating up on him, his terrified Ego attempts frantically to defend itself against the onslaught.

q. A river always takes the easiest way—downhill. So do most men.

r. A king must have nerves of iron and a will of steel; he must be both a lion and a fox.

18. Ambiguity:

a. Blackbirds, robins, thrushes . . . —different kinds of birds, or different senses of the word "bird"?

b. Tabby, tiger, leopard, puma . . . —different kinds of cats, or different senses of the word "cat"?

c. Fishing for trout, fishing for compliments—different kinds of fishing, or different senses of the word "fishing"?

d. A strong man, a strong tobacco, a strong character—different kinds of strength, or different senses of the word "strong"?

e. A sharp knife, a sharp cheese, a sharp sound-sensation, a sharp smell—different kinds of sharpness, or different senses of the word "sharp"?

19. Is the word "color" ambiguous because it can denote red, green, and so forth? Is the word "pleasant" ambiguous because what is pleasant to me may not be to you? Is the word "fast" ambiguous because what is slow for an airplane is fast for an automobile and what is slow for an automobile is fast for a bicycle?

20. Defining and accompanying characteristics. Which of the following state defining characteristics (and thus are statements about what the word means) and which state accompanying characteristics (and thus make statements about the thing named by the word)?

a. Triangles have three sides.

b. Tigers are native to India.

c. Dogs are carnivorous.

d. Steel is used for purposes of construction.

e. Books contain paper.

f. Swooning isn't the sort of thing you can plan in advance.

g. Human beings are less than twenty feet tall.

h. A good player seldom loses a game.

i. An axe is an instrument used for cutting.

j. When you run you always go fast.

k. Ladies don't use vulgar words.

21. Assume that A is a defining characteristic of class X, and B an accompanying characteristic. Which of the following statements is/are true?

a. It wouldn't be an X if it didn't have A.

b. It wouldn't be an X if it didn't have B.

c. If it weren't an X, it wouldn't have A.

d. If it weren't an X, it wouldn't have B.

22. Show how the denotation of two words or phrases can be the same while the designation of the words is different. Use examples.

23. Consider the following verbal issues, using your knowledge of defining and accompanying characteristics to clarify the controversy in each case:

a. Is this still a table if I cut off its legs? if I cut it up for firewood?

b. Is it still water even if it's not liquid now?

c. Is it still wood after I've burned it?

d. Is he an adult before he is 21 years old?

e. Is this still the same train, even though it's a different set of cars?

f. Is this still the same train, even though it leaves the station at a different time each day?

g. Is this iron even though it's not magnetic?

h. Is this a zebra even though it has no stripes?

i. Am I the same person as ten years ago, though all the cells that were then in my body have been replaced by others?

j. Is this a watch even though it has no dial?

k. Is this a hill or a mountain?

l. Is it still grass after the cow has eaten it?

24. Are the following disputes verbal? How would you proceed to settle them?

a. You have an old Ford car. One part is defective and you get a new part to replace it. The next day you do the same with another part, and so on for each part until you have replaced every part in the entire car. Is what you have left at the end of this process the same car as when you began the replacements?

b. Jack said to his brother Dick, "When I die I'll leave you my money." Next day he changed his mind and decided to leave it to his wife instead, so he wrote in his will, "All my money I leave to my next of kin" (his wife). But unknown to Jack, his wife had died. Next day Jack himself died, and his money went to his next of kin, his brother Dick. The question is: did Jack keep his promise to Dick or didn't he?

25. People *found* that whales are mammals (contrary to what was originally thought). Moreover, being mammalian is a defining characteristic of "whale." Thus, don't we *find* defining characteristics rather than give them?

26. To discover what characteristics a word designates, it is a common practice to list as many instances as possible of what the word denotes and then discover what characteristics all these particular things have in common. These common characteristics are then called the defining ones, and the list of all of them constitutes the definition. Why is this method not a safe one? Can you think of any word in which using this method would lead to inaccurate results?

27. Does it make any difference as far as the denotation of the word "man" is concerned whether "man" is defined as a rational animal, a' featherless biped, or a laughing animal? Try to state as accurately as you can a reportive definition of "man" (in the generic sense of "mankind"), the way the word is actually employed in common usage—that is, what are the characteristics which a creature could not do without and still be called "man"? (If someone suggested another definition, would you call it the wrong definition? a false definition?)

28. Would you define the following words in terms of intrinsic character-

istics or relational characteristics (and which ones)? "Chair," "box," "saw," "automobile," "camel," "vehicle," "edible," "king."

29. Show how the word "word" is ambiguous in the following dialogue: "Shakespeare used more words than any other poet in English—over 15,000." "But the average novel contains at least 60,000 words!"

30. Show how the word "is" (together with all forms of the verb "to be") is ambiguous here: "A yard is three feet"; "The chair is yellow." What does "is" mean in each case?

31. Try to translate the following assertions into clearer language:

    a. I want to discover the *nature* of this plant.

    b. What is the *essence* of living things?

    c. I insist that rationality is the *central core*, the *inmost essence*, of man.

    d. What is the *nature* of goodness? I want to know what goodness *really is*.

32. Distinguish carefully between ambiguity and vagueness. Can you mention some words which are not vague at all?

33. Which of the following words, in your opinion, share with the word "gold" the fact that no characteristics by themselves are defining, but the greater number of a cluster of characteristics must be present? Chair; run; eat; house; book; dog; radio; circle; smoke.

34. "Is this a fox or a wolf?" Is this question verbal or factual, (a) when you see the creature in the forest at some distance in the early morning mists and cannot make it out distinctly? (b) when you have the creature before you, examine it in detail, make chemical tests, and so on, and after doing all these things, still ask the question?

35. Cite five examples, either actual or of your own invention, in which failure to specify meanings of an ambiguous word caused confusion in a discussion.

36. Evaluate each of the following assertions. Clear up whatever confusions they may contain.

    a. Controversies about the nature of beauty or the nature of justice are silly and futile. People can define the words "beauty" and "justice" any way they want to, can't they? They have freedom of stipulation, so what are they arguing about?

    b. "This author defines one's religion as whatever values one holds highest in life. This of course is a *false* definition; this isn't what religion really is at all." "But a person can use the word 'religion' to mean that if he wants to. Nor is his statement false; for he is stating a definition, and definitions can't be true or false."

    c. For generations scientists tried to discover what pneumonia really is. At last they discovered it. It is a special kind of virus disease. So now at least we have the true definition of "pneumonia."

    d. No one has yet found an answer to the question: How can a human being change and yet remain the same human being that he was before?

e. You can't step into the same river twice; for the water that was there the previous time has already flowed downstream.

f. This egg before me would not be the egg that it is if it had not been laid by this hen, at this time, at this place, if it were not being seen by me now, and about to be eaten by me. (Everything is what it is because of *everything* that ever happened to it and *all* the conditions under which it exists.)

37. "How do you know that the laws of nature will still apply tomorrow?" "But they have to—it's a part of *the very meaning* of the word 'law' that the law never changes." Of what fallacy is this disputant guilty?

38. Explore the following line of thought: "Words don't stand for things. They stand for *concepts* in people's minds, and the concepts in turn stand for the things. There must be a concept, if the word is to mean anything, but there need not be a thing; for example, there are no centaurs, but there must be the concept of a centaur if 'centaur' is to be a word and not just a noise."

39. What reply can be made to anyone who holds that the word "red" is definable in terms of wave-lengths of light?

40. Socrates, in Plato's dialogues, was often concerned with such questions as: Can we know anything about virtue without first knowing what virtue is? Discuss this question. (See pages 63–64.)

41. Compare and discuss the following questions for cognitive meaning. (Some of them will come up in later chapters.)

a. Is there a shed behind the house? Is there a reality behind experience?

b. The geologist, in digging into ever deeper levels of rock . . . The philosopher, in digging into ever deeper levels of reality . . .

c. Pillars support roofs. Substances support qualities.

d. Examine the foundations of this building. Examine the foundations of your reasoning.

42. List ten words which are often employed persuasively; then state what you think some of their persuasive definitions might be.

43. "The only *true* criminal is the one who commits crimes, not in the heat of passion, but calculatingly, cold-bloodedly." Show how persuasive definition enters here, as into the use of "insane," "neurotic," "man." (Can you think of a case in which the use of a persuasive definition caused a human life to be lost?)

2

Necessary Knowledge

Having passed through the vestibule of philosophy, let us now prepare to enter the mansion itself. Some of the questions we have discussed in the first chapter may give us a clue as to what the mansion itself will be like, and most of them should be helpful in keeping our minds clear concerning the problems we are about to consider.

It would be tempting to begin by plunging at once into the questions to which most of us who are just entering upon philosophy desire answers—questions about human life, freedom, God, right and wrong. But there are many distinctions to be made and many hours to be spent in reflection before we shall be in a position to talk intelligently about these things. It behooves us to ask ourselves which are the problems which require the most preparation, the largest background for their development. It will be to our advantage in the long run to wait with these problems until our discussion has reached a point at which they can be adequately treated.

Let us begin by asking simply, "What do we know?" and "How do we know it?" More specifically, what statements are there whose truth we can be said to know? What are the tests of this knowledge? And how did we arrive at it—are there different kinds of statements whose truth must be apprehended in different ways? A consideration of questions such as these brings us at once to a controversy between two rival points of view: *rationalism* and *empiricism*.

I. RATIONALISM AND EMPIRICISM OF CONCEPTS [1]

The terms "rationalism" and "empiricism" stand for different

[1] This first section is included for the sake of completeness, but it can be omitted without harm to an understanding of the remainder of the chapter.

views, depending on what the questions are to which they each claim to give the answer. (1) The question "Whence come our ideas or concepts?" receives two answers, sometimes called "concept rationalism" and "concept empiricism." (2) The question "By what criterion are we to test our judgments to determine whether they are true?" also receives two answers, sometimes called "judgment rationalism" and "judgment empiricism" (or more usually, simply "rationalism" and "empiricism"). It is with the second of these two questions that we shall be primarily concerned. Yet the two are related, since we use concepts in the formation of judgments. Accordingly, before we embark on the second question, we shall very briefly consider (though only as a kind of backdrop for it) the first.

Concept empiricism is the view that all the ideas, or concepts, which human beings possess come from experience. Concept rationalism denies this; it agrees that many or most of them may come from experience, but insists that we do have some concepts which are either innate or somehow a part of the fundamental structure of the mind, so that they do not depend for their existence on the kind of experience we have had, there are some concepts we would have even if the world we experience were utterly different from what it is.

Concept empiricists, beginning with John Locke (1632–1704), have held that all our ideas come from experience, but they have usually distinguished between *simple* ideas and *complex* ideas. Simple ideas are those which we can have only if certain experiences (traditionally called "impressions") have occurred to us in the past: thus if we had not experienced any instances of the color red on particular occasions in our lives, we could now have no idea of redness. A man born blind could have no color-ideas; a whole "dimension" of ideas would be lacking to him, and he could not obtain these ideas until he regained his sight and thus experienced the colors for himself. Again, the idea of pain is a simple idea: to have the idea of pain we must have experienced pain ourselves. We must have seen visual shapes in order to have the idea of visual shapes, and touched things in order to have the idea of tactual shapes (the "idea of shape" being in fact two ideas, one of sight and the other of touch); and we must have experienced bitter tastes in order to have the idea of bitterness. In general, the words that are definable only ostensively, the so-called "indefinable words" (see pp. 59–62), are the ones naming the things of which we have simple ideas. Since we cannot break up the idea of redness into simple ideas, we cannot define the *word* "red" in terms of other words which together mean the same thing that it does. Redness is unique, and nothing will give you the concept of redness except your having visual experiences of red things.

Need we have seen a million-sided polygon in order to have the idea of a million-sided polygon? Need we have seen a dragon in order to have the idea of a dragon? Not even the empiricist would answer yes. But he would add that the ideas of these things are *complex* ideas, and that they are built out of simple ideas which do come directly from experience. Thus, *indirectly*—via the simple ideas which compose them—the complex ideas too come from experience. If a dragon is a fire-breathing serpent, we can form the idea of a dragon by putting together the idea of a serpent with the idea of breathing fire. Each of these ideas in turn is complex; but ultimately they break down into simple ideas—for example the idea of yellowness (in flames), the idea of shape (both flames and serpents have shape), the idea of heat (produced by the flames), and perhaps others. For our present purposes it does not matter what the simple ideas are into which the complex ones break down. What matters is the principle that all complex ideas break down into simple ideas, and that these simple ideas must come to us directly through experience. (The source of the experience need not be our "external" senses: the ideas of pain and pleasure, hope and fear, love and hate, thought and passion, are all simple ideas known through our "inner" senses. But both give us experiences from which we derive our simple ideas.) [2]

Nearly everyone, probably including the concept rationalist, will

---

[2] To this view the concept empiricist sometimes appends a criterion for the cognitive meaning of words: Words which stand for things of which we have no simple ideas, and of which therefore (according to the concept empiricist) we can form no concepts, are words which are without cognitive meaning. The concept rationalist rejects this criterion.

The introduction of this criterion places an interesting restriction on cognitive meaning over and above the general criterion discussed on pages 64–70. We shall have much to say in Chapter 3 about criteria of meaning, but we shall do so not in terms of words and concepts but of whole sentences (pages 192–207). This problem is almost always discussed in terms of sentences, and it is in these terms that we have already discussed cognitive meaning in Chapter 1.

concede that the ideas we have just mentioned come through experience. But there are more controversial ones. The idea of cause, or causality, according to the concept empiricist, is a complex idea composed of simple ones—which ones they are we shall see in Chapter 4—but concept rationalists have held that the idea of causality is a simple idea which is an innate feature of the human mind. The concept of cause is thus, so to speak, built into our make-up, so that even if we never ran into a single instance of causality during our entire lives we might still have the idea of causality.

The idea of God is another example. According to concept empiricists, the idea of God is a complex idea composed of the ideas of moral goodness, benevolence, power, incorporeality, and others. (Whether each of these in turn is a simple idea would take considerable time to determine.) According to concept rationalists, however, the idea of God is generally conceived to be a simple idea which the human mind possesses as part of its fundamental constitution (sometimes as an idea implanted in us directly by God), not a complex idea built out of simple ones which must be known to us through experience.

There are other ideas with which the concept empiricist has a harder time. (1) Whence come the ideas of straightness, circularity, and other geometrical ideas, since we never see perfectly straight lines or perfect circles? Perhaps these are complex ideas, composed of simple ideas which we get from experience; but if so this must be shown. (2) Whence come our ideas of logical and mathematical relations, such as that of implication? When we say that "A is larger than B" implies "B is smaller than A," we do seem to employ the notion of implication, but whence comes this idea? Where in experience do we find it? and if it is complex, out of what experienced simple ideas is it built? [3]

At the same time, there is a natural tendency for everyone to be a concept empiricist. Where *else* could we have got our concepts, we

[3] The rationalist may even go so far as to say that our having an idea of redness does not depend upon having previous visual experiences of red things. He will say that the empiricist is confusing tne *idea* of redness with a mental *image* of red things, and that it is indeed true that we cannot *imagine* anything red without having seen red somewhere. But, he will add, even the man born blind can have an idea or concept of redness, in the sense that he will be able to use the word "red" correctly in sentences, and even to make uniformly true judgments about red things—for example by using his sense of touch to read instruments which register wave-lengths of light.

are tempted to think, except from experience? Surely they are not innate. Three hundred years ago this might reasonably have been held, but with psychologists telling us that there are no innate concepts, what room is there for the rationalist's position? Must we not somehow be able to work out an account of the origin of *all* concepts in terms of experiences which directly or indirectly enabled us to have these concepts?

A full appreciation of this issue would require a detailed acquaintance with the history of philosophy, and we cannot enter upon it here. We have considered these two views chiefly to distinguish them from another set of views sometimes called *judgment rationalism* and *judgment empiricism.* "How do we know that our judgments are true?" Experience and experience alone enables us to know, says the empiricist, and the rationalist denies it. But neither side will say this without qualifications and amendments, and to state what these are, we must first make some very important distinctions.

II. ANALYTIC AND SYNTHETIC STATEMENTS; TAUTOLOGIES

Analytic statements. If someone said, "Black cats are fierce," or "Black cats bring bad luck," one might question whether his statement was true; but probably no one would question that, whether true or false, it is a genuine statement. However, if someone said, "Black cats are black," we might be tempted to say that he was saying nothing, or that he was saying something true but so utterly trivial as to be not worth saying.

"Black cats are black" is an example of an *analytic* statement. The term is perhaps unfortunate, because the word "analytic" means other things as well. Nevertheless, it is now well established in common usage among philosophers, and it runs constantly through the literature of the subject. The use of this word originates in the fact that you have only to *analyze* a statement of this kind in order to know whether or not it is true. For example, you can analyze "All black cats are black" into the general form "All AB is A"—and you find that the term "black," what is called the "logical predicate" of the sentence, merely repeats what is already contained in the subject of the sentence. You would not even have to know what the word "black" means: it would be enough to know that, whatever it means, it is repeated with the same meaning in the predicate.

"Black is black" would also be analytic, although it is slightly different in form. Instead of "AB is A," it is "A is A." Again we have the predicate merely repeating the subject term, only this time it is a complete repetition rather than a partial one.

If in the predicate there is something *other* than what is contained in the subject—if, for example, instead of "Black cats are black" we have "Black cats are fierce"—the statement is said to be *synthetic* rather than analytic. Here the pattern is "AB is C," or sometimes merely "A is B" ("Men are selfish"). Almost all the statements we utter in daily life are synthetic.

Tautologies. Are all statements either analytic or synthetic? Not quite. It would be true if all sentences were in the subject-predicate form, but not all sentences are. For example, "Either you leave this house or you don't leave it" is not a subject-predicate sentence as the earlier examples were; nor is "If you're here, then you're here." These are *tautologies*.

In their general character, tautologies are much like analytic statements. Indeed, for all purposes in this book it will not matter whether we call something an analytic statement or a tautology. Only for certain purposes in the study of logic will it make a difference. (The one is analyzed in logic as "atomic," the other as "molecular.") Far more important for our purposes will be what they both have in common: namely, that *to deny them is to contradict oneself;* in other words, *their denial results in a self-contradictory statement.*

A *synthetic* statement, by contrast, can now be defined as one which is neither a tautology nor an analytic statement. Whether true or false, it can be denied without self-contradiction.

Explicit vs. implicit. Often a statement is *explicitly* analytic, such as "Black cats are black," or an *explicit* tautology, such as "If you're here, then you're here." Such examples are easy to recognize but tautologies may also be *implicit:* "All brothers are males." "If he's a brother, then he's male." [4] There is no obvious repetition of

---

[4] But beware: not every statement that looks analytic really is. "Blackbirds are black" is not analytic, for being black is not a defining characteristic of the class of blackbirds. The word is used because most of the birds in this class happen to be black. Zoologists usually define words designating species by structure, not by color. And "All (or most) birds of structure X are black" is synthetic, not analytic.

words here. Yet both statements are self-contradictory to deny, as we can see when we analyze the meaning of the word "brother." If a brother is a male offspring of the same parent, then "male" is a part of the very meaning (definition) of the word "brother." So it would be self-contradictory to say that somebody was a brother but was not a male.

Most of the analytic statements and tautologies you will come across are implicit ones. Consider, for example, the statement "All matter occupies space." It is implicitly, not explicitly, analytic. For what do we mean by "matter"? Neither common usage nor physical science agrees on all the details of the definition, but it is fairly certain that they would all agree that in order to be matter something must occupy space. This is not as true of weight—something weightless might be called matter if it possessed other characteristics associated with the word "matter," but occupancy of space would seem to be an indispensable defining characteristic: something that failed to occupy any space would not be called matter regardless of what other characteristics it possessed. Therefore, if you state that matter occupies space, you are only stating part of what you mean by the word "matter"; and thus, your statement is analytic: "Everything that occupies space, and so on, occupies space."

Many statements which first appear to be synthetic are found to be analytic or tautological, on further examination. "Anybody who doesn't believe in free elections doesn't believe in democracy." This looks synthetic; but if the speaker *means* by "democracy" a form of government that has free elections, then of course it is *not* synthetic at all; to assert that you believed in democracy and deny that you believed in free elections would be a self-contradiction. "If you study this chapter long enough, you'll understand it" sounds synthetic too; but how long is long enough? You read it once, twice, ten times, a thousand times; each time you say, "I still don't understand it," you are told, "you haven't read it long *enough*." The speaker is using "long enough" so as to be identical with "until you understand it." No one could possibly refute it, for the very good reason that the denial of it involves a self-contradiction. As it stands it is a tautology: "If you read it till you understand it, you'll understand it." You may try in vain to refute it until you realize that it is nothing more nor less than a tautology.

Two points should be brought out in this connection:

1. Since the usage of words is not uniform, different people attaching different meanings to one and the same word, a statement may be analytic in one usage and synthetic in another. For example, "If you study it long enough, you'll understand it" *need* not be a tautology. If you study it for hours and still don't understand it the speaker may say, "Well, I guess I was wrong. You've read it long enough now, and still don't understand it." In that case the prediction he uttered was a false synthetic statement.

2. Often it is impossible to say whether a given statement is synthetic or not because the speaker himself is not clear about the meanings of his own words. He does not know whether what he is doing is stating a defining characteristic of a word (at least as *he* is using the word) or asserting something about the thing named by the word. As we saw in Chapter 1, this is a very frequent occurrence. "A good man doesn't break his word"—synthetic or not? The speaker himself may not know whether he is stating a defining characteristic of a good man, or stating a fact about men whom he judges to be good or bad on other grounds.

(To know whether a statement is analytic you don't have to know its *whole* definition, but only whether the characteristic being asserted in the statement is defining or not. Thus, "Tables are solid objects" is analytic, though the statement is not a definition: other defining characteristics are required also.)

Are definitions tautologies? Complete definitions, as well as statements of defining characteristics, are also tautologies: for example, "A yard is three feet." Substitute the defining phrase for the term to be defined, and we have "Three feet is three feet," which is clearly a tautology. The implicit tautology has been rendered explicit by the substitution, as in the cases above.

But does not this conflict with what we said in Chapter 1? We distinguished there between stipulative definitions and reportive definitions. Stipulative definitions are not tautologies, because they are not statements at all, but proposals for using a word. Neither are reported definitions tautologies: they only report how a word is used by human beings. This report is always a synthetic statement: "People use the word 'yard' to mean . . ." Though this may be a true statement, it would certainly not be self-contradictory to deny it, and hence it is synthetic.

In neither case, then, is a definition a tautology. In the case of a stipulative definition we have

Let us use "yard" to mean . . .

which is not an assertion at all, and therefore neither true nor false; and in the case of a reportive definition we have

English-speaking people use "yard" to mean . . .

which is a true synthetic statement. In the first case a meaning is assigned; in the second case it is reported. But in the present case it is *presupposed*. In other words, if we presuppose the truth of the synthetic statement that people use "yard" to stand for three feet, then we get, by *substituting* the defining phrase for the word to be defined, a tautology: "Three feet is three feet."

III. POSSIBILITY

We have just been considering kinds of *statements*, or propositions. In this section we shall be considering situations or *states-of-affairs*. But there is a close connection between them. A state-of-affairs is said to be *logically possible* whenever the *statement* that this state-of-affairs exists is not a self-contradictory one, and logically *im*possible when the statement *is* self-contradictory.

It is logically impossible for there to be a square circle. If we mean what is conventionally meant in English by the words "square" and "circle," the definitions of the two words contradict each other. A circle is, by definition, something which (among other things) is not four-sided; hence, saying that a circle is square would be saying that something not four-sided is four-sided, which of course is a self-contradictory statement. It is logically impossible for there ever to be a square circle: if it's a circle it can't be square, and if it's square it can't be a circle. The "can't" here is a *logical* "can't," meaning that it is *logically* impossible for it to be so.

On the other hand, it is logically possible for you to jump ten thousand feet into the air by your own unaided muscular power. If you said that you had done so, you would be making a false synthetic statement, but your statement would not be self-contradictory. There is nothing self-contradictory about "I jumped ten thousand feet into the air." The state of affairs described by the statement is *logically* possible.

If this seems strange, it is because we often confuse logical possibility with another kind of possibility, the *empirical*. A state of affairs is empirically possible when it is not contrary to laws of nature. Thus, it is empirically, not logically, impossible for you to jump ten thousand feet in the air, or to jump out of a tenth-story window and not go downward.

As far as we know, laws of nature do not change; hence, what is empirically possible at one time is empirically possible at any other time. What we *thought* a hundred years ago to be empirically impossible may have turned out to be empirically possible after all; but in that case we were simply mistaken about the laws of nature. At one time no one suspected that phenomena such as radioactivity and atomic fission were empirically possible, but they were wrong. Nature works in ways with which even now we are far from completely acquainted, which only means that more things are empirically possible than we now know.

What does change from one age to another is *technical* possibility. Technical possibility involves not merely the laws of nature but our ability to make use of these laws to produce conditions which we were unable to produce before. A hundred years ago the making of jet aircraft was not technically possible, but now it is. A space ship to Mars is today not a technical possibility, but a few years hence it may be. The laws of nature themselves have not changed; what has changed is our knowledge of them, which renders technically possible many things that were not technically possible, or even imagined, a few years ago.

Relation among the types of possibility. If a state of affairs is logically impossible, then it is impossible in the other senses too. For example: it is logically impossible to fall upwards, because "fall" means to go downwards; so falling upwards would be going downwards upwards, which is a self-contradiction. It is, then, logically impossible to fall upwards, and of course empirically impossible and technically impossible as well.

But this does not work the other way around: what is technically impossible (at any given time) need not be empirically impossible at all, for example, photographing a galaxy 500 million light-years away; and what is empirically impossible need not be logically impossible, for example, light becoming stronger with increasing distance from its source. Traveling from New York to California in three minutes is not now technically possible, but who can say that there is anything empirically impossible about it? A body not subject to gravitation is (as far as we know) empirically impossible, but it is not logically impossible because there is no contradiction in asserting it. Thus we have:

Logically possible _____   _____Logically impossible
Empirically possible_____   _____Empirically impossible
Technically possible ____   _____Technically impossible

It is for science to tell us what is empirically possible. It is for *applied,* or practical, science to tell us what is technically possible. Our chief concern here is what is logically possible. The others are brought in here only to distinguish them from logical possibility. The question that will confront us many times in the coming pages is, "Is or is not this or that state of affairs logically possible?" In doing this, we must be careful not to give a premature answer of "No" by confusing logical with other types of possibility. For example, it is *logically* possible for objects to fall faster or slower depending on their color; for you to chin yourself six million times in quick succession; for you to drink a thousand gallons of water in ten minutes without your stomach being distended; for a man to live to the age of a million years; for cats to give birth to pups, and dogs to give birth to kittens. As far as we now know, none of these things is empirically possible. When we say that they are logically possible we do *not* mean that we expect them to happen, or that we think there is the remotest *empirical* possibility that they will happen; we only mean that if we asserted that they did happen, or would happen, our assertion would *not* be self-contradictory, even though it would be false.

Another way of expressing the same idea is this: what is logically impossible could not be the case in any universe (at least not in any universe conceivable by the human mind); what is only empirically impossible might be the case in *some* universe, but does not happen to be the case in ours. For example, it seems to be empirically impossible for living things to exist without oxygen, nitrogen, carbon, and hydrogen. But it is logically possible that life in some form could exist without one or more of these. It is logically possible that Newton's law of gravitation might not apply to such a universe: that whereas actually "every particle of matter attracts every other particle with a force varying inversely as the square of the distance . . ." it might vary inversely as the cube of the distance, for example. Such a law would not describe the universe we live in, but the situation it describes is just as *logically* possible as the one in our present universe. A universe in which the attraction varied inversely as the cube of the distance is logically possible; it does not happen to be actual. On the other hand, a square circle, or a male aunt, or *falling* upwards, could not occur in any universe; the state-of-affairs asserted is logically impossible. We shall have abundant occasion in the coming pages to refer to states of affairs in (logically) possible universes which are not actual.

Conceivability. If some state of affairs is logically possible, is this the same as its being conceivable? It might easily seem so: "It's logically possible for you to jump out of a tenth-story window and not go downward" would then be equivalent to "It's *conceivable* that you might jump out of a tenth-story window and not go downward" (even though of course we don't expect it to happen). Of course we *can* define "conceivable" so that it means the same as "logically possible"; this is indeed one of the most common usages the word "conceivable" has in philosophy.

"Conceivable" is ambiguous, however. It may also mean "imaginable," and in this sense it is *not* equivalent to "logically possible." A thousand-sided polygon is surely logically possible; I cannot imagine one (form the image of one); what I am tempted to call my mental image of a polygon with 1000 sides is no different from that of a polygon with 999 sides, but I would not want to deny categorically that somebody, somewhere, can form the image of a thousand-sided polygon. People's powers of imagination vary. What is imaginable depends on who is doing the imagining. You may be able to imagine things that I cannot. What is logically possible does not have this variability. Whether I can imagine it or not, a thousand-sided polygon, an animal that's a cross between a walrus and a wasp, and a color different from any we have ever seen, are *all logically possible;* we need not stop to ask whether we can *imagine* them. Something can be logically possible and yet unimaginable (by you or by me, or even by everybody) because of the limitation of our powers of imagination.

On the other hand, if a state of affairs is really logically *im*-possible, it is not imaginable by anybody: no one can imagine a tower that is both 100 and 150 feet high, or a circle that is square. If someone says he *can* form the image of a square circle, he is probably forming the image of a square, then of a circle, then of a square in rapid succession. But he can hardly imagine something that is both round and not-round. (If he still says he can, let him draw one on the blackboard.)

There is even a *sense* in which a square circle is conceivable: namely that the words in the expression "square circle," though they contradict each other, have a definite cognitive meaning. If they did not, you couldn't know that what it designates is logically impossible. In this rather strained sense, a square circle is conceivable, but a glaminated sirophent is not, because "glaminated sirophent" is a (cognitively) meaningless expression, designating nothing logically possible *or* impossible.

"Conceivable" is used in other senses as well. Whether or not a certain state of affairs is conceivable will then depend on the sense of "conceivable" which is being employed at the time. But until the sense is clearly stated, one should not be satisfied with the simple equation "The logically possible = the conceivable."

Examples. Let us now run through a few examples of logical possibility and impossibility. There is an almost ineradicable tendency at the start to confuse logical impossibility with empirical impossibility, which only time and numerous examples can dispel; yet it is essential that it be dispelled.

1. Is it logically possible for a solid iron bar to float on water? Of course it is. There is no contradiction at all in it. It is a law of physics that objects with a greater specific gravity than water (i.e., weighing more than an equal volume of water) do not float on water (with certain exceptions such as the phenomenon of "surface tension"). There is no *logical necessity* about this—that is to say, it is logically possible for it to be otherwise. You can even imagine it now (remember, if you *can* really imagine it, it is logically possible, but if you can't, it may only mean that your powers of imagination are limited): you take a piece of iron (a chemist has verified that it really is iron), you weigh it, then you plunge it into a vessel of water, and behold, it floats. You have also verified that it is a solid iron bar, not hollow inside with large air-filled

spaces like a battleship; indeed, you have weighed it and measured it so as to make sure that its weight is really greater than that of an equal volume of water. This is a logically possible state of affairs; it does not actually occur, but there is nothing *logically* impossible about it.

2. Is it logically possible to remember something that never happened? As in so many cases, the answer is "Yes" in one sense and "No" in another, depending on the sense of the word "remember" that is employed. It may be used in a "weak" sense, so that you remember something whenever you have "that recollective feeling" about it, regardless of whether it really happened or not. In this sense, clearly, people often remember many events which, as it turns out, never really happened at all.

Here someone might object, "Then you didn't *really* remember it, you only thought you did!" This person is using "remember" in the "strong" sense, in which remembering involves not only "having a feeling of recollection" but also that the event about which you have this feeling really did occur. If it didn't really occur, then "you don't really remember it, you only *think* you did." In this sense, it is a defining characteristic of "(really) remembering" that the event actually occurred; therefore, in this sense it is logically impossible to remember something that never happened.

3. Is it logically possible for a cat to give birth to pups? Biologically impossible, doubtless (and hence empirically impossible), but logically possible. It is a fact of nature that like produces like, but there is no logical necessity about this.

"But isn't anything that a cat gives birth to, by definition, a cat?" You need only think this through for a moment to see that it is false. Suppose that what the cat gave birth to barked, wagged its tail, had all the contours of a dog, exhibited typical dog-behavior, and was unhesitatingly identified by everybody as a dog. Would you still call it a cat? In such a situation no one would say that the offspring was a cat—rather, they would be astounded by the unusual phenomenon that a cat had produced, not another cat, but a dog.

"But if a pup was the offspring, the mother must not have been a cat!" Not even if it looked like one, meowed, purred, and had all the other characteristics which cause us to call it a cat? Would you have hesitated to call it a cat *before* the strange birth took place? Must you wait to see what the creature's offspring look like (if it has any) before being able to identify it as a cat? Once again, cats are distinguished from dogs and other creatures (somewhat vaguely, as we saw in Chapter 1) by their general appearance, and it is logically possible for something with all the feline appearances to give birth to something with all the canine appearances. That nature does not operate in this way, that like produces like, is a fact of nature, not a logical necessity.

4. Is it logically possible to go from Chicago to New York without traversing the distance in between? Unless some unusual sense of the word is being employed, it is logically impossible to go from Chicago to New York (or anywhere else) without traversing distance, for to *go* from one place to another *is* to traverse distance; this is what "going" means. To assert that you went from one place to another place, and yet deny that you traversed distance, would be self-contradictory.

The word "between," however, may cause difficulty; it all depends on what it is taken to mean. One may take the word strictly, so that you are not going *between* A and B unless you are taking the shortest possible route from A to B. In this sense, you can surely go from Chicago to New York without traveling the distance *between* them. Indeed, no one has probably ever gone the distance between them in this sense, for the shortest route would be through the interior of the earth. At the other extreme, you might use "between" so loosely that *any* route you would take to get from A to B would be called "between" A and B—so that if you went from Chicago to New York by way of New Orleans or San Francisco, or by way of Shanghai, or by way of Mars, these places would be said to be *between* Chicago and New York. In this sense, of course, it would be logically impossible to go from Chicago to New York without traversing the distance in between, for any route you would take to get from the one place to the other would *ipso facto* be said to be between them.

Common usage of the word "between" seems to lie somewhere between (!) these two extremes. In common usage, any route that is within certain vague limits of the shortest distance, and especially any route that is on a standard air or railroad route from the one place to the other, is said to be between the two places. But as we have already seen (page 40), the distinction is a vague one, and one could easily be pushed down the "slippery slope" of vagueness: "Cleveland is between New York and Chicago? Very well—then what of Cincinnati? It is too? What about Memphis? New Orleans? Mexico City?" Here the familiar pattern is exhibited: probably most people would say that Cleveland is between Chicago and New York, and no one would wish to say that Mexico City is, but they would not know where to draw the line, nor would they probably wish to draw it at any specific point. In any *common* usage of "between," then, it *is* logically possible to go from one place to another without traversing the distance *between*.

5. Is it logically possible for a creature to see without eyes? (Here we do not mean "see" in the metaphorical sense of "understand," but in the ordinary *visual* sense of "see.") This is a more difficult example. To bring out various facets of the issue let us imagine the following dialogue:

A. Of course it's logically impossible. Seeing is by definition what comes by means of eyes, and through eyes.

B. Let's be careful here not to oversimplify the issue: let's not confuse a definition with a causal relation. When I say I see, I mean that I have a visual experience, probably indefinable in character; at any rate, when I say I see I am only referring to this experience, this awareness, but I am not saying anything about the sense organ which makes it possible for me to have this experience. Without rain there wouldn't be crops, and yet rain isn't crops. Without eyes there wouldn't be seeing, but seeing isn't having eyes. Isn't it an empirical fact, a fact of nature, that we have the kind of experience called visual only if we have eyes, and, in fact, when our eyes are open?

A. I see your point. In that case it's logically possible to see (have visual experience) without eyes; indeed, doesn't it sometimes happen? When your eyes are shut someone may give you a blow on the head and you may "see stars"—that's one visual experience. And the bat sees, but it doesn't have eyes at all.

B. Perhaps so, but isn't that being incautious too? How do you know that the bat *sees?* It does something that keeps it out of the way of passing objects—but the blind man does this too. Aren't you begging the question (assuming the point at issue) when you say the bat sees without eyes?

A. True, we have no direct way of knowing what the bat's experience is like. So let's go back to human beings: suppose *you* had your eyes taken out, and then suddenly found (which is logically possible, isn't it?) that you started to *see* things above you—you could see the sky above your head, the trees, and so forth, and you could distinguish colors accurately; and you found that if you bent your head downward you could see things in front of you, and they looked the way they did before you lost your eyes. That is, you could have the same visual experiences you had before but no eyes!

B. What then would you be seeing with? New eyes?

A. Not necessarily. An antenna perhaps, or something quite unique never before existing on land or sea.

B. Well, perhaps those would be called eyes—*whatever* you saw by means of would be called eyes.

A. Would they? Even if they didn't look like the eyes of a man, or of a dog, or of a fly? Even if they looked exactly like ears, would they still be called eyes? If you saw through ears at the top of your head, would you have to call them eyes, even if they resembled ears in every respect? Wouldn't you say "I saw through my (new) ears"? Surely if you said "I see through my eyes" and then people looked at the top of your head they would exclaim, "Why no, those aren't eyes up there, they're ears!"

B. As long as you had visual experiences by means of them rather than auditory experiences, they would be eyes, no matter what they looked like.

A. Would they, necessarily? That would depend on whether you defined "eye" by the organ's *appearance* or by its *function*. If the function is made the defining characteristic, then the earlike-thing-on-top-of-the-head would be called an eye because you see by means of it. But if it's the appearance (which it probably is in common usage), of course it would be called an ear, for it looks exactly like other ears, although it's in an unusual place. Now, if you called it an ear, then you couldn't say that you always see by means of eyes, for in this case you would be seeing but by means of ears. So in this case it's clearly logically possible to see without eyes. If, however, because of its function you called it an eye (even though it exactly resembled an ear), then in this case you would still be seeing by means of an eye—a very unusual eye, but still an eye; and then the question would still remain, Is it *logically* possible to see without eyes?"

B. And the answer would be No, for whatever it is you see by means of, no matter what it looked like or where on the body it was located, would be called an eye.

A. Ah, but suppose there were *no organ at all* which you had the visual experience "by means of"? not even a hole in the head? Suppose that your seeing or not seeing (having the visual experience or not having it) didn't depend on any physiological or psychological condition that even the most expert physicians could trace? Indeed, suppose you possessed no *body* at all? This is a logically possible state of affairs. At least, believers in immortality hold this. We know that the body rots away in the grave, and the eyes along with it (indeed they are the first to go), and yet we speak of a life hereafter. So here's a case of no eyes, no organs, no body at all, and still seeing! Our question here is not whether this immortality exists; the point is rather that it is *logically possible;* for in this hypothetical case, whether it actually exists or not, there is seeing but no eyes. This is the clearest way I know of to bring out the difference between the logical order and the empirical-causal order. The way our world is constituted, it may well be that seeing occurs only when the following causal conditions are satisfied: that there be an organism and that it possess eyes. But the world *might* (in the logical sense) be constituted differently, and the believer in immortality is convinced that heaven at any rate *is* constituted differently. Even the unbeliever, though he would deny that the state of affairs we have just described ever *exists*, here or anywhere else, would probably not deny that it *could* (logically) exist, that it is logically possible. The situation then is this: in our world, as far as our experience goes, seeing takes place only if there are eyes (or at least *some* sense-organ); these two things always go together. But it is a *fact of nature* that they go together, not a *logical necessity*. Or to put it differently, seeing is *causally* but not *logically* dependent on the presence of eyes; thus it is logically possible for seeing to occur without them.

IV. NECESSARY AND CONTINGENT STATEMENTS

Let us now consider the entire range of statements, true or false, that could be made: "Grass is green in summer," "I have a headache," "Crime is on the increase," "Cats are cats," "Water flows downhill," and so on. Are there any of them that are *necessarily true*, that (to put it in common language) "just *have* to be true," that "couldn't be any other way," that must hold true, always and everywhere, for example, a million years ago, or on a far distant planet in a far distant solar system?

Before we try to make the notion precise, let us try to gain a feeling for it by means of a few examples. Assuming that we believe that all crows are black, let us ask ourselves whether we think they *have* to be. Perhaps they all do happen to be, but we do not feel that it is *necessarily* so, nor would we stake our lives on their being so. Indeed, even if no exception has yet been discovered, we would probably not be too surprised to learn tomorrow that an albino crow had been discovered. But now let us examine the statement "Everything that has shape has size." We would feel much surer about this; we would feel that it "just has to be that way," that it holds not only on the earth but on Mars and everywhere else. Even if there were no objects at all, we might feel sure that *if* there were any object that had shape, then it would also (necessarily) have size. We would be less uncomfortable about staking our lives that it always held true, that there would never be any exceptions to it. Indeed, we would probably not be able to imagine what an exception would be like. What would it be like for something to have shape but no size at all? Can you draw a picture of it, for example, the way you could of a white crow? We would all feel that there is a great difference between the two statements.

The statement which "has to be true," which necessarily holds, is called a *necessary* statement; the one that does not is called a *contingent* statement, since its truth is contingent upon what the universe happens to be like. If someone said, "People can't run as fast as jack rabbits," this would be called a contingent truth; but "You can't be in New York and in California at the same time" would be called a necessary truth.

One interesting feature of necessary statements (i.e. necessarily true statements) is that *we do not need to test them further* to see whether they always hold, because they *necessarily* hold for all cases, be it tomorrow, the day after that, or a thousand years hence. If something has shape, we need not investigate further to discover whether it also has size. If someone is in New York, we do not need to investigate further to discover whether he is also (at the same time) in California. Any statement which we *do* have to test in future cases to see whether it holds of future cases as well as present ones is not a necessary statement.

With this in mind, let us ask whether the very general statements we sometimes make about the workings of nature (laws of nature, which we shall discuss in more detail in the next chapter) are necessary statements. "All water boils at 212° F. under standard conditions"; "All water flows downhill"; "All white tomcats with blue eyes are deaf"; "All solid objects whose weight per unit of volume exceeds that of a liquid will sink in that liquid"; and so on. At first we may be inclined to think that such statements are necessary, that these states-of-affairs could not be otherwise than they are. We have become so accustomed to them that we are inclined to take them for granted. Let us, however, reflect on this a moment. These are all statements of *uniformities* we find in nature. Have we any guarantee that a uniformity that has held yesterday and today will continue to hold tomorrow and forever afterwards? Don't we have to *observe* the world to test whether this uniformity holds? But if we have to observe nature to discover whether the uniformity holds, then surely it is a contingent truth (if it is a truth at all) and not a necessary one. We may be quite convinced that iron will continue to sink in water, so convinced that we may not bother to investigate any more. But *would* we not have to look to be really sure? (Could there not be a miracle, perhaps?) And would we have to look, or observe in any way at all, to be sure that A is A, or that something having shape also has size?

A priori knowledge. Another way of expressing this idea is that we can know *a priori* (prior to experience) that A is A and that everything that has shape has size, but we cannot know *a priori* that all crows are black or that iron always sinks in water—such statements can be known only *a posteriori*. Strictly speaking, the word "necessary" applies to the *statement* and the phrase *"a priori"* applies to our *knowledge* of its truth. An *a priori* statement (that is, one whose truth is knowable *a priori*) is one whose truth needs no verification by experience—we can know it to hold of all instances, everywhere and always.

There are several common misunderstandings of the *a priori* against which we should guard ourselves at the outset.

1. If a man undermined the foundations of his house, wouldn't he know *a priori* that the house would collapse? No, not in the sense philosophers employ when they speak of *a priori* knowledge. At best it can be called *relatively a priori* knowledge, or knowledge *relative to* a certain body of statements *which are not themselves knowable a priori*. Relative to certain general gravitational and architectural principles—that is, assuming them to hold in all cases—a man would know that his house would collapse if he uprooted its foundations. Relative to the principle that all stones fall, he would know *a priori* that the stone he now holds in his hand will fall if he lets go of it. But the principles on which he rests this knowledge are not themselves knowable *a priori:* only by means of observation of the world around us do we know that stones fall rather than rise when we let go of them, and that houses depend on what is below them (for support) rather than on what is above them. What we shall be discussing in this chapter is not relatively, but absolutely, *a priori* knowledge: that which we can know *a priori*, not on the basis of other pieces of knowledge which are *a posteriori*, but on the basis of no *a posteriori* knowledge whatever—prior to all experience of the world.

2. This last phrase leads us to a second distinction. It is clear that *chronologically* nobody knows anything prior to all experience.

Your experience began even before you were born—a time when you can hardly be said to have *known* anything. Surely all knowledge comes posterior to experience, in the sense that if you had experienced nothing there would be nothing you could know. So how could anyone seriously suggest that anything can be known absolutely *a priori?*

The answer is that in calling it *a priori* we do not mean that a person's knowledge of it occurred prior in time to all his experiences. In calling it *a priori* we are not referring to the time of origin at all. We are referring, not to the way of coming by the piece of knowledge in question, but to the way in which it must be *verified.* For example, you can know *a priori* that thunder is thunder, but not that thunder follows lightning. Even in the case of "Thunder is thunder" you can hardly be said to have known this before you had any experiences, before you knew what thunder was and knew what word was used to refer to it. It was not *a priori* in *that* sense; but what *is* true is that in the case of "Thunder is thunder" *you do not have to await the verdict of experience to find out whether the statement always holds true.* You do not have to investigate every instance of thunder to see whether it is really thunder. On the other hand, you cannot safely say that thunder follows lightning without experiencing instances of this relationship. There lies the difference: not in the amount of experience required prior to uttering the statement, but in the process required to verify it, to ascertain whether it is true. When a statement is known to be true *a priori*, one does not need to experience any further instances of the classes of things in question in order to know that the statement always holds. "Black cats are black" does not need to be verified by examining instances of black cats, but "Black cats are fierce" does.

Are there synthetic necessary statements? At this point one might remark: "Of course there are necessary statements, knowable *a priori*—plenty of them. But they are all analytic statements or tautologies; the denial of any of them would result in a self-contradiction. In other words, none of them is *synthetic.* A is A, cats are cats, you can't be both here and not here at the same time, cats are mammals (since being a mammal is one of the defining characteristics of being a cat), and so on. I don't deny that all these statements are necessary, and it would be foolish indeed to feel that you had to verify them by observing the world. The reason that we don't have to test them by observation of the world, and the reason they are necessary, is simply that they are empty of any real content; they are all analytic or tautological. This is very obvious in the examples just given, but it holds also of cases like 'Everything that has shape has size.' This statement is necessarily true, and knowable *a priori*, but again it turns out to be merely analytic, as you can see when you analyze the notions of shape and size. Whether something is two-dimensional like a square, or three-dimensional like a cube, its shape is only the total configuration of the *boundary* of its spatial extension, and its size is only the total *amount* of this spatial extension. A mathematical point has no shape (unlike a chalk-mark on the blackboard which is made to represent it), but then, it has no size either. The two are just two sides of the same coin."

It does, indeed, seem to be true that all the instances of necessary statements which we have examined thus far are also instances of analytic statements or tautologies. They are certainly the most obvious instances of necessary statements. But are they the only ones? Are there any necessary *synthetic* statements?

Let us pause for a moment to grasp the full import of the question. Early in this chapter we distinguished analytic statements and tautologies on the one hand from synthetic statements on the other. Later we distinguished necessary statements, knowable *a priori*, on the one hand, from contingent statements, knowable only *a posteriori*, on the other. Our present question has to do with the relation between these two sets of distinctions. There is little doubt that whatever the synthetic statements are which we can be said to know, most of them are contingent: "The desk is brown," "There are six cars in the yard," "I feel drowsy," "Nineteen-hundred fifty-six is a presidential election year in the United States"—all these are synthetic statements, and none of them is necessary. Moreover, there is little doubt that analytic statements and tautologies are necessary: "A is A," "If you're here, you're here," "You can't be both here and not here," "Cats are mammals," and so on. The interesting and tantalizing question is, Can we break these pairs? Can we cross the boundaries? Are there some statements which are synthetic, not "empty of content" but convey genuine information about the world, which yet are *necessarily true,* and do not have to wait for verification by experience of the world to be known to be so?

To many persons this will seem like trying to have one's cake and eat it at the same time. If a statement gives genuine information *about* the world, how can one know that it is true except by verifying it through observation *of* the world? And if one doesn't have to do this, but can know *a priori* that it is always true, must this not be the kind of truth that is contained in analytic statements and tautologies? How can you have the advantages of both sides at once? Can you run with the hare and hunt with the hounds?

There are those who declare flatly that there are no synthetic necessary statements, and that every alleged instance of a synthetic necessary statement turns out on analysis to be either (1) synthetic and contingent or (2) necessary but analytic. They declare that the hybrid, synthetic *and* necessary, is a myth. On the other hand, there are those who insist that there are statements which are both synthetic and necessary—that there is necessary truth about the world—even though the question of *how* we know them may be a difficult one to answer.

Here are some examples of statements that are sometimes said to be both synthetic and necessary:

A straight line is the shortest distance between points.
The sum of the angles of a triangle is 180°.
Parallel lines never meet.
All cubes have 12 edges.
Everything that is colored is extended.
Everything that has volume has shape.
A whole is the sum of all its parts.
All sounds have pitch, volume, and timbre.
If one event precedes a second, and the second precedes a third, then the first precedes the third.
Man is a rational animal.
Human beings are mortal.
It is always one's duty to do what is right.

Of these and many other statements, it is said, they are neither analytic nor tautologous (denying them does not involve one in self-contradiction) and yet we *can* know them to be true, not only in all present and past instances but for always in the future; we can be just as certain of their truth as of the truth of tautologies.[5]

Whether there are synthetic necessary statements is still a disputed question in philosophy, and we cannot hope to settle it definitely here. Nevertheless, let us consider the issue a bit further, by examining some of the more interesting candidates for the position of synthetic necessary statements.

V. MATHEMATICS

The statements of arithmetic. Let us take a simple arithmetical statement, such as $2 + 2 = 4$. Is it synthetic and necessary? It might be argued that it is. It does not look like a tautology, and surely it is necessarily true. Are we not certain that 2 and 2 make 4, and that this has always been so and always will? Must it not be as true on Mars and the farthest star in the universe as it is here, and as true a million years hence as now? Surely it is not like "All crows are black," which you could not know to be true until you had examined every crow that existed. Is the statement, then, both necessary and synthetic?

There are two possible ways of combating this conclusion: (1) that it is synthetic but not necessary; (2) that it is necessary but not synthetic.

According to the first, statements such as "$2 + 2 = 4$" are really no different from such laws of nature as "Every particle of matter in the universe attracts every other particle . . . " or "Water boils at 212° F. under standard conditions." No exceptions to these laws of nature have ever been found (we shall have much more to say about these in Chapter 3), and similarly no exceptions to these "laws of arithmetic" have ever been found: for instance, we have never come across any group of two plus two that did not equal four. The mathematical laws are more general than are the laws of physics and chemistry, in that they apply to *everything*, not only to physical bodies, but to thoughts, images, emotions, or

---

[5] These statements are usually considered to be *hypothetical* rather than *categorical* in their meaning: for example, "There are cubes" is not a necessary statement, but "*If* there are cubes, *then* they have 12 edges" may nevertheless be necessary; and it is in this latter, hypothetical way that the above statement about cubes is to be interpreted. Similarly, it cannot be known *a priori* that there are any sounds, but only that *if* there are, *then* they all have a certain pitch, volume, and timbre.

gods. It is true of absolutely everything that two of it and two more of it makes four of it. The mathematical laws are, moreover, better *established* than even the laws of physics and chemistry; if the latter have been verified in millions of instances, the former have been verified in billions or trillions of instances, and not a single exception to them has ever been found. That is why we are even surer about these laws of mathematics than about the laws of physics and the other natural sciences. However, the laws of the natural sciences and those of arithmetic are of the same fundamental sort: they are both synthetic but not necessary. We can know them to be true only by observation of the world. Just as it is logically possible that we might find exceptions to laws of nature (for instance, it is logically possible that sometimes when you heat water it boils, and at other times it turns to ice, or into something else), so it is also logically possible that we might find exceptions to the laws of arithmetic. Of course we never have, in spite of an almost infinite multitude of instances, and that is why we are so sure that the laws always hold. There is overwhelming affirmative evidence for them, and none against them. This, then, is the chief difference between laws of arithmetic and laws of the sciences: the former are more thoroughly verified by instances. If we are more certain of "$2 + 2 = 4$" than we are of "All crows are black," it is only because we have had evidence to support the former statement hundreds of times a day every day of our lives, while our experience of crows is occasional and intermittent.

Almost no one now holds this interpretation of arithmetical statements. It is held that they are fundamentally different from those of the natural sciences. The statements of arithmetic are *necessary*, while those of the sciences are not. They would hold true in all possible worlds; the laws of the sciences need not do so at all. There might be white crows on Mars (or even on the earth); there might be vast reaches of the universe in which certain well-established physical laws do not hold (and even if not, a universe in which they did not hold is logically possible); but always and everywhere and forever, $2 + 2 = 4$. There may somewhere be creatures so different from ourselves that we cannot even imagine them; the biological laws that would describe them might be far different from those in our biology textbooks; but this much is sure, if there are two of such organisms, and then two more, then there are four.

Could anything be more certain than that? And do we not know it *a priori?* Does anybody really think that we have to wait for observation to decide the matter in every subsequent instance—that there is any danger whatsoever that in the next instance 2 plus 2 may *not* equal 4? The first alternative, which says that the propositions of arithmetic are not *a priori,* is accordingly rejected.

The second way of attacking the synthetic and necessary character of mathematical statements is to hold that they are necessary but not synthetic. Certainly they can be known *a priori,* but this is nothing to shout about, any more than knowing *a priori* that black cats are black. For these statements are nothing but tautologies. What does "4" mean? "2 + 2." And what does "2" mean? "1 + 1." When we say "2 + 2 = 4," what are we saying? Merely that "1 + 1 + 1 + 1 = 1 + 1 + 1 + 1." And this is just as much of a tautology as "Black is black." The statements of arithmetic, then, are tautologies. This is the only reason we can be so sure that they always hold, and this is the explanation of the fact that they hold necessarily and that we can know them *a priori.*

Let us now consider several questions about this interpretation:

1. "I *learn* that 2 + 2 = 4 and I learn it from particular instances, first about 2 + 2 houses, then 2 + 2 apples, and so forth. Isn't the general statement that 2 and 2 always make 4 then a generalization from experience, like the generalization that all crows are black?"

Of course I learn that 2 + 2 = 4, and probably we all learned it from examples such as the above. But what is it that we learned, precisely? Is it not that the symbol "4" is equivalent in meaning to the symbols "2 + 2," and that "2" again is equivalent to "1 + 1"? In learning that 2 and 2 is 4 (it would be argued) I am not learning a fact about the world, as I am when I learn that water boils at 212° F., but I am learning what verbal symbols are equivalent in meaning to what other ones.

We do indeed learn the meanings of words and phrases through experience—how else? But this does not make the statements in which they occur *a priori.* What makes them *a priori* is our way of knowing that they are true. In the case of arithmetical propositions, we do not have to verify that 2 and 2 make 4 for every successive case any more than we do for "Black cats are black."

2. "I can think of 2 and 2 without thinking of 4." Probably I

can, or at any rate I could before I learned that $2 + 2 = 4$. This makes no difference, however. The statement that $2 + 2 = 4$ is not a law of psychology; it does not state that when I think of this I also think of that. It states that this *is* that, whether I think so or not. I may think of "brother" without thinking of "male sibling," and yet the statement that brothers are male siblings is a tautology.

3. "But even if '$2 + 2 = 4$' is a tautology, what about more complex calculations such as '40694 plus 27593 = 68287'? Surely the principle of the two is the same, so that if the first is a tautology, so is the second. Yet it is difficult to believe that the second is tautological."

The principle of the two *is* the same; both are tautologies. It would take a long time to write out the second into a series of 1 plus 1 plus 1's, but if we did so we would find that it is the "2 plus 2" story all over again, only with more 1's. Of course if we made a mistake in addition, our statement that the two figures added together equals that sum would be self-contradictory: we would be stating that $1 + 1 + 1$ . . . does *not* equal $1 + 1 + 1$. . . .

Of course the answer to the larger problem is not as *obvious* as is "2 plus 2 = 4." Again, all of this makes no difference. It is not a defining characteristic of a tautology that it must be obvious. What is obvious to one person is not so to another; and what is obvious to a certain person at one time may not be so at another time. Obviousness is a psychological characteristic which is in no way involved in the conception of a tautology. Statements of arithmetic are tautologies because their denial is self-contradictory, whether this self-contradictoriness is immediately obvious, or whether (because of our human limitations) it can only be recognized after a more lengthy computation.

4. There is a more fundamental objection than any of these, namely that the propositions of arithmetic are not even true in all cases. "2 and 2 doesn't always make 4, for example. If you add two quarts of alcohol to two quarts of water, you don't get four quarts of the mixture, but a little less than that because of a certain interpenetration of the molecules of the two. Or again, put together two lions and two lambs, and in a short time you will not have four animals, but only two—two lions! Or take two amoebas: when they subdivide, the two amoebas become four—not two plus two is four, but *two* becomes *four!* Thus "2 plus 2 = 4," far from being known *a priori* to be true, is often false!"

This objection, which is sometimes made, is the result of a mis-understanding. The principle that 2 plus 2 makes 4 does not deny that what *was* one thing can *become* two; but surely this does not mean that 1 equals 2! It only says that *if* you have two, *then* at that same moment you have 1 plus 1—that having *two* of some-thing is *the same as* having *one plus one* of that something. Of course, by subdivision (as in the case of the amoeba), what *was* one can *become* two, and what was two can *become* four. This is not denied by the statement "2 + 2 = 4." The point is that *nothing is being asserted about the world* when it is asserted that 2 plus 2 is 4. It is not even being asserted that there *are* two things in the world: it is logically possible that there might be just one thing in exist-ence—or for that matter, no universe at all. It only says that *if* there are two and two, *then* there are four: that *to say that there are two and two, and to say that there are four, is to say the same thing.* Thus, when there are two lions and two lambs, there are two plus two, i.e., four; and when the lions have eaten the lambs (at any rate when they have digested them), there are one plus one, i.e., two. It would not violate the principle "2 + 2 = 4" if two things gave rise to a million things (as it is popularly believed to happen in the case of rabbits), or split into a million things, or ex-ploded into a million things or into nothing at all. What turns into what, what becomes what, how one thing changes into another—these are matters for empirical science to investigate; these are all a part of what happens in the world, something for scientists to observe and try to discover laws about, and it is all synthetic and contingent. The statements of arithmetic, however, say nothing about the changes that go on in nature; they have nothing to do with the kind of world we live in, and they would be unchanged if the world we live in were quite different from what it is, precisely because they are *not descriptions of the world at all.* What the statements of arithmetic are concerned with is the equivalence of numerical symbols which we use to talk about the world. Arithmetic does not say that the numeral "4" *applies* to anything, but rather that *if* it applies, then "2 plus 2" also applies, because the *two sym-bols mean the same.* To use the metaphor employed in Chapter 1, they are two labels for the same bottle. Therefore, they can be used interchangeably.

The same analysis can be used for the example of the water and the alcohol. The principle says only that *if* you have 2 plus 2 quarts, *then* you have 4 quarts. It does not tell you that if you mix 2 quarts of one thing with 2 quarts of another, you will end up with 2 plus 2 quarts. What happens when you mix A with B is something arithmetic will never tell you: anything might happen! Having less volume than the total you started with is a mild result compared with what is logically possible. It is logically possible that both might expand to a million times their normal size, or turn into elephants, or be annihilated altogether. And in the case of some liquids, it is not only logically possible but empirically the case that when you get them together there is an explosion, and no four quarts of liquid at the end of it—rather, no liquid at all (and perhaps no people left in the vicinity to observe it if it *were* there). In other words, what happens when you bring two volumes of one thing together with two volumes of another has nothing to do with arithmetic: it belongs entirely to the physical sciences of physics and chemistry.

The second alternative, the one we have just been considering, is today the most widely held view about the statements of arithmetic. There remains the possibility that they are both synthetic and necessary. The defenders of this view are committed to showing that these statements are not, after all, tautologies: that "4" does not, for example, by definition mean the same as "2 + 2." There are many believers in synthetic necessary statements—and we shall advance arguments for this belief in subsequent sections—but the domain of arithmetic is not one of those in which belief in synthetic necessary statements is popularly held.

Classification of views about synthetic necessary statements. Our discussion of the statements of arithmetic has given us a background against which to make a general classification of views about synthetic necessary statements. This classification is a bit oversimplified, and it will have to be refined a little later, but in the meantime it will be a useful and convenient outline to carry in mind. In general, then, there are three types of view about synthetic necessary statements:

1. The *rationalist's* view, namely that there are synthetic necessary statements. Adherents of this view do not always agree *which* statements are synthetic and necessary: one may, for example, hold that some statements of geometry are, but deny it in the case of

statements of arithmetic. Nevertheless a person is called a rationalist if he believes that there is even *one* statement which is both synthetic and necessary.

2. The *traditional empiricist's* view, namely that there are no synthetic necessary statements because there are no necessary statements at all: the allegedly necessary ones, such as those of arithmetic, are really contingent. The only exceptions are outright tautologies and analytic statements such as "Black is black" and "This is not both a chair and not a chair." How far this list of exceptions is to go is not clear; probably no defender of the view would go so far, however, as to deny that "Black is black" is a necessary statement, and hence it would be inaccurate to say that according to the traditional empiricist there are *no* necessary statements. But at any rate the statements of arithmetic, of geometry, of logic, and all the statements we shall be considering (which are of interest to philosophers) are not considered necessary. All of them are synthetic and contingent.

3. The *logical empiricist's* view, namely that there are no synthetic necessary statements because all statements without exception are *either* necessary and analytic *or* contingent and synthetic. Even if a person says that all the statements of one domain, such as arithmetic, fulfill this requirement, he is not a logical empiricist unless he holds this of *all* statements. Thus he agrees with the traditional empiricist that there are no synthetic necessary statements, but disagrees on the reason why: unlike the empiricist, who holds that there are no necessary statements, he holds that there are, but that all of them are analytic (or tautologies).

The statements of geometry. Let us now consider a few instances of geometrical statements: "The sum of the angles of a triangle = 180°." "Two parallel lines cannot be drawn through a point." "A straight line is the shortest distance between two points."

Imagine someone arguing as follows: "Don't you *know* (at least after you've studied a little geometry) that the angles of a triangle necessarily add up to 180°? Surely you don't have to examine every triangle to see if it comes out this way; you don't have to test it by observation, you know it *a priori*—or surely so it seems. Do you really have to examine every triangle and measure its angles to see if it comes out right, the way you have to examine all crows if you want to know whether they are all black? Of course not. At the

same time, the statement seems to be synthetic also: there is nothing in the definition of 'triangle' about the angles adding up to
180°."

Now let us examine the matter a little more closely. The statement about the sum of the angles is what is generally known as a
theorem in geometry. You remember from courses in geometry that
you begin with certain *axioms,* or unproved statements at the beginning of the course, and from these axioms you begin proving
theorems by showing that they can be deduced from the axioms
(i e., that the theorems logically follow from the axioms). After we
have proved the first theorem, we get the second by means of certain
axioms plus the first theorem. We do not use all of them all of the
time: perhaps we get Theorem 50 from Axioms 1, 4, and 6, plus
Theorems 3, 13, 42, and 49.

You need one thing more besides axioms and theorems, namely,
a means for getting from the one to the other: *principles of inference.* (You may not have known when you studied geometry in
high school that you were using them, but you were.) These principles are generally taken for granted; they are principles of logic,
which we shall examine in the next section of this chapter. For example, one of them would be that if A implies B and A is true, then
B is true. Here we need only point out that they are employed in
geometrical reasoning, and that they are important, because without them we could not get from the axioms even to the first theorem.

Now the theorems, including the one about the sum of the angles
of a triangle (a comparatively simple one), do follow logically from
the axioms plus theorems which have been proved earlier. Given
these, the theorem follows as the night the day—even more surely
than that, for the night follows the day only chronologically, while
the theorem follows logically.

What does it mean to say that one statement follows logically
from others? It means that it can be *deduced* from them. It means
that *if* the axioms and previously established theorems (at least the
ones used to prove this proposition) are true, *then* the new theorem
must be true; and that it is *self-contradictory* to assert that the
premises (in this case axioms and previously proved theorems) are
true and the conclusion (in this case the new theorem) is false. It is
just like "*If* all the members of the crew were drowned and Smith
was a member of the crew, *then* Smith was drowned." It is not as-

serted that the premises are true, but only that the conclusion follows logically from them, so that *if* the premises are true, then the conclusion must be true also. The geometrical example is more complicated than the example about the crew members; there are many more steps in the proof; but the principle of it is the same: you cannot hold, without self-contradiction, that the premises of the argument are true and the conclusion false.

Thus, the theorem about the angles of the triangle can be proved, not proved to be *true* unless the premises from which it is deduced are true (we shall examine this in a moment), but proved in the sense that it can be *deduced* from them, so that *if* the premises are true *then* the conclusion must be. Of course premises are often false, and the arguments may still be valid ones even though the conclusion that follows from the false premises is also false. For example: "The animal in front of me is green" is false, but it can be proved (deduced) from the premises "All cows are green" and "The animal in front of me is a cow." The premises are false, but the argument is a valid one—that is, the conclusion still follows logically from the premises.

Very well then, are the premises true in the case of geometry? Maybe the theorem we have been considering does follow logically from the axioms and previous theorems, but are *these* then true?

Let us first note that the "pure geometrician" cares nothing about whether they are true or not. He is concerned only with whether the conclusions in some particular proof follow logically from the premises of that proof. He is not even concerned with whether the axioms, the very beginnings of the whole deductive system of geometry, are true. He investigates only what can be deduced from them, and is concerned that there shall be no logical fallacy in deducing the theorems from them. He does not care what kind of meat goes into the grinder, but only that it is ground well. A better comparison would be this: When your grocer hands you his bill at the end of the month, you may check up on his figures. There are two kinds of mistake he may have made. He may have added up the figures wrong, or he may have put in some wrong entries in the first place. The "pure geometer" (or "pure mathematician" or "pure logician") is concerned only with whether the figures have been added correctly; he cares nothing for whether the figures were the right ones to begin with. When a logician criticizes an argument, he does not, as a logician, consider the truth or falsity of the premises of that argument, but only whether the conclusion really follows validly from them. One could criticize the entries too, but that is not the mathematician-logician's business.

Either kind of error, whether in the original entries, or in the process of adding them, may be responsible for an erroneous bill. In surveying the bill, you probably look for both sources of error. As for the logician, however, it is not his business (though it is the scientist's) to ascertain the truth of statements; it is his business to see whether conclusions are validly inferred from them. Deductive logic is the study not of true and false statements, but of valid and invalid inference.

Now what about geometry? What, first of all, about "The angles of a triangle = 180°"? Is it a tautology? Yes, together with the premises from which it is deduced, it is a tautology. "Fido is a mammal" is not a tautology; but the whole proposition "*If* Fido is a dog and *if* all dogs are mammals, *then* Fido is a mammal" is a tautology, as we shall see more clearly in the next section. Similarly, "*If* . . . (certain axioms and theorems used in the proof), *then* the sum of the angles = 180°" is also a tautology.

But what about the axioms of geometry themselves? Are they left hanging in the air? How do we know that *they* are true, if the truth of the theorems deduced from them depends on them? Maybe it is not the business of the "pure geometer" to investigate this question, but it seems to need investigating.

Not all the axioms are of the same nature. Some are disguised definitions; others are partial or implicit statements of laws of logic, and the discussion of such statements will occur in the next section. The ones that do not fall under either of these headings are the ones that concern us here. Let us consider, for example, the axiom of parallels: that given a straight line and any point outside the line, there is one and only one straight line that can be drawn through that point, in the same plane, which does not intersect the line (i.e., is parallel to it). How do we know that this axiom is true? Some have thought that it should be classified as a theorem that could be deduced from axioms plus other theorems, although no such attempt has ever succeeded. Others, seeing this task fail, have concluded that the axiom was just a self-evident truth, or, more specifically, a synthetic statement which could be known to be true prior to an examination of all instances, in other words, *a priori*. Still others declared that it was indeed synthetic, but not *a priori;* rather, that it is a contingent statement which gives information about space.

For a long time it was usual to hold that the statement is synthetic and necessary. But more recently it has come to be considered not only not necessary, but perhaps not even true! It was only when the geometry of Euclid became generally accepted that this statement was considered both synthetic and necessary. This is the system of geometry you learned in high school, not as Euclid presented it to the world more than two thousand years ago, but as it has been refined by later geometers. It is a perfectly consistent system, with certain axioms and theorems, each of which can be deduced from prior statements within the system. In this system, the statement about parallels is an axiom. But this system is not the only possible system. In the geometry of Lobachevsky, *more than one* straight line can be drawn through a given point, and yet fail to intersect the other line. And in the geometry of Riemann, *no* such lines can be drawn. Each of these three systems of geometry is perfectly consistent within itself. In each of them, theorems are validly deduced from axioms, and no logical fallacies can be shown. As deductive systems, there is nothing to choose between them. Each one begins with a somewhat different set of axioms, and hence the later statements which are proved by means of the axioms differ also.

If we cannot criticize the addition on our bill from the grocer, maybe we can criticize the entries. Both of the following arguments are logically valid,

All spiders are reptiles.	All men are organisms.
You are a spider.	You are a man.
Therefore, you are a reptile.	Therefore, you are an organism.

but the premises in the second are true while in the first they are false. Now which of the axioms about parallels is *true*—Euclid's, Riemann's, or Lobachevsky's?

The first conclusion you might draw is that while each of the systems is consistent and free of fallacies in deduction, the geometry of Euclid is the only one whose axioms are true: that for example, the Euclidean axiom of parallels is true but that of the other systems false. This, however, would be a mistake. It is not as simple as that. The current scientific judgment on the matter is that the system of Euclid is only *approximately* true; for short distances such as we find in surveying on the surface of the earth, there is no appreciable difference between the surveyor's measurements and what the Euclidean geometry requires. But in the vast reaches of the universe measured by the astronomer, this does not seem to be the case: here the Riemannian system is nearer to the truth.

To pursue this complex matter further at this point would take us too far afield. The important point for us to grasp here is that the scientist's observations *are* relevant to determining the truth of axioms (in the present case the axiom of parallels) just as they are in the case of statements in chemistry or biology. This being so, it is difficult to hold that it is a necessary statement. It seems clearly to be synthetic but not necessary. It is the natural scientist who tells us whether or not a non-necessary (contingent) statement, in this case an axiom of a geometrical system, is true. He does this by observing the universe, not simply by making calculations on paper as the pure mathematician does.

With this point in mind, let us return for a moment to our example about the angles of a triangle. Suppose a surveyor found time after time that the angles in the triangles of land he was surveying did not add up to 180°. Would this show that Euclidean geometry was mistaken? This all depends. If you are considering Euclidean geometry as a deductive system, it would not; the system remains as logically flawless and as internally consistent as ever. But if you are considering Euclidean geometry or any statement in it as a description of a state of affairs in the universe, then the answer is yes. The mathematician can go on elaborating a geometry as a deductive system no matter *what* discoveries a scientist might make. As a description of the universe, however, a geometry is true or false. If surveyors constantly found in their own measurements ("surveyors" instead of "surveyor" because if it were only one surveyor his observations would probably be put down as erroneous) that the angles never added up to 180°, no matter how many times they repeated their measurements, they would conclude finally that space is not Euclidean, and that however self-consistent the Euclidean system of geometry is, its statements are not a true description of the physical universe.

Most of the errors in our conception of geometry arise from confusing these two very different aspects of geometry: one as a consistent deductive system, and the other as a scientific description of our universe. The statements of geometry in the first sense are necessary, but they are also tautologies.[6] The statements of geometry in the second sense are synthetic, but not necessary. It is usually when we obscure this distinction and confuse the two with each other we tend to look upon geometry as a body of statements which are both synthetic and necessary.

Our general conclusion thus far, then, is this: The statements of Euclidean geometry, when considered by themselves, are neither synthetic nor necessary; their truth or falsity is a matter of whether the Euclidean geometry is a true description of the universe in which we live. "The angles of a triangle equal 180°" is just one of these statements. But this statement, and all the derived statements in the system, are necessary and tautologous in relation to the preceding statements in the system from which they are deduced—precisely as "Jack is in the room" is tautological when it is a part of the argument "Jack is a member of the committee, and all members of the committee are in the room; therefore Jack is in the room."

Now let us examine, finally, the axiom "A straight line is the shortest distance between two points." Don't we know *a priori* that this axiom is true? But isn't it also synthetic? Where would be the self-contradiction in denying it? You might say, "A straight line is *defined* as the shortest distance between two points—that's what a straight line is, by definition." But is this really so? Is it not true, as the philosopher Kant pointed out, that the notion of length is a *quantitative* notion, which can be measured, while the notion of straightness is a *qualitative* notion, and thus the two can never be identified with each other? If so, it would be a fallacious oversimplification to say that they are identical by definition. Or one might ask: isn't being the shortest distance between two points an *accompanying* characteristic of a straight line rather than a defining characteristic—a *universally* accompanying characteristic (p. 30)?

Does it just happen to be so, and might it be otherwise? Or is it *necessarily* so? Is the case of the straight line like the case of the crows which, as a matter of fact (as far as we know), are all black

[6] In the sense we considered above: assertion of the premises on which the statement is based (axioms and theorems), together with the denial of the statement itself, yield a self-contradiction.

but *might* easily be otherwise? Some would say that it *is* like this, only perhaps better established because of the number of instances. Others, however, would say that it is different: that we *do not* have to examine every straight line to see whether it is the shortest distance between two points, the way we have to examine crows to see if they are all black. In other words, they would say that the straight-line statement is necessary. In this case, if it is not a tautology or analytic, is it not synthetic and necessary?

It is sometimes said that just as Euclidean geometry has been outmoded in other ways (as we have just seen), so it has been outmoded with respect to this statement: that a straight line is really not quite the shortest distance between two points, since space is curved, and the shortest distance is a curved line, just as the shortest distance from one point to another on the surface of the earth is the arc of a great circle. But if this is so—if the statement, far from being necessary, is not even *true*—it clearly cannot be *necessarily* true. It must be, then, synthetic and contingent.

Before we can decide, however, whether "A straight line is the shortest distance between two points" is synthetic, we must decide precisely what is meant by the word "straight." This is not as easy as it may seem. It does no good to say "A straight line is a line no part of which is curved," for this lands us in a circle: what is a curved line but "a line not all of which is straight"? Much controversy has taken place as to just how to define "straight." Perhaps it is indefinable: in that case one can go ahead and say that the statement is synthetic and necessary, and that we just *know* it to be true. (The dangers of this kind of approach will be discussed in Section VIII.) On the other hand, some have endeavored to define "straight line" in a convenient and checkable way, for example by defining it as "the path of a ray of light." If this definition is used, then it is synthetic and contingent that the path of a ray of light is the shortest distance between two points; for this is known only by observation of the universe.

To define "straight" thus may seem a neat way out of the difficulty; but there is something about it that is discomfiting: Is this what is really meant in speaking of "a straight line"? Maybe it is true that rays of light do travel in straight lines; but isn't this a fact of nature, rather than a definition? Isn't it logically possible that rays of light might travel in curved or jagged lines, so that we could see around corners, for example? If the world were like this, then the statement "The path of a ray of light is always a straight line" would be false: a false statement about the world, a false synthetic statement. In this case, however, it can hardly be a *definition*. If it were, the statement "The path of a ray of light is always a straight line" would become "The path of a ray of light is always the path of a ray of light," which, being a tautology, could never be false.

The outcome of this controversy, then, depends on how the word "straight" is defined.

VI. LOGIC

We come now to a far more controversial subject: the principles of logic. In a sense, nobody doubts them; we all use them every day, and they are the very rock-bottom of our everyday discourse and argumentation, although until we study logic we have probably never heard or seen them formulated explicitly. But what kind of statements they are, in what sense they are true, and how they can be proved or justified, are questions about which there has been a great deal of controversy.

Here are some typical examples of statements (or propositions) in logic: (The letters p, q, r, and so on, stand for propositions, any propositions whatever that one cares to assert.)

1. If p is true, then p is true. (Or sometimes: All A is A.)
2. Not both p is true and p is false. (Not both A and not A.)
3. p is either true or false. (Either A or not A.)
4. If p implies q, and p is true, then q is true.
5. If p implies q, and q is false, then p is false.
6. If either p or q is true, and p is false, then q is true.

Anyone who has studied logic will be able to add indefinitely to this list. The first three listed above are the so-called Laws of Thought (though this is a misnomer, for they are certainly not laws of psychology) made famous by Aristotle (384–322 B.C.): they are, respectively, the Law of Identity, the Law of Non-contradiction, and the Law of Excluded Middle. The second three are samples of rules of inference.[7] They may seem to be so obvious that when put down

---

[7] The first three are also used in inference, or rather presupposed in inference. For example, consider the first one. You could not get far in reasoning if a proposition p were not that proposition p but some other, q, instead!

baldly in black and white they may arouse contempt: "What news can *they* be to anybody?"

Indeed, the first thing one might be inclined to say about them is that they are self-evidently true, or more briefly, *self-evident*. This, however, raises a difficulty at once: What are you saying about a statement when you declare that its truth is self-evident? Aren't you merely saying that it *seems* evident, or obvious, to you? What may seem evident to you may not seem so to your neighbor. Still, you will want him to accept it as well as you do—at least, you will say it is true whether it seems self-evident to him or not. So you cannot use its "self-evidence" as any basis for asserting its truth. If you are asked "How do you know it's true?" and you reply "It's self-evident," you are not backing up your statement at all, you are more probably revealing your inability to back it up. Moreover, would you wish this criterion universally accepted? Would you believe something because it seemed self-evident to your neighbor? Or would you believe it just because it has seemed self-evident to somebody or other at some time? But that would include thousands of statements which you would almost certainly reject, and many of which would flatly contradict each other. There are many who have thought it self-evident that they should burn at the stake everybody who disagreed with them. Is it not unhappily near the truth to say that we give the name "self-evident truths" to whatever prejudices we cannot defend? At the very least, it does not help our understanding of a statement to be told merely that it is a "self-evident truth."

The problem of establishing these statements is perhaps the most pressing in the case of logic because these are the most general of all the statements that there are. If the foundations of geometry were insecure, there would still be areas of existence that would remain untouched by this. Even the statements of arithmetic have to do only with quantities. The statements of logic, however, apply to everything that can be talked about: whether a statement is about quantities or qualities, about animals or vegetables or minerals, about numbers or lines, thoughts or emotions, imaginary things or real ones, or even about statements themselves, the same thing holds: p is p, p is not not-p, and p and not-p can't both be true.

Yet, when we come to give an account of these statements, when

we ask how we know them to be true, and what kind of statements
they are, we seem absolutely stymied. How can we ever prove that
if p is true it isn't also false, or that it cannot be both true and false
at the same time? It just seems too self-evident(!) to need proof.

Objections to the principles of logic. Occasionally it has been said
that even such seemingly unquestionable statements as those of
logic are false, or at least do not always hold true. It is pretty generally agreed by those who have considered these objections, however, that they result from misunderstandings of the principles
themselves. Here are some of the most typical objections:

1. "A statement *is* sometimes both true and false—true at one
time and false at another. For example, the statement 'Chicago has
over three million people' is true today but was not true fifty years
ago."

It is true that the population of Chicago has increased, but this
does not disprove the Principle of Identity. The fact is that "The
population of Chicago is over 3,000,000" is not a complete statement. The question is, When? "The population of Chicago was over
3,000,000 in 1950" is true. "The population of Chicago was over
3,000,000 in 1900" is false. However, these are two different statements, and not the same one at all. They are only made to seem so
because of ellipsis, or incomplete specification of meaning (failure
to put down the whole sentence explicitly).

For some statements it is necessary to specify time as well as
place. Thus: "The Missouri River overflowed at Omaha, Nebraska
(place), during April, 1952 (time)." It overflowed at some places
but not at others, and at some times and not at others. In cases
where one does not specify, this is usually because the unexpressed
part of the statement is understood: it is uttered in the present tense
and made to apply at the time and place of the speaker when he
makes the utterance. Thus "It's raining" probably means where the
speaker is, at the time he is speaking. If one then objects, "The
statement 'It's raining' is true at some times and places and not at
others," he can be told that his objection arises only because the
assertion is considered out of its context, and considered apart from
the conditions of its utterance, which were themselves not uttered
because they were assumed to be already known or taken for
granted by the listener.

2. "The same statement may be both true and false—true for

you and false for me, for example. 'I had lots of headaches in 1952'
may be true for you but it's false for me."

Again, this is due to incomplete specification of meaning. It depends on who the "I" is that is being referred to. Smith and Jones
may both say "I'm going home," but the statement is a different
one in each case: in the first case it means "Smith is going to Smith's
home" and in the second case it means "Jones is going to Jones'
home." And if Smith had many headaches but Jones didn't, this
only means that the following statements are both true:

(1) Smith had many headaches in 1953.
(2) Jones did not have many headaches in 1953.

It's not that (1) is true for Smith and (2) is true for Jones. Both
are true, for Smith or Jones or anybody else. If you are Smith, it is
true that Smith had many headaches in 1953, and if you are Jones,
it is still true that Smith had many headaches in 1953. A statement
is not "true for one person but false for another"; this is a fallacy
caused by incomplete specification of meaning. The statement is
either true or false regardless of whether or not anybody knows it
or even thinks it. This is so even if the statement is *about* somebody's state of mind. Thus, "Smith is thinking of Paris" is as true
for Jones as for Smith, although it is *about* Smith's state of mind;
indeed, the phrases "for Smith," "for Jones," "for you," "for me"
are redundant. They add nothing to the issue except confusion.

3. "Some statements are both true and false, depending on how
you look at them. Thus, 'Sounds don't exist unless someone is present to hear them' is true if you mean by 'sound' auditory experiences
but false if you mean sound-waves."

After our discussion in Chapter 1 you should be able to answer
this for yourself. The answer, of course, is that what is true and
what is false is not the same statement. The true statement is
"Sound experiences don't exist unless somebody experiences them"
(many would say this is a tautology); the false statement is
"Sound-waves don't exist unless they're experienced." As always
happens in the case of ambiguity, using the same succession of words
often conceals more than one meaning. But it is the meanings, not
the words in which they are clothed, that constitute the propositions.
Words are put together to form sentences, and sentences, as we saw

in Chapter 1, express or state propositions. More than one sentence can be used to state one proposition ("A is larger than B," "B is smaller than A"), and one sentence can be used to state more than one proposition (as in the example of the sound).

4. "At least the third 'law of thought'—the Law of Excluded Middle—is false. It says 'Either *p* or not-*p*.' But this need not be so; in fact it often isn't. The water in the bowl may not be hot, but that doesn't mean that it is cold. It may be lukewarm."

This is a common objection, but quite unfounded. The objector should examine the sentence again. It doesn't say "Either *p* or *q*"; it says "Either *p* or not-*p*." Substituting, it doesn't say "Either the water is hot or the water is cold"; it says "Either the water is hot or the water is not-hot." Wherever you place the boundary-line of the hot, the not-hot covers *every* temperature that's not included under the hot. Thus "not-hot" isn't the same as "cold"—it *includes* "cold," as well as "lukewarm." "Not-hot" is the *negative* of "hot"; "cold" is the *opposite* of "hot." Much mischief has been caused by this confusion of negatives with opposites. Thus people have interpreted the Law of Excluded Middle to mean that if something is not hard it is soft, that if it is not easy it is difficult, if it is not long it is short, and so on.

5. "Even 'He's in the room or he's not in the room,' though it is not guilty of the fallacy exposed in (4), may be false. Suppose he's half in the room and half out?"

This will trouble you only as long as you do not make clear exactly what you mean by being *in* the room. If you consider a person to be in the room only when *all* of his body has crossed the threshold, the statement applies: either he's in or he's not (either all his body has crossed the threshold or it hasn't). The same is true, of course, if you consider him to be in the room even if only a small part of his body has crossed the threshold, or if more than half of his body has. No matter how narrow or broad the definition of "in the room" which you settle upon, the statement holds: either he is in the room (in that sense) or he is not.

6. "Even granting all the above points, the statements still don't hold for all cases! For example, a man may love his wife and hate her at the same time. I don't mean that the statement that he does this is true for one person and false for another, or that it's true at one time and false at another, or any of the things treated above. I

mean that it is a true fact about the man, call him Smith, that at 8
p.m. Eastern Standard Time on the twentieth of September, 1953,
he both loves her and hates her; and since hating means (or at least
involves) not loving, he loves her and doesn't love her, both at the
same time."

This is the most intelligent of the charges that have been brought
forward. The usual answer to it is this: "You must specify the respect in which these things are the case. For instance, at one and
the same moment he may love her with respect to her attractiveness
and hate her with respect to her selfishness. Or perhaps even this is
not specific enough: he may love her and hate her at the same time
with respect to her attractiveness: love her for it because it arouses
his passion and hate her for it because it enslaves him to her emo-
tionally. But here again there is no contradiction: he loves her for
her attractiveness in one respect and hates her for it in another.
You have to be very careful in specifying the respect in which the
statement applies. But actually it's just the business of incomplete
specification over again: specify exactly the respects you mean,
and you will find that there is no contradiction."

That is one way of getting around the objection. Here is another:
"Love and hate aren't really opposites. Push them far enough, as
Dostoevsky and others have clearly shown in their novels, and
finally, like the sequence of sharps and flats in music, they come
round full circle, together again. If this is so, love and hate may
exist together, but this isn't love and not-love existing together, or
even love and a *part* of not-love existing together (as would be true
in the case of opposites like hot and cold). In emotional states of
great intensity, hate has become a form of love and perhaps love a
form of hate; or perhaps neither, and the names just aren't applicable any more. In either case, 'I hate her' doesn't contradict 'I love
her,' any more than 'This is round' contradicts 'This is red.' "

Justification of the principles of logic. Let us turn back, then, to
the principles of logic, and ask how they can be proved to be true.

Is it not enough to say that to deny them is to contradict oneself?
Surely if you denied "If p, then p," you would get a self-contradictory statement, and so on with the rest of the list. Thus we could
say that the principles of logic are all tautologies; and is this not
as good a proof as we could want?

Thus far we have assumed that if a statement is self-contradictory, this is enough to refute it, and that if its negative is self-contradictory, this is enough to prove it true. But how is this in turn to be established? What is wrong with being self-contradictory? Suppose somebody wanted to be obstinate and decided that self-contradictory statements were all right; how could we prove that he was wrong? Granted that denying the laws of logic yields self-contradictions, how does this disprove them? True, some of the laws of logic themselves prohibit self-contradictions (for instance, the Law of Non-contradiction says that if p is true, the statement that contradicts p [not-p] cannot also be true) but can we use the Law of Non-contradiction to establish itself? Can we use any statement to establish itself? Is this not like a religious document declaring that it itself is divinely inspired? You cannot rise by your own bootstraps. You cannot establish the principles of logic by using those same principles of logic to do it. Then how, *other than by the laws of logic*, can we establish the laws of logic?

The answer is, of course, that it cannot be done. Even if it could, it would hardly help us. For suppose we found a body of other statements, K, by means of which the laws of logic, L, could be validly deduced. Then (1) how would we prove K? By something else, J? Then how prove J? The question here is infinitely self-repeating— we are lost in an *infinite regress*. Moreover, (2) how could we prove anything except *by* the principles of logic? These are themselves the very principles of proof. If something else, K, could be used to establish the laws of logic, L, then K would be the principles of proof and not L. Finally, (3) we cannot use them to prove themselves, for if we do so we beg the question (assume at the outset the very thing we set out to prove).

We cannot establish them by means of themselves; we cannot establish them by means of principles of proof other than themselves, for they themselves are the principles of proof. Therefore, we cannot establish them at all.[8]

It may take some time to overcome a feeling of dissatisfaction with this result. Perhaps you will never overcome it. You have come across so many statements that can be proved by the laws of logic that you will want the laws of logic themselves to be proved. You may want it done *by* the laws of logic themselves, like the snake

[8] Even in this argument we are using a principle of logic: "If p, then q or r; not q; not r; therefore not p."

swallowing its own tail. Perhaps you want it done by something other than the laws of logic, as in this example: The earth rests on an elephant; what does the elephant rest on? A rock. What does the rock rest on? Another rock. What does that rock rest on? Another rock . . ., and so on, ad infinitum. A lady in the audience keeps asking this question over and over again; finally in exasperation the speaker says to her, "Lady, it's rock *all the way down!*" All the way down—to what? The speaker can stop her endlessly repeated question only by teaching her a little astronomy and curing her of naive notions of up and down—though perhaps she will never quite overcome a feeling of dissatisfaction with the explanation. You too may remain dissatisfied with our conclusions about logic unless you get over the idea that the ultimate principles of proof must themselves be proved.

But just as the lady in the example feared that without another rock the earth would hang suspended in mid-air, so you may fear that without proof the principles of logic will remain suspended and without support. We have just seen that the principles of logic cannot be proved as other things can be proved by means of them. Is there anything other than proof that would satisfy us?

The principles of logic can be given what is generally called a *pragmatic justification*. We can show that a denial of them is *self-stultifying*, and would indeed make all discourse impossible. For example, suppose that somebody says that this object is a box, and then in the same breath denies that it is a box. "This box isn't a box!" We could then say, "But haven't you admitted that it's a box in the first two words of your sentence? How can you call it a box if you say it isn't a box? The end of your sentence gives the lie to the beginning! Your statement is self-contradictory!" "Well, what's wrong with self-contradictions?" "A self-contradiction is a self-contradiction, isn't it?" "Yes." "Then S is S, and at least one law of logic (Law of Identity) holds after all! And it's not both a self-contradiction and *not* a self-contradiction, is it?" And so on until we have the laws of logic granted after all.

Of course, our opponent may not grant as much as this. He may say, "No, a self-contradiction *isn't* necessarily a self-contradiction." "You mean when you call it a self-contradiction, you *aren't* calling it a self-contradiction? Then what *is* it you are talking about? a self-contradiction or not?" and we can get him to the point where he cannot admit to talking about anything that he can name (a self-contradiction or anything else), for the moment he gives it one name, he is excluding the thing he is talking about from areas *not* covered by that name. Thus he cannot meaningfully assert anything at all; he has passed beyond the pale of significant discourse. We cannot strictly disprove him, but we can show him that if he makes a single assertion and he means *that* assertion and not some other one, he is by that very fact committing himself to that assertion and thus denying any assertion that contradicts it.

Another example: "I deny that if *p*, then *p*." "I see. Do you think that your denial is true?" "Of course." "And if your denial is true, then your denial is true?" "Yes." "Then if *p*, then *p*. You've assumed the Law of Identity in the very act of denying it! If you didn't assume it, you couldn't even state the propositions that you just did!" In other words, *without assuming the law he could not assert anything, not even a denial of the law itself.* It is in this way that the denial of the principles of logic is self-stultifying.

Do we gain new knowledge from deductive reasoning? Although we may grant the truth of the principles of logic and the disastrous results of denying them, we may feel qualms about their usefulness. This difficulty is particularly felt in the case of the principles of deductive inference, such as "If *p* is true and *p* implies *q*, then *q* is true"—those principles of logic which enable us to go from the premises of an argument to its conclusion.

We have already observed (see pages 116–119) that rules of deductive inference do not enable us to know whether the premises from which we reason are true; they only enable us to decide whether our reasoning is valid, or in other words whether we have committed a fallacy in drawing the conclusion from the premises. But a question often arises in the minds of students concerning this whole procedure: when we validly deduce a conclusion from a set of premises, do we know any more than we already did when we started the premises? What has been gained in the process?

> All human beings have heads.
> John Stewart is a human being.
> Therefore, John Stewart has a head.

The conclusion (one might remark) is already contained in the premises, and therefore the conclusion tells us nothing new. Indeed, in order to know the major premise—that all men have heads—we already have to know that John Stewart has one! What, then, is the use of deductive argument, and of rules of deductive inference?

When it is said that the conclusion is already contained in the premises, the word "contained" is ambiguous. The conclusion is not literally contained within the premises as a marble is contained in a bag. Nor is it contained in the sense that it *occurs* in the premises, for the statement "John Stewart has a head" does not occur in the premises. The conclusion is, however, contained in the premises in the sense that it is *deducible from* the premises. But to say this is only to repeat what we said at the start. The question, then, still faces us (and we shall phrase it now without using the word "contain"): When the conclusion is deducible from the premises, are we learning anything from the conclusion that we did not already know in stating the premises?

We can answer this quite simply: sometimes we do and sometimes we don't. It all depends on the complexity of the argument and the intelligence of the individual. The question "Do we learn through deductive reasoning what we did not know before?" is a psychological question, the answer to which varies from person to person. In the case of the syllogism given above, the conclusion probably does not give us any new information; before we get to the conclusion we already know what it is. Sometimes, however, even in simple arguments, we do not immediately draw the required conclusion,

> Everyone on board the ship was lost.
> Mabel was on board the ship.

and then it may come to us with a sudden shock that if these statements are both true, Mabel was lost. Here already we may be said to have learned something. We were told nothing about Mabel except that she was on board the ship; we then learned that everyone on board was lost; we are thus enabled to deduce validly that Mabel was lost, *without ever having been told this fact about Mabel*. In coming to know this fact about her, were we not acquiring new knowledge?

This becomes more apparent as the complexity of the argument increases. The conclusion to the following argument would probably constitute new knowledge to most people:

> If the guard was not paying attention at the time, the car was not noticed when it came in.
> If the witness' account is correct, the guard was not paying attention at the time.
> Either the car was noticed or Jones is hiding something.
> Jones is not hiding anything.

Therefore, The witness' account is not correct.

To a person with perfect reasoning powers, who could instantly see the implications of every statement or combination of statements that he uttered, doubtless no conclusion would come as new information; but since human beings are not thus gifted, there are many conclusions of valid deductive arguments which do come as new information, in spite of the fact that "the conclusion is contained in (deducible from) the premises."

Classification of the principles of logic. Let us, finally, ask our now-familiar question of the principles of logic: are they synthetic, and are they necessary? If any class of statements is necessarily true, it would seem to be those of logic. "If p, then p," "If this is a cat, then it is a cat," "If p implies q, and p is true, then q is true," "If cats are mammals, and this is a cat, then this is a mammal," and so on. Surely we do not have to wait for further instances to know that these principles hold for all cases. We know them to hold for all instances—past, present, and future. A person who said that p might not be p in another instance would look even more foolish than one who said that 2 and 2 might not equal 4 in another instance. Do you have to examine cats to see whether any of them are also *not* cats? Indeed, what would it be like to examine a cat to see whether it was a cat? You might examine an animal to see if it was a cat; but when you have already declared, in the first part of the sentence, that it is a cat, what would it mean to proceed then to "see whether it is a cat"?

The principles of logic, then, are necessary and the traditional empiricist view falls by the board. To the question, "Are they synthetic?" again the answer may seem plain: "Of course they aren't. If you deny 'If p then p,' don't you contradict yourself? for aren't you then saying 'p but not p'? (If you deny 'If it's an oyster then it's an oyster,' aren't you saying 'It's an oyster but not an oyster'?) Similarly, if you admit that being red implies being colored and also that this thing is red, and then proceed to deny that this thing is colored, aren't you contradicting yourself?" (If you come to study formal logic, you will be able to show in detail that it is indeed self-contradictory.)

Now, if the rationalist is one who holds that there are necessary propositions which are synthetic, and the logical empiricist is one who holds that there are necessary statements but none of them is synthetic, isn't the outcome all on the side of the logical empiricist, at least as far as the principles of logic are concerned? Not quite; for the issue is not so simple. At this point the rationalist may take either of two views:

1. He may assert in spite of everything that the principles of logic are not tautologies, but synthetic statements; but, he will add, unlike laws of nature, they are necessarily true, and can be known *a priori*, without examination of instances. They are very general characterizations of reality—general because they apply to everything that could ever be embodied in a statement, and are not restricted to any particular subject-matter, not even to such wide fields as physics or mathematics. Not only are the statements of logic more general than any other (the empiricist would hold this too) : they are *necessary*, and they would hold in all possible worlds.

Some rationalists, however, object to the view that the principles of logic are synthetic, and their recourse is as follows:

2. Of course it is self-contradictory to deny "If *p*, then *p*," "If *p* implies *q* and *p* is true, then *q* is true," and the rest of them. In this sense, then, these statements are tautologies. But not all tautologies are alike. "A triangle is a plane figure" is a tautology because it states a defining characteristic of triangles. As we saw in Chapter 1, it is *we* who make a characteristic defining, and by using the word with a different meaning we could keep it from being defining, and then the statement would no longer be a tautology (nor would it be the same statement, for the meaning of one of the words would be different). This all depends on the way we use words. Other tautologies, however, reflect the *ultimate nature of reality;* and our verbal conventions, making some expressions self-contradictory and not others, are patterned after this reality. The Law of Identity, for example, comes down to this: that everything is what it is, and not something else. This, when stated explicitly, turns out to be a

tautology. But it is a very significant tautology. It tells us something about what reality is like, although, to be sure, it is a very general characterization. Not only does it tell us what our universe is like (if it did only this, it would be a contingent proposition) but it tells us what every logically possible universe *must* be like, for it *necessarily applies* to any logically possible state of affairs.

We indicated in defining "rationalism" that the definition would later be refined. The second view stated on page 134 would seem not to be a rationalist view at all, for it admits, in the case of the laws of logic at any rate, that these propositions are tautologies. And yet this view would generally be classified as a rationalist view. A rationalistic view will then be one which *either* (1) asserts that there are synthetic necessary statements, as in our initial classification, *or* (2) admits that necessary statements are tautologies, but distinguishes between tautologies which are mere verbal conventions and those which "reveal fundamental aspects of reality."

In order to clarify the issue, let us imagine a conversation between a rationalist of this second type and a logical empiricist, about the laws of logic:

Empiricist: I maintain that the laws of logic are tautologies, pure and simple.

Rationalist: Very well, if you like, they are tautologies; but to call them such and let it go at that makes us forgetful of their real importance. They do not merely state verbal conventions as some tautologies do. They give us important truths about this world and about all possible worlds. No matter what conditions may prevail beyond the furthest galaxy our telescopes will ever discern, if there is an object A there, then we know that A is A, and that A isn't something other than A.[9] This is an absolutely fundamental law of reality. Suppose it didn't hold! Neither science nor any other human enterprise would then be possible. Fortunately it does hold: everything is what it is. This is perhaps the most fundamental law of all reality —at least the *sine qua non* for all others.

Empiricist: I deny that this is a law about reality. It states nothing about the world. It only states a requirement of language: that when a certain symbol "s" applies to something, the symbol "not-s" does not also

[9] This is not quite the form in which the Law of Identity has been presented so far. We have presented it as being about propositions: "If proposition p is true, then proposition p is true." Here it is about things: "If this is an A, then this is an A." But actually the latter can be converted into the former: If proposition p (that this is an A) is true, then proposition p (that this is an A) is true. We are using the thing-formulation rather than the proposition-formulation because it is less cumbersome.

apply to it. To deny this, is to contradict the verbal conventions we ourselves have laid down.

Rationalist: But don't you see, the whole significance of it falls out on
your interpretation. When we say that *p* is *p we are bowing to a reality
which is not of our own making. We* did not make it so. Our verbal convention only reflects, as it were, the reality which it did not make. Take
the Law of Non-contradiction: "Not both p and not-p." This *tells us something* about the nature of things. "This is not both a table and not a
table" [10] may sound trivial, but that is only because we are so used to it;
everything we've come across has fulfilled this law. We are so familiar with
instances of it that we tend to take it for granted or overlook it. But it *is*
a fact about the table: it isn't both a table and not a table.

Empiricist: I don't think it's a fact about the table at all, not even a
very general kind of fact. The proposition *tells us nothing* about the table.
From being told it, I know no more about the table than I did before.

Rationalist: Not specific information, I grant you. Not if you want to
know its color or size or weight or what's on top of it. That, of course, is
all contingent. But behind all that specific information lies a fact for which
you may always be thankful: that when it's a table it's not simultaneously
not a table.

Empiricist: But what kind of fact is this? Surely not a fact about the
table. Substitute any noun for the word "table" in the sentence, and it
would still hold.

Rationalist: Ah, that's precisely my point! Of course it would—that is
what we mean by saying that the laws of logic give you only very *general*
information—they apply to *everything.* This isn't both a table and not a
table, that isn't both a dog and not a dog, and so on. Of course it applies
to everything, and has universal application. But a fact which has universal
application is still a fact; it's just a more general fact than the specific
facts in which we have a practical interest and think about every day.

Empiricist: Very well; but I still insist that it gives *no information.*
"This isn't both a table and not a table" gives no information about this
table or about tables in general, and "This isn't both a dog and not a dog"
gives no information about this dog or dogs in general. A principle such as
the Law of Non-contradiction is entirely *empty of content.* It says nothing
about anything in this world or any other world. The formulation is misleading, I admit, because in one case the word "table" is used in the sentence, and in the other case the word "dog" is used, and so on, so that you
may be misled into thinking that the statement is *about* tables or dogs. But
this is a delusion. All the statement reveals is a *verbal convention* about the
use of the word "not." Take any group of things, call them A; then everything outside that group will be called not-A. This is no cosmic truth, it's
simply an explication of our use of the word "not." The Law of Non-

---

[10] Again we are employing the thing-language for the sake of convenience.
But again it can be translated: "This is not both a table and not a table" becomes "Not both proposition *p* (that this is a table) and proposition *not-p*
(that this is not a table) are true."

contradiction says in effect that to call some things A is to refrain from calling them not-A, because "not-A" is the label we've given to whatever is outside the area covered by A. Similarly with the Law of Excluded Middle: it states that whatever *isn't* A is not-A, so that absolutely everything is included in the two classes, A and not-A, there is no third possibility, there is nothing that is *neither* A nor not-A. But this again is only an explication of the word "not," just as "A triangle is a plane closed figure" is a (partial) explication of our use of the word "triangle."

Rationalist: I see you miss the whole spirit of what I'm trying to say. Let me try with one more example, one of the principles of inference: "If p implies q and p is true, then q is true." Now I hold that this statement is a necessary truth which reveals something about the nature of things. After all, it does apply to the world and to everything in it without exception. If being red implies being colored, and this thing is red, then presto, we *know* that this thing is colored. If being a man implies being mortal, and Smith is a man, we *know* that Smith is mortal. And so it goes for every example. It never turns out any other way—try it out in as many cases as you like, fill in the form of this argument with any content you please, and if the premises are true so is the conclusion. And not only does it turn out always to be so (the traditional empiricist would grant this too), but it *necessarily* does so, it *must*, and hence would do so in every possible universe. Thus the principle is more significant than any law of science, which holds for the actual universe only.

Empiricist: I agree that the principle is necessary, but that's only because it's a tautology. Oh, I know that you agree now to that too, but you say it's a different kind of tautology. I deny even this. Like the cases we've just considered, the principle of inference which we're now considering only explicates a verbal convention—that is, it makes clear part of what we mean by the word "implies." Suppose you say that p implies q and also that p is true—and then deny that q is true! You must not really mean then that p implies q! In other words, you don't really mean the first premise. In the first premise you say that p implies q; this means that if you accept p, you are committed to accepting q too. Then in the second premise you accept p. Very well then, you are already committed to saying that q is true. If you deny it, you must really not have meant one of the premises you just uttered—that p is true, and that p implies q. So once again, the principle says nothing about the world; it only explicates the language with which you talk about the world. It says, in this case, that if you say p implies q, it must *really* imply it; that is, that the relation of implication really is the relation of implication and not some other relation.

Rationalist: Ah, it is what it is—everything is what it is and not another thing. Here we are back again at the Law of Identity, which I hold is a fundamental truth about reality.

Empiricist: And I hold that it is no such thing . . . but we have argued this point already.

VII. FURTHER CONTROVERSY BETWEEN RATIONALISM AND EMPIRICISM

To conclude our account of this controversy, let us examine several propositions which have often been employed to support the rationalist's position, though they do not fall within any of the fields we have been considering in preceding sections.

1. *You can't smell a taste or taste a smell.* What can you taste? Bitter, sour, and so forth, and combinations of these. What can you smell? Pungent smells, fragrant smells . . . (there is no simple classification of them, but each is easily definable ostensively). But what would it be like to smell a taste, or taste a smell?

A traditional rationalist might say that while you cannot *imagine* it, this only testifies to the limitation of human imagination. Doubtless it is empirically impossible to smell a taste, but logically possible: logically possible because a proposition such as "I smelled a taste" would not be self-contradictory, however false it might be. Doubtless it is a necessary truth, knowable *a priori;* but it still is synthetic.

A logical empiricist would reply: "Of course you can't smell a taste. But the 'can't' here is a logical 'can't'; it is logically impossible that you should do so, for to say that you smelled a taste would be self-contradictory. You'd be saying that you smelled what wasn't a smell. The very meaning of the words standing for tastes and smells is such that they exclude each other. Therefore, there is no great mystery about this impossibility: the way we use the words involved, it would simply be a self-contradiction to speak of smelling a taste or tasting a smell."

Here the modified rationalist, whose position was brought out in the preceding section, might come in: "True, you *would* be contradicting yourself. You would be violating a verbal convention. But now look behind this verbal convention. It reflects a fundamental fact about reality: in this case, that there are certain categories, one for each different sense-modality, which cannot be crossed: 'No trespassing.' And the fact that they cannot be crossed is a *necessary* fact."

(Does this hold for all the sense-modalities? Someone might object that science has enabled us to see sounds. But this would be a mistake. What science has enabled us to see are waves which aren't themselves sound-waves, but are correlated with them in a regular way. Moreover, as we saw earlier, even the sound-*waves* are not the same thing as the sounds we experience. So the case of sights and sounds is no different from that of smells and tastes.)

2. *If event A precedes event B (in time), and B precedes C, then A precedes C.* "What could be more elementary than this? Every child knows it. Wouldn't a person be crazy who said that A happened before B did, and B happened before C, and yet insisted that A happened *after* C?"

Perhaps. The question is not whether the above statement is true. It is whether the rationalist position or the empiricist position with regard to it is the true one.

Let us pause first to see how inadequate the traditional empiricist position is to take care of a proposition like this. It would go something like this: "The statement is synthetic but not necessary; it is a generalization from experience, just like 'All crows are black,' albeit a generalization which has been confirmed millions of times over and never violated even once, as far as we know. The cars were approaching each other before the collision, the collision occurred before the occupants were taken to the hospital; and, of course, the cars approached each other before the occupants were taken to the hospital. Queen Elizabeth reigned before James I, and James I before George III; and we find also that Queen Elizabeth reigned before George III. This sort of thing has been confirmed so many times in our experience that it never occurs to us that it might not always hold. There is, however, a possibility that it *might* not hold in some future instance. No matter how uniformly something may have occurred in the past, it might be different in the future, so as to upset our prediction. This is true even of the statement we are now considering. There *may* sometime be an event that occurs before a second event, and the second event occurring before a third, with the first nevertheless occurring *after* the third. Perhaps something like a football team beating a second one, which in turn beats a third, and the third turns around and beats the first. May not the time-sequence be like that, at least in some instances thus far unknown to us, far off in the future perhaps? Empirically impossible—very well; that only means that it is not the way nature works; however, it is *not* logically impossible. The statement that such a thing occurred would be false, but there

is no contradiction in it. And there is no *necessity* about it either—
that is, you cannot know it to be true *a priori* for all cases everywhere and always. In my opinion, there is no necessity about *any*
statement about the world. It is just an unusually well-founded empirical generalization, and the verdict of any empirical generalization may be reversed by subsequent experience."

This is the position the consistent upholder of the empiricist view
would maintain. Few persons do hold it because they are sure that
there is a difference between the example of the football-team sort
and the example of the time-sequence sort. Could anything be more
preposterous than to believe that ever, anywhere, nine o'clock came
before ten o'clock and ten o'clock before eleven, but eleven came
before nine? (We mean, of course, the same nine o'clock, not the
nine o'clock half a day later.) Isn't it true that if you know that
event A occurred before event B and event B before event C, *you
can be absolutely sure* that A occurred before C?

Both the rationalist and the logical empiricist will reply with a
Yes; but they will give different accounts of the matter.

Traditional Rationalist: We can be sure, and yet there's no contradiction
in denying it. It's synthetic and necessary. Here is just another instance of
synthetic necessary truth, something we can know to be true about the
world (and all possible worlds), but which we don't have to verify by
observation of the world. The traditional empiricist is right in saying that
the statement is synthetic; but he is wrong in saying that it isn't necessarily true. On the other hand, the statement "If team A wins over team B
and team B wins over team C, then team A will win over team C" is *not*
necessary.

Logical Empiricist: You and I both agree, against the empiricist, that
the statement is necessary. But we give different accounts of the necessity:
you say it's also synthetic, while I say that it's necessary for the pure and
simple reason that it's a tautology. If you said A was prior to B and B to
C, and yet said A wasn't prior to C, you'd be caught in a contradiction.
Consider the *meaning* of terms having to do with time. Isn't part of the
very meaning of "precede" its transitivity? Let me explain: A relation is
transitive when, if it holds between a first term and a second, and between
the second and a third, it then necessarily holds between the first and the
third. It's intransitive if it necessarily fails to hold. It's non-transitive if it
isn't necessary the one way or the other. Now, we both agree that the temporal relation is transitive: if A is before B and B is before C, then A is
before C. And we agree that its transitivity is *necessary,* and can be known
a priori to hold for all cases. But I say that it's transitive *by definition,*
and that its transitivity is just a part of the definition of a term like "pre-

cedes." When you *say* that A precedes B and B precedes C, you just implicitly *mean* by this that A precedes C. If you do go on and say explicitly that A precedes C, *you are adding nothing to the content of the statement;* you are saying *no more* than you said before! And everybody recognizes this. Suppose you said to someone: "Here's a piece of information: she struck him before he shot her, and he shot her before the neighbors ran in." And then you turned around to add: "Oh yes, another bit of information: she struck him before the neighbors ran in." Your listener would laugh at you. He would say, "But I knew that already! That's a part of what you told me in the first place!"

Modified Rationalist: I agree that if you denied the statement we are considering, you would contradict yourself. Hence I agree that it is necessary because it's a tautology. But what I want to insist is that something of the nature of reality is revealed in this fact. Consider: Would you say that *whenever* A has a certain relation to B, and B to C, A has that relation to C? Of course not. You wouldn't say that if A is the father of B and B is the father of C, then A is the father of C. Indeed, he couldn't be, could he, for this relation is intransitive. Or again: if A loves B, and B loves C, then A loves C? It doesn't work, does it? (This one was non-transitive.) Now, don't we *know* that some relations are transitive and others are intransitive or non-transitive? and don't we know that they are *necessarily* so, for instance, that the time relation we are now considering is necessarily transitive? You can say, if you like, that it is so by definition, that "part of the meaning" of the time relation is its transitivity and of the father-relation its intransitivity. But doesn't this strike you as a bit superficial? Why have our verbal conventions been ordered the way they are? *Why haven't we defined these two the other way around?* Because the one relation simply *is* transitive and the other is not. This is a fact which was not of our own making, and our verbal conventions (about "part of the meaning of") only reflect this antecedent and necessary fact. Perhaps I can best illustrate it this way: Can you conceive of a relationship, exactly like the time-relationship, *except that it's intransitive*—the same, with that one characteristic omitted? You see, *it's no accident that its transitivity is "part of its very meaning" and hence tautologous. Our verbal conventions reflect the way reality goes.* So even this statement, which it's self-contradictory to deny, tells us something about the world: namely that the time-stream is (necessarily) a one-way stream, and is irreversible in its direction.

3. *All colors are extended.* The word "colors" here refers to experienced colors, not to light-waves; and "extended" means simply "spread out." The statement is not restricted to saying that all colored *physical things* are extended (though this is doubtless true enough), for colors are sometimes experienced without the presence of physical things, as in hallucinations, after-images, spots before your eyes, dreams, and the like. What is asserted is that all the

colors, in all these experiences, are extended. Nor need they be extended in *physical* space: if you see red spots before your eyes, or see stars when somebody hits you on the head, it is doubtful whether these colors are locatable in physical space, but still they are spread out, or *extended*.

We might try to interpret the statement as the traditional empiricist would—synthetic but not necessary. "Isn't it just a fact of nature that colors are all extended, just as it is a fact of nature (as far as we know) that crows are all black?" Again this alternative is easily attacked. Is there really a danger that "All colors are extended" will be met with an exception in the next instance, the way there is with "All crows are black"? Don't we know, and know *a priori*, that all colors, past, present, and future, are extended? If someone says he saw a color, must we ask, "Was it extended?"

The logical empiricist's answer is easy: "All colors are extended" is analytic. Extension is a defining characteristic of color, and anyone who spoke of an unextended color would be contradicting himself. Thus we can know *a priori* that all colors are extended, and for the simple reason that it is an analytic statement.

Perhaps this is the answer; but there are many who say that it is not so. Traditional rationalists will say that the statement is not only necessary but synthetic, and that it is synthetic because "being extended" is not a defining characteristic of color. To put it another way: the concept of color is one thing, and the concept of extension is another; they are not the same concept, nor is the one even a part of the other. Thus you cannot say that extension is "a part of the very meaning" of color: out of the concept of color you can never draw the concept of extension. Rather, being colored and being extended are *two different* characteristics, and it is *logically possible* that they might occur separately; however, they do not, and we can *know a priori* that they never will. (The problem of how we know this will be discussed in the next section.) This is just another of the synthetic statements that we know *a priori* to be true.

It is also possible to take a modified rationalist view of the statement, but on this issue the usual position is the "orthodox" or traditional rationalist one presented above.

'4. *No object has two different colors at the same place at the same time.* Suppose you have a box which is painted red all over its surface. Can it also be blue all over? Of course not. How do we know this? Suppose someone said, "No boxes *you* have ever seen are both red and blue all over, but *I* have seen such boxes." Would this be like a report of a new kind of beast on a strange and unexplored island? Would it not be stranger, far stranger, than that? Do you believe there could be such a box even on Mars?

The traditional empiricist position is that it is just a fact of nature that there are no such boxes; the statement that nothing has two colors at the same place at the same time is just another law of science describing our world, but there is no necessity about it, and it might well not hold in the next case.

The rationalist position is that the statement is synthetic and necessary. We know it to be true *a priori*, but it is not a tautology or an analytic statement. (Of course, we could first paint the box red and then paint it blue, but that is not what is meant; we mean the color of the surface, not of what is just under the surface. We can paint it red and blue striped, but this again is irrelevant: no one denied that it could be red in one place and blue in another. Or we can mix red and blue paints and paint the entire surface with this; but this again is irrelevant: we do not mean reddish blue or bluish red or any other color that might result from the mixture, but we mean pure red all over *and* pure blue all over.)

The logical empiricist will say, "Of course we know *a priori* that the box can't be pure red and pure blue all over at the same time. But no wonder, the statement is a flat tautology. Why? Because 'red,' whatever else it means, and whether or not it is definable other than ostensively, means at least this, that it is *not* some other color—for example, not blue. If you said the box was both red and blue, you'd be saying that it was both red and not-red at the same time, which would be manifestly self-contradictory."

This may sound quite satisfactory: "red" means, among other things, not blue, and "blue" means, among other things, not red. Is not the logical empiricist then clearly right? But before we assent, let us try the same analysis on another adjective, "hard." If "red" means not blue, doesn't it also mean not hard? Redness is as different from hardness as it is from blueness. Yet something can be both red all over and hard all over at the same time!

Here a logical empiricist may reply, "True, the meaning of 'red' is different from that of 'hard' as it is from that of 'blue.' But the meaning of 'red' *excludes,* or is *incompatible with,* that of 'blue,' whereas it is simply different from (but not incompatible with) that of 'hard.' "

Here the rationalist interjects: "But *why is the one excluded and not the other?* Did we just *make* redness incompatible with blueness but not with hardness? No; it is a necessary fact about reality, a fact not of our own making. Our verbal usage—making 'This is red and blue all over' self-contradictory, but not 'This is red and hard all over'—simply recognizes and falls into line with this necessary fact about reality. To say 'This marble is red and blue all over' is indeed self-contradictory; but the reason for the self-contradictoriness does not lie merely in a verbal convention; it is rooted in a necessary fact about reality. We implicitly recognize this necessary fact in making our verbal conventions, which determine self-contradictoriness: for instance, in determining that 'It's red and blue' will be self-contradictory but not 'It's red and hard.'

"Actually," the rationalist continues, "the red-blue example is just one instance of a general necessary principle, the Principle of Determinables: At any given place and time *there can be only one determinate under a given determinable.* Red and blue are determinates under the same determinable, color. But hardness, being a tactile quality, does not come under the color-determinable. Therefore redness and hardness can co-exist at the same place, but not redness and blueness. The coexistence of redness and blueness would violate the Principle of Determinables. This principle is a necessary fact about reality, of which the red-blue example is merely one instance."

VIII. INTUITION AND KNOWLEDGE

A priori assumptions. Thus far we have been concerned with the question of whether there are synthetic statements which are necessary and therefore can be known *a priori* to be true. Such statements, whether there really are any or not, are small in number compared with statements that are *assumed a priori* to be true; in many cases, in fact, they are false. In ordinary life we are confronted with this every day: a person with deep prejudices will simply *assume a priori* that a certain statement is true, and he will reject any evidence that may turn up against the statement, or he will discount it or distort it to serve his ends. In other words, *prior* to an examination of the merits of the statement, he will simply assume it to be true (or false, as the case may be). To take an example outside the fields of politics, morals, and religion, which are perhaps the principal fields in which such assumptions occur: a Scotsman says that all great poets are Scottish. You then mention Shakespeare, who was not Scottish. He will then either deny that Shakespeare was a great poet, or he will reject all the historical data about Shakespeare being born in Stratford-on-Avon, and so on—not because he has any counter-evidence of his own, but because *a priori* he will admit nothing that contradicts his statement that all great poets are Scottish. In all fields of inquiry in which feeling runs high, the ideas of countless numbers of people are dominated by *a priori* assumptions.

Although *a priori* assumptions are extremely common in life, they do not have much interest for philosophers, and we only mention them here so that there will be no confusion between *a priori* assumptions and the *a priori knowledge* (real or alleged) which we have been discussing. Philosophers are not particularly interested in what statements can be *assumed a priori* to be true; there are probably very few statements about things that matter to human beings that have not at some time or other by somebody or other been assumed *a priori* to be true. What does matter is whether any synthetic statements can be *known a priori* to be true and whether any can be known *a priori* to be false, though less interest has centered on the false ones.

The analysis of knowing. If there are synthetic statements we can know *a priori* to be true, *how* do we know them?

Let us first ask ourselves what it means to know something. Consider knowing in comparison with wondering, thinking, believing, wishing, and the like. All these last-mentioned are states of mind. At first you may be inclined to think that knowing is also a state of mind (that knowing X = being in a certain state of mind or attitude toward X): that when you wonder whether proposition p is true, you are experiencing one mental state; when you believe p is true, you are experiencing another; when you doubt whether p is true, still another; and when you *know* p is true, this is yet another. Each of them, or more precisely the words standing for them, may well be indefinable except ostensively; still they are distinguishable from each other and each of us recognizes in his own experience the difference among them, for example, the difference between believing and doubting.

A bit of reflection should convince you that knowing is different from the others in a way other than the rest are different from one another. True, when you *know* something to be true you also *believe* it to be true (you don't wonder about it, or doubt it); indeed, the *state of mind* involved in knowing is probably the same as that involved in strong belief. How then are they different? They differ in this: that in believing that *p* is true we are *merely* having a certain state of mind or attitude toward the statement we are believing; but when we *know* that *p* is true, a *further condition* must be fulfilled: *p* must really be *true*. When we say that we know *p*, we are not saying merely that we feel a certain way toward *p*, for instance that we believe *p*. We are saying also that *p* is true.

Thus we have two defining characteristics of knowing *p*. We know *p* when (1) *p* is true and (2) we believe *p* to be true. Both of these are necessary conditions for knowing. In the absence of even one of them, the word "know" would cease to be applicable. Both are essential:

The first condition is essential: It would be fortunate, perhaps, if we could know whether *p* was true just by asking ourselves whether we really believed *p*. Sometimes we can tease or rationalize ourselves into thinking that we know that *p* is true when all that is really the case is that we believe *p* very strongly. Much alleged knowledge is really only strong belief, based usually on wishful thinking. But believing does not make it so: if you have invested in the stock market and confidently believe that the stocks will go up on a certain day, you know full well that believing it does not make it so.[11] You may even have been extremely confident about it and said to yourself and others, "I *know* that they will go up." But

[11] While believing *p* is not the same as knowing *p* (believing *p* does not make *p* true), it does sometimes happen that believing *p* very strongly may enable you to fulfill the conditions that would make *p* true. Thus, believing that you will pass a course may motivate you to hard study, which in turn will enable you to pass the course and thus render the statement true. That is to say, the psychological fact of believing something may have effects, among which are the fulfillment of the conditions that make *p* true. This of course does not mean for a moment that believing *p* is the same as knowing *p*.

unfortunately knowing is not merely a state of mind: the stocks may go down regardless of what you believe, and when they *do* go down you will have to retract your statement that you *knew* they would go up. What you do *not* have to retract is the statement that you *believed* that they would go up. What does this show? That if *p* turns out to be false, you cannot have *known p* to be true, because one defining characteristic of knowing *p* is that *p* be true; but you can still have *believed p* to be true, because it is no defining characteristic of believing *p* that *p* is true.

The second condition is essential: It is equally essential that you believe *p* to be true. *P* may be true without your believing it; in that case, you do not know *p*. There may be all sorts of true statements, but if you do not believe them you can hardly say you now know them. In the Middle Ages very few people would have said the earth was round, and they surely did not *know* that it was—not because the statement that the earth is round was not true, but because they did not believe that it was.

Are these two enough? Can we say that we know *p* to be true when (1) it is true and (2) we believe it to be so? We might be inclined to answer yes. But let us consider a hypothetical example: Suppose it is true that there are mountains on the other side of the moon, which no one on the earth can ever see because the moon always turns the same face toward the earth. Suppose also that you believe strongly that there are mountains on the other side of the moon. Are these two conditions sufficient to enable you to say you *know* that there are mountains on the other side of the moon? Or suppose someone who is inclined firmly to believe (at least for the moment) almost every idea that pops into his mind suddenly gets the idea that there are 2,594 books on your library shelves; then the books are counted and behold, it turns out there really are 2,594 books there. He may not get it right again in a million trials; but he got it right this time. Now, can you say he *knew* (even though he'd never been in the room before) that there were 2,594 books on these shelves? Is it not more like a wild guess that he suddenly believed in, which just happened to turn out all right? (Of course he may later tell his friends, "I *knew* there were that many," thus mystifying them as to how he could have known it; but the fact still remains that it was a guess that turned out in this instance to be right.)

What further condition do these examples suggest? That there must also be *evidence* for *p*; that in addition to *p* being true, and your believing *p* to be true, you must also believe it on the basis of *evidence*—not, for instance, a wild guess.

How much evidence is needed before you can know *p*? All the evidence there is. All the evidence that is possible at the time? No, that may not be enough. All the evidence available to us now does not enable us to *know* that the star Sirius has planets. The evidence must be complete. If we have only 99 per cent of it, the other 1 per cent may not bear out the 99 per cent, and the statement will then turn out to be false after all, or at least doubtful. We may think that every one of the 100 marbles in the bag is black after looking at 99 of them, but the 100th may turn out to be a white one. Surely we cannot *know* that they are all black until we have examined the entire 100.[12] So we now add a third condition of knowing: (3) There must be complete evidence that *p* is true. When is the evidence incomplete? When there is any further observation or calculation to be made which might render *p* more probable. Adding this condition makes it apparent that there are many statements we do not really know to be true because we do not have complete evidence for them ("all the evidence isn't in yet") which still seem very *likely* to be true. Indeed, one may well ask, after this third condition has been added, whether I really *know* the truth of any statements at all, except perhaps tautologies and analytic statements. What about seemingly obvious synthetic statements such as that I have two hands, that I am now awake, or that I am sitting on a chair?

These are all synthetic statements which are known to be true, if at all, by observation; that is to say, they are *empirical statements*. As such, they will be discussed in the next chapter. Among the many questions that will be asked about empirical statements is the question of whether any of them can be *known* to be true, as opposed to merely being *probably* true.

We are here concerned with necessary statements—those which we can know *a priori* to be true without observation of all cases. These statements are not empirical because they need not be veri-

---

[12] There are other difficulties here, such as, When do we know for sure that even *one* marble is black? or that it's a marble at all? that we aren't having a hallucination or dreaming it? These questions will be discussed in Chapter 6.

fied by empirical means (by observation of the world); they can
be known directly, without recourse to the processes of testing and
verifying that are required in the natural sciences. If we know a
synthetic statement *a priori* (although empiricists say we never do),
we can know it to hold true for all cases, even future cases which
we have never examined. This is far more than a scientist will usually claim for the statements asserted in his science; at best he will
"confidently expect" that the generalizations about nature that he
has asserted will continue to hold in the future. But he must wait
for future observation to see. The believer in synthetic necessary
statements, however, is not limited by this need: his statements
necessarily hold, and thus he knows *a priori* that they are true. Or
does he? How does he know?

Intuition. One common answer is, "By intuition. He *intuits* that
these statements are true." But what is this intuition by which
a person is alleged to know these things? What is this intuition that
can leap across gaps which scientists with the most careful instruments of verification cannot bridge?

It is not easy to say exactly what people mean by "intuition."
You have been working on a difficult problem, without getting anywhere with it, and all of a sudden the answer comes to you, or the
whole issue suddenly comes together and makes sense "in a flash
of intuition." It need not, perhaps, be a flash, as if a light suddenly
went on inside but the more gradual the process of clarification is,
the less likely it is to be called "intuition." We need not, however,
try to describe the feeling precisely. As long as it is a feeling, the
inevitable question arises: How does *it* prove that the statement
which you "intuit" is true?

This is a serious difficulty; for if the mere fact that you "intuit"
p proves that *p* is true, what about somebody else who has a different feeling about *p* and "intuits" that *p* is false? Can the same
statement be both true and false? Suppose, to take a simple example, you "intuit" that your cousin in Australia died two minutes
ago, while your brother "intuits" that he did not. You cannot both
be right. One of your intuitions must be wrong, and time alone will
tell which. Hence *the mere fact that you "intuit" that* p *is true is
no guarantee that* p *really is true.*

"But of course," one might object, "some intuitions are right and
some are wrong!" In that case, how does one *know* by intuition? Is

not intuition at best an *indicator* of what must later be found to be true *by other means?* Take the proverbial "woman's intuition": in the present case the lady is gifted with a sense of direction. When you are lost on an unfamiliar road far from home, she, without examining the stars or the compass, will tell you in what direction you are going. Suppose you want to go to Crippled Canyon, knowing only that it lies somewhere to the south, but you don't know which way south is. It is a cloudy starless night, and she says, pointing, "Go that way and you'll be going toward Crippled Canyon." You take her advice, and behold, you get to Crippled Canyon. How did she know? She has never been in this region before, any more than you have. By intuition, you say.

Let us first ask, not *"How* did she know?" but *"Did* she know?" (Remember our analysis of knowledge on pages 145–148.) Was the fact that she had a certain feeling (which we cannot easily describe) enough to enable us to say that she *knew?* Suppose that she had had the intuition, but this time it had gone wrong, and by following her advice you did not get to Crippled Canyon but to Buzzard Gulch instead. Did she still *know* by intuition that Crippled Canyon was in the direction she said it was? Of course not: then we say, "Her intuition went wrong," or "She thought she knew but actually she didn't"; she *believed p* but she didn't *know p,* because of course in order to know *p, p* must be true, and this time *p* turned out to be false.

Her "intuitive feeling" was no different when it turned out wrong from what it was when it turned out right. If it were, she would have been aware of the difference and said, "I'm not so sure . . ." If there were some warning signal in consciousness that always accompanied unreliable intuitions, she would take full advantage of this, for it would prevent her from giving voice to them. In fact, would they then be intuitions at all? If one aspect of an intuition is the feeling of certainty that it is true, then the warning signal would keep her from *having* this feeling of certainty in the first place, and so she would not even be said to "intuit" that *p* was true. And of course the notorious fact about intuitions is that the state of feeling (including the certainty of conviction) is the same whether or not the statement "known intuitively" is true. Once again, merely having an intuition alone is no guarantee that what is "intuited" is true.

What then does guarantee it? The finding out, *through means other than intuition*, that the statement is true: in the present case, by riding in the direction indicated and seeing whether the road leads to Crippled Canyon. It is not by intuition that you know that it is true—*the intuition itself provides no check* as between the true ones and the false ones. By intuition you may guess, or have a strong "hunch," or even be "utterly convinced," that *p* is true. But you do not *know* that it is true until you have amassed the evidence—in this case by riding in the direction indicated, finally seeing the sign "Crippled Canyon, population 384," talking with residents, and so forth.

One can make a strong case, then, for holding that the whole idea of *knowing* by intuition is a mistake. We have a conviction that some statement is true. But until we have at hand all the evidence for it, we cannot be said to know it. How *could* we know it as long as the evidence, when we did come to examine it, might turn out to indicate that it was false? Probably, if we take the total "intuitions" people have had throughout the ages, more of them have turned out wrong than right.

But even if this last point were not so—even if, for example, *all* the intuitions of the woman with a sense of direction were right— still, would it be the intuition that gave the knowledge of the direction of Crippled Canyon? Would it not at best be a good *indicator?* If every time someone "intuited" which horse would win the next day's race, and it turned out that that horse did win, and this had already happened a hundred times, you might not know anything about how the predicter got this feeling, but you would still be inclined to lay odds on his "intuitions." Remember D. H. Lawrence's remarkable story, "The Rocking Horse Winner." Even so, could you say that he *knew* by intuition which horse would win— even before the race occurred? Remember (1) one thing essential to knowing *p* is that *p* be true, and if, the next afternoon, the horse in question does not win, then *p* is not true, and one of the defining characteristics of knowing is not present; and (2) even if this never happened, it seems that the intuition, being a feeling only, is not knowledge; it therefore violates one of the requirements of knowing (the third one listed above). That you feel that *p* is true is never any guarantee that you know *p*, even though *p* may really happen to be true; what is further required is the verification (such as watching the races) *after* you or somebody has had the intuition.

After the person has had his "intuition," and after the placing of the bets, you still want to see the race, to observe whether the horse wins. By this fact you admit that "the evidence isn't yet all in"— and that *it won't be all in until the race is over* and the judges have made their decision. We all do in fact use this as the final criterion, no matter how much we may talk about "knowing by intuition." We use the observation of the actual race as the test, the real means of knowing. No one thinks for a moment that the preceding intuition provides this test. On the day you will be willing to say that Prancer won the race *because your wife or somebody intuited it, even though* when you were at the race your eyes told you that Beauty Queen won it, the newspapers said that Beauty Queen won it, the motion picture films showed Beauty Queen ahead of all the other horses at the last lap, those who had bet on Beauty Queen emerged with lots of cash, and you yourself had to pay out money because you bet on Prancer, and you *still* say that Prancer won because your wife intuited it—on that day you can be said to have accepted intuition as the criterion of knowledge rather than empirical evidence.

The case against knowledge by intuition is not, however, quite so easily settled. "This is all very well for empirical statements. But what about non-empirical ones? I don't mean tautologies or analytic statements; these we know to be true by analysis. I mean synthetic necessary statements. To know that these are true, we don't *need* empirical evidence the way we do to discover who wins the race. To know these statements, empirical evidence is neither necessary nor appropriate."

Now, many alleged synthetic necessary propositions are *about* empirical subject-matter and are of the sort that *can* be verified empirically, only, if the rationalists are right, they *do not have to be*—they can be known to be true without this. If you decided "No man lives to be 200 years old," and that you knew this a priori, you would be saying that you would not have to go about examining actual instances of men or even historical records to find out that it was so. In this particular example, the discomfiting possibility of finding somebody over 200 years old would probably make most persons pause before declaring that they knew it *a priori*. In other cases rationalists are more confident: "All colors are extended"; "Everything that has shape has size"; "All sounds have pitch"; and so on. Here, rationalists say, we *could* examine the matter empirically—we could examine every color to see whether it was extended. But, they add, we *do not have* to do this, for we know it *a priori*. And, rationalists would add, these statements are at the same time genuinely synthetic.

"But *how do you know a priori* that these synthetic statements are true? You don't need the evidence afforded by observation of the world. But doesn't this violate the third condition of knowing: the one requiring evidence?" As a rule the rationalist will assent to this third condition, acknowledging that the first two alone are insufficient; but he will say that not all evidence is *empirical* evidence; he will say that in some cases, notably synthetic necessary statements, the intuition itself constitutes the evidence. In the case of contingent statements we always need empirical evidence to know whether the statement is true, but in the case of necessary statements we do not; here we *can* know by intuition. He will say, for example, that there is "in the nature of things" a necessary connection between color and extension, sound and pitch, duty and rightness, and so on; this connection is *discovered* by intuition, and we did not put it there or make it that way. But we do not discover it by a successive examination of instances, that is to say, empirically.

What we *did* become acquainted with empirically are the *concepts* of color, extension, shape, size, and so forth. The judgment rationalist may well be a concept empiricist (see pages 86–90). Without experience we would never have come by such concepts; but, once experience has given us the concepts, we do not need any further experience to know that *the judgment involving these concepts is true*. We think about these concepts and we just see that there is a connection between the two of them which holds necessarily. The word "see," of course, is being used figuratively here, since it does not refer to visual experience. Presumably it refers to intuition. In the final analysis the rationalist holds intuition to be a method of knowledge: he "sees," "intuits," that all A is B and always will be, and that it is necessarily so.[13]

---

[13] This is not to say, however, that he merely "intuits" truths and lets it go at that. He employs both empirical observation and reasoning; for example,

In doing this, of course, he encounters from his opponents all the criticisms of intuition that have been made in the preceding pages. On the other hand, he will say to the empiricist: "You are placing too much emphasis upon empirical evidence. There are other ways of knowing than the scientist's way of observing and investigating. It is true that intuition is a method fraught with danger and easily misused; one is tempted to cut the Gordian knot and say that he knows something by intuition, thus avoiding the long hard road of empirical investigation which may take the human race thousands of years. But there are some truths, nevertheless, that do not have to be discovered empirically. Once one has come to understand what the statements mean, one can simply know them to be true for all cases."

Our immediate concern in the next chapter, however, will be with empirical statements—statements about our universe which are synthetic and contingent. There are many problems of the first importance which arise in connection with them. To these, then, we now turn.

SELECTED READINGS FOR CHAPTER 2

Friedrich Waismann. "Analytic-Synthetic," a series of articles in *Analysis*, beginning in Dec. 1949 issue. See especially III and IV in the series (Jan. 1951 and June 1951).

Norman Malcolm. "Are Necessary Propositions Really Verbal?" *Mind,* 49, 1940.

Bertrand Russell. *The Problems of Philosophy.* New York: Oxford University Press. Chapters 7, 8, 11.

C. E. M. Joad. *Guide to Philosophy.* New York: Random House, 1936. Chapter 5.

Brand Blanshard. *The Nature of Thought.* London: Allen & Unwin, 1939. Vol. 2, Chapters 28–30.

David Pears. "Incompatibilities of Colors." Included in *Logic and Language, Second Series* (ed. Anthony Flew). Oxford: Basil Blackwell, 1953.

Douglas Gasking. "Mathematics and the World." Included in *Logic and Language, Second Series* (ed. Anthony Flew). Oxford: Basil Blackwell, 1953.

Arthur Pap. "Are All Necessary Propositions Analytic?" *Philosophical Review,* 58, 1949.

he tries to deduce his conclusions from premises which his opponents too will accept. It is only when all this fails that the appeal to direct intuition is made.

C. I. Lewis. *Mind and the World Order*. New York: Scribners, 1929. Chapters 7 and 8.

A. J. Ayer. *Language, Truth, and Logic*. London: Victor Gollancz & Son, 1936. Chapter 4.

Morris R. Cohen. *Reason and Nature*. New York: Harcourt Brace & Co., 1931. Especially Book 2, Chapter 1.

John Locke. *Essay concerning Human Understanding*. Many editions. Especially Books II and IV.

Gottfried W. Leibniz. *New Essays concerning Human Understanding*.

David Hume. *Enquiry concerning Human Understanding*, Section II (1751); *Treatise of Human Nature*, Book I, Part I (1739). (Many editions.)

Carl G. Hempel. "Geometry and Empirical Science," *American Mathematical Monthly*, 52, 1945. (Reprinted in Feigl and Sellars, *Readings in Philosophical Analysis*. New York: Appleton-Century-Crofts, 1949.)

Carl G. Hempel. "On the Nature of Mathematical Truth," *American Mathematical Monthly*, 52, 1945. (Reprinted in Feigl and Sellars, *Readings in Philosophical Analysis*.)

Hans Reichenbach. *The Rise of Scientific Philosophy*. Berkeley: University of California Press, 1951. Especially Chapters 3 and 8.

Bertrand Russell. *Introduction to Mathematical Philosophy*. London: Allen and Unwin, 1919.

EXERCISES

1. Label each of the following as (1) analytic propositions or tautologies or (2) synthetic propositions. Give reasons.
   a. All swans are white.
   b. All blackbirds are black birds.
   c. All matter occupies space.
   d. You're either in this room or not in this room.
   e. You're either in this room or in that room.
   f. If A is larger than B, then B is smaller than A.
   g. All fathers are males.
   h. All human beings are selfish.
   i. All human beings are mortal.
   j. All water (under standard conditions) has a boiling point of 212° F.
   k. Normal persons behave like the majority.
   l. 2 plus 2 equals 4.
   m. Adding 2 quarts of water to 2 quarts of alcohol yields 4 quarts of the mixture.

2. What is the difference between an explicit and an implicit tautology (or analytic proposition)? How do you make an implicit one explicit?

3. What is the difference between logical possibility, empirical possibility, and technical possibility? Give examples.

4. Is the logically possible the same as the conceivable? Explain.

5. Are the following *logically* possible? Justify your answer in each case.

   a. To jump 1,000 feet into the air?

   b. To fall upwards?

   c. To see a sound?

   d. To see an object that doesn't exist?

   e. To remember an event that didn't happen?

   f. To have an unconscious desire?

   g. To go from point A to point B without traversing the distance in between?

   h. To be certain of something that isn't so?

   i. To cross a river and be on the same side you started from?

   j. To read tomorrow's newspaper today?

   k. To see without eyes?

   l. To be knocked into the middle of next week?

   m. For a solid iron bar to float on water?

   n. For a sound to exist that no creature in the world can hear?

   o. For a color to exist that no creature in the world can see?

   p. For a cat to give birth to pups?

   q. For a table to eat the book that's on it?

   r. For a box to be pure green and pure red all over at the same time?

   s. For Thursday to follow Tuesday without Wednesday in between?

   t. For a straight line *not* to be the shortest distance between two points?

   u. For there to be no world at all?

   v. For a thought to weigh five pounds?

   w. For a person in the twentieth century to go back five thousand years and live among the Egyptians of 3,000 B. C.?

   x. For a part of space to move to some other part of space?

   y. For a thought to exist without someone to think it?

6. What is the difference between the analytic and the *a priori?* between the synthetic and the *a posteriori?*

7. To be sure that the conclusion of a deductive argument is true, what two conditions must be met?

8. Which of the following, if any, are in your opinion necessary synthetic propositions? Give reasons for your answer. Classify those that are not necessary synthetic propositions as either (1) synthetic but not necessary or (2) necessary but not synthetic. Explain.

   a. Everything that has volume has shape.

   b. $40694 + 27593 = 68287$.

   c. If you undermine the foundations of your house, it will collapse.

   d. No mammals grow feathers.

   e. All colors are extended.

   f. Every particle of matter in the universe attracts every other particle with a force varying inversely with the square of the distance and directly with the product of the masses.

g. A straight line is the shortest distance between two points.

h. The sum of the angles of a triangle always is 180°.

i. Given any line L and any point P (not on that line), only one line can be drawn through P parallel to L.

j. It is right to do your duty.

k. If proposition p is true, then proposition p is true.

l. If p implies q and q implies r, then p implies r.

m. If A is larger than B and B is larger than C, then A is larger than C.

n. If Smith likes Jones and Jones likes Brown, then Smith likes Brown.

o. If event E occurred before F, and F occurred before G, then E occurred before G.

p. If p is true, then p is not also false.

q. Either p is true or p is false.

r. If A is north of B and B is north of C, then A is north of C.

s. If A is east of B and B is east of C, then A is east of C.

t. All sounds have pitch, volume, and timbre.

9. Evaluate the following objections:

a. A proposition (such as "It's raining") can be true at one time and false at another.

b. A proposition (such as "I have a headache") can be true for one person and false for another.

c. If a liquid is not cold, it doesn't logically follow that it's hot; so the Law of Excluded Middle need not be true in every case.

d. "He's in the room or he's not in the room"—an instance of the Law of Non-contradiction; but suppose he's half in and half out? The Law of Non-contradiction need not be true in every case.

e. A man may love his wife and hate her at the same time (love and not love her?); so again the Law of Non-contradiction does not always hold.

f. At one time or another we all learned the propositions of arithmetic, such as that 2 and 2 make 4. So how can they be *a priori*?

g. In drawing logical deductions, we may learn in the conclusion things we did not know when we stated the premises. So we have drawn new knowledge out of the situation. Accordingly, how can the principles of logical inference be tautologies?

h. Two quarts of water added to 2 quarts of alcohol does not make 4 quarts of the mixture; it makes slightly less. So "2 and 2 make 4" isn't always true.

i. An amoeba splits into two and we have two amoebas. So $1 = 2$.

10. How can the principles of logic be justified? How can you prove, for example, that p is p? or that if something is a table it is not also *not* a table? Can you prove it by means of the principles of logic themselves? or by means of something else? But if you can't prove them to be true, how can you justify using them?

11. Distinguish between rationalism and empiricism of concepts and rationalism and empiricism of judgments (or propositions).

12. Distinguish (within judgment empiricism) between traditional empiricism and logical empiricism.

13. Distinguish (within judgment rationalism) between traditional rationalism and "modified" rationalism. In what respect do they both oppose the empiricisms of the preceding question?

14. What are the defining characteristics of knowing? Show how each of the three characteristics is essential, and that it would fall short of knowing if any one of them is missing.

15. Examine the justifiability of each of the following statements:

    a. I know it will be nice weather tomorrow.

    b. I knew you would say that.

    c. Don't you know that there will never be peace in the world?

    d. I know something that you don't know—Stalin is dead; I just heard the news over the radio.

    e. I know that $2 + 2 = 4$.

    f. I know which horse will win the race tomorrow.

    g. I know which horse won the race today.

    h. I know that I am looking at a piece of paper. (See Chapter 3.)

    i. I know that you never think ill of me. (See Chapter 5.)

16. Examine the notion of "self-evident truths."

17. Examine the concept of knowledge by intuition. Consider first some of the allegedly synthetic *a priori* statements of question 8, and then such propositions about the empirical world as "I know that you are thinking of me" and "I know that Chimney Sweep will win the race tomorrow."

3

Empirical Knowledge

In Chapter 2 we considered a number of *necessary* statements. In most of this chapter we shall confine our attention to statements which almost everyone would agree to be not necessary but *contingent*. The truth or falsity of the statements we shall be considering can be known, if at all, only by empirical means—by observation of the world. Let us first ask whether there are any such statements that can be *known* to be true, and of which, consequently, we can be certain. Whether or not there are synthetic necessary statements of whose truth we can be certain *a priori*, how does the matter stand with synthetic statements which are *not* necessary and for which there is no *a priori* knowledge-claim?

I. CERTAINTY AND EMPIRICAL STATEMENTS

If there are empirical statements of which we can be certain, it seems more likely that they will be found among those that assert one thing than among those which assert many things at once. "This crow is black" asserts far less than "All crows are black," for the latter includes this crow along with millions of other ones. The first statement may well be true even if the second one is false. We would have to know much more before we were entitled to assert the second than we would the first. Accordingly, it is among statements of the first kind that we shall inquire whether certainty can be found. If it cannot be found here, it can hardly be found among statements of the second class.

First we should clear up an ambiguity in the word "certain." When we asked just now whether any empirical statements are certain, we were not asking whether we (or someone) could *feel* certain, that is, have the feeling of certainty about them. People have feelings of certainty about hundreds of statements that often turn out to be utterly false. I may be quite certain that a given statement is true, and you may be certain that it is false. My certainty does not make the statement true any more than your certainty makes it false. The question we are asking is not a psychological question about people's states of mind. The answer to that question would in most cases be yes: there are very few statements indeed which somebody or other at some time or other has not felt certain about. But we are not using certain in the sense of "I *feel* certain," but rather in the sense of *"It is* certain." And to say that it *is* certain means that I *know* it to be true.

What empirical statements, then, can be known to be true? Remember our analysis of knowledge in Chapter 2. To know p, p must be true, I must believe p to be true (have the feeling of certainty about p), and there must be evidence for p. How much evidence? All of it; complete evidence; it must be "all in," otherwise the failure of the last detail might falsify the whole statement. This is the crucial condition. The controversy about certainty in relation to empirical statements is the controversy about whether the evidence is ever really "all in."

One view (sometimes known as *fallibilism*) is that every empirical statement is fallible, that no empirical statement is certain. Even "I am looking at a sheet of paper" is only probable, but never known for certain to be true. If we want knowledge, certain knowledge (the word "certain" here is redundant), then, according to fallibilism, we shall be restricted to analytic statements and tautologies.

Opponents of fallibilism declare that some empirical statements *are* certain. They are not *logically* certain, for a logically certain statement is by definition one which it would be self-contradictory to deny, that is to say, an analytic statement or a tautology. And, by definition, an empirical statement is neither an analytic statement nor a tautology. To say that an empirical statement is *logically* certain would be to say that it is not an empirical statement at all, and it would be self-contradictory to assert that an empirical statement is non-empirical. But many empirical statements are nevertheless known for certain to be true.

The main line of anti-fallibilist argument runs something like this:

"What is the meaning of saying that a statement is not certain when you don't know what would make it more certain? Suppose I raise my hand before me and you say, 'I doubt that that's a hand.' Now what more evidence would you want? You don't believe your eyes, perhaps? Very well, then come up and touch the hand. You still aren't satisfied? Then keep on looking at it steadily and touching it, photograph it, call in other people for testimony if you like. If after all this you admit it's certain that this is a hand, very well. But if you still think it isn't certain, then pray tell me what you mean by 'certain'?"

"I doubt," it may be replied, "that even if these conditions are fulfilled, you really *know* that this is a hand."

"But then what can you mean by 'really know'? What logically possible state-of-affairs does that phrase stand for, if nothing that you could describe will be admitted by you to be an instance of really knowing? And if you doubt, after all these tests, that this is a hand, what is it that you are doubting? What now *could* satisfy your doubt? Aren't you just repeating the words 'I doubt' as a kind of formula, without knowing any more what it is that you are doubting? When you first said 'I doubt,' it was a genuine empirical doubt; perhaps you were doubting whether *if* you tried to touch my hand, there would be anything there to touch. But then you did touch it and you resolved that doubt. You resolved further doubts too, by calling in others; whenever you thought of a further test, you made that test. But now, when *you yourself cannot specify any further test which, if performed, would resolve your doubt,* you still 'doubt.' But what is 'doubt' now but an empty word? You're not doubting now that *if* you raised your hand to touch mine, you could do it; you're not doubting now that *if* Smith and Jones were brought in, they would also testify that this is a hand. Then what is the content of your doubt? What possible test is there now *the negative result of which you fear?* I submit that there isn't any, and that you are confusing a situation in which it makes perfectly good sense to doubt (when the evidence is incomplete) with one in which no real doubt is logically possible because all the tests have been satisfied and the defining conditions for doubting are no longer present. It makes sense to doubt as long as there is some fact which you might still discover which would remove the certainty of the statement you are doubting. But when you have all the facts, when all the tests are in, then what are you doubting when you doubt the proposition? There is no longer any content to your doubt!

"This is the way of the skeptic. The skeptic says 'I doubt *p*.' Now you go through the series of tests for verifying *p*. But after all these are carried out, he still says he doubts *p*. Now what does he want? The skeptic confuses a state of real doubt with a state which isn't doubt at all, but simply a stubborn attachment to the words 'I doubt' without being able to state the content of this doubt. The physician examines the patient, takes his blood count, and so on, and says, 'It's probable that you have an inflamed appendix.' Here one can still doubt, for the signs may be misleading. A, B, C, and D may always have pointed to E, but it's at least logically possible that they don't do so in this case. But now suppose the physician operates and finds the inflamed appendix and removes it, and the patient gets better. Can one still doubt the physician's diagnosis? Isn't it silly to doubt any longer? and not only silly but meaningless—I mean it isn't really doubt any longer, is it, even though you may keep on repeating the verbal formula 'I doubt'? You are driving along and you hear a rapid regular thumping sound and you say, 'I think I've got a flat tire.' The thumping of course may be caused by something else, perhaps not just *that* kind of thumping, but anyway you go out to look. There it is—flat. Almost no space at all between the rim of the wheel and the ground. The person who is riding with you steps out and sees it too. Then you both get to work and change the tire, after which you can ride smoothly again. Now, are you still going to doubt that the tire was flat? And if you did, what would you be doubting? Are you still going to say that it's not certain, but only 'highly probable,' that you had a flat tire? To say this made sense before you went out to see what the trouble was; but now, what would it mean to say it? If this isn't being certain that the tire is flat, what in the world *would* be? Isn't this the kind of situation we label with the word 'certain' rather than with the word 'probable'? If the word 'certain' doesn't belong here, where does it? Has it no possible domain of application?

"In common usage we have a way of distinguishing the one kind of situation from the other, or more precisely, of characterizing the statements designating the situation. We use the word 'probable' for the one and the word 'certain' for the other. True, we sometimes mistakenly use the word 'certain' when we should use 'probable,' either because of our determination that something shall be so ('It's certain I'll get a letter tomorrow') or a mistake in checking facts ('It's certain you turned in a joint income tax return'). Nevertheless, we have the distinction and it is a useful and important one. You want to destroy the distinction entirely, at least with regard to empirical statements. You would use 'probable' and 'improbable' to cover all cases, so that 'certain' would have no domain of application at all. You would use the word 'certain' in such a way that *it never attaches to any empirical statement whatever.*

"You are like the person who ignores the distinction between vague words and precise words, saying 'All words are really vague.' Let us adopt this word-usage for a moment: vagueness now characterizes all words without exception. But now within this all-inclusive category of vague words we have to make the same distinction we made before, between words like 'two' and 'triangle' and words like 'fast' and 'bald.' Only now we can't use the words 'vague' and 'precise' to label the distinction, because we've already thrown out the word 'precise' and made the word 'vague' cover the territory of both of them. So we'll have to devise some new words. And what has been gained by this procedure? Nothing. The new words still label the same distinction we made before by using the words 'vague' and 'precise' (though admittedly this is itself a *vague* distinction—see pages

40–41). We have not changed things a bit by these verbal gyrations. We have changed only the words which stand for the things. Now isn't the same true of the distinction between 'certain' and 'probable'? Call every empirical statement 'probable' (or 'improbable') if you like, and throw out the word 'certain'; now where are you? You will still want to refer to the distinction between the kind of situation *before* the physician has operated, *before* you've looked into the gas tank, and the kind of situation *after* these things have been done. The distinction is usually marked by the words 'probable' and 'certain.' If you want to change this, what is it but a *verbal manipulation* and nothing more? You have changed nothing; you have only put new labels on the same old bottles (or put the same new label on both of them!), and less convenient and understandable labels than you had before.

"One final point: if *after* the verification process you still say it's not certain that p is true, or if you say that you doubt whether p is true, isn't your assertion *self-contradictory?* Suppose you doubt that this thing before you on the kitchen table is a piece of cheese. You admit it smells like cheese, looks like cheese, tastes like cheese. Now you submit it to a chemical analysis (or give it to a chemist for analysis) and the verdict is that it really is cheese. But you still doubt. In other words, it has characteristics A, B, C, D and you still doubt whether it's cheese. But suppose 'cheese' is defined in terms of just these characteristics? The defining characteristics of cheese are A, B, C, and D; this has A, B, C, and D; and yet you doubt that this is cheese! But isn't this to doubt whether it has A, B, C, and D, although it *has* A, B, C, and D? and isn't this clearly self-contradictory? To such a pass has the doubter come who continues his 'doubting' past the point where it ceases to be doubt!"

The fallibilist, however, is not without a reply to these arguments. Right or wrong, his reply runs somewhat as follows:

"I am afraid you have misunderstood my point. I grant that to say that it has characteristics A, B, C, and D and then deny that it is cheese *is* self-contradictory if 'cheese' is defined in terms of those very characteristics. '*If* it is cheese, it has A, B, C, and D' is in fact a tautology and not an empirical statement at all. But what I say is that you can always doubt whether this thing *really has the characteristics* A, B, C, and D—for instance I can always doubt whether it has A."

"But," comes the objection, "the same thing applies to A as applies to cheese itself. If the word 'certain' is to have any meaning—as it must have if your statement that no empirical propositions are certain is going to have any meaning—then there must be *some* conditions of applicability. If there are *no* conditions which would render the occurrence of A certain, then what does 'certain' mean?"

"Ah, but there *is* a meaning of 'certain,' and there *are* conditions of its applicability. P is certain when all the evidence for p is in, as you yourself said. But my contention that no empirical proposition is ever certain really reduces to the contention that *all the evidence is never in*. This is where I object to the examples you give: you assume that at least some empirical statements can be known for certain. Thus, in the appendicitis example you assume that I can know at least some empirical statements for certain, namely that the physician has examined the patient and that the patient has a certain blood count; more crucial still, you assume it as certain that the physician sees the inflamed appendix. In the example of the car you assume it to be known for certain that there is really a thumping sound (that the driver isn't having hallucinations), that the driver's senses aren't deceiving him when he 'observes' the tire to be flat, and so forth. And all these statements can be questioned; they are all empirical statements which I hold are never certain. I am not denying that *if* the physician observes the inflamed appendix, then the patient has an inflamed appendix. But this is a tautology, isn't it? and I never denied that tautologies can be known for certain. But how about the statement that the physician really observes it?

"Every empirical statement has an infinite number of possible verifications, and you cannot make all the observations required to verify the statement completely; hence it is never certain. That is what is wrong with your examples: they *presuppose* the very thing I question, namely that *some* empirical statements (at least those used and assumed as known in the examples) are known for certain to be true, that the evidence for *them* at least is all in. That is why I must reject all the examples.

"Therefore I must even object to your example about the hand. True, *if* I admit that I'm seeing the hand, touching the hand, and so on, then I can't very well turn around and deny that the hand exists; for in saying that I am *really* looking at it and really touching it, I am already admitting that it exists. But how do I know that I am really seeing and touching a hand? or to put it in a different way, that I am seeing and touching a *real* hand? Of course if I *admit* that I am, then you have me, and I can't very well deny that no hand is there. But this initial admission, which you presuppose in all your examples, is precisely what I do not grant."

At this point the controversy must rest until we have built up more background for further discussion of it. Having carried it to this point, we shall take it up again in Chapter 6 in our discussion of our knowledge of the physical world.

II. LAW AND PROBABILITY

Most of the statements we make in daily life are empirical: "I fell asleep at 2 p.m. yesterday"; "World War I lasted from 1914 to 1918"; "Buffaloes travel in herds but wolves do not"; "I was much distressed by the letter I received this morning." The kind of empirical observation required is not in every case the same. In the case of the last statement you merely ask yourself, "Was I distressed or not?" For the first one, you must remember looking at your watch or have someone else's testimony to the hour at which you fell asleep; in the case of the other two we have probably never observed the truth of any such statements for ourselves but are repeating what books or other people have told us, and perhaps they in turn got it from others, but if these are true empirical statements, some person (or usually many persons) have observed it for themselves; the chain of hearsay evidence, however reliable, must stop somewhere with direct empirical observation.

Laws of nature. There is one class of empirical statements of special interest for practical reasons because they enable us to predict, and for theoretical reasons because they raise special problems: namely, the laws of the natural sciences, or sciences of nature: physics, chemistry, astronomy, geology, zoology, botany, psychology, and so on. The laws of these sciences are empirical, like the statements of ordinary life, but they are different in that they are *universal:* they apply to all instances without exception. They are stated in different forms: "All A's are B's," "If (certain conditions are fulfilled), then (this or that occurs)," "Whenever this happens, then that happens." But in whatever form they may be stated, they have in common this universality; without this, they are not laws. In other words, universality is a defining characteristic of a law.[1]

Not only must the statement hold without exception; it must also be *true:* in other words, it must state a uniformity that really does occur in the universe. These uniformities are not easy to find, and it has taken the cumulative efforts of centuries of scientific investigation to discover as many as we have today.

Often it is thought that a genuine and exceptionless uniformity has been found, but when it is tested further it is discovered that the statement of it is inaccurate and needs amendment or qualification in some way. Even a simple law such as "Water boils at 212° F." is not true without qualification: at high altitudes water boils

---

[1] There are many other features of laws which it is beyond the scope of this book to discuss, but which would be taken up in a textbook on the philosophy of science. Here we shall be concerned with only so much as to prevent certain widespread misunderstandings of the concept of law, and to indicate the relation of laws to other kinds of statements.

at a lower temperature. Water boils at 212° F. only at the condition of atmospheric pressure which prevails at sea level.

Even so, this is an unusually simple law, for in stating the uniformity in the behavior of water almost everything in the universe can be ignored, even the immediately surrounding conditions: the kind of substance of which the vessel containing the water is composed, its size and shape and color, the kind of heat applied under the vessel, the number of people watching, and so on. The law holds regardless of these conditions. Most laws of physics, though they may seem very technical, are simple in the sense that the uniformities they assert hold good *regardless of outside conditions:* in other words, in stating them you can disregard most of the things that go on in the universe. Often, indeed, only a very few factors such as mass and velocity need be considered; even temperature and chemical composition can be ignored. Laws of the biological sciences are less simple than those of physics and chemistry, and those of psychology and sociology are less simple still, for it is difficult here to state any uniformities that are not dependent upon a tremendous multitude of conditions. For example, what laws can be stated about the behavior of human beings? The influences acting upon them are so various, the conditions so complicated (for example, a seemingly trivial event that occurred in your childhood and which neither you nor anyone else may remember, may still influence your behavior today), that it is difficult indeed to make any true universal statement about human behavior. The best we can do is to state laws in a vague and general way, often allowing for many exceptions, so that the statement is not so much a law as a tentative blueprint for a law. For the most part, generalizations about human nature that are both true and exceptionless have not been found. Psychology and sociology are only in their infancy, and many persons are convinced that they are called "sciences" only by courtesy, or as a kind of promissory note, to be paid later when their subject-matters are more advanced. Others feel that they will never be developed to the point of becoming sciences.

Not all the statements regarded as "scientific" are universal statements about some aspect of the universe. There are, for one thing, definitions. But also there are ordinary singular statements: for example, geology books contain many facts about the past history of the earth. These are usually regarded, however, as *material* for laws, on the basis of which laws may some day be arrived at. The aim of geology (or so it is usually held) is to state under exactly what conditions such-and-such kinds of changes always take place; these are the laws of geology, and they would apply whenever these conditions are fulfilled, even on another planet. In psychology books, again, we find, for example, many case-histories of individual patients. These of course are not laws, but they supply the data out of which laws may some day be built, and, to some extent, have been built already, except that they are at this stage rather tentative and insecure, and remain to be purified of exceptions and over-simplifications. The more developed sciences of physics and chemistry no longer have to deal in singular statements: *all* bodies exert gravitational attraction in such-and-such a way, copper always behaves thus under such-and-such conditions.

Ambiguity of "law." A law in the sense in which the sciences use the word is a very different sort of thing from a law in the sense in which the word is usually employed in ordinary life. Indeed, the word "law" is possessed of a very misleading ambiguity (see page 22), and if we are not to fall into utter confusion we must keep the distinction between the two main senses of the word carefully in mind.

1. *Prescriptive law.* This is the kind of law imposed by a monarch or passed by a legislative body. It is not a statement at all, because it cannot be true or false, but an imperative (see pages 69–70), a "Thou shalt" or a "Thou shalt not." It does not state that anything is the case; rather, it issues a command, a *pre*scription, usually with penalties attached for not obeying the command.

2. *Descriptive law.* The sciences give us descriptive laws. They do not prescribe anything (Kepler's laws of planetary motion do not prescribe to the planets that they should behave in such-and-such a way and invoke penalties in case they do not) but rather they *de*scribe: Kepler's laws, for example, describe how the planets in a planetary system actually do move. All laws in this sense of the word describe some uniformity that exists in the universe. Sometimes, for the sake of simplicity, they describe only what would happen under ideal conditions; for example, the Law of Falling Bodies describes only how bodies fall in a vacuum, and in an atmosphere such as the earth's, the law requires amendment and complication. Such laws, however, are still descriptive: they de-

scribe our universe, not any logically possible universe, and they prescribe nothing.

Several confusions can be avoided if we keep the distinction in mind.

(1) "Laws should be obeyed." Whether you should obey all prescriptive laws, or whether it is right sometimes to violate them, is a question in ethics. But a law of nature is not the sort of thing of which it makes sense to say that you obeyed it. How could you obey the Law of Gravitation? Your motions are *instances* of this law, along with the fall of a stone; but since the law does not command anything, how could you be said to obey it? A prescriptive law, moreover, would still be a law even if no one obeyed it.

(2) "Where there's a law, there's a lawgiver." Again this applies clearly to prescriptive law: if some course of action is prescribed, somebody or some group must have prescribed it. "Law implies lawgiver" is thus beyond dispute where statute law is concerned. Whether the uniformities of nature have their source in a Divine Lawgiver is a controversial issue which will be discussed in Chapter 5.

(3) "Laws are found, not made." Prescriptive laws are, of course, made by the lawmakers; descriptive laws are found. More precisely: the *uniformities* in nature are found or discovered by men, not devised by them, although the *formulating* of these uniformities in statements (laws) is the work of men.

Laws involve the future. Scientific laws are *generalizations;* that is to say, from observing particular examples of nature's uniformities we *generalize* and assert that these uniformities hold in *all* cases. What is meant by all cases? Literally all—not only the present ones, but the past and the future. "All water boils at 212° F. at sea-level pressure" means all water, everywhere, any time. The laws of nature describe rather than prescribe, but what they describe is something unlimited in extent, extending indefinitely both into the past and into the future.

All laws of nature, then, in what they assert, go beyond the evidence which is available for them at any given time. This is what makes them generalizations. If I have examined all of the 100 marbles in a bag and say, "All of them are black," my statement is not a generalization, because I am not going *beyond the evidence;* the statement is merely a description of what I have already observed. But if I say "All the crows that exist are black" (not using

blackness as a defining characteristic of being a crow), my statement is a generalization, because no matter how many crows I have
observed my statement goes beyond the evidence—I am generaliz-
ing from the observed to unobserved instances.

If a law says that all A is B, how can we ever know that we have
examined all the A's in the world to see whether they are B's, no
matter how exhaustively we investigate? The record of the past is
always incomplete, even in those cases where we have historical
records to guide us. But even if we could somehow know that all A's
were B's, past and present, we would still be faced with the problem
of the future. How can we know what will happen in the future,
until it actually happens and thus is no longer future? How can we
know that even the best-founded generalizations will continue to
hold in the future? If knowing involves complete evidence ("*all* the
evidence must be in") is this not impossible in the case of the
future, for surely the evidence is not all in until the event in question actually happens, or the last instance of A's and B's required
by the law has occurred? Indeed, is it not *logically* impossible to
know the future, as opposed to having strong belief about it or
having considerable evidence now that something will happen then?
Would it not be self-contradictory to have *complete* evidence for
something that had not yet happened (and thus, surely, *might* not
happen)?

If it is logically impossible to know the truth of any statement
involving the future, and the laws of science involve the future, it
follows logically that we cannot *know* that any law of science is
true. The best we can say is that it is *probable:* that the uniformity
has occurred in all the cases we have observed, and that we have
observed it in a thousand or a million cases and never observed any
exceptions to it, and thus that there is every evidence that it always
holds and no evidence that it will ever fail to hold. Of course, even
the best of generalizations *may* be upset, and future developments
may falsify our most confident predictions; but meanwhile, all the
evidence is *for* the generalization, there is no evidence against it,
and if we had to lay a wager on whether the uniformity would hold
in the next instance, for example, whether the next kettle of water
would boil at 212° F., we would surely wager in favor of it.

Inductive reasoning. We arrive at laws of nature by means of induction, not deduction. We say, for example,

Crow #1 is black.
Crow #2 is black.
Crow #3 is black.
etc.
_____
Therefore, All crows are black.

The conclusion of this argument does not logically follow from its premises. It cannot be deduced from them; as a deductive argument, it is invalid. Rather, the premises only provide *evidence* for the conclusion; they make the conclusion probable on the basis of the evidence, but not certain. The more crows one observes, the more probable the conclusion becomes; but no matter how many one observes, the probability never becomes certainty. We can speak of laws of nature as relatively well established, but never as fully established in the way that the conclusion of a valid deductive argument is established if its premises are true. We can only investigate further and as our evidence increases, the more probable our induction becomes.

It is not only generalizations that can be the conclusions of inductive inference: singular statements are also. Thus:

Jones was found with a bullet through his heart at 9:20 a.m.
Smith's gun was found in Jones' room at 9:25 a.m.
Smith's gun had one bullet missing when it was found.
The bullet in Jones' body was of the same kind as those in Smith's gun.
Smith was seen approaching Jones' house at 9:15 a.m.
Five neighbors heard a shot from the direction of Jones' house shortly after 9:15.
_____
Therefore, Smith killed Jones.

Here again the conclusion does not logically follow from the premises; the argument is inductive, not deductive. When one says, "There was a muddy footprint on the davenport, *therefore* the murderer came in out of the rain and made a hasty exit through the window behind the davenport," he is performing an induction. Sherlock Holmes' famed "powers of deduction" were really powers of making shrewd inductions.

A conclusion such as "Smith killed Jones" is usually called a *hypothesis*. It can be utterly false or (at the other extreme) very probably true, depending on the degree of evidence. The distinguishing characteristic of a hypothesis is that it is not known to be true.[2]

_____

[2] According to fallibilism, then, all empirical statements are hypotheses.

If it is known to be true (or certainly true), it is no longer called a hypothesis but a fact. For example, if one of the premises in the above argument had been "Smith was seen firing his gun at Jones' heart," this would be tantamount to saying that Smith was seen killing Jones, and (in the sense of "see" which applies only when the thing seen really exists—remember Exercise 5-d on page 156) from this it can be deduced that Smith killed Jones. In that case, the argument would not be an inductive one at all, but deductive, and if the premise were taken as a fact, the conclusion must be also.

Hypotheses can be either particular statements (including singular statements) or universal. "Smith killed Jones" is singular; but a hypothesis such as "All men have a death-instinct" is a generalization and is universal. We usually do not refer to a generalization as a *law* until it has been fairly well established. When it is less well established, it is considered simply a hypothesis. We speak of Newton's Law of Gravitation, Kepler's laws of planetary motion, Snell's Law of Refraction, Maxwell's electromagnetic laws, but of hypotheses about the development of planetary systems and the causes of evolution. Often what was once merely a hypothesis is now, after years of accumulated evidence, considered a law. The distinction between a law and a hypothesis is a vague one, like the distinction between fast and slow (see pages 40–41); there is no point where something ceases to be a hypothesis and becomes a law. We can be no more precise than to say that at about the time when practicing scientists cease to doubt it, it is considered a law.

There are many matters concerning induction and hypothesis which we cannot consider here, which are, however, discussed in elementary textbooks in scientific method: matters such as the estimating of probability of a hypothesis, the tests of a good hypothesis, and the elimination of rival hypotheses. Our present concern is with hypotheses only in relation to laws; and we have seen that laws, though better established than hypotheses, are probable only, without guarantee that the uniformities thus far observed in nature will continue to occur in the future.

The justification of probability-statements. Thus far we have been content to say that, while we cannot *know* that tomorrow water will boil, the sun will rise, and so forth, we have considerable *evidence* that these things will happen, and that the statements asserting that they will happen are, although not certain, at least extremely *prob-*

able. At this point, however, a much more radical kind of question is sometimes raised: how does the fact that something has happened in the past constitute *any evidence whatever* that it will continue so in the future? What if someone said, "Very well—it's always happened that way in the past; so what? What has that to do with the future?"

Here is one comment we should consider first, lest it confuse the issue later: "You can't be so general about it—the occurrence of some regularities, or uniformities, in the past *is* evidence for their continuance in the future, but not so for others. Bertrand Russell uses the example of the chicken that has gone to its roost every night for several months in the belief that it will be secure there, perhaps because it has been secure there on past nights. But finally one night its owner comes into the henhouse and wrings its neck. If the chicken assumed that because it had been undisturbed in the past it would continue to be undisturbed in the future, it was mistaken. Some beliefs of this kind become *less* probable rather than more so with repetition: when you are eighty years old it's less probable that you will live till morning than it was when you were twenty, although the number of instances backing up the generalization is far greater at eighty. Whether the generalization is made more probable or less probable by the addition of repeated instances depends on the evidence we have for *other* generalizations relevant to the situation. We believe that the sun will rise tomorrow more confidently than we believe the eighty-year-old will live till morning because we know some statistics about the incidence of deaths and also some physiological laws about the human body, and we also know some things about the solar system, the earth's rotation on its axis, laws of planetary motion, principles of acceleration and momentum, and some of the other things that would have to be different if the sun were *not* to rise tomorrow. We have arrived at other generalizations about the behavior of nature besides the repeated rising of the sun; and these others all contribute, and add probability, to the statement about the continued rising of the sun. It is different with the case of the chicken, for our other generalizations—rather vague ones about the habits of chickens and farmers and the chicken market—do *not* lead to the belief that the past security of the chicken in any way guarantees its subsequent security. And the same with the example about the octogenarian: if the mere fact that he had lived so many days made it probable that he would live to see every next day that dawned, you would arrive at the conclusion that he would live forever! The mere repetition of days of life is subordinate to wider generalizations about the human constitution, which make it, every day that he lives, *less* probable that he will live to see the next day."

Both common sense and science would accept this view of the reasons for believing in continued uniformity in the case of the sun rising but not in the other cases. The same logical problem remains, however. It does not help to fortify the generalization about the sun's continued rising by appealing to *other* generalizations which are in precisely the same predicament that it is. How do we know that these other laws which are invoked to support the generalization about the sun will continue to hold? Being laws, they too involve the future, and therefore are as fallible as the generalization they are invoked to support. If the past affords us no evidence that the sun will rise in the future, how can it afford us evidence that the Law of Gravitation will continue to hold true, and that all the other laws that are used to support it will do the same? How, then, has our situation improved? It seems not to have improved at all.

One might suggest the easy way out, that of proving a law deductively. Thus:

> What has always occurred regularly in the past will continue to
> occur regularly in the future.
> The sun's rising has occurred regularly in the past.

Therefore, The sun's rising will continue to occur regularly in the future.

Here we have proved our conclusion deductively. The trouble is, of course, as we saw abundantly in Chapter 2, that you cannot prove the *truth* of a conclusion by valid deduction from premises; the premises must themselves be true. And if we do not know that our present conclusion is true, because it involves the future, how can we know that the major premise (the first line) is true, since it too involves the future? It is, in fact, a bigger generalization than is the conclusion. This is clearly no way out: if you want to deduce a conclusion which makes some reference to the future, there must be some reference to the future in one or more of the premises from which that conclusion is deduced. In that case the same skeptical questionings that can be made about the conclusion can be equally made about that premise (or those premises). The question has merely shifted; it has not been resolved.

The general principle, the one that covers all cases, that is usually invoked as a major premise in arguments of this type is the *Principle of Uniformity of Nature*. It is not always formulated in the same way, but it comes to this: "If Nature has always been uniform in the past (generalizations have held good), then Nature will continue to be uniform in the future." Some particular uniformity in the past will then be stated in the minor premise, and the continuance of that uniformity in the future will be deduced in the conclusion. From the Principle of Uniformity of Nature, then, we can deduce the desired conclusion. But how does one establish the Principle of Uniformity of Nature? From what true premises can *it* be deduced? "Well, the Principle of Uniformity of Nature has been true of the past; therefore the Principle of Uniformity of Nature will continue to be true of the future." But this conclusion does not logically follow. It does not follow unless we add another premise:

> What has held true of the past will hold true of the future.
> The Principle of Uniformity of Nature has held true of the past.
>
> Therefore, The Principle of Uniformity of Nature will hold true of the future.

And thus we are back in the same situation: how are we going to prove *this* major premise?

Or we could put the problem this way: "In the past, our predictions about the continued uniformity of nature have turned out to be true; in other words, our past predictions of the future have been verified. Thus we have considerable evidence that nature will continue to be uniform. After all, it's not as if we had never observed our predictions turning out right." "But that's not the question. I grant that our past predictions have been verified by the facts. In other words, our past predictions about the then-future were verified when that future was no longer future but became past. Now I'm not asking about past futures; I'm asking about future futures! What have the past futures to do with it? The fact that past futures turned out to be so-and-so doesn't prove that future futures will turn out to be so-and-so. If you assume that because past futures were so-and-so therefore the future futures will be so-and-so also, you are again assuming the very point to be proved!"

In other words, every time we try to prove the Principle of Uniformity of Nature we assume the principle in the very process of the proof. We cannot prove the principle by means of itself; and yet without doing this we cannot prove it at all. We are in a situation similar to the one encountered in Chapter 2 in connection with the principles of logic. No statement about nature being uniform in the past will prove that nature will be uniform in the future unless we assume that the fact of uniformity in the past proves future uniformity. Yet clearly it does not; from "The uniformity of nature has held in the past" we cannot deduce "The uniformity of nature will hold in the future."

If deduction fails us, how about induction? Induction, as we have seen, is not a method of proof, but only a method of estimating the probability of a conclusion; and it is the very basis of induction itself that is being questioned here. What we are examining is our very right to use inductive procedure in making generalizations. We cannot, therefore, justify this inductive procedure on the basis of inductive reasoning.

Our question, then, still remains: Can the uniformities of the past and the present render uniformities in the future any more probable? Does the fact that the past has turned out a certain way render even probable the statement that the future will turn out that way too?

There is much more agreement on the nature of the problem than on the solution of it. Unfortunately most attempted solutions become too technical to be discussed here. Nevertheless, two comments can be given which may alleviate the pressure of the problem:

1. If someone seriously says that the way things have occurred in the past affords *no* evidence whatever about the future, we can ask him what he means when he uses the word "evidence." A million times in the past when I have let go of a book or a stone it has fallen; never once has it risen into the air. This, and all the other things I know about the behavior of material objects, lead me to believe that it will fall when I let go of it this time. Is there really *no* evidence either way as to what the stone will do next time? To say this is to abandon all prediction and all science, and, more important here, *all meaning for the word "evidence."* For if the fact that it has fallen a million times is *not* evidence, what *would* be? If you so use the word "evidence" that *nothing* that ever happened

could be evidence, what would you mean by the word "evidence"? Would it not just be a meaningless noise? (You could not even say, "There is *no* evidence that X will happen," for that sentence contains the word "evidence," which must be given a meaning before it can meaningfully be used.)

The same point could be made regarding the word "probable." If the fact that the stone has always fallen and never risen, together with all the other things we have observed about stones and other material objects, does not even render more *probable* the statement that the stone will fall the next time, what in the world *could* make it so? And if nothing could, then what meaning can be attached by the speaker to the word "probable," or for that matter the word "improbable"? Remember that it would be just as meaningless to say "It is *im*probable that X will occur" as it would be to say "It is probable that X will occur"—for if the word "probable" has been deprived of all possible application to the universe, its opposite, which acquires meaning only by contrast with it, suffers precisely the same fate.

2. If the question is still asked, "How are we going to prove the Principle of Uniformity of Nature which is required to establish our inductions?" the answer is of course that we cannot. It cannot be proved by means of itself, and it cannot be proved without itself. As we have already seen, to prove (deductively) a conclusion involving the future we must have a proposition involving the future in the premises. In other words—as in the case of the principles of logic—we cannot give a *logical* justification for the Principle of Uniformity of Nature; we cannot give a logical basis for the very principle which is itself the logical basis for the deduction of laws.

It would seem, then, that to demand a logical basis for the principle is as unreasonable as to demand it in the case of the principles of logic themselves. Yet the principle is needed if our inductive conclusions (laws) are to be proved, since they involve the future. Laws are the basis of our predictions. "Why do you think that stone will fall?" "All unsupported bodies fall." If this last statement did not involve the future, it could not be employed to predict anything about the future, which it clearly *is* being employed to do.

What, then, can we do under the circumstances? As in the case of the principles of logic (see pages 128–131), we can give a pragmatic justification for our *adoption* of these principles. In the case

of the principles of logic it was the impossibility of any coherent discourse without the use of them; in the present case the situation is
not quite so radical: it is the fruitlessness of any scientific procedure
without the adoption of the Principle of Uniformity of Nature,
which alone enables us to make inferences from past and present to
future. We cannot prove that the principle which enables us to do
this is true, but *if* we want to attempt any predictions at all—and
as human beings we must all do this if we want to stay alive (do
we not refrain from going to the street via the fifth-floor window
because we are convinced that the uniformity of behavior of freely
falling bodies will continue?)—then the laws of nature are the only
sound basis for such prediction. It is these or nothing. We cannot
prove deductively that these laws are true, for we cannot prove that
the uniformities will hold in the future, and this is what every law
implicitly asserts; but *if* nature is uniform, and *if* there is an order
of nature which extends into the future, then the inductive method
is the way in which to gain knowledge of this order. We want successful prediction; we cannot prove that our predictions, however
well they may have worked out in the past, will be successful in the
next instance; but if successful prediction is to be possible at all, it
will be so only by means of these laws. This is our pragmatic basis,
our practical justification, for asserting these laws, in spite of the
fact that we cannot prove that the laws are true, or can prove them
only by using an unprovable principle as a premise.

There is, to be sure, another way out of the situation: we can
assert that the Principle of Uniformity of Nature is a synthetic
necessary statement, something which *necessarily* holds of the universe. But here again, of course, there are difficulties: what entitles
us to say that the principle is necessary? How do we know this, if
we know it? To many it would seem that this way of resolving the
Gordian knot is not by unraveling it but by cutting it with a knife.

III. EXPLANATION AND HYPOTHESIS

What is explanation? One of the chief functions of laws is to serve
as *explanations*, or in other words, as answers to questions about
why events occur as they do.

When we are asked to explain something, this request may be for
any of a number of different things. Sometimes we are being asked

merely to make something clearer to the listener, to say it in different words, as in "Explain the meaning of this passage." Sometimes we are being asked to explain how, or when, or whence, or whither. But we shall be concerned here only with explaining *why*, and even here only with regard to the occurrence of events or processes in the universe (roughly, with why things happen the way they do) and not, for example, with why the square on the hypotenuse of a right triangle is equal to the sum of the squares of the legs.

Even here we must be careful to distinguish between *explanations* and *reasons*. Often when we ask questions beginning with the word "why," we are not clear which of these two things we are asking for. To give a reason for a belief is to give one or more *statements* which are intended as *evidence* for the belief, in other words, which are intended to make the belief more probable.[3] To explain a belief, however, usually means to state why the person *holds* the belief. This may or may not (depending on the person) be because there are reasons (evidence) for it. If someone is asked why he believes in divine Providence, he may cite statements as evidence for his belief, such as the teleological argument or other arguments to be considered in Chapter 5. But the explanation of his holding the belief may have nothing to do with evidence at all; it may simply be the fact that he wants a father-substitute or wants to feel secure in an otherwise hostile or indifferent world. (If he does not have much insight into his own motives, he may be quite unaware of what the explanation is.) The giving of reasons, then, is not the same thing as the giving of explanations, although the two are often confused with each other because both of them are answers (in different senses of course) to the question "Why?"

Why (in the sense of explanation) do events occur as they do? For example, why do balloons rise? Why do birds migrate? Why does iron rust? Why does sugar dissolve in water although stones do not? Why do I have a headache this evening? Why do people read murder mysteries? What we want in these cases is an *explana-*

---

[3] It should be added that this is not the only sense in which the word "reason" is used. Indeed, the word is used very loosely and confusingly. When we ask, for example, "What was his reason for doing that?" we may be asking for his *purpose* in doing it. It would be much clearer if the word "reason" were not used in such a case as this, for what is being asked for here is an *explanation* (a purposive explanation—see pp. 185–187) for his behavior.

tion of the phenomenon in question. What precisely is involved in such explanation? What do we do when we explain why something happens?

As scientists use the word "explanation," an event is said to be explained when it has been "brought under a law." This is true whether the thing to be explained is a particular event or process, such as the occurrence of a headache, or whether it is itself a law, such as the rusting of iron; the law is then explained by being brought under a wider law. In either case, some reference to law is involved in every explanation of events. "Why doesn't the red liquid mix with the transparent liquid?" "Because the red liquid is colored water, and the transparent liquid is gasoline." The law involved here, of course, is simply the law that water and gasoline do not mix; our acceptance of the explanation depends upon our explicit or implicit acceptance of this law. If the answer given had been, "Because it's red," we would not have accepted it as an explanation, because we do not believe in any law of nature according to which transparent liquids will not mix with red ones.

In actual practice, there are many occasions when we know of no law (exceptionless uniformity) that would explain the event or law in question, but know only of general tendencies or uniformities with exceptions; these cases are usually extremely complex ones in which an occurrence depends on a multitude of conditions, not all of which we are acquainted with, so for lack of anything better we state the general tendency, though it is not strictly speaking a law. "Why does Johnny have a cold?" "He's been playing with Roger, and Roger has a cold." It is not a law that everyone who plays with someone who has a cold also gets a cold; but there is more uniformity here than with any other factor in the situation, and we cannot state any laws under which people invariably get colds. "I have a headache because I've been reading fine print." Yet people do not always get headaches under those conditions; what is needed is something more specific such as "People in such-and-such physiological states always get such-and-such headaches when exposed to such-and-such conditions." But medical science is not yet in a position to state such precise uniformities. Failing this, we must be content for the time being with the vague generalization, hoping some day to be able to state the law precisely.

What is the relation of the explanation to the phenomenon to be explained?

1. The statement of the phenomenon to be explained (whether a single event or a law) must be *logically deducible* from the statements which give the explanation. Thus, to take a very simple case involving only one law, let us ask "Why does this substance conduct electricity?"

> All copper conducts electricity.   (Explanation)
> This substance is copper.
> _____
> Therefore, This substance conducts electricity.   (Thing to be explained)

Here a particular (i.e. a non-universal) statement is required in the premises to establish the particular conclusion, since in this case the thing to be explained is a particular occurrence or state-of-affairs. But in other cases the thing to be explained is itself a law; then we explain the law in terms of other laws. Thus, "Why does iron exposed to air turn reddish in color?"

> All iron when exposed to oxygen combines with it to form iron oxide.
> (All) iron oxide is reddish in color.
> _____
> Therefore, (All) iron exposed to oxygen turns reddish in color.

Many explanations, such as some of those shortly to be discussed, involve a large number of laws and are thus much longer and more involved than the ones illustrated above. They are more complex in their structure, but the principle is nevertheless the same: the statement about the phenomenon to be explained is deduced from the statements (all the premises together) which constitute the explanation. And in every case at least one universal statement, a law, is required. (Those who have taken elementary logic will remember that from two particular premises no conclusion can be deduced.)

It is, of course, essential that the statements in the premises be *true*. As we saw on pages 116–119, it is easy to deduce any conclusion in the world as long as we can choose any premises we please without regard to whether they are true or false. But of course statements which are not true cannot be genuine laws, since they do not describe actually existing uniformities.

Sometimes one or more statements in the explanation are only probably true, or not even fairly well established. When this happens, of course, the claim of these statements to constitute an explanation is correspondingly jeopardized. If it is not true that contact between two persons, one of whom has a cold, always results in the other's catching cold, then Johnny's cold *may* not be correctly explained by reference to his contact with Roger; the explanation may lie elsewhere.

2. An equally indispensable condition for scientific explanation is that the explanation must have *predictive* value, or, what comes to the same thing, it must explain *other* phenomena besides the one it was invoked to explain. For example, the fact that your water-pitcher breaks if you leave it full of water on the outside window-sill on a very cold night is explained by the law that water expands when it freezes. (Other statements are also required: laws about the breakage point of the material of which the pitcher is composed, and at least one particular statement about the pitcher being where the temperature was below the freezing-point of water.) This same law *also* explains other phenomena, such as the formation of ice at the top of lakes and ponds rather than at the bottom. Knowing that water expands on freezing, we now know *why* these things occur as they do.

Newton's Law of Universal Gravitation is an instance of a law with remarkable explanatory power. It brings the fall of an apple to the ground together with the motions of the planets in the solar system and the furthest star in the heavens under one mighty generalization. On the basis of it, one is enabled to predict (together with other laws and particular statements about particular states-of-affairs, called "initial conditions") such diverse phenomena as eclipses of the sun and the spiral structure of galaxies. Similarly, the reason why laws about electrons and similar unobservables (see page 190) are so universally accepted among scientists is that, as explanations, they have such remarkable predictive power. On the basis of certain laws of atomic structure, one can predict many of the chemical properties of substances, such as density and combinations with other substances, even before they are discovered. Or again, psychoanalytic theory, though far less advanced than physical theory, has remarkable predictive power even today: on the basis of your past history and general laws, the psychoanalyst can not only explain why you have the dreams you do, why you feel aggression toward this person and affection toward the other, and why you feel guilt in the situations you do, but also predict what conflicts will arise, what course the therapy will take, and whether it will achieve certain desired results. (That *exact* predictions cannot be made is not so much the result of lack of well established laws as of lack of knowledge of "initial conditions," the tremendous quantity of singular statements about the patient's history, including seemingly trivial details which have long since been forgotten.)

There are many explanations which fulfill both these requirements, which may nevertheless not strike everyone as equally satisfying or equally informative. Thus, in the case of the pitcher breaking, we probably feel more satisfied with the explanation given than we do in the example of copper conducting electricity. It is not that the one is predictive but the other is not; the law that copper conducts electricity is as predictive of the future behavior of copper as the law that water expands on freezing is predictive of the future behavior of water. One might say that logically both are perfectly satisfactory explanations, yet the one about water strikes us as better, or at any rate more satisfying, than the one about copper. There may be several reasons for this. (1) It *may* be because the inquirer already knew that copper conducts electricity but not that water expands on freezing. In other words, in asking the question about copper he was not asking the question he really meant to ask; what he really wanted to know was "Why does copper conduct electricity?" This, of course, is a different question, one which may easily arise after the first has been answered, but nevertheless a different question. He was asking for an explanation not of the original phenomenon, but of the law that explained *it*. (2) Even if he did not know that copper conducts electricity, he might still not feel as content with the explanation here as in the example about the water. He might be more satisfied with the latter because, as a result of it, he is able to *bring together under one law a whole range of phenomena,* such as the bursting of his water-pipes in winter and the formation of ice at the top of ponds, which had previously seemed unrelated to each other. It is not so much the sheer quantity of predictions made possible by the law, as the range and variety of phenomena covered by these predictions, that makes a person satisfied with an explanation.

Unsatisfactory explanations. Why do we need this second requirement for explanations? Why should an explanation have predictive power, and the ability to explain other phenomena than the one it was invoked to explain? Let us see what happens when this requirement is not met, beginning with rather crude and obvious cases and proceeding to others that may not be so immediately apparent.

1. "Why do these pills put people to sleep?" "Because of their soporific power." Now what is soporific power? Nothing more or less than the power of putting people to sleep. Clearly something can put you to sleep if it has the *power* of putting you to sleep. But what does it mean to say that it has the power of putting you to sleep, except simply that under certain circumstances it *does* put you to sleep? The "explanation" is only the fact to be explained all over again, in a somewhat disguised form. The fact to be explained has only been restated, and nothing has really been explained. We still want to know what it is about these pills which, unlike other pills, puts people to sleep.

2. "Why does hydrogen combine with oxygen to form water?" "Because hydrogen has an *affinity* for oxygen." This again explains nothing. To say that X has an affinity for Y is only a less specific way of saying that under certain circumstances X combines with Y. Similarly, why does the north pole of a magnet approach the south pole but not another north pole? Because it has an *attraction* for it. But speaking of affinities and attractions is only an animistic [4] way of restating the fact to be explained, although sometimes people are actually led to believe that some genuine information has been given.

3. "Why do seeds in the ground sprout upwards rather than downwards?" "Because they have a *tendency* to go upwards." This is like the other examples. To say that something has a tendency to do X is only to say that under certain conditions (which may or may not ever be fulfilled) it *does* do X. Doing X is hardly explained by the fact that under certain conditions it does X, even though the former statement can be deduced from the latter, together with the statement that these conditions are fulfilled.

4. "How did that door get open? I shut it a minute ago." The wind may have done it, or someone may deliberately have closed it from the other side, or someone may have leaned against it, or any number of other things. If you do not know what it was you may safely say, "A door-opening force caused it to open." Doubtless this is true enough; something that caused the door to open (no

---

[4] The concept of animism will be discussed in detail in the next chapter.

matter what it was) caused the door to open, but this, of course, is
a tautology.

5. "Why does the mother cat take care of her kittens, fight to
defend them, and so on?" "Because she has a *maternal* instinct."
This is not utterly useless, for it tells us something, namely, that
the behavior is not learned; but for the rest it is much like the
previous examples. No matter what an animal does, we can lay
investigation at rest by saying that the creature has an instinctual
drive toward that type of activity. The same questions that existed
before still remain to be answered: What are the empirical laws
about the physiological constitution of cats which are concealed by
this glib reference to "instinct"? Is there any characteristic of their
genes or chromosomes, for example, which helps to explain why cats
have an "instinct" for this but not for that, or why the maternal
instinct, for example, seems to disappear a few weeks after a litter
is born? Maybe robins do have a "migratory instinct," but why
robins and not sparrows? Instead of information, which is admittedly difficult to come by in this subject, we are given merely words:
"instinct," "affinity," "power," "faculty."

6. "Why did the radio stop working just now?" "Because there is
a gremlin in it, and whenever a gremlin gets into the radio it won't
run." Here again the phenomenon to be explained is deducible from
the explanation. Yet the explanation offered is so obviously unsatisfactory that it would not ordinarily be offered except in jest. The
"explanation" here offered has no predictive value whatever. If we
had said, "The radio won't run because it was unplugged," our explanation would have predictive value, and if we put the plug back
in and the radio works again, the explanation is correct. If there
were visible gremlins and we could watch them going into radios,
and when they did the radios would not run, the situation would be
quite different—indeed, it would be no different in principle from
the explanation in terms of the plug being out; in the one case we
plug it in, and in the other, we chase out the gremlins to make it
work again. Because the gremlins are invisible, our sole test of their
presence is simply the fact that the radio will not work. Every time
the radio does not work, we can say, "The gremlins are at it again,"
but, if we intend this statement to be taken cognitively and not just
pictorially (see pages 73–74), we shall have given not one iota of
explanation of *why* the radio does not work.

We shall have a good deal more to say later in this chapter about entities like gremlins which make no difference at all to our experience. The relevant point here is that as explanations they are unsatisfactory, for we can predict nothing by means of them. Our sole test for the presence of the gremlins is simply that the radio does not work; our sole test for the affinity of hydrogen and oxygen is that they actually combine; our sole test for the soporific power of the pills is that they put people to sleep; and so on. But it is *not* the case that the sole test for the unplugged condition of the radio wire is that the radio does not work, nor is our sole test for the expansion of water on freezing the fact that the pitcher breaks. The scientific explanation covers more ground than the fact to be explained; but these fictitious explanations are in effect no more than a different (sometimes a pictorial) way of restating the same fact which needs to be explained. They do not solve the problem, but merely restate it.

Or we could put the matter in the following way: The scientific explanation has predictive value, and whenever there is a prediction there is a risk of error, for the prediction may be falsified by the facts. A scientific explanation can always be *put to the test,* and when it is it may be found wanting, so that another explanation will have to be sought. The false explanations we have been considering, which are often referred to as *"ad hoc"* explanations, predict nothing, and so nothing could possibly falsify them; they could never be laid low by a false prediction. Because they can never be put to a test, they can never fail to pass a test. Circumstances might require you to abandon the view that the wind blew the door shut, but nothing could force you to abandon the view that a door-opening force did so, for the latter "explanation" is compatible with anything that might have happened to cause the door to close. You may be able to show that the radio's failure to work was not caused by its being unplugged, because it was plugged in all the time; but you can never show that its failure to work was not caused by invisible gremlins. Since the *ad hoc* explanation does not predict any future events, it cannot be falsified by any future events.

Purposive explanations. It has sometimes been said that when you explain something you say what its *purpose* is. Thus, "What is the purpose of that contraption?" "To stamp labels on cans." How does this fit in with the scientific account of explanation we have just considered?

When you speak of purpose you usually refer to *conscious intent*. If someone asks you why you planted soybeans on your front lawn, you may say "In order to attract attention," if that was your *purpose* in doing it. Or if someone asks, "Why do you study until such a late hour?" you may reply, "In order to get good grades in my courses."

Sometimes we speak of purpose in senses derived from these but not quite the same: (1) Psychoanalysts speak of people as having *unconscious* purposes; but if "purpose" means conscious intent, this is a contradiction in terms. Actually what is meant is roughly that you *behave as if* your conscious purpose was to do so-and-so although the conscious purpose is not present. (2) We speak of machines as having purposes (thus, airplanes are for flying) but we do not attribute to them either conscious or unconscious purposes. Rather, what we mean is that they reflect the conscious purposes of their makers: in other words, *we* had a conscious purpose in making the machine, and whatever that purpose was is called the purpose of the machine. Strictly speaking, then, the purpose is ours and not the machine's.[5]

In every case, then, a purpose implies a purposer. If something happens because of a purpose, we can always ask, "Whose purpose was it?" A purpose which is nobody's purpose is not a purpose at all, any more than there can be a thought which is nobody's thought.

Often when people ask for explanations of things they are vaguely dissatisfied unless they have some answer in terms of purpose. "Why did he die?" "Well, the car hit him as he was crossing the street and . . ." "No, I mean *why* did he die?" If a complete account of what happened (the particular series of events) and the laws involved does not satisfy the questioner, what he is probably after,

---

[5] We may use "purpose" in a still more diluted sense, as when we ask, "What is the purpose of the appendix?" Here we *may* be asking what conscious intent a Creator had in creating the human organism with an appendix, and in this case of course it is the primary sense of "purpose" over again, with the difference that it is God's purpose and not human purposes about which the question is asked. But more usually when people ask such a question they mean merely something like "What does it do?" or "What part does it play in the functioning of the body?" and this can hardly be called a question about *purposes* at all.

perhaps without being clearly aware of it himself, is a statement of purpose: in this case a Divine purpose or intent in bringing about the person's death. If this is what is meant, the principle "Purpose implies purposer" is not violated, although it may be difficult or impossible to determine what the Purposer's purpose was in this case. (We shall discuss explanations in theological terms in Chapter 5.) In every case we should remember: Wherever there is a purpose, there must be a conscious being to have the purpose.

Now, what of purposive explanations in the sciences? Are they accepted as explanations? The answer is that explanations in terms of purposes are only special cases of explanations as already analyzed above. Explanations require laws, and if there are laws *about* purposes, there is no reason why they cannot figure in the explanation just as well as laws about falling bodies figure in other explanations. To the extent that laws about purposes have been established, they can be used in explanations like any other laws. Explanations in terms of divine purposes are not employed in the sciences because no laws about such purposes have ever been established. Even explanations of biological events in terms of animal purposes is frowned upon: we do not account it an explanation if it is said that the hen sits on her eggs *in order to* hatch chicks, because we have no indication that the hen does so with this conscious intent; even if this is true we do not know it, and therefore we cannot use it as a law in our explanation. Only in the human realm do we know purposes to exist, and there we do employ them in explanations. For example, "Why did you go shopping this morning?"

> People act so as to fulfill their purposes unless prevented by external circumstances.
> My purpose was to go shopping this morning, and I was not prevented by external circumstances.

Therefore, I went shopping this morning.

This example is precisely like the others given in our analysis of explanation, except that the law which is the major premise of the argument is a statement about human purposes, and when there is a conscious being to have the purpose there is no objection to explanation in terms of purpose.

Many purposive explanations, however, along with explanations of many aspects of human behavior, fall short of being genuine explanations because the universal statements which are used as the laws are not true without exception. Thus, "Why did Smith become annoyed just now?"

> All people become annoyed when they are criticized.
> Smith was criticized just now.
> Therefore, Smith became annoyed just now.

It is very unlikely that the major premise here is true. Some persons are criticized but do not become annoyed. Yet this premise is required if the argument is to yield the desired conclusion. Of course, there is a general tendency for people to become annoyed when criticized, but in order to state the generalization in such a way that it will be both true and exceptionless, it has to be qualified: "All persons of such-and-such types are annoyed when criticized in such-and-such ways under such-and-such conditions (physical and psychological). . . ." Psychology is not yet sufficiently far advanced, if indeed it ever will be, to entitle us to utter many true and exceptionless universal statements about the behavior and tendencies of human beings.

Does science describe but not explain? It is sometimes remarked that science does not tell us *why* things happen, but merely *how* things happen. What the person who says this expects in answer to the question "why" is often not very clear; sometimes, as we have seen, he seems to want an explanation in terms of purpose, which alone is conceived of as answering the question "why." Of course, a person can arbitrarily define "explanation" in such a way as to exclude everything that is now called an explanation but is not in terms of purpose. But in the way in which the words "why" and "explanation" are employed, both in science and in daily life, science does explain and does answer the question "why": the law that water expands on freezing explains why your pitcher broke when it did. Part of the explanation is a description of the relevant conditions (temperature was below 32° F.), so that explanation involves description; but by means of this description it explains. If someone says that the law of expansion of water on freezing and the fact that the pitcher was full of water and at a temperature below the freezing point of water does *not* explain why the pitcher broke, what then *would* explain it? what sort of thing is he asking for?

Ultimate laws. Often it happens that an event can be explained by means of a law, and the law in turn can be explained by another law or laws, and this in turn by others. We may sometimes be dissatisfied with the explanation of an event because what we really wanted was an explanation of the laws involved in it, and thus we are asking for two explanations in one. The wire conducts electricity because it is made of copper, and copper conducts electricity; but perhaps what we really wanted to know was why copper conducts electricity and other things do not. That the pitcher of water breaks when the water freezes is explained by the expansion of water on freezing; but why does water expand when it freezes, whereas most liquids contract on freezing?

Once we have explained A in terms of B, we can always ask for an explanation of B. And having received this, in terms of C, we can ask for C in turn to be explained; and so on, indefinitely. That is, we can ask indefinitely, but we cannot receive an answer indefinitely. Sooner or later we reach the level of ultimate laws, where we cannot explain any more. As a rule, this level is reached fairly soon. We explain the breaking of the pitcher by the expansion of water on freezing; but why does water expand when it freezes? We try to explain this in terms of theory: the atomic structure of the water molecule. But we can repeat the question: how do you explain the structure of the water molecule? If it is explained in terms of laws about the constituents of the atoms, we can ask again, but we can get no more answers. We can only say, "That's *it*—this is the way nature is, this is a basic law of the constitution of matter beyond which we cannot go; things just *are* this way; this is just an ultimate law about the universe." Many phenomena can be explained in terms of laws, and these in terms of other laws, but if a law is really an ultimate one it cannot itself be explained by other laws.

However, we can never be certain that the law in question really *is* an ultimate one; tomorrow it may be explained in terms of something more ultimate still. It was long thought that Newton's Law of Universal Gravitation, though it had such remarkable explanatory power, could itself not be explained, and was therefore ultimate. Perhaps it is, but attempts have been made to explain even this all-inclusive law in terms of a space-time curvature imposed by all the matter in the universe. We cannot be sure at any given time what the ultimate laws of the universe are and whether the laws thus far

considered ultimate are really so. But it does seem that there must
be such basic laws, if we are not to be involved in an infinite regress.
Just as we cannot go on forever proving one statement by means of
another, as we saw in Chapter 2 in discussing the principles of logic,
so we cannot go on forever explaining phenomena in terms of other
phenomena without coming finally to rest with some basic laws
which, though the ultimate sources of explanation, cannot themselves be explained. These are the ultimate laws of nature.

Kinds of hypotheses. We cannot, as we have seen, know *a priori*
what the particular phenomena of nature are, nor what the uniformities (laws) among these phenomena are. Anything that is logically possible is *a priori* equally probable or improbable. Logically
speaking, the facts could as easily be one way as another; it is only
through empirical observation that we discover what they are, or,
in other words, which of the logical possibilities are actual in our
world.

But if it is by means of empirical observation that we discover
the facts of the world, it would seem as if the natural sciences would
have nothing to do with the unobservable, so that every word used
in the sciences would stand for an "observable." Indeed, would it
not seem as if the distinction between scientific hypotheses and
hypotheses outside the sciences should rest upon this fact? How
otherwise could it be true, as scientists claim, that their discoveries
are "public property" for everyone to test and check and examine,
so that anyone who went through the same process of detailed observation of empirical facts would arrive at those same conclusions
for himself? Is not science's concern with observable empirical facts,
and are not these empirical facts there for everyone to see?

Yet scientists talk a great deal in terms of "unobservables." We
cannot see magnetic fields, we can see only the behavior of magnets
and magnetic substances. We cannot see electrons (only, as we say,
"their effects"), but yet we talk about them as familiarly as if we
could see them, if not with the unaided eye then at least through a
powerful microscope; but in fact we cannot see them, or perceive
them through the other senses in any way at all. We talk about
entropy and unconscious minds, but these have never been observed,
nor are they the sort of things that ever can be observed. Yet concepts such as these are constantly employed in the sciences.

If science can bring in unobservable entities like these, what is to keep it from bringing in invisible elves and brownies and gremlins, which cannot be observed either? If we desert the empirically observable, are we not free to introduce anything that whim or fancy may dictate? Is not the invisible brownie hypothesis as plausible as the magnetic field hypothesis? If the unobservability of the first deprives it of a place among scientific hypotheses, why does not the same hold true of the second?

In order to answer questions such as these, let us distinguish three kinds of hypotheses:

1. Hypotheses about the observable but not at the moment observed. A simple example would be: "What is causing that meowing sound outside the door?" "I think there is a cat in the hall." That a cat is causing the sound is a probable hypothesis on the basis of our knowledge (from past experience) of the behavior of cats, even though we are not at the moment observing the cat. By opening the door we can observe it, and thus we can discover whether or not our hypothesis was the true one.[6]

2. Hypotheses about the observable in principle but not thus far observable in fact. The other side of the moon is an obvious example. It is technically impossible (see page 95) at this time to observe it, but the day may not be far off when we shall land on the moon and observe the other side of it for ourselves. A hundred years ago many tiny organisms were not observable through microscopes, but increased miscroscopic power has made it possible to observe them. There are many things which we shall probably never observe, such as planets circling around a star in another galaxy 500 million light-years away,[7] but still there is nothing *in principle* unobservable about such a planet, any more than there is about a planet in our own solar system. It happens that most of the planets in our own solar system are only a few hundred million miles away from us, while the other planets in our hypothesis (if they exist) are many millions of times farther away than that. The principle of the two is, however, the same: if we *could* get close to the planets

[6] Such questions as "How do we know we are observing a real cat? How can we be sure we are not the victims of a hallucination?" will be discussed in Chapter 6. For the present, in order to avoid discussing every problem at once, we shall have to assume what we have believed all our lives anyway: namely, that we do observe physical objects such as cats, tables, trees, and so on.

[7] A light-year is the distance which light, traveling at 186,000 miles per second, travels in a year ($186,000 \times 60 \times 60 \times 24 \times 365$ miles $= 6 \times 10^{12}$ miles).

in the distant galaxy, we *would* be able to see them, at least by the light of the star to which they belonged, and if we could get closer still we could touch them and indeed land on them. There is nothing unobservable in principle about things like planets.

3. Finally, there are hypotheses about that which is unobservable in principle. Both magnetic fields and invisible brownies are unobservable in principle. It is here that our problems arise; for the magnetic field is universally acknowledged to be a scientific reality and the brownie is dismissed as a mere flight of fancy.

Where lies the difference, since neither can be observed? One might be tempted to say, "There is *evidence* that the first exists, but no evidence for the second. There are tests for the presence of the magnetic field, but not for the brownie." This is true enough, but to put the question in this way is to sidestep the basic question at issue here. Instead of asking, *Is there evidence for X?* let us ask, *What is the X for which there is or is not evidence?* What exactly does the term "magnetic field" stand for, and what does "invisible, intangible brownie" stand for? Here lies the nerve of our problem.

The impact of this question will become clearer when we reflect on the contrast in this respect between the third and the first two types of hypothesis. We know what it is like to see the cat as well as to hear it meowing outside the door. We know what it *would* be like to see and touch the distant planet even though we shall never do so. But what would it be like to observe invisible brownies or magnetic fields as opposed to observing *nothing at all?* How in the world are we to distinguish "nothing observable" from "nothing at all"? To say that there is or is not empirical evidence pointing to the *it* in question is hasty in this last case, whether the "it" be a brownie or an electron or a magnetic field, because it presupposes that we know what the "it" is which the evidence points to; and how can we know this if the "it" is unobservable? Our principal question, then, will be not "Is there evidence for it?" but "What is the 'it' that there is supposed to be, or not to be, evidence for?" This takes us squarely into one of the most controversial issues in modern philosophy, the criterion of empirical meaning.

IV. THE EMPIRICAL MEANING-CRITERION

In the last section of Chapter 1 we said that just as words and phrases are merely labels for things, sentences are labels for states-of-affairs. To know the cognitive meaning of a sentence is to know what states-of-affairs it stands for: more precisely, (1) what states-of-affairs it denotes and (2) what characteristics it designates, in other words what characteristics some state-of-affairs must have for the sentence to apply to it, just as knowing the meaning of the insignia on a pharmaceutical label is knowing what the bottle must contain in order for the label to belong to it. If we know what "A cat jumps on the table" means, we know what conditions must be fulfilled (whether actually fulfilled or not) in order for the statement to be applicable to a particular situation. If these conditions are the same, the criterion of the application of the two sentences is the same, and their cognitive meaning is the same. The same situation that makes "Cats eat mice" true also makes "Mice are eaten by cats" true; they are two labels for the same bottle. It is well to remind ourselves of this simple criterion of all cognitive meaning at this point so that we may compare it with different versions of a somewhat narrower criterion which we are now about to consider.

This criterion of meaning is usually stated in terms of verifiability, and in practice it is often called the *Verifiability Principle*. But it is not always stated in the same way. Here are a few ways in which it has been put:

1. *"The meaning* [8] *of a statement is the method of its verification."* As it stands, this is difficult to defend. Meaning is not a *method.* In order to verify the proposition that this page is 5⅝ by 8⅜ inches long, you employ a method, possibly the use of a footruler. But the statement about length is not itself a method. You only *use* a method in order to verify the statement.

2. *"A statement has meaning only if it is verified."* [9] Here "meaning" is not defined, but an allegedly necessary condition for it is stated. It would usually be objected, in fact, that the condition specified is not even really necessary. Does not the sentence "An inkbottle is on my desk" have meaning whether or not one bothers to verify it? No one would seriously wish to insist that a statement, in order to have meaning, must actually be verified. If we did not already know its meaning, how would we know what to verify?

3. *"A statement has meaning only if it is verifiable."* This formu-

---

[8] Cognitive meaning is what is being referred to in all these versions.

[9] This version is not actually held by anyone, but is easily confused by the beginning student with versions that are held, so it is inserted here for the sake of completeness.

lation takes care of the objection to (2). The statement "There is a deposit of coal 100 feet below the spot where I am standing" is verifiable, and I could verify it by digging to a depth of 100 feet; but it is meaningful, and I know very well what it means, even though I have never bothered to verify it and never will, and even if nobody else ever does. No one need verify it; it is enough that it is *verifiable.*

But to say that it is verifiable is not quite clear. Must it be *technically* possible to verify it, as it is in the case of the coal or the ink-bottle on the desk? Surely not. It is not now technically possible to verify the statement that there are mountains on the other side of the moon, and yet we know perfectly well what the statement means. Moreover, in a day or a year or a decade it may be technically possible.

What about *empirical* possibility? Is there anything in the laws of nature that prevents us from verifying a proposition? This is not always easy to say because we do not know exactly what the laws of nature are; but if it is a law (and scientists today seem agreed upon this) that nothing can travel faster than light (186,000 miles per second), then it is empirically impossible for us to verify what is now going on at the surface of a distant star. The light of a star that is a thousand light-years away will still reach us for a thousand years even though the star explodes today, and we on earth will not see the explosion through our telescopes for a thousand years. So it is empirically impossible to verify now what is happening now on the star.

It is still, however, *logically* possible to verify it. Empirically we cannot, but after all there is no logical necessity about the speed of light. The speed of light is an observed phenomenon which could conceivably be different. If light traveled the distance from the star to the earth in one second (which is logically possible), we could verify today a statement about what is happening on the star today.

The meaning of a statement (or meaningfulness as it is sometimes called) is usually identified with the *logical possibility of its verification.* The statement need not be verified, nor need it be verifiable in any but the logical sense. We should distinguish this version of the Verifiability Principle from a variation of it which is a bit more demanding:

4. *"In order to know what a statement means, we must know how to verify it; we must know what operations we would have to go through in order to determine its truth or falsity."* This version of the principle is sometimes known as *operationalism,* because it demands of each statement we make that we be able to state the operations by which it is verified. One need not go through the operations, but he must be able to say what they would be.

One may object to this demand: Don't we know what it means, for example, to say that Polaris (the north star) is 450 light-years away? and yet we may have no idea how we would verify this statement. Astronomers determine the distances of the stars by various operations: the method of parallactic displacement (an extremely intricate and exacting procedure requiring observations over many months), by the method of Cepheid variables (which again presupposes considerable technical training and knowledge of astronomy), and in the case of the most distant galaxies, by the red shift in the spectral lines shown by the light of the stars in a spectroscope. All these operations are extremely complex, and we may well ask whether we really have to know what they are like in order for us to know the *meaning* of a statement about a star's distance?

An orthodox operationalist will say yes. Indeed, he will say that the operations we go through to verify the statement determine the very meaning of the statement itself. For example: some distances are computed with a yardstick; others, somewhat greater, are computed by triangulation; still greater ones, such as those of the stars, are computed by methods such as those listed above. Now we must not assume, says the operationalist, that in all these cases we are using different methods of computing *the same thing,* distance. Instead we should say "distance-computed-by-triangulation," "distance-computed-by-foot-rule," and so on. The word "distance" does not mean the same thing in any of these hyphenated phrases. The meaning of the word "distance" is determined by the method you employ to measure it. (Even this statement is misleading, because it assumes that there is one single unambiguous "it," namely distance, to be measured, which is what operationalism denies.)

Does the ordinary person who knows nothing about how to compute the distances of the stars, then, not know what statements about the distances of the stars mean? A forthright operationalist may say that he does not. On the other hand he may say that the ordinary person does mean something, but not the same thing that the astronomer means when he talks about distance. Perhaps the ordinary person means (though he may never have thought of this explicitly—see pages 74–76) that *if* you laid foot-rulers end to end all the way from you to Polaris, there would be as many foot-rulers required to bridge the distance as there are miles between you and Polaris times 5,280. Needless to say, we cannot carry out this process of verification; we cannot climb up into the earth's atmosphere to lay the rulers end to end in the air, nor could we keep them there if we did; still less could we rise above the atmosphere while remaining alive to continue the process of verification, escape the earth's gravitational field and that of the other bodies we would approach on our long journey, and live the length of time required (many thousands of years); moreover, the star would be in a different place by the time we got there. But of course this does not matter: we are not required to carry out the verification, but only to know how we *would* carry it out; carrying it out is here at least *logically* possible. And perhaps this *is* what we mean when we say that the star is 450 light-years distant. Only then the operationalist will remind us that the meaning of the statement "Polaris is 450 light-years distant from the earth," as verified by foot-rule measurement, is not the same as when verified by parallactic or other methods; indeed, he will say that they are not the same statement at all, but different propositions expressed (misleadingly) by the same sentence.

Operationalism is a subject of controversy in the philosophy of science. Discussion of it, however, requires considerable acquaintance with the techniques of the sciences, and becomes too technical to pursue here. We shall return our discussion, then, to the version of the meaning-criterion we were considering, namely that a statement is meaningful only if it is logically possible to verify it, whether or not any given individual knows by what specific operations the verification takes place.

Even this version of the principle, however, is often rejected as being too stringent. It is said that many statements are not verifiable, even in the logical sense, and yet are meaningful; and that we should restate the principle by substituting for the word "verifiable" the word "confirmable."

5. *"A statement has meaning only if it is confirmable (specifically, if it is logically possible to confirm it)."*

What is the difference between verifying and confirming? Confirmation is incomplete verification; or, put the other way round, verification is completed confirmation. Let us suppose for the sake of simplicity that there are ten statements which together would verify a given statement. Suppose you verify *one* of these ten. Then you have *confirmed* your statement but not verified it. Each of the ten that you verify adds some confirming weight to it, until you have verified all ten. Then you have completely confirmed it: that is to say, you have verified it.

Why should one wish to substitute confirmability for verifiability? The chief motive for doing this has been that there are some classes of statements which it is *logically* impossible to verify but are easily confirmable. Let us consider some of these statements.

(1) *Statements about the past.* Can you verify today a statement about the Egyptians building pyramids four thousand years ago? You can confirm it by means of historical records, by going to Egypt and investigating ruins, and so on; but if verifying a statement involves getting *all* the evidence for it, it would involve the most direct way of getting it, namely being right there and watching them at the time they were being built. This, surely, would be the crucial, the decisive, evidence for the statement. But it is precisely this evidence that we cannot get *now*. The past is gone forever. And is it not *logically* impossible to get it back? Even if a series of events were exactly repeated now, it would not be the past recurring now, but a series of events in the present precisely similar to a series of events in the past.

Thus it could be argued: "In order to get the final, the decisive verification, wouldn't you have had to *be* there at the time? and isn't it self-contradictory for you, now, in the twentieth century A.D., to be in Egypt in 2,000 B.C.? Wouldn't this involve your existing at two different *times* at one and the same time? and isn't this tantamount to saying that you are existing in the twentieth century A.D. and *not* in the twentieth century A.D. at the same time? and isn't this a self-contradiction?" It is, of course, logically possible—and empirically possible as well—to be in the Egypt of 2,000 B.C. in your dreams or in your imagination; it is even logically possible to overtake the light-waves, now 5,000 light-years distant, and see for yourself what went on then, just as we now do for distant stars. The question is whether it is logically possible for you really and literally to *be* there, then, and to be here, now, both at the *same time!*

(2) *Statements about the future.* The skeptic in our argument about probability (see pages 172–177) would deny that any observation you can make now even *confirms* the proposition that some future event will occur. But it needs no skeptic to be convinced that you cannot verify today a statement about an event tomorrow. However the signs may point to an event, call it X, occurring tomorrow, it is always at least logically possible that it will not occur. In order to verify whether X occurs tomorrow, we at least have to be there tomorrow to see; and is it not logically impossible for us *today* to witness *tomorrow?* We may witness today a vision of what tomorrow will be like, or we may look into a crystal ball that foretells tomorrow; but the event we are witnessing, such as the picture in the crystal ball, is occurring *today.* Only tomorrow can tell whether what the crystal ball foretells today turns out to be so.

(3) *Laws of nature.* Since laws involve both the past and the future, they cannot be verified, but only confirmed. You cannot today observe the crows of tomorrow or of a thousand years hence; and yet these crows are covered in the generalization "*All* crows are black." And the impossibility of verifying a law is a logical one; for as we have just seen, it is logically impossible to verify an event of the future, or for that matter of the past. Moreover, the application of a law is infinite in extent: verifying it would mean making an infinite number of confirmations; and it would generally be held that it is not logically possible to perform an infinite number of acts of confirmation in a finite length of time. Laws of nature, then, are not verifiable; it is not even *logically* possible to verify them.

Fallibilists (see pages 160–164) would go further than this: according to them, not only these classes of statements, but *all* empirical statements, are confirmable only. Why? Because every empirical statement has an infinite number of possible confirmations, exactly as in the case of laws. "All crows are black" would require an infinite number of confirmations, but so would "This crow is black." According to the fallibilist, *no* empirical proposition is verifiable.

Thus there is considerable pressure to substitute the confirmability criterion for the verifiability criterion—at least if we do not want to dismiss the three classes of statements above (and others as well, as we shall see later) as meaningless. The pressure is greatest of all on the fallibilist, unless he wants to hold that all empirical statements are meaningless!

Considerations such as these have led many philosophers to accept the confirmability rather than the verifiability version of the criterion. It can be argued, however, that the situation is not as desperate as the arguments in the above paragraphs would seem to indicate. Perhaps the three classes of statements we have been considering are not really as badly off as they seem to be on the verifiability version. For example: it is, admittedly, logically impossible for us to verify *now* a statement about the past or the future; and it is logically impossible in a finite length of time to verify a law. But we know what *would* supply the missing condition; in the case of the pyramids, for instance, it would be being there at the time specified and observing in detail the whole operation. It is logically impossible to do this now, but it was possible *then*, so we know at least what the *conditions of verification* are; we know *what it would be like* to verify the statement even though it is logically impossible to do it *now*. It is logically impossible for you to verify now the proposition that tomorrow you will have a headache; but tomorrow you will be able to verify it, and *you know now* what the conditions for verification are, even though you will have to wait until tomorrow for those conditions to be fulfilled. Even in the case of laws, you know what would be required to verify them: namely, the observation of everything in the universe, past, present, and future. You would have to be an omniscient being, a god, in order to do this; but, granted omniscience and an infinite length of time, there would be nothing to prevent it. You know in each case *what it would be like* for you to find the statement to be true (verify it) or false (falsify it).

Whatever the outcome of this particular controversy, let us consider the Verifiability Principle a little further. In considering it we shall have particularly in mind Version 3 (logical possibility of verification) and Version 5 (logical possibility of confirmation), these being the most liberal of the group, without going into specific additional requirements of others such as operationalism.

The Verifiability Principle is much used by philosophers of science and by scientists themselves, although the latter do not usually formulate it explicitly. Sometimes it is extended so as to be a criterion for *all* synthetic statements.

Same verification, same meaning; different verification, different meaning. Let us first notice one important consequence, or corollary, of the Verifiability Principle in all its forms: If two statements have the same verification (or confirmation), they have the same cognitive meaning; and if they have different verifications (or confirmations), they have different cognitive meanings. In order for the meanings to be the same, *all* the verification-tests (whether actually made or not) must be the same; *almost all* will not do. The tests for "This is glucose" and "This is sucrose" are *almost* the same; the two sugars look alike, taste alike, and have many other characteristics in common, but the process that will produce the one will not produce the other, and chemical actions of one are not quite the same as those of the other. Therefore, the first sentence has a meaning different from the second.

Let us consider some examples of statement whose verifications are the same, and which, therefore, according to the Verifiability Principle, have the same meaning.

1. "Johnny is taller than Billy" means the same as "Billy is shorter than Johnny." This is a very obvious example. Actually these two sentences are interchangeable. They are verified in the same way, and confirmed in the same way. If you have confirmed the one, you have automatically confirmed the other; nothing could give evidence for the one that would not also give the same evidence for the other.

2. Someone says, after being chided for sleeping too long, "I don't really sleep longer than other people, I only sleep *more slowly.*" We know what it means to sleep longer than others, and how to verify the statement that a person does this. The other sentence is not so clear, because "sleeping more slowly" is not a phrase that has been *given* a meaning in our language. Of course one could give it a meaning so as to make it mean something different from "I sleep longer than others"; for example, one might make it mean the same as "I breathe more slowly." But as a protest against sleeping too long, such a remark would hardly seem appropriate. One would surely be tempted to ask, "Isn't 'I sleep more slowly' just another

way, a euphemistic way perhaps, of saying 'I sleep longer'? Perhaps the two have different emotive meaning or pictorial meaning, but surely their cognitive meaning, which is what we are talking about here, is the same." Indeed, this would seem to be sufficiently clear to most people so as to recognize this utterance for what it is: an attempt at humor.

3. "Twice last year my radio wouldn't work." "Twice last year invisible gremlins got into my radio." These two statements sound quite different, but yet according to the Verifiability Criterion there is no distinction in cognitive meaning between them. They both stand for the same set of facts: the failure of the radio to work. The second adds nothing to the first. To see whether the radio was in working order you would turn the knob, wait to hear any sound that was forthcoming, and so on. To see whether there were invisible gremlins in it, *what more could you do?* There is no more; the two statements are verified in exactly the same way, so they have the same cognitive meaning. The second is, indeed, a very misleading way of stating the first, unless it is understood (as it probably would in ordinary discourse) that the second is not intended cognitively at all, but pictorially, and hence is not an assertion about any state-of-affairs existing in the world.

4. A wire gives off sparks, gives you a shock when you touch it, runs electric motors, charges batteries, and the like. Suppose you admit all this, but add, "I doubt whether there's a *current* in the wire." Now it may be objected, "When you say that the wire does all these things, you are in effect saying that there is a current in it. To speak of a current in the wire is just a shorthand way (not a pictorial way this time) of referring to a rather vague *collection* of characteristics exhibited by the wire. (It need not be these particular ones, such as giving off sparks.) Thus, to say that the wire does these things, and at the same time to doubt or deny that there is a current in the wire, is to contradict oneself. It is logically impossible for these manifestations of current to occur without the current itself occurring. And why? Because the first statement (or rather series of statements) about how the wire behaves is just a more specific way of saying the second, 'There's a current in the wire.' "

Suppose now that you have verified that the wire does all these things. What *in addition* would you be verifying if you verified the statement that there is a current in the wire? Their verification is the same, and their meaning is accordingly also the same.

"But the first contains only statements about the *manifestations* of the current; the second is about the current *itself*. Surely then the second contains more than the first. In addition to the manifestations of the current, there is something, the current, which does the manifesting!"

The defender of the Verifiability Principle (let us call him the verificationist) replies: "Of course there's an *it* that does the manifesting: namely, a current. Nobody denies that there's a current. But what is the meaning of 'current' here? Isn't 'the current itself' just the sum of the behavior-characteristics of the wire in this state? When we use the word 'current' aren't we just using a shorthand way of referring to all these characteristics? You can talk about a current and its manifestations if you like, as long as you realize that the current is nothing more nor less than the sum total of the manifestations." [10]

The difference between the example of current "flowing" (quotation marks are used here because the word is clearly metaphorical) through a wire and water flowing through a pipe is instructive here. We may say that there is evidence that water flows through a pipe if we see it come in one end and go out the other end. But we can, or could under specifiable circumstances, observe not only the water coming in one end and going out the other end but also the water *flowing through the pipe;* this would be easy, for example, if a segment of the pipe were made of glass. Let us note, too, that it is *logically possible* for water to go in one end and come out the other and yet not *go through* the pipe; we should be much surprised if it happened, and we might wonder how the water could disappear once it entered the pipe and suddenly reappear at the other end while no water flowed past the glass segment, but the logical possibility exists: no matter how constantly A (water flowing into and out of the pipe) and B (water flowing through the pipe) have oc-

---

[10] The issue is complicated a bit but no different in principle if one says that when he is speaking of the current itself he is speaking of a stream of electrons flowing through the wire; for this stream of electrons is itself an unobservable which is known only through "its" manifestations, and the same questions that were first asked about the current can now be asked about the electrons. On the other hand, if it is held that the movement of electrons is itself only another "manifestation" of the current, the question again recurs: "Very well, what is the current as opposed to all these manifestations?"

curred together, as long as they are distinguishable phenomena they can be conceived to occur separately.

But in the case of the current (the verificationist will point out) there is *nothing in addition to* the observable characteristics of the wire which we can call the current. There is no test for the presence of current *except* the behavior of the wire; but there are tests for the presence of water in the pipe other than observing it flow in and out. To say "Water flows in and out of the pipe but not through it" would not be self-contradictory; but to say "The wire gives shocks, affects voltmeters, etc., but has no current in it" would be, for speaking of the current is just a way of speaking of these other things.

Thus, the verificationist concludes, the meaning of "The wire gives off sparks" and "There is a current in the wire" is the same, because the verification of the two is the same; and the meaning of "The water goes in one end of the pipe and comes out the other" and "The water flows through the pipe" is different, because their verifications are different; in principle, at least, one can observe the former without the latter.

5. The workings of the Verifiability Principle, and the controversies it engenders, are clearly shown in an issue from physical theory: the controversy about the ultimate constituents of matter.

As late as the nineteenth century the ultimate constituents of matter were conceived to be extremely small particles, far too small to be seen even with powerful microscopes, but still not really different from small bits of matter that we *can* see; the only difference was in size. And it seemed possible that further technical advance in science would enable such particles to be seen. Even then it seemed clear (as indeed it did 500 B.C. to the Greek philosopher Democritus) that there must be such particles. Stone steps wear down gradually from year to year, though from day to day the change is imperceptible. How could this change come about if there were not very small particles successively being removed by the tread of human feet? A lump of sugar is put into a vessel of water, and we cannot see it any more; yet it is still there, for we can taste it in the water. What could have happened except that it has dissolved into particles too small to be seen?

These same arguments still hold good as evidence for the existence of what science today calls molecules; and there is no impossibility in seeing some of these in extremely powerful microscopes. But molecules are not regarded as being the ultimate particles of matter. They are composed of atoms; and atoms in turn are composed of protons and electrons. Whether or not these are the ultimate constituents of matter need not concern us at this time. The important point here is that whether these are ultimate or whether they break down further into others, the ultimate particles are not conceived as being anything like the "tiny marbles" of previous ages; indeed, it is misleading to call them "particles" at all. For they have no temperature, no texture, no color; they are surely not particles in any sense we can imagine. (The phenomena of temperature, texture, and color occur only when large aggregations of them are present, so single "particles" could hardly possess them.) We must, according to contemporary physical theory, abandon any conception of the ultimate constituents of matter as being remotely like the things we are on the macroscopic level, that is, the level of ordinary human perception.

How, then, are we to conceive of them? At this point the views diverge:

1. *The phenomenalistic view*, so called because the meaning of sentences about unobservables is rendered in terms of sentences about observable phenomena. This view is sometimes characterized by saying, "Electrons [11] don't really exist." This, however, is a misrepresentation. It is not denied that they exist; the only question is, What does it mean to say that they exist? The answer given by phenomenalists is that statements about electrons have meanings no different from the meanings of statements which are adduced as *evidence* for the electron-hypothesis. Take any statement about electrons; suppose there are a hundred statements set forth as evidence for the truth of the electron-statement. The electron-statement is then equivalent in meaning to the hundred statements together, or as it is usually put, to "the sum of the evidential statements."

This is, quite naturally, the verificationist view. For how do we verify (or confirm) statements about the existence of electrons, which are unobservable? By verifying statements about what we *can* observe, namely those statements which are set forth as evi-

---

[11] From this point on in our discussion, for the sake of brevity, we shall use electrons as typical of the ultimate constituents of matter, whether they are or not.

dence for the electron-statements. This is all we can verify, so this is all we can (cognitively) mean. It is like the case of the current in the wire; the statement about electrons is only a shorthand way of referring to a large range of phenomena. (But the meaning of statements about the water flowing into and out of the pipe is not the same as that of the statements about the water flowing through the pipe, for they are verified differently.)

The cognitive meaning of electron-statements, then, according to the verificationist, is the same as the combined meanings of the *evidential* statements. So are statements about magnetic fields, currents "flowing" in wires, and so on; but not, again, of water flowing through pipes. The statements about these entities may have *pictorial* meaning which the evidential statements do not have: when we talk about electrons we may have many accompanying images in our minds, probably (whether we want to or not) the images of small marble-like particles whirling around in orbits like planets in the solar system. This imagery does no harm if we do not take it seriously; but we must not imagine for a moment, says the verificationist, that when scientists speak of electrons they can really mean anything like tiny marbles or miniature planets. If they did, electrons would be in principle observable.

What, then, are electrons? According to phenomenalism, they are *logical constructions:* which means only that to say something about electrons is only to say something about (in principle) observable phenomena. It is in the cognitive meaning of statements about these observable phenomena that the only cognitive meaning of electron-statements lies. You can verify (or confirm) the existence of electrons only by verifying (or confirming) the occurrence of these phenomena; the verification is the same, hence the cognitive meaning is the same. Any dispute about the nature of electrons, if it is not verbal, is a dispute about phenomena which are observable in principle—phenomena that have occurred, now occur, will occur, or would occur under specifiable circumstances. To assert that the phenomena occur and deny that electrons exist would be self-contradictory, because the statements about electrons mean (cognitively) no more or less than the statements about the phenomena. All the rest is picture-thinking.

2. *The realistic view,* so called because of its contention that electrons are "really there" in some sense denied by phenomenalism.

The phenomenalistic view, as we have seen, does not deny that there are electrons, but gives an analysis of the meaning of electron statements in terms of the statements which are their evidence. Realism says that they mean more: that the cognitive meaning of a statement about electrons is *not* exhausted by the total cognitive meaning of the statements which are their evidence. The realist declares that he is just as opposed to the macroscopic picture-thinking in dealing with this sub-microscopic subject-matter as the phenomenalist is. Nevertheless, electrons exist in some sense as *things* (perhaps even particles, though this comes too close to the objectionable macroscopic associations), not merely as logical constructions. Speaking of electrons is more than using a shorthand way of referring to observable phenomena. What the something more is, we do not know. How to conceive them we cannot say. We surely cannot imagine them, for our imaginal equipment depends entirely on what we can perceive with the senses. But there is something more to them than the phenomenalist says; and there is something more to the statements dealing with them than there is to statements about any observable phenomena whatsoever.

A full airing of this controversy would require considerably more acquaintance with physical theory than can be presupposed here. But we mention it here because it affords an excellent illustration of the verificationist position together with its opposition. The verificationist says, "What more *can* you mean? You verify the two in the same way, the conditions under which you assert the two are the same, and so they mean the same." The anti-verificationist—in this case the realist (in one of the thousand and one senses of that much-abused term)—says, "I do mean more, and the more is not just pictorial."

It would be easy to make out of this controversy an illustration of a metaphysical and anti-metaphysical controversy, which we shall take up in the next section. While the argument we are now considering may well illustrate this kind of issue (depending on how "metaphysical" is defined), what keeps it empirical in practice is the fact that even in the case of the realist, empirical evidence is what he goes by. The realist, while insisting that there is a surplus of *meaning* in electron-statements over and above what is empirically observable, holds that at any rate the sole *evidence* for electron-hypotheses is the empirically observable behavior of material things. (In the issue to be considered in the next section, no empirical observations are even considered relevant.) Thus, of two philosophically minded physicists, one may be a phenomenalist and the other a realist, but this difference will not interfere with their scientific endeavors; both will agree that the "cash value" of their hypotheses is to be found in their empirically observable consequences.

V. METAPHYSICAL ISSUES

We are now in a position to state one of the most fundamental distinctions in philosophy. One might well say that in philosophy there are two prevailing types of approach: the metaphysical and the anti-metaphysical. The advocate of the metaphysical approach is usually called the *metaphysician.*

It is not easy to give a coherent account of what the metaphysician believes or of what the metaphysical approach is, for the words "metaphysics" and "metaphysician" have been used to stand for related but overlapping sets of philosophical positions. Perhaps the clearest and briefest account we could give of the distinction is as follows: We distinguished in Chapter 1 between verbal and factual issues: for example, whether there are black swans and whether rings around the moon are signs of rain are factual questions; on the other hand, whether the man goes around the squirrel (see page 32) and whether there is a sound when a tree falls and nobody hears it (see page 23) are verbal questions. Thus far, everyone is in agreement. But now comes the distinction: the verificationist is the one who says that all factual issues are empirical ones, issues which *in principle* could be settled by some kind of observation or other (even if only by a person possessing ten more senses than human beings have): "No conceivable way of verifying it, then no cognitive meaning." On the other hand, the metaphysician is the one who says that there are *two* kinds of factual issues: issues which could in principle be resolved by some empirical observation or other, and issues which could not. Those which could not the verificationist would hold to be verbal; but the metaphysician would still hold them to be factual issues, albeit factual issues of a peculiar kind: a kind, namely, which no empirical observation in any circumstances could settle. Indeed, in some cases no empirical observation would even be in any way relevant to the outcome of the dispute. According to the metaphysician, even if we were acquainted with every empirically observable fact in the universe, there would still be *other* facts.[12] (Sometimes it is alleged that we can know them, through intuition or through reasoning about the matter; sometimes it is alleged that there are such facts even though we can never know them at all.) But according to the verificationist, if by "observable" we mean "observable in principle," the observable facts are all the facts there are; anything outside this realm does not even pass his meaning-criterion.[13]

We shall now enter upon a controversy in order to sample the distinction between the metaphysician and his opponent: the controversy about substance. It has a long history in human thought, although most persons have never thought of it or known of its existence before they came to study philosophy, for the problem is not one that arises in connection with the affairs of everyday life or of science.

The problem of substance. We find that in the world there are many substances. Some hold that there are substances other than physical substances, but let us confine ourselves here to physical substances, since our problem is just as well illustrated by them. The ultimate substances, chemists tell us, are elements, of which almost a hundred are known, and these cannot be broken down into other substances, although different combinations of substances (compounds and mixtures) can be formed from these elementary substances.

Each substance has many different qualities, or characteristics. Gold, for example, is yellow, has a certain weight per unit of volume, melting-point, spectral lines, and so on. In Chapter 1 (see pages 42–45) we asked how many of these qualities could be removed while the substance still remained gold. This, we saw, is a verbal question, a request for those characteristics in the absence of

---

[12] Other than tautologies and analytic statements. It is a fact that black is black, and that we do not discover this empirically. But this is such a different and peculiar kind of fact that it seems a bit strange to refer to it as a fact at all. At any rate, the metaphysician is referring to facts asserted in *synthetic* statements.

[13] "But doesn't the verificationist believe in in-principle-unobservables, such as electrons?" A little reflection should assure you of his answer: he does believe in them, and he does use these words, but all he means by them (and all he believes to exist when he "believes in" them) is the occurrence of phenomena that *are* in principle observable.

which we would no longer apply the word "gold," in other words for its defining characteristics. We saw also that even in the case of a comparatively precise word like "gold" the answer is not entirely clear because our usage of the word "gold" is not entirely clear: most of the time we are not sure ourselves which characteristics we would take to be defining. But whatever defining characteristics we may decide upon, remove any of these characteristics and the substance is no longer gold; that is to say, we would no longer use the word "gold" to apply to it.

In all this, however, we never doubted that if we removed one or more of the defining characteristics we would have left *some substance or other*. If it were no longer yellow, it would still be something, whether we called it by the name "gold" or not. But now let us ask: Suppose we removed *all* the qualities—not just the qualities peculiar to gold, but all of them, including extension, mass, and shape? Wouldn't we then be left with *nothing at all?* Not only would it not be gold (we would be inclined to say), it would not be anything. Not only would there be no qualities left, there would be no "it" to *have* the qualities.

Yet is this true? Surely gold is one thing, and its qualities are something else. "Gold isn't the same as the qualities of gold," the common-sense metaphysician might argue. "Doesn't gold have to exist in order for the qualities-of-gold to exist? Is substance not prior (logically, not chronologically) to its qualities?"

The verificationist replies along lines similar to the previous example. What is the proper analysis of "gold" and other substance-words? That gold, a substance, exists, is true enough; but saying that gold exists is the same as saying that *a whole group of qualities co-exist.*[14]

"If you verify that this is gold," he says, "aren't you verifying the presence of a certain group of qualities, namely those that define gold? Substances do exist, but they are no more than the sum of their qualities."

"*Their* qualities! Doesn't that give away the whole case? There is an *it* that has the qualities!"

"Of course there is. But the *it* simply *is* the sum of the qualities. You

---

[14] Even this is not quite accurate; for qualities are timeless and do not *co-exist* with anything. Qualities are *exemplified* by particular items in the world, i.e. by instances. The instances co-exist with other instances. Thus, an instance of gold will be *instances* of the qualities yellowness, malleability, and so on, coexisting in the same area of space at a given time.

verify the presence of the it by verifying that all the qualities co-exist. Verifying that there's gold isn't any *more* than this. It's true that my contention sounds as if I'm throwing out an *it* and leaving only qualities, like a bare stage without actors. But this is because of the grammatical division of our language into nouns and adjectives, the adjectives usually designating qualities and the nouns substances (bundles of qualities). This fact, which is not a feature of all languages, may blind us to the fact that substances really are no more than bundles of qualities; or rather, that substance-*words* designate bundles of qualities."

It happens to be the case that we cannot, in our language, refer to the sensible ,properties [qualities] of a thing without introducing a word or phrase which appears to stand for the thing itself as opposed to anything which may be said about it. And, as a result of this, those who are infected by the primitive superstition that to every name a single real entity must correspond assume that it is necessary to distinguish logically between the thing itself and any, or all, of its sensible properties. And so they employ the term "substance" to refer to the thing itself. But from the fact that we happen to employ a single word to refer to a thing, and make that word the grammatical subject of the sentences in which we refer to the sensible appearances of the thing, it does not by any means follow that the thing itself is a "simple entity," or that it cannot be defined in terms of its appearances. It is true that in talking of "its" appearances we appear to distinguish the thing from the appearances, but that is simply an accident of linguistic usage. Logical analysis shows that *what makes these "appearances" the "appearances of" the same thing is not their relationship to an entity other than themselves, but their relationship to one another.*[15]

"Moreover," the verificationist will persist, "if one still says that substance is more than a sum of qualities, *what is the more?* How could it possibly be verified or confirmed? Could you, *in addition* to verifying that this is yellow, malleable, has a certain weight, and the like, verify that it is gold? Its being a piece of gold just *is* its instancing all these qualities together. You verify the statement 'This is gold' and the statement 'This has qualities A, B, C, D . . .' in exactly the same way. The verifications are the same, therefore, the meanings are the same."

"But this," says the metaphysician, "assumes the Verifiability Principle, which I do not accept. I grant that there is no empirical difference between our two assertions; we agree on all the *empirical facts*. What I insist on is a *metaphysical fact*, not an empirically observable fact. You cannot have bare conjunctions of qualities; you must have a something, in-principle-observable or not, to hold the qualities together."

"Here you are picture-thinking," charges the verificationist. "You think of the substance as if it were a pincushion, and the qualities are the pins. Obviously if you remove all the pins you still have a pincushion left. But

[15] A. J. Ayer, *Language, Truth, and Logic* (London: Victor Gollancz & Son. 1936), pp. 32–33. Italics mine.

the relation of substance to qualities is not like this. Don't let your thought be dominated by this bit of picture-thinking."

"I'm not," the metaphysician will say. "I do not use the picture to support my argument. But may it not be that in this case the picture is a good one? There may well be a similarity between the empirical reality described in the picture and the metaphysical reality about which I am speaking. At any rate, it is the metaphysical reality which I am asserting to exist, and it does no good to say 'But I can't observe it' because I never pretended that it could be observed, even in principle; if it could, it would be an empirical reality."

The word "metaphysics." We shall have further occasion, especially in the next two chapters, to examine metaphysical issues. Meanwhile, a word of caution about the use of the term "metaphysics."

The words "metaphysics" and "metaphysical" have been used to mean many things, usually closely related and often extremely vague. The words have acquired many suggestions, both favorable and unfavorable (depending on the sympathies of the persons using them), and more often than not they are used as emotive words, either of praise or of abuse. Since the cognitive meaning of a word tends to become less precise the more it acquires emotive meaning, and since everyone wants to use his own persuasive definition of "metaphysics" (attaching whatever cognitive meaning he thinks will accompany the desired emotive meaning), it is extremely difficult to pin down the word with any precision. Indeed, we might be best advised to avoid the use of the word entirely, but for the fact that it occurs all the time in philosophical discourse and the student should probably be familiar with it.

Sometimes a metaphysical statement is interpreted to be the same thing as a necessary synthetic statement. In this sense, all the necessary synthetic statements there are constitute the domain of metaphysics, and the question "Is there such a thing as metaphysics?" is the question "Are there necessary synthetic statements?" We have already considered this question in Chapter 2.

More often, however, metaphysical statements are identified with statements about things that are in principle unobservable and for which there is no empirical test to confirm or disconfirm [16] the statement: in other words, not only is the thing that is alleged to exist

---

[16] Disconfirm, not unconfirm. To confirm a statement is to give evidence for its truth; to disconfirm it is to give evidence *against* its truth. An unconfirmed statement is one for which no evidence has been given one way or the other.

an unobservable, but there are no empirical consequences of the
statement which would distinguish it from other statements by
means of the Verifiability or Confirmability Principles. In this
sense, "Trees exist" is not metaphysical because we can all see
them; "Electrons exist" is not metaphysical because, even though
electrons are in principle unobservable, electron-statements have
observable consequences which are different from the observable
consequences of other statements. "Substances exist" (in the sense
discussed in this section) is metaphysical because there is no observable difference between this and "Substances do not exist, only
collections of qualities exist"; there is no observation which would
confirm the first statement without also confirming the second.

Synthetic necessary statements are universal: they assert an invariant relation between two classes of things: "All colors are extended," "If something is a sound, then it has pitch," and so on.
They assert that the relation between these two classes holds *necessarily,* so that we can know *a priori* that it holds for all cases and
do not need empirical confirmation by means of instances. Further-
more, they are usually thought of as being *hypothetical:* they do
not assert that anything exists, but that *if* it exists, then (necessarily) something else (some other thing, or some characteristic of
the same thing) also exists. Metaphysical statements, in the sense
discussed in this chapter, need not do any of these things. They
assert the existence of, or characteristics of, unobservables (in the
sense we have described). Necessary synthetic statements need not
do this at all: there is no unobservable in "All colors are extended."
The two do indeed have something in common, namely their non-
empirical character, and this is what may lead us to confuse the one
with the other. Universal statements which do not stand in need of
confirming instances are not statements we *need* to verify empirically. And statements about unobservables (having no observable
consequences) are not statements we *can* verify empirically. Persons who hold to the first are likely to hold to the second also, and
vice versa.

It is in the second sense that we shall speak in this book of metaphysical statements and metaphysical issues. Chapters 4 and 5 will
contain examples of these issues.

Status of the verifiability principle. We have examined many
statements and pairs of statements in the light of the Verifiability

Principle in one or another of its formulations. Now what are we to say of the principle itself? It is not difficult to attack.

"According to the principle," one might say, "all statements to have cognitive meaning must be verifiable or at least confirmable. Very well; is the principle itself verifiable? How could one ever proceed to verify it? If it is not verifiable, then according to the principle itself it has no cognitive meaning. The principle has chopped off its own neck."

Or one could take a different line of attack: "What kind of a statement is it? If it is put forth as a *definition* of cognitive meaning, then one is welcome to reject it; why should we accept somebody's stipulative definition of 'cognitive meaning'?" But perhaps it is not a definition but an empirical generalization: "Every statement that has cognitive meaning is verifiable." Such a generalization, of course, is always in danger of being upset by the next instance. But this is not the worst consequence: if the statement is an empirical generalization about statements and not a definition of "cognitive meaning," then it should certainly be made clear what *is* meant by "cognitive meaning," because the verificationist has left it undefined. Or perhaps the statement is to be taken as a synthetic necessary truth, with all the difficulties attendant thereupon.

Usually the defenders of the principle do not interpret it as a *statement* at all, but as a kind of *procedural rule* in discourse. We shall have more to say about procedural rules in the next chapter; it is enough to point out here that a rule is not true or false, any more than "Don't park on the left side of the street" is true or false; it is a rule, not a statement, and it is justified not by its truth but by its usefulness. The usefulness of the Verifiability Principle is to be found (according to its adherents) in the fact that it enables us to talk sensibly, to avoid nonsense, to pinpoint our meanings clearly and not get ourselves into trouble because of the assertions we make. It puts to us the challenge: "If two statements are verified by precisely the same set of observations, what difference could there be in their (cognitive) meaning? Do they not then describe the same situation? If the one describes more than the other does, what is the more?" And it makes us ponder over the question: "If there is a statement which you haven't the faintest idea how you would proceed to verify or even to confirm, how can you say that you know what it would be like for it to be true or false? Can you know what situation the statement labels? And if you don't know this, can you honestly say that you know what its meaning is?"

In the final analysis, the value (if any) of the Verifiability Principle is like that of a purge, neither true nor false but very effective in eliminating waste. The metaphysician, for his part, declares that what is "purged" is not waste but an important part of the body itself which the verificationist, like a sadistic surgeon, is ripping out wilfully.

We shall not attempt here to decide the issue between them, nor for that matter shall we in subsequent chapters. But we have not seen the end of this controversy. In the next two chapters in particular, we shall be concerned with issues which illustrate admirably the main centers of contention between these two opposed approaches in philosophy. In doing so we shall develop many points which, it is hoped, will give pause to dogmatists on both sides of the issue.[17]

SELECTED READINGS FOR CHAPTER 3

Norman Malcolm. "Certainty and Empirical Statements," *Mind*, 51, 1942.
————. "Knowledge and Belief," *Mind*, 61, 1952.
Moritz Schlick. "Meaning and Verification," *Philosophical Review*, 1936. (Reprinted in Feigl and Sellars, *Readings in Philosophical Analysis*. New York: Appleton-Century-Crofts, 1949.)
Monroe C. Beardsley. *Practical Logic*. New York: Prentice-Hall, 1950. Chapter 15.
Norman Campbell. *What Is Science?* London: Methuen & Co., 1920.
Columbia Associates. *Introduction to Reflective Thinking*. Boston: Houghton Mifflin Co., 1923.
Morris R. Cohen. *Reason and Nature*. New York: Harcourt Brace, 1931. Especially Book 2, Chapters 2–3.
Ernest Nagel (ed.). *John Stuart Mill's Philosophy of Scientific Method*. New York: Hafner Library of Classics, 1950.
Alfred N. Whitehead. *Science and the Modern World*. New York: Macmillan, 1925.
L. Susan Stebbing. *Philosophy and the Physicists*. London: Methuen & Co., 1937.

[17] For presentations of the Verifiability Principle, see, for example, A. J. Ayer, *Language, Truth, and Logic,* Chapter 1; Moritz Schlick, "Meaning and Verification," reprinted in Feigl and Sellars, *Readings in Philosophical Analysis*. For criticisms of it, see, for example, A. C. Ewing, "Meaninglessness," *Mind*, 46; Paul Marhenke, "The Criterion of Significance," *Proceedings and Addresses of the American Philosophical Association*, 1949–1950, Vol. 23; J. L. Evans, "On Meaning and Verification," *Mind*, 62, 1953.

A. J. Ayer. *Language, Truth, and Logic.* London: Victor Gollancz & Son, 1936. Chapters 1–3.

Friedrich Waismann. "Verifiability," *Aristotelian Society Proceedings,* Supplementary Vol. 19, 1945. (Reprinted in Anthony Flew (ed.), *Logic and Language,* First Series. Oxford: Basil Blackwell, 1952.)

Hans Reichenbach. *The Rise of Scientific Philosophy.* Berkeley: University of California Press, 1951. Especially Chapters 5, 6, 7, 10.

P. W. Bridgman. *The Logic of Modern Physics.* New York: Macmillan, 1927. Especially Chapter 1.

John Hospers. "On Explanation," *Journal of Philosophy,* 43, 1946.

Paul Edwards. "Bertrand Russell's Doubts about Induction," in *Logic and Language, First Series* (ed. Anthony Flew). Oxford: Basil Blackwell, 1951.

William H. Hay. "Bertrand Russell on the Justification of Induction," *Philosophy of Science,* 17, 1950.

Henri Poincare. *The Foundations of Science.* Lancaster, Pa.: The Science Press, 1913.

C. I. Lewis. *Mind and the World Order.* New York: Scribners, 1929. Especially Chapters 9–11.

C. D. Broad. *Scientific Thought.* London: Kegan Paul, 1923. Part I.

David Rynin, Part II of Critical Essay in Alexander B. Johnson, *A Treatise on Language.* Berkeley: University of California Press, 1947.

Paul Marhenke. "The Criterion of Significance," *Proceedings and Addresses of the American Philosophical Association,* Vol. 23, 1949–1950. (Reprinted in Leonard Linsky (ed.), *Semantics.* Urbana: University of Illinois Press, 1952.)

C. I. Lewis. "Experience and Meaning," *Philosophical Review,* 43, 1934. (Reprinted in Feigl and Sellars, *Readings in Philosophical Analysis.* New York: Appleton-Century-Crofts, 1949.)

Arthur Pap. *Elements of Analytic Philosophy.* New York: Macmillan, 1949. Chapters 9, 11, 15, 16.

Herbert Feigl and May Brodbeck. *Readings in the Philosophy of Science.* New York: Appleton-Century-Crofts, 1953.

EXERCISES

1. What distinguishes empirical statements from all other statements?
2. What conditions must be fulfilled in order for an empirical statement to be a law of nature?
3. Distinguish laws of nature from statute laws (two different senses of

the ambiguous word "law") as clearly as you can. In the light of this distinction, evaluate the following comments critically:

   a. We shouldn't disobey laws of nature.

   b. Laws of nature have pre-ordained what I shall do tomorrow.

   c. When there's a law, there must be a lawgiver.

   d. We don't make laws, we find them.

   e. Laws of nature control the universe.

   f. Our behavior must conform to psychological laws.

4. Which of the following statements would you consider to be laws of nature? Why? Can you think of any narrower sense of the word "law" than we have employed in this chapter, in which some of these statements would not be laws but would be in the sense we have employed?

   a. Gold is malleable.

   b. All human beings are mortal.

   c. All electric radios require tubes.

   d. If you press the lever of the candy-machine, a candy bar will come out.

   e. When organisms reproduce, the offspring is always of the same species.

   f. All white tomcats with blue eyes are deaf.

5. Consider all the arguments you can think of, first for and then against the view that no empirical statement can be known for certain to be true—not even such statements as "I am sitting on a chair" and "I am looking at a sheet of paper."

6. What does the word "prove" mean in each of these sentences?

   a. Prove to me that I'm sitting on a chair.

   b. Prove that the angles of a Euclidean triangle add up to 180°.

   c. Prove that if p implies q and q implies r, then p implies r.

   d. He was able to prove that he had not been near the theater on the night that his friend was murdered there.

7. Can the Principle of Uniformity of Nature be proved? Explain.

8. State the view according to which no statement about the future can even be probable. What reasoning can be used to support it? to attack it?

9. Under what conditions is an event said to be explained?

10. Examine the following why-questions. Are they requests for a reason or an explanation, or could they be both? Defend your answer.

   a. Why do you believe there will be a Third World War?

   b. Why did the water boil? Because I lighted the burner under it.

   c. Why did you flatter the boss? Because I wanted to get ahead in the office.

   d. Why do you think it will rain this afternoon? Because dark clouds are gathering in the sky.

11. Give some examples of your own of unsatisfactory explanations, and show why they are not acceptable as explanations.

12. When is explanation in terms of purpose acceptable and when is it not? Why?

13. Evaluate the following as explanations:

a. Why do birds build nests? Because they want to have a place to lay their eggs and to house and bring up their young.

b. Why do birds build nests? Because it's their instinct to do so.

c. Why does this drug produce sleep? Because of its soporific power.

d. Why do most creatures lay more eggs than can possibly develop into full-grown offspring? Because they want to protect the species from extermination by competing organisms, cold, storms, and other destructive agencies.

e. Why does hydrogen combine with oxygen to form water? Because hydrogen has an affinity for oxygen.

f. Why does this wire conduct electricity? Because it's made of copper, and copper is a conductor of electricity.

g. Why did the Allies win World War II? Because they wanted to do so, and people generally do what they want to do.

h. Why does this substance become lighter (per unit of volume) as it becomes hotter? Because it contains an invisible substance, phlogiston—the more of this it contains, the hotter it becomes; and it is so light that an object is heavier for losing it.

i. Why did he arrive last night? Because God willed it so, and whatever God wills happens.

14. "Why did she stab him?" Answer #1: "Because she hated him intensely and wanted more than anything else to see him dead." Answer #2: "Because, as a result of the motion of certain particles of matter in her brain, electrochemical impulses were discharged along certain neuronic pathways, stimulating certain efferent nerves, activating the muscles in her hand and arm, causing them to move in a certain way . . ." Do these two explanations conflict with each other? Does purposive explanation necessarily conflict with such "mechanical" explanations as given in Answer #2? How do you conceive the relation between them?

15. Examine the following dialogue, noting what you consider to be its good points as well as its bad points.

A. Did Newton discover any hitherto undiscovered empirical facts?

B. Yes, he discovered gravitation.

A. But we didn't need Newton to tell us that apples fall.

B. He explained *why* apples fall. They fall because of gravitation.

A. But gravitation isn't an explanation of *why* they fall. It is simply a fancy word stating a familiar fact, namely that things *do* fall. It is not an explanation, but simply a re-description in more general terms of the familiar fact that they do fall. (Compare the physician's statement that you are in this physical condition because you are run down.) What *is* gravitation but the fall of apples and the like?

B. Ah, you have admitted my point: gravitation is, indeed, much more than the fall of apples—it is the fall of apples *and the like.* Newton connected apples in orchards with stars in heaven. He brought seemingly disconnected events together under a general law, and to do this is to have explained them. Of course, if you think animistically of gravitation as a pull exerted as if by some super-giant, you are mistaken. Gravitation is not a pull; the word is simply a name for the fact that matter behaves in a certain definite and specifiable way. But the law that it does behave in this way is a genuine explanation, and it explains a vast number of phenomena, including the revolution of planets and the fall of apples.

16. We can explain some laws by deriving them from other laws; the uniformities referred to in the laws in the first group are as they are because of the uniformities described in the laws in the second group. But what about the laws in the second group—the basic, or underived, laws? Does it make sense to ask why the uniformities described in these are as they are? What would you do with the question "Why are the ultimate laws of nature as they are?"

17. Which of the following alternatives would you prefer, and why?

a. We can't explain why the basic uniformities of the universe are as they are. This is a mystery we cannot solve.

b. To explain a law is to place it into a context of a wider law or laws. If a law is a basic or underived law, then by definition this can't be done—it is logically impossible. The request to explain is, therefore, illegitimate: to explain (subsume under a more basic law) a basic law is self-contradictory.

18. Under what conditions is a sentence cognitively meaningful? First state the general criterion laid down in Chapter 1. Then distinguish the various versions of the Verifiability Criterion set forth in this chapter.

19. Which of the following statements would pass some version or other of the Verifiability criterion, and which would not? Justify your answer.

a. There is a deposit of coal 500 feet below where I am now standing.

b. The temperature at the center of the sun is 40,000,000° Centigrade.

c. The earth is 2,000,000,000 years old.

d. A hermit, in the middle of a wilderness 500 miles from the nearest other human being, has just sneezed.

e. The hydrogen atom has one electron.

f. Ghosts exist.

g. There are cosmic rays even in the enormous interstellar spaces which contain no matter.

20. Consider each of the following pairs of statements. Do they have the same cognitive meaning according to the criterion of cognitive meaning laid down in Chapter 1? Then determine which, if any, of them have different cognitive meanings according to this criterion but different ones according to some version or other of the Verifiability criterion. Justify your answer in each case.

a. A is larger than B.
   B is smaller than A.

    b. A is larger than B, and B is larger than C.
      A is larger than C.
    c. She is sleepy.
      She is drowsy.
    d. This is a mammal.
      This is an animal.
    e. I like custard pudding.
      I do not dislike custard pudding.
    f. Little green elves live in the forest.
      Little blue elves live in the forest.
    g. Invisible elves live in the forest.
      Invisible brownies live in the forest.
    h. Perceivable chairs are in this room.
      Unperceivable chairs are in this room.
    i. Ghosts exist.
      Ghosts do not exist.
    j. The wire gives off sparks, gives electric shocks if one touches it, and affects the voltmeter.
      There is a current in the wire.
    k. Water comes in at one end of the pipe and goes out the other.
      Water flows through the pipe.
    l. Oxygen has a valence of 1.
      Oxygen has a valence of 2.
    m. She has strong unconscious guilt-feelings, which demand punishment.
      She acts (without consciously intending it) in such a way as regularly to bring upon herself unfortunate accidents, disapproval of her friends, loss of her job, and other misfortunes.

21. In which of the above examples (question 20) is it self-contradictory to assert the first statement and deny the second?

22. Which of the statements in question 20 are, in your opinion, metaphysical and which are not?

23. Discuss the following hypotheses in the light of the Verifiability Principle (preferably in its most limited form, that of confirmability).

    a. Imagine that during the night while you slept everything in the universe has expanded to twice its previous size. You cannot detect the change by means of measuring instruments because they too have expanded at exactly the same rate as everything else. Is such a hypothesis meaningful according to the Verifiability Principle? (Is there any empirically discoverable consequence of "Everything has expanded"?)

    b. Is it meaningful to talk about other people, perhaps conscious beings on Mars, having senses which enable them to perceive in ways of which we human beings on earth have no conception?

    c. "Imagine a community of men living on a cell in the blood stream of one of us, but so small that we have no evidence, direct or indirect, of their existence. Imagine further that they themselves are provided with scientific instruments of the type we use, and possess a method of science and a body of scientific knowledge comparable to ours. One of the bolder of these thinkers proposes that the universe they inhabit is a Great Man. Is this hypothesis admissible on scientific grounds or is it to be laughed down . . . on the ground that it is 'metaphysical'? . . . Why at our own level cannot a similar hypothesis be raised: namely, that *we* are parts of a Great Man, the whole of our known universe being perhaps but a portion of the Great Blood Stream?" (Charles W. Morris, "Empiricism, Religion, and Democracy," in *Conference on Science, Philosophy, and Religion*, New York, p. 219.)

24. What would you say of the following criterion of meaning? "Any statement is meaningful to me if it makes (or can make) some difference or other in my subsequent experience."

25. Are self-contradictory statements cognitively meaningful? Can you think of things that might be said on *both* sides of the issue?

4

Law, Cause, and Freedom

In this chapter we shall be concerned, as we were in Chapter 3, with empirical knowledge. We shall consider one aspect of it in particular, namely, our knowledge of causes and effects. Since there are metaphysical interpretations of causality, we shall also have occasion to remind ourselves of the distinctions made in the last section of Chapter 3. We are considering this issue—causality— partly because it is an excellent illustration of the conflicting approaches discussed in the preceding chapter, but chiefly because it is associated with other issues, especially determinism and freedom (which we shall also be considering), and these are the objects of a great deal of popular interest. Indeed, you have probably thought about some of these issues yourself, perhaps before you knew that there was a subject named "philosophy" which dealt with them systematically.

I. WHAT IS A CAUSE?

When we say that drafts cause colds, or that striking a match causes it to light, or that taking arsenic causes death, what do we mean by the word "cause"? What, precisely, are we saying about the relation of the cause, C, to the effect, E, when we say that C causes E?

Our first reaction may be to say, "Why, that's easy. To cause something is to *produce* something, to *bring about* something." Doubtless this is true, but it hardly answers the question; it only shifts it: what does "produce" mean? It means the same as "cause," and thus we are back where we started, having run around in a circle. "Produce" and "cause" are synonymous terms, and instead of defining them in terms of each other, we should state what they

221

both mean. We do not want a word-word definition, we want a word-thing definition (see pages 54–55). We want to know what characteristics a C must have in order to cause an E.

Temporal precedence. The simplest empirical statements are those which can be verified by direct observation: "I am sitting down," "Three books are on my desk." We can also observe that some events occur before or after other events: for example, that smoke issues from my pipe after I have lighted it but not before, and that intoxication follows the consumption of liquor but does not precede it. But do we also observe that one event *causes* another? and if so, what is it that we are observing when we observe this? We observe that someone scratches a match, and that the match lights; but what do we observe when we observe (if we do) that scratching the match *causes* the match to light?

To say that C causes E is not merely to say that C precedes E. Many events occur before others without causing them. Perhaps a moment ago the President of the United States sneezed; but this is in no way a cause of the fact that I am now entering my car. If I ate breakfast at 7:30 this morning and you ate breakfast at 7:31, my eating did not cause yours.

When C causes E, can we say even that C always precedes E?[1] Your standing in front of a mirror is the cause of your reflection appearing in it; are not the two simultaneous? Not quite: light travels at 186,000 miles per second, but it is not instantaneous; so the cause of your reflection now is your standing there an infinitesimally small fraction of a second earlier. In the case of most causes and effects, at any rate, the cause precedes, though perhaps ever so slightly, the effect.

Does the cause ever occur *after* the effect? Suppose I have in mind a goal that I want to attain, such as passing an examination; will this cause me to do certain things in the present, such as study harder? If we reflect even briefly about the matter, we shall probably see that it is not really the future event that does the causing. The future event has not yet occurred and is not yet there to *do* any causing; indeed, it may never occur at all. What causes you to behave a certain way in the present is the *vision* or *thought*

[1] Strictly, that events belonging to a certain class, C, always precede other events of a class E. This distinction will become important later in the chapter. Until then we shall not burden our discussion with the rather technical way of speaking which the distinction will require.

of the goal to be attained in the future. The vision or thought exists now, though the goal itself does not.

Can we be quite sure that no instance will ever occur of a cause that follows its effect rather than precedes it? Probably here almost everyone would be willing to say that the characteristic of not occurring after the effect is a *defining* characteristic of a cause. Of any two events, one the cause and the other the effect, the one we call the cause is simply the one that comes first. Thus we never speak of a rain falling today as reviving the crops yesterday, or of a person's swallowing poison on Tuesday causing him to die on Monday of that same week.

A cause, then, never occurs after its effect. But this has not taken us very far. We need to know much more than this. A cause is not just any event that occurs before another event or at any rate fails to come after it. What, then, distinguishes events that precede others and cause them from events that precede but do not cause?

An attempt to answer this question plunges us at once into the central controversy in this whole issue: between necessary connection and constant conjunction.

Necessary connection. The traditional metaphysical view on this issue is that there is some kind of *necessary connection* between C and E when C causes E; that it is not enough to say that E follows C in a certain way, but that C *must* be followed by E. To assert a causal relationship between C and E is to assert that C and E are *necessarily connected* and could not occur apart. When C occurs, E *has to* occur; it is necessarily the case that C is followed by E. C and E, as it were, are forged together by chains of necessary connection.

The principal attack on the doctrine of necessary connection, together with the first searching analysis of the idea of causality, was made by the Scottish philosopher David Hume (1711–1776). He tried to show that the doctrine was false, because another was true in its stead.

Constant conjunction. What is it, Hume asked, that entitles us to say that C causes E, that friction causes heat, that lightning causes thunder, that windstorms cause trees to blow down? Empirical observation, he replied. And what is it that we observe? Well, we observe that C precedes E, but that of course is not enough. What observation is it then that entitles us to say that C causes E? Is it observation of a necessary connection among events in nature? No, said Hume, for we never observe any such thing. What we observe is always that things *do* occur in a certain way, never that they *must* occur in that way. Try as we will, we never find a "must" in the workings of nature. Empirical observation gives us no justification at all for using expressions such as "C is *necessarily connected* with E," "E *must* occur," "E *has to* occur."

But if causality is not necessary connection, what is it? What is it that we observe when we observe that C causes E? Let us see: When we observe the world around us, at any given moment we find many events occurring; some happen simultaneously with others, some earlier, some later. As we observe this shifting panorama of events around us, we begin, however, to notice certain *repeating sequences* of events—some C's which are *regularly* followed by certain E's. C is followed by E once, twice, ten times, a thousand times —and when we find that C is *regularly* followed by E, we say that C *causes* E. In other words, causality is *constant conjunction* among events. Observing a causal relation between C and E is merely observing that C and E regularly go together—that they are *constantly conjoined*. One observation, of course, is not sufficient to entitle us to say that C causes E; before we can say that we must have observed many conjunctions of C with E, the more the better. (Strictly speaking, we could never *know*, but only have increasing probability of evidence, that C causes E; for we can never know that C is *always* followed by E, that it always has been and always will.) The difference between C being followed by E on one occasion and C causing E is that in the second case the conjunction between C and E is *regular*, or *constant*. In other words, "Always, if C, then E." As a modern Humian puts it,

> To say that the electric current causes a deflection of the magnetic needle means that whenever there is an electric current there is always a deflection of the magnetic needle. The addition in terms of *always* distinguishes the causal law from a chance coincidence. It once happened that while the screen of a motion picture theater showed the blasting of lumber, a slight earthquake shook the theater. The spectators had a momentary feeling that the explosion on the screen caused the shaking of the theater. When we refuse to accept this interpretation, we refer to the fact that the observed coincidence was not repeatable.

Since repetition is all that distinguishes the causal law from a mere coincidence, the meaning of causal relation consists in the statement of an exceptionless repetition—it is unnecessary to assume that it means more. The idea that a cause is connected with its effect by a sort of hidden string, that the effect is forced to follow the cause, is anthropomorphic in its origin and is dispensable; *if-then-always* is all that is meant by a causal relation. If the theater would always shake when an explosion is visible on the screen, then there would be a causal relationship.[2]

Volitions as causes. The following objection to the foregoing account has sometimes been made: "What you say is true enough of events in external nature; but there *are* some events in which we are aware of a necessary connection, namely those involving our own will, or volition. I am not aware of any necessary connection between lighting the fuse and the explosion, only of constant conjunctions between these two events;[3] but I *am* aware of it in the case of willing something and then doing it. Here there is real necessary connection between the cause and the effect."

Hume replies to this explicitly: the example of an act of will causing a motion of your body is no different from any of the other examples. The only difference here is that there is included in the cause (the volition) an *idea* of the effect to be produced. But we still have to know what causes what by observing constant conjunctions. I know from experience that willing to move my arm is followed by moving my arm, but that moving my liver, or my car, or the moon, does not occur upon my willing to do these things. The new-born baby may assume that everything is under the control of his will, but many *failures* of constant conjunctions to occur teach him the bitter lesson that it is not so. What things he *can* do he finds out by noting what acts are constantly conjoined with their volitions: for example, bending his lower legs backwards, but not forwards.

Moreover, another condition is required, namely that one's limbs be in good working order, for if one is spastic or has suffered a paralytic stroke, no amount of willing will enable one's limbs to move in the desired manner. The real constant conjunction, then, is between C-1 (willing to raise the arm) *plus* C-2 (limbs in good work-

---

[2] Hans Reichenbach, *The Rise of Scientific Philosophy* (Berkeley: University of California Press, 1951), pp. 157–158.

[3] One might say that even here there is necessary connection; but the sense in which this can be meant is discussed a few paragraphs below.

ing order) and E (raising the arm). How then can there be a necessary connection between the volition and the event, when in some cases the event does not even follow upon the volition?

> A man, suddenly struck with palsy in the leg or arm, or who had newly lost these members, frequently endeavours, at first to move them and employ them in their usual offices. Here he is as much conscious of power to command such limbs, as a man in perfect health is conscious of power to actuate any member which remains in its natural state and condition. But consciousness never deceives. Consequently, neither in the one case nor in the other, are we ever conscious of any power or necessary connexion. We learn the influence of our will from experience alone. And experience only teaches us, how one event constantly follows another.[4]

Metaphysician vs. verificationist on cause. "True," the metaphysician objects, "one does not *observe* necessary connection, either in external nature or in human volitions. But such a connection exists all the same. When C causes E, there is a *bond* uniting C with E."

Hume and his followers reply, "What is this bond? What we see is that C is regularly followed by E; that is all. What more are you looking for? What do you want? Do you expect C to be connected with E in the way that the links of a chain are connected? This of course we don't find; we find friction followed by heat, but no literal bond or connection between them. What do you mean when you ask for it? Either you are asking for something that just isn't there, or you are being misled by picture-thinking (see pages 73–74)."

The same applies if the language is changed a bit so that one wants not a link, but a kind of *glue* that pastes events together. No such thing of course is found; and surely, Hume says in effect, this is not what we really want. But if not this, what do we want, and what *are* we asking for?

> A. Of course I expect nothing like this. These would be visible bonds, and I am holding that there are *invisible* bonds. There is something there, not observable, not even in principle observable by means of the senses, and hence not discoverable empirically and of no consequence to the scientist. Still, it exists, and it is not merely constant conjunction. Rather, the occurrence of constant conjunction among events is merely a *sign* that necessary connection exists. I cannot describe this necessary connection in empirical terms, because it is not an empirical phenomenon. Necessary connection, then, is the essence of causality, and constant conjunction is merely a sign of its presence.

[4] David Hume, *Enquiry concerning Human Understanding*, Part VII.

B. But how do you know that constant conjunction is a sign of necessary connection? How can a person know that one thing is a sign of another unless he has observed them going together, like twisters and tornadoes? And in this case, by your own admission, the thing of which constant conjunction is a sign can never be observed.

A. True, we observe only constant conjunction. But it is unfair to ask me to give empirical proof of a reality that is non-empirical—just as it would be unfair to demand to *see* a piece of invisible glass.

B. But why multiply entities beyond necessity? Both of us are viewing the same reality—the ever-shifting scene of nature. We both note constant conjunctions of events in this scene. I use the obvious label for it: "constant conjunction." You take the same situation and give it another label: "necessary connection."

A. The same *observable* situation, you should have said. But there is also the unobservable situation, and it is here that necessary connection belongs. Necessary connection is a fact, but not an observable fact.

B. Consider: how do you verify the statement that C causes E? By observing that C and E are regularly conjoined. Now how do you verify the statement that C is necessarily connected with E? In precisely the same way; there is no difference. Let me quote a contemporary philosopher:

> The difference between a mere temporal sequence and a causal sequence is the regularity, the uniformity of the latter. If C is *regularly* followed by E, then C is the cause of E; if E only "happens" to follow C now and then, the sequence is called mere chance. And since (as we just saw) the observation of the regularity was the *only* thing that was done, it was necessarily the *only* reason for speaking of cause and effect, it was the *sufficient* reason. The word "cause," as used in everyday life, implies *nothing but* regularity of sequence, because *nothing else* is used to verify the propositions in which it occurs.[5]

A. But to say this, of course, is simply to assume the verifiability criterion of meaning, which I refuse to do. If you invoke it here, you merely beg the whole question.

What is to be done in this baffling situation? When the metaphysician asks for *something more* than constant conjunction in the causal relation, and calls it "necessary connection," his opponent disagrees: first (1) he tries to show that all we really want to assert in the causal relation can be stated in empirical terms—constant conjunction is what we find in nature, it is perfectly sufficient, and we do not *need* any concept of necessary connection; then (2) he makes a more radical criticism: the so-called concept of necessary connection is not really a concept at all—the phrase "necessary con-

---

[5] Moritz Schlick, "Causality in Everyday Life and in Science," *University of California Publications in Philosophy*, Vol. 15, 1932.

nection" designates nothing, but is merely a way of using *words* based on fundamental confusions. This is his program. Whether he is successful in carrying out his program is something that each reader will have to judge for himself; in any event, the greater part of this section will be devoted to showing what that program is.

The attack on necessary connection: 1. Its existence. "Conjunction is not enough," says the metaphysician. "Events are not merely conjoined, they are *connected*. In other words, there is something *more* than constant conjunction required." Here the empirically-minded philosopher begins his critique. According to him, when we ask for more, we either get constant conjunctions all over again, or we get something else which, however, is no metaphysical unobservable like necessary connection.

(1) **Connection as more detailed constant conjunctions.** Suppose that your willing to raise your right arm is regularly followed by your raising your right arm. We say that the willing *caused* you to raise the arm. (This is an oversimplification, as we have seen, but let us assume it here for the sake of simplicity.) Now, between the volition and the movement of your arm there are other events occurring, in your brain, in the efferent nerves carrying impulses from the brain to your arm, and in the muscles of your arm. Perhaps the metaphysician is thinking (even though not explicitly) of *these* when he thinks of a necessary connection between the volition and the motion? These do provide a connection, of course, both in space and in time, between the volition and the motion—not a necessary connection, not even a *literal* connection like the interlocking links of a chain, but rather *more detailed constant conjunctions:* now it is no longer volition-motion but volition-brain event-brain-event-
. . . -nerve event-nerve event- . . . muscular event, and so on. (The situation resembles one in which you have twelve dominoes, each so placed that it will knock over the next one in line. You knock over the first one, which knocks the second, and so on, until the twelfth falls. You have caused the fall of the twelfth, but only by means of the intermediary eleven. The constant conjunction between your push and the twelfth domino falling is broken down into a series of constant conjunctions occurring in between.)

If it is said, "Surely there is more than constant conjunction between volition and motion!" one may answer, "Yes, there are lots of causally related events occurring in between—but these turn out to be more constant conjunctions of the same kind. A and B are connected by events in between, but the connection is more constant conjunctions. When someone asks for a connection between two events, we can tell him what these connections (i.e., more detailed constant conjunctions) are.

If some of these are still separated, we have to look for new events between them, and so on, until all the gaps are filled out and the chain has become perfectly continuous in space and time. But obviously *we can go no further*, and it would be nonsense to expect more of us. If we look for the causal link that links two events together, we cannot find anything but another event (or perhaps several). Whatever can be observed and shown in the causal chain will be the links, but it would be nonsense to look for the linkage.

This shows that we are perfectly right when we think of cause and effect as *connected* by a causal chain, but that we are perfectly wrong when we think that this chain could consist of anything but events, that it could be a kind of mysterious tie called "causality." . . . After the scientist has successfully filled up all the gaps in his causal chains by continually interpolating new events, the philosopher wants to go on with this pleasant game after all the gaps are filled. So he invents a kind of glue and assures us that in reality it is only his glue that holds the events together at all. But we can never find the glue; there is no room for it, as the world is already completely filled by events which leave no chinks between them. Even in our times there are some philosophers who say that we directly experience causation, e.g., in the act of volition, or even in the feeling of muscular effort. But whatever such feelings of willing or of effort may be, they are certainly events in the world; they can be glued to other events, but they cannot be the glue.[6]

(2) **Connection as explanation of constant conjunctions.** There is another (but related) sense in which one could demand connections in nature, saying that connection is *more than* constant conjunction: the sense in which a connection is supplied by *explaining* a constant conjunction by means of a *law*. (Remember our discussion of explanation in Chapter 3.) Thus, one may discover a constant conjunction between the use of a certain kind of gas in one's stove and a discoloration of the walls of the room in which the stove is located. One need not be satisfied with this "bare constant conjunction"; he may ask "*Why* does this constant conjunction take place?" Here he is not asking for the metaphysician's necessary connection; he is asking for an *explanation* of the occurrence in

[6] Moritz Schlick, *op. cit.*, pp. 108–109.

question. Suppose that a component of the gas, such as sulphur, combines chemically with a constituent of the paint on the wall to form a compound which is dark in color. Now the constant conjunction has been explained. If the request for a connection between A and B is really the request for an explanation of the constant conjunction between A and B, this explanation can be given without appealing to the metaphysician's "necessary connection."[7]

Thus, if one asks, "Are events in nature *connected?*" the answer depends on what one means by the question. The verificationist will say, "If it means 'Is there a link or a glue?' the answer of course is no. If it means simply 'Are there constant conjunctions among events?' the answer is yes. If it means 'Are there more detailed or minute constant conjunctions?' again yes. If it means 'Can such constant conjunctions be explained?' again the answer is yes. But if it means "Is there necessary connection in the metaphysician's sense?' the answer is no. It all depends on what you mean by the question. If such questions as 'Are events in nature connected?' puzzle us and make us inclined to answer both yes and no, it is because we haven't analyzed the question. We must separate it out into the various things that it could mean, and answer each of these questions separately."

The attack on necessary connections: 2. Its meaning. So much, then, for the first step in the criticism of necessary connection. Its conclusion is, "We never find such a thing; what we do find is constant conjunctions." But now let us ask, What is the nature of *that which we do not find?* When we assert that it exists, what are we asserting, and when we deny it, what are we denying? Our critic thus far has denied that there is necessary connection; but did he go far enough? did he know what he was denying? If we know what it means to *deny* that X exists, then we must surely know what it means to *assert* that X exists. But what does it mean either way, the assertion or the denial? Granted that the expression "necessary connection" may have emotive and pictorial meaning (at least to

---

[7] One could make a case for saying that these two empirical senses of "connection" come to much the same thing. You have explained the occurrence of the discoloration, but you have done so *by means of* saying what occurs between the appearance of the gas in the room and the discoloration of the walls. Doubtless this is true; but the second includes something that the first does not, namely reference to *laws,* which, as we saw in Chapter 3, are indispensable in all explanation.

certain people), what is its *cognitive* meaning? What does the term stand for?

The metaphysician, of course, says that it does stand for something, but that what it stands for is unobservable in principle. The verificationist agrees that it is unobservable in principle, but adds that this only shows that the phrase stands for nothing at all, and is therefore cognitively meaningless.

Having reached this impasse, let us examine this issue in the light of concept empiricism and concept rationalism (see pages 87–90). If we have an idea of necessary connection, how did we get it?

Origin of the alleged concept of necessary connection. According to the concept rationalist, there is of course a concept or idea of causality, and it is identical with the concept of necessary connection; the two terms are synonymous. There is a concept of constant conjunction too, which comes from experience; but the rationalist holds that this is not the concept of causality, but is merely a sign or indication that the causal relation is present. Where then does the idea of causality, or necessary connection, come from? The concept rationalist is not committed to the view that it is derived from experience at all. He can perfectly well agree with Hume that experience reveals to us the "is" of nature and never a "must" or necessary connection, but then the concept of necessary connection is not derived from experience. When asked to analyze the concept, he will usually say that it is a simple concept or idea, and that the word or phrase naming it ("necessary connection") is accordingly indefinable.

On the other hand, the position of the concept empiricist is as follows: There is no idea of necessary connection; all our ideas are derived from experience, and experience only reveals to us what events *do* happen. We do, of course, have an idea or concept of causality, but this is merely the concept of constant conjunction or regularity of succession among events; and both the idea of regularity and the idea of temporal succession are derived from experience.

But if there is no idea of necessary connection, how can we talk about it? When we dispute about it, surely we are disputing about something? When we deny that there is such a thing, surely there is something we are denying? Have we no idea what we are disputing about?

No, says the concept empiricist, there is literally nothing (no thing) that we are disputing about. The term "necessary connection" designates nothing,[8] and hence it has no cognitive meaning, though it may have emotive or pictorial meaning. It is only a confusing and misleading *use of words*. We import the words "necessary" and "connection" from logic and from empirical contexts, where they each have different meanings but perfectly clear meanings, and we use them here in a context in which they are literally meaningless. (Similarly, it would be cognitively meaningless to say "2 plus 2 equals 4 hastily." See pages 68–69.) If we think that in the present context these words literally mean anything, we are deluded. Thus he will speak of "the *so-called* idea of necessary connection."

All we are entitled to say is that events regularly *do* occur in a certain regular sequence, not that they *must* do so. Our knowledge of causality is derived from experience, and experience never tells us what "must" happen, but only what *does* happen. Indeed, what does it mean to say that events *must* occur in a certain way? We do sometimes talk in this way: we say that stones must fall, that water must flow downhill, that organisms must die. What account are we to give of such a way of speaking? It is a result of at least three distinct but related confusions.

1. Confusion of causality with logical necessity. When we draw a conclusion from premises in a deductive argument, we use the word "must" in a very specific way. Thus, if *p* implies *q* and *p* is true, then it *must* be that *q* is true. This entire statement, moreover, is *necessary*, as we saw in Chapter 2. The words "must" and "necessary" are here used in their *logical* sense: there is a logical inconsistency in asserting the premises and yet denying the conclusion.

It is only statements, or propositions, that are necessary in this sense. Some of them are necessary all by themselves, such as "Cats are cats," "If all cats are mammals and this creature is a cat, then this creature is a mammal." Others are necessary only *in relation* to other statements: "This creature is a mammal" is not a necessary statement, but it is necessary in relation to "All cats are mammals and this creature is a cat," which is just another way of saying that it is logically deducible from them. In every case, however, neces-

---

[8] Remember that a word is cognitively meaningless only if it *designates* nothing; it need not *denote* anything. See pages 25 ff.

sity belongs to *statements* and not to *events*. The word "necessary" here has been given a meaning only in the context of statements (see pages 68–69). It is not false but cognitively meaningless to speak of *events* as necessary.

Of course we can *describe* the events in nature in statements. Are these statements, then, necessary statements? Once again, it seems quite clear that they are not. "Friction causes heat" is not a necessary statement; it is, on the contrary, an empirical statement. It is logically possible that friction might have produced magnetic disturbances instead. It is only by means of empirical observation that we discover what causes what. There is no necessity about statements concerning causes as there is about "$2 + 2 = 4$." We can never, by merely analyzing statements about causes, discover whether those statements are true.[9]

There is one point of particular importance here because failure to be aware of it may lead us to ascribe logical necessity to the causal relation in spite of everything. Consider the statement "Johnny is taller than Billy." It is an empirical statement and in no way a necessary statement. The same is true of the statement "Billy is shorter than Johnny." We have to see Billy and Johnny to discover whether these statements are true. But the statement *"If Johnny is taller than Billy, then Billy is shorter than Johnny"* is a logically necessary statement (indeed, it is a tautology), and we need not know anything about the Johnny and Billy in question in order to know whether it is true. The same holds true for the uniformities of nature. "Whenever friction occurs, heat occurs" is an empirical law of nature. "Friction occurs" (at some particular place or time) is an empirical statement, and so is the conclusion that is logically deduced from these two statements, "Heat occurs." But the statement *"If whenever friction occurs heat is produced, and* friction occurs, *then* heat occurs" is a logically necessary statement. In other words, the statement that heat is produced in any specific instance when friction occurs *can be deduced from a general law of nature* asserting the constant conjunction of friction and heat. The statement *by itself* is not necessary, but when it is the "then" part

[9] The statement "C causes E, but C is not always followed by E" is, of course, self-contradictory *if* "C causes E" means the same as "C is always followed by E." But this, of course, does not make it logically impossible for C *not* to be followed by E; if this happened it would only mean that this C was not the cause of this E.

of an "if-then" statement of which the "if" part asserts a law of nature plus some particular circumstance, *the whole statement*, the hypothetical or if-then statement, is a logically necessary statement.

Now, how is this apt to confuse us if we are not careful? In the following way: We can say "When there is friction there is always heat, and here there is friction, so it *must* be that there is heat." This is the *logical* sense of the word "must," which only means that the conclusion in question can be logically *deduced* from the premises. The same would apply even if the premises were false: "If all reptiles are green and my dog is a reptile, then it *must* be that my dog is green." The conclusion of a deductive argument can always be prefaced with the word "must," to indicate that the conclusion logically follows from the premises. The danger is that we are apt to put in the "must" and then forget about the empirical premises from which the conclusion is deduced. Thus we say, "Stones *must* fall," "Water *must* go downhill," "Organisms *must* die," and so on, forgetting that these are not necessary statements at all, but that they can be deduced from general laws of nature. These general laws of nature, however, are empirical; and the conclusions can be called necessary *only with respect to* these non-necessary empirical laws.

But isn't it true that water must flow downhill, that organisms must die? If we still ask this question we have not grasped the above analysis. What we can observe at best is that water always *does* flow downhill and that all organisms *do* die, and that the statements stating these facts can be deduced from general laws of nature and must (*in the logical sense*) be true *if* the laws are true. Only in this derived sense, then, can we speak of events in nature as if they *must* occur: they, or rather the statements asserting that they occur, can be deduced from general empirical laws, and are necessary only in relation to them, just as "Billy is shorter than Johnny" is necessary only in relation to the premise "Johnny is taller than Billy."

2. Confusion of laws of nature with prescriptive laws. Another familiar sense of the word "must" is the *imperative* sense. "You must be home by eleven o'clock or else . . ." means in effect that **if** you are not home by eleven o'clock, certain penalties will be imposed. The command imposes upon you a certain *compulsion*. You **are** not strictly compelled as you are when you are bound and gagged and have no control over your movements; it is always open to you to disobey the command and receive the penalty; nevertheless you are compelled in the sense that you have no choice but to obey the command or accept the penalty; and to this extent, compulsion is being exerted.

Prescriptive laws (see page 167) are of this same general sort. The law commands you not to drive over 25 miles per hour in a certain zone, and in doing so it compels. Here again we say, "You must obey the law or risk the penalty." The word "must" in the imperative sense usually carries a strong emotive meaning, in this case evocative (see pages 69–70); it is intended to act as an influence upon the person being commanded, in the direction of obeying the command.

People who do not clearly distinguish descriptive from prescriptive law are all too inclined to talk about the laws of nature and the laws of a statute body as if they were the same. In doing so, they may use words like "must," which are legitimate enough when one is talking about prescriptive law, to apply to descriptive laws as well. But if we take such assertions literally, they make no cognitive sense. "Water must flow downhill," we say; but the water is not being commanded. The law simply describes a uniformity that occurs in the order of nature. It prescribes nothing, commands nothing.

> The laws of celestial mechanics do not prescribe to the planets how they have to move, as though the planets would actually like to move otherwise, and are only forced by these burdensome laws of Kepler to move in ordinary paths; no, these laws do not in any way "compel" the planets, but express only what in fact planets actually do.[10]

Historically, the two senses of the word "law" were not distinguished. (The ambiguity occurs in most languages.) The uniformities of nature were conceived as the expression of the will of the gods, or of God. God *commands* the forces of nature to operate in certain ways, *compelling* every event to occur. Since He is far more powerful than any government, His laws are inviolable. Moreover, since God is good, His laws are so also: the laws of nature are the expression of a *moral order* supernaturally imposed upon the universe. The workings of this order *must* be as they are because they

---

[10] Moritz Schlick, *The Problems of Ethics* (New York: Prentice-Hall, Inc., 1939), p. 147.

are the expression of divine will. Effects follow causes much as punishment follows forbidden acts and reward follows approved acts; they follow *necessarily*, because the laws are enforced by an all-powerful Deity. With this conception of the universe, it is no wonder that words such as "must" and "necessary" came to be attached to statements about causes and effects.

It is not relevant at this point to discuss whether this view of the universe is true; the question is whether the truth of this view is presupposed in every statement we make about causes or effects. When we say "Friction causes heat" or "The appearance of the lion caused the antelope to flee," do we really mean to imply this view of nature, so that if this view of nature were not true, we would not be entitled to make any statements at all about causality? Surely this is not the case. Whether we view nature as a manifestation of divine will or not, this is *no part of what we mean* when we make causal statements in everyday life. We would wish to argue this view of nature *separately:* we would first utter the causal statements (about friction, the antelope, or about anything else) in any case, and then go on, *in addition,* to defend this view of nature.

> The question which must be put to those who speak as if there were necessity in nature is whether they really mean to imply that the laws of nature are normative rules, enforced by a divine will. If they do not mean to imply this, their talk of necessity is at best an unfortunate metaphor.[11]

3. Confusion resulting from animistic use of language. One may object that the view of nature just described does not literally make sense: do not words like "command" and "compel" and "necessitate" have meaning only within the context of human beings, beings who have wills and can thus be made to do things against their will? Stones and waterfalls have no wills, and therefore they can hardly be said to be *commanded* or *compelled*.

This, of course, is true, *unless* stones and waterfalls *are* conceived as having wills. In the primitive view of things called "animism," this is precisely the case. Animism is the tendency to confer upon inanimate objects characteristics which belong only to animate beings.

Today people are no longer animistic in any literal sense: we do not believe that the mountains and trees are spirits, nor even that

[11] A. J. Ayer, *Foundations of Empirical Knowledge,* p. 198.

they contain spirits; we do not believe that the tree feels pain when
it is cut down or that the stone is animated by a desire to get to
the center of the earth; we do not believe that water is compelled
to do anything, because only animate beings can have compulsion
exerted upon them and water is inanimate. Nevertheless, we often
talk *as if* we believed these things. We "read our feelings into
nature." We speak of the sky as gloomy, though it is we who feel
gloom and not the sky; we speak of the chasm as yawning, of the
earth as smiling, of the train as "steaming away impatiently."
Poetry is filled with animistic language, and the poetic quality is
often enhanced by it: it adds immeasurably to the pictorial and
emotive meaning. But when we are concerned (as we are in philosophy) with cognitive meaning, it is important that we weed out as
dangerous many things that for other purposes and in other contexts would be advantages. Animistic language can be misleading.
Let us see how, by means of a few examples.

Originally the word "resistance" stood for a certain kind of feeling people had, for example when trying to move a boulder or hold
a heavy door open. Now we speak of resistance even when no animate beings are involved: we say that the object resists pressure,
resists our attempts to move it, and so on, although we do not mean
that it *feels* resistance. The word "resistance" has become trans-
ferred from the feeling to the thing which occasioned the feeling.
We impute resistance to the doorstop that holds the door open because if *we* were in the position of the doorstop we would feel
resistance. "Resistance," "force," "energy" and other animistically-
tinged words are constantly used in the physical sciences. Here,
however, they are comparatively harmless, for they are given special
and precise meanings within these fields.

You push a large ball and start it rolling toward the place where
you want it. On another occasion you see another ball strike it,
thereby imparting the motion to it. The work done is approximately
the same. But since on the first occasion you pushed to get the ball
where you wanted it, you incline to say, when you see the other ball
doing the same work, that the first ball *pushed* the second, or *forced*
it to go in the path it took, or even *compelled* it to go. This language
is, of course, somewhat misleading. If these expressions refer simply
to what you observe, namely that one ball makes contact with another and the other starts moving in a certain direction (what a

motion-picture camera would record), then you have not gone beyond the empirically observable facts. But the words you use to describe the situation *seem* to import into the situation something that is not there at all; they seem to imply that the first ball had a feeling of effort or strain in "pushing" the second one, and that the second felt "resistance" to the motion of the first. We do not really believe this, but our language leaves the impression that we do.

The same is true even when we say that the first ball *makes* the second one move. If this means merely that when the first ball hits the second the second moves, and that this regularly occurs, then we are merely describing what we observe. But there is an animistic ring about the word "makes," which seems to hint at some kind of compulsion. In using all these words, let us remember that what we observe is simply that when the first ball strikes the second the second moves, and that this regularly happens. There is no more. We probably do not seriously demand more; but our linguistic habits, a carry-over from primitive times when animism was literally interpreted, do not render this instantly evident, and they are apt to confuse us. Probably there is no objection to using this kind of language, provided that we are clear about what we are doing; but our language is so full of animism that *unconsciously our thought becomes so,* and we are left with verbal expressions which we have the impulse to defend even though we cannot seriously take them literally. That is why we often resist the tendency to describe causal relations simply in terms of regularity of succession. We want to keep on saying, "The first billiard ball *compels* the second one to move," and "When the first hits the second, the second *must* move, or even "When the first hits the second, the second *can't help* moving" (as if it were a conscious being that could avoid doing things if it wished to) or "The first ball *forces* the second to move" (note the implicit comparison with a quite different kind of situation, such as a robber forcing you to give up your money). These are the ghosts of animism which haunt our everyday language. We have been so accustomed since childhood to talking in these ways that we come to feel we have lost something when we have translated "The first ball caused the second one to move" into "When the first ball contacts the second, the second regularly moves." We do not feel quite so much at home with this straightforward, nakedly empirical, studiedly non-animistic language; and so we feel that we mean more than this, even though we cannot discover what the more is. When we have reached this stage, we are ready to begin using such terms as "necessary connection," whether they stand for anything or not: they "have the right kind of sound," they fill the vacuum created by the removal of the animistic overtones from our everyday causal language.

Do causes always operate by contact? So much for the ways in which the anti-metaphysical philosopher explains how people came to defend the "so-called idea of necessary connection." He himself analyzes causality, as we have seen, into constant conjunctions among events. There is, however, a qualification which we would do well to investigate before proceeding further. Is not the constant conjunction which occurs always of a certain definite kind? Specifically, is it not true that whenever C causes E, C is in *contact* with E, or as Hume put it, *contiguous* to E? When C causes E, is it not always the case that two things are in contact with each other? This is the question of "Is there action at a distance?" (There are many examples of contact without causality; our question is, when there *is* constant conjunction, is not contact also required before we can truly say that a causal relation is present?)

At first it may seem that the answer is not in favor of action at a distance. You hold a poker in the fire and the handle gets hot. But of course this is because the rapid motion of the molecules that are in the fire is transmitted along the poker until it reaches your hand. There is no action at a distance here—unless, of course, molecules never touch each other as we believe that they do. Another example: A bell rings a mile away, and produces a disturbance in your ear and, via your ear, in your brain. The bell is not contiguous to your ear. But the bell and your ear are connected by particles of air which transmit sound-waves from the one to the other, by immediate contact of the molecules. If between the two there were a vacuum, in other words, no particles to transmit the motion, the sound-waves would never reach your ear. Thus, while bell and ear are not contiguous, what happens to the one causes what happens to the other by virtue of a more detailed series of constant conjunctions in between, in which there *is* contiguity.

So far, it seems as if all causing occurs by contact. There are other examples, however. Consider the sun: it gives heat and light to the earth. Undoubtedly there is a causal relation between them. But where is the contact? There is nothing, not even air, between them. "But surely there is some medium to transmit the radiation from sun to earth!" How does the person who says this know that it is true? All empirical evidence has failed to reveal any such medium. The Michelson-Morley experiment and others ingeniously devised to detect the existence of any such medium, called the ether, failed utterly, and the notion of the ether has dropped out of science. If one says that it is there anyway, that it *must* be there (in what sense of "must"?), this looks suspiciously like an attempt to introduce it just in order to save the principle that all causes operate by contact. In other words, the existence of the ether has now become an *a priori assumption* (see pages 144–145); regardless of all evidence, it is assumed to be there throughout all space. Why this assumption? Because "all causes operate by contact"! But this, of course, begs the whole question.

May it not be, however, that the principle of no action at a distance (all causes by contact) is false? Here we have C causing E, and no contact of anything that we have ever been able to discover. If this is so in the case of radiation, what of gravitation? Surely this is action at a distance if anything ever was: one star may affect the course of another many hundreds of light-years away; unless, again, one brings in a medium simply in order to save the principle.

It seems, then, that if we are not to introduce an *a priori* assumption we shall have to abandon the principle that all causes operate by contact. It seems that not all causes are contiguous with their effects, nor can they be traced through a series of more detailed causes and effects which *are* contiguous. But if there are instances of causality without contact, contact can hardly be necessary to causality. In other words, contact is not a *defining* characteristic of causality. It is an accompanying characteristic, and no more.

Even if it were a universally accompanying characteristic, it would still be accompanying, for we could still ask, "*If* sometime an instance of constant conjunction should arise but no contact, *would* it be an instance of causality?" And would not the answer be that it would? If the prime minister of India had a fit of palsy every time you stumbled while walking, and this happened millions of times, and *only* when you stumbled, would you not say that the

two events were somehow causally related, whether or not you or
anyone else could ever trace a chain of more detailed constant conjunctions between them? It is true, of course, that the most *familiar*
mode of operation of physical causes is by contact; but we should
not make that which is most familiar the model for all causal relations everywhere.

Can we have *a priori* knowledge of causes? As a rule, even the
metaphysician will assert that we cannot know *a priori* what causes
what in the universe. Even if he interprets causality as necessary
connection, he holds that the only way we can *know* whether necessary connection is present in any given case is by observing constant conjunctions. And we cannot know in advance of experience
what events will turn out to be conjoined with what other events.
"There are no objects," writes Hume, "which by the mere survey,
without consulting experience, we can determine to be the causes of
any other; and no objects, which we can certainly determine in the
same manner not to be the causes."

When we see two trains rapidly approaching each other a hundred feet apart on the same track, can we not say *a priori* that they
will have a collision? Even here the answer is no. Prior to experience
of how solid objects behave, we could have no idea what would happen when they approached each other. It is always *previous experience* that enables us to predict what will happen. Since long before
the time we began remembering events we have been acquainted
with the behavior of moving bodies; but if we were opening our eyes
on the world for the first time and saw the trains approach each
other, we would have no more evidence that they would collide than
that they would swerve apart, explode, turn to gas, dissolve, be
annihilated, or fly to the moon. Experience and experience alone can
tell us what causes what. *A priori*, any conjunction of events is
equally probable; we have to learn through experience which are
the ones that actually occur.

The meaning of "constant conjunction." According to Hume, when
C causes E there is a constant conjunction between C and E. Before
we can give a final clarification of the notion of causality, we must
analyze this further. Exactly what does it mean? Does it mean that
every time C occurs, E also occurs? Does it mean that if E occurs,
we can infer that C has occurred? Does it mean that if C does not
occur, E does not occur either? Here we come to a distinction which

is well known in discussions of causality and elsewhere: the distinction between a necessary condition and a sufficient condition.

1. Necessary condition. When we say that C is a necessary condition for the occurrence of E, we do not mean that there is a "necessary connection" between C and E, although we sometimes say "In order for E to occur, C *must* occur." What we mean (or should mean) is simply the empirical fact that in the absence of C, E never occurs. Thus, in the absence of oxygen, we never have fire. The presence of oxygen is in no sense a *logically* necessary condition for the occurrence of fire; indeed, it is conceivable that something quite different from oxygen, say the presence of an elephant, would be a necessary condition of fire. Only by experience can we know what the conditions are, the absence of which is followed by the absence of the event. "Oxygen is necessary for fire" is thus a simple empirical statement, verifiable or at least confirmable by experience.

If oxygen (C) is necessary to fire (E), we can also say that if there is fire there is oxygen present. Thus we can say that when C is a necessary condition for E

If not C, then not E,

or, what is the same thing,

If E, then C.

But we cannot say either of these things:

If C, then E.
If not E, then not C.

2. Sufficient condition. C is said to be sufficient for the occurrence of E if, invariably, whenever C occurs, E occurs. "If rain is falling on the street, the street is wet." The occurrence of the rain is sufficient for the street's being wet. It is not necessary, however: the street might be wet even if it had not rained at all, for example if a water-sprinkler had just passed. To say that C is sufficient for E is to say

If C, then E,

or, what is the same thing,

If not E, then not C.

But we cannot say either of these things:

> If not C, then not E.
> If E, then C.

Thus, necessary condition and sufficient condition are the reverse of each other.

Cause as necessary condition. When it is said that C causes E, which of these things is meant? or perhaps both? or neither?

We say that scratching the match caused a flame. Was it a necessary condition? Surely not—one can produce flame in other ways. Drowning caused somebody's death. Was it a necessary condition? No, for death occurs in many other ways. We commonly speak of causes when we do not mean necessary conditions at all.

The reverse is also the case. There are many necessary conditions which we would not call causes. There are thousands of necessary conditions for your being here at this moment: it is necessary that you have been born, that your parents have met and their parents before them, and so on. But if someone asked you for the cause of your being in this room at this moment, you would hardly reply, "Because I was born," or "Because Mother met Father on board ship." We may sometimes mean by "cause" simply a necessary condition, but for the most part we do not.

Cause as sufficient condition. When we say that scratching a match caused a flame, we do not mean that this is a sufficient condition for the occurrence of the flame. Other things are required also: one must scratch against the right kind of substance, with a certain degree of vigor, without too much moisture, not in a high wind, in the presence of sufficient oxygen. If even one of these conditions is absent, the flame will not appear. No one of them alone is sufficient, but there is a set of conditions *all of which together are sufficient* (though the list would have to be much longer than the one just given here). The entire group constitutes the sufficient condition. And even in the case of a comparatively simple occurrence like the lighting of a match, the conditions constituting the sufficient condition are so numerous that it is difficult to list them all, and so complex that it is difficult to list them precisely.

One way of defining "cause," then, is as sufficient condition: the cause of an event is the whole set of conditions sufficient for its occurrence—so that the fulfillment of these conditions is always followed by the occurrence of the event. If the event does not always occur upon the fulfillment of these conditions, we have left out one or more of the conditions that together make up the sufficient condition. The cause, the *whole cause*, is the sufficient condition.

In common usage, however, we often employ the word "cause" when referring to just *one member* of this group, of which the entire group constitutes the sufficient condition. It is seldom indeed that when C is sufficient for the occurrence of E, C is just *one* event; but we often speak as if it were so. We say that taking arsenic was the cause of someone's death, though it is surely not sufficient; a person whose stomach walls were made of iron would not be affected by arsenic. Ordinarily we fail to mention this condition, because we take its existence for granted. We do not deny that it is a causal factor, but since we do not mention it explicitly it *seems* as if we do not consider it part of the cause. When we say that the cause of a man's injury was that the ladder on which he was standing slipped, we do not mention (because we presuppose) that he had weight, even though the event in question would not have occurred without this condition. In short, we often talk as if a *part* of the sufficient condition were the cause, though we realize well enough that until we have stated the entire sufficient condition we have not stated the *whole* cause.

When the causal factors are extremely numerous, as they are in the realm of human behavior, we are more than ever inclined to speak in this way. What is the cause of this burglary? "The lock was easy to break open," says one person. "Everyone living in the house was out," says another. "The house was set fairly far back from the street." "It was a dark moonless night, in which detection and identification would have been difficult." "The burglar had just escaped in the prison break." "Consider his family background— there lies the *real* cause." All of these are causal factors; all of them may have had something to do with the effect in this case, but we single out one of them and talk as if it were *the* cause. The one we single out for special attention may be the last one among the group to occur, or the one whose occurrence is in some way the most spectacular, or the one in which we happen at the moment to be the most interested.

Often we call that one factor the "cause" and all the others the "conditions." But there seems to be no basis for such a distinction; all of the factors are causally relevant to the occurrence of the effect.

Nothing can better show the absence of any scientific ground for the distinction between the cause of a phenomenon and its conditions, than the capricious manner in which we select from among the conditions that which we choose to denominate the cause. However numerous the conditions may be, there is hardly any of them which may not, according to the purpose of our immediate discourse, obtain that nominal pre-eminence. This will be seen by analyzing the conditions of some one familiar phenomenon. For example, a stone thrown into the water falls to the bottom. What are the conditions of this event? In the first place, there must be a stone and water, and the stone must be thrown into the water; but these suppositions forming part of the enunciation of the phenomenon itself, to include them also among the conditions would be a vicious tautology . . . The next condition is, there must be an earth; and accordingly it is often said that the fall of a stone is caused by the earth, or by a power or property of the earth, or a force exerted by the earth . . . or, lastly, the earth's attraction, which also is only a technical mode of saying that the earth causes the motion, with the additional peculiarity that the motion is towards the earth, which is not a character of the cause, but of the effect. Let us now pass to another condition. It is not enough that the earth should exist; the body must be within that distance from it in which the earth's attraction preponderates over that of any other body. Accordingly we may say, and the expression would be confessedly correct, that the cause of the stone's falling is its being *within the sphere* of the earth's attraction. We proceed to a further condition. The stone is immersed in water; it is therefore a condition of its reaching the ground that its specific gravity exceed that of the surrounding fluid, or, in other words, that it surpass in weight an equal volume of water. Accordingly any one would be acknowledged to speak correctly who said that the cause of the stone's going to the bottom is its exceeding in specific gravity the fluid in which it is immersed.

Thus we see that each and every condition of the phenomenon may be taken in its turn, and, with equal propriety in common parlance, but with equal impropriety in scientific discourse, may be spoken of as if it were the entire cause. And in practice that particular condition is usually styled the cause whose share in the matter is superficially the most conspicuous, or whose requisiteness to the production of the effect we happen to be insisting on at the moment.[12]

Plurality of causes. Is every member of this group of conditions, all of which together constitute the sufficient condition, also a necessary condition? In other words, is a sufficient condition made up *only* of necessary conditions?

Let us take a simple example to illustrate the question, and even this simple example will be somewhat oversimplified. In order for

[12] John Stuart Mill, *A System of Logic* (New York: Longmans, Green, 1843), Book 3, Chapter 5, pp. 215–216.

something to burn, what conditions must be fulfilled? It must be something that *will* burn—in other words, it must be a combustible object. Second, it must be heated to a certain temperature (the temperature differing with different materials). Third, oxygen must be present. The word "must" in these sentences refers to necessary condition. Each condition is necessary, for in the absence of it no combustion would occur. Moreover, these three conditions together are sufficient; when they are fulfilled, combustion always occurs. Thus we have three necessary conditions which together constitute the sufficient condition for the occurrence of combustion.

Let us number these conditions 1, 2, and 3. Now *suppose* that combustion occurred also whenever an entirely different set of conditions—call them 4, 5, and 6—were fulfilled, whether 1, 2, and 3 were fulfilled or not. Thus we could say that 1, 2, and 3 together constitute C_1, a sufficient condition for the occurrence of E; and that 4, 5, and 6 together constitute C_2, another sufficient condition for the occurrence of E. E occurs whenever 1, 2, and 3 are all fulfilled, but also whenever 4, 5, and 6 are all fulfilled. In that case, E would be said to have a *plurality* of causes (in this example, two).

In the case of combustion, there does not seem to be a plurality of causes. The question is, Is there ever? Does it ever happen that more than one set of conditions can invariably lead to a given effect? Probably nothing like the above hypothetical example occurs, for in it there are *no* necessary conditions for E whatever. If there are actual cases of plurality of causes, they are more probably like this: 1, 2, and 3 are invariably followed by E; and 1, 2, and 4 are also invariably followed by E. In this scheme, 1 and 2 are necessary conditions for E, since E never occurs without them; but 3 and 4 are not, for E sometimes occurs in the absence of 3, and sometimes in the absence of 4.

In daily life we tend to assume that plurality of causes exists: we can remove a stain from a garment by using gasoline or carbon tetrachloride or perhaps any of a number of other chemical reagents; we can produce certain organic compounds either by inducing chemical reactions in living organisms or by synthesizing them out of their elements or simpler compounds. Often many different causes appear to produce the same effect. On the other hand, it often happens that an *apparent* plurality can be reduced to unity: (1) Irrelevant factors are sometimes included among the causal conditions on the list. Thus we may say that the second billiard ball can be made to move in a certain direction, not merely by being struck by another billiard ball, but by being struck with your elbow or by jiggling the table. Quite clearly this is not a genuine case of plurality: what is necessary and sufficient for the movement of the ball in this direction is that a certain force be applied upon it in that direction; it does not matter who or what wields the force, and consequently no mention of it should be made in the list of causal conditions. Thus, in the numbered conditions we considered in the last paragraph, to include 3 and 4 among the conditions is to include too much: what really does the causing is a component, X, which both 3 and 4 have in common. If this is so, plurality has been eliminated, because the total set of conditions is in both cases 1, 2, and X. (2) Sometimes the name we give to an effect is an extremely vague and general one applying to many unlike things: thus, death can have many causes—cancer, pneumonia, poisoning, shooting, and so forth—but death by one means is a different sort of effect from death by another, and we should give each class of events a more precise classification: the word "death" is merely a blanket term covering them all.

Whether all cases of alleged plurality can be eliminated by these means is a matter we shall not attempt to settle here. Whether plurality of causes exists is after all a matter for the sciences to determine. What is important here is that we keep clear as to what the term means. Remember that if there is plurality of causes, there are components of sufficient conditions that are not also necessary conditions, but if there is no plurality every component of a sufficient condition is also a necessary condition.

From here on we shall formulate the issues in such a way as to leave open the question of plurality. When we say that C is sufficient for E, we shall not, then, be committing ourselves as to whether it is the *only* set of conditions, C, which is invariably followed by the E in question.

Apparent constant conjunctions. Does it not happen, however, that there are C's which are invariably followed by E's but yet are not sufficient conditions for their occurrence? Day follows night in unvarying succession, but no one would say that day causes night. The red and green traffic lights go on in succession, but one does not cause the other.

The succession of day and night depends, of course, upon the continued rotation of the earth on its axis and the continued shining of the sun. These conditions are necessary and (if we are careful to add a few others, such as the absence of material between the sun and the earth that would obstruct the sun's light) sufficient. These would be said to be the *causes* of the succession of day and night. The trouble arises here when we ask, "Isn't this a case of constant conjunction but not causality? Accordingly, isn't it incorrect to define 'cause' in terms of constant conjunction?"

But *is* there really constant conjunction between day and night? There seems to be; but so may there seem to be between heating a combustible material and burning. A person could repeat the experiment thousands of times and conclude that heating the material to a certain temperature was sufficient for the occurrence of combustion. And yet he would be mistaken; for these conditions are not sufficient at all. What is needed to make them together sufficient is the presence of oxygen. Just because oxygen was present every time the experiment was conducted, the combustion occurred, and the person may never have thought of including it among the conditions in his experiment; yet it would be easy to show that the presence of oxygen does belong among the conditions, as one could do if he tried to induce combustion in a chamber from which the oxygen had been removed. The real constant conjunction, then, is between all three of the conditions (temperature, combustible material, oxygen) and combustion, even though the person may fancy that the three are only two. Without the oxygen the uniformity would not be exceptionless, and if it were not exceptionless, the conjunction would not be really constant.

Let us return to the case of day and night and the case of the traffic lights. Are we to say that there is a constant conjunction between day and night, or between the red and green traffic lights flashing, even though there is no causal relation? No: there is only an apparent, not a real, constant conjunction in these cases. Remember, the constant conjunction must be genuine, and to be genuine it must be *exceptionless*. In other words, it must occur *no matter what else happens*. In the case of the traffic lights, we can remove the bulb from the green light, and the red one will continue to flash intermittently as before, thus showing that *it* was not the cause of the flashing of the green one. What then is the cause? The automatic mechanical device that controls them both. Put it out of commission, and the red-green succession stops entirely: in other words, the real constant conjunction is between the working of the machine and the flashing of the lights.

The same analysis applies to the case of day and night. The rotation of the earth, plus the continued presence of the sun, causes the succession of day and night. In this case we cannot perform the experiment that would decide the issue, extinguishing the sun and stopping the earth's rotation. But there is nevertheless considerable empirical evidence for it. In any case, our belief that these things cause the succession of day and night is nothing more nor less than the belief that these things are constantly conjoined with that succession: or, in the more precise terminology we have now developed, that these conditions are together sufficient for the occurrence of that succession.

II. THE CAUSAL PRINCIPLE

Does everything that happens have a cause?

Let us continue to take "cause" to mean sufficient condition. Our question then becomes, Is there, for every event in the universe, a set of conditions such that if the conditions, C, are all fulfilled, the event, E, invariably occurs? The sets of conditions may be ever so complex and ever so difficult to discover, and perhaps we shall never discover them all, but the question remains all the same: *is there, for every event, such a set of conditions?* To answer yes to this question is to assert the Principle of Universal Causation, or, more simply, the Causal Principle.

When we try to answer this question, there is a difficulty right at the start. "Every time all the conditions in C are fulfilled, E occurs." But E is a particular, individual event, and *particular events never recur*. Events *like* them may occur, but the particular event E, once it has occurred, is gone forever. How, then, are we going to interpret the specification that E recurs?

If E does not occur a second time, an event *like* E may do so. The same, of course, applies to the C's. The principle is usually formulated approximately as follows (formulations vary somewhat): "For every class of events E in the universe, there is a class of conditions C, such that whenever an instance of each member of class C occurs, an instance of E occurs." For example: whenever an instance of the first class of conditions (combustible material) occurs, plus an instance of the second class (temperature), plus an instance of the third class (oxygen), all of which together constitute C, then an instance of class E (combustion) occurs.

Let us then restate our question: Is it true of *every event that occurs in the universe* (past, present, and future) that it is a member of a *class* of events which is related to a class (or classes) of conditions in such a way that every time a member of this class (or these classes) of conditions is fulfilled, a member of the class of events occurs? (The question is now far more complex, but complexity is often the price we have to pay for accuracy.) If the answer is yes, the Causal Principle is true; if the answer is no, it is false.

1. The empirical interpretation. We have never observed every event in the universe and we never shall. We can observe only an infinitesimally small fraction of the events now taking place in the universe, and even if we could observe them all, there is an infinite reach of past events forever beyond recall, and of future events that have not yet taken place. It would seem, in fact, that we can be far less sure of the principle than we can of any ordinary empirical law, such as those of physics and chemistry, for it is more inclusive than any of them. Both the person who asserts the principle and the person who denies it are going far beyond what is empirically observable.

It would seem, indeed, that about all we can say is that as we examine nature we find some uniformities in it, some classes of events invariably related to certain classes of conditions, and that the more carefully we look, the more of these uniformities we find. There are many investigations, of course, from which no discovery of uniformities results at all, and in which even the most exhaustive attempts to find them have failed. Sometimes we make tentative formulations of such conditions—such as the conditions under which cancer invariably develops in an organism—and sometimes our hopes of finding the causal conditions are confirmed by experience, and sometimes falsified by it. When the latter occurs, we simply try again, and see whether, by introducing other factors into the situation or qualifying our statements about the old ones so as to make them more precise, we can arrive at statements which *will* assert an invariant relationship that really holds between the events and their conditions. Sometimes we succeed in this and sometimes we do not.

At any rate, the search for genuinely invariant relationships between events and conditions is a most difficult one. Consider a class of events which is perfectly familiar: trees blowing down. Is it true that whenever a member of a class of conditions C (wind blowing against tree) is fulfilled, a member of class of events E (tree falling down) invariably occurs? No; we must add endless qualifications: the wind must blow hard enough (and how hard is that?); the tree must be fragile (at least more than *so* fragile—and how is fragility to be defined?); and so on. Whether or not the event occurs depends on a multitude of factors such as the velocity and direction of the wind, the shape of the tree, its position among other trees and buildings, its relation to the surrounding terrain, and many others. It would be difficult indeed to lay down any set of conditions, no matter how numerous, upon the fulfillment of which a member of the class-of-events tree-falling-down *always* occurs.

If it is difficult to state the conditions in the case of a tree, how much more difficult it is in more complex cases! What are the conditions under which the hearing of the *Eroica* Symphony of Beethoven is always followed by a certain kind of feeling-state, for example? Even if we have succeeded in pinning down in words what kind of feeling-state we mean, our troubles have only begun; for what possible account can we give of the conditions under which such a feeling always occurs? We may ordinarily like the symphony but may not be in the mood for it now, perhaps through concentration on other things, or through having already heard it several times the same day; and those who have never heard it before respond quite differently from those who have. What we feel when we hear it depends on such a bewildering array of factors that it would seem that we never shall be able to relate this class of events to any finite set of conditions. (We may some day be able to relate this kind of feeling to a definite kind of neurological state in the brain, but the same question could then be asked about the relation of this kind of neurological state to the conditions under which *it* always occurs.)

Would it not seem, then, that the Causal Principle is more likely to be false than true? If we despair of ever finding such a set of conditions for every class of events, may we not suspect that *there isn't any?*

At this suggestion, however, many persons will rebel at once: "The fact that these conditions are very hard to find doesn't mean that there *aren't* any. Some of them we have tried for generations to find, and finally succeeded; some we shall find in due time; some we shall never find. But even if we never find such conditions for every class of events, they do exist. Nature is uniform through and through, even though her uniformity is a bewilderingly complex one. Every event in the universe is related to a set of conditions in the way the principle specifies. The fact that we may never find it testifies only to our ignorance."

What are we to say of such an assertion? We may ourselves agree with it; and yet we shall be hard put to it to defend it on empirical grounds. After all, how in the world do we know that it is true? What justifies our certainty, or at least the certainty of many persons, that it always holds?

There is another curious circumstance about the whole matter. With any empirical generalization, there is a possibility of refuting it by empirical facts. Thousands of generalizations have been devised and then abandoned because they failed to pass this test. The discovery of one white crow would wreck the generalization that all crows are black. But what would, or possibly could, wreck the generalization that every event is related to a set of conditions in the way stated by the Causal Principle? The more causes we find, the more we say we have confirmed the Causal Principle; but if in some cases we do not find any, do we say, "For these events there are no causes?" We never do; instead we say, "We haven't *found* any," or, "There is a cause, and some day we may find it; but even if we don't, we have not shown that no cause exists, but only that our powers of detection are limited." In other words, the Causal Principle *can never be disproved.* The discovery of more causes is taken as confirming it, but failure to find causes disturbs it not a whit. *What kind of a principle is it that can be confirmed by empirical observations but not disconfirmed by them?*

2. The *a priori* interpretation. As many persons hold the Causal Principle, then, it is not empirical at all but necessary and knowable *a priori.* When one states the principle, it sounds like any ordinary law of nature; but as one begins to consider it, he begins to sense that it operates quite differently from empirical laws. It is not open to disproof as empirical laws are.

Are there any conditions at all under which we would say that the Causal Principle had been disproved? Many of us would go quite far, perhaps further than we are now aware, before we would say such a thing. This can be shown in the following way:

Thus far we have discussed only the form of the Causal Principle which is actually employed in the sciences: we have talked about classes of conditions and classes of events; and presumably the individual conditions and events need be only similar enough to each other to be placed in the same classes. But now let us be far more exacting, and speak for a moment in terms of identical conditions and identical events.[13] Let us suppose that two events occur which are *not* identical to each other. Shall we not say that the conditions leading up to them were not identical either, even though they may appear to be so? And if two sets of conditions are identical, shall we not say that the events which they cause will also be identical? Yet the empirical grounds for saying these things are slenderer than in the case of the earlier version of the Causal Principle, which spoke only in terms of classes of events and conditions without demanding that any two events or conditions be identical. Perhaps no two events or sets of conditions that have ever occurred have been absolutely identical. At any rate, science does not speak in terms of them, because either they do not occur or we do not know that they do. There is no pair of events or conditions between which further investigation *may* not reveal a difference. Yet even here *we are just as confident as before* that the Causal Principle holds. "It *must* hold," we say (what kind of a "must" is this?). "If what happened is different in two cases, then one or more of the

13 The word "identical" has two meanings: "one and the same" and "exactly similar." We say that the morning star and the evening star are identical—the same identical star, actually the planet Venus. We also say that two marbles are identical, namely that they are precisely similar to each other—same shape, same size, same color, and so on—although probably they are not actually *precisely* similar. In this discussion we shall use the word "identical" in the second of these two senses.

Even here there is one qualification. It is logically impossible for two things to be precisely similar in the sense of having *all* their characteristics in common. Two marbles could not be at the same place at the same time; they would then be one marble, not two. We shall say, then, that two things are identical if they are precisely similar *except* in respect of spatial and/or temporal position.

conditions leading up to it must have been different too. How *could* the events have turned out differently if the conditions had been exactly the same?"

Suppose we performed an experiment twice and found that the results were markedly different even though the conditions were, to the best of our knowledge, exactly the same. What would we say? Would we abandon the Causal Principle, even in its precise form (identical conditions, identical events), saying that here was an exception and hence the generalization did not hold? In all probability we would not. We would always find some way to get around it. Specifically, what would we say?

We could say that we had not observed all the relevant conditions. *"If* we could observe (or have observed) them all, then we could have detected a difference in the C's; if all the known causal factors were the same in the two cases, the difference must be due to other factors which we had not previously considered which *were* different in the two cases."

This sort of thing, of course, often happens. If you thought that two clocks, in the same room, in the same atmospheric conditions, of the same make and construction, were identical in every respect, and it developed that the one kept perfect time and the other started to run fast, you inferred that there was some difference in the causal conditions, and then you found it, perhaps in some detail of their construction which you had previously overlooked. After some experience with this we say, even without further evidence, that if there was a difference in the E's there must have been a difference in the C's. *We take the very fact of there being a difference in the E's as evidence that there was a difference in the C's.*

Nor will we admit any exceptions to this principle. If two E's turned out to be quite different and we could find no difference in the C's, and we looked again and again and then some more and still found no difference in the C's, would we abandon the Causal Principle and conclude that, after all, even when the conditions are identical, the events may sometimes be different? Probably not. We would still keep on saying, "There was a difference between the two E's. Now, *something or other must have caused that difference,"* even though a million years of investigating had not revealed any such difference.

Similarly, although we never find identical C's, do we not believe that *if* identity in the C's were attainable, there would be identity in the E's too? A boy is bouncing a ball against a wall, catching it and bouncing it back again. The ball never lands at the same spot on the wall twice; nor does it ever bounce back to him in quite the same way on any two occasions; every time the direction, speed, and distance are slightly different. But do we not believe that *if* on any two occasions the conditions could be made exactly the same (identical)—speed, direction, point from which it is thrown, etc.—then it would bounce against exactly the same spot and rebound back to him in exactly the same way? If you could only throw the dice tonight in exactly the same way you did last night, with each die in the same position, then surely the same sevens you threw last night would turn up again. If something else turns up this time, is it not because the conditions are different? The conditions are so intricate that we cannot be sure that they are even approximately the same on any two successive throws; but *if* they were exactly the same, would not the same thing have happened?

How far would we go in defending this contention?

Let us return to the case in which the E's are different and the C's appear to be identical. Suppose now that we have sub-microscopic eyes which can peer into every atom of matter involved in C; there is not a single aspect of C which is not visible to us. This being done, we find that the C's are identical; yet the E's are different. Would we not have to abandon the Causal Principle?

No; we could say, "All *these* conditions are identical in the two cases, but the fact that the E's are different only shows that we haven't included enough in the conditions. Some hitherto unconsidered factor was different in the two cases, and this difference accounts for the difference in the E's. So we must look around, outside the circle of factors we examined so exhaustively before."

Suppose now that we do this; we look outside the factors we originally considered, and still find no difference. So we look outside this in turn, to still other factors, hoping to find a difference there. Still we find none. We continue this process indefinitely.

Where must we stop in investigating this ever-enlarging circle of conditions? Only with the whole universe. And you could never find the universe as a whole to be in an identical state on any two occasions; *you* at least would be different on the second occasion, since you would remember that the universe had been like this on the previous occasion.

But even waiving this, even assuming that the total state of the universe (you included) to be identical on the two occasions, and two non-identical events nevertheless followed, would we take this to be an exception to the Causal Principle? Probably not even then. One thing would be different, namely that the events took place at *two different times*. *This difference could never be overcome.* We could always hold that the mere fact that time had elapsed, and nothing else, was responsible for the difference. (If the two events are imagined as occurring at the same time but at two different places, the same objection can be made about space: the fact of being in two different places, even if all the other conditions were the same, was what made the difference.)

This is not a sort of thing which has ever been held, because in formulating scientific laws it has never been found necessary to introduce such a factor. Always when events were different, some differences could be found (or were assumed to exist) in the conditions themselves, *other* than the mere fact of the passing of time. Nevertheless, it is logically possible that the time-factor would have to be considered in formulating laws: it is conceivable, for example, that water boiled at 212° in 1952, at 213° in 1953, 214° in 1954, and so on, not because of any difference in the conditions other than the lapse of time. This would be a highly peculiar state of affairs, and would excite much surprise simply because as far as we now know nature does not work this way; scientists would cast about desperately in search of conditions to account for the difference in the boiling-point *other* than the time-factor. But if they were forced to the wall, if they had to abandon the one principle or the other, the Causal Principle or the time-makes-no-difference principle, they would very probably abandon the time-makes-no-difference principle. They would rather say that *the mere fact that time had elapsed* caused the difference between E_1 and E_2 than say that E_1 and E_2 were different although there was *no* cause for the difference.

So far, then, we would probably go in defending the Causal Principle. We would hold to it *a priori*. We do not put it to an empirical test: the minute we find that the E's were different, we say that the C's were, whether we observe it or not. Perhaps they were different in some way we do not know about; perhaps years of research will not unearth the difference; perhaps we never shall discover it; but still, we feel, if we could examine the C's long enough and thoroughly enough, we would find *some* difference between them, and thus account for the observed difference between the E's.

How long is long enough? Until we had found such a difference. That is, "If you look till you've found a difference, you'll find a difference"—a flat tautology. And yet, until we had found such a difference, we would not say that we had looked long *enough*. It is no wonder that we can find no exceptions to a principle which requires us to refute a tautology before we can attack it!

What kind of *a priori*? If we take the position that the Causal Principle is *a priori*, our next question is, What kind of *a priori* is it?

(1) If we could show that the Causal Principle is a tautology or an analytic statement, we should have no difficulty in persuading ourselves that we can know its truth *a priori*. But it seems quite clear that it is synthetic. The concept of an event in no way involves the concept of a cause. The idea of an event is simply that of something happening: someone running, a shot being fired, and the like. They do not involve the idea of what *caused* them or brought them about. In a highly chaotic universe in which no uniformities had ever been discovered, there would still be events occurring, but the concept of causality might not even have arisen. If the principle were "Every *effect* has a cause," it would indeed be tautological, for "effect" and "cause" are correlative terms: an event would not be called an effect unless it had a cause. But the Causal Principle states that every event, in addition to being merely an event, is also an *effect* of something, in other words, it was caused by something. And this assertion is clearly synthetic.

(2) If it is synthetic and also *a priori*, perhaps here at long last we have a case of synthetic *a priori* knowledge. According to this view, our knowledge of particular causes and effects (for example, that drafts cause colds) is not *a priori* knowledge; it is empirical. But the general statement that every event that occurs, whatever it is, has some cause or other (whether we ever discover it or not), is what is held to be both synthetic and known *a priori*.

We have already considered at some length (Chapter 2) the matter of synthetic *a priori* knowledge. Any considerations which may have operated for or against them would apply here also, and we need not raise the question again. But, lest a person call the Causal Principle synthetic and *a priori* simply because he feels that it is not empirical and yet is not tautological either, he may be invited to consider other possibilities:

(3) It may not be a case of knowledge at all, but merely an *assumption*. We have already considered *a priori* assumptions (see pages 144–145), and perhaps the Causal Principle is one of them. Rather than know it to hold true for all cases, past, present, and future, we simply *assume* that it does; we refuse to grant even the possibility of any contrary evidence. Without further investigation we take the very fact of the E's being different as proof positive that the C's are different too. This sounds very much indeed like an *a priori* assumption.

Yet this interpretation too should not be accepted without further reflection; for surely the situation is not one in which we stubbornly refuse to accept any exceptions to the principle in the way in which people stubbornly refuse to accept any statement which conflicts with their pet prejudices. After all, we might say, are there not good empirical grounds for accepting this principle rather than some other? Have we not some evidence for it? Did not empirical observation lead us to state it in the first place? And has not the principle proved its worth in so many cases that we have some justification in trusting it beyond the extent to which it has actually been confirmed?

Difficulties in all the preceding interpretations. Thus we seem once again to be led back toward the empirical view of the Causal Principle. Yet before we do so, let us once again remind ourselves that it is different from the empirical generalizations of which science is chiefly composed. In any empirical generalization—all A is B—there is always the possibility of disproof by counter-instances; even if no counter-instances actually occur, the fact is that *if* an A turned up that was not a B, the generalization would be upset. And no matter how many favorable instances one has observed, there is always this possibility. But the Causal Principle is not like this: there seems to be no possibility here of disconfirming instances; it is forever protected against them.

To be quite clear about this, let us contrast for a moment how the Causal Principle operates with how the generalizations of science operate. Suppose a student in freshman chemistry reports (and he is not deliberately lying) that when he tested for the melting-point of lead it turned out to be different from what the chemistry book said. His teacher without further ado would say that he was wrong; the teacher would not grant for a moment any alleged exception to this generalization. Is this not an *a priori* assumption on the teacher's part? No, for the teacher is resting his claim on empirical evidence: all things considered, there is more evidence that the student made a mistake in his experiment than that the melting-point of lead is not what the chemistry book says it is. Students have been proved wrong before, and the melting-point of lead is something that has been tested empirically thousands of times. We tend to dismiss all alleged exceptions as errors simply because we have already amassed so much empirical evidence supporting the law. Without doubt the law is empirical: if not only the freshman but trained chemists kept reporting that the melting-point of lead was different from the figure given in the textbooks, a thorough investigation would be conducted and, if further tests bore out the student's claim, the generalization about the melting point of lead would be revised.

Similarly, a law such as the Law of Conservation of Energy is empirical. It is a more fundamental law and much wider in the scope of its confirmation. If a particular experiment yielded a result that was incompatible with the law, we would probably attribute the difference to an experimental error or postulate a new and different kind of energy of such a quantity as to close the gap between the experimental results and the figure required by the law. Still, even here, the generalization is clearly empirical. If our experiments repeatedly came out wrong, and if we had to keep on postulating kinds and quantities of energy *ad hoc*, we would reluctantly abandon our hard-won generalization. It is empirical observations which led us to believe in the generalization in the first place, and it would be the occurrence of other empirical observations which would lead us to abandon it. The same remarks hold also of the principles of Euclidean geometry when interpreted as descriptions of physical space (see pages 120–121). Our entire basis for holding to these generalizations is empirical observation, and they should dissolve if once that basis were removed.

Now what of the Causal Principle? Is it empirical in the same way? Probably it is empirical observation that led us to formulate the principle in the first place; had we never observed any uniformities in nature, the principle would never have occurred to us. But the peculiarity is that *no empirical evidence would lead us to abandon it:* we would keep on holding to it no matter what we found in nature. We know what observations of the universe would lead us to abandon generalizations about the color of crows, the melting-point of lead, action at a distance, and even the Conservation of Energy. But what observations of the universe would ever make us abandon the Causal Principle? Apparently, none at all. If the universe were far different from what it now is, if few or no uniformities were discoverable in it, would we have to reject the principle as false? We would not. Instead of saying, "The generalization has now been refuted," we would probably say, "Events still have causes, they are just so much harder to discover these days." We would not say that there were non-identical events occurring with identical conditions, but rather, "The conditions differ in mysterious ways which we just can't seem to locate." In other words, we would hold to the Causal Principle no matter what happened, no matter how chaotic the universe became, *no matter how hopelessly our attempts at detecting causes failed.*

This, then, is the strange situation in which we find ourselves. This case is not like that of empirical generalizations, yet we cannot dismiss it as *a priori* either. We have a statement which empirical evidence can confirm but which no empirical evidence can disprove. What kind of hybrid is this anyway? The Causal Principle does not seem to fit into any pigeonhole we have prepared for it.

3. The Causal Principle as a leading principle of scientific investigation. There is a view of it, which at first blush may seem strange, but which, nevertheless, has won a considerable acceptance. The Causal Principle is neither *a posteriori* (an empirical statement) nor *a priori*, because *it is not a statement at all,* and, not being a statement, it is *neither true nor false.*

Surely this requires an explanation. How can it be neither true nor false? Does it not state something, whether we know it empirically or *a priori*, or indeed whether we know it at all? A full discussion of the status and function of the Causal Principle, according to the present interpretation, would take us far beyond an introductory account. Briefly, it comes to this: The Causal Principle is neither true nor false, for it is not a statement (proposition) about the world at all. Rather, it expresses a resolve, *"Let us find uniformities in the world."* It is sometimes called a *leading principle*, because it leads or guides us in our empirical investigations. Scientists, bent on the discovery of causes, utter the principle, *not* as a true description of the universe, but as a way of eking out of nature as many uniformities as possible. The Causal Principle is not a statement of fact about the world, it is something we *bring to* the world; it is not something we read on the fact of nature, it is something we *read into* nature; it is not something we find in the world, it is more like a demand, or a hope, which we put to the world. There may even be in it something of "whistling to keep your courage up," as if to say, "Never fear, these uniformities will yet be found." The important point, in any case, is that it is not a description of any state of affairs in the universe.

But if it is not a description of anything in the universe, it cannot be a *true* description of anything in the universe. The Causal Principle, on the present interpretation, is not a *truth* about the universe at all, not even an *assumed* truth. As we have seen, we would hold to it regardless of what kind of a universe we lived in; and something that we would defend *no matter what* the universe was like is not something that in the next breath we can call a *truth about this universe.*

Even here there is one possible qualification. Conceivably, we *might* abandon the Causal Principle *if* uniformities now observed did not continue and the universe became hopelessly chaotic. But even if we did abandon it, this would have nothing to do with the principle's being *true* or *false;* we would abandon it because the uniformities had been dismissed as so complicated that it would no longer be worth our while to try to track them down. We would abandon it as we might abandon a mine, not because of a conviction that it contained no gold, nor yet that it did, but because of a conviction that, whether it did or not, the gold was so scattered or so hard to reach as to make it not worth the mining. Our abandonment would express the resolve, "Let's give it up."

Whichever interpretation of the Causal Principle we may adopt, let us be consistent in our application of it. Let us not first refuse to abandon the Causal Principle under any circumstances whatever, and then turn around and look upon it as a true description of the universe. If it is taken strictly as empirical, then the failure to find uniformities will have to count as heavily against it as success in finding them will count in favor of it, and we shall have no comeback to the person who doubts its truth. But if we then adopt our last interpretation, and say that it is not a true statement about the universe at all (nor for that matter a false one), we cannot then reverse our position and say that it always holds, and make this the basis for assertions of determinism or denials of free-will—to which, at last, we now turn.

III. DETERMINISM AND FREEDOM

Discussions of causality usually go hand in hand with discussions of determinism and freedom. The connection among these three concepts is not always made clear, but as a rule it is conceived in this way: If everything that happens has a cause, then we live in a deterministic universe, or in other words, *determinism* is true; and if determinism is true, then there is no room for freedom of the human will. Having arrived at this point, people commonly take one of two views: either "There is freedom, and therefore determinism is false," or "Determinism is true, and therefore there is no freedom."

Consider the following argument:

With every day that passes, science is able to tell us more about the causes of things—the *determining* factors which *make* things happen the way they do. This includes human actions as well as events in the physical world: we know more than ever before about what makes people behave as they do.

Consequently, more and more people's actions are becoming predictable. Once eclipses were not predictable; now we can predict their occurrence to within a tenth of a second ten thousand years in advance. Once the path of a projectile could not be predicted; now it can be mapped out with such precision that we know how to make it hit a certain distant target at just the right moment. Even when we don't know exactly what a thing will do, for instance just how a stone will roll downhill, this isn't because its path is not completely determined by the forces acting upon it, but because we don't know what all those forces are: just where the stone will hit this crevice, whether the slippery side of the stone in rolling down the hill will be against the smooth part of the ground on this part of its journey downward, and so on. We know the laws, but not all the initial conditions. But nobody imagines—at least, no one who has the slightest acquaintance with science—that its path *couldn't* be calculated if we knew, or bothered to acquaint ourselves with, all the million and one factors that would have to be considered in computing its course down the slope.

Now, nobody ever pretended that stones have freedom, or free-will. But it *has* been contended that human beings have, and science is gradually showing up this claim for what it is—a mere superstition. We know far more today than ever before about people's hereditary constitution and environmental conditions, the laws of how people behave, all the factors that make people act as they do. The person is becoming more and more like the stone. He may fancy that he is free, but this is a delusion: he is no more free than the stone is. The forces acting on him are more *complex*, and therefore far more difficult to discover, than those acting on the stone, but they are there just the same. Whether he knows what they are or not, they are there, and they inevitably make him what he is and make him do what he does. Anyone who had knowledge of the laws and of his total state at any given moment would be able to predict everything that he would do in response to every future situation; he would, in short, be able to show how every moment of the person's life is determined.

The above argument is an imaginary one, but it closely resembles many arguments that take place around us every day. If anything, it is probably more clearly outlined than most of them are. Yet it is full of confusions. (Before reading further, you will do well to spot as many errors in it as you can.) For example, three of the concepts used in it—causality, compulsion, and predictability—are treated as if they were the same. Let us, then, endeavor to see what can be said about human freedom in the light of the preceding sections. This task will consist chiefly of trying to dispel confusions which are almost always made in discussions of this issue. We shall begin, as it were, at the bottom of the ladder of clarity, beginning with a rather uncritical use of the animistically tinged language of ordinary life, but making the distinctions that bear upon the topic at hand, until we have cleared up the whole issue as much as we can.

A. Determinism and Fatalism

Determinism. The word "determinism" usually stands for the view that everything that happens is determined. The word "determined," however, is not very clear. In the context of everyday usage "to be determined" usually means "to be resolved," as in "I was determined to arrive there on time no matter what the cost." But in the context of the problem of freedom, "to be determined" usually means "to be caused." Determinism, then, is the view that everything that happens has a cause. The determinist argues: "Everything that happens has a cause; we may not know what it is, but there *is* one all the same. Whenever you do something, there is some cause for your doing that rather than something else. Every event that occurs, whether in your history or that of a stone, is a link in an unbreakable chain of cause and effect. There are no 'loose ends,' no 'gaps' or breaks, in the constitution of the universe; there are no broken links in the iron chain." When asked how he knows that everything has a cause, the determinist replies, "I don't; but more causes are being discovered all the time. I don't claim that we'll ever discover all the causes that there are, but at any rate when I have found the causes of events A, B, and C, I know that *they* at any rate have causes; whereas my opponent can never prove even of one event in the whole universe that it is causeless. At best he can only say that we haven't yet *found* a cause for it."

The determinist is not always as crude as this, nor does he always fall victim to the animistic language used here. At his clearest, the determinist is simply the person who holds to the Causal Principle in one or another of the forms discussed in the preceding section.

Indeterminism. The indeterminist denies that everything has a cause. Indeterminism, like determinism, can be either a confused, animistically tinged view like determinism at its cloudiest, or it can be a denial of the Causal Principle in one of the forms stated in the preceding section. No matter which version he takes, however, he is at a disadvantage from the start: he cannot point to any causeless events, but only to events for which no cause has been found. With regard to these, he can say, "Not all of them are determined. For many events we have found determining causes, but not for all; may it not be that the reason for this is that they (some of them, at any rate) *have* no causes? If you can't find gold, this may be because it has escaped your scrutiny, but it may also be because there is none there to be found."

As for the events in inorganic nature, the indeterminist is likely to leave these entirely to the determinist, without a battle.[14]

---

[14] Unless, that is, he is convinced, by conclusions that are sometimes drawn from scientific developments such as Heisenberg's "Principle of Indeterminancy," that indeterminism holds even here. The discussion of this principle, to be accurate at all, involves complexities far beyond the level of this book. It must suffice here to say that this controversy has no bearing one way or another on the problem of free-will. See the bibliography at the end of the chapter.

"Maybe the path of projectiles and planets is determined," he says, "but with events on a higher level it is otherwise. This is particularly true of human behavior. There is surely no conclusive evidence for determinism in the realm of human actions. We have never found any exceptionless generalizations about human actions, and those we have formulated are so vague and general that almost any kind of behavior could occur without falsifying them. Human behavior is predictable to only a very small degree. The 99.99 per cent we can't predict *may*, as the determinist says, be due to the complexity of the causes, but it may also be due to a genuine indeterminism in human beings themselves. If this is true, then even a *complete* knowledge of the causal factors influencing a person would not enable us to predict whether, in a situation of choice, he would choose A or B. That decision remains free."

One might object that if there is no conclusive evidence for determinism in the realm of human actions, neither is there evidence against it. Why then does the indeterminist hold to his position? The chief motive underlying this conviction, in almost every case, is the belief that human beings have freedom of choice—"free-will" is the usual term for it—and that if determinism were true they would not have this freedom. Not all human actions are free, of course, but (according to the indeterminist) some are. You are faced with a difficult moral choice, between two alternatives, A and B. Morality makes no sense unless you are really *free* to choose between them. Freedom of choice is the most precious of human possessions. Determinism, if it were true, would make freedom impossible. Determinism, then, is false, for free-will does exist.

(Sometimes the determinist points to the occurrence of *chance* events as evidence for his view. But ordinarily when we speak of events occurring "by chance" we do not mean that they are uncaused; or, if we ever do, there could be no evidence in favor of our view, for, as we saw in the preceding section, there could be no evidence for uncaused events. We do speak of events as occurring by chance, and by speaking in this way, we may mean any of several different things, none of which implies the absence of cause. [1] We may mean that an occurrence was unplanned or unintentional, as when we say, "We met by chance downtown this morning." We do not deny that there were causes for our respective trips downtown, but only that we planned the meeting. [2] We may mean to refer simply to our ignorance of the causal factors, either because they are so complex or simply because we do not consider it worth while to track them down. "I don't know what will happen," we say; "it's all a matter of chance." [3] We may mean to refer to *probability:* "There's a 50-50 chance that when you toss the coin it will turn out to be heads." Again, we are not denying that either outcome would be caused by something, principally by the way we tossed the coin.)

Fatalism. At this point, another distinction becomes important: the distinction between determinism and fatalism. Determinists do not declare that all events are beyond human control, or that things will happen in a certain way regardless of what we do. This belief is *fatalism.* Seizing upon some future event, the fatalist says, "If it's going to happen, it's going to happen"—which he does not intend as a tautology; he wants to say that all human efforts are futile, that the event will happen (or fail to happen, as the case may be) regardless of what he or other human beings may try to do about it. The determinist says nothing of this kind; he insists only that if the event does occur, there will be causes leading up to it, and that if it does not occur, its failure to occur will also be caused. He will not for a moment deny that human beings themselves are often causal influences which help to determine whether events will or will not occur.

The members of a certain congregation were opposed to having a liquor store brought into their small town, but decided that if it was fated to happen (in this case, if God so willed it), it would happen regardless of human efforts; accordingly they decided that there was nothing they could do. The thing they feared came to pass. Their efforts might have prevented it; but they made no effort, and as a result, the thing they disapproved of occurred. They were fatalists about the matter. Had they been merely determinists, they would not have been committed to such a policy; they could then have said, "Whichever way it turns out will be the result of determining causes; but *we* can be a part of those determining causes; because of the causal influences *we* exert, we may be able to bring about the event or prevent it, as we wish." Determinism merely says that all events have determining causes; fatalism says that all events have causes *outside of ourselves,* in other words, that everything that happens does so regardless of what we do.

Probably no one is a fatalist with regard to every event that occurs; at least, such a view could not be put into practice. Nobody says, "If I'm fated to have my lunch today, it will be given to me, regardless of what I do or don't do," and then take no steps to prepare lunch or go to a restaurant. People know well enough that there are *some* things they can do which will make a difference to what happens later. Thus the doctrine that what we do *never* makes a difference is as manifestly false as any doctrine can be. Determinism is, at least, not easily refutable; fatalism is refuted by hundreds of events we all observe and take part in every day.

Freedom. Having now eliminated the confusion between his own view and fatalism, the determinist asserts that he is in as good a position to believe in freedom as anyone else. "Doesn't my view," he asks, "leave human beings as much freedom as they would ever want? You are free to do something when you can do it *if* you want to: more precisely, when your willing to do it is actually followed by the thing's occurring. I am free to move my arm (if I don't get a paralytic stroke), because I can do it if I will to; but I am not free to lift the house, for no amount of willing or wanting can enable me to achieve this result. We are not free to do *everything;* no human being is free in this way; but we *are* free to do a vast number of things. Our volitions, in other words, can make a considerable difference in the world; they act as causes as well as do the forces of nature. What more freedom than this can anyone ask for?

Indeed, the determinist carries the battle into the enemy's camp; he will say to the indeterminist, "Not only will my view permit freedom; yours will not! Freedom, in my opinion, is possible only to the extent that determinism is true. Suppose that some act of yours were causeless; it would not be affected by your character, your habits up to now, in short by *you.* Don't you want your acts to be determined *by you?* Can you really call them free if they are determined by *nothing*—are cut off from all roots whatever? In that case how could they even be called *your* acts? Suppose you had a friend whom you had known for years and trusted implicitly; if he were to be cut off from all causal conditions, in other words if he were seized with an attack of indeterministic free-will, there would be nothing to determine his action, and no grounds whatever for trusting him. Education, reformation, advice, reward, and punishment would be useless, for, in the absence of causality, there would be no chance that they might *cause* a change in the person's character and determine his future actions. In education and reformation, do we not assume the truth of determinism? What would be the use of these things if they could have no influence in determining subsequent behavior?"

The indeterminist, on the other hand, will reply: "Don't make my position absurd. No indeterminist believes that all events are uncaused. If there were only a small amount of indeterminism in the universe, say in a small range of human behavior, this would not interfere with the regularity and uniformity in the universe to any appreciable degree. Nor would it interfere with our powers of prediction: there are enough things that are unpredictable now, and always will be. Human behavior, in particular, is notoriously unpredictable; the causal factors here are so infinitely complex that they will surely never all be known, and the introduction of a bit of indeterminism here would not be noticeable any more than a drop of water in the sea. You need not feel that all is lost if the universe is not rigidly deterministic. There are still plenty of causal factors for the sciences to unearth."

"Nevertheless," comes the determinist's reply, *"to the extent* that we do admit indeterminism, to that extent we admit chaos. It is simply a mistake to admit it at all. You admit that your position is without evidence in its favor; your sole motive for introducing it is to give grounds for freedom. I hold that this is unnecessary, for freedom occurs without it."

"But neither do you have evidence for your view. You have found causes for some events, but not all. You simply assume that the rest have."

"No, I say it is probable on the basis of evidence. The area of events known to be caused constantly increases as scientists discover more causes. But there is no area of events *known not* to be caused; there is merely an area of events *not known* to be caused, and that area is constantly diminishing in size."

Thus, at this level, rests the controversy between determinism and indeterminism. The proponents of each view hold that they make room for free-will. However, we have scarcely yet begun to examine the confusions that beset this controversy.

B. Freedom and Compulsion

To say that an event is determined is not, as we have seen, to say that it is determined in spite of us, or that we can have no effect upon it if we try. But, someone may reply, even though our volitions can cause events, this very fact is determined also: we are determined to will the way we do, so we "can't help" it.

It is time that we took a little of the sting out of the word "determined" and its synonyms. Our previous discussion has already paved the way for this. Specifically, when we say that an event is determined, let us not confuse this with saying that it is *compelled*.

Let us remind ourselves once again (page 167) that laws of nature do not prescribe, but only describe. Accordingly, there is no excuse for saying that we are not free because our behavior is determined by the laws of nature. Once again, the laws of planetary motion do not force the planets to move. Exactly the same consideration applies to the laws of psychology. It is sheer confusion to say that a person's will *obeys* psychological laws. Laws of psychology do not compel you to behave as you do; they only describe how you (and others) do in fact behave. If you did not behave in that way, the law in question would be false; your behavior would then falsify the generalization.

Do causes determine in the sense of *necessitate?* Not in any usual sense, but the word is ambiguous: (1) In the logical sense—the sense in which "Fido is a dog" necessitates "Fido is a mammal"— the answer, as we have already seen in the case of the word "must," is clearly No. (2) It is sometimes said that an event occurs necessarily, in the sense that its occurrence is an instance of some law; in other words, the proposition stating that it occurs can be *deduced* from a law. If this is meant, it is probably true enough, but the word "necessitate" in this context is misleading, since the law from which it is deduced is simply an empirical generalization. (3) If one says in turn that the law itself is necessary, this (if it is not merely a confusing and misleading way of using words) means that it holds in all cases, or in other words that it has no exceptions. And to say this is merely a tautology, for a defining characteristic of a law (see pages 165–166) is that it be exceptionless. (4) The only other clear sense of "necessitate" seems to be merely "compel." And in this sense, again, events in nature are not necessitated. They simply occur. They occur as a result of causes, to be sure, but this is only to say that they occur in a uniform sequence and not chaotically.

Indeed, it would seem that to speak of events as being compelled has (cognitive) meaning only in the context of conscious beings who can be made (compelled) to do things against their will. It has no more application outside that context than do words such as "above" and "below" outside the context of physical bodies such as the earth (see pages 68–69). When I stab somebody as a result of a decision to murder him, I am not compelled, though doubtless my act has causes. But when a powerful arm grips mine and forces me to wield the dagger, my act is not only caused, but compelled. When I am physically able to do X, and I do X as a result of a decision to do it, I would usually be said to be free in doing it.

To say, then, that something is compelled is to say something over and above merely that it is caused. Compulsion is a certain specific kind of causality: all compelled events are caused, but not all caused events are compelled. To say "Everything is caused, therefore everything is compelled" is as much a mistake as to say "Everything is colored, therefore everything is red." True, the concept of compulsion is sometimes extended so as to include events in which the person himself does not know that he is being compelled: the kleptomaniac is, in a sense, compelled as surely as if someone were taking hold of his hand and physically forcing him to steal. Still, if the presence of certain characteristics are what entitle an act to be called "compelled," then the absence of those same characteristics entitle it to be called "uncompelled," or free. Freedom is the opposite of compulsion, not of causality.

> That all causes equally necessitate is indeed a tautology, if the word "necessitate" is taken merely as equivalent to "cause"; but if, as the objection requires, it is taken as equivalent to "constrain" or "compel," then I do not think that this proposition is true. For all that is needed for one event to be the cause of another is that . . . there is an invariable concomitance between the two classes of events; but there is no compulsion, in any but a metaphorical sense.[15]

The words "determine" and "determinism" have a decidedly animistic suggestion about them. Somehow "Is X caused?" sounds less strong than "Is X determined?" Perhaps the ring is merely fatalistic, and "Is X determined?" is taken to mean "Is X determined

---

[15] A. J. Ayer, "Freedom and Necessity," *Polemic*, September–October, 1946.

(caused) in spite of me (against my will), so that I can do nothing about it?" But even if we are aware that events are often caused *by* us, we may still feel that "determined" is stronger than "caused." It is the old carry-over from animism with us once again. We tend to think of events as *forcing* each other instead of simply following each other. Perhaps we form a mental picture of an unhappy effect trying in vain to extricate itself from the clutches of an overpowering cause. Probably we do not do this consciously, but the effects of such picturing continue to linger in the mind and give an emotive and pictorial charge to the meaning of "determine," which is not present in its cognitive meaning. Once again, however, if we wish to be clear what our cognitive meaning is, let us reflect on the situation: some events regularly follow others, and the fact that they do is what entitles us to speak of causes and effects. The rest is picture-thinking. The picture-thinking in this case can be dangerous, for without our knowing it, it may lead us to think that there is an antithesis between causality and freedom.

Ambiguity of the word "free." Freedom, we said, is the opposite of compulsion, not of causality. But of course we *can* use the word to mean whatever we like. We can use the word "free" to mean the same as the word "uncaused," if we like. But this would be extremely confusing, and it would be complicating even if we specified in advance that we were so using it. If we mean "uncaused," why not say so? It would be far less confusing. Using "free" to mean the same as "uncaused," moreover, has no basis on common usage; the last thing people have in mind in calling an act free is that it is uncaused. They probably would not deny that it has causes, but they would still assert that it is free. When they assert that it is free they *would*, however, deny that it is compelled. In ordinary usage, "free" (in the context we are now considering) means approximately the same as "uncompelled." To say that free acts are uncompelled acts, then, is to give a true reportive definition of "free," and to say that they are uncaused acts is to give a false reportive definition.

There are other senses of "free," however, even in fairly common usage. We speak of political freedom, economic freedom, freedom of religion, freedom from fear, and so on. There are also numerous persuasive definitions (see pages 71–73) of the word: the psychiatrist may say, "A man is not truly free unless he has been successfully treated for his mental quirks," and a preacher may say, "A man is not truly free unless he has faith in God," and so on.

But no matter what sense of "free" (and indeed of other words) you are using, always remember that if there are certain characteristics the presence of which (as you are using the word) make the word applicable to a thing, then the absence of those same characteristics make the same word inapplicable to the thing. This basic principle, set forth in Chapter 1 (see pages 25–27), is nowhere more important to keep in mind than in the present controversy. You cannot have your cake and eat it both: you cannot say that a person is not free when certain restricting conditions are present, and then when those restricting conditions are no longer present, say that he is still not free. The word "free" would then have no criterion of applicability, and no characteristics would be designated by it. If you refused to call anything a triangle, whether it had three sides or not, whether it was a plane figure or not, and so forth, then the word "triangle" (as you were using it) would have no application to the world, for even when the criteria of its use were fulfilled you would refuse to use it. Some persons are in precisely this position with respect to the word "free." If the word is to designate a set of characteristics, then when those characteristics are present in some situation the word is applicable to that situation. Otherwise the word "free" is being used (cognitively) meaninglessly. If you so use the word "free" that no act which anyone might ever perform is to be called "free," you are ruling out *a priori* the applicability of the word to the world. In such circumstances it is no surprise to learn that "nobody is ever free"—though it may be something of a surprise (to those who talk thus) that in such circumstances it is meaningless even to say so, for the word "free," having no criterion of applicability, is not being used as a symbol for anything.

C. Freedom and Uniformity

As we have treated the matter so far, to speak of determinism is only to speak of uniformity; in uniformity there is no compulsion, so in determinism there is no compulsion either. Since it is only compulsion that is opposed to freedom, determinism, being cleared of compulsion, is simultaneously cleared of opposition to freedom.

Strictly speaking, then, our task is completed: not all events are compelled, so freedom exists. But let us pursue our question one step further, for some may feel that even in the fact of uniformity there is something hostile to freedom. Let us then ask, "If we could not find any uniformities, could we still say that every event is determined (caused)?"

Here we touch upon ground already made familiar on pages 249 to 262. According to the empirical interpretation of the Causal Principle, the Causal Principle is simply a super-generalization about nature: that for every event there is a set of conditions . . . and so on. Whether every event is thus correlated with a set of conditions, we simply do not know. If determinism and indeterminism are, respectively, the doctrines that there is, and that there is not, such a universal correlation, there is no basis for deciding between them. Determinism has a methodological advantage in that we can know when events have causes (are related to conditions in the way specified) but not when they do not. But, taken empirically, the issue is one that will never be settled; nor, apparently, can we settle it if we take it as an *a priori* truth not in need of being established empirically.

If we take the *a priori* interpretation, we must hold to the principle even in the absence of discoverable uniformities: we would then say, if we could discover no uniformities, that causes are very hard to find, but holding the principle would express our resolve to find them. If, however, we hold to the principle no matter what the facts are, the principle is not a description of any facts. In this case, we cannot even look upon the Causal Principle as *true*, or, for that matter, false. It is not a description of the universe at all, but rather a demand-hope-request which we put to the world. Accordingly, if we cannot speak of determinism as being true or false, *we can hardly base a theory of freedom on its truth or falsity.* Here, then, we have the final blow to the interconnection between determinism and freedom.

Not only does uniformity not compel; on this interpretation at least, the absence of uniformity is quite compatible with the acceptance of the Causal Principle.

An illustrative dialogue. It is not easy for linguistic habits of many years to be changed by argument. Difficulties and questions will still crop up, even after the principles relevant to the issue have been explained. The following imaginary dialogue illustrates the most typical of these—questions and difficulties that come up regularly when one is first grappling with this issue. The dialogue could perhaps be continued indefinitely, but with a brief reference to the most typical difficulties we shall close our analysis of the present controversy.

A. I don't think people are free. Take any particular occasion in your life: I don't think you *could* have done anything other than what you did.

B. Does this mean that I couldn't have acted differently even if I had wanted to? That is what such a question usually means. "Could you have done it?" means "Were you able to do it?" and in this case, could I have acted differently? Surely I could, if I had wanted to. I couldn't have lifted a ton if I'd wanted to, but I could have lifted ten pounds if I'd wanted to. In this sense I was obviously free to lift it. My wanting to can make all the difference between my doing it and not doing it. Maybe a thousand factors predisposed me toward lifting it on both of the two occasions; but one time I *wanted* to and the other time I didn't want to—so the one time I lifted it and the other time I didn't. But I was free to do either one.

A. Very well, you *could* have lifted the ten pounds if you had wanted to. But you *couldn't* have wanted to, since you didn't do it. Your precise "mental set" at that moment—the result of hereditary and environmental influences—prevented the occurrence of anything except what you actually did do.

B. Couldn't I have wanted something different? If I had developed a taste for Y instead of X, I would surely have wanted Y. Wouldn't I?

A. No, you *couldn't* have. Your background being just what it was, you *had* to do X, or will X, or want X, as the case may be.

B. You mean my background *compelled* me? Do backgrounds compel? Is causality compulsion? Don't fall victim to the very fallacy we spent so long trying to expose.

A. All right. But I still say you couldn't have acted differently. I'll put it this way: Could you have acted differently, *even if everything else in the universe had been the same?*

B. "Couldn't." Again, do you mean I couldn't even if I had wanted to? I was compelled? But that's not so. No one did. Yet how else are we to render the force of "couldn't"?

A. All right then, you *wouldn't* have acted differently. That takes out the animistic "couldn't" and makes it purely empirical. I say then that you never *would* in fact have acted differently, if all the circumstances had been exactly the same.

B. Well, if all the circumstances were exactly the same today as when some decision was before me two years ago, I would act differently now; experience has taught me that what I did then was foolish.

A. Yes, of course; but I mean by "all the circumstances" *really all* the circumstances, not just the external ones; you yourself and your state of mind must be included among the circumstances. You of course are different now; lots of things have happened to you in the meantime. But suppose that you were exactly the same? This never happens, of course, but suppose that it did: the external circumstances are identical with those two years ago, and you have no recollection of facing those circumstances on a previous occasion, and everything that has occurred in the meantime has been blotted out, not a brain-trace left. Then you'd just be repeating yourself! You'd do the same thing you did then. What else *could*—I mean *would*—you do?

B. Well, how do you know I'd do the same thing? Suppose I *did* act differently this time; suppose I didn't do the same thing on this hypothetical identical second occasion? Then you would automatically say that something *had* been different in the circumstances and that if nothing had been different I wouldn't or couldn't have acted differently! Your resolution not to admit exceptions is what makes your rule exceptionless. No matter how I act, no matter how definitely I might seem to demonstrate an exception to your principle, you would take the very fact of my behaving differently this time as evidence that the circumstances (internal or external) in which I acted this time were different. Under such circumstances, of course, I'm licked at the start. But it's a mock battle. You won't make it an ordinary empirical battle because there are too many chances that you'd lose—or in this case, perhaps, that it would never end; and you want a quick victory, now. And so, perhaps without even knowing it, you switch the rules of battle in such a way as to guarantee yourself a victory—hoping that your opponent will be unwary enough not to notice the switch. Dropping the analogy, you keep on acting as if it is a true statement about the universe which you are defending, while actually it turns out not to be a true statement at all, for only a statement can be true, and what you are defending is only a resolve, and not a statement at all.

SELECTED READINGS FOR CHAPTER 4

John Stuart Mill. *A System of Logic.* London: Longmans, Green & Co., 1843. Book 3, Chapter 5, and Book 6, Chapter 2. (Also in Ernest Nagel [ed.]., *John Stuart Mill's Philosophy of Scientific Method.* New York: Hafner Library of Classics, 1950.)

David Hume. *Enquiry concerning Human Understanding.* Sections 7 and 8. Many editions.

A. J. Ayer. "Freedom and Necessity," *Polemic,* 1946.

R. E. Hobart. "Free-will as Involving Determinism and Inconceivable without It," *Mind,* 1934.

Moritz Schlick. "Causality in Everyday Life and in Science." University of California *Publications in Philosophy,* 15, 1932.

————. *The Problems of Ethics.* New York: Prentice-Hall, Inc., 1938. Chapter 7.

G. E. Moore. *Ethics*. Oxford University Press, Home University Library. (Originally published 1912.) Chapter 6.

California Associates. "On the Freedom of the Will," in *Knowledge and Society*. New York: Appleton-Century, 1938. (Reprinted in Feigl and Sellars, *Readings in Philosophical Analysis*. New York: Appleton-Century-Crofts, 1949.)

C. L. Stevenson. "Ethical Judgments and Avoidability," *Mind*, 47, 1938. (Reprinted in Sellars and Hospers, *Readings in Ethical Theory*. New York, Appleton-Century-Crofts, 1952.)

L. Susan Stebbing. *Philosophy and the Physicists*. London: Methuen & Co., 1937. Part 3.

A. J. Ayer. *The Foundations of Empirical Knowledge*. New York: Macmillan, 1940. Chapter 4.

Hans Reichenbach. *The Rise of Scientific Philosophy*. Berkeley: University of California Press, 1951. Chapter 10.

G. J. Warnock. "Every Event Has a Cause," in Anthony Flew (ed.), *Logic and Language, Second Series*. Oxford: Basil Blackwell, 1953.

A. C. Ewing. *The Fundamental Questions of Philosophy*. New York: Macmillan, 1951. Chapters 8 and 9.

EXERCISES

1. Are the following logical inferences or causal inferences? (When the inference is logical, you can substitute the words "logically deduce" for "infer.")

    a. From the tone of your voice I infer that you are angry.

    b. He had only $100 left at the beginning of the month, and I know he has received nothing since then, and he paid the grocer $50 yesterday, so I infer that he has no more than $50 left.

    c. From these footprints in the mud I infer that a bear has been here.

    d. From the fact that something is a circle I infer that it encloses a larger area than does any other perimeter of the same length.

2. What is wrong with saying that the causal relation is simply the relation of temporal precedence?

3. Are causes always contiguous to their effects (a) in space? (b) in time? Give examples.

4. "Events in nature are not merely conjoined, but connected." State as many things as possible that "connected" could mean here. In each case, do you consider it applicable to the causality controversy? Why?

5. "There is no necessary connection among events." "There is no such thing as a *concept* of necessary connection." Explain the difference between these two statements.

6. Explain the sense in which the word "must" is being used in each of the following sentences:

    a. You must do as you're told or you'll be punished.

    b. It simply must be nice weather tomorrow or our picnic will be ruined.

    c. If I had $10 yesterday and haven't lost or spent any nor received any since, I must still have $10.

    d. In order to catch a walrus, there must first be a walrus.

    e. If we want to understand Topic B, we must first discuss Topic A.

    f. If you want this cake to turn out well, you must have three large well-greased cake-pans. . . .

    g. Why must you say such things?

    h. He must have been pretty thoroughly intoxicated or he never would have done it.

    i. Oh, you must be a mind-reader!

    j. You must have your yard looking quite beautiful by this time.

    k. It's a law of human nature that people must be selfish.

    7. Explain the principal confusions responsible for the attribution of the word "must" (and along with it, "necessary connection") to the processes of nature.

    8. Analyze critically the following expressions; if you find them faulty, indicate how they could be amended.

    a. The first billiard ball *compelled* the second billiard ball to move.

    b. When the first ball hits the second, the second one *can't help* moving.

    c. The motion of the second ball is *inevitable* when the first one hits it.

    d. The first ball hitting the second *made* the second one move.

    e. The first ball hitting the second *produced* the motion of the second one.

    9. Evaluate the following assertions:

    a. It's not enough to say that A causes B; more than this, A produces B.

    b. There is a bond or link between cause and effect which a Humian view of causality does not take into consideration.

    c. When I press the button, the light goes on. This regularly happens. I need not be satisfied with this constant conjunction. I can go further and ask, "Why is this so?" In other words, I can ask for the connection behind the constant conjunction, and need not rest satisfied with the mere constant conjunction.

    d. Water must flow downhill—it's a law of nature.

    e. I can disprove the regularity view of causality very easily. I can truthfully say that the unexpected arrival of my sister from India (whom I hadn't seen for thirty years) at the front door caused me to run to greet her. Now there is no constant conjunction here at all. I almost never run, and I have never before done so on an occasion such as this one. Yet I can safely say that her appearance is what caused me to run as I did.

10. List, if you can, some (a) necessary conditions which are not sufficient conditions, (b) sufficient conditions which are not necessary conditions, (c) conditions which are both.

11. Assuming "cause" to mean the same as "sufficient condition," examine the following assertions:

    a. Striking the match caused it to light.

    b. Taking arsenic caused his death.

    c. Pressing the button caused the light to go on.

    d. The fire was caused by an overheated furnace.

    e. An unhappy childhood caused him to be bitter all his life.

    f. The Darwinian theory of the survival of the fittest caused the first World War.

12. Assuming "cause" to mean the same as "necessary condition," examine the assertions in the preceding question.

13. In the following examples, is the relation of A to B that of necessary condition, sufficient condition, both, or neither?

A	B
a. overeating	illness
b. deciding to raise your hand	raising your hand
c. the writing of an essay	the reading of that essay
d. running	feeling fatigued
e. plug pulled out of socket	radio not working
f. plug inserted in socket	radio working
g. a foot of snow falling on the ground	ground being white
h. rock hitting window	window breaking
i. occurrence of friction	generation of heat

14. In each of the following examples the relation of A to B is that of necessary condition. State whether it is a *causally* necessary condition (the kind we have been considering in this chapter) or a *logically* necessary condition.

A	B
a. presence of oxygen	occurrence of combustion
b. having three angles	being a triangle
c. having extension	having shape
d. existence of sodium	existence of salt
e. presence of moisture	growth of crops
f. being a mammal	being a cat
g. presence of a non-opaque object	looking through that object
h. presence of heat	occurrence of flame

15. "To say that C causes E is no different from saying that C is the *explanation* of E." Recalling Chapter 3, do you think that this statement is true? (When you state the cause of something you normally state one

or more antecedent events or conditions. Is this what you do when you give an explanation? Is it a part of what you do?)

16. According to the regularity ("constant conjunction") view of cause (e.g. Hume, Reichenbach, Schlick) "there would be no more special connection between the striking of a match and the flame which followed it than between the striking of a match and an earthquake which might also occur just afterwards. It would merely be that the striking of a match is usually followed by a flame and not usually followed by earthquakes, and that would be all. We could not then say that the striking *made* the flame follow . . . On this view to give a cause . . . does not in the least help to explain why the effect happened, it only tells us that it preceded the effect." (A. C. Ewing, *The Fundamental Questions of Philosophy*, page 160.) Evaluate this passage sentence by sentence. (For example: Does the regularity interpretation of "C caused E" render it impossible to explain *why* C caused E? See pages 229–230.)

17. Evaluate this statement: "That C is regularly followed by E is our means of knowing that C causes E. But this is not what the causal relationship consists in; it is the mark but not the essence of the causal relationship."

18. "I said that because it's true." Can the truth of a statement be the cause (or a causal factor) of your uttering it? (Remember that the truth of a statement is a non-temporal fact, while a cause is always a temporal event or condition.) What change of formulation would make the statement more accurate?

19. Are the following examples, in your opinion, genuine cases of plurality of causes, or can the plurality be reduced to unity? Defend your answer.

a. There are several causes of fires: arson, lightning, overheated furnace, spontaneous combustion of fuel in the basement, and so on.

b. There are many causes of death: heart disease, cancer, pneumonia, automobile accident, drowning, poisoning, stabbing . . .

c. There are many ways of taking a stain out of a garment; many different chemicals will produce the same effect, namely the removal of the stain.

d. There are various possible causes of erosion: wind, rapid drainage of water, failure to adopt contour plowing . . .

e. There are many causes of headaches: eyestrain, improper diet, nervous tension, and so on.

f. There are many causes of expulsion from school: low grades, failure to attend classes regularly, repeated intoxication, planting a time-bomb in the president's office, and so on.

20. "There is constant conjunction between day and night, yet neither of them causes the other. Causality, then, is not constant conjunction of either the necessary condition or sufficient condition variety." Evaluate this argument. Give examples of other apparent constant conjunctions.

21. Distinguish clearly the various interpretations of the Causal Principle. Write a defense of one of them, with criticisms of all the others.

22. Examine some characteristics that the Causal Principle, in the last

interpretation of it considered in this chapter (as a leading principle but not a statement), might have in common with (a) the Verifiability Principle, (b) the Principle of Uniformity of Nature, (c) the principles of logic.

23. Can you think of any empirical observations which might cast doubt on the Causal Principle? Does your answer to this question help you to decide which interpretation of the Causal Principle to accept?

24. Distinguish determinism from (a) indeterminism; (b) fatalism.

25. Indicate some ambiguities in the word "freedom."

26. A student who had long been troubled by the problem of free-will and determinism reasoned as follows: "Science has pretty clearly shown that everything that happens is determined. If this is so, it includes everything that I do. In that case, I have no free-will. If I have no free-will, I'd rather not live." So he committed suicide. Of what errors in reasoning was he guilty?

27. Examine critically the following assertions:

a. Determinism can't be true because there is chance in the world. We all speak of this or that event as happening "by chance."

b. If everything we are going to do is determined, we may as well sit back and take things easy (or break loose and do whatever we please); our own efforts are useless if everything is determined anyway.

c. "What significance is there in my mental struggle tonight whether I shall or shall not give up smoking, if the laws which govern the matter of the physical universe already preordain for the morrow a configuration of matter consisting of pipe, tobacco, and smoke connected with my lips?" (Arthur E. Eddington, in *Philosophy* Magazine, January 1933, p. 41.)

d. Determinism can't be true because we don't know the causes of everything that happens.

e. Determinism can't be true because it is essential to the very existence of science that every event have a cause.

f. Determinism can't be true, because people aren't just machines.

g. Determinism can't be true, because I *feel* that I'm free; I know this by introspection. This is a much better proof than any arguments.

h. Free-will is incompatible with determinism.

i. Free-will is incompatible with fatalism.

j. Free-will is incompatible with indeterminism.

k. Laws of nature make everything happen the way it does.

l. My background compels me to behave as I do.

m. If I had been under different influences I would have acted differently; and if the set of influences acting upon me on two occasions had been exactly the same I would have acted the same way the second time as the first—I couldn't help doing it. So I'm not free.

n. I couldn't have acted differently from the way I did act. No matter what the act was which I contemplated doing, there was only *one* road open to me (though I didn't know it at the time), only *one* thing that under those peculiar circumstances I *could* have done: namely, the one I did do.

28. Write a paragraph or two on the meaning (or meanings) of the italicized word or phrase in *one* of the following sentences:

    a. I *can* do this.

    b. I *could have* done otherwise.

    c. I have the *power* to do this.

    d. I was *compelled* to perform this act.

(You will find the reading of the article by Hobart, referred to in the reading list on page 275, extremely useful in this connection.)

5

Life, Mind, and Deity

In the past two chapters we have considered various problems connected with empirical knowledge; in this chapter we shall consider still others—problems that arise when we reflect on some of the most pervasive features of the universe in which we live. Here more than ever, the cleavage between metaphysical and non-metaphysical interpretations will be apparent.

I. MECHANISM AND VITALISM

Among the inexhaustible multitude of inorganic objects which constitute the earth, the other planets, and the stars and galaxies, there are objects which are conspicuously different from the rest: they are *living organisms*. As far as we know, they exist only on the earth, and even there they are present only on or near its surface; they are not found more than a few miles below its surface or more than a few miles above it. In the total amount of space they occupy, they are about as small in relation to the entire volume of the earth as the earth is in relation to the entire solar system. Yet they are quite different from the objects which surround them in a number of remarkable ways: (1) The matter of which they are composed is constantly changing; new matter is assimilated and old matter is excreted. What persists throughout this continuous process of change is the *form* of the organism, until the organism dies and loses its characteristic form.[1] (2) Even the form changes somewhat, though in a regular way: until it reaches its maturity, an organism *grows*. (3) Moreover, the organism *reproduces*, producing other organisms

[1] We saw in Chapter 1 (see page 39) that the defining characteristics of organisms have to do with their form rather than with the matter which assumes the form.

of the same kind or species as itself; this is something which does not happen in the realm of inorganic matter. (4) Finally, organisms (animal organisms, not plants) display varying degrees of *impression-reaction* activities. They respond to stimuli, and not merely in the way in which certain chemicals respond to the presence of other chemicals; they do not always respond the same way each time, but they learn through experience. This phenomenon occurs to a far larger extent in the "higher" and more complex organisms, but it happens to some extent even on the humblest levels of animal life. A tiny organism is hit by a stream of water and it shrinks and curls up into its stalk; a minute later it expands to its normal size; when the stream of water strikes again, precisely as before, the creature pays no attention to it—the creature has already adapted itself to the harmless stimulus. Sticks and stones do not do this.

The boundary line between the living and the non-living is not in every case clear and sharp. (For example, some crystals duplicate part of the behavior of living organisms in that, in some sense at least, they *grow*.) Between the most complex phenomena of inorganic matter and the simplest phenomena of the organic realm, there is no clear-cut boundary. But this, of course, does not destroy the distinction between organic and inorganic, any more than the fact that red shades into orange shows that there is no distinction between red and orange (see page 40).

Perhaps the most remarkable feature of the behavior of living things, something to which all the four characteristics listed above contribute, is the *teleological,* or purposive, behavior of living organisms as opposed to rocks and rivers. Their behavior seems to be directed to some *end*, to be animated by a *purpose*. Specifically, living things behave in such a way as to keep themselves alive, and if this is impossible, to keep their offspring alive and thus assure the perpetuation of the species. Most of their activities seem to be directed toward this end.

But if it is true, as we said in discussing explanation (see pages 185–188), that "when there is a purpose, there must be someone to have the purpose," are we to assume here that even the least complex organisms have purposes, and act from a conscious intent to keep themselves and their species alive? Are we to assume that the hen has a conscious intent in setting patiently on her eggs until they hatch? is she animated by visions of motherhood and the chicks that will later hatch? Is the squirrel who stores nuts for the winter doing so with the conscious purpose of eating them after the snow falls? Perhaps some will answer these questions with a Yes. But then what of examples such as that of the complex and intricate embryonic development of an organism, in which organs are developed for future use, though they have not yet been used?

> In the case of the human eye, for example, 120 million rods, more than one million cones, and 400,000 ganglionic cells must be developed and brought into functional alignment prior to the functioning of the eye and in order that the normal functioning may be possible at all. These cells cannot be arranged under the influence of external stimuli which might facilitate the division of labor or determine the alignment, but must be produced, coordinated, and connected with the sensory centers of the brain entirely from within the growing embryo and prior to, yet for the sake of, their balanced functioning.[2]

Surely in this case the embryo has no conscious purpose in growing thus; yet it behaves exactly as if it had the conscious purpose of being able to see when once confronted by the outside world. Or consider the development of antitoxins in the human blood stream when toxins are introduced—a different specific antitoxin for each toxin, as if the organism *knew* that it needed just this antitoxin in order to survive and regain health. Digestion is another case in point. The highly complex carbohydrates which enter the stomach are broken down by complex organic compounds (the diastatic ferments) secreted by the pancreas, and are transformed by them into glucose. In this form the food enters the blood stream and is carried to the cells, particularly in the liver and muscles, which store it. The storage is an extremely complicated process requiring many different cells, each with a specific function. Special chemical agents produced in different regions of the body are then transported to the scene and build up the glucose into a more complex compound, glycogen, and store it. In case of need, however, the glycogen is transformed back into glucose and is liberated into the blood stream. "In case of need!"—it is as if each of the cells knew what it was doing, as if each had been assigned its specific task to perform, and all were working together to produce the desired end, like the people in a well-organized state.

Now, it is not the aim of a book in philosophy to regale the reader

___

[2] W. H. Werkmeister, *A Philosophy of Science* (New York: Harper & Bros., 1940), p. 332.

with facts of biology, however fascinating these facts may be. There are hundreds of books in which these facts are available to any reader who is interested. What we are concerned with here are questions about what to make of these facts, or how to interpret them. Does life, so different from non-life, require a special act of creation to bring it into being? Is there a special Life-force, or *élan vital*, present in living things which makes their behavior different from that of non-living things? Are living things merely complicated machines? Do living things exist somehow in a higher "level" of existence, and is there more to them than the physicist and chemist could ever possibly discover? Are biological phenomena reducible to those of physics and chemistry? These questions, though related, are not quite the same; indeed, some of them at least are by no means clear, and it is the question of what they mean which has first to be clarified.

On all of these questions there are two opposing points of view, known as *mechanism* and *vitalism,* mechanism emphasizing the continuity and likeness between living and non-living things and vitalism the discontinuity and difference. But since both these terms are used to tag now one doctrine and now another, and since many of the doctrines themselves are not very clear, the terms "mechanism" and "vitalism" are both vague and ambiguous.

Let us consider several of the ways in which it is possible to state the issue between mechanism and vitalism.

1. A divine creator of life. This could be stated as an issue between those who assert a divine creation of living things (whether by special creation or by the slow process of evolution) and those who deny it. This issue properly comes under another heading which will be discussed in the last section of this chapter. Moreover, the dispute between those who believe in a divine Creator of life and those who do not is not the dispute to which the names "vitalism" and "mechanism" are *usually* attached, although whether or not a person believes one way or the other on this issue has much to do with whether he is a mechanist or a vitalist in one of the more usual senses of those words.

2. A non-material life-force. A very common way of distinguishing between mechanism and vitalism is this: according to vitalism there is a special *non-material life-force,* or *élan vital,* which is present in living things but not in non-living things. Its presence in living things explains the difference between the behavior of living things and that of the non-living.

If one asks *where* this force is, the answer is that it is no*where,* for it cannot be pinned down to any place in space, not even inside the organisms, for no observation has ever revealed such a thing there, nor is it expected to. It is not located in space any more than numbers or thoughts are. It is something that can never be discovered by the methods of the empirical scientist, but nevertheless it exists, and its existence explains the remarkable differences that can be observed between living and non-living things. The mechanist is the one who denies these contentions.

Now, if the issue is put in this way, there are very strong arguments that can be brought to bear against the vitalistic position. (1) If the non-material life-force is set forth as an *explanation* of the observed behavior of living organisms, one can reply that it is surely not an explanation in any sense that a scientist would accept. It can be made to satisfy the first criterion of explanation (see page 180), that of deducibility:

> Whenever a Life-force is present, things exhibit the properties of life.
> In this thing a Life-force is present.

Therefore, This thing exhibits the properties of life.

But it fails to satisfy the second criterion. It does not enable us to predict a single observable phenomenon; in no way whatever does it extend our knowledge. "The behavior of living things, as opposed to non-living things, is explained by the presence of a non-material Life-force," we are told; but having been told this, we are confronted with the same questions as before. Consider some particular phenomenon, such as the ability of some pigeons to find their way back home after being released from an airplane in unfamiliar terrain hundreds of miles away. The scientist, being told that this is explained by the presence of a Life-force, still wants to know by exactly what means the pigeons are enabled to do what they do, while other birds cannot: is the pigeon sensitive to magnetic stimuli radiating from the earth's magnetic poles—is it equipped with "built-in compasses?" In short, even if a scientist assented to the vitalist's account, he would say that it was useless: the vitalist's claim, even if true, would be empty. Indeed, the vitalist could invoke the same "explanation" for every remarkable new bit of organic behavior that turned up; and each such "explanation" might be equally true, but equally useless.

The mechanist's objection to a Life-force, or *élan vital,* is not that it is unobservable, not even that it is unobservable in principle. For that matter, as we have already seen (pages 190–192), there are many entities which the scientist accepts, such as electrons and magnetic fields, which are unobservable. But for each of these there is empirical evidence, for the hypotheses in question have *definite empirical consequences,* and if observation shows that the predicted consequences do not occur, the hypotheses must be abandoned or altered. A person who disagrees with the present electron-hypothesis and submits another in its stead can put the matter to the test of observation: are the consequences which he predicts actually forthcoming? are there consequences of the present hypothesis which are *not* forthcoming? The vitalist, however, is able to submit nothing like this; the only things he can point to as evidence for his hypothesis are *the same facts of organic behavior* with which the mechanist is already familiar and readily admits to exist.

(2) But the vitalist may take another line of defense. "Perhaps the *élan* does not give an explanation in the scientist's sense," he may say, "but still, it may exist. The *élan* is a reality, but not the kind of reality which the scientist's method permits him to discover. Not being the sort of thing which is available to empirical observation, it is no wonder that he cannot discover it by empirical observation. Why should you assume that all realities are realities that the scientist can discover?"

What can the mechanist say in reply to this charge? First, he can appeal to the Law of Parsimony, or the principle sometimes known as Occam's Razor: "Do not multiply entities beyond necessity." "If the behavior of living things, or some aspects of them, is a mystery," he may say, "then by accepting the *élan* we have two mysteries on our hands instead of one. Surely this does not help the situation!" But the vitalist may question this principle. "This may be a very convenient methodological procedure for you to use," he may reply. "But if there *are* two entities and not one, whether mysterious or not, there is no point in trying to talk the second one out of existence. And you still haven't proved to me that the second— the non-material Life-force—does *not* exist."

The mechanist will then reply along the following lines. "Pray tell me *what* precisely it is that you believe exists when you say that a Life-force exists. I first objected that the concept had no explanatory power, and that accordingly there was no evidence in favor of the view that any such mysterious entity exists. But this objection did not go deep enough. Indeed, it was misleading: it assumed that we do have a concept of an *élan vital*, and that the only difficulty was that we had no evidence that anything of the kind actually existed. My real objection is that '*élan vital*' is a mere phrase, standing for nothing whatever. All you have given me is a phrase, not a thing for which the phrase stands. And if the phrase stands for nothing, it is cognitively meaningless. In that event, the statement "There is an *élan vital* is cognitively meaningless, and, correspondingly, the statement "There is no *élan vital*" is cognitively meaningless too; hence I cannot consistently hold it. What I am now saying, therefore, is not that no *élan* exists; it is that you haven't told me what it means even to say that it exists, or for that matter to deny it.[3] After all, what is the phrase the label of? What *does* it stand for? If it stands for merely the observed facts of organic behavior which we all agree upon, and is simply a convenient shorthand way of lumping these bits of behavior together and talking about them, then there is no disagreement among us: we all agree that organisms behave in these ways. But if it stands for something *more*, as you vitalists say, then please tell me what the something more is. What would you say to someone who agrees that this organic behavior occurs but denies that there is an *élan vital?* What are you asserting to exist over and above the organic behavior which your opponents too are asserting to exist?

"The fact is," the mechanist concludes, "that the vitalistic argument is an argument from ignorance. You say, 'Here is all this behavior of living things which you cannot explain!' I reply that some of it we *can* explain, and the amount being explained is increasing all the time. But let that pass; even where I cannot yet explain, you are in no better position; *all you offer is a mere word.* But the addition of a word can no more assure that a reality corresponding to it exists than you can furnish your house with the *names* of various items of furniture." As one writer puts it, vitalism "simply fills

[3] The parallel between the argument here and the one on necessary connection in Chapter 4 (see pages 226–229) will be apparent.

up the gaps in mechanistic descriptions after the fashion of Columbus' map-maker, 'Where unknown, there place Terrors.' " [4]

The mechanism-vitalism controversy, however, can take other forms than the one we have just considered.

3. Emergence. It is said that vitalism asserts that the characteristics of living things are *emergent*, while mechanism denies it.

Before we can argue this position we must be clear about what is meant by calling a characteristic emergent. An example may give the best preliminary indication—an example, moreover, drawn not from the biological sciences at all but from chemistry: Water is composed of hydrogen and oxygen. Hydrogen is gaseous at ordinary temperatures and is highly combustible; oxygen is also gaseous at ordinary temperatures but is incombustible; instead, it is a necessary condition of combustion. The two together form water, which is not gaseous but liquid at ordinary temperatures, and is neither combustible nor a necessary condition for combustion; on the contrary, it is used to stop combustion. Is it not strange that two elements should combine to form something with such utterly different chemical properties? Examples of this in chemistry could be multiplied: for instance, the combination of sodium, which is highly corrosive when exposed to air or water, with chlorine, a semi-poisonous greenish gas, to form ordinary table salt. The question arises, If we had never had any experience of water or salt, *would we be able to predict* what properties they would have just from knowing the properties possessed by hydrogen and oxygen alone, or sodium and chlorine alone? If we would *not* be able to predict the existence of these properties, then they are emergent; but if we would be able to predict them, they are not emergent. (The word "emergent" here is metaphorical, but it seems to arise from the fact that the properties of a compound seem to *emerge* from the elements without having been apparent in the elements themselves.)

At this point it may appear that whether the answer is yes or not is simply a question for empirical observation to decide. If this were so, philosophy would have no business with it and it would be left to the natural sciences, which handle such questions on the basis of empirical evidence. However, this is not the case, at least on the level of clarification we have reached thus far. Let us ask: *On the*

---

[4] J. Needham, *Science, Religion, and Reality* (New York: Macmillan, 1925), p. 245.

basis of exactly what are the qualities of water and salt predictable or non-predictable? On the basis of a knowledge of the properties of the elements of which they are composed. But on the basis of *how much* knowledge of these properties? Presumably on the basis of complete knowledge. But what would a complete knowledge be? Would we not say our knowledge was incomplete *until it did enable us* to predict the properties of water or salt? In this case, however, the statement is a tautology: "A complete knowledge (i.e. a knowledge that will enable us to predict X) will enable us to predict X." Anyone, vitalist or not, who denied this tautology would be foolish indeed!

Clearly, then, if we include among the properties of hydrogen the property of combining with oxygen to form water (and this *is* undeniably one of its properties), then we can predict that it will combine with hydrogen to form water, for the very simple reason that the statement follows tautologically. But surely this is not what the mechanist is concerned to assert or the vitalist to deny. Let us amend the statement, then, to read: "A complete knowledge of the properties of hydrogen *except* for the property of combining with oxygen to form water would enable us to predict the formation and qualities of water," or (the more usual formulation) what is similar but not the same thing, "A complete knowledge of the properties of hydrogen and oxygen *in* isolation, i.e., *not* including their relational properties (what they combine with to form compounds), would enable us to predict the properties of water."

If we apply this to the case of living organisms, the question becomes, "If we had a complete knowledge of the physical and chemical properties of every cell (including that of every molecule composing these cells) within a living organism, except the relational properties of combining in certain ways to form organisms, would we be able to predict what all the properties of the organism would be?" In the case of some properties, we already can; the weight of the organism, for example, is merely the weight of its constituent cells, which are in turn the aggregate weight of their constituent molecules. Similarly, much of the digestive behavior of organisms is predictable on the basis of a knowledge of the chemistry of the extremely complex compounds involved in the digestive process. What is *not* predictable on the basis of our present knowledge of physics and chemistry is the *teleological* (purposive) behavior of the organism—for example, red blood cells going "in case of emergency" to parts of the body where they are needed to keep the organism alive. How in a million years, one may ask, would a phenomenon like the complex and intricate group behavior of wasps and bees— such as scouting around through a neighborhood to familiarize themselves with the terrain, so as not to forget the location of the nest or hive—be predictable on the basis of even a complete knowledge of the physical and chemical properties of these organisms?

Even at this point we should not rest content with a definite yes-or-no answer, not because the empirical sciences have far from completed their investigation of the properties of organisms (though this is true enough), but because there is still a further source of unclarity to be removed: What is meant by "predictable"?

When we say that a certain property, say of water or of a living organism, is predictable on the basis of a knowledge of the properties of its constituents, what do we mean? When we say it is predictable we surely do not mean merely that someone can volunteer a prediction about it; we mean at least that he is in a position to volunteer a prediction that will turn out to be correct. Probably or certainly correct? Doubtless we can mean either one, but probability is not usually what is intended in discussions about this issue. For example, if we knew the properties of sodium chloride (salt), sodium iodide, and sodium bromide (chlorine, bromine, and iodine are all members of the halogen family of elements), would we be able to predict, without observing them, what the properties of sodium fluoride (fluorine being also of the same family) would be? We might volunteer a prediction, and say that it was probable on the basis of previously observed similarities in the properties of the compounds formed by these elements. But we might well be mistaken: we sometimes are in such matters. We could say, "The other compounds of fluorine have turned out to be like the corresponding compounds of chlorine, and so forth, so *probably* this one will be too," but even if such a prediction turned out to be correct, the participants in the mechanism-vitalism controversy would not be inclined to say that this constituted predictability, thus proving that the mechanist was right. What is wanted is certainty, specifically logical certainty: the issue is whether, from statements about the constituents, we are able to *deduce logically* statements about the wholes which they form. "*If* such-and-such physical and chemical properties, *then* such-and-such behavior." [5] If the statements about the wholes cannot be so deduced, the properties of the whole are emergent; if they can, these properties are not emergent.

4. Reducibility. But if this is so, the controversy about emergence has become one with the controversy about *reducibility*, which is another form which the mechanism-vitalism dispute may take.

One science is said to be reducible to another science, or one part of it reducible to another part, when all the statements in the one science can be logically deduced from statements in the other. The mechanism-vitalism question, in this guise, is: "Is biology reducible to physics and chemistry?" If it is, mechanism is true, and if it is not, vitalism is true.

This sounds like an outright empirical question; but our formulation is not yet quite accurate. If it is taken as it stands, the answer is definitely in favor of vitalism, for the simple reason that the biological laws we now have cannot possibly be deduced from laws of physics and chemistry; and they cannot be so deduced because biological laws contain references to entities such as cells which are never mentioned in physics and chemistry, and of course a statement about cells cannot be logically deduced from any number of statements which do *not* contain any reference to cells. This is true not only of the relation of biology to the other physical sciences; it is also true within physics itself. For example, the laws of thermodynamics are not reducible to those of mechanics, because thermodynamic laws involve the use of concepts such as heat, while in mechanics no reference to heat occurs. In this strict sense, then, neither the sciences nor the various branches of the sciences are reducible to each other; the irreducibility is by no means peculiar to statements about living things.

Yet it is usually agreed among physicists that thermodynamics, for example, *is* reducible to mechanics, and in fact has already been so reduced, while it is not yet certain whether biology is reducible to physics and chemistry. What then is meant? The answer is that *by introducing as premises* hypotheses which permit us to omit all references to heat and to substitute only references to things which *are* a part of the subject-matter of mechanics (such as the motion

---

[5] This, of course, in no way affects the issue of certainty and empirical statements discussed in Chapter 3. "*If* this is salt, it contains sodium" is certain, for it is a tautology, even though "This substance here is salt" may never be certain.

of molecules), we *can* deduce all the statements in thermodynamics from statements of mechanics. In this example, the hypothesis is the kinetic theory of heat; once this is used as a premise in the deduction, the laws of thermodynamics are deducible from those of mechanics, and thus thermodynamics is reducible to mechanics.

Similarly, there are good grounds for saying that all of chemistry is reducible to physics, and that in the course of time a complete reduction will have been achieved. Statements about the color, weight, melting-point, and other chemical properties of elements and compounds can be deduced (again, together with certain hypotheses, usually involving molecular structure) from statements about the intra-molecular properties of these elements and compounds. Another way of saying this is that chemistry is becoming explainable in terms of physics; for explanation, as we have seen (pages 180–181), involves deduction of the statement about the phenomenon to be explained from the statements which do the explaining.

Now, in this sense, is biology reducible to physics and chemistry? If this means, "Has it now, at the present time, been reduced?" the answer is no. If it means, "Will it ever?" the answer is that of course we do not know, but that it is quite possible that it will. A great deal of it already is. The part that resists reduction is chiefly the part having to do with the teleological behavior of organisms. What further reductions can be made as biological science advances is something which only time can tell. Here, then, we shall leave the matter to the empirical sciences.

Whatever be the outcome of this controversy, vitalism in the sense of irreducibility is a far different thing from vitalism in the sense of a special non-material Life-force which we considered earlier. There is nothing unscientific about irreducibility. It may well be that the laws of some sciences will never be reduced to the laws of other sciences at a "lower" level; yet each will continue to operate thoroughly and systematically. The only persons who will be disappointed at irreducibility will be those who are monists by temperament and have a burning desire to "reduce everything to unity." Such are those who say that fundamentally there is only one science, physics, and that all the others are only more complicated special cases of this one basic science. (In other words: basic laws [see pages 189–190] are found only in physics, not in chemistry or biology.) The hopes of such persons may in time be dimmed by our continued failure to work biology into this neat scheme; and if they are dimmed by biology, they may well be dashed to the ground when we consider a still "higher" level of existence, namely mind. To this we now turn.

II. THE MENTAL AND THE PHYSICAL

In historical succession, mind follows upon life. Just as life did not occur on our planet until inorganic matter assumed forms of great complexity, so mind did not arise until organic matter had reached a still further degree of complexity, involving sense-organs, nerves, and brains.

It is often said that within the realm of the empirical we find three levels: matter, life, and mind. Living things, though remarkably different from non-living things, are still material, or physical, things: they are composed of matter, albeit organic matter. But now we come to something that, in the opinion of most philosophers at least, is not material at all: the organic bodies which are apparently necessary conditions for the occurrence of minds are material, but minds themselves are not. If this is so, we have a wider "gap" between life and mind than we had between inorganic matter and life.

Our first task will be to show that there is such a thing as the mental as opposed to the physical. Not everyone will agree with the distinctions we are now about to draw, but every student should at least be thoroughly familiar with them, not only because most persons who have spent considerable time with the subject would assent to them, but because without them one is apt to commit some easily detectible errors.

Mental events. What happens when you hear a noise? Unless you are just "hearing things," in which case the auditory sensation is generated from within the brain itself, something first happens outside your body: sound-waves, alternate condensations and rarefactions of the air, cause air-particles to strike repeatedly on your ear drum, so that it vibrates. The ear drum is connected by three small bones to a membrane that covers one end of a spiral tube in the inner ear. The vibration of your ear drum is transmitted through this chain of three bones to the membrane at the end of the tube. The tube is filled with a liquid, perilymph, so that the vibration in the membrane attached to these bones causes a corresponding vibration to pass through this liquid. Inside the first tube is another one, filled with a liquid called endolymph; vibrations in the perilymph cause vibrations in the membranous wall of the inner tube and waves in the endolymph. Small hairs stick out from the membranous walls into the endolymph, which are made to vibrate by the vibrations in the endolymph. The auditory nerve is joined to the roots of these hairs. The vibration of the hairs causes impulses to pass up the auditory nerve to a part of the brain called the auditory center. Not until the auditory center is stimulated do you hear a sound.

So far all the events described have been physical; they have been minute changes going on inside your head. They are extremely difficult to observe, even with cleverly devised instruments, since people's heads are not transparent and it is difficult to open a person's head while the person remains alive with his brain functioning as usual. Nevertheless, these minute physical changes have been observed and measured. (Even if this were not so, they would still be *logically* possible to observe; the impossibility would be merely technical.)

The entire process just described takes only a small fraction of a second; but now, when the auditory nerve has carried the stimulus to the appropriate portion of the brain, something new and different occurs: you *hear a sound*, you have an *auditory sensation*. This is "something new under the sun." It is something quite different from anything that went on earlier in this brief but complex process. The auditory sensation is a *mental event,* not a physical event like the preceding ones. It is an *awareness*, a state of *consciousness*. The same holds for visual sensation and all other kinds of sensation: kinesthetic sensations, smell-sensations, taste, touch, heat, cold, pain, and so on; and also for states of consciousness not directly associated with the senses, such as thoughts, memories, images, emotions. Let us see in what ways they are different from physical events:

1. We can always locate physical things, events, and processes in space. They take place some*where*. The sensory and neural processes associated with sensation take place inside the person's head. But where is the sensation? Suppose you hear a bell ringing; where then is your auditory sensation? It is not the physical sound-waves

—these are in space outside your body, between the bell and your ears. Still less are they in the bell, which is a physical object which you can locate in space. But the auditory sensation—where is it? Inside your head somewhere? Would a surgeon cutting open your head ever find it? If your skull were transparent and a surgeon with a powerful microscope could see what was going on inside it, he might see the stimulation of the auditory nerve, but would he see or hear your *sensation?* (And if he did would it not be his sensation rather than yours?)

Or take the case of vision. Light-waves impinge upon the retina of your eye, producing there an inverted image of the object seen. This is physical; the inverted image can be observed (though it is not what *you* are seeing). The optic nerve is stimulated, a chemical-electrical impulse passes along it, and finally, in a very small fraction of a second, the occipital lobe of the brain is stimulated; then a *visual sensation* occurs. Up to the occurrence of the sensation, every step of the process can be located in space, somewhere inside your head. But, supposing you are looking at a solid green wall, where is your sensation of green? Is it in your head? inside your brain somewhere? If so, where? Would someone opening your head or looking at it through a super-X-ray microscope find the green you were seeing? Would it make sense to say that the green was four inches behind your eyes? (But it *would* make sense to say of a neural process that it was going on four inches behind your eyes.)

This applies equally if the sensation is not caused by objects outside your body. Suppose you are, as we say, seeing red spots before your eyes. Where are the spots? Before your eyes, literally? Six inches in front of your eyes perhaps? You cannot locate them there, and neither can anybody else. These spots do not exist in space at all. You may say, "They aren't real; they don't really exist at all." But don't they? They do not exist as physical spots, like the spots on a dog, but you *do* see spots and that is an inescapable fact of your experience, just as inescapable as your visual sensation of the dog's spots. By saying that they are not real you may mean that they do not form part of the physical world, but they do certainly exist—you are seeing them right now. Perhaps they exist only as mental events, but they still exist. Because they are not physical, however, you cannot locate them in the physical world, in front of your eyes or behind your eyes *or anywhere else.* Mental events are non-spatial; physical events are spatial. It makes no more sense to ask "Where (in space) is this mental event occurring?" than it does to ask "Where is the number 4?" (as opposed to the *numeral* "4" which I have just written on the blackboard and which certainly *is* located in space). Do not assume that because it is false that a mental event occurs outside one's head it therefore occurs inside one's head. A physical event or process would have to go on in the one place or the other, but not a mental one: the category of space, or spatiality, just does not apply to them at all. That is one thing that distinguishes them from physical events and processes.

If mental events (states of consciousness), then, are not locatable in space, then neither are they *extended* in space. You cannot meaningfully ask how much space they occupy. How much space do the red spots before your eyes occupy? Two inches? Three feet? (And if you did make some such assertion, how would you go about verifying it?) Suppose you form an image of the Empire State Building, or, more precisely, an image shaped so as to represent the Empire State Building. How tall is, not the Empire State Building itself, but your image of it? What is the tallness of the image as compared with the tallness of the Empire State Building itself? Is it one-tenth as tall, perhaps? If so, how could it possibly be squeezed into your brain, whose dimensions are only a few inches? If you constructed a *model* of the Empire State Building, you could meaningfully say that your model was one-tenth as tall, or one-thousandth as tall, as the building itself, for your model is a physical object located at a definite place in the physical world. But the image you have in your mind is not like the model you have before you on the table: the image is not inside your head (no one opening your head or looking at it from the outside would ever find it there), but neither is it outside your head, say on the table. It is not in space at all, and consequently it has no extension in space either.

2. Physical objects, physical events, and physical processes are publicly observable; but mental events (states of consciousness) can be experienced by only one person.

It may be technically impossible now (though possibly not fifty years from now) for me to observe what is going on inside your head, say at the midpoint of a straight line connecting your two ears. But whatever it is, it is some physical process taking place in your brain. *If* I had an instrument (as some day I may have)

through which I could see it, others could look through it and see
your brain-processes also. For that matter, so could you, by means
of a set of mirrors between the instrument and the space in front of
your eyes. In principle, all physical occurrences are publicly observable, inside your head just as much as inside your house. Any
impossibility in the former case is only *technical*. But what kind of
impossibility is it when I say it is impossible for me to have your
sensation of green, or to feel your pain?

In ordinary life we sometimes say "I feel your pain," by which
we only mean that we sympathize very strongly, sometimes so
strongly that we too may feel a pain, but then of course the pain
we feel and the pain the person with whom we are sympathizing
feels are two different pains, not one. But we are not asking here
whether a person can sympathize strongly with another person; we
are asking whether two persons can feel literally *the same pain*,
the way they can see the same head or the same house. Is it logically
impossible, or is it logically possible but not actual?

Suppose that the world were different from the way we now find
it, with biological laws quite different from the ones that now describe it. Suppose, specifically, that every time your finger was
pricked with a pin, I felt a pain but you felt none; and that every
time I was hit, you felt a blow, and so on. This is a logically possible
state of affairs. It is not actual, for in actual fact my pains are dependent on the state of my organism and your pains on yours. As
far as we know, it is empirically impossible for the situation we
have just described to occur; but it is logically possible, and in fact
easily imaginable. Suppose that this state of affairs occurred; would
we then say that I felt your pain and that you felt mine?

It all depends on what we mean by the phrases "your pain" and
"my pain." If "your pain" means "the pain that occurs when your
body is injured" and "my pain" means "the pain that occurs when
my body is injured" ("injured" here does not carry any connotation
of *feeling* the injury, it refers only to the physical state of the
body), then the answer is yes. In the situation we have just visual-
ized, this is actually the state of affairs: I feel the pain that occurs
when your body is injured, and you the pain when my body is injured.

But the answer may also be no: even if I felt the pain when *your*
body was injured, I might (and probably would) still call it *my*

pain; and the pain you felt would be called your pain even though it occurred when my body was injured. In other words, whose pain it is would be determined by *who feels it*, not by whose body is injured. In this case, it is *logically impossible* for me to feel your pain. If I feel it, *ipso facto* it is my pain; if you feel it, it is your pain. If we both feel pain, it is not the same pain we feel: you feel yours and I feel mine.

If any pain that you feel is thereby your pain, no matter what are the causal conditions under which it is felt (even if it is caused by injury to *my* body), then it is logically impossible for you to feel anybody else's pain. Thus the statement "I can feel only my own pain" means "I can feel only the pain I feel"; and "I can't feel your pain" becomes "I can't feel a pain that I don't feel" both of which are tautologies, and to deny them involves self-contradiction. This much is agreed, though the basis for it may be disputed: the empiricist (pages 134–144) will declare that it is only a verbal convention that determines this self-contradiction, while the rationalist will contend that it reflects a profound, far-reaching, and necessary fact about reality.

Our knowledge of other minds. If I can have access only to my own states of consciousness, my own sensations, thoughts, emotions, pains, and pleasures, how can I ever know about yours, or even whether you have any? I can now see the outside of your head, and some day I may be able to see what is going on inside it, but as we have just concluded, even then I shall not be able to experience your pains, your feelings, your thoughts. Lacking direct experience of these things, the best I can do is to *infer* what you are thinking or feeling. In other words, I can *confirm* statements about what you are feeling, by watching your facial expression, your gestures, your activities; but I cannot *verify* them, because verification requires complete evidence and in your case I can never have that complete evidence, for example, feeling the pain. In my own case I can (1) look in a mirror and see my tooth, and (2) feel my toothache. In your case I can see your tooth, but I cannot feel your toothache. I can only see the decayed tooth, watch your agonized expression, see you wring your hands, and hear your cries. From all this behavior I *infer* (never directly observe) that you feel pain. To ascertain whether or not you have a toothache I have to resort to methods that I do not have to use in my own case. Of course, I can look into a mirror and see my tooth, watch myself wringing my hands, and so on, but *I do not have to do this* in order to know that I have a toothache; the whole procedure is superfluous when it is *my* toothache that is in question. Watching my own gestures in a mirror would do nothing to help me confirm the statement that I feel pain (though watching yours would help me confirm the statement that *you* feel pain). I need no such confirmation, for the statement that I feel pain is completely verified by my feeling it.[6]

Let us examine this situation in the light of the Verifiability Criterion. "If the verification (or all the confirmations) of two statements is the same, then the (cognitive) meaning of the two statements is the same." Let us consider these two statements:

> A. I have a pain.
> B. You have a pain.

The first statement is about me and the second statement is about you; but apart from this, is there any difference in meaning between the two statements? There does not appear to be; yet the way in which I would go about finding whether the first is true is utterly different from the way in which I would go about finding whether the second is true. What, then, shall we do? Shall we say that because the verifications are different the meanings are different, or shall we say that the meanings are the same although the verifications are different?

1. We can say that because the verifications are different, the meanings are different. When I say "I have a pain" I am talking not about my overt behavior but about my state of consciousness, my pain; but when I say "You have a pain," my statement is not about your state of consciousness at all but about your behavior, since this is all that I can verify.

This is very curious indeed: it is saying that I am not really talking about your *pain* at all, but only about the physical events that accompany your pain. Is this alternative, however, acceptable? Am I not talking about your *pain* rather than your accompanying behavior when I say "You have a pain," just as much as I am talking about *my* pain and not my accompanying behavior when I say "I have a pain"?

---

[6] In fact, when a statement "is its own verification" we do not usually speak of verification at all. This point will be discussed in Chapter 6.

Perhaps when I talk about your pain I am just using a shorthand way of talking about a whole cluster of behavior-characteristics, just as in talking about the current in the wire I am talking about a cluster of characteristics exhibited by the wire. This may sound like a simple and neat solution; but is it really true? When I talk about my own pain I am not talking about my facial expression, my gestures, or my screams; and talking about my own pain is clearly *not* just a shorthand way of referring to all these phenomena. Sometimes I may use expressions, such as "current," as shorthand ways of referring to a group of diverse phenomena, but not in this case. I am talking about my pain, which is a different thing from the *causes* of pain or the *effects* of pain. And why should it be different with *your* pain? When I am talking about your pain, am I not talking about your *pain* and *not* about all the accompanying physical events—even though all I can possibly verify in your case is the occurrence of these accompanying physical events?

When I say you are color-blind I am not saying merely that you fail to pass the color-blindness tests and that you get your signals mixed up in your job as railroad switchboard operator. I do not even mean that you are in a certain retinal state or brain-state. I mean that you *do not see the variety of colors* that I do, that your color-sensations are less varied than mine. These bits of your behavior that I observe are *effects* of your color-blindness, and they are what I verify (or confirm), but they are not what your color-blindness is: your color-blindness is the fact that you can not see certain colors.

Similarly, when I say you have a toothache I mean that you *have an ache,* just as I do sometimes if I have a decayed tooth; I do *not* mean that your face is contorted in pain (this is only an effect of your pain) or that your wisdom tooth is in a decayed condition (this is only a cause of your pain). This can be brought out most clearly as follows: Suppose I predict, "At 11 A.M. you will pull a wry face and announce that you have a pain"; or suppose that instead I predict, "At 11 A.M. you will *feel a stabbing pain,* pull a wry face, and announce that you have a pain." Don't you expect something different in the second case from what you expect in the first? Don't you dread the occurrence of the second set of circumstances more than you do the first? *I* may observe no difference and may confirm the two statements in the same way; but nevertheless there is a great difference in the *meaning* of the two statements, as you will be the first to insist!

2. So we come to the second alternative: we can say that the meanings are the same although the verifications are utterly different. When I say you have a pain I am not talking about your behavior or your brain-state *any more than I am talking about my own behavior or brain-state when I say that I have a pain.* When I say that you have a pain, and that I have a pain, I mean the same in every respect except that the one proposition is about you and the other is about me. That is, when I say that you have a pain *I mean to assert the same thing about you that I assert about myself when I say that I have a pain,* in spite of the fact that the verifications (or confirmations) of the two statements are so different from each other.

Of course, "I have a pain" is verified *by me* in the same way that "You have a pain" is verified *by you.* In this sense the two statements are verified in the same way. But as long as I am doing the verifying (or confirming), it surely seems to be the case that if I can verify or confirm the statement "You have a pain," the verification or confirmation *is not different* from my verification of "Your body is in a certain physical state" (brain-state, behavioral manifestations), and therefore, if the verificationist is right, *they ought to mean the same.* Yet it seems quite clear that they do not; "You feel pain" is quite different from "Your body is in a certain physical state"; the one seems to be just as clearly *not* about your physical state as the other one *is.*

This entire issue is still in a state of controversy, and we shall leave it here.[7] If our discussion of it has accomplished nothing else, it has sharpened our awareness of the distinction between physical states and states of consciousness.

The reductive fallacy. States of consciousness, then, are closely correlated with neural processes in the brain, but they are not the same thing as these processes. When two things, A and B, always or almost always occur together, there is a great temptation to try to

[7] For a penetrating and challenging discussion of this issue (and its relation to many other issues in philosophy), see John Wisdom, *Other Minds* (Blackwell, 1952). To any reader who is able to grapple with the arguments, the essays contained in this book cannot be equaled for clarity, depth, and incisiveness. In addition, they convey a sense of "philosophical analysis in action" which it would be difficult to match anywhere in the literature of philosophy.

"reduce the one to the other"—to say that one of them is "nothing but" the other. To do this is to commit the reductive fallacy (or nothing-but fallacy).

"Thoughts are nothing but electro-chemical impulses through neural pathways to the brain." "Pain is nothing but (a certain kind of) stimulation of the nerve-endings." "Sounds are nothing but alternating condensations and rarefactions of air (or some other medium)." "Colors are nothing but wave-lengths of light." "Heat is nothing but the motion of molecules." Let us reflect for a moment on statements such as these.

When thoughts occur, neural processes are going on in the brain; indeed, it seems to be the case that thoughts never occur in the absence of neural processes; in other words, the neural brain-processes are a necessary condition for the occurrence of thoughts. But if A is a necessary condition for B, A and B are not one and the same thing; A could hardly be a necessary condition for itself. If B is causally dependent on A, then *ipso facto* there are two things, A and B. In general, it seems to be an empirical fact that mental life is utterly dependent on brain-activity. If certain parts of the brain are damaged or removed, certain aspects of conscious life never occur. But to say that consciousness is utterly dependent on brain-activity is a far cry from saying that consciousness *is* brain-activity. It may be, for example, that the occurrence of the sensation of pain is causally related to the stimulating of nerve-endings, but again this is not to say that it *is* this stimulation. You can know that you feel pain without knowing anything about your nerve-endings, or even that you have any. You do not need to study physiology to know that you feel pain, though you do in order to know the causal conditions of pain.

In the case of colors, there is not even a perfect correlation between the wave-lengths of light and the color-sensations we have. In general, we see red when the wave-lengths of light are between 550 and 700 Angstrom units. However, if you are blind, or have your eyes shut, or are color blind, you do not see red at all, even in the presence of light of this wave-length. And if you are having the hallucination of a red dragon, or seeing red spots before your eyes, or seeing red objects in your dreams, you are having the experience of red in the absence (at that moment at least) of light of the required wave-length. If there is any correlation between seeing red and some physical state, it is between the sensation and a certain specific brain-state (we do not yet know which)—the brain-state which normally (but not always, as we have seen) follows upon the stimulation of the retina of the eye by light of the required wavelength.

The physicist, of course, *defines* color-words in terms of wavelengths. This he has every right to do, since he has freedom of stipulation (see page 6). But this does not for a moment imply that the sensation of red does not exist. No definition can subtract a jot or a tittle from what exists (see pages 36–37). The physicist is merely ignoring the sensation; it is his business to study physical conditions, not sensations, so he defines "red" in terms of the physical conditions under which we normally see red. The wave-lengths, of course, are not what we see; red is what we see, and the physicist is giving us a useful bit of information when he tells us that we normally see it under such-and-such circumstances. What he is defining is not the word naming the sensation, but the word naming the conditions under which the sensation normally occurs. (The word naming the sensation may be verbally indefinable—see pages 59–62). We knew what the sensation was like, and people knew it for centuries, before we knew that it usually occurs under these specific physical conditions. Exactly the same analysis applies in the case of sounds.

The same analysis applies also if we use the concept of heat as our example. "Heat is the motion of molecules." If this means the sensation of heat, it most assuredly is not the motion of molecules; what *is* true is that, normally, when molecules are in more rapid motion we have a more intense heat-sensation, and (up to a point, at any rate) the more the one increases the more the other increases. But this is not to say that the experience is the same thing as the motion.

Suppose now that someone says that heat is the degree of expansion of a column of mercury in a tube. Again, he can define "heat" in this way if he likes; but it legislates out of existence neither the motion of molecules nor the sensation of heat. Since we cannot examine molecules directly, we use the height of the mercury column as a *measure* of the rapidity of the motion of molecules; we do this because, for good empirical reasons, we believe that there is a close and reliable correlation between the rapidity of this molecular motion and the height of the mercury column. At very high temperatures we no longer use the mercury column as an indicator of molecular motion because (we believe) the correlation breaks down. In other words, no one, on reflection, would *identify* heat with the height of the mercury column; he would use the latter as an *indicator* of the former. *Both* of these, of course, are physical, and are distinct from the heat-sensation. Between the molecular motion and the sensation, and also between the mercury column and the sensation, the correlation is far less reliable: for example, if you have a fever you may feel boiling hot in a room even though the thermometer registers less than 60° F.

Which is *the real meaning* of "heat"? What is heat itself? The foolishness of such questions should be apparent after our study of Chapter 1. The word "heat," like any other word, has no more meaning than its users have given it; and the meaning which is first chronologically is the sense in which "heat" stands for a certain kind of sensation familiar to all of us; this is still the sense we use most in daily life, the one we use before we know anything about thermometers or molecular motions. The sense in which "heat" means molecular motion arose only after the rise of modern science in the seventeenth century. Neither is "the real" meaning; both are legitimate meanings, harmless enough as long as we do not try to use the word to deny the existence of any phenomenon in the world. This is precisely what happens in the case of the reductive fallacy, particularly with people who know a little about physics and nothing whatever about semantics: "Heat just *is* molecular motion; that's all there is, there is nothing more to it." As if people could not talk meaningfully about heat for centuries before anyone had ever heard of molecules! No one denies that there are such things as molecules; no one denies (or should deny) that there are such things as heat-sensations. *Both* these things exist, and it appears that there is a causal relation between them. No amount of defining can put either of these phenomena out of existence.

The fallacy, however, in our century at least, is as widespread as it is simple. It shows up again in the view known as *materialism.*

Materialism. The word "materialism" is often used to stand for the view that everything is material, and that there is nothing mental at all: "All matter, no mind." Here again the familiar question arises: what exactly does this mean?

1. If "mind" is defined in metaphysical terms, as something more than the totality of mental events, or as some substance in which mental events inhere, then every anti-metaphysical philosopher would be inclined to agree that there is no such thing, or even to declare that the word "mind" in this sense is cognitively meaningless. Still, most such persons would not call themselves materialists, for they would still believe in mental events. Let us turn, then, to another meaning.

2. One could mean that there really are no mental events: no thoughts, no sensations, no emotions—no states of consciousness at all. But this view is so preposterous that it is difficult to believe that anyone could ever have held it. Imagine a person who thinks that there are no thoughts: does he not think that his view is true? But then there is at least one thought after all, namely the thought that this view is true. If this is what is meant by "materialism," materialism is self-refuting.

3. A more likely meaning, then, is this: thoughts, sensations, and so forth, do occur, but they are physical in nature, not mental at all. Here, of course, everything depends on how broadly one is going to use the word "physical": if he uses it so broadly as to cover every phenomenon, no matter what it is like, then he has won an easy but empty triumph in concluding that everything is physical— like that of a person who says that everything is blue in color, using the word "blue" so broadly as to cover not only what we now call "blue" but also what we now call "red," "green," "white," and so on. The relevant question, then, is this: Are there not some events that are different enough from events which we ordinarily call "physical" to deserve another name? Is it not true that some events and processes, such as thoughts, are not publicly observable, not locatable in space? And do we not have these characteristics (perhaps among others) in mind when we call something "physical"? But if this is so, it is mere verbal obstinacy for us to keep calling them "physical" even though they do not possess the distinguishing characteristics by virtue of which we now call something "physical." To call these things physical would be just as misleading as to call a person a humorist if he tells one joke every twenty years.

In common parlance, however, the word "materialism" is not used to name the view that denies the mental in any of these senses. It is used to name either the view that mental life is *dependent upon* physical conditions and would not exist without it—this will be discussed further when we take up the theories of mind-matter relationship—or, more popularly still, the view that human beings either *are* or *should be* exclusively interested in material things, such as money or possessions; this in the one case is a psychological doctrine and in the other case an ethical one, and in either case is not relevant here.

Behaviorism. Behaviorism in psychology is often thought of as the twin or counterpart of materialism. As a rule, however, those who call themselves behaviorists do not wish to deny the mental in any of the three senses listed on the preceding page. (If they do, the same remarks made in connection with materialism will apply here.) Rather, the word "behaviorism" generally names a kind of *method* employed in psychology, a method characterized chiefly by the refusal to use introspection of one's own mental states as material for arriving at laws in psychology. Its chief data consist of overt and publicly observable behavior, introspection and even introspective reports being considered too misleading and insecure to constitute data of the required scientific exactness. With behaviorism as a method of procedure in psychology, of course, we are not here concerned.

Even here, however, we should be on our guard not to define "behavior" so broadly as to include consciousness, lest the word lose all distinctive meaning; nor should we identify behavior with the consciousness that goes along with it.

Wherever there is consciousness there is behavior. Even in thinking, or in dreaming, we are reacting, though merely in slight, tentative ways, not visible to a spectator. Whatever we are conscious of (whether in perception or in conception, with our eyes open or in a brooding reverie) we are reacting *to*. The behaviorists have dragged to light these multitudinous, minute, incipient reactions, and shown us that all organisms, and especially the higher organisms, are incessantly performing these delicate reactive movements, and, in that way, keeping in touch, as it were, with their world. Since all definition is, at bottom, arbitrary, we might be content to call this incessant play of reactions, incipient and overt, the organism's consciousness of things, *except that we need the term "consciousness" for something else!*

When I look at a red flag, my head turns, my eyes focus themselves at the proper distance, certain tensions and inhibitions are produced which I call "paying attention" to it, incipient reactions of various sorts are engendered, according to what the flag means to me, and what thoughts, or esthetic feelings, or purposes, or emotions it arouses. All this is grist for the behaviorist's mill. But *in addition* to all this, I have the sensation *red*. The behaviorist who is studying my reactions cannot find that sensation red anywhere in me. He may have a similar sensation himself if the flag is within his field of vision; but we are talking, not about his sensation of red, but about mine. The completest possible account of my bodily reactions leaves out of account what I *see*, my sense-data; and, likewise, what I *hear*, and so on. Nor can the behaviorist discover my feelings and emotions, my thoughts and dreams. He can guess at them, from studying my reactions; but the quality of my feeling eludes him. He may see me writhing, but he cannot feel my pain. He may see my smiles, measure my muscular tensions, count my heartbeats, discover what my glands are doing, but he cannot feel my happiness. That, and all the rest of my conscious experience, is private.[8]

The mental without the physical. It seems to be a matter of empirical fact that states of consciousness occur only when a multitude of physical conditions (having to do with brains, sense-organs, and nerves) are fulfilled, and that one person's state of consciousness does not affect that of any other person without the fulfilment of intervening physical conditions. But if this is so, it is a matter of empirical fact, not of logical necessity.

1. It is logically possible for a state of your consciousness to affect mine without physical intermediaries. Ordinarily I do not know what you are thinking about unless you tell me or express it in your face and gestures. But suppose that every hour I suddenly had an idea, the contents of which I would write on paper, and that you did the same every hour, and that on consulting each other later we found that our accounts corresponded exactly, and that this occurred even if we were thousands of miles apart. We might try to find some hitherto unsuspected intermediary in the physical world, some ray or some type of radiation perhaps, but if we found none, we might well (pending further investigation) arrive at the conclusion that there was a direct causal relation between one person's states of consciousness and another's. At any rate, whether anything like this ever occurs or not, there is nothing *logically* impossible about it.[9]

[8] Durant Drake, *Invitation to Philosophy* (Boston: Houghton Mifflin Company, 1933), pp. 329–330.
[9] This example would constitute one kind of "mental telepathy." Whether such things really occur is, of course, a matter for investigation by psycholo-

2. It is logically possible for the mind of a human being to occupy (literally, for one person's states of consciousness to be associated with) the body of, say, a dog. Indeed, it is logically possible for me (that is, my body) to change into a dog at this very moment, though of course it is empirically impossible, which is only to say that there are no empirically known conditions under which it ever happens. But even a small child can imagine it. It would be very strange for me to find myself suddenly possessing four paws, fur, and a long cold nose, yet retaining all the recollections of my state in a human body, especially when I tried to talk about it but found myself unable to utter anything except barks and growls; but there is nothing logically impossible about it. The universe of fairy tales in which creatures are transformed into other ones at the wave of a wand, or for that matter parts of Dante's *Inferno* and of *Here Comes Mr. Jordan,* is a logically possible universe which, fortunately or unfortunately, does not happen to be actual.

3. It is logically possible for states of consciousness to occur without a body of any kind. As far as we know empirically, disembodied minds do not exist. Yet is it not logically possible that you might awaken sometime, remember the experience of dying and many other memories of your life when you had a body, but be bodiless? Believers in personal immortality must hold something like this, for it is as certain as any empirical statement can be that the body disintegrates after death; belief in personal immortality is the belief that consciousness goes on in spite of the disintegration of the body. Whether this happens or not, it is *logically* possible.

Is the self the same as the mind? When I speak of myself, I usually mean to include both my mind and my body. There *are* times when only my body is meant: "I am six feet tall" means the same as "My body is six feet tall." If I said, "I am six feet tall but my body is not six feet tall," I would be guilty of a self-contradiction. When we are speaking of physical characteristics, it is the body (or some aspect of it) of which we are speaking.

But "I feel happy" is not the same as "My body (or some part of

---

gists. It may be worth pointing out that even in cases such as these psychologists would not have to talk in terms of mental events. They might well describe their work in this case as an attempt to investigate the relation between one bit of behavior (your writing some words on a piece of paper) and one bit of my behavior (my writing the same words on a piece of paper at the same time).

it) feels happy," and "I am thinking about Paris" is not the same as "My body is thinking about Paris." The latter assertion in each pair would generally be held to be not false but (cognitively) meaningless. Ordinarily we would not even say "My mind is thinking about Paris"; we would say "I am thinking about Paris." Whether we would mean the mind (even though we do not say it) is not clear in this example, but there is one kind of case in which the self is identified with the mind, namely in discussions of immortality: when we speculate about whether we live after the body dies, we are not speculating about the survival of the body, but about the survival of consciousness (what we have thus far called "the mind") after the body has "returned to dust."

Analysis of mind. Can we identify the mind simply with states of consciousness? It has sometimes been held that a substance-word like "gold" stands for something over and above the sum total of its qualities (see pages 208–211). Similarly, it has often been held that mind too is a substance, not a physical substance, of course, but a non-material something "holding together" the states of consciousness—sensations, emotions, thoughts, pains and pleasures—just as the physical substance, gold, is supposed to "hold together" all the qualities of gold. On the other hand, it has been held that your mind is nothing more or less than the sum total of your experiences: all your thoughts, pains, and sensations (as well as your dispositions to think, feel, and so on, a certain way).

> There are some philosophers who imagine we are every moment intimately conscious of what we call our *self;* that we feel its existence and its continuance in existence. . . . For my part, when I enter most intimately into what I call *myself* I always stumble on some particular perception or other, of heat or cold, light or shade, love or hatred, pain or pleasure. I never can catch *myself* at any time without a perception, and never can observe anything but the perception.[10]

Moreover, it would be added, any conception of the self as *more* than this introduces something logically impossible of verification, just as in the case of physical substance. The verificationist does not object to talking about a self, just as he does not object to talking about gold, but he would insist that statements about the self must not be thought to mean any more than empirical statements about mental states. "There is a mind over and above all these

[10] David Hume, *Treatise of Human Nature,* Bk. I, Pt. IV, Chapter 6.

states" should be amended to read "The mind is *composed,* or *constituted,* of these states." In other words, the word "mind" is simply a shorthand way of referring to all these states, but nothing more.

Whichever alternative is adopted, problems arise. If we take the substance-alternative, we can ask, What is this "something more" than the mental states we can introspect? It could never under any circumstances be observed, so what could "mind" or "mental substance" as opposed to all the mental phenomena even mean (exactly as in the case of physical substance)? There were similar difficulties encountered in discussing vitalism. The metaphysician, however, holds the view nevertheless.

On the other hand, if this view is rejected, the pressing question becomes, What then makes all your mental states *your* mental states rather than somebody else's? What unites a whole series of mental status into the *history of one self?* Aren't we left with a series of states not united together by the fact of belonging to one self?

The most usual answer to this question is that *memory* is the unifying factor. If you had no memory, even from one split-second to the next, it would not be a continuing entity, *you,* existing. There would be a body but no personal identity. Memory is what connects one momentary state with other, preceding, momentary states.

One may, however, object that this is insufficient: we can use the word "self" as we please, and refuse to apply it when memory ceases, but still, if Smith loses his memory completely, isn't he still Smith, whether he knows it or not? We still say he is *the same person* (metaphorically only do we say "He's a different person now," as we shake our heads over his amnesia). And by virtue of what is he the same person? The fact that Smith's body continues to exist and function; *bodily continuity* can be invoked as a criterion for the continuance of a self even if memory is absent.

As a rule we speak of the same person as continuing to exist when *either one* of these criteria is fulfilled. We speak of a person as surviving the loss of his memory as long as his body continues to exist. We even speak of a person surviving the loss of his body whenever we speak of life after death. We may not be sure whether this occurs, but we are sure that *if* it does, it is *the same person* that continues to exist *without a body* as long as there are memories of his state when associated with a body.

What would it mean to speak of a person who had survived the extinction of *both* body and memory? He no longer has a body, and he remembers nothing of his former state; but it is difficult to see what one could mean if he spoke of *the same person* continuing to exist. How would "the same person" be distinguished from "a different person" if both memory and bodily survival were absent?

The relation between mental states and physical states. Physical events and processes occur, and mental events and processes occur, regardless of how we may interpret substance-words about the physical and the mental. What, then, is the relation of these events and processes to each other? Do they affect each other, and if so, how? Here are perhaps the two principal and rival traditional theories on this question:

1. *Interactionism.* Interactionism begins as a simple "common-sense" view. What could be more obvious than that physical events cause mental events and that mental events in turn cause physical events? You receive a blow on the head (physical event) and you feel pain (mental event); light-waves impinge upon your retina (physical event) and you experience a visual sensation (mental event). Every time a physical stimulus causes something to register in consciousness, we have proof positive that physical events cause mental events. It is equally clear that mental events cause physical events: you feel frightened (mental event) and your heart beats faster (physical event); you decide to step outdoors (mental event) and you step outdoors (physical event). Every time a volition (act of will) results in your doing what you willed to do, we have proof positive that mental events cause physical events. In other words, mind and body *interact*. True, as far as we know body never acts on mind except by means of the brain, nor does mind affect body except through the intermediary of the brain. The brain, which itself is physical, is the connecting link between other physical states and mental states. Thus the interaction takes place only under very specialized conditions; but it does take place.

The chief defect that has traditionally been found with interactionism can be put as follows: How does the body affect the mind, or the mind the body? When we become aware of a light flashing, what happens? Most of the story is plain enough, even though its details are extremely complex: it is the old story of retina, optic nerve, brain. We can trace a continuous series of physical impulses.

But now what happens when we get to the brain? As long as we stay in the brain, there is no difficulty: what happens in the brain is extremely difficult to discover, of course, but this is a technical difficulty only. But what of the mental event which is supposed to occur *as a result* of a brain-event, say the last (or terminal) brain event before the mental event occurs? It cannot even be spatially located! How does the brain-state bring it about?

This difficulty is even more keenly felt when we consider a mental event (such as a volition) causing a physical event (such as a bodily movement). Nerve pathways are stimulated from the brain; but how do the brain-centers get stimulated by the volition? The volition, being a mental event, can hardly *touch* any physical particles in the brain to give them the appropriate stimulation; but how else can they be caused to move? "By the mental event," the interactionist says; but the critic who tries to visualize this state of affairs (volition, non-spatial, affecting a spatially locatable part of the brain) finds himself baffled. "Of course," the interactionist reminds him, "you can't visualize it because mental events are not spatial, not extended, hence not visualizable to begin with!" But the critic remains dissatisfied. He wants to know more of the *how* of this relation; how could a mind act upon a body to produce a physical event?

We turn, then, to another theory, *psycho-physical parallelism*.

2. *Parallelism*. Parallelists object to the interactionists' view that physical events *cause* mental events and vice versa. They contend that there is no *causal* relation between the two at all. It is as if mental and physical events occurred along two parallel tracks without ever touching each other. For every mental event that occurs there is a physical event corresponding to it, taking place in the brain;[11] but it is not true the other way round: there are many physical events that occur, such as ice breaking at the south pole, to which no events in anybody's consciousness correspond.

How can any hypothesis deny that physical stimuli have mental effects and vice versa? Is this not going flatly contrary to the most

---

[11] In the brain, not in the sense-organ, even in the case of sensations. For example, the eye may be open and an image may be on the retina, but if the optic nerve is atrophied, there will be no visual sensation. The sensation invariably occurs only when the brain-state (which itself is usually the result of a state of the sense-organ) occurs, not necessarily when a certain state of the sense-organ occurs.

obvious empirical facts that we experience thousands of times a day? No: parallelism is not denying any fact of experience; it does not deny the truth of a statement such as that the strong light caused you to get a headache; it only says that strictly speaking the relation is not a causal one, and that common-sense is using language loosely when it talks as if the relation were causal. What causes a physical event, according to parallelism, is always another physical event, and this in turn is caused by another physical event, and so on, the chain of physical events being unbroken. When physical events of a certain highly specific nature occur, however (namely, events in the cerebral cortex of a brain), then mental events occur as a kind of *running accompaniment* to them. But the physical does not *cause* the mental. Rather, there is a *one-to-one correlation* between them. Between certain physical states of the brain and mental events there is a one-to-one correlation, so that if a certain brain-state were repeated exactly, the corresponding mental event would be repeated exactly; and the physical brain event and its corresponding mental event always occur simultaneously.

What, then, according to parallelism, is the true account of what happens in the process of sensation? Light-waves impinge upon the retina (in the case of vision); an impulse is carried along the optic nerve to the brain. All this is physical. Does this not *cause* a mental event to occur? No. What is caused is always another physical event. In this case what is caused is a brain-event, which in turn causes another brain-event, and so on. But, along with these brain-events, events in consciousness (mental events) now occur, and invariably occur; but they are not *caused* by them.

Neither does a mental event ever cause a physical one. Suppose the visual sensation referred to in the preceding paragraph is one of seeing the words in a recipe book, "Add a pinch of cinnamon"; don't you then *will* to walk over to the spice cabinet? and don't your legs move in that direction as a *result*, an *effect*, of your volition? Again the parallelist's answer is no. Your legs move—granted. What causes this motion is not a mental event at all but a series of brain-events (the last ones in the series described in the preceding paragraph), which in turn stimulate certain nerves ("efferent nerves") going all the way from the brain, through the spine, to the feet; these in turn affect the muscles, and you walk.

The entire series of causes and effects can be traced in the physical realm. For a complete causal account of what happened from the time of stimulation of the retina to the time of walking (perhaps just a fraction of a second) you can trace an unbroken series of causes and effects in the physical realm. A causal account need include nothing more. A complete description of what happened, of course, would include more; it would have to include the mental events, since of course parallelism does not deny that they occur. It is only their acting as causes and effects that is denied by parallelism.

According to parallelism, is not the mind in the position of a mere passive spectator of the physical, unable to *do* anything in the physical world? No, says the parallelist, not if the situation is properly understood. For suppose that the chain of physical events described in the previous paragraphs is labeled P-1, P-2, P-3, and so on. This chain of physical events is uninterrupted. Now, at a certain stage, namely when brain-events of a certain kind occur, mental events occur simultaneously with them. Suppose this starts at P-12. Then corresponding to P-12 we have M-12; corresponding to P-13 we have M-13, and so on. The relation between M-12 and P-12 is invariable: if P-12 were to occur again, M-12 would occur again simultaneously with it. (Probably this outright repetition would never occur, because memory-traces in the brain would make the second brain-state different, even if the external stimulus were exactly the same; and the consciousness of previous occurrences of the same kind of event—memory—would make the mental event different the second time.) Now let us assume that P-25 is the legs moving, or more precisely one event in that process; and that M-15 is the volition (act of will) and P-15 its corresponding brain-event, about which at present we really know nothing. Now P-15, a brain-event, *is* in the causal chain of events leading up to P-25, and without which P-25 would not have occurred. M-15 is not in this causal chain; P-15 is M-15's *representative,* as it were, in the causal order; it is only by means of P-15 that any effect is caused in the world. Nevertheless, *M-15 is essential to the process: P-25 would no more have occurred without M-15 than it would have occurred without P-15.* In other words, M-15 is just as much a *necessary condition* (and part of the sufficient condition) of P-25 as P-15 is.

No house was ever built, no book was ever written, without the occurrence of mental events. The parallelist does not deny this. He only insists that what did the actual *work* in the physical world was never the mental event itself but its representative in the physical realm, not M-15, but P-15.

If this is so, what is the difference between saying that M-15 is a necessary condition but *not* a cause, as the parallelist does, and saying, as the interactionist frankly does, that it *is* a cause, at least *one* causal factor in the occurrence of P-25? There does not seem to be any. If M-15 always occurs before P-25, and P-25 never occurs without M-15, then is not M-15 just as much a cause of P-25 as P-15 is? Is not the difference between parallelism and interactionism a difference of language—in other words, a *verbal* difference, the one applying the word "cause" in a situation where the other refuses to do so? Is not the whole issue, then, a *verbal* one? According to both views, a physical stimulus is part of a sufficient condition (and in most if not all cases, a necessary condition as well) of a mental effect; and according to both views, a mental event such as a volition is part of a sufficient condition (and in most cases at least, a necessary condition as well) of a physical effect, or series of physical effects such as building a house. The interactionist calls this a *causal* relation, as indeed we do in ordinary life. Is not the parallelist then merely being stubborn in refusing to call the relation a causal one, while accepting the same empirical facts about constant conjunctions in the matter? Why *not* call the relation causal, seeing that there is constant conjunction between physical causes and mental effects, as well as between mental causes and physical effects? Is this anything more than terminological obstinacy on the part of the parallelist?

Surely the parallelist would have to agree that if constant conjunction (sufficient condition or necessary condition or both) is all that is intended by "cause," then the relation is a causal one. But he is aware (or at least "has the idea in the back of his mind") that in ordinary life, at any rate, the notion of causing has to do with *a particular kind* of constant conjunction in which one body *acts upon* another ("all causation by contact"), such as in the example of the billiard balls. This is, as we saw on pages 239–241, the most familiar kind of causality in daily life: not only is there a constant conjunction between the first ball striking the second and the second moving, but the motion is brought about by direct impact. Doubtless the parallelist's disinclination to use the word "cause" in speaking of the mind-brain relationship results from the difficulties he sees the interactionist getting into when the latter tries to show *how* consciousness acts upon brain or brain upon consciousness.[12] Mind and body (or that part of body which is the brain) are not like two bodies. How can mind states of consciousness act upon matter the way one bit of matter acts upon another bit of matter? Does not acting upon involve *touching*, and is it not nonsense to say that a non-spatial mind can *touch* matter at any point, in the brain or elsewhere? Thus, if saying that A causes B carries with it any implication at all of A acting upon B, the parallelist, seeing that the mental cannot literally act upon the physical, will shy away from the use of the word "cause" in referring to the relationship. Moreover, he will add, if the interactionistic doctrine *is* committed to that, it is plainly false.

How then is the relationship between them to be conceived? We may refer again (see pages 239–241) to instances of causal operation without contact. A magnet causes iron filings to move in a certain way, though there is no contact of particles. Heat and light from the sun reach the earth, even in the absence of contact of particles. Again, one may invoke the ether in order to rescue the principle that all causation is by contact; but this of course assumes the very point at issue, in addition to using the word "particles" in a metaphorical way. And again we may refer to gravitation, which operates over thousands and millions of light-years; here is one of the most pervasive causal agents known to man, and it operates without contact. True, none of these events are mental, but at any rate there is ample evidence of causation without contact of particles of matter. There seems to be no reason, then, why the same should not be true of the relation between the mental and the physical.[13]

This, then, is the situation: If the parallelist in denying a causal relation between mind and matter is merely denying that mind can touch (or make physical contact) with matter at any place, and vice versa, then his contention is undoubtedly true, and the view of any interactionist who contests this contention is false. On the other hand, if the interactionist in asserting a causal relation is merely

[12] For a systematic exposition of this point, see G. S. Fullerton, *A System of Metaphysics*, Chapter 17.
[13] For a more closely reasoned suggestion of the possibility of this, see C. D. Broad, *The Mind and Its Place in Nature*. Chapter 3.

asserting constant conjunctions between mental states and physical states, his contention is also undoubtedly true, and the view of any parallelist who denies such constant conjunctions is false. There is constant conjunction, but no contact. Once it is agreed that (1) there is constant conjunction and that (2) there is no contact, no literal acting-upon, there is no difference left (other than a verbal one in the use of the word "cause") between the interactionist and the parallelist.

Before turning to the remaining theories, let us pause over one question: Even now, with the interactionism-parallelism issue resolved, has the relation between the physical and the mental been *explained?* Isn't it simply left "hanging in the air," with nothing to account for it? If we are troubled by this, let us stop once again to review the concept of explanation (see pages 189–190). An event is explained when it has been subsumed under a law (or set of laws), and a law, or uniformity of nature, is explained when it has been shown to be a consequence of some other (more basic) law, or uniformity of nature. When we explain, we explain in terms of something else, which is a more basic law than the first. But when we arrive at an ultimate, or "really basic," law of nature, we can do no further explaining (what would it mean to explain a basic law? what would we explain it by?); we can only assert the uniformity. The peculiarity of the mental-physical relations seems to be that the laws of these relations are all basic laws. We cannot say *why* this particular physical state should be invariably associated with this peculiar sensation (which we call "red") rather than with that one (which we call "yellow"); we know of nothing more ultimate than this in terms of which to explain it; we simply assert the uniformity.[14]

Let us now turn briefly to the other theories concerning the relation of physical states to states of consciousness.

3. *Epiphenomenalism.* According to this view, the mind is nothing but an *epiphenomenon* of the body. Its relation to the body is like that of the smoke to the locomotive from which it issues, or like that of a person's shadow to the person himself. The motions of the person cause the motions of his shadow, but the motions of the

[14] In this connection read John Stuart Mill, *A System of Logic,* Book 3, Chapter 14, Section 2. In his opinion, all laws stating correlations between physical states and states of consciousness are basic laws.

shadow do not in turn cause the motion of the person. Similarly, the physical causes the mental but the mental never in turn causes the physical. It is strictly a one-way causal relationship.

The great disadvantage of this view, once we get the interesting bits of picture-thinking (see pages 73–74) out of it, is that it combines whatever difficulties can be found in both the previous views. Whatever reason can be found for saying that the physical causes the mental (physical cause and mental effect) will *also* hold good for saying that the mental causes the physical, as in volitions causing bodily movements. And whatever reasons can be found *against* saying that the mental causes the physical, as the parallelist does if he interprets causation as implying contact, can *also* be found against saying that the physical causes the mental, such as "How do motions in particles of matter bring forth mental events?" Thus, caught between the two other views (which do remain two different views if the interactionist means to imply contact, as he traditionally does), epiphenomenalism tends to drop out of the picture.

4. *The double aspect theory.* According to this view, mental and physical events are merely two aspects or manifestations of one and the same "underlying" *substance.* The substance itself is generally conceived to be unknowable by human beings, but two of its aspects, the mental and the physical, are known to us. (This was the view of Spinoza, 1632–1677.)

The usual objection to this view rests on its metaphysical nature, and will not appeal to metaphysical philosophers: that in its attempt to weld the mental and physical more closely together—to "put them under the same roof," to use one metaphor, or to "make them two different sides of the same coin," to use another—it creates more of a mystery than the one it set out to resolve. For if the substance of which the mind and the body are both aspects or manifestations is unknowable to us, how can we know that it exists, and in any case how can its presence constitute an explanation of the relationship to be explained? One can speak of a person's figure being reflected in two mirrors, one on each side of a corridor down which he is walking (the one mirror corresponding to the physical, the other to the mental), but this is mere picture-thinking unless one first gives an account of *what* exactly it is that is being reflected in these two mirrors. Better indeed, some would say, to call the conjunction of the mental and the physical one of the ultimate laws of nature, than to create a substance and make it not only ultimate but unknowable as well!

5. *The identity theory.* According to this view, mental events *are* physical events; they are two words for the same thing. A sensation is nothing but a physical event in the brain. A thought is another physical event, or physical process, in the brain. The contention here is not merely that sensations and thoughts are correlated with physical events or processes in the brain, but that they literally *are* these processes.

How does it come about that we have two names for the same thing? We systematically use one word for the mental phenomenon —be it a thought, a feeling, or a sensation, and another word for what we have thus far called its physical correlate, such as some kind of stimulation of neural pathways in the brain. Why this systematic doubleness (one might even say duplicity) of language, if what is being talked about is "really the same thing" in both cases?

This depends (so the answer runs) on whether we see the event "from the inside" or "from the outside." We see it from the inside when we are experiencing it in ourselves, for example, thinking a thought; we see it from the outside when we examine somebody's brain while he is thinking, or for that matter our own (if we could, perhaps by means of a set of mirrors). Now, what do these phrases "from the inside" and "from the outside" literally mean? Inside the brain? Moreover, if we get two different "views" as a result of seeing it in these two ways, perhaps it is not two different *things* we are viewing, but at least there are *two different views* which cannot be identified with each other, and we are back with the double-aspect theory. Once there, we again must ask, clearly though perhaps ungrammatically, "What is it that the two different views are views *of?*"

The identity theory appeals to the impulse to "reduce everything to one thing," in this case to make everything physical after all. There is a certain esthetic neatness and tidiness in this, though what this has to do with the truth of the theory is difficult to see. But once we have overcome the fascination exerted by a monistic account of things, there are very powerful objections which can be brought against this theory. Are there not mental events and physical events, distinguishable by the criteria that we mentioned earlier? How does the identity view propose to dispose of these distinctions? Indeed, can we not know a good deal about our mental life but little or nothing about our corresponding brain-states? and if we can know about A but not about B, must not A and B be distinct entities, however regularly they may occur together?

The champion of the identity view may say that sometimes we talk about two things only to discover later that they are one and the same thing. The ancients talked about the Morning Star and the Evening Star, thinking that they were two different objects; they did not know that the two stars were the same object, namely the planet Venus. An explorer in the wilds of Africa may approach a mountain from the north and give it one name; another explorer may approach the same mountain from the south and give it another name, and the two explorers may think that there are two different mountains until by comparing notes more carefully they come to realize that it was the same mountain that they were talking about, employing two names for it.

The most usual objection to this contention is that this is all very well for the morning star and the mountain, but that this hardly proves that the same consideration holds for the relationship between mind and matter. How can your thought about Paris and a certain complicated brain-state inside your head be literally *the same thing*, since the one has characteristics which the other has not?

However completely the behavior of an external body answers to the behavioristic tests for intelligence, it always remains a perfectly sensible question to ask: "Has it really got a mind, or is it merely an automaton?" It is quite true that we have no available means of answering such questions conclusively. It is also true that, the more nearly a body answers to the behavioristic tests for intelligence, the harder it is for us in practice to contemplate the possibility of its having no mind. Still, the question "Has it a mind?" is never silly in the sense that it is meaningless. At worst it is silly only in the sense that it does not generally express a real doubt, and that we have no means of answering it. It may be like asking whether the moon may not be made of green cheese; but it is not like asking whether a rich man may have no wealth. . . .

Let us suppose, for the sake of argument, that whenever it is true to say that I have a sensation of a red patch it is also true to say that a molecular movement of a certain specific kind is going on in a certain part of my brain. There is one sense in which it is plainly nonsensical to attempt to reduce the one to the other. There is a something which has the characteristic of being my awareness of a red patch. There is a something which has the characteristic of being a molecular movement. It should surely be obvious even to the most "advanced thinker" who ever worked in a psychological laboratory that, whether these "somethings" be the same or different, there are two different *characteristics*. The alternative is that the two phrases are just two names for a single characteristic, as are the two words "rich" and "wealthy"; and it is surely obvious that they are not. If this be not evident at first sight, it is very easy to make it so by the following considerations. There are some questions which can be raised about the characteristic of being a molecular movement, which it is nonsensical to raise about the characteristic of being an awareness of a red patch; and conversely. About a molecular movement it is perfectly reasonable to raise the question: "Is it swift or slow, straight or circular, and so on?" About the awareness of a red patch it is nonsensical to ask whether it is a swift or a slow awareness, a straight or a circular awareness, and so on. Conversely, it is reasonable to ask about an awareness of a red patch whether it is a clear or a confused awareness; but it is nonsense to ask of a molecular movement whether it is a clear or a confused movement. Thus the attempt to argue that "being a sensation of so and so" and "being a bit of bodily behavior of such and such a kind" are just two names for the same characteristic is evidently hopeless.[15]

III. DEITY

Having considered the concepts of life and mind, we now turn to that of Deity, or God. The transition is a natural one, for God is usually conceived to be a mind, but a mind unaccompanied by a body; moreover, God is conceived as a limitless, or infinite, mind—infinite in power, infinite in goodness, and so on. Let us consider, then, what philosophy has to say about the concept of Deity: what kinds of belief in a Deity are possible, which of them if any is justified, and what arguments have been advanced on this subject.

Studying the concept of Deity is not the same as studying religion. (1) Religion covers much more ground in one way: religion is a many-sided phenomenon including matters such as prayer, ritual, and ecclesiastical organization. (2) In another way religion *may* cover less ground: there are religions which make little or no use of the concept of Deity, and may even (implicitly or explicitly)

---

[15] C. D. Broad, *The Mind and Its Place in Nature* (New York: Harcourt, Brace & Co., Inc., 1925), pp. 614, 622–623.

deny the existence of a Deity. Of course, one may take the presence of belief in a Deity (or deities) as a defining characteristic of religion, and in that case it will be a tautology to say that all religions hold to belief in God: anything which did not would not then be called a religion regardless of what other characteristics it had, such as the kind of feeling among its adherents which ordinarily is called simply "religious feeling." But if Buddhism, for example, is to be called a religion, as it usually is, one must grant that there are religions that do not contain what many persons in the Western world would regard as the irreducible minimum (defining characteristic) of religion, namely belief in some kind of Deity, or God.

What kind of belief is belief in God? The word "God," of course, can be and has been used in as wide a diversity of ways as the word "religion." "Your God is whatever you value most highly in life," it is sometimes said; and if money is what some person values most highly, then money is that person's God. ("Therefore everybody believes in God," is the conclusion sometimes drawn from this—switching the meaning of "God" by a conscious or unconscious verbal sleight of hand to a more traditional meaning of the word.) It may be that such statements are not intended literally, but only "poetically"; in that case they may or may not be satisfying, but cognitively they are dangerous and misleading. If they are intended literally, they are only persuasive definitions (see pages 71–73) of "God"; and while there is nothing wrong with persuasive definitions as instruments of discourse, they can be highly misleading if one is not aware that that is what they are. For example, one might be convinced by such verbal chicanery that everybody believes in God in *another* sense (such as "supernatural being") from that being employed in the persuasive definition; and thus would be just as misleading as to define (usually without saying so) a physician as anyone who can cure all diseases, and then conclude from this that there are no physicians in the world.

Traditionally, and in common usage of the word, "God" has stood for a *supernatural being*—supernatural not in the literal sense of being *above* nature, which after all is metaphorical, but in the sense of being *other than* or *more than* nature ("outside" nature, though this again is metaphorical), and thus distinct from nature or the totality of natural objects and processes (including human minds) in the universe. The doctrine sometimes known as *pantheism* holds that God is not transcendent (does not transcend nature) but is merely *immanent* in nature; in other words, that God is no more than nature itself, so that the words "God" and "nature" are words for the same thing. When we investigate the concept of God in the coming pages, we shall not mean a God that is identical with nature, but something which is super-nature, or supernatural.

This, however, leaves plenty of room for a wide diversity of beliefs. We can believe in a God that is all-knowing (omniscient) and all-powerful (omnipotent), or one whose knowledge and power are limited. We can believe in a God that is loving, beneficent, and merciful, or one that is jealous, cruel, and tyrannical. We can believe in a God that is physical, larger and more powerful than we, and governing our destinies perhaps, but still possessing a physical body and presumably bodily organs (primitive religions sometimes possess this kind of belief), or in a God who, while having complete control over the physical order, is in no sense physical. We can believe in a God who is much concerned with the affairs of the world, such as the Christian God, or is quite indifferent to its welfare, like the gods of the ancient Epicureans or the God of Aristotle. For that matter, we can believe in one God (monotheism) or in many gods (polytheism). Finally, we can believe that there is no God (atheism) or that we are not entitled on the basis of evidence to hold either to belief in God or to disbelief in God (agnosticism).

Which of this vast variety of possible beliefs is the true one? Or, if we cannot know any of them to be true, which is the most probable on the basis of the available evidence?

A number of arguments have been advanced, most of them many centuries old, to establish, or at least to render more probable, the existence of God. Most of them have been devised to establish the Christian God or a God similar to this—one conceived as omniscient, omnipotent, and benevolent. But not all the arguments specifically require such a God: in the case of the causal argument, for example, any divine Cause is sufficient, be it a personality or not, good or bad, concerned with the world or indifferent to it. Let us, then, briefly examine some of the principal arguments which have been advanced to show that a God exists, as well as some of the principal objections to these arguments.

A. The Ontological Argument

The ontological argument (from the Greek "ontos," *being*), though it has not carried much popular appeal since the Middle Ages, should be stated because it is the only argument which attempts to establish the existence of God entirely *a priori*. The argument proceeds as follows: We have the idea of a completely perfect Being. Now, *existence* is necessary to complete perfection; anything that did not exist would be less perfect than if it did exist. And since God is completely perfect, He must exist; if He did not, He would lack complete perfection.

Two main criticisms have usually been made of this argument:

1. Even granting (which many persons would not) that we really do have an idea of a completely perfect Being (the phrase "infinitely perfect" has not been added here because it would raise more difficulties still) the idea of existence *adds nothing* to the concept of a thing. If I first imagine a horse and then imagine the horse *as existing, what* I imagine is no different in the two cases—if it were different, if something were added in the second case, then I would not be imagining as existing *the same thing* that I had previously imagined.[16] The notion of existence adds nothing to the concept of the thing. Indeed, it is not a part of the concept of the thing at all; rather, to say that something exists is to assert a relation *between* the concept and the world. But if existence is no part of the concept, we cannot use the ontological argument, which tries to extract the notion of existence from the very concept of God.

This is sometimes expressed by saying that "existence is not a predicate" or "existence is not a property," in the way squareness,

---

[16] This point was expressed more precisely, but more technically, by Kant: "By whatever and by however many predicates we may think a thing . . . we do not make the least addition to the thing when we further declare that this thing *is*. Otherwise, it would not be exactly the same thing that exists, but something more than we had thought in the concept; and we could not, therefore, say that the exact object of my concept exists. If we think in a thing every feature of reality except one, the missing reality is not added by my saying that the defective thing exists. On the contrary, it exists with the same defect with which I have thought it, since otherwise what exists would be something different from what I thought. When, therefore, I think a being as the supreme reality, without any defect, the question still remains whether it exists or not." Immanuel Kant, *Critique of Pure Reason*, Norman Kemp Smith translation, pp. 505–6.

redness, and the like, are properties. The difference between statements about existence and statements about the properties of a thing can be shown as follows: "Horses are herbivorous" means "If there is (exists) anything that is a horse, then it is herbivorous." On this analysis, "Horses exist" would become "If there is (exists) anything that is a horse, then it exists," which is a flat tautology and is obviously not what the statement means at all. Moreover, "Horses do not exist" would become "If horses exist, then horses do not exist," which is an outright self-contradiction, whereas the original statement is merely false. Thus, beneath the grammatical similarity of the two statements lies concealed a great difference in type, and the two must be analyzed quite differently. The same applies, of course, to the difference between "God is benevolent" and "God exists." The details of the analysis are too technical to concern us here; it is sufficient to grasp the point that existence, unlike benevolence, power, and so on, is no part of the concept of the Deity, and is not a property of the Deity as the others are.

2. Let us assume that existence *is* included in the concept of perfection; even so it does not follow that the perfect thing we imagine actually exists. At most it shows only that in order for us to imagine it as really perfect, we must in so doing imagine it as existing. Having one horn is a necessary condition of being (i.e., is a defining condition of) a unicorn; but this does not prove that any unicorns exist. *A priori* we cannot say what does or does not exist. We can have a word and define it ever so precisely, but this goes no distance at all toward showing that there is in the world anything that corresponds to this word (see pages 36–37).

If the argument were valid, we could prove the existence of a perfect island in the same manner. "I imagine a perfect island," we could argue; "now you see it is *really perfect,* and it wouldn't be really perfect unless it existed. If it didn't exist it would be less perfect than if it did; existence, you see, is a necessary condition of perfection. Hence this perfect island must exist." And so on for a perfect automobile, a perfect razor-blade, a perfect system of taxation, and the like.

B. The Causal Argument

The argument for the existence of God which most often occurs to people is the causal argument, sometimes called the *cosmological* argument, or the argument from *origins*. Look around you at the universe, says the argument in effect—the millions of stars and nebulae, the vast panoply of living things, the whole panorama of human life. It must have come from somewhere. Some great Cause must have produced all this. And what could this Cause be but God? Belief in God, then, is required to account for the very existence of anything at all.

Are there any objections which can be given to this argument, which carries such a strong appeal?

1. A preliminary caution about the argument: If it establishes the existence of a Deity, it establishes nothing whatever about the Deity's characteristics except the characteristic of being the Cause of the universe. It enables us to say nothing about whether God is good or evil, whether God is concerned with the problems of human life or indifferent to them, or whether the God of any particular religion is the true one, or indeed whether there is one God or many gods (the divine power could conceivably be a *collective* power). The argument cannot be used to establish any particular kind of Deity.

2. The most usual objection to the argument is that it leads to an *infinite regress;* the question it answers in terms of God can be asked of God in turn. If everything has a cause, including the universe, and God caused the universe, then what caused God? What is to prevent us from asking about God the same question we asked about the universe?

But if this is so (so runs the criticism), what have we gained by postulating God as Cause-of-universe to begin with? Haven't we now two mysteries on our hands instead of one: the universe, and the Deity that we allege to cause it? What have we gained by our procedure?

> How therefore shall we satisfy ourselves concerning the cause of that Being, whom you suppose the Author of Nature, or . . . the ideal world, into which you trace the material? Have we not the same reason to trace that ideal world into another ideal world, or new intelligent principle? But if we stop, and go no farther, why go so far? Why not stop at the material world? How can we satisfy ourselves without going on *in infinitum?* And after all, what satisfaction is there in that infinite progression? Let us remember the story of the Indian philosopher and his elephant. It was never more applicable than to the present subject. If the material world rests upon a similar ideal world, this ideal world must rest upon some other; and so on, without end. It were better, therefore, never to look beyond the present material

world. By supposing it to contain the principle of its order within itself, we really assert it to be God; and the sooner we arrive at that Divine Being, so much the better. When you go one step beyond the mundane system, you only excite an inquisitive humor, which it is impossible ever to satisfy.[17]

3. The causal argument is usually presented as an empirical argument, an argument from experience. How do we know that everything has a cause? From experience, seems an innocent enough answer. However, we have already seen considerable reason (in Chapter 4) to object to this. Perhaps it is a synthetic *a priori* statement, as some claim, though this interpretation has difficulties shared by all claims to a synthetic *a priori;* or perhaps it is just an assumption, in which case we can hardly speak of *evidence* that it is true; or perhaps it is a procedural rule, in which case it is not a statement at all, and thus neither true nor false.

But even supposing that the Causal Principle is an empirical statement, which holds true of all events, past, present, and future, we must still ask how it is that we know this. The most that experience could tell us would be that all the events we have observed in the empirical world have causes. Experience tells us nothing about causality in any non-empirical realm. To extend the principle is to desert the ground of experience entirely. Indeed, one might well go further and ask what meaning it has outside the realm of observable constant conjunctions.

> The principle of causality has no meaning and no criterion for its application save only in the sensible world. But in the cosmological proof it is precisely in order to enable us to advance beyond the sensible world that it is employed.[18]

Volition as ultimate cause. In the minds of many persons lingers the idea that somehow volitions (acts of will) have a peculiar and ultimate place in the sphere of causation. We do not see sticks and stones coming together of themselves to form mechanical objects; we contrive them, we *plan* them, then *will* to arrange the matter of which they are to be composed into certain arrangements or structures so that the mechanical object will be formed. How else, indeed,

[17] David Hume, *Dialogues concerning Natural Religion*, Part IV. (Pp. 714–715 in E. A. Burtt's *English Philosophers from Bacon to Mill.*)

[18] Immanuel Kant, *Critique of Pure Reason* (Edinburgh: Nelson & Sons, 1935), Norman Kemp Smith translation, p. 511.

could the universe have come into existence except as a result of God's will?

The whole conception of the universe as the product of a *plan* or *design* will be discussed under the heading of the teleological argument. But it may be worth-while to stop for a moment over the question, To what extent does experience entitle us to say that volition is a more ultimate cause of things than are physical events and processes in the universe? (1) Many movements of matter, such as arranging pieces of wood into a house, are indeed the result of will, and without volition they would never occur. (2) But in no case are we entitled to say that the will *creates*, or brings into being, the matter; it merely changes the position of particles of matter which already exist. (3) Neither does volition create force or energy. The will does originate motion, for example when a bodily movement follows upon an act of will; [19] but it does so only by means of innumerable brain-events, in which one form of energy is converted into another (energy of motion); energy itself the will does not create. Far from creating energy, the behavior of the brain-particles (which must occur if consciousness is to occur at all) is itself an instance of the law of Conservation of Energy, and presupposes it. In all cases of which we have had experience, energy is prior to volition and not the other way around; volition (or its bodily concomitant, depending on one's theory of mind) is just one of thousands of manifestations of energy. So volition is hardly in a position, in an empirical argument, to be an Ultimate Cause. (4) It seems quite certain that volition did not come into being for countless ages—during all of which the law of Conservation of Energy was nevertheless in operation—until during the long evolutionary process it finally arose. Matter and energy are, so far as we know, eternal; volitions are not, for we can trace their beginning in time.

The idea of a first cause. "But surely the universe must have had a cause. It didn't just come into existence of itself!" "Now suppose we say that God caused it; remember that now we can keep asking the same question—what caused God? You may be satisfied that when you have reached God you have come to a *stop*, and indeed your own *mind* may have come to a stop at this point. But the answer is no more satisfactory in the one case than in the other: in

[19] See, however, the interactionism-parallelism dispute in the preceding section.

both cases you can ask, 'And what caused *that?'* " [20] Are we to be
left with such an impasse?

The idea of a First Cause, in the sense of First Event, has always
been troublesome. May we not ask, What existed *before* the First
Event? Nothing? Not even space and time? How did a First Event
come into existence? "Of itself?" But does it not make sense of *any*
event to ask what preceded it, and how it was brought about? Did
it just pop into existence, and before it—a blank? These problems
are the same whether the First Event is thought of as a volition of
God or as something else.

Alternatives. It would seem that no matter how far back, we can
always (like the child being told a bedtime story perpetually asking, "What happened *then?*") ask, "What happened before *that?*"
Astronomers trace the history of the earth back for about 2,000,-
000,000 years to its common origin with the sun and the other
planets of our solar system. But before that? The sun along with
millions of other stars condensed from the huge nebulous mass
which is now our galactic system, or galaxy; thousands of other
galaxies, or star-cities, can be seen through powerful telescopes,
often many millions of light-years away. And before that? We do
not know—in the same way that we do not know who walked in
this sand a year ago: the traces are just too faint. There *are* traces,
which have led to different empirical hypotheses on this matter,[21]
but the evidence is not yet sufficient to enable us to decide among
them even with reasonable probability. But none of them involves
the concept of a First Cause, for, at least in the opinion of some,

> To ask how matter was generated from nothing, or to ask for a
> first cause, in the sense of a cause of the first event, or of the universe
> as a whole, is not a meaningful question. Explanation in terms of causes
> means pointing out a previous event that is connected with the later
> event in terms of general laws. If there were a first event, it could not
> have a cause, and it would not be meaningful to ask for an explanation.
> But there need not have been a first event; we can imagine that every
> event was preceded by an earlier event, and that time has no begin-

[20] It does not help, of course, to say, "God caused Himself." When God
caused Himself, did He already exist? If so, He did not need to cause Himself, for He already existed. But if He did not already exist, how could He
cause anything?

[21] See, for example, Fred Hoyle, *The Nature of the Universe;* Sir James
Jeans, *The Universe around Us.*

ning. The infinity of time, in both directions, offers no difficulties to
the understanding. We know that the series of numbers has no end,
that for every number there is a larger number. If we include the negative numbers, the number series has no beginning either; for every
number there is a smaller number. Infinite series without a beginning
and an end have been successfully treated in mathematics; there is
nothing paradoxical in them. To object that there must have been a
first event, a beginning of time, is the attitude of an untrained mind.
Logic does not tell us anything about the structure of time. Logic
offers the means of dealing with infinite series without a beginning as
well as with series that have a beginning. If scientific evidence is in
favor of an infinite time, coming from infinity and going to infinity,
logic has no objection.[22]

It is still possible, however, to hold this view and at the same
time to believe in God: not as a First Cause, but as a Being entirely
outside the infinite time-stream, as non-temporal as mathematical
entities such as numbers and circles. God (or gods) as conceived by
most worshipers is temporal—God does this, then does that; God
creates mankind, then repents the act; God looks down on human
beings and sometimes answers their prayers, and on occasion performs miracles. Such a God is temporal, He is actively in the midst
of the time-stream; even if it is asserted that He is everlasting, this
only means that He lasts an unusually long time—infinite time. But
the God we are now considering does not exist in time at all, not
even infinite time. He is not *everlasting*, but *timeless*. Such a God
does not have a history, since history is temporal; He cannot do
things, initiate events, and so on, for all these are in time; to say
that he did them would be to say, "At such-and-such a time God
did so-and-so," which would put Him squarely in the midst of the
time-stream. Such a God could not be conceived anthropomorphi-
cally; indeed it is difficult to see how He could be conceived at all,
and hence to know what we meant by the word "God" when we
used it. Nevertheless, theologians have sometimes conceived of God
(if this is a genuine concept) in this way. In regard to the causal
argument, in any event, the relation of God to the temporal universe is what constitutes the main problem: however a timeless God
(or any timeless entity) might be related to the temporal universe,
the relation could hardly be a *causal* one, for the causal relation is
a relation among temporal events.

[22] Hans Reichenbach, *The Rise of Scientific Philosophy* (Berkeley: University of California Press, 1951), pp. 207–208.

C. The Argument from Miracles

One of the most popular arguments for the existence of God has always been the occurrence of miracles. The argument runs as follows: Miracles have occurred at various times in human history. (There is much disagreement, however, as to just which events were miraculous and which were not.) And how could you account for a miracle in any other way than by saying that God intervened in the natural course of events (took nature into His own hands, so to speak), and made the miraculous event occur? The occurrence of miracles, then, proves that God exists.

1. The most usual way of attacking this argument has been to try to show that none of these happenings ever took place. It is pointed out, for example, that our accounts of such events usually come from primitive and credulous people—people with vivid imaginations who perhaps hope for and expect mysterious events, or those in whom the feelings of awe and wonder are pleasant, and who seldom have the impulse to check up on interesting stories. It is pointed out that it is more probable that certain people lied or were deluded (these things happen every day and are familiar to all of us) than that an event (such as water being turned into wine) ever actually occurred. It is pointed out, further, that miracles that have been affirmed by many have been denied by many more; the testimony of one group to the occurrence of a miraculous event is counterbalanced by the contradictory testimony of another group, to the effect that they did not occur but that quite other miracles (those of the religion of the second group) did occur.[23]

All of this, however, is a matter for empirical evidence to decide. The investigation of what did or did not occur in past history belongs in the hands of those who, like detectives, are trained in making probable inferences about past events from their present effects.

2. The first objection was simply, "Miracles have not occurred." The inference, "*If* they occurred, *then* God's existence would be established" was not questioned. It is this second, hypothetical statement which constitutes the second (and philosophically more

---

[23] For a famous discussion of this approach to the question, see David Hume's essay "On Miracles," in his *Enquiry concerning Human Understanding.*

interesting) criticism of the argument. Let us suppose that all the events labeled as miracles actually happened; what then? Assuming that these irregularities in the course of nature occurred,[24] do they constitute an argument for the existence of God? Suppose that at this moment a solid iron bar is thrown into water and it floats. Many persons see this happen, and the event is photographed. Is it a miracle? Clearly, the question involved here is "What is a miracle?" What must an event be like in order to be miraculous?

(1) Everyone would probably agree that a miracle must be an unusual event; something that happened all the time or even once a year would not be considered miraculous, unless we extended the word to include such uses as "the miracle of sound," "the miracle of the 1954 Chrysler," and so on. A miracle can hardly be just any unusual event. The earth passing through a comet would be an unusual event, but it would not be considered miraculous as long as it could be accounted for (as it could) by known laws of nature. Perhaps an object may drop from an airplane and in falling strike a telephone wire outside your window and sever the wire, and the segment of wire on its way to the ground may strike a passing cat and electrocute it. This is surely unusual—"it wouldn't happen again in a million times"—but it would not be considered miraculous, since everything that occurred in this unusual sequence of events is explainable by known laws.

(2) It would seem, then, that no event would be called a miracle as long as it is an instance of some known law or laws of nature. But is this enough? Suppose that an event occurred which could not be accounted for on the basis of any *known* laws of nature. Would it then be a miracle? Probably it would make us suspect that there were some laws of nature we did not yet know, or that some of those we were already familiar with had been inaccurately formulated and must be revised or qualified in such a way as to admit the new occurrence. When it was first noticed that photographic plates were exposed although they had been in complete darkness all the time, this could not be accounted for on the basis of any known law of nature; but men soon came to realize that there were other laws they had never suspected which did account for

---

[24] It is interesting to note what different grounds are given for belief in God. In at least one version of the teleological argument it is the orderliness of events that is taken to prove a Deity; but in the argument from miracles it is the non-orderly events that are taken as evidence for the same belief.

this curious phenomenon, and in so doing the science of radioactivity was founded. When comets' tails were found to be repelled by the sun, it was not assumed that the universal attractive power of matter stated in the Law of Gravitation had gone berserk; new laws were discovered which took care of cases like these.

(3) Under what conditions *would* an event be considered miraculous? We cannot now say "when it isn't an instance of any *known* law"; shall we say "when it isn't an instance of *any law at all,* known or unknown"? This would seem to be more satisfactory; at least it escapes the objection to the previous view. Of course, on this conception of a miracle, we could never definitely state that any event was miraculous. For how could we ever know that the event in question could never, even in millions of future years of scientific investigation, be explained on the basis of some law of nature, however complicated and elusive? We could not, and therefore we could never know an event to be miraculous. If the iron bar suddenly floated, we would indeed be surprised; but who knows after all exactly what complicated sets of circumstances may cause matter to behave as it does? We judge what is probable or improbable by the kind of behavior Nature has exhibited in the past; but, if we may use a metaphor, there may be a good many springs in Nature's depths which only occasionally, or under very special conditions, bubble up to the surface. The surprising behavior of the iron bar might turn out to have something to do with the moisture in the air, or some law of radioactivity not now known, or even the mental state of observers. Such things would be unexpected because they are not in accordance with the way Nature generally works (as far as our present knowledge goes), but they would certainly not be without precedent in the history of science. It was a surprise to learn that profuse bleeding could result from a mental condition and not from any of the physiological causes so earnestly sought for, or that a perpetual hand-tremor could result from a forgotten aggressive act committed in early childhood in which no physiological damage was done. Many persons are still suspicious of such phenomena because they feel that "Nature just doesn't work that way"; but we should have learned enough by now in the hard school of scientific experience to know that Nature "has a few tricks up her sleeve" that we never suspected, and which will

certainly seem strange as long as we judge "how Nature ought to behave" by laws which are already familiar to us.

The important point for us here is that, on this definition of "miracle," we could never be sure that any event, no matter how bizarre or unusual or contrary to the regular course of our experience, was a miracle; we could never know that the event could not be subsumed under some laws. However, let us *suppose* that we could be absolutely sure that some such event was *not an instance of any law at all, known or unknown.* Would this show that God must be invoked to account for it? The answer seems almost inevitable: of course it wouldn't; it would only prove that some events are not instances of laws. But to establish this and to establish God are, of course, two entirely different things.

(4) According to others, for example, John Stuart Mill (1806– 1873), an event cannot be considered a miracle no matter how strange it is, if it would occur again if the same set of conditions were repeated. (This comes to much the same thing as the preceding sense.) In order to constitute a miracle, an event must take place *without* having been preceded by a set of conditions which are sufficient to make it happen again. The test of a miracle is: Were there present conditions such that whenever these conditions reappear the event will recur? If there were, the event is no miracle. Once again, of course, we could never be sure that an event was a miracle in this sense—we could never know for sure that if the same conditions were to recur, the "miracle" would not recur; at best we could only know that when the conditions were the same *as far as we knew* (and taking into account only those conditions which we thought to be causally related to the event, we have to add this provision or else the conditions to be included might be extended to cover the entire state of the universe, which of course can never repeat itself), the allegedly miraculous event did not occur. But there might always be other conditions that never occurred to us to consider, which were yet causally relevant, and if added to the set of conditions to be repeated, the event *would* recur. Moreover, just as on the preceding definition of "miracle," even if somehow we *could* know that we had all the relevant conditions, and that they were all the same, but the event did not recur, what would this prove? Only indeterminism—that is, that two identical sets of conditions may yet be followed by non-identical events. This might be a surprise,

but would it force us to invoke God to account for it, any more than a completely deterministic state of affairs would do so? After all, one might ask, why shouldn't we be indeterministic rather than deterministic?

(5) There is still another meaning of the word "miracle," according to which a miracle would be *defined* as an intervention of God into the natural course of events. Now if it is asked whether a miracle in this sense would entail [25] the existence of God, the answer of course would be yes—an intervention of God would indeed entail the existence of a God that could intervene! But this definition, of course, begs the whole question. The question would now become, "*Are* there any miracles in this sense? *Is* there in fact anything to correspond to this definition?" *If* there are miracles in the sense we are now considering, then of course God exists, but to say this is only to utter a crass tautology; it is only to say, "If God intervenes, there is a God." But what would establish the statement that God intervenes? The existence of unusual events, as we have just seen, would not prove it.

Thus the argument from miracles encounters the following dilemma: if miracles are defined in any of the ways other than the last one, their occurrence could at best prove indeterminism, but not God; while if miracles are defined in the last way, they do require a God to cause them (indeed it is tautological to say so), but there is no way of showing that any event exists to correspond to the definition.

D. The Utility Argument

The argument which often goes by the name of "the utility argument" is strictly irrelevant to the present discussion, and is never, in fact, used in philosophical circles. But since it is an extremely popular one in the public mind, perhaps it should receive a brief mention here. The argument runs somewhat as follows: Belief in God is a great and indispensable moral influence. Without it, human beings would not live good lives. Therefore, it must be true. (The

---

[25] The word "entails" is being used here, as it usually is in philosophy, to mean "logically implies." A logically implies B when it is self-contradictory to assert A and deny B. But some implication is not of this sort. "X has just been bit by a cobra" implies (but not logically) "X will soon be dead"; but "X owns a dog" entails (logically implies) "X owns a mammal."

argument is not usually stated in this bald fashion, but its validity is often presupposed in popular reasoning.)

If this is intended as a serious argument, several obvious considerations present themselves:

1. Of which religious belief is the argument intended to establish the truth? All of them? But they contradict one another, and cannot all be true. If only one of them is established by the argument, why not the others?

2. Is it really the case that religion is indispensable to good conduct? To determine this, of course, we would have to conduct a detailed survey of the *mores* of all tribes and nations in order to know whether there were fewer murders, acts of deceit, and so on, and more kindness, fair play, and honesty (or whatever we had in mind in speaking of "good conduct"), when religious belief was present than when it was not. We would have to make sure whether all moral acts that were done in the *name* of religion were done *because* of religion; whether the effects of early religious training were the result of being religious rather than of merely being early; whether the influence of religion was more powerful in shaping a moral life than the influence of parental authority or public opinion, even when these were divorced from religion.[26] Such an investigation, however interesting, would hardly belong in philosophy; it would be a purely empirical investigation: in this case, whether religious belief was correlated with a marked increase in good conduct and a decrease in bad, independently of other possible influences, such as law and public opinion.

3. More relevant here, however, is the question: What does the utility argument prove? Let us assume for the moment that people live better lives if they possess religious beliefs and worse ones if they do not. Would this show that the beliefs were *true?* If people could be made to behave only if they believed in ghosts, would this make the belief in ghosts true? The moment this question is asked there seems little doubt about the answer. Beliefs are not rendered true or false by the fact that people want to believe them, or are persuaded to believe them, or need to believe them. Belief in Santa Claus or in "good luck just around the corner" does not make such beliefs true, however much they may buoy up one's spirits; and re-

---

[26] John Stuart Mill's essay "The Utility of Religion," in his volume *Three Essays on Religion.* is a classic study of this question.

fusal to believe in any unpleasant facts does not make them any less facts. You might, of course, have a "moral right" to hold to a belief, whether true or not, if highly desirable consequences resulted from believing it (this is a moral question), but saying that a belief is true and saying that you will be better off for believing it are, unfortunately, two different things. If a particular religious belief has a good moral influence, this does not prove it true, and if it has a bad moral influence, this does not prove it false; it is simply irrelevant either way.

Many persons, indeed, have been much concerned to disengage morality from any dependence on religion. They have felt that it is a dangerous thing for religion and morality to be closely intertwined in the public mind, the survival of morality being made dependent on the survival of religion; for in that case, if the religious belief should ever collapse, the morality which has been made dependent upon it may collapse with it.

E. The Argument from Religious Experience

The argument from religious experience is not always clearly stated, and it is more often not stated at all, but is held implicitly as a kind of unspoken proof that never reaches the stage of outright verbal presentation. This is approximately what it comes to: I (and other persons) have experiences of a peculiar nature, which are so profound, so meaningful, so valuable, that they cannot be explained on any natural hypothesis; they must then be due to the presence of a Supernatural Being, God, who inspires such experiences.

Let us first consider the expressions "God" and "religious experience." The word "God" *may* be used synonymously with "religious experience," simply as a label for the experience itself. There are those who would accept this meaning of the word "God"; and in this sense, of course, it is simply a tautology to say that religious experiences prove that God exists, for it is no more than saying that religious experiences prove that religious experiences exist. In this sense, it would be self-contradictory to say that God exists even when religious experiences do not, just as it would be self-contradictory to speak of a pain existing unfelt. For a pain to exist is simply for it to be felt, and for God to exist (in this sense) is simply for religious experiences to occur.

Most persons, however, would not attach this meaning to the word "God." They would not say that when they assert that God exists they are asserting merely that religious experiences exist. They would say, rather, that the experience is merely an *indicator* of something *beyond itself*, namely of a Being who exists just as objectively as the tree out there exists. The religious experience points to a Deity but it is not the same thing as a Deity.

What of the term "religious experience"? Why not simply define it as "an experience of God"? Thus defined, the occurrence of religious experiences would prove the existence of God, since by definition a religious experience *is* an experience of God. In this case again the existence of religious experiences proves that God exists; indeed it is a tautology to say so. But, as in cases we have already considered, it hardly establishes what people may want it to establish; it only shifts the question. The original question was, "Religious experiences exist; does God exist?" whereas the question now becomes, "On this definition of 'religious experience' (on which God must exist in order for the experience to be a *religious* experience), *are* there any religious experiences?" We cannot, after all, define anything into existence (see pages 36–37).

Usually when we talk about religious experiences we mean (and shall mean here) experiences (whose precise quality is hard to describe, partly because of lack of words for describing what it is like, partly because the quality of the experience itself varies so much from person to person) which cause those who have them to attribute them to a deity (or sometimes, to deities) and increase one's tendency to worship, adore, reverence, or fear the Deity allegedly revealed in the experience. Conceived in this way, religious experiences are, as the name implies, simply experiences of a certain special kind (admittedly difficult at times to mark off from other kinds), and the question then remains, Can we infer from the occurrence of these experiences that a deity or deities exist to cause these experiences?

Let us see what happens if the inference is granted. It seems that if the argument proves anything it proves far too much. There are multitudes of religious experiences, and if in one case we can infer from a religious experience to a deity of which it is the experience, we can do the same in another case. If the religious experience of A, a Christian, proves the existence of the Christian God, it would

seem that the religious experience of B, a Mohammedan, would
prove the existence of Allah, the Mohammedan God. People use the
argument from religious experience in support of their own religious
experiences, being unaware perhaps that the same argument, if admitted, would permit the same inference for the religious experiences
of persons embracing different religious faiths. If we admit one, we
must admit all.

Why not admit them all? Because, of course, they contradict each
other and cannot all be true. Each religion claims to be the only
true one, and it is logically impossible to have a number of religions
each of which is the only true one.

In order to ameliorate this situation, the following argument is
sometimes used: All religious experiences are of the same Being;
people disagree only in the way they describe the object of these
experiences, for this depends on their particular environment and
upbringing; they are at a loss for words and use language in loose,
misleading, and even contradictory ways when they talk about it.
The Deity experienced is the same in every case; only the historical,
"accidental" features are different. Purge the religions of their historical features, in which Mohammedianism and Christianity for
example do contradict each other, and take only the essence or kernel common to them both, and they do not contradict each other
because they are one.

This may seem an easy way out of the situation; but there are
several points that should be considered before it is adopted. (1) In
this process you have taken away the God of every *particular* religion. Christianity declares, for example, that God is revealed in
the Holy Scriptures, and manifested in Christ, and that any view
which denies this is false. Remove these beliefs and you do not have
"the essence of Christianity" left; you have something left that can
hardly be called Christianity at all, whatever else it may be. Purge
Christianity of its "historical features," and you have purged away
virtually all of Christianity. Some may consider this all to the good,
but let us not then say that we have "true Christianity" left when
we have done this. (2) Let us try to imagine such a Being as the
God who is supposed to possess only the features shared by all religions, and none of the peculiarities of any particular religion. Such
a God could not be loving (for the gods of some religions are not),
nor brutal (for the gods of some religions are not so), and so on,

such a God could hardly possess any characteristics whatever, so few are the characteristics which the deities of all, or even a small fraction, of the religions of the world possess in common. About all such a Deity would have left is power. Strictly speaking, he would not even possess unity, for many religions are polytheistic—but at the same time he could not be multiple either, for some religions are monotheistic. What kind of Deity would it be that is neither one nor more than one? (3) Neither could such a Deity be given "more character" through the *addition* of certain characteristics—he could not be the God of various specific religions "all rolled up into one," as has sometimes been suggested; for then he would be loving like the Christian God, vengeful like Yahweh, demanding human sacrifices like Baal, prohibiting it like the God of Christianity, and so on. These characteristics are logically incompatible with each other. Clearly *some* of these beliefs must be wrong; hence it would appear that religious experience alone cannot guarantee the truth of the God of any religion.

"But some religions must be excluded—the obviously barbaric ones, such as Baal-worship . . ." Where, in this case, are we to draw the line? What kinds of religious experiences are going to establish the God in question, and which are not? What is the criterion? More important still, how is this criterion to be justified and defended against others? If the occurrence of one religious experience really establishes the existence of the Deity believed in by this person, what is to exclude another from doing so? One may, indeed, employ some question-begging use of the term "religious experience," so that only the experiences of one religion or denomination are "truly religious," the others being "mere deceptions." But the opponent of one who argues thus can simply return the compliment. Logically there is nothing to choose between them. Each side can use its own persuasive definition (see pages 71–73) of the word "religious"; and there, perhaps, ends the argument and begins the fight.

It would seem, then, that having a certain kind of experience is not *by itself* a guarantee that an objective thing corresponding to that experience exists. Let us compare the present situation for a moment with a situation encountered in perception. Suppose a person were to argue, "Of course ghosts exist; how else could I have seen one last night?" One need not deny that the person had a *visual experience* of a certain kind, which led him to declare the existence of ghosts; but having the ghost-experience is perfectly compatible with having a hallucination. A traveler in the desert may "see" an oasis in the sense of having a visual experience which leads him to judge that there is an oasis not far off; but of course he can judge wrongly. The existence of the experiences is not denied—the persons in question are not deliberately deceiving others when they report thus, but what can be denied is that an objective ghost or oasis exists which is the object of these experiences. If the occurrence of these experiences were sufficient to insure the existence of the alleged objects of these experiences, we would have to say that every dream-object or hallucination which anyone ever experienced had an objective existence.

Religious experiences are, of course, very different from these ghost-experiences and oasis-experiences. They are far more intense, more deep-seated, more valuable, and they "mean more" to the experiencers. As far as the inference from experience to object is concerned, however, the same consideration applies: one cannot, merely on the basis of having the experience, admit any one of the alleged objects of the experience without admitting them all. The fact of religious experience alone cannot guarantee the truth of a religious belief. When we assert that something objective exists, the mere fact of having a (subjective) experience is not enough; there must be some *criteria of objectivity* for distinguishing what has objective existence (as opposed to existence merely as an experience, like the oasis in the hallucination) from what does not have objective existence.

In the case of perceiving physical objects, we do have such criteria; here we do bridge the gap between subjective and objective. Here we not only have experiences, we can tell by means of them (not always right away) whether or not there is a real oasis, a real unicorn, and so on. How do we do this? The criteria by means of which we distinguish cases of "truly perceiving" from "falsely perceiving" (veridical and non-veridical perception) will be discussed in Chapter 6. It must suffice here to note that there are such criteria and that in fact we use them every day of our lives. In most cases, at any rate, a hallucination does not deceive us very long; in general, we know how to distinguish a real oasis from an oasis-hallucination. A single experience does not suffice for this, but a number of them, of a certain variety and in a certain order, do.

Why can we not do this in the case of religious experiences? There is no reason in principle why we cannot; but in fact no set of criteria in this field has ever been set forth which enables us to distinguish veridical from non-veridical religious experiences. No matter what criteria have been suggested—such as number of people having the experiences, repetition of the experiences, intensity, duration, or some other—various conflicting religious views are admitted by these criteria. There is no means, at least not by the argument from religious experience alone, of admitting any one religious hypothesis while rejecting the rest.

In one sense of "see," when we say we see an oasis we are asserting no more than that we are having a certain kind of visual experience; but in another sense of "see," we are asserting in addition that a real physical oasis exists, and in this second sense, having the visual experience does not ensure that the oasis exists. When we say that we experience God, in one sense of "experience" we are asserting only that we are having a certain (indescribable) kind of feeling; in another sense, we are asserting in addition that an objective Being, God, exists, and in this second sense, having the feeling does not ensure that such a Being exists. We should not confuse these two senses; else we may slip from the first sense to the second and make an inference from experience to object which we are not entitled to make. When a statement which seems to be simply about an experience asserts, however covertly, the existence of something beyond the experience itself, then the occurrence of the experience alone can never guarantee that the thing beyond it exists.

F. The Teleological Argument (Argument from Design)

The most popular of all the arguments for the existence of God is the teleological argument, or argument from design. This argument attempts to arrive by empirical means at the conclusion that God exists, by examining the world and trying to show that it points to the existence of a God. Look out upon the world, says the argument, and you will find that it shows many evidences of order and design. If you reflect on the way the universe is arranged, you will find it difficult to avoid the conclusion that there is a purpose in it, that a Master Architect has been at work. Not blind chance, but purpose, governs the universe. And where there is a purpose, there must be a Purposer.

The first question on which we should be quite clear is just what kind of Deity the teleological argument is intended to establish. It can be used to show that there is a Deity who is omnipotent and benevolent, or one who is omnipotent and malevolent, or one who is benevolent but not omnipotent, or even more than one Deity. The arguments in each case are somewhat different.

[1.] *An omnipotent, benevolent Deity:* in other words, a God who is both good and all-powerful. This is the conception of a Deity which the argument has most often been employed to establish. And the principal arguments that have been used in its favor are the complexity and teleological character of living things—the same phenomena discussed earlier in this chapter in defense of vitalism. We need not repeat here any of the examples of organic behavior that were mentioned there.

In a universe composed chiefly of inorganic matter, the existence of both life and mind seemed a mystery that could be explained only on the hypothesis of a divine Designer or Artificer who planned and created, either from nothing or from inorganic matter, the ancestors of the living organisms we see around us. How otherwise could living things have sprung into being on the earth?

Theories about the evolution of organic from inorganic matter sprang up in many times and places to challenge this belief. Such theories are at least as old as Anaximander (611–547 B.C.), but no comprehensive theory with the full weight of detailed and painstaking empirical observation behind it arose until the nineteenth century, with the publication of Charles Darwin's *The Origin of Species* in 1859. Since then, the teleological argument has rapidly declined, in spite of the many hundreds of books written on it pro and con shortly after Darwin's publication. Though amended in some respects, the main contentions of Darwin's work are still accepted by biologists today, and the hypothesis of evolution, including a struggle for existence and survival of the fittest, is considered as well confirmed as any hypothesis about the distant past can be.

It is for biologists and not for philosophers to judge whether the empirical hypothesis advanced by Darwin is true or false, probable or improbable. It is of relevance here, however, to point out that, strictly speaking, Darwin's hypothesis did not rule God out of the picture at all. Most persons heretofore had believed that God had created living things instantaneously by an act of special creation for each species. Now they were free to believe instead that God had chosen the slow and gradual process of evolution as a *way* of bringing the higher forms of life into being. No scientific doctrine of evolution by itself contradicts the notion that God is the designer of life; it can be considered simply a reinterpretation of God's methods in executing that design.

In spite of this, however, the teleological argument has fallen into eclipse since Darwin. Why? Chiefly because Darwin's hypothesis "filled the gap": there seemed no longer any *need* to account for the origin of life in supernaturalistic terms when Darwin had given a clear and coherent account of the matter without using such terms at all—much as the hypothesis that the ghost of a departed spirit is knocking at your door is no longer needed when the knock turns out to have been caused by a salesman making a call.

Before Darwin, the existence of life seemed to indicate intelligence and ingenuity in the Designer, for how otherwise than by intelligence could such complex structures have been formed? But after Darwin, and more than ever through his successors, the whole process seemed explicable enough without bringing in design. Large numbers of mutations occur in every species, most of which die out in the struggle for existence; the individuals (and the species) which win out are not the ones appointed for that purpose by a divine design, but merely the ones which natural selection, and the conditions of environment, have rendered most capable of surviving. (The vast proliferation of living things from comparatively simple beginnings in the pre-Cambrian era is a long, complex, and fascinating history, but of course it belongs to biology and paleontology rather than to philosophy.[27])

Not only did the evolutionary hypothesis seem to render the belief in an intelligent Designer unnecessary; it also seemed directly to contradict the belief in a *benevolent* Designer. The spectacle of evolution itself seemed difficult to interpret as an unmixed work of benevolence. Through countless ages animals evolve; those that are able to adjust themselves to changing conditions, and to find food, and to kill and eat other animals, survive; the rest are blotted out

[27] Perhaps the clearest brief account of this is to be found in George G. Simpson, *The Meaning of Evolution* (New Haven: Yale University Press, 1949).

in the struggle for existence, living in constant danger and dying in torment. Many living things, such as tigers and constricting snakes, are so constructed that they can live only on other living things as food, squeezing them to death or tearing them to pieces in the process. Death is the necessary condition, the *sine qua non*, of the very existence of life. Seldom are living organisms (except some human beings and their animal pets) permitted to die a "natural" death; and even when they are, dying is often painful and protracted. In addition to this, the environmental conditions are so undependable and quixotic, and the life of the organism so dependent on the fulfillment of such a vast multitude of conditions, that even a comparatively small change in the environment or disorder in the functioning of the organism may cause the extinction of its life, and often that of the entire species. "A single hurricane destroys the hopes of a season; a trifling chemical change in an edible root starves a million people." [28]

There are, of course, benevolent adaptations in nature. "What marvelous design exists," one might argue, "in a young kitten; it leaps and runs, and responds to impulses which even we do not; and its body, a vast complicated network of tiny nerves and muscles and bones, regenerates with such smooth efficiency that it knows nothing of how wonderfully it is cared for and constructed." But on the other hand, "With what wonderful craftsmanship the cobra is designed; out darts its forked tongue, and with lightning-like speed it infixes its fangs with their deadly poison into its prey; the victim swells, goes blind, undergoes the most indescribable pain, and in twenty minutes dies an agonized death." (If the victims were always rats or even goats, we human beings would not consider this so evil; but human beings equally are the victims.) Or: "What wonderful forces are at work in the human body, so complex that centuries of biological investigation have not yet enabled us to understand it fully, every part helping and protecting every other part to work together for the maximum health of the organism." "Ah, but not always! In such a complex and delicate mechanism things are often going wrong, causing great anguish; often no cure is possible, and even when it is, it involves much more suffering; surgeons have to

[28] John Stuart Mill, "Nature," in *Three Essays on Religion* (London: Longmans, Green Co., 1874), p. 30. See also Part XI of David Hume's *Dialogues concerning Natural Religion* (written before Darwin), and parts of Tennyson's poem *In Memoriam* (contemporary with Darwin).

get at our internal organs as one would open a can of sardines, since the Designer has seen fit to put these complex and vulnerable organs inside of us without even the convenience of a zipper-like opening in the abdomen. Would it have been much trouble for the Designer to make our arteries out of durable elastic tubing so that they would not harden with age? Would not people be happier if brain-power and energy-drive lasted throughout a lifetime instead of reaching a peak at about forty and then declining? Why should people have to be born with incipient weaknesses and congenital diseases—many of them condemned to physical agony or idiocy or crime before they even start in life? One of the most unfortunate features of all is that the parts cannot be replaced when they go wrong; what would you think of an automobile manufacturer who failed to supply new parts even though his automobiles were constantly needing them? And observe how a cancer works away at the victim organ, silently and unnoticed, as if to escape detection by anyone who wants to discover it before it is too late, tearing away at the vital parts, draining the patient of precious life-fluid, then making him suffer by degrees, passing through every stage of torment until death comes as a relief."

There is a well-nigh endless array of empirical facts about the world which has been employed in defense of this version of the teleological argument, and an equally endless array of empirical facts which has been employed to attack it. But there is a logical point in these controversies which many participants do not observe, a rule of consistency: If one group of empirical facts seems to point toward the hypothesis of a benevolent designer, then an opposing group of empirical facts must in consistency be used against the hypothesis. *If* the presence of soil, moisture, etc., in suitable quantities in some regions is really evidence for benevolent design, *then* the absence of these things in other regions is evidence against benevolent design. We cannot have it both ways. If the fact that the legs of a lobster grow back on after being cut off, is evidence for benevolent design, then the fact that people's legs do not do so, cannot also be taken as evidence for benevolent design. If the expansion of water on freezing is evidence for design because it promotes marine life, enabling fish to swim about under a layer of ice which forms at the *top* of bodies of water, then the fact that life is *not* possible under other conditions (such as extremely high temperatures) must not be ignored on the other side of the issue. Suppose that we lived in a world in which water did not expand on freezing, but continued to contract as it became colder, and that as a consequence fish could exist only in tropical climates. Would we have used this as an argument *against* design? "All we can say with certainty is that life is possible under certain conditions and not under others. Naturally those conditions under which life is possible can be called favorable to life. But this is an analytic proposition and can hardly support a proof that life is the result of design." [29]

The problem of evil. The most insistent objection to the kind of deity we are now considering has always been the problem of evil. Epicurus (342–270 B.C.) put it as follows: Is God willing to prevent evil, but not able? Then he is not omnipotent. Is he able, but not willing? Then he is malevolent. Is he both able and willing? Then whence evil? (As we shall see below, the problem can be escaped if other kinds of deity are assumed.)

The existence of this dilemma has often been considered fatal to the hypothesis of a Deity that is both omnipotent and benevolent. At any rate, the popular "escapes" from the dilemma are quickly open to objection:

1. "The evil in the universe is caused by man's wickedness." But this does not account for the physical evils (earthquakes, hurricanes, plagues, and the like) as opposed to the moral evils, which men inflict upon men. Even with moral evils there are objections: They are the result of the divine gift of free-will, it is said. But is it worth the price of preserving a dictator's free-will if millions are tortured and slaughtered in concentration camps? And if the Deity cannot give us free-will and avoid these evils, He is not omnipotent as the argument says He is. Moreover, if the evils are inflicted as a punishment for sin, would they not be more equitably distributed? Is every disease, every bereavement, a punishment? For what is a child being punished when he is left alone in a room and burns to death on a hot stove, or when he is stricken with poliomyelitis or spinal meningitis?

2. "Good often comes out of evil." If this is true, it is equally true that evil comes out of good. The general tendency, however, is for evils to breed more evils and goods more goods. Moreover, would

[29] Morris R. Cohen, *Reason and Nature*, New York: Harcourt, Brace & Co., 1931, p. 291.

the fact that good might come out of it excuse the committing of an evil—such as killing a stingy old woman so that her granddaughter, inheriting her money, could go to school? In any case, does not the use of such means, no matter how desirable, cast doubt on either the omnipotence of any Deity who employed them (since, being omnipotent, He could achieve the end without them) or on the Deity's benevolence (in not wishing to do so)?

3. "The world is a moral training-ground for the building of character, and evils are here to discipline us rather than to punish us. Their object is to make us virtuous; the infliction of evil is necessary to achieve this end." But again, for a Deity that is both omnipotent and benevolent, there are difficulties. The world seems to be as ineffectual a moral training-ground as it is a haven of happiness; many persons never receive those "jolts" which would be most efficient in improving their character, while evil is piled upon evil to no effect in countless cases where it is not needed or positively interferes with the person's moral development. Moreover, a really omnipotent Deity would not need to adopt any means (certainly not means involving the slow death or slaughter of human beings) to this or any other end: omnipotence could achieve the end directly.

4. "God does not approve evils, but permits them, because every possible alternative would involve even greater evils than the present scheme of things." But

> . . . did I show you a house or palace, where there was not one apartment convenient or agreeable; where the windows, doors, fires, passages, stairs, and the whole economy of the building were the source of noise, confusion, fatigue, darkness, and extremes of heat and cold; you would certainly blame the contrivance, without any farther examination. The architect would in vain display his subtlety, and prove to you that if this door or that window were altered, greater ills would ensue. What he says, may be strictly true: the alteration of one particular, while the other parts of the building remain, may only augment the inconveniences. But still you would assert in general, that if the architect had had skill and good intentions, he might have formed such a plan of the whole, and might have adjusted the parts in such a manner, as would have remedied all or most of these inconveniences.[30]

A good architect would have designed the house in such a way as to avoid these disadvantages, so that one would not have to choose

[30] David Hume, *Dialogues concerning Natural Religion*, Part XI (Edinburgh: Nelson & Sons, 1935), p. 204.

between a bad plan and one that was still worse. Moreover, as we have seen earlier, the employment of evil as a means to attaining a good end (permitting evils so that worse ones would not occur) is justifiable, if at all, in human beings, who cannot attain worthy ends without employing means toward them; but an omnipotent Being would not need to employ such means, nor any means at all. A surgeon is justified in inflicting extreme pain by the fact that in no other way can he achieve for his patient the goal of recovery and health; if he could achieve it otherwise, his infliction of pain would not be excusable. What would we think of a father who first infects his child's leg and then decides to amputate it although a complete cure was within his power to give, and the infection was of his own giving to begin with?

5. "Perhaps what we call evil is really good: God's goodness is of a far different nature from ours, and beyond our comprehension." But again it is objected: Considering the spectacle of the world as we find it, there is no judgment of which we are more certain than that it is not perfectly good. If we distrust this judgment, we have no reason to trust any moral judgment, including the one that what is evil to us is good to God. Even if everything we think evil is really good, we still think it an evil, and this would be an error; then this error, hiding from us the perfect goodness of the universe, would be at least one evil; so there is evil after all. Finally, what can we mean in calling something or someone good if it is not the same sort of thing we mean in calling other human beings good? Unless this is what we mean, how can we be entitled to use the word "good" at all? We are told that this goodness is infinite, and therefore we cannot understand it; but infinite goodness is still goodness.

> Among the many who have said that we cannot conceive infinite space, did anyone ever suppose that it is *not* space? that it does not possess all the properties by which space is characterized? Infinite space cannot be cubical or spherical, because these are modes of being bounded; but does anyone imagine that in ranging through it we might arrive at some region which was not extended; of which one part was not outside another; where, though no Body intervened, motion was impossible; or where the sum of two sides of a triangle was less than the third side? The parallel assertion may be made respecting infinite goodness. What belongs to it as infinite I do not pretend to know; but I know that infinite goodness must be goodness, and that what is not consistent with goodness, is not consistent with infinite goodness.

If in ascribing goodness to God I do not mean what I mean by goodness; if I do not mean the goodness of which I have some knowledge, but an incomprehensible attribute of an incomprehensible substance, which for aught I know may be a totally different quality from that which I love and venerate . . . what do I mean by calling it goodness? and what reason have I for venerating it? If I know nothing about what the attribute is, I cannot tell that it is a proper object of veneration. To say that God's goodness may be different in kind from man's goodness, what is it but saying, with a slight change of phraseology, that God may possibly not be good? To assert in words what we do not think in meaning, is as suitable a definition as can be given of a moral falsehood.[31]

The power of the Deity, by contrast, is always interpreted in a completely human way: it is never thought to mean that we could not be killed or thrown into hell-fire, in spite of the fact that the power of the Deity is conceived of as far greater than ours. Greater power means more of the same thing that we experience and call "power." Does not the same remark apply to "good"? But this is often spoken of, unlike the power, as inconceivable, perhaps because so many of its manifestations conflict so strongly with anything we would ever call goodness.

Several alternative hypotheses, however, are open to us:

[2.] *An omnipotent, malevolent Deity.* This view has not been nearly so popular, though it has occasionally been suggested, sometimes half-humorously, in the suggestion that the world was created by the Devil. The problem of evil would not exist on this view, for according to it the world was designed by a Being who wanted to promote evil. (Rather one might say there would be a "problem of good.") The support alleged for this view would be the very facts that created the indictment against the previous one: the law of the jungle—"nature red in tooth and claw," seeming to maximize the amount of torment among living things; the ineffectiveness of man's efforts compared with the magnitude of the obstacles which nature sets in his way; the amount of useless pain, poverty, and suffering in the world, and so on.

[3.] *A benevolent but not omnipotent Deity:* one well-intentioned but limited in power, like human beings themselves. Again, this view avoids the problem of evil: it is there because God is limited in power and cannot help it. Perhaps human beings can struggle to-

---

[31] Mill, *Examination of Sir William Hamilton's Philosophy* (London: Longmans, Green & Co., 1865), p. 101.

gether with Him in overcoming it. (One reason for the comparative unpopularity of this view may be that people desire a God who will be sure to have power enough to give them heavenly rewards when the time comes.)

[4.] *Two deities:* one might say there is a struggle between good and evil going on in the world, which might be interpreted as a struggle between a benevolent and a malevolent deity competing for control, as the ancient Manichaeans and Zoroastrians conceived it. Does not the universe (one might argue) look more like a battle-ground for conflicting deities than the work of a single Deity with one purpose in view and all things tending in one direction? Again, of course, there is no problem of evil: the evil is all attributable to the evil deity. (Christian thought at times almost has two deities, God and the devil: only the battle is a sham-battle because the good Deity created the bad one and is guaranteed to win over him in the end; indeed, He could destroy him at any time. But why, then, the battle, with all the evils thus involved, if they could be avoided? For a genuine religious dualism, both deities must be limited in power, and the outcome genuinely in doubt.)

[5.] *More than two deities: polytheism.* When we look at a ship or a house, we may marvel at its craftsmanship, only to find that it was built, and sometimes even designed, by a large number of individuals.

> If we survey a ship, what an exalted idea must we form of the in-genuity of the carpenter, who framed so complicated, useful, and beautiful a machine? And what surprise must we feel, when we find him a stupid mechanic, who imitated others, and copied an art, which, through a long succession of ages, after multiplied trials, mistakes, corrections, deliberations, and controversies, had been gradually im-proving? Many worlds might have been botched and bungled, through-out an eternity, ere this system was struck out; much labor lost; many fruitless trials made; and a slow, but continued improvement carried on during infinite ages in the art of world-making.[32]

[6.] *A cosmic organism.* Thus far we have considered only design-ing minds in our hypotheses. "But," one might ask, "why take mind, which as far as we know is limited to human beings and per-haps higher forms of animal life, as the model for the entire uni-verse? It may reflect merely our own egotism. Since what we are doing in the teleological argument is looking at the empirical world

[32] Hume, *Dialogues concerning Natural Religion,* Part **V.**

to glean hints about the nature of the Deity (or deities), let us observe that nowhere in the universe do we find examples of minds occurring without bodies; yet this is what we have been assuming all along to exist in the case of the Deity. We find two primary principles of order in the universe, generation (by which a tree confers a certain order on its offspring, via seeds) and design (by which human beings make machines). Thus far we have given design priority; let us now give generation a hearing. Some would object, of course, that the principle of generation in all organisms must have been designed by a Deity, so all order stems from Deity after all. But if he can go beyond the observed facts to assume that generation stems from design, I can go beyond them too and assume that design stems from generation: after all, I *see* much order stem from generation (in the case of organisms), and though I see some stem from design also—principally in human constructions—I note that designs take place in minds, and minds occur only in conjunction with bodies, and bodies are living organisms which stem from generation; so generation is the prior principle after all."

Thus encouraged, one might say that the universe, like an organism, seems animated with life and motion; the parts remain in contact with each other (at least gravitationally); and a constant circulation of matter in it appears to produce no disorder. Therefore, the universe is an animal. Or more unusual still,

> The Brahmins assert, that the world arose from an infinite spider, who spun this whole complicated mass from his bowels, and annihilates afterwards the whole or any part of it, by absorbing it again, and resolving it into his own essence. Here is a species of cosmogony, which appears to us ridiculous; because a spider is a little contemptible animal, whose operations we are never likely to take for a model of the whole universe. And were there a planet wholly inhabited by spiders (which is very possible), this inference would there appear as natural and irrefragable as that which in our planet ascribes the origin of all things to design and intelligence. . . . Why an orderly system may not be spun from the belly as well as from the brain, it will be difficult . . . to give a satisfactory reason.[33]

The teleological argument as an argument from analogy. Are all these weird hypotheses equally probable, or equally improbable? Is there nothing to choose among them? Let us examine the logic of these arguments a bit more closely. They are all *arguments from*

---

[33] Hume, *Dialogues concerning Natural Religion,* Part VII.

analogy. In an argument from analogy, there are two things, A and B, which have a certain relation to each other: A is the cause of B, or A is larger than B, or A constructs B, etc. There is a third thing, C, which is very similar to A. From this it is inferred that there is a fourth thing, D, which holds the same relation to C that B does to A.

As a deductive argument the argument from analogy is always invalid, for nothing about the relation of A to C and A to B proves anything about the relation of B to D. If in empirical fact, however, A were *identical* with C (in the sense of "identical" discussed on p. 253 n.), we might be justified in holding that D would be identical with B, at least if the relation in question were a causal one and if the Causal Principle in some form is accepted. But of course, A and C, whatever they are, are never exactly alike, so the argument never strictly proves anything about D. The argument, though never conclusive, is at its strongest when (1) there have been many observed instances of the A-B relation, so that there is *some* evidence for a law connecting phenomena of type A with those of type B; if such a law were established, the C-D relation would then be merely another instance of it; and (2) when C is as much like A as possible. For example, I have seen hundreds of eggs (A) which I have found to possess yolks (B), so I infer that this egg (C) which is like the previous ones will also have a yolk (D). Of course I cannot be sure: it *may* turn out not to have a yolk at all.

In most cases the argument is much weaker than the one in this example. If the epiphenomenalist argues, "The smoke (A) that issues from the locomotive is in no way a cause of the motion of the locomotive (B); hence, the mind (C) is in no way a cause of the motion of the body (D)," the argument is very poor indeed: perhaps the mind-body relationship *is* like the smoke-locomotive relationship (that is not at issue here), but the argument from analogy does not prove it: the fact that A is an effect of B does not prove that C is an effect of D. Indeed, the differences between the mind (A) and smoke (C) are so immense that when we examine the argument even for a moment it crumbles into dust. We can only say, "Assuming that the smoke-locomotive relationship is like that, what in the world does that prove about the mind-body relationship?" The fallacy in such arguments is known as the fallacy of *imperfect analogy.* When the argument from analogy is explicitly stated, people generally agree that it proves nothing; but as a rule they do not state it outright, and are merely taken in by it. Often they are the victims of picture-thinking (see pages 73–74): they have a vivid mental picture of smoke issuing from a locomotive and their minds become so dominated by this image that they assume without even being aware of it that the relation of the mind to the body is like this. Arguments from analogy are thus psychologically very powerful, but logically very weak.

The teleological argument in all its forms is an argument from analogy. In each case some feature of the empirical world is taken as the basis for the analogy; that is why it is called an empirical argument. But the features selected in each version of the argument are different. If the argument is for a divine Designer, as most versions of it are, the basis for the analogy is the human mind, which designs mechanical objects. Thus we are told, "If we found a watch in the middle of a desert (A), we would infer that there was a watchmaker (B); similarly, we find a universe (C) (or some aspect of it, such as living organisms), and we infer that it too had a maker (D)." Psychologically this strikes many persons as a powerful argument; but its success depends on the similarity of the universe to a watch, which many other persons do not find to be very great. Remember that even the smallest dissimilarity between A and C can make for the most radical disparity between B and D: a gentle breeze can cool and refresh you, but a slightly stronger one may give you pneumonia. Between a watch and a universe there are hundreds of differences. One of the most striking of them is that we have seen not only watches but their makers and designers—or at any rate we *can* see them, even if we have not taken the trouble —while in the case of the universe this is not so.

The opponent of the Designer-hypothesis, of course, seizes upon *other* features of the universe on which to build his argument. "If the similarity of the universe to a watch proves that the universe, like a watch, is the result of design," he says, "then the similarity of the universe to a plant or living organism proves that, like an organism, it is the result not of design but of generation." If the argument from analogy is permitted in the first case, it should consistently be permitted in the second; if it is not permitted in the second, neither should it in the first. Each of the arguments is on the same footing: each one seizes upon some observed aspect of the world and takes it as a model for the whole.

The same consideration applies, of course, to the benevolence-malevolence versions of the argument. Agreeing on a Designer, the two factions here disagree on the nature of that Designer. The one takes benevolent adaptations in nature as grist for his mill, and the other returns the compliment by taking the maladaptations. Each goes far beyond the empirical facts in the inference he makes.

What is the result of all this? The teleological argument cannot establish any of the hypotheses whatever. If the argument from analogy were accepted in one example, it would have to be accepted in others as well. If we argue that the existence of order in the universe proceeds from design, on the analogy with machines, others can argue that the existence of order in the universe proceeds from generation, on the analogy with organisms. We have not *observed* that all order proceeds from design; we observe at least as many instances of order to result from generation. We cannot therefore argue that *all* order, including generation itself, results from design. What we tend to forget is that order is empirical evidence of design *only insofar as order has been observed to proceed from design.* We have observed it to proceed from design in the case of watches and houses, but not in the case of organisms. Therefore our argument that *all* order proceeds from design is inconclusive. (It is equally inconclusive, of course, to argue that some order is observed to result from generation, and that therefore all order, including that brought about by design, results ultimately from generation.)

Is the teleological argument an empirical hypothesis? The teleological argument has usually been advanced as an empirical argument. Its evidence (it is said) is probably inconclusive, but nevertheless it does provide *some empirical evidence* for the belief in a Designer. True, the empirical evidence cuts both ways, like a double-edged knife: it can be used against as well as for any given position. If you use the good in the world as evidence for a good Designer, your opponent can use the evils in the world as evidence for an evil Designer. But the important point is that, inconclusive and ambivalent as the evidence is, there *are* empirical facts which we can adduce as evidence *relevant* to the hypothesis of a Designer.[34] This being the case, the belief in a Designer is an empirical

[34] We say "Designer" here instead of "God" because a Designer is all that

hypothesis, just like the belief in mountains on the other side of the moon or the belief in magnetic fields or unconscious motivation. Doubtless it is less well attested than they are, because whatever evidence there is points both ways, like clues pointing to both Smith and Jones as the murderer of Brown. But still, it is a hypothesis *in the empirical domain.*

But let us review again the types of hypotheses we considered in Chapter 3 (see pages 190–192). The Designer-hypothesis is not like that of the cat in the hall, where we can go out and look to see whether a cat caused the sound. Nor is it like the other side of the moon, which it is at least in principle possible to see, and which one day we may see for ourselves. Like the electron and the unconscious mind, God is *in principle* unobservable. Yet no science investigates the God-hypothesis, while the sciences do investigate in detail the other hypotheses. Where lies the difference?

1. It lies partly in the fact that every empirical hypothesis about in-principle-unobservables has definite empirical consequences: *If* Hypothesis H is true, *then* empirically observable consequences A, B, C. . . . If A, B, C . . . are not then observed, we conclude that hypothesis H is inadequate to account for the empirical facts, and we try to replace it with another. In the case of the Designer-hypothesis, this is not what people usually do. People do not say, "If the Designer-hypothesis is true, then the world will have features A, B, C . . ." for even when it is shown that A, B, and C do not occur, they do not on that account abandon the hypothesis of a Designer. They then take refuge in saying, in effect, "My hypothesis is still true, but His purposes are mysterious and His ways are not our ways (although I know enough about them to know that my hypothesis is true). Even if the world is very bad, the beneficent Designer hypothesis still holds." But in this case the hypothesis *is compatible with the existence of any empirical state of affairs whatever.* If no facts about the world could contradict the hypothesis, what would? Presumably nothing. But an empirical hypothesis must be compatible with some empirically observable states of affairs and incompatible with others. The physicist would be laughed out

---

the argument usually attempts to establish. It does nothing, for example, to help the First Cause argument. The argument from design would apply just as well to the hypothesis of a God whose function was not to create matter but to impose a certain form or order on it, just as a sculptor imposes form and order on a block of stone but does not create the stone.

of court who said, "If a magnetic field is present there, iron filings
will arrange themselves in this way. You've tried it and they don't?
Oh well, there's a magnetic field there anyway." But we cannot
have it both ways: if we adduce the presence of certain conditions
as evidence for a hypothesis, then the absence of these same conditions will be evidence against it. It is because the proponents of
the teleological argument are not usually willing to accept this consequence—because they accept certain facts as evidence *for* the
hypothesis but will accept no facts as evidence *against* it—that
their hypothesis is dismissed by scientists as unempirical.

2. But let us suppose that we do not fall into this error, and that
we are willing to put the hypothesis to some empirical test and
abandon it if it fails to pass that test. At once we are faced with the
question, What would constitute such a test? When A is evidence
for B, is it not because A has been observed to go along with (cause,
accompany, vary with, or have some regular relation to) B? If the
chattering of jays is evidence for the passing of a fox, is it not because the former has been observed to occur regularly with the latter? But in the present case—empirical facts about the universe
(A) and God (B)—we cannot observe both the terms of this relation. So how do we know in this case that the observed facts, A,
constitute evidence for the hypothesis, B? Indeed, what does the
so-called hypothesis itself *mean?*

According to the Verifiability Criterion, the cognitive meaning
of a hypothesis about unobservables is simply the total cognitive
meaning of the empirical statements which constitute its evidence.
In the case of the benevolent Designer hypothesis, this would be,
for example, the fact that there is good in the world (assuming that
this can be given empirical meaning), that there are adaptations
which enable organisms to survive, and so on. Now, according to
the Verifiability Criterion, of the two alleged hypotheses, (1) that
there is a Designer manifested in empirically observable phenomena
A, B, C . . ., and (2) that there are simply the empirically observable phenomena A, B, C . . ., how do they differ? Not at all: their
verification is the same, therefore their (cognitive) meaning is the
same.

Almost everyone, however, would object to this analysis in the
case of the Designer hypothesis. By saying "A Designer exists" they
mean something *more* than the existence of these phenomena in

nature. Perhaps in the case of the magnetic field they do not, but in the case of a Designer they do. The verificationist will say that they have no logical right to, but they will say that they do mean more all the same. "Same verification, then same meaning," he will insist; and they will respond that this may be a convenient principle to employ in science, but it does not work here. Anyway, they will add, what proof is there of the Verifiability Principle itself? If the verificationist says that only such hypotheses as he admits can be distinguished from each other, the metaphysician replies that they cannot *empirically* be distinguished from each other, and that this is a tautology: he for his part does mean more by the one than by the other. The verificationist in turn will want to know what is the more, exactly as in the case of vitalism (see pages **285–289**).[35]

Verificationist: We agree on the existence of certain phenomena such as benevolent adaptations, religious experiences, human virtue, and the like. Now in addition to all this you say that a Designer exists. What are you offering, however, but a mere *word?*

Metaphysician: The phenomena you cite are all I can empirically *verify;* but you are assuming the Verifiability Principle itself if you assume that therefore there *isn't* any more.

Ver: Very well; for the time being I shall not appeal to the principle at all. I shall rest my case on an elementary semantic principle, namely that every word to be cognitively meaningful must stand for something. You hold that the terms "God" and "Divine Designer" stand for something, don't you?

Met: Of course I do; but they don't stand for anything visible, tangible, or in any other way available to the senses, otherwise it would be available to empirical observation. Now what do you expect me to do—state the empirical meaning of a word that designates something admittedly not accessible to sense-perception?

Ver: I expect you to give some meaning to the noise "God," which is generally taken to mean something; at any rate you use it, so you should know what you mean by it. Now let's see: suppose I said to you that there are six invisible chairs between you and the wall. You would look at me askance, then start walking between your own (visible) chair and the wall to try to verify my statement—by stumbling against the invisible chairs. But then I say to you, "Oh, I forgot to tell you, these chairs have an additional peculiarity, they are intangible also—they cannot be touched." Then perhaps you will wonder, look at me more askance than ever, saying

[35] It is important to follow every step of the following imaginary dialogue, not only to appreciate fully the ins and outs of the arguments on the issue, but to test your mastery of distinctions that have arisen in the preceding chapters.

"Peculiar chairs indeed!" Perhaps you will say, "What's the difference be-- tween such chairs and no chairs at all?" Perhaps you will say, "How can I ever *know* whether such chairs exist?"

Met: Well, isn't it a possibility? Maybe they do; maybe there are thou- sands of such chairs in this room and we'll never know it. It's true that as practical human beings we don't care whether the answer is yes or no, be- cause we are generally concerned with the kind of chairs we can see and touch—but still, as a non-practical question, how do you *know* that they don't exist? How can you prove that there aren't invisible brownies in your watch, invisible spirits in the wind? How can you prove it either way— that there are or that there aren't?

Ver: Before I can prove a statement true or false, I must first know what it means. I want to know what this one means—what actual or possible state-of-affairs your sentence is a label of. I know, and you know, what it means to say that there are visible, tangible chairs in the room. But I do not know what it means to say that there are invisible, intangible ones. How would I ever detect them?

Met: But that's just the point—you never *could* detect them. (You're slipping back into the Verifiability Principle—be careful.) You may never know whether they are there, and yet *they may be*. Perhaps you'll never know whether a God is there, but perhaps He may be.

Ver: But please, *what's meant by saying* that they may be? When you speak of ordinary tangible chairs, I know the difference between the state- ments "There is a chair there" and "There isn't a chair there." I can draw two pictures, the first of which shows the type of situation that the first sentence is a label of, the second of which shows the situation corresponding to the second label. Even if I can't draw a picture, I can recognize the dif- ference between the two—the situations are different, what the two sen- tences stand for is different, hence the meanings are different. Similarly, I know the difference between "There is a ghost in this room" and "There is not a ghost in this room." Yes, these are both perfectly meaningful sen- tences. If the first statement were true, an eerie white hooded shape (or whatever it is a ghost is supposed to look like) should be visible; if not, the second statement is true, that is, the second sentence is the label by which I would identify that situation. And I say the second sentence is the correct one to use because nothing answering to the description of a ghost is found, no matter how closely we examine the room. I know what situa- tions are labeled by these sentences, even if there are no actual instances of ghosts in the world. But I do *not* know how "There is an invisible, in- tangible chair" is different from "There is no chair at all"; the two sen- tences seem to me to label precisely the same situation, with the second sentence being preferable because it is the more usual and less misleading way of referring to this familiar sort of situation. Similarly, I do not know how the situation labeled by the sentence "There is a God" is different from the situation labeled by the sentence "There is no God," or for that matter, "There are empirical phenomena A, B, C . . ." (those adduced as evidence for God).

Met: A ghost is an observable; God is not.

Ver: Neither is an electron or a magnetic field. But there is nevertheless a big observable difference between the presence and the absence of a magnetic field. If iron filings did not arrange themselves in a certain way in the presence of a magnet, we would have to say, "No magnetic field here." Similarly with unconscious motivation: If certain facts about the way people behave are not as they are, we would have no title to make any such statements; and there *is* a difference between "There is unconscious motivation" and "There is none": if the observable facts that make the first statement true were not as psychoanalysts say they are, then the second statement would be the true one. With an electron-hypothesis the case is more complex because the observable phenomena are more complex, but the principle is the same. Any scientist defending his theory can tell you, if you understand his vocabulary, the observable differences between his hypothesis being true and its not being true. You see what I am asking: what is the difference between the state-of-affairs labeled by one sentence and that labeled by the other? Wherein do they differ? *Of what state-of-affairs is "There is a God" the label, of which "There are such-and-such observable phenomena" is not?*

Met: Well, first let me demonstrate conclusively that we *are* talking about something more than the observable phenomena. When people give arguments for the existence of a benevolent Designer, they are not arguing merely that the benevolent adaptations in nature occur; for they know that already. Indeed, they may realize that the world is not on the whole benevolent, and yet they may declare that a benevolent Deity exists—which would be self-contradictory if "benevolent world" and "benevolent Deity" meant the same thing! They hold that certain empirically observable phenomena *point to* the Deity's existence, but do not constitute that existence. When A points to B, A must be different from B; A could hardly point to itself. Moreover, if the empirically observable phenomena were all that were meant by the statement that a Deity exists, there would be no controversy about it, for these phenomena are there for anyone to see who wants to take the trouble. No, people will readily agree that the empirical phenomena occur, but will *still dispute about whether a Deity exists.* What could show more clearly that by the God-hypothesis they mean something more than, something over and above, what they mean by any conjunction of statements about empirically observable phenomena?

Ver: I agree with you; most people would not say that the two statements mean the same. But now suppose you tell me *what the difference is.* What does the one assert that the other does not?

Met: That a Supernatural Being exists, of course.

Ver: Of course, but this doesn't help, does it? What does "cause" mean? "Produce." What does "produce" mean? "Cause." The terms "God" and "Supernatural Being" are used synonymously. But I want a word-thing definition, not a word-word definition. *What is the thing, existent or not, that both the word "God" and the phrase "Supernatural Being" stand for?*

Met: "Here we are again; I can't draw you a picture, for God, at least any God that isn't a crudely anthropomorphic super-organism (which would be in principle observable), is not visible. What else can I do? I can describe intense religious experiences, but you will agree that I have these experiences and still deny that God exists, won't you?

Ver: No, I won't deny it—that would imply that I knew what I was denying, and I still don't know that. I still want to know *what* you use the expression "God exists" to stand for.

Met: I hold that it stands for something in principle unobservable. Nor is it observable in terms of empirical phenomena as in the case of the magnetic field. Like the invisible intangible chairs, you cannot list anything whatever as empirical evidence; but both the chairs and the Deity may still be there.

Ver: But in that case the difference between you and me is merely verbal. We agree on the same empirical facts. You give me a word, "God," as a shorthand way of referring to this string of facts.

Met: That is not true! I am not merely giving you a shorthand way of referring to the old facts; I am talking about *other facts*. That is the real difference between us; you do not agree to the other facts. True, I am not giving you any new *observable* facts; but why should all facts be observable ones? I hold to something more than the observable (even the in-principle-observable) facts, and it's a tautology to say that *they* don't make any observable difference. What I am insisting on is that the word "God" stands for something, though of course not an observable something, nor on the other hand an unobservable like a magnetic field whose existence can be asserted in terms of that which is observable.

Ver: And I insist that if that is the case it's the same as not standing for anything at all; you are merely giving a word—rather, a noise that is not even a word because it stands for nothing. Thus you are violating the semantic rule we both agreed on: that a word, to be a word and not a mere noise, must mean something, and that a sentence, to be a sentence and not just a string of words, must mean something too.

Met: I don't think so. Do you really think you are invoking merely the semantic rule we both agreed on?

Ver: Yes. A word must stand for something, and I want to know what the word "God" stands for.

Met: Suppose I tell you, what I think is true, that the word "God" does stand for something—something that is in principle unobservable. Then what do you tell me? You tell me that in that case *it doesn't stand for anything at all*. But in doing this you are invoking the Verifiability Principle, don't you see? If you merely insist that the word must stand for something, I agree, and I say that it stands for an unobservable something, and, moreover, something like the invisible chair, not like the magnetic field. But since it does stand for something, I am satisfying the semantic rule on which we both agree. Now: if you object that I *haven't* satisfied it because the word "God" doesn't stand for something observable (or translatable into observable terms) and *therefore* it doesn't stand for anything at all, I insist that you are *going beyond the semantic rule and invoking the Verifiability Principle.*

Ver: Yes ... I see. The statement "The word doesn't stand for anything" doesn't follow from "The word doesn't stand for anything observable" *unless* I supply a premise that every thing is an in-principle-observable thing.

Met: Precisely. And I would question the principle—not in science, but in religion and in metaphysics generally. So, by invoking it—which you must do if your inference is to stand—you are begging the question at issue.

Ver: So it looks as if I had better try to make you accept the principle.

Met: That I shall never do. You may tell me that it is the principle of Occam's Razor—"don't multiply entities beyond necessity"—but I'll not accept that principle either. You may tell me that introducing unobservables like this without any empirical check is of no use, and I'll say it may be of no *scientific* use, but there are non-scientific uses too. You may tell me that if I accept an unobservable God, I can also accept unobservable brownies, elves, and for that matter our invisible chairs; and I agree; we should be cautious in introducing these things, but we cannot rule out the possibility of them. You will say that we believe in the same empirical phenomena and since I can't indicate anything more, our dispute is verbal. I think it is not verbal at all, though it is not empirical either, for we both agree on the empirical facts of the case. But *it is still a factual dispute and not a verbal one, for there are other facts than empirical ones;* metaphysical facts are still facts. What I am insisting on is an unobservable difference between us, not an observable one.

Ver: You put the conflict between us dramatically at least. But I must insist that here we should apply the same analysis to the words "unobservable difference" that we formerly did to "unobservable chair" and "unobservable God." I said there was no difference between an unobservable chair and no chair at all. Now I say that there is no difference between an unobservable difference and no difference at all. We know what it means to speak of a difference that is observed, or even one that has not yet been observed but which *may* be (an anticipated difference can be labeled with words); but this is different. In this case what would it mean to speak of a difference? Could we label the situation expressed by "There is a difference between these two" and distinguish it from the situation expressed by "There is no difference between these two"? With two empirical objects, no matter how similar, say two sugars, there is still a difference, even though not observable at every moment. But here we cannot do this. Here "unobservable difference" and "no difference at all" are merely two labels for one and the same state of affairs, namely the indistinguishability of the two things being referred to. After all, what criterion have you for distinguishing these two situations—unobservable difference and no difference—from each other?

Met: I have an answer for you, but let us pursue this possibility first: Perhaps we just don't know; perhaps the criteria are beyond us—we don't

have them. There is a difference between the two situations, but discovering
it is beyond our mortal ken.

Ver: Ah, I was looking for that one! But it won't work. No one denies
that there may be many things we shall never know or discover. But the
semantic point remains nevertheless: just as words are labels for (actual
or possible) things, so sentences are labels for (actual or possible) situations. Complicated situations, sometimes, but still they must label *some*
possible situation or they stand for nothing. If you do not specify what this
possible state-of-affairs is which a sentence you utter stands for, it is just
as meaningless as if you said "Pirots carulize elatically" or uttered a random
row of nonsense-syllables.

Met: But here you are using certain criteria, such as perceivability,
though you don't say this, and rejecting all others. This criterion works out
all right for the entities of physical science, but not for those of religion.

Ver: I stack no cards for science; I don't care what kind of statements
come out of the hopper unscathed, whether they are scientific or religious
or magical. My discussion has no particular end in view. I only insist on
the *sine qua non* for *all* discourse, whether scientific or religious or anything else. I insist that words, to be words and not mere noises, must have
meanings, and the same for sentences; also that meanings are *given* to
noises by their human users and that if one of these human users does not
know what meaning the persons who speak his language have given to a
word or sentence, and if he has given none himself, it is as meaningless as
the wind whistling past your window. If this is the fate that befalls religious statements, I'm sorry, but so much the worse for religion. The criterion must be fulfilled if we are not to talk noises rather than words. You
see, I am only invoking the semantic rule again, which you assent to as
well as I.

Met: Ah, but you are not—and here comes my real answer to you.
Earlier you said that the word "God" doesn't stand for anything observable and concluded that therefore it doesn't stand for anything at all; I
rejoined that this conclusion logically follows only if you bring in as a
premise that a statement stands for nothing if it stands for nothing observable or something that can't be rendered in terms of observables. I make
exactly the same answer now. You challenged me on the word "difference,"
asking how to distinguish a forever indiscernible difference from no difference at all. My reply is exactly the same: there *is* a difference between an
unobservable difference and no difference at all (though not an observable
one, of course). You say, "There is no observable difference between the
two alleged kinds of difference, therefore there is no difference between
them at all." But this again begs the question. You have to invoke the
Verifiability Principle to make that one stick. The semantic rule alone
won't do it.

Ver: But if you have *no criteria* for the detection of that difference
under any conceivable circumstances, how can you speak of a difference?
You are again only giving me a word, not a thing that word stands for.

Met: No observable thing, you mean. That is the difference between us. I say that the word stands for an unobservable thing.

Ver: How are you to distinguish God from other unobservable things, or unobservable differences from no differences? Invisible leprechauns in your watch are just as likely.

Met: I can't distinguish them in terms of observables; as I said before, the observable situation is the same whether my hypothesis is true or not.

Ver: How then do you know whether it is true or not? What other means have you?

Met: Insight, intuition perhaps . . .

Ver: Ah, but you know how easily intuition is attacked. (See pages 149–152.)

Met: Well, what do you want me to say, empirical observation? I have already granted that the two sides to the quarrel agree on the same empirical facts.

Ver: But what other kinds of facts are there? I still haven't the faintest idea, and you haven't offered me a bit of evidence.

Met: Empirical evidence? Not for metaphysical facts.

Ver: When you speak of "metaphysical facts" I just don't know what you mean. If you could only give me some indication . . .

Met: And nothing but an empirical indication would satisfy you.

Ver: Perhaps, for in no other terms can I understand what sort of thing you could possibly mean.

Met: True; then so much the worse for you; I mean something that isn't empirical at all, even in its evidence, and I'm sorry if you don't understand what it is.

Ver: How can I understand it if you don't even give me an "it" to understand? You still haven't shown me that you mean any*thing* at all. Your utterances have all been much beating around the bush, to hide the complete emptiness inside. Cognitively there is nothing in your assertion; the meaning of the utterances is all emotive and pictorial, not cognitive.

Met: And I say that they do have cognitive meaning, but I don't hope to make *you* understand what that meaning is.

Most conversations on the subject, of course, proceed on a much more superficial level than the imaginary one just given. Both sides present their arguments far more vaguely, without a sense of exactly what they are arguing for or against or the basis upon which they are taking certain statements as evidence for their position. Moreover, each of the participants in the above dialogue has been made to present his position in a state of almost naked purity, without shading or compromise. Many philosophers, however, would not be willing to go all the way with either of these disputants.

The issue is such a tangled web of overlapping and conflicting points of view that it would be difficult to disentangle them or to list them clearly. But two points of view may be briefly outlined before we conclude this account.

1. God as cosmic mind. Let us listen for a moment to the following line of reasoning: "Is it not possible that there may be a Mind greater than any of our minds, which designed the whole scheme of things? Granted that the universe doesn't much look like the result of design by an omnipotent and benevolent Being, still, is not the hypothesis meaningful? I am not worried about its truth, but about its meaning. And surely there is no difficulty in knowing what it means to speak of a mind powerful enough to design and rule the world. We cannot observe it; we could only observe the body associated with it, and in the case of the Deity there is no such body. But we do know what a mind is like from being acquainted with our own minds. There should be nothing objectionable, then, in the idea of a mind far more powerful than ours, a mind whose will was able to do anything it chose. Such a mind is not, of course, the same thing as its effects in the universe; but may there not be such a mind? and may not the nature of the effects give us some empirical evidence, some clue to its nature?"

Let us take a parallel case which does not involve divinity to see what sort of clue this might be: Could there not be evidence for the existence among us of disembodied human minds? Suppose that before he died your grandfather said, "After I die, if my consciousness persists I'll try to get into contact with you. I'll sound middle C on the living room piano three times, and if I can I'll speak a few words." After he dies, you hear middle C on the piano sounded three times (others hear it too, and you make a record of the sound, so that there is no danger of hallucination) and then you hear your grandfather's voice. (You play the record back on your recording device later as often as you wish.) The voice is exactly his, you would recognize it anywhere, and he first says things that you alone knew, which you told to him and to no one else. The voice then says, "Don't worry about me, I'm all right." If this occurred, would you not take it as evidence that your grandfather still survived and was now talking to you? Would you be content to say merely that you heard these noises, and no more? Is there no difference in meaning between these two statements?

A. Middle C was struck three times, followed by the utterance of
     words in a voice exactly resembling my grandfather's. . . .

B. My grandfather, who died last week, spoke to me from the spirit
world, striking middle C three times, speaking to me. . . .

There is no *empirical* difference, granted. The sounds are the same
regardless; yet will you not suspect that this curious juxtaposition
of circumstances is the result of your grandfather's disembodied
existence? (Is it not true of all statements about other minds that
there is difference in meaning between consciousness-statements
and behavior-statements, but no difference in verification? See pages
299–302.)

Now let us suppose that the world were quite different from what
it is, and that people who committed murders were suddenly punished or struck to death, that people who were kind to their neighbors were rewarded, and so on. Suppose also that if someone
expressed doubt that God existed, iron would suddenly float or
tables would rise to the ceiling; or suppose a voice should suddenly
sound from the clouds, saying, "I am God, and I hereby command
you . . ." and that after investigation it was shown that nobody
had done this as a joke, and so on. Would you not say that this lent
some plausibility, at any rate, to the hypothesis that a Deity exists
who rewards kindness and punishes murder? or would you be content to say merely that these strange things were happening, and no
more? (Of course, things do not happen in this way, and so perhaps
there is no evidence for such a God, but that is not the point here:
if they happened, *would* we not consider it as evidence?)

It can be contended, then, that the God-hypothesis is an empirical
hypothesis in the sense that empirical facts would make it more
probable or less probable. Still, there would be no empirical difference between the person who asserted and the person who denied it;
they would both assent to the same empirically observable facts
about the voice, the striking down of murderers, and so on.

Or suppose that we could not possibly account for the origin and
development of living things in terms of evolution. Suppose that
man were the only species, and there was no fossil record of any
other. How then did man come into existence? Would this situation
not make it probable, or at any rate plausible, that God was the
cause? True, perhaps we do not need that hypothesis because we
can account for these things in naturalistic terms, but *if* we could
not, would not a supernaturalistic hypothesis then gain plausibility?
and would not the existence of man count as empirical evidence for

it? If this is so, we have a hypothesis about something in principle unobservable, but having empirical consequences; the statement of the hypothesis, however, is not reducible to statements about these consequences.

2. Mysticism. There is, however, another kind of view which proceeds along quite different lines. It does not conceive of God as having human characteristics, or even as being a mind. None of these concepts, indeed, no concept at all, applies to God. The argument runs as follows:

Traditional religions are full of anthropomorphic expressions which are bound to result in contradictions if we take them literally. There are countless examples of this. Here is one: Traditionally people refer to God as "He." Do they really mean that God is of masculine gender? Perhaps some people do: this may be a hangover from the days when the man was undisputed master of the household. Most reflective persons, however, would probably deny that they mean it literally: they would say that they do not mean that God is male rather than female. In denying that God is male they do not mean, of course, that God is female. Nor does the neuter "it," which would liken God to an inanimate object, render what they want to say. None of the personal pronouns seems appropriate. So the masculine pronoun continues to be used in spite of the fact that it is not, and is not meant to be, literally accurate.

This is a fairly crude bit of anthropomorphism. But there are many others which are not quite so evident to most of us. We speak, for example, of God as thinking, willing, desiring, hearing our prayers, finding ways to do things in the world; and many persons do take this quite literally. Some of these conflict with other things they say about God: for example, how can someone desire something unless there is something that he does not have? yet in the next breath they say that God, being infinite, has everything or even *is* everything. Or why is it necessary to find ways to accomplish things in the world (what this amounts to is finding means to achieve certain ends) when an omnipotent being could achieve ends without means (see pages 349–350)? But, whatever difficulties we may be led into by attributing these characteristics to God, there is one which is shared by all of these operations (thinking, willing, and so on); they are all *temporal* processes. Is not thinking necessarily in time? Would it make sense to speak of thinking of something but not for a definite length of time, indeed not in time at all? Is not willing something an event, and are not events necessarily in time? If it is really true, as theologians assert, that God is non-temporal, and that "with God there is no before and after," how can we escape contradiction when we attribute to God these mental processes? We cannot; we cannot consistently say that God does these temporal things and yet is non-temporal, any more than we can consistently speak of a circle that is not round.

Yet it is precisely of these temporal events that a *mind* is constituted. To speak of a mind without thoughts, without volitions, without events and processes taking place in its history, indeed, to speak of a mind *without* a history, what is this but to speak of no mind at all? [36] One cannot get out of this by saying that it is still a mind, but a mind of a very different kind from ours, such that we cannot conceive it; for if we cannot conceive it, what entitles us to call it a mind at all? What enables us to say that it is a *mind* rather than something else, or even to say that there *is* an "it" which we can call "mind"? It is much as if we were told that there exists a book, only a very special kind of book, without pages, without cover, without print—in fact, a red liquid. Whatever it is, it is not what we mean by the word "book" when we use this word in the English language, since it lacks the defining characteristics (see pages 26–28) of books. Just as surely does the "timeless mind" lack the defining characteristics of mind. And if something lacks the defining characteristics of X, we are not entitled to call it an X. It is mere sophistry and double-talk to do so.

According to the mystic, we are driven into the same difficulties no matter what characteristics we attribute to God: when we say that God is masculine, that God created the world or man, that God sent out angels, that God loves or hates or commands or prohibits. The moment we attribute a certain characteristic to God, we are *conceptualizing* God, for we have a *concept* of something and we attribute to God the characteristic of which we have the concept. And this, according to the mystic, is just what we cannot do, for God *cannot be conceptualized*. To refer to God as masculine is to bring God under a concept, but to speak of God as a mind, or as having wisdom, power, or goodness, is to do so not a whit less. All

---

[36] See on this point David Hume, *Dialogues concerning Natural Religion,* end of Part III and beginning of Part IV.

of these are conceptualizations, and as such all of them are equally illegitimate.

Where then does this leave us? What *can* we say about God? According to the mystic, nothing at all. Indeed, to say anything about God is to *limit* God. To say that God possesses characteristic A is to say that God lacks the characteristic not-A, and to say this is already to limit God's nature, which transcends all such distinctions. Since God is limitless, it is a mistake to say anything that would limit God's nature; and any characteristic we attribute to God does precisely this.

But if this is so, must we not carry the same reasoning on to its full conclusion? Can we even speak of God as *limitless?* for surely to say this is to attribute a characteristic. The same reasoning which would prevent calling God a mind would prevent calling Him limitless. Could we even speak of God as *existing?* Would not this limit God in the same way? [37] Indeed, to be rigidly consistent we would have to take the ultimate step: we would have to cease even to use the word "God," for to use the word and to mean something by it is already to conceptualize.

Having come to this impasse, one might well ask, "How is mysticism to be distinguished from agnosticism or skepticism? The consistent mystic must be silent—he says that God is beyond any description, that no words can be used to characterize God, including, ultimately, even the word 'God' itself. Is this not, if anything, more radical than the position of the skeptic who doubts that God exists, or of the agnostic who says that he does not know?"

At this point the mystic offers an answer: he says that the religious statements that he utters—such as "God is the ultimate Unity of all things," "God's goodness is an infinite outpouring from an infinite vessel," "God overflows all existence, transcends all distinctions, obliterates all boundaries"—are *not literally true at all,* and not intended to be so; rather, they are *symbolically* true. On the literal level, these statements (as well as more traditional and orthodox religious statements, such as "God is benevolent," "God is powerful, wise, and so on") are all vulnerable, and justly so, to

---

[37] Even if existence is not an attribute (see pages 325–326), it is still true that to refer to God as existing is to say something about Him, to use a concept to refer to Him, and thus to fall prey to the mystic's objection. If God transcends all description, this would seem to include describing God as *existing*

the criticisms of the skeptic: he has an easy time refuting the literalist and exposing his fallacies and contradictions. Nevertheless, if taken symbolically rather than literally, many religious statements may be true.

How can such a claim be justified? Let us recall our discussion of figurative language in Chapter 1 (see page 24). When we say, "She is but a walking shadow," we are using figurative language, for we do not literally mean that she is a shadow; nevertheless we are able to back up the check of metaphor with the cold cash of literality: we can say, "What I mean is that she is very thin, she is pale, she looks anemic . . ." The same can be done for most of the figurative expressions we employ in ordinary life; we can produce a literal meaning when we are called upon to do so. But what is the literal meaning when we say "God is the ultimate Unity of all things," "I am *one with* God," "God overflows all boundaries," and the like, if these are not intended to be literally true? What *are* the literally accurate expressions into which we could translate them? We cannot produce any. Then what could justify us in using such expressions, seeing that we cannot say what they mean? What, indeed, justifies us in saying what we do say rather than something else, for example the opposite?

The only answer that seems possible is that there is a certain *analogy* [38] or *resemblance* that is felt to exist between the things referred to in the symbols and the inexpressible, non-conceptualizable X which the symbols are said to be symbols *for*. If this were not so, there would be no grounds for saying that the expression "God is love" is a better symbol for an inexpressible truth than the expressions "God is hatred" or "God is pink fortitude."

To say even this much, however, is already to compromise the purity of the mystic's position. Using one expression, X, is a symbolic way of referring to an inexpressible, non-conceptualizable X', and using another expression, Y, is a symbolic way of referring to an inexpressible, non-conceptualizable Y'. Now why—on the basis of what—is X a better symbol for X' than Y is? Surely it is because there is some *likeness* of X to X' that X does not bear to Y'. If there were not some affinity between X and X', however tenuous,

[38] "Analogy" here means only *resemblance* or basis of *comparison*. It is not to be confused with an *argument* from analogy (see pages 353–356), i.e., an argument from resemblance.

the use of one expression rather than another, even symbolically, would be indefensible. Even if the statement, X, is not literally true, and what *is* literally true is inexpressible, one statement is taken as a better symbol for the inexpressible than another one is; and if one knows this, is one not already knowing something about the inexpressible?

But if we can go so far, if we can know that one statement is a better symbolic rendering of the inexpressible than another statement is, and if knowing this is knowing something about the inexpressible, then can we not ask the mystic what his inexpressible is like? can we not inquire, honestly but ungrammatically, what sort of thing his symbolic expression is a symbolic expression *of?*

(1) *Of an inexpressible reality.* It is usual for mystics to say that what the expressions they use refer to, not literally but symbolically, is some reality (for which they ordinarily use the word "God") the nature of which cannot be communicated in words. In a strict sense, this is, of course, incompatible with their own position. Suppose, for example, that this reality is called "objective"; is the word "objective" being used literally? If so, the reality is not inexpressible, for one is expressing something about it by calling it objective. Moreover, its title to be called this (if literally intended) can be attacked (see pages 342–343). If, on the other hand, the word "objective" is not intended literally, what entitles us to use it at all? Indeed, we can go further: what entitles us to call this reality "God"? Is this not almost deliberately misleading—leading us to associate it with the non-mystical God of traditional religions, while at the same time this association is declared to be irrelevant and mistaken? What, in fact, entitles us to say that it is a "reality" at all? If the "reality" is inexpressible, how are we enabled to express anything at all about it, including the assertion that it is a reality? Once again, it would appear, we are in consistency reduced to silence.

(2) *Of the mystic's inner experience.* An alternative which is more easily defended logically—one that would ordinarily be opposed by Christian mystics, because Christianity is committed to saying definite things about a God which it asserts to exist objectively, but would not be opposed by Buddhist mystics—is simply that what the statements of the mystic symbolize is nothing more than the mystic's own religious experiences. At first this view may seem to be

both unsatisfactory and pointless. Do we not already have a psychological language for referring to our inner experiences? "Yesterday a feeling of utter panic overwhelmed me, I felt paralyzed, afraid . . ." and so on. This is a description, though perhaps a crude one, of feelings. Why, if the mystic is referring only to his feelings, does he employ misleadingly objective terms, such as "God," and statements which are literally nonsense?

One might defend the mystic's use of such language in this way: With us the sight of a cat ordinarily evokes in us the utterance of the word "cat." The word refers to the thing. But suppose (to take an extreme case) that a person, and not only one person but thousands of persons separated by thousands of miles of space and years of time (many of whom could not have influenced each other or even known of each other's existence), regularly and spontaneously uttered the exclamation "Square circle!" We could dismiss this utterance as literal nonsense, but yet it would be a correct enough *symbol* of the experience of those who uttered the expression. Those who used it might not be able to describe to us what the feelings were which evoked from them this curious exclamation. Yet those who had the experience would understand the expression well enough, *not* as a symbol for square circles (which *would* be nonsense) but as a symbol for the peculiar kind of *experience* they had which brought forth in all of them this peculiar verbal response. Now, if we change the words from "square circle" to words which mystics of all ages typically use—about the oneness of the worshiper with the Ultimate Reality, about the infinite and overflowing character of God's nature, and the like—we have in a nutshell the situation of the mystic. His expressions are nonsense as long as they are taken literally, just as "square circle" is nonsense if taken literally; but if taken to be symbolic ways of referring to his own experiences, they may be as revealing (at least to other mystics) of the nature of his experience as the phrase "square circle" in our fictitious example.

On this interpretation, then, a deeply religious nature, and a capacity for the most exalted religious experiences, are quite compatible with a philosophical naturalism. Buddha, for example, combined both of them. Perhaps the language of the mystic, nonsensical though it may sometimes be, and unintelligible to non-mystics, is of great value, not because it stands for anything as the symbol

"cat" does to what it stands for, indeed not because it stands literally for anything, but because it helps to lead people to, and finally
to evoke within them, certain *experiences* which those who have had
them consider to be the most worth-while of all experiences available to human beings.[39]

SELECTED READINGS FOR CHAPTER 5

Mechanism and vitalism:

Durant Drake. *Invitation to Philosophy*. Boston: Houghton Mifflin Co.,
1933. Chapter 18.

Morris R. Cohen. *Reason and Nature*. New York: Harcourt Brace & Co.,
1931. Book 2, Chapter 3.

George G. Simpson. *The Meaning of Evolution*. New Haven: Yale University Press, 1949.

D. Needham. *Man a Machine*. London: Kegan Paul, 1926. (Psyche Miniatures.)

Eugenio Rignano. *Man Not a Machine*. London: Kegan Paul, 1926.
(Psyche Miniatures.)

Henri Bergson. *Creative Evolution*. London: Macmillan, 1911.

Ernest Nagel. "Mechanistic Explanation and Organismic Biology," *Philosophy and Phenomenological Research*, XI, 1951.

C. D. Broad, *The Mind and Its Place in Nature*, Chapter 2. London,
Kegan Paul, 1925.

The mental and the physical:

G. S. Fullerton. *An Introduction to Philosophy*. New York: Macmillan,
1906. Chapters 8 and 9.

Peter Laslett (ed.). *The Physical Basis of Mind*. Oxford: Basil Blackwell,
1951.

Durant Drake. *Invitation to Philosophy*. Boston: Houghton Mifflin Co.,
1933. Chapter 19.

G. S. Fullerton. *A System of Metaphysics*. New York: Macmillan, 1904.
Part 3.

[39] We have treated here the logic of the mystic's position, without going
into a psychological description of the mystic's experiences. For these fascinating pieces of descriptive psychology, see for example Evelyn Underhill, *Mysticism* (London: Macmillan, 1930); William James, *The Varieties of Religious
Experience* (New York: Longmans, Green & Co., 1902), especially Chapters
16 and 17; W. T. Stace, *Time and Eternity* (Princeton: Princeton University
Press, 1952), especially Chapters 2, 3, and 4. The book by Stace contains an
extended discussion of the notion of symbolic truth and the logic of mysticism
in general, in addition to its description of mystical experiences.

Rene Descartes. *Meditations* (1621); *On the Passions of the Soul* (1630). Many editions.

C. D. Broad. *The Mind and Its Place in Nature*. London: Kegan Paul, 1925. Chapter 3.

John Wisdom. *Other Minds*. Oxford: Basil Blackwell, 1952.

The concept of deity:

John Stuart Mill. *Three Essays on Religion*. ("Nature," "The Utility of Religion," "Theism"). London: Longmans, Green & Co., 1874.

David Hume. *Dialogues concerning Natural Religion*. Numerous editions, the best of which is probably that of Norman Kemp Smith. Edinburgh: Nelson & Sons, 1935.

J. MacTaggart. *Some Dogmas of Religion*. London: Edward Arnold & Co., 1906.

Curt J. Ducasse. *A Philosophical Scrutiny of Religion*. New York: The Ronald Press, 1953.

W. T. Stace. *Religion and the Modern Mind*. Philadelphia: Lippincott, 1952.

W. T. Stace. *Time and Eternity*. Princeton: Princeton University Press, 1952.

William James. *The Will to Believe*. New York: Longmans, Green & Co., 1897.

John Wisdom. "Gods," in *Logic and Language, First Series*, ed. Anthony Flew. Oxford: Basil Blackwell, 1951.

W. T. Stace. "Naturalism and Religion," *Proceedings and Addresses of the American Philosophical Association*, 23, 1949–50.

George Santayana. *Reason in Religion*. New York: Scribners, 1905.

William James. *The Varieties of Religious Experience*. New York: Longmans, Green & Co., 1902.

James Ward. *Naturalism and Agnosticism*. 2 vols. London: Adam & Charles Black, 1899.

Samuel Alexander. *Space, Time, and Deity*. 2 vols. London: Macmillan, 1918.

Evelyn Underhill. *Mysticism*. London: Macmillan, 1930.

EXERCISES

1. Discuss and evaluate the mechanism-vitalism issue as set forth in one of the following:

    a. Morris R. Cohen, *Reason and Nature*, pp. 241–282.

    b. C. D. Broad, *The Mind and Its Place in Nature*, Chapter 2.

2. Evaluate the following statements:

    a. Organisms are just complex machines.

b. Biology can be reduced to physics and chemistry.

c. On the basis of what was taking place on the earth 1½ billion years ago (before life existed on the earth), the advent of life could not possibly have been predicted.

d. What's the vitalism dispute all about? Everyone knows that organisms behave differently from rocks and rivers.

3. State as many ways as you can in which the mechanism-vitalism controversy can be formulated.

4. List as many things as you can that can be said about states of consciousness that cannot be said about brain-processes, or vice versa.

5. Describe the notion of mind as set forth in one of the following:

    a. C. D. Broad, *The Mind and Its Place in Nature*, especially Chapter 3.

    b. C. A. Strong, *Why the Mind Has a Body*.

    c. G. S. Fullerton, *A System of Metaphysics*, Part 3.

    d. Gilbert Ryle, *The Concept of Mind*.

6. If mental telepathy should turn out to be a fact, would it still be true to say that mental events are private?

7. How can I know (or can I know at all) that the color-sensation I have when I say "red" is similar to the color-sensation you have when you say "red"?

8. According to Descartes (*Les Passions de l'Ame*, Art. 34 ff.), an interactionist, the point of contact between mind and body lies in the pineal gland of the brain, by which physical stimuli cause states of consciousness and volitions are carried into action. "Let us . . . conceive of the soul as having her chief seat in the little gland which is in the middle of the brain, whence she radiates to all the rest of the body by means of the spirits, the nerves, and even the blood, which, participating in the impressions of the spirits, can carry them through the arteries to all the members . . ." Evaluate this view.

9. Evaluate each of the following statements:

    a. Mental events are nothing but brain-events.

    b. Whether or not life is emergent, mind certainly is.

    c. According to parallelism, mind exerts no influence over matter.

    d. The brain secretes thought as the liver secretes bile.

    e. What I see is always something going on in my own brain.

10. Change each of these figurative expressions (involving the use of physical metaphors for the mental) so that they are literally correct:

    a. You didn't really see it—it's all in your mind.

    b. She has too many ideas in her head.

    c. This strange notion kept cropping up in the back of her mind.

    d. She was a scatterbrain—her thoughts just went flitting this way and that through her mind.

    e. Having so many responsibilities put too much pressure on his mind.

11. On the basis of the discussion of logical possibility in Chapter 2 and of mind in Chapter 5, would you say it is logically possible (and why)

a. for one mind to affect another mind without the intermediary of matter?

b. for a mind to exist without a body?

c. for a mind to *touch* a body?

d. for a person to have two bodies?

12. Do you think that the hypothesis of life after death is in any way incompatible with the Verifiability Criterion? (Read on this, first, A. J. Ayer, *Language, Truth, and Logic,* page 198; then Moritz Schlick, "Meaning and Verification"; then V. C. Aldrich, "Schlick and Ayer on Immortality." The last two readings are included in Feigl and Sellars, *Readings in Philosophical Analysis,* New York: Appleton-Century-Crofts, 1949.)

13. Machines now being constructed are said to have memory. But doesn't memory imply a mind? Do these machines then have minds? Explain.

14. Evaluate the following arguments from analogy:

a. When I behave in this way, I am angry. You are behaving in this way, therefore you are angry.

b. If we found a watch, we would infer that its parts didn't come together by accident, but were the result of design. Similarly, we find a universe, and may infer that its parts didn't come together by accident, but resulted from design.

15. Consider the following pairs of statements in the light of the Verifiability Criterion of meaningfulness. Do the two members of each pair mean the same? Why?

a. Living things exhibit teleological behavior.

There is a Life-force, or Vital Principle, in living things.

b. He flunks the color-blindness tests and gets traffic signals mixed up, and so on.

He is color-blind.

c. At 11 o'clock your muscles will contract, you will show all the symptoms of pain, you will shout that you are in pain, and so on.

At 11 o'clock you will feel a stabbing pain.

d. Organisms exhibit benevolent adaptations, things work together for good in the world, and so on.

There is a benevolent Deity running the world.

16. Discuss the following allegations with reference to the problem of evil:

a. All evils occur for wise and good ends.

b. Evil is justified by the good that comes out of it.

c. The evil in the universe is the result of man's wickedness.

d. Perhaps everything we think evil is really good.

e. God permits evil even though He does not condone it; not to permit it would involve even greater evils than those that now exist.

17. What are some religious hypotheses for which the traditional problem of evil does not constitute a problem at all? Why, in each case?

18. Evaluate the status of statements about God as explanation (see Chapter 3) of particular events in the world.

19. "No scientific argument—by which I mean an argument drawn from the phenomena of nature—can ever have the slightest tendency either to prove or to disprove the existence of God." (W. T. Stace, *Religion and the Modern Mind*, page 76.) Do you agree with this statement, and why? Discuss the general question of the relevance of empirical facts to religious belief. (Read Chapter 5 of Stace's *Religion and the Modern Mind*, the chapter from which the above quotation was taken, for more material on this question.)

20. Which of the following statements could be taken, in your opinion, as literally true? When words or phrases in them cannot be taken literally, try to translate the sentences in which they occur into sentences which *can* be taken literally. Examine those that can be taken literally, for internal consistency.

    a. God is above the stars.

    b. God is above human concerns.

    c. God existed before time began.

    d. "And God said . . ."

    e. God exists throughout all space and all time.

    f. The earth is God's footstool.

    g. God caused the world.

21. Discuss the criteria for the use of the word "exist" with reference to each of the following:

    a. "Tables exist."

    b. "Headaches exist."

    c. "Magnetism exists."

    d. "Ghosts exist."

    e. "God exists."

6

Perceiving the World

We are now ready to consider a problem which our discussion in previous chapters has been leading up to for some time: the problem of how the human mind can have knowledge of a physical world which exists and (so we believe) continues to exist whether minds exist or not.

The need to consider this problem has doubtless been increasingly apparent to many readers as our discussion advanced. Thus far, whatever statements we may have doubted or analyzed, we have not questioned the truth of statements about the existence of physical objects. We have assumed merely that we know by means of empirical observation that a physical world exists: "How do you know there are trees?" "I see them, of course." We considered the phenomenalistic reduction of statements about electrons into statements about physical objects; but we have performed no analysis at all upon statements about physical objects. Again, when we considered empirical doubt we said that (according to one view at least) if seeing and touching a hand does not remove the doubt that a hand is there, nothing would remove it and the doubt is empty. But even here we assumed that seeing and touching do suffice to show that a hand is really there. What would happen if one questioned even this?

It is time now to consider such questions as these. How do we know that our senses give us information about a world which exists whether we do or not? Indeed, how can we be sure that there is such a world at all? In practice, of course, we never doubt it; still, it would be interesting to know how we would go about trying to establish it. The fact that we never doubt something surely does not prove that that something is true.

I. NAIVE REALISM

It may not seem obvious to everyone that there is a problem here. Many persons would be inclined to hold that where unobservable entities are concerned, such as electrons, there *is* a problem: how can we know (since we cannot observe electrons) that such statements are true? Or, if we are more sophisticated, how do we determine what they mean? But once we have given their meaning or determined their truth in terms of what we do observe, that would seem to solve the problem. In other words, this chapter would seem to them quite superfluous.

Moreover, this agrees with the way we "naturally" tend to look at the matter. When I survey the scene before me, I would ordinarily describe it by saying that I see a desk, with some papers on it, books on a shelf, several chairs, walls, a window, and outside the window, houses and trees in the distance. I see these things, and I never doubt that all these things exist (after all, don't I see them?), and that I see them as they are. In other words, I am a *naive realist*. If I were uncorrupted by philosophy and were asked "How do you know that these things exist?" I would say, "Because I see them, of course! How could I see them if they weren't there to be seen?" If I doubted such statements as these, I would soon be considered a candidate for an institution for the mentally deranged.

In all of this, then, what is there that constitutes a philosophical problem? If I were told that a considerable portion of the energies of philosophers for several hundred years had been expended on analyzing beliefs such as those in the existence of chairs and people and trees, I would be inclined to make certain remarks which would hardly be in praise of the philosophic enterprise.

Yet we do not have to probe very deep beneath the surface of the subject to have doubts about the matter.

1. Isn't what we perceive dependent, at least in part, on the nature of our organs of perception? If our eyes were different, what we see would be different; if our taste-buds were different, so would be the tastes we have. What right then have we to assume that we see or taste things the way they really are? In fact, how could we possibly know "how things really are," or "what they are really like in themselves"? Suppose our two eyes did not focus into one image

and we saw everything double. Or suppose we had one eye on each side of our heads, like horses, so that we could see almost 180° of an arc but (probably) no spatial depth. Or if the rods and cones in the retina were different or nonexistent, we would not have the color-vision we now have—indeed, most mammals do not have color-vision, and cannot distinguish one color from another, only degrees of lightness and darkness (as in a black-and-white movie); bees, on the other hand, can see ultra-violet, which we cannot even imagine. Or suppose we had a thousand eyes, like some insects; would not the world look very different to us?

Thus far we have considered only vision; similarly, our senses of hearing, smell, taste, and touch might be quite different from what they are. We might have other senses, too, the nature of which we cannot now even imagine, which would reveal to us things we cannot now imagine either. Would not the world then look very different to us? (We can't even say "look," for this implies vision; and we have no names for the hypothetical other senses we are now discussing.) How would things look—or shall we say appear—to the inhabitant of Mars, for example to the "very intelligent cuttlefish" that H. G. Wells conceives as inhabiting that planet? As long as the content of our perceptions depends so much on the nature of the perceiving organ, and as long as we are unable to shed our perceiving organs as we do spectacles to try out other ones, how can we be so sure that we are perceiving things as they are? (We use the general word "perceiving" to cover hearing, seeing, smelling, etc., the "etc." covering also whatever senses there may be available to living creatures elsewhere in the universe.) Indeed, do we have any right to say what the physical world is *really* like at all?

2. Even with our present organs of perception, there are perfectly familiar cases of not perceiving things as they are. These we call *illusions*. The stick looks bent when it is half immersed in water, though it is really straight. The trees on the distant mountainside look grayish-blue, though ordinarily we would say they are dark green. The two lines in the Müller illusion (one with arrows pointing inwards, the other with arrows pointing outwards) look different in length, though they are equally long. In yellowish artificial light the blue dress looks black. The train whistle seems to be higher in pitch as the train approaches and lower as it recedes, though the pitch (so we believe) is the same all the time. The vessel of luke-

warm water feels cold to one hand (which has just been near a hot stove) and hot to the other (which has just been in ice water) although the temperature of the water is the same throughout the vessel. Surely it is a matter of common knowledge that our senses sometimes deceive us. Everybody makes the distinction between how things seem, or *appear*, and how they really *are*. We often "perceive things the way they aren't." (Sometimes the causes of such phenomena lie within us, sometimes without; but they are all classed together here as illusions.)

3. Indeed, often there is an appearance when there is no reality at all; we "perceive things that aren't even there." This is a more radical way in which our senses deceive us. The drunken man sees pink rats going up and down the wall, but there are no pink rats there. Press your eyeball and you will see two candles, but only one is there. If you are anxiously waiting for someone you may hear a knock on the door ten times throughout the evening, though no knock has really occurred. A man may feel intense pain in his leg although that leg has been amputated some time before.

This is a more misleading kind of perceptual error than illusion. So far we have assumed that, although we perceived certain things wrongly, and that the nature of our perceptions depended on the nature of the perceiving organ, there were nevertheless things to be perceived. In hallucination, however, we seem to perceive what does not even exist, at least not at the time and place we perceive it.

4. Having thus prepared the ground, we can be much more radically skeptical than this. Our senses sometimes deceive us. Very well; how do we know they don't deceive us all the time? If sometimes, why not always? Maybe the whole world is one gigantic hallucination; maybe it isn't there at all; maybe we are constantly being deceived. A much more skillful deception, no doubt, than pink rats or oases in the desert when you are thirsty and they suddenly disappear; but isn't it possible? How do we know that it isn't so?

Descartes (1596–1650) told himself that perhaps there was an evil demon at work, arranging things in such a way that he would *believe* there was a world of real physical objects, when in fact there were no such objects at all. It would be just *as if* there were—so much "as if" that he could never tell the difference. Thus, Descartes decided that he could never know that what was before him was really a table, that there were real trees outside, and so on. All these things he could doubt. What could he *not* doubt? Only that he, the doubter, existed, at least while he was doubting.

What then about the physical world? How do we know that the demon is not constantly deceiving us? Descartes tried to show that God is not a deceiver and therefore would not play us false on so important a matter as this. But, beginning with only oneself and one's doubt, how can one bring in God, much less prove that God is not a deceiver? These issues carry us outside the confines of the present chapter; here we can only comment that no one believes Descartes was successful in his attempt to make our knowledge of the physical world depend on the goodness of God. (The doubts about the physical world could also take the form of suspecting that it is all a dream—that perhaps we shall even awaken the next minute and find it so.)

Suggestions such as these will be discussed in this chapter. We cannot face them all at once, but only gradually. And as solutions (we hope) gradually appear, other difficulties will appear also, which are too technical to set forth until we have developed a more precise vocabulary with which to deal with the issues that are now confronting us.

II. REPRESENTATIVE REALISM

The man in the street, though he would probably not be able to disprove the proposition that "it's all a dream," would dismiss it as absurd. "Of course it's a real tree I'm seeing"—and he would ask us to touch it if we doubted it, thus referring us once again to the evidence of our senses and assuming the very point at issue.

The "man in the street" is sometimes called a naive realist. But if the expression "naive realism" is construed to mean the doctrine that "things are always as they appear," even he would have to deny it. He too believes in illusions and hallucinations; at least *some* things are not as they appear, and some things that appear aren't real *things* at all. This is already an opening wedge. From this point on it is not difficult to get him to believe, not only that we *sometimes* don't perceive physical things, but that we *never* perceive physical things at all.

Let us consider the following line of thought: we begin with certain scientific statements about perception such as would be found in psychology and physiology books. There is a tree out there; light-waves emanate from the tree, and some of them impinge upon the retina of your eye. This (in a way we do not exactly know) causes an electro-chemical impulse to be conveyed along the optic nerve going from the eyes to the brain. A very small fraction of a second later this impulse reaches what is known as the occipital lobe of the brain; then and only then are you visually *aware* of the tree, and a *sensation* occurs. If anything went wrong along the way—if no light were illuminating the tree, if the eyes were shut or blind, if the optic nerve were cut or atrophied, if a portion of the brain were removed—there would be no sensation. All these prior events are necessary conditions for its occurrence; and the sensation occurs *only* when all these conditions have been fulfilled.

Knowledge is limited to sensations. Now, this opens up an alarming possibility: what we are acquainted with, what we "know in perception," is never the object, for instance the tree, itself. What we are directly acquainted with is only the sensation we have. At time t_1 an explosion occurs; at time t_2, an infinitesimally small fraction of a second later, we see it (we have a visual sensation); at time t_3, a small fraction of a second later still (since sound does not travel as fast as light), we hear it. We have no knowledge of the event until the sensations occur; everything we know about the world is through sensations. And not only this: not only do we know events *through* or by means of sensations, but it now appears that *the sensations themselves are all we really know.* We say we are aware of the explosion; but what we should say in strict accuracy is that we are aware only of our own sensations of sight and sound (visual and auditory sensations). What goes on at the other end of the wire (nerve) connecting the brain with the outside world we do not know; we only know what occurs at the brain-end, or rather (if mental events are non-spatial), what occurs when the impulse has reached the brain-end. More than this we know nothing. If there were something in the nerve, for example, which distorted all the impulses that traveled along it, we would never get a correct impression of the thing. All we can be *sure* of is our sensation, not the *thing of which* it is a sensation. Sometimes we have sensations that have no things as their causes at all: cases of hallucination, such as hearing the knock on the door, were not caused by any events in the outside world at all; they were, as we say, "just in your mind," or caused by complicated events going on in your brain, although the sensation occurred just *as if* it had been caused by a real knock on the door. Indeed, it is possible to imagine our sensations occurring just as they do and having the characteristics that they have, even though nothing outside our bodies caused any of them at all! As long as the sensations themselves were the same, the rest would make no difference.

It would be easy to reply, "But we couldn't have any sensations if there were no real physical objects outside of us to cause them!" If we are acquainted only with our own sensations, how can we know this? By being acquainted with physical objects too, namely things that are *not* sensations? But this, on our present hypothesis, is impossible. If you are acquainted only with your own sensations, you cannot smuggle in something which is *not* sensations in order to prove that something other than sensations exists to cause the sensations.

The analogy of the telephone exchange. The following analogy has sometimes been used to illustrate the situation: The mind is like a telephone exchange; you are the telephone operator, or clerk; messages come in to you along the wires (nerves) from the outside world. You do not see the people who do the telephoning; you do not even hear them as you would if you were in the same room with them; you hear only the sounds of their voices as they reach your end of the wire. You receive their incoming calls via the incoming wires (afferent nerves) and you connect them with their proper parties via other wires (efferent nerves), but you yourself never get outside the exchange.

This situation has been very vividly put by the scientific writer Karl Pearson, in the late nineteenth century, in his book, *The Grammar of Science:* [1]

> We are accustomed to talk of the "external world," of the "reality" outside us. We speak of individual objects having an existence independent of our own. The store of past sense-impressions, our thoughts and memories, although most probably they have beside their physical element a close correspondence with some physical change or impress in the brain, are yet spoken of as *inside* ourselves. On the other hand, although if a sensory nerve be divided anywhere short of the brain, we lose the corresponding class of sense impression, we yet speak of

[1] Quoted from Everyman Library edition, pp. 56–58.

many sense-impressions, such as form and texture, as existing outside ourselves. How close then can we actually get to this supposed world outside ourselves? Just as near but no nearer than the brain terminals of the sensory nerves. We are like the clerk in the central telephone exchange who cannot get nearer to his customers than his end of the telephone wires. We are indeed worse off than the clerk, for to carry out the analogy properly we must suppose him *never to have been outside the telephone exchange, never to have seen a customer or any one like a customer—in short, never, except through the telephone wire, to have come in contact with the outside universe.* Of that "real" universe outside himself he would be able to form no direct impression; the real universe for him would be the aggregate of his constructs from the messages which were caused by the telephone wires in his office. About those messages and the ideas raised in his mind by them he might reason and draw his inferences; and his conclusions would be correct—for what? For the world of telephonic messages, for the type of messages that go through the telephone. Something definite and valuable he might know with regard to the spheres of action and of thought of his telephonic subscribers, but outside those spheres he could have no experience. Pent up in his office he could never have seen or touched even a telephonic subscriber *in himself.* Very much in the position of such a telephone clerk is the conscious ego of each one of us seated at the brain terminals of the sensory nerves. Not a step nearer than those terminals can the ego get to the "outer world," and what in and for themselves are the subscribers to its nerve exchange it has no means of ascertaining. Messages in the form of sense-impressions come flowing in from that "outside world," and these we analyze, classify, store up, and reason about. But of the nature of "things-in-themselves," of what may exist at the other end of our system of telephone wires, we know nothing at all.

But the reader, perhaps, remarks, "I not only see an object, but I can *touch* it. I can trace the nerve from the tip of my finger to the brain. I am not like the telephone clerk, I can follow my network of wires to their terminals and find what is at the other end of them." Can you, reader? Think for a moment whether your ego has for one moment got away from his brain exchange. The sense-impression that you call touch was just as much as sight felt only at the brain end of a sensory nerve. What has told you also of the nerve from the tip of your finger to your brain? Why, sense-impressions also, messages conveyed along optic or tactile sensory nerves. In truth, all you have been doing is to employ one subscriber to your telephone exchange to tell you about the wire that goes to a second, but you are just as far as ever from tracing out for yourself the telephone wires to the individual subscriber and ascertaining what his nature is in and for himself. The immediate sense-impression is just as far removed from what you term the "outside world" as the store of impresses. If our telephone clerk had recorded by aid of a phonograph certain of the messages from the outside world on past occasions, then if any telephonic message on its receipt set several phonographs repeating past messages, we have an image analogous to what goes on in the brain. Both telephone and phonograph are equally removed from what the clerk might call the "real outside world," but they enable him through their sounds to construct a universe; he projects those sounds, which are really inside his office, and speaks of them as the external universe. This outside world is constructed by him from the contents of the inside sounds, which differ as widely from things-in-themselves as language, the symbol, must always differ from the thing it symbolizes. For our telephone clerk sounds would be the real world, and yet we can see how conditioned and limited it would be by the range of his particular telephone subscribers and by the contents of their messages.

So it is with our brain; the sounds from telephone and phonograph correspond to immediate and stored sense-impressions. These sense-impressions we project as it were outwards and term the real world outside ourselves. But the things-in-themselves which the sense-impressions symbolize, the "reality," as the metaphysicians wish to call it, at the other end of the nerve, remains unknown and is unknowable. Reality of the external world lies for science and for us in combinations of form and color and touch—sense-impressions as widely divergent from the thing "at the other end of the nerve" as the sound of the telephone from the subscriber at the other end of the wire. We are cribbed and confined in this world of sense-impressions like the exchange clerk in his world of sounds, and not a step beyond can we get. As his world is conditioned and limited by his particular network of wires, so ours is conditioned by our nervous system, by our organs of sense. Their peculiarities determine what is the nature of the outside world which we construct. It is the similarity in the organs of sense and in the perceptive faculty of all normal human beings which makes the outside world the same, or *practically* the same, for them all. To return to the old analogy, it is as if two telephone exchanges had very nearly identical groups of subscribers. In this case a wire between the two exchanges would soon convince the imprisoned clerks that they had something in common peculiar to themselves. That conviction corresponds in our comparison to the recognition of other consciousnesses.

The view set forth by Pearson in this passage is sometimes called "epistemological dualism": "epistemological" because it has to do with epistemology (theory of knowledge, from the Greek *episteme,* "knowledge"); "dualism" because it asserts the existence of *two* kinds of entities: sensations and physical things. It is also called "representative realism": "realism" because it asserts that physical things do exist, "representative" because the sensations *represent* them (symbolize them, stand for them). One might say that it would be more consistent if the view held *only* to sensations, inasmuch as this is all that (according to the view, at least) we can be acquainted with; but nevertheless the theory does go on to assert that physical things, as well as sensations, exist.

Physical things, on the view we are considering, exist at least as the *causes* of sensations, just as the people at the other end of the wires cause us to hear what we do through impulses carried along the wires. But the cause itself, of course, cannot be known, and each person is shut up within the charmed circle of his own sensations.

Do we know anything about the things other than that they cause the sensations? Some versions of the theory have gone on to suggest that the relation, in addition to being causal, is also one of *resemblance;* the sensations are *like* the things, at least in some respects. The view of Democritus, a Greek philosopher who lived in the fifth century B.C., is an instance of this: he held that all things, such as trees, constantly give off effluvia which are tiny replicas of the trees themselves; some of these, flying about through the air, get into the head via the eyes, and in this way we see things. Sometimes they get battered about and distorted along the way; in this way Democritus tried to account for perceptual error. A crude theory, no doubt; but already human beings were bothered by the problem of how a thing, a tree for instance, outside of us, somehow gets *inside* in order that we may be acquainted with it. And the theory of images (replicas) was the simplest, even if not the most accurate, way in which to account for this.

Representative realism is a kind of "enlightened common-sense" view; it is the next step from naive realism. Once throw overboard the view that we are directly acquainted with physical objects, the next most attractive view is that we are never acquainted with them but only with sensations, but that the sensations somehow represent the objects. Unfortunately, however, there are objections to it which are very difficult to overcome:

1. How could we know that the sensations resemble, or are like, the things? We could know this, presumably, by observing them both to see whether they were, just as we look at two curtains to see whether they are really the same shade. But *ex hypothesi* this

is impossible; we can be acquainted only with our own sensations. And we can never know whether there is a certain relation between two entities if we can observe only one of the two terms in the relation.

2. Nor could we know that the thing is a *cause* of the sensation. If causality has anything to do with observable constant conjunctions, then we never *could* observe A, the thing, and B, the sensation, to discover whether the thing (or some aspect of it, or something happening to it) was regularly followed by the sensation. Thus, even if there was such a causal relation between thing and sensation, according to the theory itself we could never know it.

3. The theory breaks down when it comes to the "connecting links" between the sensations and the physical world outside: the sense-organs and nerves. For how can we know that *they* exist? If we can be acquainted with them, they must, according to the assumption of the theory, be sensations also. But a *sensation* can hardly carry an impulse from the tree to the brain. If, on the other hand, we are *not* acquainted with them, then we are hardly in a position to assert that they exist at all; and yet the theory does assert this. (And if we can never be acquainted with them, what can terms such as "tree," "nerves," and so on even mean?) The telephone operator can be acquainted only with the sounds that come in along the wires of the exchange; but how can we know that there are *wires?* or that he is in an exchange at all? If he knows this, then, just as in the case of tables and trees, they must be sensations also; in which case they can hardly be external objects that connect the things with the sensations. Sense-organs, nerves, and brains seem to be in the same boat as tables, chairs, and trees. If the one is unknowable, so is the other. If it isn't, then it is sensation too; and then the whole telephone exchange collapses into the operator and the analogy breaks down.

In our analogy the telephone operator is in an exchange, and we are supposed to know this. *We* know that he is getting messages from the outside along the wires. *We* distinguish between the exchange and the messages received. But, if we are like the operator in the exchange, have we a right to do this? How can we speak of an exchange at all? If all we can know is the messages that come in, how can we know that there is an exchange at all through which they come? And how can we know that messages come in from the outside? How can sensations come in along nerves that must really be inside too? (If they're not inside we have no right to say they exist at all, since we can know only what is inside.)

But if the only nerves and sense-organs we can know are sensations too, in the mind, then we cannot say that sense-impressions come "flowing in" along these nerves (wires). Nor can we speak of sensations as being nearer to the brain-end of the nerve than to the eye-end. How could the mind, placed at the brain terminals of the sensory nerves, place itself at the end of a nerve which (as it now turns out) it must have constructed within itself? And how can we speak of something existing at the other end of the nerves that is completely unknowable? Moreover, since the nerve to be known must be in the mind, can anything be at the end of it which is not also in the mind?

If the analogy of the mind (here the word can refer simply to the sensations) with the operator in an exchange is to hold, the entire exchange must be collapsed into the mind of the clerk. This breaks down the analogy itself: it becomes senseless when we have placed the telephone exchange inside the operator. (We can not even speak of two operators as connected by a wire, if every wire must really be in some operator.)

What has happened? The theory seems to assume that it itself is not true. It is self-contradictory. *In the very process of showing* that we can have no knowledge of an external world, but only of our own sensations (messages at the end of the wire), *we have assumed that there is an external world and that we have knowledge of it,* at least enough knowledge to know that there are things in the world which stimulate sense-organs, which in turn stimulate nerves and send "messages" to the brain. *Only* if we know these things can our analogy get into operation; but, if the theory is true, we can never know these things! The sounds we hear are causally related to the exchange—later the very existence of the exchange (at least the possibility of knowing it) has to be denied, but not before it has played an indispensable part in the analogy. Thus, in the very attempt to deny any possible knowledge of an external world, we unconsciously assume all the while that it does exist and that we know some things about it.

III. SUBJECTIVE IDEALISM

The view which is almost an inevitable "next step" from representative realism is called *subjective* idealism to distinguish it from the view sometimes known as objective idealism, which is a view of a different kind. It is called "idealism," somewhat misleadingly, because of its derivation from the word "idea"; it might better be called "idea-ism." John Locke (1632–1704) used the word "idea" to cover not only what we use it to cover (such as when we say "I now have an idea of Paris") but also what we have called "sensations." Any immediate experience—a color, a sound, a smell, a taste, a thought, a pain, a stab of jealousy or anger, an image—all these are ideas in Locke's sense. And in this broad sense of the word "ideas," idealism is the view that nothing exists except minds and their ideas. The theory is most closely associated with the name of George Berkeley, Bishop of Cloyne (1685–1753).

Idealism builds on the basis of the theory of representative realism and is most easily made plausible with reference to it. Assuming the main contentions of representative realism, idealism modifies it in one important respect: it denies that there are external physical objects to cause our sensations. We could never know them if they did exist; they are just so much excess baggage. We have certain sensations—this we know for sure; but if we can be acquainted only with these sensations of ours, how could we possibly know that there is an "external world" to cause them? Of course we couldn't. Realism itself admits this: it admits that all we can know about physical things is that they cause the sensations that we have; what they are like in themselves we can never know. But even this, says idealism, is asserting too much: we could never observe such a causal relation; we must observe both C and E if we are ever to know that C causes E. And if one goes on, as some realists do, to assert that our sensations, or some of them, are *like* objects, idealists object at once that even if this were true, we could never know it. Once again, we must be able to examine both A and B directly in order to know that C is like E. (Moreover, said Berkeley, how could an idea possibly be like anything else that is not an idea?) By realism's own admission, we cannot observe one of the terms in this relation—we can't compare the chair with our sensation of the chair to see whether they are alike, or indeed whether there is any other kind of relation between them. All that is accessible to us is our sensation of the chair. Therefore, let us do away with the chair itself, and retain only the sensations. This is all we can be acquainted with; and all that we are being deprived of is something we could never be acquainted with anyway, so we could hardly miss it.

In what sense do physical objects exist? We can never be acquainted with the chair itself, only with our sensations of the chair. But when we say we have a sensation *of a chair,* doesn't this imply that there is a chair for us to have a sensation of? It surely seems so; and to remedy this situation, in the future we shall not call it "sensation of a chair" but rather "chair-sensation." Why is this an improvement? Simply because it does not carry with it the implication that the thing really exists. When I have a chair-sensation I am only having a sensation of a certain kind: I am only referring to the qualitative character of the sensation itself, not making any assertion as to how it came about or how it is related to anything else; indeed, I can have a chair-sensation even if I am the victim of a hallucination. Some sensations of a similar nature occur often enough for me to give them names; thus, one kind of sensation I call "chair" and another I call "table." All I know is that I just do have these different kinds of sensations; and I can classify these sensations according to their similarity to each other. Some sensations are similar enough to each other to receive the same name, "chair"; and the same for "table." I do not imply by this that anything other than sensations exists, but only that sensations occur in certain regular patterns, certain *groups of similars,* to which I then give names. And of course the names are given not just to the recurring groups of visual sensations, but to the touch-sensations as well. The word "chair," for example, names a group (or in other words, a complex) of similar touch-sensations as well as sight-sensations.

Nor do "sight" and "touch" imply sense-organs. When I say that I have visual sensations, auditory sensations, tactual sensations, and so forth, I imply nothing about the origin or causal genesis of the sensations; I only assert that the sensations are of different types. There is a respect (which everyone who is not blind recognizes) in which all visual sensations are alike and quite unlike any auditory sensations. The two classes are just qualitatively different, that's all; and in practice no one would ever confuse the one with the other.

What about sense-organs themselves? Eyes and ears are no different from tables and trees. I am having table-sensations right now; I can have eye-sensations by looking at your face, or by looking in a mirror. And I can have brain-sensations by opening up somebody's head. What about the mirror? what about the head? These are just sensations too. *All* physical objects are just groups or *complexes* of sensations, and *nothing but* that. No physical objects exist as something other than sensations. All there is is sensations; they occur in fairly uniform groups, to which we give names; but strictly speaking they are sensation-names and not physical-object names.

If one still insists on using the phrase "physical object" to name something *other* than a sensation-group, one must grant that it names something nonexistent (existent but unknowable according to representative realism, nonexistent according to idealism); and in that case there would be no possible application for physical-object names. Yet physical-object names *do* clearly have application; therefore, they apply to sensations, or to complexes of sensations. It is to these complexes that we give names. Indeed, the account we gave of common names in Chapter 1 can be accepted here, with the provision that the word "sensation" be used instead of "thing."

Physical objects exist, then, according to idealism, but not in the sense of something other than sensations. Most idealists, however, are not content with asserting that *as a matter of fact* physical objects do not exist as something over and above sensations; they say that it would be *self-contradictory* to say that they do. For is not a physical object, by definition, something that is capable of being perceived, something at least available to perception? and the unknowable physical objects of realism, as we have just seen, do not fulfill this requirement. Chairs and tables are what we *perceive;* and if you use physical-object words in the way realism does, you will get "Physical objects (unobservables) are observed," which is self-contradictory. What we experience are sensations; now, surely we do experience chairs and tables; therefore chairs and tables are sensations, distinguished by certain defining characteristics from other sensations.

Thus, if an idealist were asked, "Are there physical objects or aren't there?" he would reply, "That depends on the sense you mean. If you mean in the realist's sense, as something unknown and unknowable, no. Even to assert that they do is, in my opinion, to contradict yourself. But if you mean in the ordinary sense, in which chairs and tables are *experienced* entities, then by all means yes: they exist *as* sensations. Sensations are all we are acquainted with; chairs and tables are among the entities we are acquainted with; therefore, chairs and tables are sensations. The class of chairs is a class of sensations grouped together by similarity from the totality of sensations; the class of tables is another such class; and so on."

But do only sensations exist? Don't *things* exist? It is indeed a peculiarity of language, the idealist replies; but it only *sounds* strange. Actually idealism comes far nearer to common sense than does the representative realist's position. Whatever common sense means by words like "table" and "chair," it does *not* mean something unknown and unknowable; it means something *experienced*. Now, only sensations are experienced. Thus chairs and tables are sensations; it's as simple as that. True, common sense would say we know things, not sensations; in fact, most people wouldn't even know what the word "sensation" (in this sense) means. People do not realize, however, what the difficulties in realism are; once they are made aware that *things* are unknowable in realism, they would become idealists; for people are sure of one thing: that they *are* acquainted with tables and trees, woods and fields. If to be knowable they must be sensations, then very well, they are sensations.

Tables and trees, then, in the sense of complexes of sensations, do exist and are experienced. For them to exist *is* for them to be experienced. *Esse est percipi* (to be is to be perceived). Apart from experience, they have no existence; in fact, as we have seen, to assert that they exist but are never experienced, as realists must say, is to assert something self-contradictory: namely, that something unexperienceable can be experienced.

Experiences other than sensations. For the sake of simplicity of exposition, our account thus far has contained an inaccuracy. We are acquainted only with sensations. But no—we are acquainted, indeed, only with our own experiences—but not all of these are sensations. There are also images, thoughts, feelings, pleasures and pains. Idealism does not deny the existence of any of the experiences we have. Strictly speaking, however, not all experiences are sensations. There is a difference, for example, between the *sensation* of a chair (a chair-sensation) and the *image* of a chair (a chair-image). There is some controversy as to just how to state this difference; we cannot say "Sensations come through sense-organs and images don't," because sense-organs themselves are only complexes of sensations, and thus our definition would be circular. There is some qualitative difference between the class of experiences we call sensations and the class of experiences we call images, just as there is between the sub-class of sensations we call tables and another sub-class we call chairs. Hume said that images were less vivid than sensations; others say that the difference lies in the dependence on, or independence of, the will; still others assert that ideas are distinguished from images not by their intrinsic nature but by their context and relations (e.g., you can have a visual image with your eyes closed but not a visual sensation). However this difference is analyzed—and we shall be in more of a position to say something about it as our discussion develops—there *is* a difference between sensations and images which we all recognize; we can tell the difference between seeing red and imagining red. Both the sensation and the image, however, are experiences; and idealism's thesis is that nothing exists outside *experiences,* not outside sensations.

If we keep this in mind, we shall see that the popular objection to idealism, "According to idealism, chairs and tables don't really exist; they are only imaginary," is quite mistaken. Samuel Johnson did just this in reply to Berkeley; asked how he would refute Berkeley's view, he kicked his foot against a stone and said, "I refute it thus!" But it was no refutation. Berkeley never declared that stones are imaginary; we can, of course, imagine stones, but there are real stones as well as imagined ones. And this difference is a difference within experience. Stone-sensations are different from stone-images. Berkeley's idealism does not ignore the difference between sensation and imagination; rather, it insists upon it; but it insists, also, that they all fall under the general heading of experiences, and that outside this category there is nothing even imaginable.

Idealism and science. What is the fate of science if idealism is correct? Doesn't it deal with the physical world that Berkeley denies? No, says Berkeley; science deals with things in the same way that common sense does (only more precisely), and things are reducible to complexes of sensations for science as well as for common sense. Fortunately for us, there are many uniformities traceable in the experiences we have; one sensation is followed by another regularly, at least in many instances; this is the basis for our laws. However, the laws of nature are really nothing but laws of succession of sensations. All we have to do is translate the thing-language into sensation-language, as we did in the case of chairs and tables.

Thus, science traces uniformities in experience, say between C and E. Suppose C and E are events and that C causes E. (We have seen in Chapter 4 that *one* event can seldom be said to cause another; the situation is more complex than this; but the principle is the same, so for the sake of simplicity we will suppose that event C causes event E.) Now, how will we formulate this? We see event C, say, the lighting of a fuse, and then event E, the explosion. But both of these are experiences. The law connecting C with E is merely the law connecting the C-sensation with the E-sensation. (Sometimes C and E can be observed only under difficult or highly specialized circumstances; but these circumstances can in turn be stated in terms of experiences.) It is on the basis of this regularity that we are enabled to predict. And the prediction is of course the prediction of experiences: specifically, of sensations.

What about scientific constructs, such as electrons? We can't perceive electrons, and yet we wouldn't want to say they don't exist. Here again, the principle is no different from what it is in the case of tables and trees. As we have already seen in Chapter 3, electrons are not perceived, but they are *constructs* out of what we perceive. If we are to talk meaningfully about electrons, we must, in the final analysis, talk about experiences. (We shall consider electrons and their ilk again later in this chapter.)

God as cause of sensations. But aren't our sensations caused? Surely they must be caused by something, and by what else but physical things?

This question does not always receive the same answer from idealists. One might argue as follows: What is the causal relation? Unless all our previous reasoning on that subject was on the wrong track, causality has something to do with repeating sequences of events. And we are entitled to make statements that C causes E only when we can experience both C and E. Now all we experience is sensations (and images, and so on); so statements of causality, if we are entitled to make them at all, must be statements of observable constant conjunctions among sensations. One thing seems certain: experience could never justify you in asserting that something you couldn't possibly experience was the cause of your experiences; thus, even if the realist's physical objects did cause experiences, you could never know this fact, and would never be entitled to assert it.

But idealism, at least in the case of Bishop Berkeley, makes another answer. Without trying to analyze the meaning of "cause," he did assert that our experiences had a cause—God. God, not material objects, is the source of all our experiences (including sensations). And if they occur in a fairly orderly and predictable way, so that we can formulate laws of succession by which to guide our actions and predict the future, this is something for which to thank God— He has made it so that we can do this, by giving us experiences in an orderly manner. He *might* have arranged matters so that we had such a chaotic succession of experiences that we could never predict what was going to happen next; then laws could not be formulated, and science would be impossible. Instead, He has made our experiences orderly. According to Berkeley, God does not need the realist's physical objects as intermediaries to give us our experiences; instead, He "feeds" us our experiences directly. This includes, of course, all our physical-object-experiences, including our eye-experiences, brain-experiences, mirror-experiences, and nerve-experiences (although we do not usually have these latter experiences unless we first have other experiences which we call dissecting a body). None of these things exist apart from minds as the realist says they do, and even if they did they would be unknowable. They exist only as sensations in minds—your mind, my mind, Smith's mind, and so on. And where do these sensations come from? Directly from God.

God as correlator of sensations. But why is it that the experiences of different minds are so much alike? When you say, "Look, there's a house over there on the hill," I look and also have sensations which I describe in the same way that you do; the presumption is then that our sensations are similar. Why not account for this similarity of our sensations by the simple hypothesis that there *really* *is* a house there, as the realist says there is?

Let us stop for a moment to examine this assertion. Would an idealist deny that "there really is a house there"? Certainly not. He would grant that there is, but he would add once again that it exists only as *sensations in minds*. *To say* that there is a house is merely *to say* that you, I, and other centers of consciousness have similar sensations. ("What else *could* it mean?" the idealist asks us.) We cannot say, then, that we have similar sensations *because* a house is there, if by referring to the house we are referring to nothing more or less than these similar sensations! It would make no sense to say that we see A because we see A.

"But why is it," the questioner may persist, "that we all have similar sensations—that we all agree that there is a house, six trees in front of it, and so on? Isn't this a remarkable coincidence?" Here the unrelenting idealist will charge that this is the same question over again, and that the objector has not yet grasped the point of the reply. That sensations occur in resembling sequences in different minds will simply have to be taken as a basic and ultimate fact about nature (remember our discussion of basic laws on pages 189–190), just as the *dis*similarity of our sensations would have to be taken if *that* were the fact.

Again, however, Berkeley has a different reply: The explanation of this remarkable similarity is that God works in an orderly manner in "feeding" us our sensations. He gives you certain sensations from moment to moment, and He gives me others which resemble them, and by this means we are enabled to communicate with one another. If God did not providentially "feed" us similar sensations we would not be able to converse with each other about objects in a common world. Our living in a common world, indeed, *is* nothing but the fact that we have similar sensations under similar circumstances. And this fact is the result of divine providence. The function of God, then, with regard to human sensation, is not only that of *cause* of sensations but that of *correlator* of sensations. Because of this divinely ordained correlation when you have a house-sensation I have a house-sensation also. God *might* have arranged things so that I had a sensation utterly unlike yours.

The introduction of God by Berkeley has often been objected to by his critics as inconsistent with his basic view. (This is not an objection to God as a theological doctrine, but as a solution to the present difficulty.) If I can be acquainted only with my own experiences (this premise of idealism Berkeley inherited from representative realism) then I cannot be acquainted with God, who surely is more than the totality of my experiences, any more than I can with the realist's physical objects to which Berkeley so violently objects. If my experiences are all I can know, and God is not merely my experience, then I cannot know that God exists, much less that He causes my sensations and correlates your sensations with mine.

Other selves. Even if we do not bring in God, haven't we brought in more than the theory strictly permits by bringing in other persons? It is all very well to say that the chair is nothing but chair-sensations in minds; but what about the minds themselves? *I* am acquainted only with *my* experiences, not with yours; how then am I entitled to say that you have any? I can see you, touch you, watch you behave (i.e., I can have certain visual and tactual sensations). Your body is nothing but my sensations; and as for your mind, it is forever inaccessible to me (I can only watch your gestures and so on), and since I cannot experience your states of consciousness, how am I entitled to say that you have any consciousness at all? If *esse* is really *percipi*, you are only a series of sensations in *my* mind. This role may seem too humiliating to you; if so, you can turn the tables on me: *I* am only a part of *your* consciousness.

"Well, what's wrong with that? *To me*, you are only a part of my consciousness; and *to you*, I am only a part of yours." But what do the phrases "to you" and "to me" add? (See pages 125–126.) What is the actual situation: that you are merely a part of my consciousness, or that I am a part of yours, or neither? *Both* assertions cannot be true: you cannot both be *merely* an aspect of my consciousness and *also* a mind which contains all of me as a part of *its* consciousness. Either I am more than merely an aspect of your consciousness, or I am not.

The idealist replies: "It's true that I can have acquaintance only with my own experiences, but I never said that only my experiences *exist*. I said that only *minds*—many minds—and their experiences exist. Physical objects exist only as sensation-groups in different minds; but minds exist quite independently of each other." This, indeed, is the idealist's picture of reality—a vast collection of minds (centers of consciousness) and their states of consciousness, including sensations, images, thoughts, emotions, and so on; and (according to Berkeley at least) another Mind, God, causing all these experiences and correlating them. God exists independently of these minds, and these minds exist independently of each other. But chairs and tables do not; they exist only as contents of minds.

But how, one might object, does this square with the idealist's motto, *"Esse est percipi"?* For something to exist is for it to be perceived; I do not perceive your pains, so am I not committed to saying that they do not exist? No, says the idealist; to be is to be perceived, but not necessarily to be perceived *by me.* There are other centers of consciousness besides myself, and they can have experiences as well as I. (Berkeley declared that *esse est percipi* was true only of physical objects, but that of minds it would be more accurate to say that *esse est percipere*—to be is to perceive, not to be perceived.)

The objector, however, is not necessarily content with this reply. "Doubtless you idealists do hold that other minds exist," he will say, "but how can you know that they do, since you can know only of the existence of your own? You can experience your own states of consciousness, but how can you have any reasons to believe that there are other states of consciousness?" Indeed, there are those who say that the logical resting-place of idealism is *solipsism* (literally "oneself-alone-ism"), the view that only I and my experiences exist. Solipsism has never been seriously held by anyone (a solipsist who tried to defend his view against attack must presumably believe that other people exist to do the attacking), but it has sometimes been alleged to be the inevitable end-result of a consistently held idealism.

Do physical objects exist when we don't perceive them? Another difficulty is also pressing: Physical objects are complexes of sensations. Now, your sensations do not exist when you are not sensing anything. And if physical objects are simply complexes of sensations, the conclusion seems inescapable that they, too, cease to exist when they are not being sensed.

This conclusion seems extremely strange; so much so that most persons would dismiss it at once as absurd. Let us not on that account, however, dismiss it. A conclusion may be strange but true; and if anyone thinks it is too absurd to argue about, let him try to refute the doctrine. Someone said of Berkeley that his doctrine was "utterly absurd—and utterly irrefutable." If the view is so absurd, how can we refute it?

Let us first try to see exactly what idealism says. "There is no reality apart from experience"—this is the oft-repeated motto of idealism. What does it come to? Tables, trees, and other physical objects are complexes of sensations (which are themselves one class of experiences), and since sensations can't exist unsensed (to say that they *could* would be self-contradictory), therefore complexes of sensations can't exist unsensed. To say that sensations exist unsensed, or that experiences exist unexperienced, would surely be self-contradictory.

Does the table cease to exist when I go out of the room? No, not if you stay in the room and keep on seeing (or touching) it; there are still tactual sensations even though I have my head turned or my eyes closed so that there are no visual sensations. But suppose I leave the room. Does the table cease to exist? No, you are still having table-sensations. But suppose we both go out. Does the table then cease to exist? Not necessarily: if we think no one is in the room any more, we stay out for 15 minutes, and then come back, we may find someone saying, "It existed all the time. I was looking at the table through a hole in the floor above, and I assure you that I had table-sensations while you were gone just as I did when you were in the room." None of this is doubted by idealism.

But suppose that *no* one is in the room—no one, not even an animal, no organism whatever that could possibly have table-sensations. Does the table cease to exist then? Yes. "No experience, then no existence." For physical objects, *esse est percipi.*

Some persons will be wildly opposed to this conclusion. Others will say, "Well, what difference does it make? As long as the table is there in the same condition when I get back, what do I care if it's not there when I'm gone? The question whether it's there when I and everyone else are gone is of no practical interest." And the idealist would be the first to say Amen to this; as long as yours and mine and everybody's sensations keep going on just *as if* the table keeps on existing, it makes no difference to experience, does it? so who cares? [2] Still, whether it is a practical question or not, it would

___

[2] Strictly speaking, we cannot say that sensations go on *as if* the table continued to exist. While sensations go on, the table is there. When sensations do *not* go on but are interrupted, what sense does it make to speak of them as nevertheless "going on" as if there were a table?

be interesting to know whether the idealist's conclusion is true.

At first it might seem that refutation is simple. "Bring a motion picture camera into the room, set it going, then have everybody leave. Come back a few minutes later, develop the film, and project it on a screen. It will show that the table was there all the time." But the matter is not so simple as this. The camera is itself a physical object, hence is itself a complex of sensations, hence is itself non-existent when it is not being perceived. What about the showing of the film? Idealism does not deny a single experience which we have: we leave the room at time t_1 (have no more table-experiences), then come back (have table-experiences again at time t_2), then see the film (have more table-experiences at time t_3 except that only the visual and not the tactual ones occur—or, if you prefer, we have experiences *much like* table-experiences). And this is all we perceive. Hence it is all that exists. The succession of experiences is just what we experience it to be (this is a tautology); and "that's all there is." Indeed, what need is there for more?

At this point we may feel like the boy who was told by his brother that the street light went out whenever his eyes were shut. He watched the street-lamp intently, studiously shut his eyes, then furtively opened them again for a moment. The street-lamp was shining as usual. "But you told me it went out!" "No," said his brother, "I said it goes out only when your eyes are shut. Now that your eyes are open again, of course it's on." Utterly absurd—but utterly irrefutable?

"But if it went out, there would be traces of some sort!" Take an obvious example such as the fire in your fireplace. You light a fire, you watch it burn down partway. You leave the room for half an hour. No one else is in the room. When you come back, nothing is left in the fireplace but a pile of ashes. What can you infer except that the fire kept on burning while you were gone? How else could the wood have been transformed into ashes? And in order to burn while you were gone, it must have existed while you were gone!

But the idealist has us again. He does not deny that we have a fire-sensation at time t_1. We leave at time t_2. At time t_3 we return and have no fire-sensation but ashes-sensation. That is all. It is all that we experience, and it is all that has occurred.

"But the fire *must* have existed! How else could the wood have burned down?" Ah, but *did* the wood burn down? This is to assume that a uniformity, which admittedly holds when we do observe it, *also* holds when we do not observe it. But why can't *"esse est percipi"* hold for uniformities too as well as physical objects? If uniformities of nature do operate in our absence as well as in our presence, how can we know that they do? (1) We don't *perceive* that they do—we can only perceive X when X is present. (2) We don't *infer* that they do either: for how can we infer? Either deductively or inductively. (a) We can't do it deductively—we can't deduce a statement about what happens at time t_2 from any statement about what happened at time t_1 or t_3—except by *assuming* (as a major premise) a law connecting them, which is the very thing to be established in this instance. (b) And we can't infer it inductively either, for to establish a conclusion inductively we have to argue from instances that we observe: we observe A followed by B once, twice, a thousand times, and infer inductively that A is always followed by B; but in this case, of course, we can't observe that in addition to existing when experienced (A) an event, or a uniformity among events *also* exists when unexperienced (B). Of this *we cannot observe even a single instance,* and hence we have no basis whatever for an induction. Therefore, since we can neither perceive nor infer (either deductively or inductively) that something exists unperceived, we have no reason whatever for saying that it continues to exist when everyone is gone. "Even if physical objects continue to exist when no one perceives them," writes W. T. Stace, "we can have no good reason for supposing that they do; for no one can observe them existing unobserved."

Weak vs. strong idealism. So speaks one idealist. Other idealists would go even further. They would say, not only that there is no *evidence* that physical objects and uniformities continue to exist unobserved—let us call this the "weak" version of idealism—but that there *could not* in the nature of the case be such evidence (and the "could" here is a *logical* "could")—this we shall call "strong" idealism. According to the strong version, the weak one is inconsistent: to speak of a physical object existing unobserved is not a hypothesis for which we unfortunately lack confirmation; it is not a hypothesis at all; its very assertion is a *self-contradiction.* To speak of physical objects existing unexperienced is just as self-contradictory as to speak of experiences existing unexperienced; and physical objects, remember, are complexes of experiences; therefore it is *logically* impossible for them to exist unexperienced. When we assert that physical objects do not exist unperceived we are uttering a tautology; and if we deny it we are uttering a self-contradiction.

Why then is a conclusion such as this so surprising? Surely no one wants to deny a tautology; and everyone wants to deny a self-contradiction. The idealist says it is surprising only because we never really have digested the initial premise of idealism, that physical objects are simply complexes of sensations. Once accept this, and all objections are irrelevant. If the idealist's account seems to make physical objects like tables discontinuous (ceasing to exist when nobody is having table-sensations), this is only because we still have lurking in the back of our minds the notion of tables as inhabiting a world of independently existing things which keep on existing regardless of percipients: in other words, of tables and so on as *not* being complexes of sensations at all. Once accept physical objects as complexes of sensations, there is no more ground to complain about the discontinuity of physical objects than there is about the discontinuity of sensations, which everyone already accepts. We feel uncomfortable only because *independent* physical objects, having been thrown out the front door with the declaration "objects = complexes of sensations," are sneaked in at the back door. Once we grant that physical objects are reducible to sensations, and really get this through our heads, we would never even bring up any question of their existing unexperienced, any more than we would in the case of sensations.

According to idealism, this answer is sufficient and decisive. Nothing more is needed. But some idealists, such as Berkeley himself, have gone on to give another answer as well. As if to prop up their position in the minds of their audience, having missed with their first shot they try a second: the audience, being astonished at the very idea that objects don't exist unperceived, is now told, "True, objects don't exist unperceived, but don't let that worry you, because in fact objects *never are* unperceived. If neither you nor I nor Smith nor the dog perceives the table, at any rate *God* perceives it. God is a universal perceiver, and He is always perceiving everything, so thanks to Him there is really no discontinuity after all. When you and I and everyone leave the room, He holds the fort, and because He does, because He is always perceiving it, the table never ceases to exist until it is chopped into kindling and burned.

Thus the conditions for the table's not existing are never fulfilled—because of God."

This addition to the doctrine is, of course, easily attacked. We have already considered some objections. If God is the cause of our experience, then we have one entity at least that is not experienced, and something does exist unperceived, namely a Cause-of-experience. This introduces something which is strictly inconsistent with idealism itself. Moreover, it does no good because it is not needed. The need is felt only by those who *have not really digested* the equation: "Physical objects = complexes of sensations." They somehow feel that it is all right for sensations to cease to exist when no one is experiencing them, but not so for physical objects—thus in actuality denying that the equation holds. Those who *have* digested it do not need the added hypothesis. It only confuses the issue.

Summary. Idealism is a doctrine which is very easily misinterpreted and caricatured, and we should not leave it without an appreciation of whatever strength it may have. It rests its case on two principal contentions: (1) Physical objects—trees, houses, rocks, and the like—are genuine objects of knowledge by human beings. This is a statement which probably no one wishes to tamper with if he can avoid it. (2) All that human beings can know is their own experiences. This statement it inherits from representative realism, by means of the line of argument considered in Section II. From these two premises it draws the inevitable conclusion: (3) that physical objects must then be experiences. A critic can rebel against this conclusion all he wishes, but it will be to no avail if he is unable to refute these two premises. He will hardly wish to deny the first; his attack, then, will be centered upon the second. But how in the world can the second be attacked?

IV. PHENOMENALISM

Phenomenalism is not in entire disagreement with idealism; one might even call it a refinement of idealism, and certainly an outgrowth of it. But at the very outset it modifies the idealist's doctrine on at least two points:

1. **The existence of physical objects unperceived.** According to idealism, physical objects do not exist unperceived—both according

to the weaker version which says we have no right to say they do, for lack of evidence, and according to the stronger version which says it is self-contradictory to say that they do. But the phenomenalist disagrees with this conclusion.

The argument of the idealist on this point is:

> Sensations do not exist unexperienced.
> Physical objects are (complexes of) sensations.
> Therefore, Physical objects do not exist unexperienced.

We can hardly attack the first premise; it appears to be a tautology. So, if we are to avoid the conclusion, we shall have to attack the second premise. How can we do this? Is not this premise invulnerable? If we deny it, are we not forced back to the untenable theory of representative realism?

No, says phenomenalism—not if we remedy it in one respect. Physical objects are complexes of sensations, but not of *actual* sensations—rather, of actual *and possible* sensations. A physical object can exist even though it is not *actually* being perceived by anybody; it is enough that it is *capable* of being perceived, or is *perceivable.* To speak of a physical object that could not be seen, heard, touched, and so on, not even under *any* specifiable conditions, this would indeed be a contradiction. Such a "physical object" would be indistinguishable from nothing at all. But why should it be necessary that it be actually perceived? Perceivability, not actual perception, is the criterion. As John Stuart Mill (1806–1873) put it, *"Matter is the permanent possibility of sensation."*

Things may exist now that are not being seen and never have been seen. When I say that there is ice at the south pole now, I do not mean that I or anyone else, even God, is actually perceiving it. What I mean is only that *if* I or anyone else were to go there, then he *would* perceive the ice (have ice-sensations). If we were to go there and yet did not have any ice-sensations, then we would have to admit that we were wrong in saying that there was ice there. Or, if I say that there is a deposit of coal 500 feet below the spot where I am now standing, I do not imply that anyone is perceiving it; I only mean that *if* I or someone dug a hole 500 feet deep, *then* we could perceive the coal deposit. In other words, there are conditions under which we *can* perceive it, though no one may actually have fulfilled these conditions. It is enough that the conditions for perception are there. Doubtless there are flora and fauna at the bottom of the ocean which no one has ever perceived; but it would be foolish to say that they are not there. We would be justified in saying they are not there only if we could somehow go down there and, having fulfilled the conditions for perception, still did not perceive any. For that matter, there were long geological ages of millions of years in the earth's history in which no one (for a long time, no organism at all) was perceiving the changes that took place on the earth's surface; and yet those changes did take place. We do not need God perceiving them all the time to be able to say that they took place. It is enough to say, "*If* a perceiver had been there, with the appropriate sense-faculties (not blind, etc.), *then* he would have perceived the changes."

2. **The introduction of sense-data.** So far, the change which phenomenalism rings upon idealism is comparatively simple. Whether it can be attacked we shall see at a later stage in our analysis; but it is doubtless much more acceptable to common sense. The next step, however, is not so easy to explain.

Phenomenalism as we have developed it so far would have seemed quite acceptable to early phenomenalists such as Mill. But almost no phenomenalist would accept it today. It is still, they would say, only a slightly modified idealism. It is too "mentalistic." It interprets reality, as idealism does, in terms of sensations; and sensations are mental, events in minds. It does not deny that there are tables and trees, but these are analyzable into groups of sensations —actual sensations for idealism, actual and possible sensations for phenomenalism. The entire physical realm, being analyzable into the mental, is then itself mental. The physical is only a part of the mental. Physical and mental are not two distinct classes of entities, but are related as part to whole.

Idealists do not try to avoid this conclusion. Indeed, they insist upon it. This is what physical objects are, according to idealists; "all reality is mental." Physical objects, to be knowable, *must* be complexes of sensations, and thus be mental. But most persons who call themselves phenomenalists think otherwise. Physical objects, they say, must be defined in terms of what is in some sense experienceable; but what is experienceable is not just *sensations*—nor even other mental events such as dreams, thoughts, pains, and the like. According to phenomenalists, what we are immediately and directly aware of is *sense-data,* not sensations.

What is the difference? The use of a different term surely cannot change things. Doesn't the term "sense-datum" (more frequently used in its plural, "sense-data") cover the same ground as is covered by "sensation"? What's wrong with the word "sensation" itself?

1. It should be mentioned first that there is a tendency to use the word "sensation" in another way: to stand not for the sensations themselves (as we have thus far been using the word) but for the *process* of sensing. (This is another instance of the process-product ambiguity mentioned on page 23.) We do not want to use the same word for both; hence we leave the word "sensation" to name the process.

2. The very notion of "sensations" seems to imply something which is not sensations. And if one were to reply, "Well, according to idealism, too, there are things other than sensations—dreams, memories, thoughts, and so on," this would be admitted; but, say phenomenalists, all this falls under the heading of the *mental.* And to speak of something as mental seems to imply the possibility of something else that is not mental. Even when you speak of sensations, don't you have "at the back of your mind" the idea of external independently existing objects, trees, eyes, nerves, brains, which are necessary conditions for the occurrence of the sensations but are not sensations themselves? One can deny it verbally, but isn't it precisely against this non-sensational background that the term "sensation" acquires its distinctive meaning? If this is so, another term is surely desirable—one which has no such associations as this, one which does not seem to commit us to any view about the cause of sensations.

3. At this point we might say, "Very well, 'sense-datum' means the same as 'sensation,' but without any specific reference to its origin." But even this is not enough. It does not yet bring out the difference between the use of the terms "sense-data" and "sensations."

We have used the term "sensations" to stand for certain mental contents, or experiences, as opposed to others such as dreams. But the term "sense-datum" is so neutral and noncommittal as not even to carry the implication that it stands for an experience. The term "sense-datum" stands not for the experience but for *that which* we experience—only it is what we *immediately and directly* experience.

But are we not taking the very ground from under us when we refuse to say that sense-data are experiences? Is this not the irreducible minimum of what the word means? Is it not obvious, in fact tautologous, that what we sense are sensations—visual sensations, auditory sensations, and the rest?

No, says the phenomenalist. The fault of idealism is to confuse an *experience* with the *object* of that experience. Suppose someone said, "What is it that people see?" Our first answer doubtless would be in terms of physical objects: "Tables, books, automobiles, and so on." But we have already seen difficulties in that in discussing naive realism. Our next answer may then be, "Only our own visual sensations." And doubtless we do *have* visual sensations; but what is it that we *see?* Suppose that now we answer, "Colors," or "Colors and shapes." (We mean here, of course, not the light-waves of the physicist—*these* are clearly not what we see—but the reds, greens, yellows, and other colors which we can distinguish but can't define except ostensively.) These are "that which we immediately and directly experience."

Doesn't this satisfy the requirement? We see colors; we hear sounds; and so on. And we *directly* see them or hear them. They are that which we directly experience. Not necessarily the real color of the physical object—that is another question. There may be no physical object at all. If there is, and we can come to know its real color, that is a question to be discussed later. But some color we do see; we see black, even though the dress may "really" be dark blue.[3]

But, once this is granted, *is* it really obvious that what we see are color-*sensations?* We *have* sensations, including color-sensations, but do we *see* color-sensations? We *sense* sense-data (such as colors); we *have* sensations. But the sensations are in no sense *what we see.*

(Consider this also: it is logically impossible for you and me to have the same sensation; at best I can have one much like yours. But it is not logically impossible that you and I might sense the

[3] Psychologically speaking, black and white, of course, are just as much colors as red and blue; they are just as much objects of immediate and direct awareness; only after a study of physics do we learn that where there is no object to reflect light, or the object absorbs all the light-waves, then we see black.

same sense-datum. Ordinarily when we speak of "seeing the same color" we often mean two instances of the same color, but may we not also mean *the same instance?* If neither of us is color-blind and we are both looking in the same direction at a certain moment, isn't it possible that we may be acquainted with the same instance of the color green?)

Now, if visual sense-data are colors directly seen, they cannot at the same time be color-*sensations*. This is the real crux of the refusal to make sense-data identical with sensations. Phenomenalists wish to use the term "sense-data" to stand for what we are immediately aware of—colors, sounds, smells, and so on, *without* meaning to imply that these are color-*sensations*, sound-*sensations*, and the like. To call something a sound is after all not the same as to call it a sound-sensation. If someone asked you what you heard, and you said, "A shrill sound," this would sound more natural than if you said, "A shrill sound-sensation." You might assent to the first without being able even to make sense of the second. You see colors; you hear sounds; whether these are real colors or sounds of real physical objects does not matter here; at any rate you are directly aware of them, and it is from these that you begin. The word that has been coined purposely to stand for these objects of immediate experience is "sense-data."

The given. According to phenomenalists, sense-data are the ultimate rock-bottom of all knowledge, that upon which all knowledge is based and from which it ultimately stems. That we see tables and chairs may be doubted; but that we see colors and shapes cannot. The colors and shapes we see may not be those of real objects (they may be, like the pink rat, no real objects at all) but they are at any rate colors and shapes, even though they are only red round spots before our eyes. It is these that we *directly* sense; and their existence is *indubitable*.

When I see a tomato there is much that I can doubt. I can doubt whether it is a tomato that I am seeing, and not a cleverly painted piece of wax. I can doubt whether there is any material thing there at all. Perhaps what I took for a tomato was really a reflection; perhaps I am even the victim of some hallucination. One thing however I cannot doubt: that there exists a red patch of a round and somewhat bulgy shape, standing out from a background of other color-patches, and having a certain visual depth, and that this whole field of color is directly present to my consciousness. What the red patch is, whether a substance, or a state of a substance, or an event, whether it is physical or psychical or neither, are questions that we may doubt about. But that something is red and round then and there I cannot doubt. Whether the something persists even for a moment before and after it is present to my consciousness, whether other minds can be conscious of it as well as I, may be doubted. But that it now *exists*, and that *I* am conscious of it—by me at least who am conscious of it this cannot possibly be doubted. And when I say that it is "directly" present to my consciousness, I mean that my consciousness of it is not reached by inference, nor by any other intellectual process.[4]

That which we directly sense is said to be *given*. Physical objects are not given; phenomenalism asserts, as we shall soon see in detail, that they are *constructs* out of the given; but the colors, sounds, smells, and so forth, *are* given. The expressions "given" and "the given" are used a great deal by philosophers. Strictly, the realm of the given is broader than that of sense-data; sense-data are a species, or sub-class, of the given. The data given in dreams, memory, or imagination are not *sense*-data, though they are still given, still immediately and directly experienced. But since it is our knowledge of the physical world that we are concerned with in this chapter, and since this knowledge (or supposed knowledge) is based upon sense-data, it is only sense-data that we shall be concerned with here.

Can anyone doubt that there are sense-data? No, say phenomenalists. To doubt that you sense sense-data is to doubt that you see colors, hear sounds, and so on. Of course it is difficult in many cases to distinguish what is *given* from what is added by the mind, by *interpretation*. But nevertheless, something is given, or there would be nothing to begin with, nothing to base the interpretation upon.

Thus, when we look at a distant mountain peak and say "It looks cold," the coldness is surely not given—the cold is not now a sensedatum the way it would be if we were sitting on the ice. The fact is that from past experience we have come to *associate* the look and the feel of the mountaintop (or of other cold things), and now, seeing the white, which *is* given, reminds us of the cold, which is *not* now given. (Perhaps it does not even remind us: it may not even be a conscious association. Association is often unconscious if it has been of long standing and often repeated in our past experience.)

[4] H. H. Price, *Perception* (London: Methuen, 1933), p. **3**.

Or again, it may well be that visual depth is not given. Berkeley declared, and many thinkers are still of the opinion that he was right, that what is given to sight is simply a panoply of colors, in two spatial dimensions only: that when we think we see *depth*, we are only interpreting what we see in the light of past experience. If we were eternally rooted to one spot, like a tree, we would have no conception of visual depth, of "in front of" or "behind"; there would just be a passing parade of color-patterns. The reason we do recognize, for example, the house as being behind the tree is that when we walk we reach the tree first and then the house. If it were not for the fact of locomotion, we would have no conception of depth in space. Vision alone would never give it to us. But, having observed how things look when we walk among them (for example, getting bigger in our visual field as we approach), we come to associate the visual with the other data and come to think that distance is apprehended by vision alone. Indeed, if it is held that visual depth *is* given, how is it that we cannot distinguish the distances of the stars? They all seem to be the same distance from us, as if fixed on the interior surface of a hollow sphere of which we are at the center. From looking at them we cannot tell how far away they are, whether any given point of light is a very distant searchlight or a very nearby glow-worm. If vision alone can inform us of spatial depth, why is it not more helpful when we look at the stars?

We are not concerned here to defend or refute this theory; the only point of interest here is that if it is true, it shows how much we *bring* to our experience, how much we import into the present from the past. We must be careful, then, to distinguish what is really given from what is not given but is brought by us from past experience. Something we may have assumed all the time to be a part of the given may really have been the result of interpretation. This, of course, does not show that nothing whatever is given. On the contrary, it shows that something must be given, else there could not be anything for what is *not* given to be associated with. It may be that "what I see is 'contaminated by' the traces of past experience, or 'overlaid with' them; I answer, that where there is contamination there must be something which is contaminated, and where there is overlaying there must be something which is overlaid." [5]

[5] H. H. Price, *op. cit.*, p. 9.

In all experience, then, something is given. And what is of particular interest for our purpose in this chapter is that branch of the given which is sense-data. What is the nature of these sense-data? The term alone does not commit us to much. It does not commit us to the belief that sense-data are mental, nor yet that they are physical. It does not commit us to the belief that sense-data can exist unsensed, nor yet that they cannot. It does not commit us to the belief that two persons can sense the same sense-datum, nor yet that they cannot. It does not commit us to any view about their causal genesis or origin. Every one of these points is hotly disputed among epistemologists. The arguments supporting and attacking each of these contentions would fill many pages, and in order to get a full understanding of the issue it would be necessary to go into them in detail. Unfortunately, there is no space for that in this chapter; nor can the arguments be easily "summarized." One must simply steep himself in the large amount of literature on the subject. (See the list of readings at the end of the chapter.) Our course here will be to inquire into the relation between sense-data and physical objects, taking up whatever of these topics may be required along the way.

If there are both sense-data and physical objects, perhaps we shall most quickly get to the heart of phenomenalism if we consider how we know that the first (sense-data) can be present when the second (physical objects) are either unlike the first or absent entirely. In other words, how does the view we are considering account for perceptual error? It has often been said that the acid test of any theory of knowledge is its ability to account for error. Where do the theories we have been considering stand on this issue?

The analysis of error: illusions. According to the theory of representative realism, whether a perception is veridical or erroneous depends on whether there is or is not a *correspondence* between the sensation and the thing. The most straightforward version holds that if your sensation has quality X and the thing also has quality X, then, in respect of quality X at any rate, you are sensing veridically. If it does not have quality X, but has Y instead (illusion), or if there is no thing to have the quality in the first place (hallucination), then you are sensing erroneously. As we have already seen, however, there is no way to observe both the sensation and the thing to see if they are both alike in having quality X.

A slightly more subtle version of the theory holds that the corre-spondence is not between the thing and the sensation but between the thing and the *judgment* about the thing. For example, if the stick in water is really straight, and you have a bent-stick sensation, you are not necessarily having an illusion—though on the strict correspondence theory you would be. According to the judgment correspondence theory, you are having an illusion only if you are "taken in": that is, if you judge that the stick is really bent. It is not an illusion if you have the bent-stick sensation but nevertheless judge that the stick is straight. It is an illusion only if you make a false *judgment*. The same objection, however, applies. How are you to *know* that it is a false judgment? As long as you have no access to the object itself, you can compare neither the sensation nor the judgment with the object, and the road to skepticism about the physical world seems to be very well paved.

Idealism denies all this: what determines whether perception is veridical or erroneous is not the relation of sensations to things other than sensations, but the relation of sensations *to each other*. The same principle is applied to sense-data by phenomenalists; and since it is chiefly the phenomenalists who have developed this notion in detail, we are discussing it at this point.

Let us begin with a few examples of how the principle operates. (We shall be using physical-object words such as "dress," "stick," and so on, but keep in mind as we are doing so that these words, according to the phenomenalist, are all definable in terms of actual and possible sense-data.) We say that a certain dress is dark blue. Under yellowish artificial light, however, it looks black, and is in-distinguishable from a dress which, as we say, is "really black." If someone were to say that the first dress was really black, we would say he was in error. How do we know this? Not by comparing the sense-data (black) with the thing (blue) to see whether they are alike—this, as we have abundantly seen, would be impossible. How then? By comparing the sense-data we sense at certain times with those we sense at *other* times. Or, to put it differently: we see a number of *appearances,* some black, some dark blue; how do we decide between them? isn't one appearance as good as another? No: out of the total set of dress-appearances we select *some* and use them as a standard or touchstone by which to test the rest. We do not compare sense-data with things; we compare some sense-data with *other sense-data.*

But on what basis do we do this? We say that the dress really is blue though it looks black in yellowish light. Why don't we say instead that the dress is really black but only looks blue in direct sunlight? Why this prejudice in favor of the blue appearance rather than the black one? Is it because we first used sunlight as a standard, and just never got out of the habit? or is it because sunlight is the most usual kind of light, the kind we encounter most often? No —this last may not even be true: people who are awake mostly at night still use sunlight as standard like the rest of us. What is crucial is the fact that in sunlight we are capable of *the maximum possible discrimination* of shades. At night the two dresses look the same color, the one dress being "really" black, the other "really" blue; by sunlight they can be distinguished from each other. We can see the difference then, and of course we want to have different color-names for what we have thus distinguished. Therefore we use the situation in which the maximum color-discrimination is possible, namely, sunlight.

The frequency or usualness of sunlight has nothing to do with it: if some other light were devised or discovered which would enable us to make more discriminations than are possible via sunlight; if, for example, something examined in sunlight looked one uniform color but in this new light broke up into different shades which the sunlight did not enable us to distinguish, then we would take the new light as standard. Just as we previously said under lamplight, "It looks black now; but wait for sunlight to see what color it really is!" so we would then say, "It looks blue now, but wait till I've shined light X on it to see what colors it really has!"

A microscope enables us to make more discriminations than does the unaided eye. Hence in this case too we say, "Blood looks red; but turn a microscope on it and you'll see that it's really partly red, partly white, partly clear, and so on."

Thus, of the total set of appearances of the object, we take certain ones and give them a privileged status, calling them the *real* quality of the thing; and we select whatever appearance or set of appearances (sense-data) enable us to make the maximum discrimination, using this as a standard by which to judge the rest of the appearances. We are driving up a blind alley if we make a distinc-

tion between "how things appear" and "how they really are" and
then conclude that, since we can only know how they appear, we
can never know how they really are. "How they really are" *is*, for
phenomenalism, how they appear, under certain privileged conditions. And we have been investigating what gives them the privilege.
(Or to put it another way: we shouldn't divorce "what they are
really like" from "how they look." What they are really like *is* how
they look, under certain conditions. The "looks" and the "is" are
not in separate realms; the "is" is a part of the "looks." The only
alternative, says phenomenalism, is complete skepticism, as must
be the case for the realist. But we do constantly make the distinction between the way things are and the way they look, thus showing that it is a distinction which is knowable. And how could it be
knowable if it weren't a distinction among the "looks"?)

But some would not be content with the principle of maximum
discrimination, demanding an explanation of it in turn. Why choose
it? The answer usually given is that it conforms to an even more
important standard, namely that of *maximum predictability* of further sense-data. For instance, if you saw the two dresses in yellowish light and couldn't tell them apart, you wouldn't be able to
predict from that situation what color each would assume in sunlight. But if you saw them for the first time in sunlight, the one
appearing blue, the other black, you would know that both would
look black in yellowish light (you would not need experience of
many instances of the phenomenon, at any rate, to be able to predict this). Using the sunlight as standard, the other sense-data are
predictable from it; using the lamplight as standard, this is not the
case.

Thus, when we say that the trees in the distance are really green
and not grayish-blue as they appear, because when we get near
them they look green, and these are the conditions of maximum
predictability. (But not *too* near—for then our eyes cannot focus,
and the sense-data are blurred, and we can make no discriminations
at all.) The world is really made up of different colors, and not all
red, as it appears through red spectacles, because the color you will
see when you put the glasses on is predictable on the basis of ordinary vision. However, if you first saw a landscape through these
glasses you would not know what colors would appear when you
removed the glasses.

It may be that even the criterion of maximum predictability is not applicable to every perceptual situation. For example, why do I say the coin is really round? From most angles it presents an elliptical appearance; only from a perpendicular does it look round. In this case we appeal to the *touch* sense-data: it *feels* round, and we make touch the standard. Or the case of the stick in water: it *looks* bent; it *feels* straight, even in the water. We take the "feels" and make that the standard for "how the stick really is." Our early examples had to do with color, which is apparent to sight only. But when we have something, such as shape, which is available to both sight and touch, we generally make the touch-datum the standard. Berkeley held that visual appearances are only the *signs* of tactual appearances: for example, to say that the stick is straight is only to say that it will *feel* straight.

All this has been argued at length. Some have adhered to the "touch" criterion; others have rejected it. But the important point for us to see is the method which they all have in common: whatever exactly the standard be, or whether there is one or more, the general procedure is the same: to relate sense-data *to each other*. *The difference between appearance and reality is not the difference between the sense-data and the realist's physical objects, but the difference between a certain selected group of sense-data and the rest of the sense-data from the same complex.*

The analysis of error: hallucinations. But what if there is no object there at all? How do we know this? Again, only by comparing certain sense-data with other ones. There are some sense-data which we dismiss as hallucinatory because they do not conform to certain conditions. What are these conditions? There are several that are generally acknowledged as minimum conditions to be met if the sense-datum is not to be hallucinatory.

One obvious test of veridicality which we constantly employ in ordinary life is reenforcing visual sense-data with tactual sense-data. Thus, no matter how clearly or vividly you "see" a tree outside the window, if you went up to it and couldn't touch it, and in fact could *walk through* the place where you declared it to be, you would not say that there was a real tree there.

But even among the visual data themselves there are ways of eliminating those that are hallucinatory. If there were not, we could never know whether the stars were hallucinations, for we surely

cannot touch them, although of course in believing they are real
stars we believe that if we were in the appropriate place in space
(some light-years away) we could touch them (if we didn't get
burned to a crisp first).

Let us consider, for the sake of simplicity, the case of looking at
a table-top. We do not touch it; our only sense-data are visual. How
can we tell whether it is real or hallucinatory? Several characteristics are apparent at once. (1) As I look, the sense-data from moment to moment *resemble* each other. If I stand still they are
exactly alike. But if I move around, changing my angle of vision,
they do not always do so (the table-top looks rectagular seen from
above, but the angles are very acute when seen almost edge-on);
but *adjacent* sense-data do—sense-datum 1 (rectangular) may not
greatly resemble sense-datum 50 (sharply diamond-shaped), but the
two are connected by a series of sense-data each of which is almost
identical with the one on each side of it. The change is gradual and
regular—so regular that we can formulate general laws about how
it will occur in each case; these are the laws of perspective. Hallucinations need not behave in this way. (2) If the *sensible environment* (surrounding sense-data) changes, it occurs in the same
regular manner. For example, the table may be moved; but if it is a
real table it does not disappear at point A and reappear at point M.
A real table is one whose motion I can follow visually through overlapping sense-fields. The table may be in the center of vision, all
during the moving, but the sensible environment changes in a gradual series of overlapping fields. (3) The series is *gap-indifferent*.
Suppose I watch a fire burn down in the fireplace. Suppose next
time I walk out during the burning and come back in. The first
series can be represented by ABCDEFG; the second by ABC . . .
FG. In the second series there is a gap, but the sense-data I experience on my return (at F) are *indifferent to the gap;* they are just
what they would be at that point if I had stayed in the room all the
time. There is no logical necessity that it should be so; it might be
that when I came into the room again the series of fire-sense-data
would resume at stage D, having left off at C half an hour before
when I left the room. The succession of our sense-data is not, however, like this (not in veridical perception, at any rate) and this is
one of the most pronounced, insistent, and recurrent facts in our

whole experience; not an hour of our waking life passes without our experiencing some instances of it.

These are not the only criteria by which the veridical can be distinguished from the non-veridical. Indeed, they are samples taken almost at random. Different writers have different lists and emphasize different ones. Perhaps the easiest course here, with only a limited amount of space at our disposal, would be to lump them all together and say that some sense-data *fit into a world-order,* whereas others are *"wild."*

It is doubtful that *all* the conditions that have been suggested for veridicality are actually essential. For example, a table that inexplicably hopped around all over the floor would still be called a real table and not a hallucination, as long as you could keep on touching it or sitting on it during its entire helter-skelter journey. Probably, as in cases already considered on pages 40–49, we have here no hard-and-fast criteria that have to be fulfilled, but rather the majority of a whole *group* (and perhaps not a very definite group at that) of criteria. Indeed, the concept of a hallucination, like the concept of gold (pages 42–45), is not a clear-cut one. We all dismiss the pink rat as a hallucination: it can't be touched, it jumps about in ways which do not conform to laws of nature, it disappears and reappears without going into a hole, and so on—there is scarcely a single criterion of veridicality that it fulfills. On the other hand, the table here fulfills all of them. There are, however, imaginable conditions in which the situation would not be so clear: suppose I saw a tree that cast no shadow even though it was past noon and the sun was shining? or suppose I could see it and touch it only two minutes out of every three, even though I continued to look in the same direction and nothing passed by in the line of sight? These things, as far as we know, do not happen, and hence we are not required to decide—we do not *have* to define "hallucination" precisely. If phenomena such as these did occur, we would probably set up more carefully a list of defining characteristics.

But the important point, once again, is that according to phenomenalism the difference between hallucination and veridical perception is a difference *among* sense-data, not a difference between sense-data and something else that is unknowable. Certain standards are set up, certain conditions (though, as we have just seen, not very precise ones) which must be fulfilled if the sense-datum is to take its place in the "world-order" as opposed to being "wild." (Fortunately, almost all the sense-data we experience *do* take their place in such an order; the majority of them are not "wild.") And the difference between hallucinations and illusions is that the hallucinatory data, being "wild," do not belong to any *family* of sense-data, while the illusions do belong to the family, but not to the standard or privileged members of that family.

The analysis of error: dreams. The difference between waking life and dream life is accounted for along similar lines. Waking-life sense-data possess a certain regularity, a certain continuity with each other, which dream-experiences lack. You dream that your wife is dead; but you awaken and there she is—you can touch her. Or, if she is not there, she appears later or she telephones you. She "fits into the order." There is sometimes—not always!—a certain continuity and regularity *within* the dream experience; but that continuity is broken when you awaken, find yourself in bed, and remember being in that bed, getting drowsy, turning off the light. A whole pattern of sense-data occurs similar to those remembered, to bridge the gap, and against this background the whole chaotic succession of dream-data stands out as an intruder. You instantly put it in a different realm or category, and call it a dream. Sometimes, to be sure, the dream has been so vivid that you may not instantly be aware that it was a dream. You may get up and think your wife is really dead, until you see her in the bathroom.

The *exact* differences between dream-experiences and waking-life experiences are difficult to state, again, partly because there is no *precise* set of criteria for distinguishing them. Some writers emphasize the qualitative nature of the two classes of experiences; others emphasize their context. But of one thing they are all sure: the difference between dreams and waking life is nothing other than the difference between two classes of data ("data" rather than "sense-data," because whether you call dream-data "sense-data" or not depends on how broadly you choose to define "sense-data"). There is a difference, sometimes an intrinsic difference but surely a relational difference, among the data themselves. If there were not, argues the phenomenalist, how would we ever be able to distinguish dreams from waking life? And yet we can and do make this distinction all the time. If the distinction cannot be made among the data of immediate experience, how could it be made? Would not the only alternative be skepticism?

At this point someone may suggest, "Maybe all of life is a dream!" Here the phenomenalist has a forthright reply: The word "dream" means something only in contrast to something else which is *not* dream. Dream-data are those which just *"don't fit in"* with the regular every-day order of our data. Now, if we said of *every* datum we ever experienced that it didn't fit in, what would this mean? Fit in with what? To say that something doesn't fit into a certain context or background is to imply the existence of the context or background into which it doesn't fit; otherwise the whole assertion becomes meaningless. To say that some things immediately experienced are dreams, then, is to imply that there are other things immediately experienced which are *not* dreams, and so it's not *"all* a dream" after all.

Or one could put it this way: Say, if you like, that it's all a dream. But this is no more than a verbal manipulation. Within that one huge dream which all of us are in all of the time, there are still distinctions to be made: some of the data don't fit in with the others; they stick out like sore thumbs. And we will still want a name by which to label those that don't fit; only we shall now be unable to use the word "dream" because this word has already been pre-empted to apply to the totality of the data. So we shall have to use a new word—to refer to exactly the same thing that we called "dream" before. Clearly there is no gain in this; in doing it we would only be substituting a new word for one that is already in current usage and which everybody understands.

Certainty and physical-object statements. In Chapter 3 we considered the topic of certainty and dubitability. According to one view, at least, we cannot rationally doubt an empirical statement when we cannot specify the empirical content of our doubt: for example, what does it mean to doubt that I have a hand, when you and I can both see it and touch it at length? What more could one desire? What is lacking which, if it were supplied, would resolve the doubt? We then indicated that more would have to be said about the problem later when we had developed a background for it. That time has now come. We can now make the fallibilist's position more plausible. It amounts to this:

How do we know there is a table there? By sensing sense-data.

If it is a real table, the visual data will succeed each other in a certain orderly way, changing as we change our angle of vision (we all know from experience *how* they change, though it is difficult to describe it in words), becoming smaller as we recede, and the like. The more sense-data we sense, the surer we can be that it's a real table we're seeing. If besides visual data we can have tactual data as well, we can be surer still. But when can we be *absolutely* sure? The fallibilist says: Never. Why? Because there is an *infinite* number of sense-data we could sense: for instance, in vision alone, between any two perspectives from which the table might be viewed there is an infinite number of other perspectives. For all practical purposes, we can be (or at any rate we are) sure after just a few looks, or maybe a look and a touch; as a rule we are satisfied with just a brief glance. But if you ask, "At what point do you really *know* that it's a real table?" the answer is, not until you have sensed the infinitude of sense-data relevant to the verification of the statement, and of course you cannot do this in a finite amount of time. At first glance the coin looks somewhat elliptical; a half-second later, from a more acute angle, it looks more elliptical; but if you hadn't blinked just at a quarter-of-a-second, you *might* have experienced, instead of a sense-datum of an ellipticity between these two, a visual sense-datum that was shaped like a cow. And in that case you would have had reason to doubt your original assumption that you weren't having a hallucination and that it was a real coin you were seeing. But this sort of thing is always a possibility; you can never be absolutely sure that it won't happen, no matter how many favorable sense-data you have experienced.

Another way of putting the matter is this: when you assert that there's a (real) table there, this is an implicit *prediction;* indeed, every physical-object statement is an implicit prediction. When you say it is a real physical object you are predicting that the visual sense-datum you are sensing now will be followed (under specifiable conditions) by *other* visual sense-data, that the visual sense-data can be "backed up" by tactual sense-data, etc. When you assert that that's a real apple, you assert in effect that the visual data will vary in certain ways (according to laws of perspective), that tactual data will follow if you reach out your hand in the right direction, that a certain indefinable taste sense-datum will occur (which we would describe as an "apple taste"), and the like. The negative result of any of these experiments would cast doubt on the hypothesis that this is a real apple. When, then, would you *know* that the hypothesis is true? Strictly, never. No matter how many apple-data you experience, you can always experience more.

By contrast, the statement that you are experiencing a red sense-datum is not predictive at all. Even if it disappears in a split-second, it still remains true that you *did* experience it. There was a red sense-datum present to your consciousness at that moment. But it is not so with the statement that this is a real apple. No matter how many apple-sense-data you have experienced, you can never be sure that the next one won't be such as to cast doubt on your whole hypothesis. Hence, it will always remain just that—a hypothesis. Between "I am sensing a red sense-datum" and "I am perceiving a real apple" is all the difference between one and infinity. In uttering a physical-object statement you are making a prediction which is infinite in its range. And it is always possible that the prediction may not be fulfilled. At any rate, if it is infinite, you can certainly never fulfill it yourself.

Certainty and sense-datum statements. What about statements concerning sense-data? Can *they* ever be certain? Whether there's a real apple there or not, isn't it indubitable that I'm directly aware of a red, roundish something? I certainly can't doubt my experience of it, can I, even though the "it" should be a hallucination? How, then, could anyone doubt the sense-datum statement, however much he may doubt the physical-object statement?

Yet there are those who argue in favor of fallibilism for sense-data too. If I say "I am now sensing a reddish color," my statement may well be false. (1) I may be deliberately lying. (2) I may have a "slip of the tongue" and get the wrong words out. (3) Most important, I may make a *verbal* error: I may be misusing a word. If I don't know what "red" means, I may say I have sensed an instance of it when I haven't. I may have said "red" as a child in many situations when later verbal experience would lead me to say "orange." This is most obvious in the case of an unfamiliar color-name. Suppose you see, for example, magenta (not necessarily a physical object possessing that color), but you don't know that there is a name for that particular shade. So you may call it something quite different, quite incorrectly. It was still magenta you were visually aware of, but you weren't aware of it *as being* magenta—that is, you weren't aware that "magenta" was the name for the color you saw. Similarly, you may sense something, perhaps just a spot before your eyes, which is elliptical in shape, but you will certainly not call it that if you don't know what the word "elliptical" means.

Now clearly there is *always* a possibility of verbal error. No statement, whether about sense-data or anything else, is immune from this. The difference between statements about sense-data and ordinary empirical statements such as "That's a tree" is that in the case of sense-datum-statements there is no possibility of *empirical* error, and there always *is* in the other cases. If you're not lying, not getting the wrong words out, not misusing any of the words in the sentence, then your report *can't* be mistaken. Your statement "I see a blue after-image" (a sense-datum statement) is then indubitable, infallible, incorrigible, because it makes no prediction about future experiences the way "I see a blue box" does; the statement about the box entails an infinite array of sense-datum statements, while the statement about the after-image, being a sense-datum statement, entails nothing whatever beyond itself.

Here many persons would rest the matter. But some would go on to make an important addition: they would say that while a sense-datum statement is certain and infallible, no sense-datum statement can ever be uttered! Every alleged report of the given (in this discussion, sense-data) goes beyond the given of the moment dealt with in the report. Why? Must it do so? Yes, for the simple reason that when statements are made, *words* are used; and when we use words, we go beyond the given, unless those words are proper names (see page 15). When you call a sense-datum "red" you are not saying something that applies only to this given sense-datum; since "red" is a class-word, it denotes not only the datum you are now experiencing but countless others you have experienced before—and by calling this one "red" you are *relating this one to those previous ones,* declaring in effect that the datum you are now aware of is *like* those you have been aware of previously, enough like them at any rate to be put in the same pigeonhole and labeled with the same class-name. And in doing this you are doing more than reporting the nature of your present datum: you are relying on *memory* (how else would you know that this datum is like others you've sensed before?), and memory of course is fallible. (In calling it red you are not *naming,* baptizing, this datum; if you were, you could never use the word again, for this datum disappears forever; rather, you are describing it, saying what it is like. And this gives the whole show away: you are indeed saying what it is *like*, and it is like other data which have gone by the same name.)

If you could give every sense-datum a different proper name, you could get round this difficulty, though it would require literally an infinite number of proper names, none of them repeatable. But aside from this possibility, language being what it is, when you use language at all, you go beyond the given of the moment and relate the present given to past givens. Hence it is impossible to report the given only: in the very act of making the report in words you are going beyond it. And in going beyond it you are involving the possibility that your report may be fallible. It is true, of course, that you sense certain sense-data—but in characterizing them with class-words, such as "red," you are placing them in the same class with other sense-data and thus involving the possibility of misclassification. A possibility of error thus arises in the very act of using language.[6]

There is no more space for further discussion of the certainty vs. fallibility issue. Suffice it to say that the center of controversy is not so much empirical statements (including physical-object statements), which are pretty generally agreed to be excluded from the promised land of certainty, but rather sense-datum statements (or, in general, statements about the given), if, indeed, pure sense-datum statements are possible at all.

Are sense-data mental or physical? It is tempting to assert at once that colors, sounds, and so on are merely the "contents of minds," and mental in nature. But this, says phenomenalism, is a hangover from the confusion of idealism. Actually, the phrase "in the mind" isn't at all clear in its meaning, unless it means what it does in ordinary conversation ("It's all in your mind" means "it's imaginary"; "It keeps running through my mind" means "I keep thinking about it"). It does not even make sense to say that the colors are in your mind, as if that were a *place*. It's not as if the green you saw were

---

[6] Some philosophers would say that calling a sense-datum "red" implies only acquaintance with a linguistic *rule* specifying under what conditions a symbol (in this case the word "red") is to be used. (And in a case like "red" the rule would have to be learned ostensively.) This may be so. But the net result is the same. For in this case also, error is possible; one may be misapplying a rule.

somehow refracted through your eyes and nerves and projected onto a screen in the back of your head. (Even if it were, this wouldn't be the green you see; for surely the green you see requires eyes as a causal condition, and the green in the back of your head would be *behind* your eyes.) The point is that the greens and blues are the objects of immediate and direct awareness; they are not the awareness itself, but *that of which you are aware.* And what would it even mean to say that not merely your awareness, but that of which you are aware is mental? [7]

Are sense-data physical? Again, no. Of course, colors, sounds, and the like in the *second* sense of those terms distinguished on page 304 are physical; light-waves are physical phenomena. But light-waves are not what we see. I am aware of colors when looking at the wall, or even in seeing spots before my eyes (when presumably no light-waves are present at all), and it is colors as the objects of immediate awareness that we mean here in this entire discussion. When we say that we see colors in this sense, we imply nothing about the "real" color of the physical object, or what kind of light-waves emanate from it, or what it would look like to the normal eye under specified conditions of light, or even whether there is a physical object at all. And our question is, are colors in this immediate sense, the colors which we see, physical? And again the answer is given, What does this mean? Does it mean that they belong to a physical object? In that case the answer is that they need not: for instance, the red spots, the stars you see when you get hit on the head, the hallucinations, images, dreams, and all the rest. But then what does it mean?

The most usual analysis of this issue among phenomenalists is that sense-data are neither mental nor physical: in fact, that it is cognitively meaningless to assert that they are either one. Sense-data are, as it were, the *raw material* out of which we *construct* both the mental and the physical realms. Sense-data are *given*, and the given—the colors, the shapes, the smells, and so on, of which we are immediately aware—is neither mental nor physical; the colors we see are not given *as* either. The green you see does not come with a tag on it labeled "mental" or "physical." The green as such is

---

[7] It might be taken to mean that it is causally *dependent* for its existence on your being aware of it. This will be discussed when we bring in the notion of sensibilia.

neither, any more than a slab of marble yet uncarved is either a column or a statue. The mental and the physical are both *constructed out of* the given, but neither itself is given: only the colors, shapes, smells, tastes, and so on of which we are immediately aware are given. *We* put the tags on the given data, at a later stage of the game; and we apply or withhold the tag depending on the context, setting, or *relations* in which the given data are sensed.

Is the green I am now seeing physical, characterizing a physical thing? That all depends. First of all, is there a physical thing? We determine that by means of the relations of successive sense-data to each other, as outlined in the section on error, distinguishing the hallucinatory from the veridical. Second, is it really green? This can mean "it looks green to the normal eye under conditions of maximum discrimination or predictability." Or it can mean "it emanates light-waves of a certain wave-length," in which case certain laboratory equipment is set up which will provide the answer. In either case, sensing further sense-data must answer the question of whether the green belongs in the physical order. If it does fulfill the criteria, it fits into the physical order, it "belongs"; and it is physical in that sense. The green itself is no different, but we call it physical now because it has passed its tests and now "belongs to the system."

Is the green I am seeing mental? Well, it is experienced, and if whatever that is directly experienced is said to be mental, then the green is—but phenomenalists would declare this to be a confusion between our sensing of X with the X that is sensed. Is the green a sensation? Again no; we *have* a sensation *of* the green, but this doesn't imply that the green itself *is* a sensation. Indeed, if we incline to view the green as mental, or as a sensation, we are viewing it *in a context* of sense-organs, nerves, and brains, and saying that —normally at any rate—you do not sense green unless certain conditions having to do with these things are fulfilled. By way of emphasizing this fact you may call the green a sensation—but, phenomenalists would say, this is sheer confusion.[8] Once again: *seeing* the green is doubtless a mental process, as any seeing is; but this does not for a moment involve that *what* is seen—the green—is mental.

[8] See **W. T. Stace**, *Theory of Knowledge and Existence* (Oxford: The Clarendon Press, 1932), pp. 88–92.

The status of sense-organs. "But if the objects of immediate experience are always sense-data, how can I know that my awareness of these sense-data depends on the existence of eyes or ears, nerves, and brains?" The phenomenalist answers that I know it, if I know it at all, as a result of the sense-data which I sense. If you can't distinguish colors, and I examine your retina with an optician's flashlight, I am sensing eye-sense-data. My information about your eye is in principle no different from my information about the tree. How do I know about nerves and brains? I don't have nerve-sense-data or brain-sense-data (at least not from you) while you are alive; but my belief that these conditions are really necessary conditions is based on experiments I have conducted or heard of in which scientists making an autopsy on a person who couldn't see *did* experience brain-sense-data or nerve-sense-data and found that they differed in certain ways from the normal. It is from experiencing sense-data under these unusual conditions that scientists conclude that nerves and brains are necessary conditions for sensing sense-data. It all comes down again to sensing sense-data. Surely such physiological knowledge is not *a priori;* if it were, we wouldn't have to undertake such labored investigation in order to determine what the exact conditions of perception are. Our knowledge of these things comes by the same sense-datum path that all empirical knowledge does; it differs only in that it is concerned with the causal conditions under which sense-data themselves are sensed. And when we investigate this, we are only investigating more actual and possible sense-data—namely, physical objects such as brains and sense-organs.

The causation of sense-data. We should be careful, however, in making statements about the causation of sense-data. Let us remember that it is occurrences, events, things happening, that are caused. The house is not caused, but the coming-into-being of the house is caused. The number 2 is not caused, but your uttering the word "2" at this moment doubtless is. Now sense-data are not caused, for sense-data are not events. But your *sensing* this particular sense-datum—in other words, your *having the sensation*—at this particular time is doubtless caused. Your sensing green at this moment may be caused by the presence of a green book (the book being itself a family of actual and possible sense-data) ; your sensing green yesterday may have been caused by hypnotic suggestion.

The causes of the *event*, sensing sense-data, are sometimes physical and sometimes not. And we determine what causes what on the basis of constant conjunctions. This holds as much of our sensing of sense-data as of anything else.

Physical objects as logical constructions out of sense-data. We have, then, as items in our sensory experience, sense-data and physical objects. Just what is the relation between these two classes of things? According to most phenomenalists, to speak of them as two classes of things is extremely misleading, as if it were like the relation of moisture to crops. Such a way of talking leads to endless puzzles, such as: Are sense-data parts of physical objects? Do they resemble physical objects? What kind of thing are they, anyway, interposed as it were between the mind and the physical world? If we view the issue in this way, we would soon be talking like representative realists. We can avoid this if we cease to talk as if the problem was that of the relation between two kinds of *thing.*

The relation between sense-data and physical objects is generally stated by phenomenalists as follows: "Physical objects are logical constructions out of sense-data." Perhaps this way of putting it is unfortunate: it makes it sound as if physical objects are constructed out of sense-data as a house is constructed out of bricks, or a patchwork quilt out of bits of cloth. But this is not so; indeed, it is (cognitively) meaningless. To say that I am eating not a tomato but a tomato-ish group of sense-data is neither true nor false but meaningless. The problem of the relation of physical objects to sense-data is conceived by most phenomenalists as the problem of the relation of two classes of *statements:* statements in which sense-datum-words occur and statements in which physical-object words occur. Phenomenalists contend that statements from one class can be made equivalent to statements from the other class, in this way: *to say* something about physical objects is really *to say* something about sense-data. Saying something about the table is equivalent to saying something about sense-data—the statement about the table is reducible without remainder to a statement (or set of statements) about sense-data. This is what phenomenalists mean when they speak of physical objects being logical constructions out of sense-data. Of course, it is briefer and easier to use the physical-object-language, and this is what we have been doing all our lives; nevertheless, according to phenomenalists, everything that can be said about physical objects can be said in terms of sense-data. Every physical-object statement is a disguised sense-datum statement.

Not every sense-datum statement can be translated into a physical-object statement. If you have a hallucination, for example, due to suggestion, you are entitled to make sense-datum statements (about the sense-data which comprise the hallucination) but no physical-object statements, for in this case there was no physical object. But every time you make a physical-object statement, you must be able to make sense-datum statements. It is the latter that are ultimate.

How is it that in addition to making sense-datum statements (about the objects of direct sensing), we also make physical-object statements? Does the nature of the sense-data we experience require this? No, phenomenalists answer, it does not *require* it, it only makes it very *convenient*. How does it happen to be convenient? This question is best answered by showing how, if the succession of our sense-data were quite different from what it is, it would not be convenient at all; indeed, the concept "physical object" would never have existed. We can show this as follows:

What entitles us to say the table is there? The fact that sense-data succeed each other in a certain order and with a certain predictable regularity. If I keep looking steadily, the visual sense-data do not change; as I move about and change my angle of vision, the sense-data change too in certain predictable ways; also if I reach out I experience tactual sense-data; and so on. But now suppose the sense-data did not succeed each other in this orderly manner: the first moment, a rectangular sense-datum; the second, a round one; the third, none at all; and no tactual datum whatever. In that event we should say it wasn't a real table but a hallucination. Of course, as we have seen, we say this, and we have the concept "hallucination," only by contrast with the regular and uniform series of sense-data we usually experience which are not hallucinatory. But suppose *all* the data we experienced were chaotic: suppose there was no order or regularity to be found among them. In that event we would have no term "physical objects," nor, of course, "hallucination." There would just be sense-data one moment, sense-data the next, and so on indefinitely, in chaotic succession, one blooming, buzzing confusion, with no order, no repeatability, no uniformity, no predictability among them. Science would be impossible, and the meagerest attempt to predict our future experiences would be impossible.

But wouldn't *we* still be there? and aren't we bodies, at least in part? Yes—in all this we have been imagining that at least *some* data remained constant—the visual, tactual, kinesthetic, and somatic data which belong to the construct which we call our body. This would be at least one physical object. But it is conceivable that even *these* data might be absent. "Very likely then *we* wouldn't be here to tell the tale." Doubtless, but this does not matter for the argument; in any case, if one admits the logical possibility of a disembodied mind, one can imagine this whole panorama of ever-shifting chaotic sense-data, lacking even the relatively stable patterns of sense-data we call our bodies which thus far in our imaginings we have conceived to be present as a center of constancy in the sense-data in the midst of the flux.

But, because of the relations of continuity, regularity, and the like, which obtain among sense-data, we do have the concept "physical object"—our bodies and other physical objects as well, other relatively stable and constant *families* of sense-data, which constitute other physical objects. And the contention of phenomenalism is that talking about these physical objects is nothing more nor less than talking about these *families of sense-data*. The former is only a logical construction, or construct, out of the latter, in the way described a few paragraphs above.

Physical objects, then, are constructs out of sense-data. Anything say-able about physical objects must be say-able in terms of sense-data. But there are also constructs out of physical objects—such as electrons: everything say-able about electrons must be say-able in terms of physical objects. These are *second-order* constructs, just as physical objects are *first-order* constructs out of sense-data. The second-order constructs do not concern us in this chapter; we discussed them in Chapter 3, though we did not use this name for them then. We are now enabled to see how they fit into the whole phenomenalistic scheme of things. Whether you are thinking of a first-order construct or a second-order construct, if phenomenalism is right there must be a path, be it short or long, from them to the given. Ultimately, any assertion you make about any empirical

matter of fact must be translatable, through one or more translations, into assertions about given sense-data.

It will be seen that this fits in very well with the Verifiability
criterion discussed in Chapter 3: that a statement is equivalent in
its cognitive meaning to the total set of statements which would
verify it. A statement about electrons means the same as, and no
more than, the entire set of physical-object-statements which constitute the evidence for this statement. And the meaning of a physical-object statement, in turn (it now turns out), is the same as,
and no more than, the meaning of the total set of sense-datum statements which verify it. The meaning of a statement is the same as
that of the whole set of evidential statements, the truth of which
together constitutes the truth of the statement in question.

Statements about unobserved physical objects. But how can physical object statements be reducible in meaning to sense-datum statements, while at the same time physical objects are held to exist even
when no member of the family of sense-data constituting it is being
sensed? We have already hinted at phenomenalism's answer
(though in misleading terms because of the word "sensation") at
the beginning of this section (pages 405–407). Though neither I nor
anyone else may be sensing sense-data of the back of my chair just
now, these sense-data are *available*—it is *possible* to sense members
of this family of sense-data even though no one is actually at this
moment doing so. When I say that it exists even though no experience of the relevant sense-data is being had, I mean only that *if*
I or any other observer were satisfying certain conditions (principally that of looking in the right direction from the right place),
then I or the other observer would be sensing these sense-data.

We do not even have to talk about *possible* sense-data; all we
have to do in our present analysis is to see to it that some, at least,
of the sense-datum sentences into which the physical-object sentence is to be translated are *hypothetical* rather than categorical.[9]
They are about sense-data which we *would* be sensing if some con-
dition(s) relating to our position in space or time or our faculties of
perception were other than they actually are. Thus, the sentence
about the table's being in the room need not be reducible entirely

---

[9] An example of a categorical statement: "I was downtown yesterday." An
example of a hypothetical statement: *"If* I had been **downtown yesterday,** I
would have seen the fire."

to categorical statements about sense-data which I or someone else is sensing—after all, the table may still be here when no one is in the room; *some* of the statements in the reduction must be *hypothetical* ones, such as *"If* I were in the room, I would be sensing such-and-such sense-data," and *"If* I were at position P (which I am not), I would sense such-and-such sense-data" (such as, rectangular if you were poised directly above the table), and so on. In fact, most of the sentences will undoubtedly be hypothetical.

How can we ever know that these hypothetical statements are true? I can be sure that I am sensing certain sense-data at this moment; but how can I know that *if* I were at a place where I am not, I *would* be sensing sense-data which in fact I am not? According to phenomenalism at least, we often have good inductive evidence for believing such statements to be true, even though of course we cannot verify them in the direct way we can the statements about what we are actually sensing. Perhaps no one is having sense-data of the coal-pile in the basement now; but I sensed some sense-data belonging to this family when I was down there ten minutes ago, and since I have heard nothing suspicious going on in the meantime (and am pretty sure that the removal of a coal-pile would occasion enough noise so that I would hear it) I conclude that it is still there—that is, that sense-data belonging to the family are available now, even though they are not being sensed now. If I had to lay a wager for or against it, I would certainly wager for it; and so would you.

Sometimes phenomenalists introduce the term *sensibile,* or (plural) *sensibilia,* in this connection. Thus far we have left open the question of whether sense-data can exist unsensed. We have used only the notion of sensed sense-data, and have not considered the possibility of unsensed ones. But in connection with the issue we are now considering, the point needs to be raised. As a rule, the term "sense-datum" is now limited to that which *is* directly sensed, so that it would be self-contradictory to speak of a sense-datum existing unsensed. But of course this does not answer the question, "Is there something just like a sense-datum except that it can exist unsensed?" It is to these entities, whether they exist or not, that the term "sensibilia" is applied. There is much to be said both for and against the introduction of sensibilia. But the point here is that *if* they are introduced, we do not need the hypothetical statements we have been discussing in this section. Instead of saying, *"If* I were poised above the table, I would be sensing a rectangular sense-datum," I can now say, "There is a rectangular sensibile existing now, whether I am sensing it or not," adding, "I have only to get to that spot above the table to sense it."

Why the translation of physical-object statements into sense-datum statements does not succeed. If phenomenalism is correct in saying that physical-object statements are translatable into sense-datum statements, it would seem that the best way to show this would be to carry out the program by providing some specimen translations. "If statements about the table are equivalent to statements about sense-data, please give me the statements about sense-data which the table-statement is equivalent to!" And yet no phenomenalist has ever done this, not even in a single case. According to many phenomenalists it can never be done. But if this is so, does it not force the entire phenomenalistic program to break down?

Phenomenalists, of course, say no. They say that while in actual practice it is impossible to give any such translations, this does not damage the phenomenalistic ideal. It does not prove it wrong, any more than our inability to count all the trees in the world proves that there is no definite number of trees. The principal reasons for the practical impossibility of making the translations are as follows:

1. *The poverty of our language.* Neither English nor any other language has the words that would be necessary for making the required sense-datum statements. The sense-data which we sense from moment to moment are infinitely various; what words can we use that will distinguish the sense-data of moment-1 from those of moment-2? I am looking at the top of the table from a certain angle; now I move a few inches and look at it from a slightly different angle; and so on. Or, I look at it in a certain light, then vary the light a bit, or wait for the afternoon sun to shine in the window, changing the quality of all the visual data. How am I to describe in words these moment-to-moment changes in such a way as to distinguish them from each other? I recognize the differences; they are an undoubted fact of my experience; but I have no words for them.

Indeed, in order to characterize sense-data we generally have to resort to physical-object words. If I want to describe the mirage that looks like an oasis, without committing myself to the assertion that there is an oasis there, I can do this most accurately and briefly by saying that I am aware of an oasis-like sense-datum, or I have to describe the sense-data in terms of "trees," "grass," "water," and the like, all of which are physical-object words. Language is used primarily for talking about physical things and events; for the "artificial" purposes of philosophy—such as talking about sense-data—we simply have to borrow that language, being careful to avoid certain of its usual implications.

This is true of any sense-data we may wish to describe, except for a comparatively small class such as "red," "round," "shrill," and similar words, which can be used to stand for sense-data in ordinary life as well as qualities of physical things. Even these are normally used to qualify physical things, but since we do sometimes see things like red spots before our eyes and do not mean to impute to them any existence in the physical order, we at least have some use for the words outside physical-object contexts. But this does not go far. Even in such a simple statement as "That's a dagger"—in the sense which does *not* commit the speaker to the assertion that a real dagger is present, as in Macbeth's hallucination, "Is this a dagger which I see before me?"—we must resort to physical-object words to describe the data: "That is a dagger-ish group of sense-data" or some such awkward locution.

And if we have such trouble with language in the case of visual sense-data, how much more do we not have with tactual data, taste-data, or kinesthetic data! In all of these we are aware of an indefinitely large number of differences; and yet how shall we state them in words? We all are acquainted with the "feel" of iron and the "feel" of wood—but how describe the difference in the tactual sense-data? Or between the "feels" of cedar and soft maple? None of these classes of sense-data have names, but only such general names as "hard," none of which would even begin to distinguish them from each other.

But suppose that someone took the trouble to name millions of different varieties of sense-data, and moreover that he could somehow communicate to others what he meant by each of them so that others too knew how to distinguish the sense-data by the words. Would he then be able to translate any statement about a physical object into statements about sense-data? And here we reach our second difficulty:

2. *We would require an infinite number of sense-datum state-*

ments. How many sense-datum statements would we need to be equivalent to one physical-object statement such as "There is a table in the room"? There is no end to them. Suppose (limiting ourselves to vision alone) you had made in the newly-formed sense-datum language of the last paragraph a thousand sense-datum statements, each describing the table-sense-data you sensed from a slightly different angle. Suppose that among them are two positions near together, Positions 1 and 2. Wouldn't a part of the table-statement be rendered by specifying what the sense-datum was like when you were in a position halfway between 1 and 2? You would need the report from that place too—Position 3. You would need another between 1 and 3, between 3 and 2, etc. The description of the sense-data from each of these angles (and there is an infinite number of them) contributes its bit to the whole meaning of the physical-object statement. Each one needs to be included. If, for example, at position 3 the sense-datum turned out to be kidney-shaped, this would *not* fit in with the family of sense-data constituting the table; and of course it is always conceivable, and surely logically possible, that this might turn out to be the case: "one never knows until he's looked." In practice, of course, we never do anything like this—we assume that the sense-data from most of the positions are "all right." But

> . . . the fact remains that however many favorable tests he may make he can never reach a stage at which it ceases to be conceivable that further sense-experience will reverse the verdict of the previous experiences. He will never be in a position to demonstrate that he will not subsequently have experiences that will entitle him to conclude that his original statement was false after all. And this implies that the content of a statement about a material thing cannot be exhaustively specified by any finite number of references to sense-data.[10]

But even this is not all.

3. *No particular sense-datum statement is necessary.* We have just seen that no finite set of sense-datum statements is sufficient to render the complete content of any physical-object statement. We must now face the prospect that no particular sense-datum statement is even necessary: that is, there is no one particular statement in the infinite series that cannot be done without. The reason for this is that

---

[10] Ayer, *The Foundation of Empirical Knowledge,* pp. 239–240.

What is required to verify a statement about a material thing is never just the occurrence of a sense-datum of an absolutely specific kind, but only the occurrence of one or other of the sense-data that fall within a fairly indefinite range.[11]

For example: though the occurrence in my experience of a particular visual sense-datum, X, does confirm the proposition "There is a table here," and make up part of its total meaning, and so also with sense-data Y and Z, still no single one of them is required; there are an infinite number of sense-data which would confirm it, and one can get an infinite series of them *without these particular ones.*

> For any test that we actually do carry out there are always an indefinite number of other tests, differing to some extent either in respect of their conditions or their results, which would have done just as well. And this means that if we try to describe what at any given moment would afford us direct evidence for the truth of a statement about a material thing by putting forward a disjunction of statements about sense-data, we shall find once again that this disjunction will have to be infinite.[12]

4. *The concept "physical object" is itself not clear.* So far all the difficulties have been on the side of the sense-data. We have assumed that the meaning of the physical-object statement was clear enough, but that for one reason and another we could not supply the sense-datum statements which were alleged to be equivalent to it. But now we face the difficulty that there is no really clear-cut meaning of the term "physical object" (we have referred to this once before in discussing hallucinations). We have, of course, stated certain general criteria for veridical perception; but this has been only approximate. They all have to do with a certain regularity and orderliness in the succession of the sense-data. But how regular is "regular," and how orderly is "orderly"? What if they are orderly in one way but not in another?

> Suppose I say "There is my friend over there." What if on drawing closer in order to shake hands with him he suddenly disappeared? "Therefore it was not my friend but some delusion or other." But suppose a few seconds later I saw him again, could grasp his hand, etc. What then? "Therefore your friend was nevertheless there and his disappearance was some delusion or other." But imagine after a while

[11] Ayer, *op. cit.*, p. 240.
[12] Ayer, *op. cit.*, p. 241.

he disappeared again, or seemed to disappear—what shall I say now? Have we rules ready for all imaginable possibilities? [13]

In other words, we are confronted once again with something described on pages 48–49: the *open texture of language*. The phrase "physical object" shares in the open texture. And, of course, we cannot give a precise translation of physical-object statements into sense-datum statements if we do not know exactly the meaning of the physical-object statements which are to be translated.

What are we to infer from all this? Must we conclude that to talk about a physical object is to talk about something altogether different from sense-data, or that physical-object statements are equivalent to statements about sense-data *and something else besides?* No, say phenomenalists. That would be

> . . . a mistake analogous to that of supposing that because sentences referring indefinitely to what is red cannot be translated into a finite number of sentences referring to particular red things; therefore "redness" is the name of an object with a distinct existence of its own; or that because sentences referring to "someone" cannot be translated into a finite disjunction of sentences referring to particular persons, therefore "someone" is the name of a peculiar being, a "subsistent entity" perhaps, who is distinct from any person that one can actually meet.[14]

We cannot produce the required translations, for the reasons given above. But it does not follow that to say something about a physical object is *not* to say something about sense-data, or to say something about sense-data and more besides. Maybe the sense-datum statements would have to be infinite in number, maybe they are indefinite in range, *but* in trying to analyze the meaning of physical-object statements, once we leave the firm solid ground of sense-data, which alone can offer this solid ground, we are off in some metaphysical realm with unknowable physical objects and in-principle-unobservable entities.

Anti-phenomenalistic objections. There is a considerable group of philosophers who oppose the whole phenomenalistic analysis in one way or another. As a rule they call themselves realists, though they do not in general hold to the doctrines we have referred to as naive

---

[13] Friedrich Waismann, "Verifiability," *Aristotelian Society Proceedings,* Supplementary Volume XIX, 1945.

[14] Ayer, *op. cit.,* pp. 241–242.

realism or representative realism. Let us examine some of the objections which they have registered against phenomenalism. We shall begin with the milder objections, and work our way into the more fundamental ones.

1. According to the phenomenalistic analysis of statements about physical objects existing unperceived, the observer is necessary to the statement. For example: "There is a desk just around the corner though no one is perceiving it" means *"If I (or someone) were just around the corner, I would sense certain desk-ish sense-data"* (*not* "I would see the desk," for this would bring in a reference to physical objects in the very attempt to eliminate such references from the sentence in favor of references to sense-data). But *what about the "I"?* I am, if nothing else, a body, which is a physical object. So reference to physical objects has not yet been eliminated from the sentence.

The phenomenalist will reply, of course, that statements about bodies, being physical-object statements, are themselves reducible to statements about sense-data; and that therefore the original physical-object statement requires two reductions: the physical object referred to (the desk), and the body of the observer. This may complicate things, but, says the phenomenalist, the principle is no different: if phenomenalism can take care of one physical object, it can surely (by repeating the process) take care of two.

2. How can laws of nature be formulated as laws of regularity among sense-data? Suppose we have the law "Whenever A happens, B happens." Now it is physical events the law is talking about, not sense-data. Can the alleged regularity between these two classes of events be translatable into regularity among sense-data? It seems not. For *there is no invariant relation, no constant conjunction, among sense-data.* Let us take a simple example. Suppose the generalization is "When you strike an elastic ball against a wall, the ball rebounds." But suppose when the ball hits the wall you close your eyes and do not see it rebound. You sense no sense-data of the rebounding. Then the law does not hold! In the past the one sense-datum was always followed by the other in your experience, but this time (because you closed your eyes) the second did not occur. Even the blink of an eye can dash the most secure generalization against the rocks. Or suppose the law is "Whenever you take this drug, you'll feel dizzy." As long as you sense sense-data in both cases, the

generalization will hold. But now suppose somebody administers the drug to you in your sleep. Then the constant conjunction between sense-data of the first and sense-data of the second is broken.

It seems undeniable that there *is* no constant conjunction among sense-data. What law is there that is so secure as to conjoin sense-data when you turn your head or choose to be absent? Any view, such as Berkeley's seems to have been, which tries to find exceptionless regularity among the data of immediate experience is foredoomed to failure. And so the notion of *possible* sense-data is brought in, or, sometimes, the *actual* existence of unsensed sensibilia. Thus, if the law says "Whenever A, then B," even though you didn't observe B happen, you *could* have. The law says nothing whatever about the sense-data you or anybody else *will* experience; that depends on too many things, such as your decision to avert your gaze. But it *does* say something about what sense-data you *could* sense *if* you were in the appropriate circumstances; and of course these circumstances too must be describable phenomenalistically.

But can this be done? This is the subject of the next difficulty:

3. How can the condition of *place* in the "if" part of the hypothetical statement be specified except in terms of physical space, and how can this be done phenomenalistically? "*If* I were in the next room . . ." "*If* I were just around the corner . . ." "*If* I were at the south pole now, I would be experiencing ice-sense-data." But the south pole, like the next room, is a place, a place in physical space, and how can you locate a place in space except by reference to physical coordinates? How can you describe the south pole in sense-datum terms? Maybe you can translate physical-object statements in a phenomenalistic manner; but when you are talking about physical objects existing unperceived, you have to specify the place at which the sense-data *could* be sensed; so the phenomenalistic physical objects must at least exist in a non-phenomenalistic physical frame!

Admittedly this difficulty is not an easy one to remedy. A reference to place is contained in the hypothetical sentence—and it is real physical place. Now, how is one to eliminate reference to this and substitute a reference to sense-data? Phenomenalists would doubtless reply that the principle of this is no different from that of the previous objections. But it is enormously more complicated.

"If I were in Paris now . . ." How reduce such a clause as this to phenomenalistic terms?

The phenomenalist would reply that phrases like "so many miles from here" and "in such and such a direction" will have to stand for the *sense-datum route* that anyone would have to travel if he were to pass from where he is to the other place (Paris). This is to be done as follows: I am now visually aware of a certain sense-datum field. If I walk a step, I am aware of a similar and mostly overlapping sense-datum field. The same happens if I walk a third step. Finally none of the sense-data I began with are in my visual field any more. But they do not change suddenly, only gradually, in an *overlapping series of sense-fields*. Let us call these S_1, S_2, S_3, etc. Then, *if* I replaced S_1 by S_2, S_2 by S_3, S_3 by S_4, and so on, I would finally be sensing the visual field of sense-data belonging to Paris. Of any place, P, P will have to be defined in terms of the sense-datum route that leads from my present sensory field to the sensory field that includes P.

This complicates matters enormously. But even this is not all. By "If someone were at place P . . ." we mean "If someone were *really* at place P . . ." He might dream he was there, or have a hallucination of being there; but this would not do. And so for the sense-datum route: he must really travel it, not dream that he was doing so. Thus the sense-datum route (the series of sense-data between the experience of being here and the experience of being at P) is more complicated than we indicated above. We require still more if's. If the sense-datum route is S_1, S_2, S_3 . . . , in saying that I am at any stage—let's say S_3—I must be able to sense *further* S_3-ish sense-data, enough to establish that I am not dreaming or having a hallucination. The same must be possible at the next stage, S_4, and at every stage along the way. At every stage of the series leading to P, there must be the possibility of another sense-datum series (or unsensed sensibilia existing at each stage), branching off from the main one, so that *if* I had obtained sense-data belonging to this branch, I would have verified the existence of a physical object located at that place. I may not experience any of these branch-series; for that matter, I need not experience the main series. But it must be *possible* for me to experience both: once again, *if* I were in these sense-datum circumstances, then I would have experienced such-and-such sense-data. After all, if it is *not* possible, then it isn't true that I might have had the experience of really moving from here to P.

4. The same problems arise about *time*. "*If* an observer had been at that place at time *t,* he would have experienced such-and-such sense-data." "Time *t*" will mean so many days or seconds or centuries ago. And this in turn the phenomenalist will have to analyze in terms of a sense-datum route by which someone could have been *going to* sense the sense-field that is being sensed by the speaker; so again it will contain a whole battery of "if's" inside itself. "Caesar sensed X 2,000 years ago" would have to be something like this: "Caesar sensed a sense-field such that *if* he had been going to sense a later one temporally adjacent to it, and *if* he had been going to sense a still later one temporally adjacent to that one, and so on, then eventually he *would* have been going to sense the sense-field that is now being sensed by the speaker."

Nor is this all. He must *really* be at time *t*—he must not dream it or hallucinate it. "Caesar was in Rome in 50 B.C." must be translatable into the sense-datum routes in time, through successive sense-fields connecting the two times; and it must *really* connect them. Some could dream of the whole series of events filling the interval between 50 B.C. and now. The sense-datum route from 50 B.C. to now must consist of normal or veridical sense-data; and again this means that there must be the possibility of experiencing innumerable branch-series, just as in the case of space.

The completion of this whole series would be a truly staggering task. And what the realist contends is that the phenomenalist *could not even begin on it if he had not already before his mind the thought of a physical world, ordered in space and time, conceived to be already there waiting to be sensed.* What else, he says, could guide us in our choice of the right if-clauses, and enable us to know which should come after which? [15]

5. It is often objected that statements about unobserved physical objects cannot be translated into hypothetical sense-datum statements at all. Here it is not the "sense-datum" part that is objected to, but the "hypothetical" part. Remember that hypothetical statements may be true even though the conditions described in their if-clauses are unfulfilled. "If you were to go to Atlantic City, you

[15] See H. H. Price, *Hume's Theory of the External World* (London: Oxford University Press, 1934), pp. 188 ff.

would see the ocean" is true even though you never go to Atlantic City. "All dodos are white" means "If there are any dodos they are white," and this may be true even though in fact there are no dodos. And "If you were at place P, you would sense such-and-such sense-data" could be true even though there is no place P, no you, in fact no world at all! The truth of the hypothetical statement is quite compatible with the non-existence of a physical universe. But no physical-object statement, at any rate one which declares that there is a certain physical object, is compatible with the non-existence of a physical universe. Therefore physical-object statements can never be equated with hypothetical statements—and this includes statements about unobserved physical objects too. Somehow we have to get rid of the hypotheticals. But phenomenalism needs them; it cannot do without them. Therefore, phenomenalism must be wrong.[16] (This objection cannot be gone into in more detail without some technical knowledge of logic.)

These are some of the principal difficulties in the phenomenalistic doctrine which realists have suggested. The word "realism" requires a word of explanation: it has many meanings, even in the epistemological problem being discussed in this chapter. It may mean something as general as that "physical objects really do exist," something which in some sense or other nobody denies. Or it may mean a specific doctrine such as the theory of representative realism discussed earlier in this chapter. The objectors to phenomenalism who call themselves realists do not necessarily ally themselves with naive or representative realists at all.

What, then, is their main thesis? It is this: that every time phenomenalists try to translate physical-object statements into sense-datum statements they *presuppose* a physical order and use the concept of it in the very attempt to make the translation. Apart from these presuppositions, say realists, the attempted translations are either unintelligible or a failure, and, they suspect, maybe they are a failure anyway. The physical order is not something arrived at on the basis of sense-data; it is implicitly present from the very beginning.

This issue is as far today as ever from having reached a settlement; it is still a hotbed of controversy. But here we must

[16] See Isaiah Berlin, "Empirical Propositions and Hypothetical Statements," *Mind*, July, 1950.

leave the matter. We cannot investigate it further without plunging into a flood of technical detail which is far beyond the scope of this book.

SELECTED READINGS FOR CHAPTER 6

George Berkeley. *Principles of Human Knowledge* (1710); *Three Dialogues between Hylas and Philonous* (1723). (Many editions available; both works are contained unabridged in one volume, the Modern Students' Library edition of Berkeley, ed. M. W. Calkins. New York: Charles Scribner & Sons.)

David Hume. *Treatise of Human Nature.* 1739. (Many editions available; most convenient is perhaps the Selby-Bigge edition. London: Oxford University Press.) Book I, Part IV, Section 2 ("On Skepticism with Regard to the Senses").

John Stuart Mill. *Examination of Sir William Hamilton's Philosophy.* London: Longmans, Green & Co., 1865. Chapters 11 and 12.

Karl Pearson. *The Grammar of Science.* London: J. M. Dent & Sons, 1892. (Available in Everyman Library edition. New York: E. P. Dutton & Co.)

G. S. Fullerton. *An Introduction to Philosophy.* New York: Macmillan Co., 1906. Chapters 3–5.

W. A. Sinclair. *An Introduction to Philosophy.* New York: Oxford University Press, 1944. Chapters 3–8

Bertrand Russell. *The Problems of Philosophy.* Home University Library. New York: Oxford University Press, 1912. Chapters 1–4.

C. H. Whiteley. *An Introduction to Metaphysics.* Boston: The Beacon Press, 1951. Chapters 5–8.

G. E. Moore. "The Refutation of Idealism." In *Philosophical Studies.* London: Kegan Paul, 1921.

W. T. Stace. "The Refutation of Realism." *Mind,* 53, 1934. (Reprinted in Feigl and Sellars, *Readings in Philosophical Analysis.* New York: Appleton-Century-Crofts, 1949.)

————. *Theory of Knowledge and Existence.* Oxford: Clarendon Press, 1932. See especially Chapter 6.

A. J. Ayer. *Foundations of Empirical Knowledge.* New York: Macmillan Co., 1940.

O. K. Bouwsma. "Descartes' Evil Genius." *Philosophical Review,* 58, 1949.

G. A. Paul. "Is There a Problem about Sense-data?" In *Logic and Language,* First Series, ed. Anthony Flew. Oxford: Basil Blackwell, 1952.

A. C. Ewing. *Idealism: a Critical Survey.* London: Methuen, 1934.

H. H. Price. *Perception.* London: Methuen, 1933.

————. *Hume's Theory of the External World.* London: Oxford University Press, 1934.

Margaret Macdonald, "Sleeping and Waking." *Mind,* 72, 1953.

Martin E. Lean. *Sense-Perception and Matter.* London: Routledge & Kegan Paul, 1953.

Arthur Pap. *Elements of Analytic Philosophy.* New York: Macmillan, 1949. Chapter 7.

H. A. Prichard. *Knowledge and Perception.* London: Oxford University Press, 1950.

Paul Mahrenke. "Phenomenalism," in *Philosophical Analysis.* Ed. Max Black. Ithaca: Cornell University Press, 1950.

Isaiah Berlin. "Empirical Propositions and Hypothetical Statements," *Mind,* 69, 1950.

C. I. Lewis. *Mind and the World Order.* New York: Charles Scribner's Sons, 1929.

―――――. *Theory of Knowledge and Valuation.* La Salle, Illinois: Open Court Publishing Co., 1946. Chapters 7 and 8.

C. D. Broad. *Scientific Thought.* London: Kegan Paul, 1923. Part 2.

―――――. *The Mind and Its Place in Nature.* London: Kegan Paul, 1925. Section B.

John Wisdom. *Problems of Mind and Matter.* Cambridge: Cambridge University Press, 1934. Chapters 9 and 10.

F. H. Bradley. *Appearance and Reality.* New York: Macmillan Co., 1893.

W. P. Montague. *The Ways of Knowing.* London: Allen & Unwin, 1925. Part II.

EXERCISES

1. "How do I know that physical objects (tables, trees, stones, and so on) exist?" "Because I see them!" How would you make clear to someone that this answer is not sufficient?

2. What line of thought would ever lead people to the conclusion that they are acquainted only with their own states of consciousness (e.g. not the table, but table-sensations; not the star, but only star-sensations reaching us perhaps years after the star has ceased to exist)?

3. Present the "telephone exchange" analogy, showing what difficulties we get into (as far as knowing a physical world is concerned) if we try to apply it literally. Show how the analogy seems to presuppose its own falsity.

4. Make as strong a case as you can for idealism. List some attacks that have been or could be made to it, and defend idealism against them.

5. Samuel Johnson, asked to refute Berkeley's doctrine, kicked his foot against a stone, exclaiming, "I refute it thus!" Refute his "refutation."

6. In what sense is the following statement true, and in what sense is it false? "Berkeley denied that there are physical objects, such as houses, trees, stars, and so on."

7. Were Berkeley's account true, would science be impossible? Explain.

8. Examine each of the following examples. Do they succeed in demolishing idealism? How might an idealist reply to each of them?

a. I'll prove to you that the table exists even when no one is perceiving it. We'll all go out of the room, but before doing so we'll set a motion picture camera going, focused on the table. Later we'll come back, take out the film, develop it, and project it on a screen. If it shows the table in the field of vision the whole time (as it surely will), that will prove that the table was there even while nobody was looking at it.

b. I leave the room while the fire is burning in the fireplace; half an hour later I come back and there are only glowing embers left. Doesn't this prove that the fire existed and went on burning while I was out? But if it burned while I was out, it must have existed while I was out.

c. If I am the only perceiver about, and I see only the top half of a building, the bottom half must be there even if I don't see it. But the idealist must believe that if no one sees the bottom half, it doesn't exist: for *esse est percipi*. The idealist must believe, then, that the top half can exist without being supported by the bottom half.

d. If I see the shadow cast by an object but neither I nor anyone else sees the object, the idealist would have us believe that the shadow exists but not the object. This, obviously, is absurd.

e. If I place a tablecloth over the table, so that no part of the table is visible, idealism is committed to the view that the table does not exist. What, then, supports the tablecloth? Is it simply suspended in the air?

f. Somebody gives me a drug and I pass out. But idealists can't admit that I pass out, for I have no experience of this, and *esse est percipi*.

9. "Idealists admit, in fact they insist, that there are sensations. Now, how can there be sensations unless there are sense-organs, nerves, and brains? But sense-organs, nerves, and brains are physical objects. So there are physical objects after all." How might an idealist reply to this?

10. Isn't the explanation for our table-sensations the simple fact that a table is really there? What would idealists say?

11. If physical objects existing independently of minds are not the cause of our sensations, what is, according to Berkeley? Explain his view on this, together with any difficulties in it that may occur to you.

12. Why, according to the idealist, can we never have any evidence for the hypothesis that physical objects exist unobserved? (We cannot observe it, because........ Nor can we infer it: we cannot infer it deductively because........ and we cannot infer it inductively because........)

13. Distinguish between (a) those idealists who say "Even if physical objects do exist when no one is observing them, we can have no reason to suppose that they do, for no one can observe them existing unobserved" (Stace) and (b) those who say "The statement that physical objects exist unobserved is not merely without supporting evidence, it is *self-contradictory*." Explain this latter view. Whence comes the self-contradiction? How, according to the latter view, is the former one in error?

14. Examine the following syllogistic arguments in defense of idealism. (The conclusion of the first argument is a premise of the second.) Do you accept the final conclusion? If not, can you find any flaw in the reasoning? any premises that you would not accept? If so, why?

> We do have acquaintance with physical objects.
> All we can have acquaintance with is experiences.

Therefore, Physical objects are experiences.

> Physical objects are experiences.
> Experiences can't exist unexperienced.

Therefore, Physical objects can't exist unexperienced.

15. Do you think that the following lines of argument would give any difficulty to idealism? Why?

a. Physical objects are sensations (or sensation-complexes); sensations are private; yet physical objects are public.

b. Physical objects are extended; sensations are unextended; therefore physical objects can't be sensations.

16. What would you say to someone who declared that he was a solipsist? Do you think that solipsism can be disproved?

17. Explain how phenomenalism departs from idealism in its account of

a. the existence of physical objects existing unobserved.

b. sense-data (as opposed to sensations) as the immediate objects of sensing.

18. What is the given? Are physical objects given? Why not? Is the coldness of the distant mountain peak given to sight? Why not? Is spatial depth, in your opinion, given? Explain.

19. Phenomenalism of the early "possible sensation" variety (Mill) ends by making the entire physical realm part of the mental. After the concept of sense-data has been introduced, how does phenomenalism avoid this result?

20. If there were no hallucinations, no illusions, and no dreams, would the introduction of sense-data be unnecessary? Defend your opinion. Do you think phenomenalism can be held in a form which does not introduce sense-data at all?

21. How many senses of the word "see" can you distinguish in the following?

a. I see green.

b. I see an oasis. (Assume that there is no oasis.)

c. I see a tree. (Assume that there is one.)

d. I hunted for my pen for an hour, and it turned out to be on top of my desk in plain sight, where I'd been looking for it all the time; I must have seen it innumerable times during my search.

22. What does phenomenalism say to such assertions as "We do not know what physical objects are like *really;* we know only how they *appear.*"

23. Explain phenomenalism's analysis of error in the case of illusions. Why do we say that the stick looks bent in water but is really straight? (Why not say it feels straight but is really bent?) From most angles a coin looks elliptical; why do we say it is really round? The dark blue dress looks black in lamplight; why do we say that it is dark blue and not black?

(See also A. J. Ayer, *Foundations of Empirical Knowledge*, pp. 263–274.)

24. If we can never "get beyond" sense-data—can never compare sense-data with anything that is not sense-data to see whether they correspond—how can we preserve the distinction between appearance and reality in perception, between how things appear and how they really are? or can we never know "how they really are"?

25. Explain phenomenalism's analysis of error in the case of hallucinations. What are the test for whether a physical object is actually present or not?

26. How do we know that we are not all dreaming right now? Explain.

27. In the light of this chapter, discuss the issue of certainty and empirical statements which was treated in Chapter 3.

28. Can sense-datum statements (reports of sense-data) be in error? According to phenomenalism, what kind of error can occur in physical-object statements that cannot occur in sense-datum statements?

29. How can it be argued that, while sense-datum statements are indeed certain and indubitable, no sense-datum statements can ever be uttered?

30. Do you think it possible that when I see green you see red, and vice versa? (I *say* "green" when we look at the grass, just as you do; but meanwhile my sense-data are red.) Could we ever discover it if such a state-of-affairs really existed? Do you think it meaningful to say that it exists?

31. What is meant by saying that physical objects are constructs out of sense-data? that every physical-object judgment is an implicit prediction?

32. Distinguish categorical from hypothetical statements, and show how the latter are brought in by the phenomenalist in discussing physical objects existing unobserved.

33. Do you think that we have inductive evidence (p. 433) or no evidence at all (pp. 402–403) that physical objects exist unobserved? Explain.

34. If all physical-object statements (according to phenomenalism) can be translated into sense-datum statements, why has not the translation been achieved, so that we can examine a few specimen translations? Discuss various reasons.

35. Name and discuss some objections that have been brought against the phenomenalistic doctrine of the reducibility of physical-object statements to sense-datum statements.

36. Some of the positions discussed in this chapter seem to be based on the premise that all we are ever acquainted with is our own states of consciousness. Can you think of any arguments that would damage or refute this view? (Would you agree with someone who said, "To say that we are acquainted only with our own states of consciousness is to say that we can experience only our own experiences; and this is a tautology. Both representative realism and idealism take this as their basic premise—so they are both based on tautologies!" Does phenomenalism share this basic premise?)

7

Problems in Ethics

In preceding chapters we have examined many kinds of synthetic statements: ordinary empirical statements, such as "It is raining" and "There is a book on the table"; reports of the given, such as "I feel drowsy" and "I hear a noise"; empirical generalizations (laws) such as "Water boils at 212° F. (under standard conditions) and "Water expands on freezing"; statements which are shorthand summaries of a large and rather indefinite range of ordinary empirical statements, such as "She is neurotic" and "She is intelligent"; statements involving unobservables, such as "The hydrogen atom has one electron," from which empirical consequences can be drawn; other statements involving unobservables, such as "Substances underlie qualities," from which no empirical consequences can be drawn; and other statements whose status is disputed, such as "A Deity exists." All of these assert, whether truly or falsely, that some state-of-affairs exists, without trying to evaluate this state-of-affairs as good or bad, desirable or undesirable. So much at least they all have in common.

But now we come to statements which seem, at least, to be of a very different kind. To say "The atomic bomb can kill millions of people" is to utter a statement of empirical fact, but to say "The atomic bomb is a bad thing for mankind to have" is to utter a judgment of value.[1] People who agree with the first statement might not agree on the second. "That book is 5 × 7 inches" is a statement of fact, but what about "That book is good"? The first can easily be verified, or at least confirmed, but how would you verify the second? There is a similar difference between "This has gone on for two

[1] It is not denied that these are also statements of fact: for instance we might say that it is a fact that atomic bombings are bad. But if so, it is a different kind of fact—a "value fact"—and the same questions we shall be asking in this chapter would still arise concerning these facts.

449

weeks" and "This has gone on too long"; between "The picture on the wall is an oil painting" and "The picture on the wall is beautiful"; between "She has red hair" and "She is gorgeous." In this chapter and the next we shall be considering two classes of these evaluative statements: the *ethical* and the *esthetic*.

I. THE MEANING OF "GOOD" AND "RIGHT"

When we begin to study assertions containing typically ethical words like "good," "bad," "right," "wrong," "ought," "duty," "obligation," and their synonyms, we encounter a difficulty at the very outset: how are we to interpret these assertions? If a person says "All acts that contribute to human happiness are right," what is he saying? (1) Is he giving a *definition* of the word "right" or the phrase "right acts," just as he would be giving a definition of "yard" if he said "A yard is three feet"? Or (2) is he making a statement of *fact* (either true or false) about right acts, i.e., about the acts to which the word "right" applies? (We have encountered this situation before; see, for example, pages 34–35.)

This is a question of the first importance, and yet many persons who discuss matters of morality are not at all clear which of these two things they are doing. Perhaps they intend an assertion such as the one above to be a definition; if so, the ethical term "right" can be omitted from the sentence entirely, and we can substitute the phrase "contributing to human happiness," just as we can omit the word "yard" from every sentence in which it occurs and substitute the phrase "three feet," without any change in meaning. More probably, however, they intend it as a statement *about* right acts: they mean to say that every act that has one characteristic or property, namely, contributing to happiness, also possesses *another* characteristic, namely, being right. These persons would also hold that every act that is right *also* contributes to human happiness, thus making the two classes of acts co-extensive (pages 28–30). In other words, they would assert that the two classes of acts have the same denotation (pp. 25–26), and that contributing to happiness is not a characteristic defining of rightness but a *universal accompaniment* of it (see pages 28–30). If this is what they mean, however, they must still face the question, "What does 'right' *mean* in the sentence? What are the two classes between which this universal correlation

holds? We know fairly well what it means to say that an act contributes to happiness, but what does it mean when someone says
that an act is right?" He surely does not *mean* by "right acts" the
same as "acts contributing to happiness," for then he would merely
be uttering the tautology that acts contributing to happiness contribute to happiness; and it is very unlikely that this is what the
person making the statement means to say.

Let us return to the imaginary example used in Chapter 1 (see
pp. 29–30): Suppose that all red things were round and that all
round things were red. If this were so, redness would still not be
roundness, in spite of the fact that everything possessing the one
characteristic also possessed the other. The presence of the one characteristic would be an *indicator,* or a *criterion,* of the presence of
the other; thus, a blind man could tell you whether something was
red by feeling its shape. Now, many statements involving ethical
terms, such as "All acts contributing to happiness are right," seem
to be of this type; they take the fact that an act contributes to happiness as a *criterion* of its rightness, not of what the rightness consists in. Our question then becomes, "What *does* its rightness consist
in?" In the red-round example, we know from direct empirical observation what it is for something to be red, and for something to be
round, quite independent of each other; but in the present example,
what does "right" mean as distinguished from "contributing to happiness?"

The difficulty becomes all the more pressing when we turn from
ethical statements asserting the coexistence of two classes to ethical
statements which simply *attribute* rightness or goodness [2] to an object or class of objects. When someone says, "It's right to keep your
promises," he pretty certainly does not mean that "right" means
the same thing as "keeping your promises." What then *does* he
mean? What are we saying about promise-keeping when we say

---

[2] In ethics the terms "right" and "wrong" are used to apply only to *acts*
("That was the right thing to do," "He acted wrongly"). The terms "good"
and "bad" are used to refer to (1) the *consequences* or *effects* of acts ("The
act accomplished good results"), to (2) the *motives* from which the act was
done ("The act was wrong but the motives were good"), to (3) the *intention*
of the person in doing the act ("His intention of returning the money was
good, but his motive—to ingratiate himself with his creditor so that he could
swindle him later—was bad"), and to (4) the person himself who performs the
act, i.e., the *agent* ("He is a good man but he sometimes does the wrong
thing").

that it is right? Presumably we are attributing to acts of this class some characteristic, or property, namely rightness. But what is this property? It certainly does not *seem* to be an empirically verifiable one like redness or roundness; but then what kind of property is it, and how are we to know when it is present in a particular case? Before we can be in a position to know that promise-keeping is right, we must first be told what is meant by calling an act right. The same consideration applies to other ethical terms like "good," "ought," "duty," and the like. The first question which we encounter, then, is simply this: What do these ethical terms mean?

It is not at all easy to give an answer to this question. Our first approach might be to employ a kind of analysis already used several times in this book: Words are conventional symbols, and when we want to ask "What does this word mean?" we should really ask "What do we mean (intend) when we use the word?" After all, words don't mean anything by themselves; they are only noises until we *give* them a meaning, *confer* a meaning upon them. What meaning, then, have the users of language given to "good" and "right"?

If we ask people, "What do you mean by 'good'?" and so on, they are generally quite unable to give a definite reply; they are usually baffled and bewildered by such a question. And no matter what specific suggestions we may make to them—such as, "When you say an act is right perhaps you just mean that it helps somebody in some way"—either they are not satisfied with our suggestions, or it turns out that the suggested usage does not work in all cases. For example, they will come across an act which fulfills this condition which they would not want to call right, or one they would call right but which does not fulfill this condition.

Are we to conclude from this that these evaluative words have no clear meaning at all, or even that they are meaningless noises that should be stricken from our vocabulary? Some persons have actually suggested such a procedure; those accustomed to the terminology of the exact sciences, in particular, are inclined to label such words "sheer confusion."

Yet the same persons who say this use these words constantly in daily life: for example, "It would be a *good* thing if such words were eliminated!" If it is difficult to ascribe any definite meaning to such a word as "good," is it not more difficult still to assert sincerely that it is meaningless, that we are talking nonsense every time we use it? How then are we to account for the fact that we find the word useful, that we keep on using it, and that we do not usually ask another's meaning when he uses it in a sentence? There *appears* at least to be no communication-difficulty when it is used in discourse.

Others have said, in effect, "Since 'good' seems to have no definite meaning, if we are to use it sensibly we shall have to *give* it a meaning; let us stipulate, therefore, that when we use the word in the future, we shall mean so-and-so by it." However, this would hardly help us. We want to discover the meaning of words that are already in use by millions of people; we are not interested in investing an old sound with a new meaning. We are not interested in getting a stipulative definition, but in a reportive definition (pages 52–53), and as clear and uniform a one as possible. We want to know what "good" and similar words mean when used in everyday life in everyday contexts. It is easy to stipulate a meaning; it is not so easy to pin down the meaning of a word already in use. To stipulate a meaning in our present situation would simply be irrelevant; we would have to say, "Very well, you can use the word to mean this if you want to; but our question still remains: what do people unacquainted with your special usage ordinarily mean when they use the word?"

Here is another possibility: "When two persons use the word 'good,' they don't often mean the same thing by it. One person means one thing, another person means another; there is no uniformity. It's not that the word is meaningless, but rather that its meaning varies from person to person." But if this is true to any considerable extent, one is led to wonder how we can communicate in using the word. If by "book" I meant any headgear with feathers, and you meant the egg of any species of reptile, and someone else meant the steering-rod of a motor vehicle, there would be no communication among us when the word was used in conversation, and from the context we would soon discover that we did not mean the same thing by it. But no such phenomenon is noticeable with the word "good" and similar words. To a certain extent there are differences, as we shall shortly see, but it can hardly be that the word is used as erratically as "book" in the fictitious example just given. (Even if it were, the question would remain, "What do you, and I, and each person individually mean in using the word?" This might be just as hard to specify as in the general case already raised.)

Perhaps, then, we should say instead, "It isn't that when you use the word you mean one thing and I mean another; it's rather that we, all of us together, mean one thing by it in one context and another thing in another context. When we call a man good we don't mean the same thing by 'good' as when we call a horse good, or a chair, or a book; and our meaning is still different when we call a painting good, or a road, or a car that travels on the road. These are not ethical usages of the word 'good,' to be sure, but the same ambiguity pervades them. It's not that you and I disagree on what makes a good road, though this may enter in too, but rather that the characteristics that make a good road aren't the same as those that make the car that rides on it good, or the man that drives the car."

It would be difficult to deny that the word is ambiguous in this way. Yet an interesting question remains: Is there any common or universal meaning of "good"? Is there any core of meaning which all the usages of "good" share in common? After all, why is it that all of these different things are called "good"? If the meaning of "good" differs for every kind of thing to which we apply it, why have we come to use this one word in such a variety of different meanings? Why not then use a different word, instead of overworking this one poor word to mean so many different things? Is it just a curious linguistic accident that it has come to be used so variously? Surely there must be some reason why we use this word rather than others in all these cases; surely there is some common core of meaning determining our use of the word "good" rather than a bunch of other words.

But if there is, what is this common meaning? We speak of a good man, a good state-of-affairs, a good motive; a good house, a good movie, a good dog. Not all of these are of relevance to ethics; yet it will be instructive to ask ourselves the question, Is there something common to all of these—some characteristic by virtue of which all of these diverse things are called "good"? If there is, what is it? and if there is not, why is it that the word "good" is used as a blanket term to cover so many meanings?

Most of those who have thought much about this question have believed that there is some common meaning. But there has been much disagreement about what that common meaning is.

A. Naturalistic Theories: [3] objectivistic

The kind of view that first suggests itself is one that seems to be implied in the very way we use ethical words in sentences. We use sentences of the form "X is good" in much the same way that we do "X is round"; when we say of an X that it is round, we mean to attribute to it a characteristic, or property, namely roundness, which we believe to exist in X regardless of our attitude toward X, our awareness of X, or even of our very existence. Since "X is good" is of the same grammatical form as "X is round," it seems natural to believe that goodness is, in these respects, like roundness, and that the word "good" names an objective property of X just as "round" does—an ethical property in the one case, a geometrical property in the other. Theories which assert this are usually called *objectivistic*, or *objectivist* theories. Our question, then, becomes: What is this property?

Utilitarianism as a theory about the meaning of "good" and "right." The view known as *utilitarianism* provides perhaps the simplest and clearest answer to this question, at least with regard to two ethical terms, "good" and "right." It first makes a distinction between *intrinsic* good and *instrumental* good. To say of some state-of-affairs that it is intrinsically good is to say that it is good "in itself"—that it is good regardless of its effects, and would be good even if it stood alone. To say of something that it is instrumentally good is to say that it is a good *means* to something else, or, in other words, that it is a good *instrument* for the achievement of something other than itself.[4]

With this distinction made, the utilitarian theory asserts (1) that happiness, and only happiness, is intrinsically good; (2) that anything is instrumentally good which leads to happiness; and (3) that an act is right if its total consequences are intrinsically better than

[3] The word "naturalistic" will be defined as the discussion proceeds. The label is attached here for the sake of completeness in the section headings.

[4] Something can, of course, be instrumentally good and yet intrinsically bad: a surgeon inflicting pain on a patient may be instrumentally good, because only in this way can recovery take place; yet, intrinsically (i.e., considered apart from its consequences) it is bad. Something can also be intrinsically good but instrumentally bad: if prisoners were made very happy in jail, the happiness would be intrinsically good, but might be instrumentally bad in that it would induce many otherwise law-abiding persons to commit crimes so that they could get themselves imprisoned.

any other act the agent could have performed instead.[5] The rightness of an act, in other words, is measured by the goodness of its
consequences; an act that is right is an *instrumental* good—instrumental to the achievement of good results. Rightness, then, is deriv-
ative of goodness; before one can know whether an act is right, one
must know what the good is, the achievement of which would make
the act right.

Utilitarianism, as thus far stated, can be held in either of two
forms: (1) It can be held that happiness is a *criterion* of intrinsic
goodness, without being identical with intrinsic goodness. This is the
way in which most utilitarians have interpreted the sentence "Being
happy is intrinsically good." In other words, they have held that a
state of happiness is *also* a state of intrinsic goodness. But this,
once again, leads us back to the now familiar kind of question:
"What, then, is meant by saying that something is intrinsically
good?" If an instance of happiness and an instance of intrinsic goodness were the same, then the statement "Happiness is intrinsically
good" would be a tautology. However, on the present interpretation,
since happiness is a *criterion* of intrinsic goodness, the two cannot
be the same, and the statement is synthetic. This is doubtless the
most natural way in which to interpret the statement, and utilitarianism is (in the opinion of most philosophers) most easily defen-
sible on this interpretation. However, as we have seen, it *presupposes*
an answer to the question, "What, then, is meant by intrinsic goodness, the thing with which happiness, on your view, is universally
correlated?"

(2) The second interpretation of utilitarianism is bolder than the
first. It does not assert merely that all cases of happiness are cases
of intrinsic goodness and vice versa; it asserts that happiness and
intrinsic goodness are one and the same thing. "Happiness = intrinsic goodness," and the equals sign is intended literally. (And the
same for rightness: to say that an act is right just *means* that it
produces the most good.) It is only this interpretation of utilitarianism that is of concern to us here, since we are concerned with the
meaning of ethical terms. We need to know what "good" and "right"

[5] This formulation is not quite accurate; for a precise account see G. E.
Moore, *Ethics* (New York: Oxford University Press), Chapter 1. The accurate
statement is somewhat more complex than this, and, since the difference in no
way affects the points under discussion here, the simpler formulation has been
given.

mean before we can discover what is being said about an act when it is asserted to be right, or what is being said about a state-of-affairs when it is asserted to be good. To be told simply that happiness always *goes along with* intrinsic goodness, as the first interpretation does, tells us only that there is an X, to which the name "goodness" is given, which is always a concomitant of happiness; and this will be informative only if we know what this X is which is the concomitant.

It is this second interpretation, then, which sets out to answer the question which is our first concern. But it is precisely this second version which is open to attacks that do not touch the first. Many people would probably assent to the statement that happiness is intrinsically good and that right acts are productive of the most happiness. But if they were asked, "Is this all you mean by 'good' and 'right'? When you say that happiness is intrinsically good, are you uttering a tautology? And if someone said that some state-of-affairs was intrinsically better than some other, but did not contain more happiness, or if he said that some act was right but not happiness-producing, would you consider his statement not merely a *false* statement but *self-contradictory*, as if he had asserted the existence of a square circle?" they would find it difficult to give honestly an affirmative answer. Yet this is precisely what, as utilitarians of the second interpretation, they would be committed to.

Criticism of all theories of this type. It is precisely this line of criticism that has often been considered fatal to all objectivistic theories, if they are taken as rendering the *meaning* of ethical terms. If the different views are interpreted as attempts to give *criteria* of rightness or goodness—for example, "Right acts always produce the most happiness," "Right acts are always manifestations of a good will," "Right acts always have such-and-such kinds of motive," "Right acts are always intended to produce such-and-such consequences, whether or not they actually do"—they are far more easily defended, although there will be a great deal of controversy as to which of them is acceptable. (If you take a course in ethics you will probably discover that the course consists chiefly of an evaluation of different criteria for determining goodness and rightness.) But, once again, our present concern is not whether the presence of a certain property, A, be it the production of happiness or anything else, is a *criterion* for the presence of rightness, but, rather, what the rightness is of which the property A is the criterion: in other words, what "right" *means*. And it is to this latter form of objectivistic theories (the "meaning" version, not the "criterion" version) that the criticisms apply. If these criticisms apply to all such theories, it would be pointless here to examine others. These, briefly, are the principal criticisms:

1. No matter what the property is which is said to constitute the meaning of "good" (or "right"), we can always ask, "X has this property but *is X really good* (or right)?" This would be a self-contradictory question if being good and having this property were one and the same thing. Similarly, one can always ask, "Are you quite sure that everything that has this property is really good?" This betrays the fact that we do not really consider goodness and the possession of this property to be one and the same thing, for we are surely not asking "Are you quite sure that everything that has this property really has this property?" Or, again, it is never self-contradictory to say, "I grant that X has this property, but I *doubt* that X is good," and yet it would be self-contradictory if having the property and being good were the same. Since we *can* always sensibly ask such questions and make such assertions as these, we must conclude that being good and having the property are two different things.

2. No matter what property of X is supposed to constitute its goodness (or rightness) two persons may agree that X has the property and *yet disagree on whether X is good* (or right). Many Nazis probably believed that killing large numbers of people in concentration camps was right, just as a utilitarian would hold that it was wrong. Both of them may have agreed on what the consequences of such acts were—they both knew how much suffering was caused, how much terror and insecurity was brought about, and so on. The Nazi and his opponent could well have agreed on all the consequences of such acts, and yet he would have said the acts were right and his opponent that they were wrong; he, that the consequences were good and his opponent, that these same consequences were bad. It would appear, then, that since they agree about the one and disagree about the other, the two cannot be one and the same thing. If calling an act right meant simply that it had such-and-such consequences, for example, then two people who agreed that it had such-and-such consequences would *ipso facto* agree about the rightness—

which they manifestly do not. What clearer indication could there be that being right and having these consequences are not the same thing? The same reasoning applies no matter what properties are supposed to constitute goodness or rightness.

3. A third criticism results from an objection to the account in the preceding paragraph. The objection runs as follows: "You draw the wrong conclusion from this situation. The two disputants agree on all the consequences of murder, including, say, consequences A and consequences B. But it doesn't follow that they are really disagreeing about the rightness of these acts. Why? Because they are using the word "right" ambiguously. When the utilitarian uses the word he means "having consequences A," and when the Nazi uses the word he means "having consequences B." Of course, the acts in question may have both sets of consequences. The two disputants are not really disagreeing about the rightness of the acts; they are just talking a different language from each other when they use the word "right."

Here the critic will seize upon the opportunity to reply. "This may sometimes happen," he will say. "But when it does, we have an even more unlikely state-of-affairs than before; for every time that this happens, one must believe that the two so-called disputants aren't really disputing at all! If what you say is so, the Nazi who says 'Killing Jews is right' is merely saying something like 'Killing Jews tends to increase the proportion of Teutonic stock,' while the utilitarian is saying 'Killing Jews decreases the total happiness of mankind.' And of course both of these statements are probably true. Why, then, doesn't the dispute cease? If your analysis is correct, there is no dispute at all. The participants, however, are quite convinced that they *are* disputing about something. And mark this: if you point out to them that they each agree on the consequences that the other insists on, they will not end their argument—they will argue all the more vehemently! The utilitarian knows that these killings increase the Teutonic stock, and the Nazi knows that they decrease the happiness of mankind. So they are not trying to convince each other of the consequences they each insist on. Indeed, each of them insists on his own case the more strongly *because* he knows that the other is perfectly aware of these consequences. Doesn't it seem absurd to insist, then, that the dispute is *about* consequences? This, then, is my point: (1) There exists between them a real disagreement about whether acts of a certain kind are right; (2) this disagreement is not about the consequences, for they agree on these; therefore (3) the disagreement about rightness is not a disagreement about the consequences. The rightness and the consequences, then, cannot be the same."

The disagreement, then, is about the rightness of X; it certainly seems to be a real disagreement—certainly the participants would laugh at anyone who said they were not disagreeing at all. Yet we have not been able to pin down any property of X in which its rightness consists. We seem to be as far from discovering it as ever. Perhaps we have been on the wrong track all along. Perhaps it is not some property of X that makes it right, but simply the fact that people feel a certain way toward X or have a certain attitude toward X. Let us see.

B. Naturalistic Theories: Subjectivistic

According to all subjectivistic theories, when you say of an act that it is right, or of a state-of-affairs that it is good, you are not saying that it has a certain objective property; you are only saying that you (or other persons) have a certain attitude toward X. Sometimes, on this account, subjectivistic theories are called "attitude theories."

Let us examine a few attitude theories. There could be as many attitude theories as there are kinds of attitudes, but most of them have never been taken to constitute the meaning of ethical terms. Let us examine a few possibilities.

1. "X is right" means the same as "I like X."

It is apparent at once, however, that there are plenty of acts we would never call right which we nevertheless like to do. A person may like to get drunk and yet never for a moment think that doing so is right. He may not like to keep promises, but he may believe that keeping one's promises is right. Saying that you like to do something and saying that it is right to do it are clearly two different things.

Even those few who would say that the right acts are those which you like to do would consider this a statement of fact, not a tautology, yet a tautology is just what it would be if saying that you liked it and saying it was right were the same thing. Similarly, "I like to do things that are right" would only mean "I like to do things I like to do," and it would never occur to anyone (outside philosophical analysis) to utter such a sentence as this.

2. For "like" let us substitute "approve." We would call some acts right (and some things good) even if we don't like them, but would we do so even if we didn't approve them? Let us consider, then, this view: "X is right" means the same as *"I approve X."*

At first this view may sound plausible enough. Yet there are well-nigh insuperable objections to it, which will become apparent if we examine what some implications of the view are.

(1) If this view is true, all you have to know, in order to be certain whether an act you are considering is right, is whether or not you really approve it. If you do, it's right, and if you don't, it isn't: that is all there is to it. And if you change your attitude from disapproval to approval, then what was wrong suddenly becomes right. In order to make an act right, simply work yourself into a state of approval toward it.

Does anyone seriously believe that he can know what is right or wrong simply by consulting an introspective report? When you inquire as to the rightness of an act, is it really sufficient to introspect and ask yourself whether you do or do not have the attitude of approval toward the act in question?

(2) If this view is true, one and the same act can be both right and wrong—right for you because you approve it and wrong for me because I don't. There are those who would probably not consider this an objection to the view at all: "Sure, what's right for you may be wrong for me, and vice versa." But when persons who say this stop to analyze it, it usually turns out that they do not mean that one specific act, such as Brutus' killing of Caesar, is both right and wrong; they mean that a certain *kind* or *class* of acts may have some instances (or members) which are right and others which are wrong. For example, they might say (and even utilitarians would agree to this) that it may be right for one person to divorce his wife but not for someone else. Perhaps there are children in the second case but not in the first, or other conditions exist which distinguish the one case from the other. Perhaps there would be more happiness all around if the first man did divorce his wife, but not if the second one did. Something like this is probably what most people have in mind when they say "What's right for one person may not be right

for another." One act of divorce may be right, another wrong (depending on the conditions); but this is not to say that one and the same act of divorce is both right and wrong. Yet if the view we are considering is true, one and the same act can be both right and wrong: right for Smith (who approves it) and wrong for Jones (who disapproves it).

(3) Whatever a person does mean when he says of X that it is right, he does *not* mean simply that he approves it. Indeed, he may wonder whether his approval of X is justified. He may question his approval; he may *wonder whether what he approves is right*. If he does this, is he doubting or wondering whether his approval is really his approval? Surely not. Being approved by him and being right, then, are two different things.

If they are not, again we have the curious situation in which his statements are either tautologies or self-contradictory. "I know I approve X but I wonder whether X is right" would become "I know I approve X but I wonder whether I approve X," and "All acts which I approve are right" would become "All acts which I approve are acts which I approve."

(4) If the view were true, the curious conclusion would follow that no one disagrees with others about matters of right and wrong. Suppose that the rightness of some act, X, is under discussion by two persons, Smith and Jones. Smith says, "X is right," and Jones says, "X is wrong." They surely seem to be disagreeing about something. But on the view we are now considering, each of them is saying only that he himself approves X.

> Smith: "I, Smith, approve X."
> Jones: "I, Jones, disapprove X."

Now, *these two statements do not contradict one another at all*. It is quite possible for Smith to approve X while Jones disapproves X; this sort of thing often happens. But they are *not* disagreeing about whether the other approves X; concerning that point they are already in agreement. Jones knows that Smith approves X, and Smith knows that Jones disapproves X. It is just *because* they realize this, and agree upon it, that they are *disagreeing* with each other on the rightness of X. When Smith is trying to convince Jones that X is right, he is emphatically *not* trying to convince Jones that he, Smith, really approves X after all; nor is Jones trying to convince

Smith that he, Jones, really disapproves X. Neither of them questions the other's introspective reports. Yet, on the present theory, this is exactly what they are doing. Accordingly, when Smith tries to convince Jones that X is right, he is trying to convince him that he, Smith, really approves X—something which Jones knows already. Surely, whatever it is that Smith *is* asserting when he asserts that X is right, he is *not* asserting that he himself approves X. Jones, even if he did not know it already, would not require much convincing on this point, and his doubts could be put at rest. Smith could bring in a lie-detector and say to him, "Now, try this on me, Jones, and you'll see that I really do approve X." Does not this example show how irrelevant the speaker's approval really is to the question of good or bad, right or wrong? Another example: Suppose Jones said, "X is wrong and you know it," and Smith replied, "But I do approve it—what ever made you think I didn't?" Everyone would consider Smith's reply quite unnatural; yet it would be perfectly in order if "X is right" meant the same as "I approve X." What Smith and Jones are disagreeing on is not what feelings or attitudes they each may have, but whether X is right or not; and whatever this may mean, it is not the same as whether they approve X, for this is not something which (in most cases at least) they would even bother to argue.

3. According to still another view, goodness and badness and right and wrong do not depend on any particular person's approval or disapproval, but on the *attitude (approval or disapproval) of one's society or social group.* But:

(1) If "X is right" just means "The majority of my society approve X," then the statement of the minority, who declare that X is not right, is not merely false but *self-contradictory:* "X is approved by the majority but is not right (not approved by the majority)." But *is* it self-contradictory to say "X is wrong although the majority of my society approve X?" If the majority of a certain society approve lynching, and a member of the minority says, "Lynching is wrong, even though the majority do approve it," is he contradicting himself? Can't a majority be wrong? Perhaps a majority can often be misled, ignorant, perverse, or degenerate.

Even members of a majority group would probably not mean by "right" the same as "approved by the majority." A member of a majority group may try to justify his convictions by saying, "Almost everyone agrees with me," but he would hardly believe that when he said "X is right" he was saying the same thing as "The majority approve X." Something may be both right and approved by the majority, but being the one is not the same as being the other.

(2) Suppose some kind of behavior is approved by 51 per cent of one's society, in which case (on the present view) it would *ipso facto* be right. Then suppose a minority campaign against this kind of behavior and the percentage drops to 49 per cent. Then, immediately, the same acts which had formerly been right would now be wrong. It is extremely doubtful whether either side, majority or minority, would say that the rightness or wrongness of the acts had changed on account of the change in percentage.

(3) According to this view, people *from different societies* could never disagree about ethical matters. The reasoning here is the same as in criticism 4 of the preceding theory. If Smith says "X is right" he means that the majority of his society approve X, and if Jones, from another society, says "X is wrong," he is saying that the majority of his, Jones', society disapprove it, and these two statements may both be true; there is nothing for them to disagree about. Thus, a Mohammedan and a Christian disagreeing on whether polygamy is right are (according to this view) not disagreeing at all; each is only declaring what the majority of his own society approve.

Within a society there can (according to this view) be disagreement. But two members of a society who disagreed about whether X is right would be disagreeing only about whether the majority of the members of the society to which they both belong really approve it. This is a disagreement which could be settled by conducting a Gallup Poll. Thus even here an objection could be made to the theory: Is ethical disagreement really the sort of thing a poll could settle? Would not the minority, as a result of such a poll, agree that X is approved by the majority, yet *not* agree that X is right? But in that event, again, being right and being approved by the majority cannot be the same thing.

4. Another possible view is that "X is right" means the same as *"The majority of mankind (past, present, and future) approve X."* According to this view, there *is* possibility of disagreement on ethical matters. Ignoring the possibility of creatures from Mars, we

cannot go outside mankind to argue ethical matters; and the majority of mankind either do or do not approve X.

All the other objections, however, still hold. Ethical disagreement is only disagreement about whether the majority of mankind really approves X. The minority statement "X is wrong, though approved by the majority" is self-contradictory. And the view probably does not represent what anyone seriously means in his use of ethical terms. Asking the question "Is X approved?" can in principle be answered empirically, while "Is X right?" it would seem, cannot. Even if it can, it is a *different* question.

Much of the superficial popularity of attitude theories rests upon a confusion. It is an empirical fact that people generally come to have the moral convictions shared by the rest of their society, and that the backing of public opinion, in addition to the disinclination of most people to think things through, keeps them holding more or less through habit whatever moral views are already current around them. Thus as a causal factor influencing people's moral convictions, the moral approval of the majority of one's society is of first importance. But to say that the approval of the majority, or of one's family, or of oneself, is the chief *causal factor* leading you to say "X is right," is not at all the same thing as saying that when you declare that X is right *what the statement itself means* is that you, or the majority, or some group, approve it. The meaning of a statement should never be confused with the causal factors leading you to utter it.

5. Still another kind of attitude theory has yet to be mentioned: the view that "X is right" means the same as *"X is approved (or commanded) by God (or by the gods)."*

(1) The obvious question that arises is, of course, Which God? On this point, of course, not everyone will agree. No matter which one is selected, some persons will reject the choice and wish to substitute another.

(2) Let us assume, however, that a deity has been agreed upon, as well as what the deity's commands and prohibitions are. It remains true that there are persons who have moral convictions who do not have convictions about any deity at all. According to the theory we are considering, however, a statement about God is *involved in the very meaning of every ethical sentence*. This, to say the least, is an astounding consequence. Even devout believers would

generally hold that non-believers can have some standard of goodness and rightness, however misguided this standard might be. They
might say that non-believers could not have true beliefs about what
things are good or right; but they could hardly deny that these persons *do* have beliefs about goodness and rightness. But if this is so,
then beliefs about goodness and rightness do not involve beliefs
about God or gods as part of their meaning. The beliefs are none
the less beliefs about morality for not being beliefs about God.

(3) Often the truth of some religious belief is appealed to as
grounds for a belief about morality. But no belief is grounds for
itself; hence a belief about morality must be different from a belief
about God.

People sometimes say, "God wouldn't command it if it weren't
right." Clearly this does not mean "God wouldn't command it if
God didn't command it." The two, then, have different meanings.
Indeed, is not the rightness of something logically independent of
God's commanding it? If God did not command it, would it not still
be right? Might one not say that God's commanding it is an effect
of its being right, rather than a cause?

Most religious persons have replied to these questions with a Yes.
Even if they replied No, however, it would still not follow that
"God commands it" and "It is right" mean the same thing. Suppose
one said that if God reversed his commands, everything that formerly had been wrong would suddenly be right. The question would
still occur, "Is saying that God commands it the same as saying that
it's right? Is an ethical belief no more than a disguised religious belief?" Possibly everything God commands is right and everything
that is right is divinely commanded; even if the two terms have the
same denotation, it does not follow that they have the same designation (pages 25–28).

6. Some would substitute for "God" "the inner voice of conscience." "To say that X is right means only that one's conscience
approves X."

But this merely lands us where we were before. What is the difference between "My conscience approves X" and "I approve X"?
And even if there is a difference, it is difficult to see how the objections could be circumvented—for example, the impossibility of ethical disagreement.

It would seem, indeed, that no matter what attitude theory is chosen—whose attitude it is, or what kind of attitude it is—it cannot escape these objections. X's being right or good, and some individual or group having a certain attitude toward X, are simply two different things which should not be confused with each other.

C. The Unique Property Theory

We have tried to equate the meaning of "good" and "right" with some property or properties of that which is called good or right, and then with some attitude toward that which is called good or right. And although many of these statements, such as "All good things are approved by God," may be true synthetic statements about that which is good or right, none of them is a definition: none of them renders the *meaning* of these ethical terms. No matter what phrase we substitute for the ethical term as constituting its meaning, we never arrive at anything which is strictly identical with it without loss of meaning. Something will always have been lost in the translation, though we may not know what it is. We may want to say that everything that has the suggested property is good, but if we are aware of the implications of so saying (which we have been discussing in sections A and B), we shall be very careful before committing ourselves to the view that "good" just *means* the possession of this property.

Yet surely the word "good" and other ethical words are not meaningless. What then are we to conclude? According to the view we shall consider in this section, "good" is an *indefinable* word, standing for a property which is not analyzable into other properties. We saw in Chapter 1 (pp. 59–62) that there are such words; according to the present view, good is one of them. "Good"

. . . is one of those innumerable objects of thought which are themselves incapable of definition, because they are the ultimate terms by reference to which whatever *is* capable of definition must be defined. That there must be an indefinite number of such terms is obvious, on reflection; since we cannot define anything except by an analysis, which, when carried as far as it will go, refers us to something, which is simply different from anything else, and which by what ultimate difference explains the peculiarity of the whole which we are defining: for every whole contains some parts which are common to other wholes also. There is, therefore, no intrinsic difficulty in the contention that "good" denotes a simple and indefinable quality. There are many other instances of such qualities.

Consider yellow, for example. We may try to define it, by describing its physical equivalent; we may state what kind of light-vibrations must stimulate the normal eye, in order that we may perceive it. But a moment's reflection is sufficient to show that those light-vibrations are not themselves what we mean by yellow. *They* are not what we perceive. Indeed we should never have been able to discover their existence, unless we had first been struck by the patent difference of quality between the different colors. The most we can be entitled to say of these vibrations is that they are what corresponds in space to the yellow which we actually perceive.

Yet a mistake of this simple kind has commonly been made about "good." It may be true that all things which are good are *also* something else, just as it is true that all things which are yellow produce a certain kind of vibration in the light. And it is a fact that Ethics aims at discovering what are those other properties belonging to all things which are good. But far too many philosophers have thought that when they named these other properties they were actually defining "good"; that these properties, in fact, were simply not "other," but absolutely and entirely the same with goodness. This view I propose to call the "naturalistic fallacy." [6]

Just as "yellow" is one of those ultimate color-terms which no further analysis can help to define, so, according to the present view, "good" is a word referring to a property which is not further analyzable, and thus the word is not definable. It is not *verbally* definable, that is; no other *words* will suffice to make its meaning clear; it is—at least "yellow" is—*ostensively* definable; one can show instances of yellow and thus indicate to someone what the word means. What the theory we are now considering alleges is that the same is true of "good." And the fallacy of believing that goodness is analyzable into non-ethical terms is called the *naturalistic fallacy;* this name, coined in the passage just quoted, has become standard in philosophical literature. All the theories thus far considered about the meaning of "good" commit this fallacy.

This fallacy can be illustrated by an analogous case, that of pleasure.

Suppose a man says, "I am pleased"; and suppose that it is not a lie or a mistake but the truth. Well, if it is true, what does it mean? It means that his mind, a certain definite mind, distinguished by certain

[6] G. E. Moore, *Principia Ethica* (Cambridge: Cambridge University Press, 1903), pp. 9–10.

definite marks from all others, has at this moment a certain definite feeling called pleasure. "Pleased" *means* nothing but having pleasure, and though we may be more pleased or less pleased, and even, we may admit for the present, have one or another kind of pleasure; yet in so far as it is pleasure we have, whether there be more or less of it, and whether it be of one kind or another, what we have is one definite thing, absolutely indefinable, some one thing that is the same in all the various degrees and in all the various kinds of it that there may be. We may be able to say how it is related to other things; that, for example, it is in the mind, that it causes desire, that we are conscious of it, etc., etc. We can, I say, describe its relations to other things, but define it we can *not*. And if anybody tried to define pleasure for us as being any other natural object; if anybody were to say, for instance, that pleasure *means* the sensation of red, and were to proceed to deduce that pleasure is a color, we should be entitled to laugh at him and to distrust his future statements about pleasure. Well, that would be the same fallacy which I have called the naturalistic fallacy. That "pleased" does not mean "having the sensation of red," or anything else whatever, does not prevent us from understanding what it does mean. It is enough for us to know that "pleased" does mean "having the sensation of pleasure," and though pleasure is absolutely indefinable, though pleasure is pleasure and nothing else whatever, yet we feel no difficulty in saying that we are pleased.[7]

What are we to say of this view?

We have already seen what difficulties are involved in identifying the meaning of an ethical word with the meaning of any non-ethical word or phrase; no matter what we try, nothing renders its meaning exactly. Thus it is welcome to have this difficulty settled for us by being told that "good" is indefinable. After all, many words— such as "yellow" and "pleasure" discussed above—share this feature with "good." We saw (page 59) that verbal indefinability is compatible with meaningfulness; so the indefinability of "good" need cause us no alarm.

Or need it? What distinguishing characteristic have all the verbally indefinable words "yellow" and "pleasure" in common? At least this: they stand for *immediately given data*—colors or sounds, pleasures or pains, thoughts or feelings. About these elementary given-words there is no particular difficulty in the communication of one's meaning. We all know what a shrill sound is, even though we cannot define in words what "shrill" means. We cannot define "pain" either (though we can state approximately the physical con-

[7] *Ibid.*, pp. 12–13.

ditions under which it occurs); yet when someone says "I have a pain" we know what he means.

However, "good" is quite different from these. The word does not even pretend to stand for anything given, as the others do. (Moral feelings are given, but the goodness of something cannot be identified with the attitude one has toward it, as the previous section has abundantly shown.) But then what *does* the word "good" stand for? A property of things. But not, apparently, a property that can be stated in terms of any other property; rather, a unique property—a property, moreover, whose presence cannot be detected by any empirical means, by any kind of scientific method.

How then could one go about settling disagreements about whether something was good or some act right? There is not the public check that there is with color-terms, for example: If you point to something and say to a child, "That's red," he will be able to recognize the color when he sees it again and will not be likely to make mistakes about it in the future. Moreover, if one is not talking about a given sense-datum but about the quality of an object, one can perform tests for the presence of light-waves within a certain span of wave-length. There is no such physical correlate in the case of "good." Its presence according to the theory we are now considering seems to be *unverifiable*. Two people disagreeing about a physical quality can find ways to settle their disagreement. If they disagree about the number of trees in the world, in principle the dispute can be settled even though it is not worth while to attempt to count the trees in the world in order to settle the dispute; nevertheless we know the kind of way in which it could be settled. But in the case of goodness we are at a loss to know even this.

Quite understandably, then, the indefinability view usually ends up in ethical *intuitionism:* we simply *intuit* the presence of a property, goodness, which no empirical method can reveal. What we cannot detect with the physical eye we can detect through the "inner eye" of intuition. And, since the presence or absence of this property cannot be detected empirically, the issue is a *metaphysical* one (see pages 207–208).

We need not review again the difficulties in the notion of knowledge by intuition (pages 149–154). It may be worth while to recall, however, that there is a great practical difficulty in settling disputes of this kind; one person "intuits" that X has the quality in question, and another person "intuits" that it does not. Beyond this there is no court of appeal.

From a methodological point of view, all this is very unfortunate. But let us not lose sight of the ground we have gained in coming upon this view. The difficulty that attended all previous theories— that no matter how we tried to translate an ethical word into other terms we could not do so, that no matter what definition was suggested we could not say "This is the very meaning of the word," that no matter what characteristics were supplied it still seemed quite certain that one could ask without self-contradiction, "It has the characteristic *but* is it good?"—is resolved for us by this theory. For goodness is unique: it cannot be identified with any natural property, simply because it is not a natural property; it is a uniquely ethical property. "Everything is what it is, and not another thing": goodness is simply goodness and not anything else, just as yellowness is simply yellowness and not anything else.[8] There is, however, another type of theory which claims to be able to resolve the difficulty.

D. The Emotive Theory

We turn now to a view of which thus far no mention has been made. Usually it is called the *emotive* theory, or sometimes the *dynamic* theory, of the meaning of ethical terms. Not all formulations of it are the same, but they agree at least in this: all other theories err in attributing to ethical terms a purely *cognitive* (sometimes the word used is "descriptive") meaning, and fail to recognize that ethical words are *emotive* in their meaning.

[8] For a further development of this view, read its original statement in G. E. Moore, *Principia Ethica* (Cambridge: Cambridge University Press, 1903), and then, for criticism, read W. K. Frankena, "The Naturalistic Fallacy" (included in Sellars and Hospers, *Readings in Ethical Theory*, New York: Appleton-Century-Crofts, 1951), and Arthur N. Prior, *Logic and the Basis of Ethics* (Oxford: The Clarendon Press, 1949).

It is not really essential to the theory described in this section that "good" be verbally indefinable. It is only essential that it not be definable in *non-ethical terms*. The point is that goodness is a uniquely *ethical* property and therefore not identical with any non-ethical property or group of properties, either objective or subjective. Defining an ethical term in other *ethical* terms would not be fatal to the theory. Thus, for example, "good" might be taken as indefinable and "right" defined as "productive of the most possible good." "Right" would thus have been defined in terms of "good," another ethical term, but rightness would still be a non-natural property.

Language, we remember from Chapter 1 (see pages 69–71), is used for purposes other than the utterance of true and false statements. The use which the present theory insists on, in the case of ethical words, is, of course, the emotive use. (1) Language is used *evocatively;* many sentences do not seem to contain definite assertions, but simply arouse, or evoke, emotions in the hearers. Even sentences which do assert something, and are therefore true or false, often have as their primary *intent* not the stating of true or false propositions but the evocation of certain emotions, attitudes, or actions on the part of those who hear them. (This is sometimes called the *directive* use of language because language is used to direct the hearers' attitudes. It is also known as the propaganda use of language.) (2) Language is also used *expressively,* or (a more accurate label) *interjectionally,* not to arouse emotions in others but to express or give vent to them in ourselves. The interjections of common speech, such as "alas" and "hurrah," are perhaps the purest examples of single words employed in this way. They certainly do not stand for things, nor are they generally employed to arouse feelings in those who hear them; they merely serve to give vent to emotions ("to let off steam") on the part of the speakers. The expressions one might employ after hitting his thumb with a hammer are typical cases of this use of language. Screams and groans are of the same kind, although they are not words. Both the evocative and the expressive uses of language (since the one is used to arouse emotions, the other to give vent to them) are grouped together under the heading of "emotive use of language."

According to the theory we are now considering, all previous ethical theories were on the wrong track in failing to recognize (not in daily life, but in philosophical analysis) the fact that ethical words are used, not only commonly but constantly, in this emotive way. Therefore they have all gone amiss in their accounts of ethical terms. All the theories have assumed that ethical words have some definite *cognitive* meaning, and have disagreed among themselves as to what that meaning is; actually, according to the emotivists, the difficulty is elsewhere: the distinctive feature of ethical terms is not in their cognitive meaning at all, but their *emotive* meaning.

Since the meaning of an ethical word is emotive, the word does not stand for a property or characteristic of things, such as the property of producing happiness. (If it did stand for something, its meaning would be cognitive.) No wonder that philosophers have puzzled themselves endlessly, and without success, trying to discover, for example, "the nature of the property of which 'good' is the name." According to emotivism, there is no such property at all. Consequently, there are no "peculiarly ethical statements." There are only (1) statements such as we have considered in previous chapters (including statements about people's motives and the consequences of acts) and (2) expressions-evocations of emotion, which are not statements at all, and thus are neither true nor false. These do indeed *look* like statements, for "X is good" has the same grammatical form as "X is round," but we should not be misled by this similarity; the fact is that "X is round" asserts that X has a certain characteristic or property, while "X is good" asserts nothing whatsoever.

If we turn to the way in which ethical words are used in daily life (say the emotivists), we shall find our best confirmation of the emotive theory. If you assume that ethical words are used cognitively, and then ask people "What do you *mean* by the word 'good'?" it is no wonder that people cannot give you a coherent answer; they may not know it, but they are not using "good" to name anything at all. For example, if you ask someone who says "Lying is wrong" just what it is he is saying about lying when he says of it that it is wrong, he will naturally be hard put to find an answer. If he assumes that we are seeking a cognitive meaning, the reason for his bafflement is, of course, that there is no cognitive meaning there to begin with. But observe his use of language; observe on what occasions he uses words like "good," and when he refrains from using them; observe when he stops insisting that something is good after he has been making heated declarations about it. You will discover that he stops using these words when he is no longer trying to evoke some favorable attitude toward that thing or to direct people's behavior.[9] The mother says, "Lying is wrong," chiefly to mould the attitudes and behavior of her child, to whom she says this. She is not really conveying any *information* about lying; she is not *asserting* that lying has some property of which "wrong" is the name; she is not asserting *anything at all,*

[9] The evocative meaning, which is the more important of the two in connection with the use of ethical terms, will sometimes be spoken of as if it were the sole component of emotive meaning.

even though her sentence has the form of an assertion. She is no more uttering a true or false statement than a person who weeps or laughs is thereby uttering a true or false statement.

Evoking an emotion is not at all the same thing as asserting that you feel one. The emotive theory is not an attitude theory. Attitude theories hold, for example, that when you say "X is right" you are *asserting* that you feel approval toward X. According to the emotive theory, you are asserting neither this nor anything else. When you say "I feel contempt for him" you are asserting that you feel contempt, but when you grunt or spit, you are expressing that feeling (and perhaps evoking it in others) without asserting anything at all.

Traditional interest [attitude] theories hold that ethical statements are descriptive of the existing state of interests—that they simply *give information* about interests. . . . Doubtless there is always *some* element of description in ethical judgments, but this is by no means all. Their major use is not to indicate facts, but to *create an influence*. Instead of merely describing people's interests, they *change* or *intensify* them. They *recommend* an interest in an object, rather than state that the interest already exists.

For instance: When you tell a man that he ought not to steal, your object isn't merely to let him know that people disapprove of stealing. You are attempting, rather, to get *him* to disapprove of it. Your ethical judgment has a quasi-imperative force which, operating through suggestion, and intensified by your tone of voice, readily permits you to begin to *influence*, to *modify*, his interests. If in the end you do not succeed in getting *him* to disapprove of stealing, you will feel that you've failed to convince him that stealing is wrong. You will continue to feel this, even though he fully acknowledges that you disapprove of it, and that almost everyone else does. When you point out to him the consequences of his actions—consequences which you suspect he already disapproves of—these *reasons* which support your ethical judgment are simply a means of facilitating your influence. If you think you can change his interests by making vivid to him how others will disapprove of him, you will do so; otherwise not. So the consideration about other people's interest is just an additional means you may employ, in order to move him, and is not a part of the ethical judgment itself. Your ethical judgment doesn't merely describe interests to him, it directs his very interests. The difference between the traditional interest theories and my view is like the difference between describing a desert and irrigating it.

Another example: A munitions maker declares that war is a good thing. If he merely meant that he approved of it, he would not have to insist so strongly, nor grow so excited in his argument. People would be quite easily convinced that he approved of it. If he merely meant that most people approved of war, or that most people would approve of it if they knew the consequences, he would have to yield his point if it were proved that this wasn't so. But he wouldn't do this, nor does consistency require it. He is not *describing* the state of people's approval; he is trying to *change* it by his influence. If he found that few people approved of war, he might insist all the more strongly that it was good, for there would be more changing to be done.[10]

The fact is (according to the emotivists) that words like "good," "ought," and "duty" have a certain *persuasive* power which no other words in the language can quite duplicate. "X is good" has a subtle persuasive power that "I approve X" seldom does. When people use ethical words, accordingly, they use them primarily as instruments of persuasion. They are not really concerned with asserting anything. If Smith, in saying that X is right, were merely asserting that he approved X, then if Jones replied, "Yes, I know you approve it," and even more if he went on to assert "I approve it too," Smith should rest quite satisfied at having communicated the information about X and then rest his case. But of course he does not. He does not really believe he has convinced Jones that X is right until he has succeeded in getting Jones to do X, or at the very least in building up in Jones a genuine desire to do X; until he has changed Jones' attitudes he will continue to press his point.

It is because of this persuasive power of ethical sentences, which, because of their grammatical form, seem to say something about X, while in reality they are saying nothing at all, but only expressing or evoking feelings, that ethical words are not translatable into non-ethical ones.

> Suppose you substitute a sentence containing only non-ethical words for one that contains an ethical word. Then the interjectional, rhetorical, or imperative force which the original sentence derived from the ethical word in it, has vanished. Suppose you have never doubted that ethical words are the names of characteristics. Then you will explain this feeling of "something missing" by saying that the proposed analysis of an ethical characteristic into purely non-ethical characteristics has missed out some essential logical constituent of the ethical characteristic.[11]

You will then find yourself, perhaps in spite of misgivings, holding

---

[10] Charles L. Stevenson, "The Emotive Meaning of Ethical Terms," *Mind*, 1937, pp. 18–19. (Reprinted in Sellars and Hospers, *Readings in Ethical Theory*, New York: Appleton-Century-Crofts, 1952.)

[11] C. D. Broad, "Is 'Goodness' the Name of a Simple Non-natural Quality?" *Proceedings of the Aristotelian Society*, 34, 1933–1934, p. 252.

the unique property theory, and saying that the word is not definable in terms of other words because the property it stands for is simple (unanalyzable) and unique. But this resort is unnecessary. The reason you cannot render the full meaning of the ethical term in any non-ethical terms is not because of any unique cognitive meaning it may have, but simply because no non-ethical words can duplicate the persuasive, imperative force of the ethical words. "X is right" cannot be translated into "X produces happiness" or "X is approved by me" for the same reason that "You swine" cannot be translated into "You member of the family 'porcus.' "

Finally, the emotivist will declare that his view gives the only true account of what all usages of ethical words like "good" have in common. If one searches for any cognitive meaning which is common to all usages, one will search in vain; but if he considers emotive meaning he will have his answer at once. What all usages of "good" and "right" have in common is their emotive meaning—the "aura of favorable feeling hovering about the words" which makes them subtle but potent instruments of persuasion; with "bad" and "wrong," of course, it is their aura of unfavorable feeling.[12] Smith and Jones may call opposite things good, they may call utterly different acts right, and yet we can truly say that they are both using these words in the same way (and in a way they both understand very well) because each of them is trying to mould the other's attitudes into conformity with the thing he favors by the means of these verbal instruments of persuasion.

E. Modifications of the Emotive Theory

The emotive theory may seem to solve the difficulties in the previous theories; yet one may not feel satisfied. "Is it really true," we may ask, "that when we say that something is good we are asserting nothing whatever about the thing, nor about ourselves, nor about anything at all, but merely giving vent to emotion, as we might when screaming, or trying to work up someone else's emotion, as in a rally, but without asserting anything whatever about the thing

---

[12] "Right" and "good" do not carry exactly the same emotive meaning, however. See C. L. Stevenson, *Ethics and Language* (New Haven: Yale University Press, 1943) on this as well as for a detailed and sensitive development of the emotivist point of view. See also R. M. Hare, *The Language of Morals* (Oxford: The Clarendon Press, 1952).

we're supposed to be talking about? It's true, of course, and the point is well made, that we do use language emotively as well as cognitively, and that ethical words are among the prime examples of words used in this way, but still this can't be the whole story. When I say that lying is wrong I'm surely saying *something* about lying, however unable I may be to tell you in other terms just what it is. To say that ethical words are used *only* emotively is doing just as much violence to their actual use as to say that they are used only cognitively."

Most emotivists would, in fact, admit or even insist that ethical words possess cognitive meaning as well as emotive meaning. It may be (they would say) that sometimes they are used in a purely emotive manner, as perhaps when the indignant mother has just caught her young son stealing from the neighbor's watermelon patch, and is interested only in changing his behavior by whatever means are available (ethical words, threats, or a spanking); but if this is true, it is equally true that there are times when we pronounce moral judgments and intend them as sober studied judgments which we believe to be true, when we are not particularly interested in giving vent to feelings (we may not yet have any on the judgment in question) or in arousing them in others, but only in "arriving at the truth." Surely it is possible to state truths in ethics? The *modified emotive* theory, then, holds that while the meaning of ethical terms is always partly emotive and, in fact, is *primarily* emotive in daily discourse, yet it is (at least in many cases) cognitive as well.

What, then, is this cognitive meaning, which we have sought after for so long? The reply is, "There is no single cognitive meaning for any ethical word." Let us take, for example, the word "good," and not restrict ourselves (for the time being) to its ethical usage, so that we can better discern what a wide variety of cognitive meanings may be attached to it. Consider the word "good" in the following phrases: "a good harbor," "a good car," "a good pianist," "a good dog," "a good moral character." In every case there is (in varying degrees) the "aura of favorable feeling about the word," and it is this that all the uses of "good" have in common. There is, however, cognitive meaning also, but it differs from case to case in each of the above examples and in thousands of others that could be mentioned. When one says that New York is a good harbor, or that he has a good dog, he is indeed asserting something; he is ascribing to the object in question a rather indefinite range of characteristics; but the characteristics he is ascribing to New York harbor in calling it good are not the same characteristics as those he is ascribing to his dog in calling it good, or to his friend Smith in calling him a good man. In each case the cognitive meaning is different; what unites them all is emotive meaning. "A good halfback," "a good movie," "a good bowl of soup," "a good dentist"—what a variety of characteristics we are ascribing to things when we call them good! Cognitively, the meaning of "good" is infinitely various.

That cognitive meaning is present, however, is as much a fact as its variability from usage to usage. If you ask someone, "Is that a good road?" and he says "Yes," and you start to drive over it and find it full of hills, dangerous corners, and deep mudholes, you will call your informant a liar without reservation. Surely this shows that you believe he was asserting something when he said that the road was good, that he was asserting the presence of some characteristics (however vague and ill-defined) by virtue of which he called it good, and that he was asserting it falsely because the road did not turn out to have any such characteristics. If the sentence "The road is good" expressed no proposition, it could have expressed no false proposition, and hence there would have been no lie. There are, then, characteristics of the thing called "good" which are being asserted to exist when a person says that the thing is good, the absence of which would make "X is good" express a *false proposition*. In most cases these characteristics are of a rather indefinite range, and using the adjective "good" is a kind of shorthand way (and possibly a careless way) of referring to them all at once.

In those cases where the cognitive meaning of "good" is the clearest and most pronounced, there is likely to be a fairly uniform conception of what constitutes a good X, whatever the X may be. There is pretty general agreement as to what characteristics of a road entitle it to be called "good"; they are the characteristics which make motorists prefer roads that have them to roads that do not. If someone asks you, "Is Road R better than Road S?" you know fairly well what he means. If you are in doubt as to just what characteristics he has in mind in calling it better, you can ask, "What do you mean exactly? is it paved? is there a minimum of cross-traffic?" and so on; but the fact that we generally do not find it necessary to ask this shows that we understand fairly well what cognitive meaning people attach to the word "good" in the phrase "a good road." In the phrase "a good pianist," we are more likely to have to ask the person what characteristics he has in mind in calling the pianist "good," unless we already know the musical tastes of the person who utters the statement.

Separation of emotive from cognitive meaning. How then shall we analyze sentences of the form "X is good"? We must first try to separate the emotive from the cognitive meaning, and then do our best to determine what the cognitive meaning is in the particular case at hand. When someone says, "She's a better pianist than he is," we must say to ourselves, "Emotive meaning aside—and there always is this element of persuasive-expressive meaning when the word 'good' is used—what characteristics of a pianist does the speaker have in mind in calling the pianist good, or better than another pianist? How would he translate his sentence into other words? He cannot translate his *entire* meaning, for, as we have seen, the emotive meaning of words like 'good' cannot be duplicated by any other words and is therefore absent from any attempted translation; but we should try to translate his *cognitive* meaning."

In most cases this will not be an easy thing to do: (1) The person in question will not usually have a definite set of characteristics in mind at all, but will be able to say only in the vaguest sort of way what he means (cognitively) by "good" in such a sentence as "She is a good pianist." (2) Even if he has definite characteristics in mind as the cognitive meaning of "good" in one case, he will often find it difficult (owing to the inadequacies of language) to state in words what these characteristics are. Most points of musical technique and expression, for example, can be grasped by sensitive listeners but cannot be easily stated in words, and when it is, one cannot be sure that one's hearer means the same thing by the same words. (3) Even if these difficulties are overcome, persons will differ widely from each other (about pianists, pickles, and moral characters if not about roads) on what constitutes the cognitive meaning of "good" in a particular case. A person who likes characteristic C in a pianist will list C among the characteristics included in the cognitive meaning of "good" as he is using it in the phrase "a good pianist," while a person who dislikes C will not include it on *his* list. (4) Even the same person may not include the same characteristics on his list at one time as he would at another; for example, his conception of what constitutes a good pianist may change. All this, of course, enormously complicates the problem of determining, in any particular case, the cognitive meaning of "good."

This is a difficult and arduous business, and yet, it is urged, we must go through with it if we want to know the cognitive meaning attached to "good" and similar words in any particular instance. Always the formula is the same: "Ignoring the emotive meaning, what cognitive meaning do you attach to 'good' in this sentence? By virtue of what characteristics it has do you call it 'good,' and in the absence of which would you no longer apply the term? In other words, what characteristics are you using as *defining* of the word 'good' in this instance of its use?" When we have done this, we have teased out, or, more likely, *tortured* out, the cognitive meaning attached by the speaker to this value-sentence at this time. We would have to start all over again for another person (who might have something quite different in mind in calling someone a good pianist, or good company, or a good man) and for the same person in his next utterance of a value-sentence (he would not attach the same cognitive meaning to "good" in "a good hospital" or "a good race-horse"), and even perhaps for the same person in using the same sentence at a later time.

(Usually the cognitive meaning of "good" in qualified statements is more easily tortured out than in unqualified ones: "a good man" usually conveys less cognitive meaning to the hearer, at least prior to questioning, than does "a good man to hire as an accountant"; "philosophy is good" is less clear than "philosophy is good as a mental discipline"; "this is a good car" is less clear than "this is a good car for going at high speed"; "he's a good baseball player" is less clear than "he's good at fast pitching." Indeed, when one is not sure what is meant by "good" in a particular sentence, he usually asks for such qualifications: "What do you mean, philosophy is good? good as a means of finding out truths about the world? good as a mental discipline?" and so on.)

The cognitive meaning of most ethical sentences, such as "Stealing is wrong," differs from that of outright empirical ones, such as "Stealing causes widespread insecurity," chiefly in the fact that the ethical sentence has a far stronger component of emotive meaning. This emotive meaning, moreover, tends to obscure such cognitive meaning as the sentence may have (as used by this speaker at this time), so that it becomes more difficult to torture out; and the more the sentence is used directively, as an instrument of persuasion, the dimmer the cognitive meaning is likely to become. In a way, the difference in cognitive meaning between "Stealing causes insecurity" and "Stealing is wrong" is like the difference between the shell of a nut and the meat: the first statement carries its cognitive meaning on its face, while that of the second statement requires some hammering before one can get at it at all.

Because ethical terms so often are used as a blanket to cover up vagueness (or total absence) of cognitive meaning, things would be much easier, *cognitively* speaking, if ethical terms were not employed at all; we would have a much clearer idea of what was being asserted if sentences contained no such words. When we have nothing clearly in mind, it is easy to be semantically sloppy and use these vague and slippery value-words in order to cover up the lack of clarity and precision in our thoughts.

Does this mean that we should abandon the use of ethical words entirely? Of course not. These words have a definite function, namely their emotive use in the directing of people's attitudes. Here lies the *principal* function of such words in actual practice. Moreover, here lies their *peculiar* function: ethical words can do this; ordinary descriptive words cannot. For conveying cognitive meaning, on the other hand, descriptive words are the proper instruments. The cognitive meaning of ethical terms is by no means so clear; cognitive confusion is often brought about when we introduce them; and, as we have already seen, such cognitive meaning as they do have must be tortured out anew for each particular instance of their use.

The primacy of emotive meaning. If the proponents of this view hold that ethical words have both cognitive and emotive meaning, why then are they still called "emotivists"? Because they hold that the emotive meaning of ethical terms is primary: in other words, that it is the emotive meaning, not the cognitive, which is the *determinant* for the use of ethical terms in particular sentences. Suppose, for example, that a man says that polygamy is right and monogamy is wrong; then he changes his mind and says that monogamy is right and polygamy is wrong. Let us suppose that in each case he is not using his ethical terms *merely* emotively but attaches cognitive meaning to the use of the word "right" in these sentences. It does not matter for our present purposes what that cognitive meaning is, but let us suppose that (in his first sentence) the cognitive meaning he attached to "Polygamy is right" was "Polygamy has consequences C," and calling polygamy wrong would have meant that it did *not* have consequences C. But now he changes his mind, and calls polygamy wrong and monogamy right. He may not have changed his mind at all about polygamy having consequences C; he may believe this as much as ever, but no longer think so highly of such consequences. So he now calls polygamy wrong, *in spite of the fact* that both the consequences of polygamy and his belief about them are exactly what they were before. Well then, if the cognitive meaning of "Polygamy is right" was originally "Polygamy has consequences C," why doesn't he stick to his original usage and *still say that polygamy is right*, since he hasn't changed his mind about the occurrence of consequences C? He doesn't, because the emotive and not the cognitive meaning of the ethical term is the determinant for its use. He doesn't stick to his original use of "right" as "having consequences C" because his attitude toward polygamy has changed and consequently the *directive influence* he wants the sentence to exert has changed. Saying that polygamy is right just would not convey his meaning any more, and it would be well-nigh inconceivable that he should continue saying "Polygamy is right" now that he feels as he does, in spite of the fact that he has *not altered his opinion one whit* as to what the consequences of polygamy are. This shows clearly that it is not the cognitive meaning which determines his use of the ethical word. If it were, he wouldn't change the adjective from "right" to "wrong," for his original cognitive meaning of "right" was "having consequences C" and he still believes that polygamy has consequences C. Yet he has the overpowering compulsion to reverse the cognitive meanings of "right" and "wrong" in this matter once his feeling toward polygamy has changed, which he would have no reason whatever for doing if cognitive meaning were what he was interested in. However, he does change the cognitive meaning with his change of attitude, for the emotive meaning of "right" remains the same, and now that it has become attached to a different cognitive meaning he must change the latter. As he well knows, or at least practices, in using ethical words he is using language emotively: he wants to express his new disapproval of polygamy and encourage others to disapprove it. The word "wrong" serves this purpose as no non-emotive word does; that is why he must use it; that is why he cannot keep his language *cognitively* consistent as he would if the cognitive meaning were the determinant of his use of ethical terms.

Ethical disagreement. Let us now reiterate a question which concerned us earlier in this chapter: what account are we to give of disagreement in ethical matters? We saw that on those attitude theories which identify a moral judgment about X with a judgment about the attitude of oneself or one's group toward X, no disagreement occurs, for each disputant is only asserting that he or his group has such-and-such an attitude toward X. On objectivist theories there is genuine disagreement (for example, about X's consequences), but we gave reasons for believing that ethical sentences do not have the same meaning as any of the sentences suggested by objectivist theories. On the unique property theory there is genuine disagreement but apparently no way of resolving it. On the pure emotive theory, there is no disagreement because there are no genuine statements (only expressions-evocations that look like statements) for the so-called disputants to disagree about. Now, how does the matter stand with the emotive theory as we have modified it thus far?

According to the modified emotive theory, there can be disagreement to the extent that cognitive meaning is present. If, on some particular occasion, the ethical term is being used without cognitive meaning, then there is no disagreement, since there is no statement which is the subject of disagreement (normally, at least, disagreement implies a *statement* the truth of which is asserted by one person, and whose falsity is asserted by another). But when cognitive meaning is present, as it usually is in varying degrees, then of course there is at least one property which the X in question is asserted to have, and then, of course, there may be a genuine disagreement on whether or not X really has this property. When this happens, there is not merely a "clash of attitudes" but a difference of opinion on some matter of fact.

Let us suppose that Smith and Jones are arguing about the rightness of euthanasia (mercy-killing), and that in addition to the emotive meaning which they both attach to the terms "right" and "wrong," some cognitive meaning can also be extracted from their assertions: in this case, that "right" means the same as "having consequences C" and "wrong" means the same as "not having consequences C." [13] Now, Smith may, through ignorance or misinformation, not be aware that euthanasia does not have consequences C (whatever they are). Thus he will say that euthanasia is right (euthanasia has consequences C), simply through lack of knowledge of the consequences, not through any conviction that it could have consequences C and still be wrong. Once Jones sets him straight on what the consequences are (which of course he will have to show empirically), the disagreement, a real one while it lasted, is settled.

On the other hand, suppose that Smith continues to say "Euthanasia is right" and Jones to say "Euthanasia is wrong" even though they both agree on what the consequences of euthanasia are? Perhaps there is some other fact about euthanasia which is the object of their disagreement; if so, then perhaps this matter of fact, too, can be settled and the argument come to rest. But what if this is not the case? What if they agree on every matter of fact and still continue to utter their respective ethical statements? In that case, says our modified emotivist, there is no disagreement between them at all. Every disagreement is about some matter of fact—about whether some sentence states a fact (and thus is true) or does not state a fact (and thus is false); and if there is no statement whose truth or falsity is in question, of course there can be no disagreement about its truth or falsity. The so-called ethical statements are then being used purely emotively, to exhort or to dissuade; there is a *clash of attitudes* between Smith and Jones, but since assertion is being made by either of them (not even an assertion *about* attitudes), there is no disagreement. "Can the disagreement be settled?" Not if there is no disagreement to begin with. The clash of attitudes will probably remain, unless the attitude of one of the participants can be changed by emotive language, screeches, groans, or armed conflict; at any rate, no *statement* will be sufficient for the purpose because there is no statement about whose truth they disagree.[14]

[13] This does not contradict the position stated on pages 458–460 that the meaning of "X is right" cannot be identified with the meaning of "X has certain consequences." The total meaning of "X is right" cannot (as the modified emotive theory insists) be thus identified. Only the *cognitive* meaning of it can. And that is the aspect of it which we are now considering. (The total meaning would also include the emotive meaning, which cannot be translated.)

[14] Cf. Stevenson's distinction between disagreement in belief and disagreement in interest. It is, however, surely misleading to call the latter disagreement at all. (C. L. Stevenson, "The Emotive Meaning of Ethical Terms," in

II. ETHICAL NATURALISM AND NON-NATURALISM

"There is genuine disagreement only if there is some matter of fact on which the disputants disagree." Very well, but what kinds of matters of fact are there? Are there peculiarly ethical matters of fact, or are all so-called ethical facts really other kinds of fact (facts about consequences, facts about attitudes, and the like) in disguise? It is on this issue that ethical theories ultimately split.

It is sometimes said that the principal ethical theories in the field today are ethical naturalism, ethical non-naturalism (or intuitionism, for reasons soon to be described), and emotivism. Such a statement, however, is quite misleading. The emotive theory, at least in its modified form, can easily be incorporated into the other two kinds of theory. Proponents of both naturalism and non-naturalism in ethics can say, "We grant, what we did not recognize before, that ethical terms possess considerable emotive meaning, sometimes *only* emotive meaning. We grant that if one is searching for the common and universal meaning of ethical terms, that meaning is emotive. We grant that the determinant for the use of ethical terms is largely emotive. We grant, too, that there is no disagreement if there is no statement which one person believes to be true and the other believes to be false." But whether any of such statements are uniquely ethical, and thus untranslatable into non-ethical statements—that is the bone of contention between naturalists and non-naturalists. Again, the two may agree that the emotive meaning of ethical terms keeps such terms from being translatable into non-ethical terms; but they will disagree on whether it is *only* emotive meaning that makes them so: the naturalist will hold that it is, while the non-naturalist will hold that even in the absence of emotive meaning there would be untranslatable cognitive meaning in ethical terms (as the unique property theory holds), untranslatable because sentences containing ethical terms simply do not have the same meaning as sentences which do not contain them. Ethical sentences are forever irreducible to non-ethical sentences, because ethical properties (such as goodness) are irreducibly different from non-ethical properties.

Sellars and Hospers, *Readings in Ethical Theory*. New York: Appleton-Century-Crofts, 1952.)

Description of ethical naturalism. The core of the naturalistic position, then, is this: Granted that the entire meaning of an ethical sentence is untranslatable because of the peculiar persuasive force of the ethical term, the *cognitive* component of its meaning *can* be translated into non-ethical terms. This cognitive meaning, when finally elicited (it usually has to be tortured out), has to do with the causes of X, or the consequences of X, on humanity or on some person or group, or with someone's attitude toward X, or with the attitude of some group toward X, and so on.[15] It is different on different occasions of the use of the ethical term, and it would be a mistake to hold (as did our original objectivistic and subjectivistic theories) that the ethical sentence is always translatable into *one* specific and unvarying non-ethical sentence. But it does insist that when the ethical sentence has cognitive meaning at all, it is translatable into *some* non-ethical sentence(s) or other.

There is, then, according to ethical naturalism, *no "peculiarly ethical" type of statement.* Insofar as ethical sentences yield statements at all, they are non-ethical statements of the kinds we have already considered in preceding chapters. The *appearance* of being a peculiarly ethical statement is due simply to emotive meaning, which makes the total meaning of the sentence untranslatable, but it does not make the cognitive component untranslatable.

Possible misunderstandings. Can there be true moral principles according to ethical naturalism? Of course there can. For example, once we have extracted the cognitive meaning of "To commit murder is wrong" and found it in some particular instance to be, let us say, "To commit acts of murder causes more unhappiness and less happiness than not to commit them," then the statement is very probably true. Many statements about the rightness or wrongness of acts cannot be known for certain to be true, simply because the statements about consequences into which they (in their cognitive

---

[15] It might even have to do with God's attitude toward X without damaging ethical naturalism. Ethical naturalism, once again, has nothing to do with religious naturalism and thus is not opposed to religious supernaturalism. All that it insists on is the *translatability* of the cognitive component of ethical sentences into non-ethical terms. Usually these non-ethical sentences will be *empirical* ones about consequences and so on. But there is no reason why they may not be sentences about a Deity. To have translated the ethical sentence into a non-empirical sentence about God is still to have translated it into a non-ethical sentence, and this is all that ethical naturalism strictly requires.

part) are translated cannot be known to be true: the consequences
of many acts are so bewilderingly complex and far-flung that one
simply cannot know what they all will be. This uncertainty, however, does not attend the statements because of any distinctively
ethical feature which they possess; it is entirely an *empirical* uncertainty (like the uncertainty as to how many blades of grass there
are in North America), the uncertainty of what the total consequences will be.

Some instances of murder may be right (for example, killing a
tyrant who is enslaving an entire population), depending on the
consequences. Clearly, if consequences are what one has in mind in
calling an act right, then an act will depend for its rightness on
what those consequences are. On the other hand, if, say, the attitude
of one's society is what one has in mind in calling an act right, then
the rightness of the act (as one is then using the term "right") will
depend on what the attitude of the society is. In every case, one has
first to translate the sentence (its cognitive component) into another sentence or sentences to see exactly what is meant by the
ethical term on this particular occasion of the use of an ethical
term; this done, one can go about trying to discover empirically
whether the proposition it expresses is true or false.

Ethical naturalism, then, is not attacking the truth of any moral
principles, much less saying that none exist. It is attempting simply
to discover, from case to case, what the ethical sentences cognitively
mean in terms of non-ethical sentences. The ethical philosopher
must try to remove the blanket of ethical terms and uncover whatever meaning may be there. Once this meaning has been elicited, it
is quite possible that the statements yielded by the analysis may
turn out to be true. There is thus nothing "morally dangerous"
about ethical naturalism, as there might be about the pure emotive
theory.

"It all depends on the cognitive meaning you attach to the ethical
term in a particular case," you say. "But aren't some meanings the
right ones, and others wrong? If a criminal attached to the phrase
'right acts' the meaning 'whichever acts get me the most financial
rewards, regardless of what other consequences they have to human
beings,' wouldn't that be the *wrong* meaning?" Meanings are not
wrong, as we already observed in Chapter 1 (pages 4–6) ; they can
only be unusual, inconvenient, or misleading. But this, of course,

does not imply that once a meaning is given to a word the statement in which the word occurs is true. If one said "Murder is right" and meant by this "Murder pleases me," his statement might very well be true, depending on who he was and how he felt. But this does not mean that the same sentence uttered by you or me would express a true proposition, for we would attach a different cognitive meaning to it: we are more likely to mean, in saying that murder is wrong, that it brings about much pain and suffering and so on to those affected by the act, and in that sense it would be entirely false to say that murder was right. If we find it surprising that "This murder is right" would be true if we meant "This murder pleases the murderer," let us remember that the same sentence does not always state the same proposition—that "This murder is right" is true enough in the murderer's meaning of it, but that *on his lips the sentence would not have the same cognitive meaning.* Our surprise at the conclusion comes from reading *our* meaning into *his* words. If someone said that oranges are blue, we might be surprised until we learned that by the word "oranges" the speaker meant what we mean by the word "bluebirds"; but on *his* meaning of "oranges" his statement would be perfectly true.

Naturalism contrasted with non-naturalism. The ethical naturalist, then, holds no brief for any one translation of ethical sentences into non-ethical ones; he merely asserts that when cognitive meaning is present some such translation can always be made. Once this is done, the statement yielded by the translation may be true or it may be false—that depends, of course, on what the statement is. Ethical sentences are indeed untranslatable, but this is only because they have emotive meaning; in their cognitive meaning they are always translatable into non-ethical sentences. Once we skim off the emotive meaning, the remainder—i.e., the cognitive part—yields only non-ethical statements such as we have considered in the chapters prior to this one: principally empirical statements such as one would find in the domain of psychology and sociology. (Statements about attitudes would be bits of descriptive psychology; statements about consequences of acts upon society would be sociological.) The import of ethical naturalism then comes to this: that insofar as cognitive meaning is concerned, ethics is not a separate field of inquiry; insofar as ethical sentences yield statements at all, these statements are psychological, sociological, and so on

The ethical non-naturalist denies these assertions. Even if there were no emotive meaning, he says, ethical sentences would still be untranslatable into non-ethical ones. The reason for this is that there are uniquely ethical properties which simply are not the same as any non-ethical properties whatever or any conjunction of such properties. Ethical terms are untranslatable not only because they possess emotive meaning, but because they refer to these ethical properties.

Translatable ethical sentences. It should not be assumed, however, according to the non-naturalist, that *every* sentence containing an ethical term is untranslatable.

1. Some sentences contain ethical words used purely in an emotive way. When this happens, of course, nothing is being asserted at all, particularly not anything uniquely ethical.

2. Some sentences contain ethical words but do not employ them in an ethical sense. "That's a good road" contains the word "good," but it is not used in an ethical sense, and no ethical property is involved. The same holds for countless usages of "good" ("a good cook," "he has one good eye," "it tastes good") and "right" ("that's the right answer," "have you got it right this time?") and "ought" ("the chair ought not to be in that corner," "there ought to be a turn in the road here"). It is not denied that such sentences as these are translatable into sentences not containing the ethical term.

3. Sentences about what is *instrumentally good* (see page 455) as opposed to intrinsically good are admitted by most non-naturalists to be translatable into non-ethical sentences. To say that A is good as a means or instrument for the attainment of B is to say nothing more than that A actually leads to B; and statements about what leads to what are empirical statements. Pulling the trigger on a loaded gun is a good means toward a man's death (it is not asserted that his death itself is good), because it is normally followed by this effect; beating him with a club, on the other hand, is not a good means—i.e., it does not usually produce death. Such statements about what causes what or what is conducive to what else are empirical statements, and this is all that statements about means turn out to be. Thus there is no difficulty about their translatability.

Untranslatable ethical sentences. Although statements about what is instrumentally good turn out on examination to be disguised empirical statements, this is not true of statements about what is intrinsically good. How would one translate, for example, "Happiness is good"?—not in the sense in which one sometimes means it, that happiness is instrumental to something else, but that happiness is good, in and by itself, considered quite apart from anything that it may lead to. Perhaps self-discipline, self-sacrifice, and courage are good only as a means to or instruments for the achievement of ends, and therefore statements about them are translatable; but what of the ultimate end itself? We need not even insist here that happiness *is* that ultimate end toward which all other good things are good as a means (though many philosophers have said that it is). What matters here is simply that it *is a statement,* and yet *not* a statement which is translatable into any non-ethical terms whatever. (Doubtless this is what John Stuart Mill had in mind when he said that statements about ultimate ends could not be proved.) You cannot say that "X is intrinsically good" means the same as "X leads to Y," for by saying that X is intrinsically good we mean that X would be good even if it did not lead to Y or Z or anything else.

Now, says the non-naturalist, what are we to do with such a statement? Surely it is not nonsensical. It is a statement about whose possible truth we can ponder, reflect, and arrive at conclusions. How can an ethical naturalist possibly account for the undoubted meaningfulness of such a statement? The possibilities open to him are not very encouraging: (1) He may say that since the sentence cannot be translated into non-ethical terms, its meaning must be wholly emotive. But this is to beg the very question which is at issue here. "It's not translatable, therefore it is emotive" is the very inference which the non-naturalist questions, and therefore it cannot be taken for granted in the argument. Moreover, it is not very likely, in any case, that a sentence of this kind is emotive even to a very considerable degree. It is not the kind of sentence which people who wield ethical terms as instruments of propaganda are ever likely to utter; it is most likely to be used by the philosopher in his study, and he is probably not trying to work on anyone's feelings or even to express his own, but rather to convince himself that the sentence does or does not state a true proposition. (2) He may also say that "Happiness is intrinsically good" is a tautology. And so it may be if he turns it into a definition—if by "intrinsic good" he just *means* happiness. But surely this is not a very plausible position: he may mean that happiness is an *instance* of intrinsic goodness (perhaps the only instance), but is happiness not merely what he denotes but what he *designates* (in the ordinary sense, what he *means*) by the phrase "intrinsic goodness"? Moreover, can one not ask himself, "*Is* happiness intrinsically good?" and one is not thereby asking "Is happiness happiness?" The statement that something (no matter what) is intrinsically good is surely a synthetic statement which one accepts, if at all, only after considerable reflection, rather than a definition set up at the beginning. There are many who believe that happiness is not the only thing that is intrinsically good—that knowledge of truth, for example, is intrinsically good also; are they believing that happiness is not the only thing that is happiness? To interpret the statement as a tautology is, in the opinion of the non-naturalist, a move of desperation.

What, then, is it? It is, according to the non-naturalist, a synthetic statement from which the ethical word "good" *cannot be removed* because nothing can be substituted for it; it is a statement which asserts that there is an invariant concomitance between two classes of things, happiness (an empirical property) and intrinsic goodness (an ethical property).

To sum up, then, in cognitive meaning *some* sentences containing ethical terms can be translated into non-ethical terms, but not all of them can. There always remain sentences about intrinsic goodness, as well as (according to most non-naturalists) sentences about duty and obligation, which cannot be thus translated. This is because they assert the existence of uniquely ethical properties which are simply not identical with any non-ethical properties whatever.

Ethical disagreement. What, then, is the non-naturalist's position on ethical disagreement? Contrary to the naturalist, he insists that ethical disagreement may remain even *after* all disagreement about non-ethical matters (such as the effects of X on society) have been resolved. The disagreement is a real one, and it concerns the presence of an ethical property. It is a caricature of the true situation to dismiss all ethical disagreement (after the non-ethical has been taken care of) as "no disagreement at all but a mere clash of interests." Some situations may be of this kind, but there are some cases, notably that of intrinsic goodness, in which there can be real disagreement about a matter of fact which is a matter of *ethical* fact, not of any non-ethical fact whatever. The emotivists have tried to explain the untranslatability of ethical statements as the result

of their emotive meaning, and they did uncover many important
truths about the way in which people in daily life use ethical terms;
but their analysis did not exhaust the uniqueness of these terms.
Even if there were no emotive meaning, ethical terms would still be
unique in their meaning, for they would stand for uniquely ethical
properties.

The problem of verification. But how are we ever to know when
and where any instances of a uniquely ethical property exist? Since
it is not an empirical property, we cannot discover its presence by
empirical means. At least, one might be tempted to remark, the
naturalist offers us hope of settling ethical questions: he translates
ethical sentences (insofar as they have cognitive meaning) into non-
ethical ones about attitudes and consequences, which we can then
set out to verify, although admittedly it is often difficult or technically impossible to do this. But the path of empirical verification
is closed to the non-naturalist where his uniquely ethical properties
are concerned. One can verify the presence of acts and consequences
empirically, but not the presence of uniquely ethical properties. How
then are we ever to settle these disagreements about ethical facts,
which may persist even after there is no longer any disagreement
about non-ethical facts?

At this point comes the reply—"by intuition"—which causes the
title "ethical non-naturalist" to be usually replaced by the title
"ethical intuitionist." Many non-naturalists hold that the human
mind has the power to know by intuition the truth of one or more
fundamental ethical principles. The application of these general
principles to specific cases is not generally held to be knowable by
intuition—for example, one can know that happiness is good but
not that this act will lead to it; it is only the "ultimate principles"
for which intuitive knowledge is claimed. Whether the ultimate
principle(s) are about intrinsic goodness or about obligations to act,
is a matter of dispute. Those who say that the only ultimate ethical
principle (knowable by intuition) has to do with intrinsic goodness,
will say that all statements about right acts, and about what one
has a duty or obligation to do, turn out to be statements about
means (and thus translatable): means to the achievement of intrinsic goodness. Those who say that the main types of duties or obligations must be intuited (instead of, or in addition to, intrinsic
goodness) are usually those who hold that certain kinds of acts are

obligatory whether or not they tend to produce states-of-affairs which are intrinsically good.[16]

How can the intuitionist defend himself in the face of the notoriously conflicting beliefs which different persons, societies, and civilizations hold about what is good, what is right, what is our duty? He can say several things: (1) Many persons and societies, now and in the past, have not been interested in discovering the truth in ethical matters. The Nazis, for example, were not trying to discover truths about what was right. One should hardly be surprised if they failed to discover truths which they were not in search of in the first place. (2) The actual disagreement among different peoples about ethical matters has been vastly exaggerated and grossly misinterpreted.[17] (3) Most disputes in this area, in any case, are disputes about what is instrumentally good, not what is intrinsically good. We may all agree that world peace would be a good thing, yet disagree violently about how it is to be achieved. Such disagreements (as we saw on page 455) are about what leads to what, and thus are about matters of empirical fact, not about ethics at all. (4) Our attempts to get at moral truths may be, and almost invariably are to a great extent, obscured by "the personal equation"—our personal desires, our human preferences in our own behalf, wishful thinking, clever rationalization, and the like. These factors constantly color and distort our moral judgments, and their elimination requires never-ending vigilance. In trying to discover ethical truth we need to be just as rigidly impartial as in trying to discover scientific truth.

In spite of all these things, disagreements may still remain. Perhaps our finite human judgments in this realm can never be entirely free from the possibility of error. But we must simply do the best we can with the moral faculties that we have. At least, argues the intuitionist, it is better to admit this and go forward in our search than to caricature the moral situation by insisting that every statement must be empirically verifiable or confirmable, and that therefore there are no distinctively ethical truths at all.

And here we must let the matter rest. The controversy still re-

[16] For a sampling from some of the most important ethical intuitionists, and their most cogent arguments, see Sellars and Hospers, *Readings in Ethical Theory* (New York: Appleton-Century-Crofts, 1952), pp. 115–249.

[17] This point cannot be developed here, but for a brilliant exposition of it see W. T. Stace, *The Concept of Morals* (New York: Macmillan, 1937).

mains, and it carries a strong appeal on both sides. We should like, if possible, for all our moral judgments to be capable (at least in principle) of empirical confirmation, and will naturally bend every effort to cast them into a form in which this will be possible. (In the case of statements about instrumental goods, it pretty clearly *is* possible.) The truth or falsity of ethical judgments will then be publicly ascertainable. On the other hand, it does seem that ethical judgments are not simply psychology plus sociology plus persuasion, and that genuine ethical disagreements can continue even after all matters of non-ethical fact have been agreed upon; moreover, the argument of the non-naturalist on intrinsic goodness (pp. 489–491) is a very powerful one.

SELECTED READINGS FOR CHAPTER 7

Plato. *Protagoras; Gorgias; Republic.* Many editions.

John Stuart Mill. *Utilitarianism.* Many editions.

G. E. Moore. *Ethics.* Home University Library. New York: Oxford University Press, 1912.

James Balfour. "On the Idea of a Philosophy of Ethics," in *A Defense of Philosophic Doubt.* London: Hodder and Stoughton, 1912. (Reprinted in Wilfrid Sellars and John Hospers, *Readings in Ethical Theory.* New York: Appleton-Century-Crofts, 1952.)

Bertrand Russell. "The Elements of Ethics," in *Philosophical Essays.* London: Longmans, Green, 1910. (Reprinted in Sellars and Hospers, *Readings in Ethical Theory.* New York: Appleton-Century-Crofts, 1952.)

C. L. Stevenson. "The Emotive Meaning of Ethical Terms," *Mind*, 46, 1937. (Reprinted in *Readings in Ethical Theory*, ed. Sellars and Hospers. New York: Appleton-Century-Crofts, 1952.)

K. Baier. "Proving a Moral Judgment," *Philosophical Studies*, 4, 1953, pp. 33–44.

Herbert Feigl. "Validation and Vindication," in *Readings in Ethical Theory*, ed. Sellars and Hospers. New York: Appleton-Century-Crofts, 1952.

W. T. Stace. *The Concept of Morals.* New York: Macmillan, 1937.

A. C. Ewing. *The Definition of Good.* New York: Macmillan, 1947.

Arthur Pap. *Elements of Analytic Philosophy.* New York: Macmillan, 1949. Chapter 2.

P. F. Strawson. "Ethical Intuitionism," *Philosophy*, 24, 1949. (Reprinted in *Readings in Ethical Theory*, ed. Sellars and Hospers. New York: Appleton-Century-Crofts, 1952.)

James B. Pratt. *Reason in the Art of Living.* New York: Macmillan, 1949.

Immanuel Kant. *Foundations of the Metaphysics of Morals*. 1785. Many editions. (University of Chicago Press, 1949.)

F. H. Bradley. *Ethical Studies*. London: Oxford University Press, 1876. (Reprinted in abridged form in Little Library of Liberal Arts edition. New York: The Liberal Arts Press, 1951.)

Henry Sidgwick. *The Methods of Ethics*. London: Macmillan, seventh edition, 1907.

G. E. Moore. *Principia Ethica*. Cambridge: Cambridge University Press, 1903.

E. F. Carritt. *The Theory of Morals*. London: Oxford University Press, 1928.

————. *Morals and Politics*. London: Oxford University Press, 1935.

————. *Ethical and Political Thinking*. London: Oxford University Press, 1947.

W. D. Ross. *The Right and the Good*. London: Oxford University Press, 1931.

C. D. Broad. *Five Types of Ethical Theory*. London: Kegan Paul, 1930.

C. L. Stevenson. *Ethics and Language*. New Haven: Yale University Press, 1943.

H. A. Prichard. *Moral Obligation*. London: Oxford University Press, 1950.

Stephen Toulmin. *The Place of Reason in Ethics*. Cambridge: Cambridge University Press, 1950.

EXERCISES

1. List and illustrate half a dozen distinctions made in Chapter 1 which have a bearing upon the contents of this chapter.

2. Explain how expressing an emotion is different from stating that you have an emotion. What is the importance of this distinction in the classification of theories about the meaning of ethical terms?

3. Discuss the role of intuition in (a) geometry, (b) logic, (c) ethics. Note any similarities and differences that may occur to you.

4. To what extent do you think emotive meaning is present in each of the following phrases? What cognitive meaning do you think is present in each of them? (It will vary, of course, in different circumstances.)

    a. a good horse
    b. a good car
    c. a good thing to keep in mind
    d. bad news
    e. a bad man
    f. a bad taste in one's mouth

5. According to Stevenson, in his essay "The Emotive Meaning of Ethical Terms," all analyses of "good" must fulfill each of the following requirements:

(1) We must be able sensibly to *disagree* about whether something is good.

(2) Goodness must have a "magnetism": a person who recognizes X to be good must thereby acquire a stronger tendency to act in its favor than he otherwise would have had.

(3) The goodness of anything must not be verifiable solely by the use of scientific method. "Ethics must not be psychology."
Which of the theories considered in this chapter fulfill these three requirements? Explain.

6. According to utilitarianism, one particular act (such as Brutus killing Caesar) cannot be both right and wrong; but of two acts belonging to the same type or class (e.g. lies, divorces, assassinations) one may be right while another is wrong. Explain why this is so.

7. The term "ethical relativism" is often introduced into discussions and is not always given the same meaning, but it is sometimes defined as the view that there is no single standard of right and wrong that is applicable to all people. In this sense, utilitarianism would not be relativistic, for it holds to one standard of rightness (promotion of maximum happiness). Yet utilitarianism is quite compatible with the view that e.g. it would be right for Smith (who has no children) to divorce his wife but wrong for Jones (who has children) to do so. Show as clearly as you can that this belief— that what is right for Smith may be wrong for Jones—is not necessarily relativistic.

8. Which of the subjectivistic theories considered in this chapter would you consider to be relativistic? Explain.

9. Can you detect any differences among the following:
   a. saying that ethical terms (at least one) are verbally indefinable.
   b. saying that ethical terms (at least one) name unanalyzable properties.
   c. saying that ethical terms are not translatable into non-ethical ones.
   d. saying that ethical properties are not the same as non-ethical ones.

10. "Ethical sentences are untranslatable into non-ethical ones." Do ethical naturalism and ethical non-naturalism agree on the reason(s) for asserting this? Explain.

11. Can you think of any arguments both for and against the view that happiness is the only intrinsic good?

12. Attack or defend the thesis that the rightness of acts is determined by the intrinsic goodness of their effects.

13. State as clearly as you can what you consider to be the strong points in both ethical naturalism and ethical non-naturalism.

8

Problems in Esthetics

Statements in ethics, such as "X is good," pronounce *moral* judgments; statements in esthetics, such as "X is beautiful," pronounce *esthetic* judgments. As we saw in the preceding chapter, there is no universal agreement as to whether "good" is the central term in ethics, as opposed to "right" and "duty"; nor, as we shall shortly see, is there universal agreement as to whether "beautiful" is the central term in esthetics. Nevertheless, we shall not go far amiss if we begin our necessarily brief inquiry into esthetics by asking, What is the meaning of "beautiful"?

I. THE MEANING OF "BEAUTIFUL"

The esthetic experience. We are generally inclined to speak of objects as beautiful when they arouse in us *esthetic experiences*. And if we had no such experiences, we would surely have no conception of beauty in objects. Let us begin, then, by asking, What are esthetic experiences? What distinguishes those experiences to which the name "esthetic" is applied from all other experiences?

Almost everyone has had experiences in the presence of the ocean or the sunset, the mountains or the forests, symphonies or poems, which would unhesitatingly be labeled "esthetic." To give an adequate description of these experiences is extremely difficult. Probably it is impossible to convey to anyone who has not had such experiences what one means by the word "esthetic," just as one cannot convey to a man born blind what he means by words which name colors (see pages 59–62). Nevertheless, it may be helpful to ask ourselves what the principal characteristics are in the absence of which an experience would not be called "esthetic"—in other words, its principal defining characteristics. The word "esthetic" is admittedly difficult to pin down to a precise meaning, but perhaps the principal necessary condition agreed upon by most or all of those who have reflected about the matter, is the *non-practical* character of the experience. When you are enjoying something esthetically, you are enjoying it "for what it is in itself," not as a means to some further end. You are not thinking of the use to which it can be put, what you can get out of it, or how you can influence others by means of it.

> The painter who, in viewing an expanse of pasture land, observes the gentle curve of the hills, the gradations of light and shade on the grass, the limbs of the trees silhouetted in intricate patterns against the sky, may be said to be viewing the scene esthetically; but not the surveyor who is interested merely in measuring its extent, or the real-estate man whose attentions are confined to estimating its value. The man who seeks a painting because it is rare or expensive, and the woman who prizes a vase because it is antique or because it belonged to her great-grandmother, are not viewing these objects esthetically any more than the person who becomes so obsessed with the nudity of a statue that he fails to regard it as a work of art.[1]

It would surely seem that if this condition at least is not met, there is not much left to distinguish esthetic experiences from other experiences. Many would insist that other conditions also must be met before the experience should be entitled "esthetic," but this one at any rate would seem to constitute the irreducible minimum.

A discussion of the esthetic experience could easily detain us for many pages;[2] but space does not permit entering upon it further here. Assuming that we have some idea of what kind of experiences are called "esthetic," our question is this: What is the relation between esthetic *experiences* and beautiful *objects?* Is every object that arouses esthetic experiences beautiful? If you enjoy something esthetically one day and not the next, is it beautiful one day but not the next? If it arouses esthetic experiences in some persons but not in others, is it beautiful and not beautiful at the same time? Can it be beautiful even if no one has ever had an esthetic experience in the presence of it?

---

[1] J. Hospers, *Meaning and Truth in the Arts* (Chapel Hill: The University of North Carolina Press, 1946), p. 6.

[2] For further analyses of the esthetic experience, see Laurence Buermeyer, *The Esthetic Experience;* Edward Bullough, "Psychical Distance," in M. M. Rader's *A Modern Book of Esthetics;* H. S. Langfeld, *The Esthetic Attitude.*

The moment we ask these questions, we are driven back to the fundamental question, What is beauty? or, less misleadingly, What is the meaning of "beautiful"? When X is beautiful, what sort of property does X have, by virtue of which the adjective "beautiful" is applicable to it?

Here, as in ethics (see pages 450–452), we must be careful to distinguish two kinds of statements: (1) statements about the *meaning* of "beautiful," and (2) statements of fact about the things to which the term "beautiful" applies—such as, for example, what properties always accompany beauty and thus can be used as an indicator of its presence. Theories which try to establish that all objects which are beautiful *also* have properties A, B, C . . . are theories about the concomitants or accompaniments of beauty, not about beauty itself. In this chapter, as in the previous one, we are primarily interested in questions of the first type, and for the same reason: until we know the meaning of "beautiful" we do not know what it is that the properties A, B, C . . . accompany.

The emotive meaning of "beautiful." What, then, is the meaning of "beautiful"? At this point the theories branch out in much the same way as in ethics. But now we can learn some lessons from our discussion of analogous problems in ethics. We need not pause long over the *emotive* meaning of the words "beauty" and "beautiful." Clearly it exists. People say "It's beautiful" when they want to "gush" or "purr," perhaps even more than they say "It's good." That the word "beautiful" is used emotively can hardly be denied. It is used in the ordinary give-and-take of daily conversation to express esthetic feeling and to evoke esthetic feeling in others.[3]

The emotive meaning of the word, then, is easily understood, and everyone who uses it is aware of this function of the word in daily conversation (although most persons have not heard that it is *called* "emotive meaning"). The *cognitive* meaning, by contrast, is extremely difficult to isolate. If you were to ask people, "When you use the word 'beautiful,' what precisely do you mean? Can you please give me a translation? What quality of a thing are you referring to when you call that thing 'beautiful'?" they would simply

---

[3] And sometimes not even *esthetic* feeling. People may speak of a portrait as beautiful when they do not react esthetically to it at all—for example, when it is simply an easily recognizable likeness of someone they know. And a man may speak of a woman as "beautiful" when he is not viewing her esthetically at all but merely finds her sexually desirable.

be nonplussed. Nor would the situation be eased if you said, "When you tell me that X is two feet long I understand what you mean— you are informing me of some fact, or alleged fact. But when you tell me that X is beautiful, of what fact, pray tell, are you inform- ing me?"

There seems little doubt that, whatever cognitive meaning we may be able to elicit from the word "beautiful" in any particular case, it is the emotive meaning which is the *determinant* (see page 481) for the use of the word. If we ask, "What is the common mean- ing which is present in *all* cases of the use of the word?" there does not seem to be any except emotive meaning; in this case the expres- sion and arousal of esthetic feeling (or feelings near enough to the esthetic to be mistaken for it). Whatever may be the objects which arouse this feeling in us, and however unlike each other they may be, and however much the feeling may vary from person to person, what makes us use the word "beautiful" is the fact that we feel a certain way about the things which we so label, and the word "beau- tiful" helps to express and/or evoke this feeling.

Some of us may wish to stop at this point. We may hold that whenever we use the word "beautiful" in a sentence we are *merely* gushing, and never are asserting anything at all—that our meaning is merely emotive and nothing more. But, just as in the case of ethics, most of us will wish to stop short of such a conclusion. What- ever may be our cognitive meaning, and however difficult it may be to isolate, and however unclear we may be about it ourselves, we still want to say that sentences of the form "X is beautiful" do state propositions; and if this is so, we shall still want to know *what* propositions they state. We shall ask, "Emotive meaning aside, what is the cognitive meaning which the word, and the sentences contain- ing the word, convey?"

A. Naturalistic Theories

When we ask, "What do statements of the form 'X is beautiful' mean?" is this the same as asking, "What do people *mean* when they utter statements of the form 'X is beautiful'?" To answer this question, read again pages 74-76 of Chapter 1. Perhaps in esthetics more than anywhere else, we cannot go much by what people *say* they mean: a man may say that when he uses the word "democracy" he means any government in which representatives are elected by the people, and yet in his actual use of the word he may contradict this: he may refer to a nation or group as a democracy even though it fails to satisfy this criterion, or deny that another nation is one even though it does satisfy the criterion. That is, he *doesn't really mean* by the word what he says he does; but on the other hand, he is not deliberately lying either; he simply has not thought the matter through. If you want to know what a person means by a word, watch how he uses it: observe in what contexts he employs it and when he refrains from employing it; notice when he shifts from the use of that word to the use of another one in its place.

This sort of thing happens constantly with "beautiful" and similar words. A man may say in haste, "When I say something is beautiful I just mean I like it," and soon afterward he may be arguing with someone about whether a certain object is beautiful—though if all he means by calling it beautiful is what he says he means, no disagreement with anyone else would ever occur (see pp. 460–461). Now, when we ask, "What is the meaning of statements of the form 'X is beautiful'?" we do indeed want to know what it is that the person who utters these statements means (after all they have no meaning in themselves, as we saw on pages 4–6) provided that this is interpreted as being what he really means, not just what he may say that he means.

According to all naturalistic theories of beauty, "X is beautiful" (in its cognitive aspect) is translatable into some other statement or series of statements. The question is, Into what statement or statements can it be translated?

Objectivistic theories. The kind of view that naturally occurs to us is that when we say that X is beautiful we are ascribing to X some property which it has—some property which all beautiful things have in common. The difficulty, of course, is to discover what this property is. Think of all the things that you would call beautiful, and ask yourself what they all have in common. "Their beauty," you may say—but of course this will not do here: we want a translation of this term, we want to be told what this beauty consists of. And the great difficulty with objectivistic theories is their inability to fix upon some property or properties of which beauty can be said to consist. Take any object you wish; if you call it beautiful, why, by virtue of what, do you call it so? In most cases it will be difficult enough to answer this question; but if you can give an answer in terms of some property of the object, turn then to another object which you also consider beautiful, and ask yourself whether the property in this case is the same. If you consider something beautiful because it has a certain shade of vivid blue, will you call everything else beautiful for the same reason? and will you call everything beautiful that has this shade? will you not call some things beautiful which are not blue at all? The frustrating fact is that no matter what properties of a thing we select as constituting its beauty, we want to call other things beautiful on the basis of other properties. It was once said that what constituted the beauty of rectangular figures was their possession of a certain linear proportion, known as that of the Golden Rectangle. But are all Golden Rectangles beautiful? and is nothing beautiful *except* Golden Rectangles—not colors, not symphonies and poems, which are not visual at all?[4] The Golden Rectangle is unable to cover such cases; and so, for similar reasons, appears to be everything else that we might suggest in its place. Even if there were no other difficulty, there is the well attested fact in esthetic experience that everything depends upon *context:* a certain kind of figure may be beautiful in one total pattern but not in another; a certain color-combination will be just right in one painting but questionable in another. A work of art is a complex interweaving of a tremendous multitude of different elements, each acting upon the other, and the absence or change of any one of them is often enough to alter radically its esthetic value. Is it not then hopeless to isolate one element in an object, or even one group of elements, and say that its beauty consists in this?

One may, indeed, offer more general criteria. "An object is beautiful if it possesses *organic unity:* if it is so arranged that every element in it is necessary to every other element in the total effect, so that the total effect would be destroyed if anything in it were different from what it is."[5] "An object is beautiful if it possesses the

---

[4] One might object further that even if all Golden Rectangles were beautiful and all beautiful things were Golden Rectangles, the property of being beautiful and the property of being a Golden Rectangle are two different properties.

[5] This is the most usual, but not the only, way of defining "organic unity." The discussion of others, however interesting, would be irrelevant here as long as the same objections apply to them.

proper *balance* (in the case of spatial arts) or *development* (in the case of temporal arts)." But here again difficult questions arise: for example, can an object be beautiful and lack organic unity, or have organic unity and yet not be beautiful? (Is it not possible for the entire esthetic effect of an ugly painting to be changed by a change of one detail, just as in the case of a beautiful painting?) Moreover, is organic unity (or any other suggested property) really an objective property of the thing? Two persons might well agree that organic unity constitutes an object's beauty and yet disagree to the end of their lives as to whether this particular object possessed it. Perhaps, then, organic unity depends on the object's *effect* on us, in which case it is not an objective property.

The same difficulty recurs if we say that a *combination* of these properties is what constitutes beauty. How many of them, and in what proportion? And even if this is agreed, may there not still be disagreement about whether they are present in any particular case? The sober fact seems to be that the sources of esthetic satisfaction are infinitely various, defying all codification. There seem to be no properties of which we can honestly say, "If X has these properties (A, B, C . . .), it is beautiful; otherwise not."

Beauty as a capacity. "Clearly," one may say, "there is no objective property which all beautiful things have in common, by virtue of which they are beautiful. But all beautiful things do have something in common, namely their capacity, or *power*, to evoke an esthetic response. This power is the common quality by virtue of which all beautiful things are called beautiful."

What does this mean? Does it mean that X is beautiful if X has the power to evoke in somebody or other, at some time or other, an esthetic response? In the last analysis, there is probably nothing in the world that lacks this power; no matter how many of us find it ugly, somebody or other, in some mood or other, may find it beautiful. "Well, why not? What's wrong with that? Everything, then, is beautiful." But must we not, for consistency, apply the same principle to the ugly, and say that X is ugly if X has the power of esthetically revolting somebody or other at some time or other? And is it not just as probable that everything has this power too? Thus we have two contradictory properties—beauty and ugliness—both possessed by everything; everything is both beautiful and ugly at the same time. Looking back to our discussion of the Law of Non-contradiction (see pages 125–127), one might still ask, "Well, why not? Something can be beautiful in one respect and ugly in another." But the same analysis holds for "the same respect." One person calls a certain pink dress beautiful, and another person calls it ugly, in both cases on account of its color; so the dress is both beautiful and ugly at the same time in respect of its color! The moral is clear: if it is really true that X has a certain property if it has the power to evoke a certain response in somebody at some time, and another property (contradictory of the first) if it has the power to evoke an opposite response in somebody at some time, then (like the hypothetical box that's red and blue all over as was discussed on pages 142–144) X is cluttered with all sorts of mutually contradictory properties, for without doubt X does have the power to evoke all these varied responses.

Transition to subjectivistic theories. After this watered-down version of objectivism, one may feel that we have been on the wrong track all along. "Beauty," we may exclaim, "is obviously not an objective property at all." The following suggestion may then appear attractive to us: " 'X is beautiful' is not like 'X is round.' A thing can't be both round and not round at the same time. If Smith says it's round and Jones insists it isn't, they can't both be right. But consider some other sentences, such as 'X is interesting,' 'X is stimulating,' 'X is strange.' X may be both interesting and not interesting at the same time—that is, it may interest you but not me. Terms like 'interesting' are relational terms: to make a sentence containing them meaningful you have to specify not only what the thing is that interests but who it is that is interested. To say merely 'X is interesting' simply prompts the question, 'Interesting *to whom?*' Perhaps X is interesting to Smith but not to Jones; in that case the statement 'X is interesting to Smith' will be true, and so will the statement 'X is not interesting to Jones'; but simply to say 'X is interesting' is neither true nor false but meaningless (unless it contains an implied reference to Smith, or to Jones, or to most people in a given society, and the like). Like 'X is greater than,' it is an *uncompleted* statement. In the same vein, I suggest that 'X is beautiful' is an uncompleted statement and should be amended to read 'X is beautiful to Smith' or 'X is beautiful to Jones,' or to some other person or group."

As we shall see, this characterization does not apply to all subjectivistic theories. However, let us explore the possibility of such an analysis.

Subjectivistic theories. When X evokes in me an esthetic response, I am inclined to say that X is beautiful. This response is (whatever else it may be) my chief *motivation* for uttering the sentence, "X is beautiful." From this fact, I may be tempted to conclude (though the conclusion does not logically follow) that *what I am saying* when I say that X is beautiful is simply that I respond to X in this way.

1. "X is beautiful" = "I *like* X." On this interpretation, "X is beautiful" requires completion—one must specify who does the liking. "X is beautiful to Smith" (according to this view) means the same as "Smith likes X" and "X is not beautiful to Jones" means the same as "Jones does not like X."

This possibility can surely be ruled out from the start. Liking is much too general: you may like something, yet never think of calling it beautiful. You may like it for a multitude of reasons which have nothing to do with its beauty: you may like a piece of furniture because it cost a great deal, or because you enjoy showing it off to your friends, or because it is very old, or because it is comfortable to sit in; yet none of these things would make you call it beautiful. So let us amend the formulation.

2. "X is beautiful" = "I *esthetically enjoy* X" (or esthetically respond to X, or am esthetically moved by X). Again, the person who enjoys it determines X's beauty for that person. If Smith enjoys it, the statement "X is beautiful to Smith" is true, and if Jones does not, the statement "X is beautiful to Jones" is false.

This version, at least, makes it clear that the response to X is esthetic. It is analogous to the version we considered in ethics (see pages 461–463) according to which "X is right" means the same as "I approve X." And the same objections apply to it. We may review a few of them here, emphasizing those that loom particularly large in esthetics.

(1) If this theory is true, all you have to do to know whether X is beautiful is introspect and find out whether you really respond to it esthetically at the moment when you put the question to yourself. This difficulty, great enough in ethics, is still more pressing in esthetics: moral approvals as a rule do not vacillate with great rapidity, but people's esthetic enjoyment from any given object tends

to vary with one's mood, environment, and other preoccupations. You may enjoy your favorite symphony more each time you hear it, *provided* that you don't hear it, say, ten or twenty times a day; few, if any, works of art can be fully appreciated when you are constantly exposed to them. Or, you may just get bored, or be in the wrong mood. But if you enjoy it at 10 o'clock and don't enjoy it at 11, and perhaps enjoy it again at 6, according to the theory it was beautiful at 10, not at 11, and beautiful again at 6. (Not just that it *seemed* beautiful—this *is* roughly the same as saying you esthetically enjoyed it—but that it *was,* or *is,* beautiful at 6 but not at 11.)

Moreover, is there no such thing as improvement or progress in matters of esthetic sensibility? At first you were very fond of Tschaikovsky and only moderately fond of Bach and Mozart. Then as you heard them more you became somewhat weary of Tschaikovsky—strains that had moved you before came to strike you as being melodramatic and exhibitionistic; even some of Brahms began to pall on you after repeated exposures; but you found new subtleties of feeling in Mozart, who had seemed merely bright and superficial before, and Bach, who had just seemed pompous and bewildering, now moved you to great depths. You feel, and on comparing notes with others who have listened to music a great deal you find that they feel too, that this change is an *improvement,* that your esthetic taste is *better* now than it was when you began. After all, if training is required in mastering the sciences, is not the same true in the arts? Is the judgment of a person who is just beginning to enjoy the arts to be accepted right alongside, and equally with, that of the experienced observer, a Bernhard Berenson or a Sir Donald Tovey, who have spent a lifetime in the appreciation of an art? Yet according to the present theory, none of this is true: when you say it is beautiful you are saying only that you, now, esthetically enjoy it.

(2) As in the case of the corresponding view in ethics, the statements "It's beautiful but I don't enjoy it" and "I enjoy it but I wonder whether it's beautiful" would be self-contradictory. And yet are not statements of this kind often made? In the first case, you may honestly think there is something missing in your enjoyment—something in the work of art that you "aren't getting"; and in the

second, you may feel that your enjoyment is misplaced, that it may be the result of irrelevant associations, and so on.

(3) The view entails also that people do not disagree on esthetic matters. Some persons may be more willing to accept this consequence in esthetics than in ethics; there are those who say that in esthetics "It's all a matter of 'I enjoy it, you don't'" whereas in ethics there is genuine right and wrong independent of one's tastes. But even in esthetics many thoughtful persons will balk at this theory: if, after being slow to appreciate the poetry of Shakespeare, and having now caught the fire of his lines, the incisiveness of his perceptions, the endless stream of full, rich metaphors, they encounter someone who says in an offhand manner that Shakespeare is no good, they are likely to reply: "But he is!" and here begins an argument. Are the opponents here really not disagreeing? Surely the burden of proof rests upon him who says this!

3. Let us then revise the statement to read "The *majority of persons* (presumably of all of the human race) esthetically enjoy X (perhaps not always, but usually)." On this view, as on all the subjectivistic theories to be considered from this point on, it will not be possible to say that X is both beautiful and not beautiful, beautiful to one person (or group) and not to another; the beauty of X is being identified with the majority's esthetic response to X, and the majority either do respond esthetically to X or they do not. (A Gallup poll might decide this.) "The majority respond esthetically to X" and "The majority do not respond esthetically to X" cannot both be true. (However, these theories are still subjectivistic, because an object's being beautiful or not beautiful depends not on the object itself but on the response of human beings to it.)

In this theory once again familiar difficulties meet us. (1) Is the minority report self-contradictory? (Read again the corresponding section in ethics, pages 463–464.) (2) Are the majority enlightened? If the majority enjoy the verses of Edgar Guest, does this make them beautiful? May not a minority perceive excellence in a work of art which the majority, without training and often without sensitivity, entirely miss? Is it any more appropriate to judge a work of art by majority consensus than it is a work of science? Persons may sometimes, to defend their esthetic judgments, appeal to the fact that a large number of others, perhaps the majority of those acquainted with the work, share their tastes and would make the same

esthetic judgments about it. But when forced to the wall, they would
very likely say that the concurrence of the majority is an *accompanying* rather than a defining characteristic of the beauty of a
work—that the concurrence reflects the excellence of the work and
the perceptiveness of the public. Put the same person in the minority, and he will not give up his view just because the majority is
against him.

4. One might change the statement to read "The majority of
esthetically sensitive persons enjoy X"—though there are doubtless
many esthetically sensitive persons whose sensitivities have never
been brought out by training, and hence cannot make mature esthetic judgments, if indeed they make any such judgments at all.
Or one might say "The majority of esthetically *trained* persons"—
but not all trained persons have esthetic sensitivity, and for them
a study of the arts becomes merely a study in terms, names, periods,
and so on, and this would hardly qualify them to judge. So let us
say, "The majority of esthetically sensitive *and* esthetically trained
human beings enjoy X."

This criterion selects from the human race a certain class: not a
very definite class, for one must still ask *how* much training, and
how esthetically sensitive. Yet many will feel that an improvement
has been made. Some people are fit by temperament and training to
judge; perhaps *their* majority judgment is the meaning of "X is
beautiful."

It is very difficult, however, to keep this criterion from being
question-begging. Perhaps one could ascertain, through checking up
on people's backgrounds, whether they had been esthetically trained
or not: even here one would be tempted to say of a person whose
tastes clashed with his own that the person hadn't been trained
properly or hadn't been *really* trained, and thus discount his vote.
But "esthetically sensitive" is particularly vulnerable. Who are the
esthetically sensitive people, and who is to judge who they are?
There is an almost irresistible temptation to say that those who
agree with you are "sensitive" and that others are Philistines, charlatans, or boors.

But let us assume that the impossible, or at any rate the difficult,
has been achieved and the esthetically sensitive persons have been
selected. One then agrees that if the majority of them oppose his
own judgment, he will defer to them and say, "I was wrong—it *is* a

beautiful concerto even though I think it's ghastly." Let us then ask, Isn't it possible, isn't it even *logically* possible, that the majority of even these people might be wrong? Might they not be wrong at least on some particular occasion? Haven't the critics and sensitive persons in general in one age sometimes looked down upon a great work of art, only to have succeeding generations revere it as among the finest, as in the case of El Greco? And who is to say that this couldn't happen today?

5. One might then revise the formulation to read, "The majority of sensitive persons, past *and* present, esthetically enjoy X." This gives a certain backing from the past to counteract any eccentric or lunatic-fringe tendencies that the present may have.

Aside from the impossibility of taking a poll about the past—we would have to rely only on those trained and sensitive individuals who wrote about the work of art in question, and, moreover, whose work has been preserved for posterity—it does not help us with the art of the present. Is the favorable judgment of the five people who have seen a painting completed yesterday a guarantee of its beauty?

6. Suppose we revise it again and say, "The majority of sensitive and trained persons, past, present, *and future*, enjoy (did enjoy, will enjoy) X esthetically."

One consequence of this, of course, is that since the future is indefinitely long we shall never know whether a given work is beautiful or not because we shall never know how the majority of esthetically trained and sensitive persons, including the future, will feel about it.

One might, however, accept this verdict: "We can only guess; now, especially with contemporary art, we just *don't know* whether it is really beautiful or not. Only time will tell. At least now we know what our judgment *means;* what we don't know is whether it is *true.* But the same holds of any judgment that involves the future."

But even here a curious consequence develops. Suppose I say, "I want to know *now* whether it is beautiful. This painting was finished yesterday. All those who have seen it thought it was beautiful. The future may not bear me out, so—I shall destroy it now! Thus there will *be* no future to refute my judgment." It is beautiful if it is destroyed now—but it may not be if it is kept for the future! Is this not a strange consequence? It is the same painting either way!

Does the truth of a judgment of its beauty really depend on how many people view it? Yet this consequence has pervaded all the subjectivistic theories thus far. Can it be amended?

7. We can say that "X is beautiful = The majority of sensitive persons, past, present, and future enjoy (did enjoy, will enjoy) it esthetically, and *would* enjoy (or have enjoyed) it esthetically *if* they were (or had been) brought into repeated contact with it."

Thus, even a contemporary painting, to be beautiful, *would* have been esthetically enjoyed by the majority of trained and sensitive persons of the past; and esthetically trained and sensitive persons today *would* enjoy esthetically all beautiful works of art *if* they were repeatedly exposed to them, and so would those of the future. All these hypothetical votes must be counted in the final poll which determines the majority.

This remedies our difficulty. Even if you destroy your painting now, it is condemned as long as the esthetically trained and sensitive persons who never did see it *would* have failed to give it a favorable verdict *if* they had seen it. Your destroying it makes no difference to its beauty. (Indeed, the painting's beauty would be unaffected even if there were no esthetically trained and sensitive persons in the world, never had been, and never would be. The statement would still be, *if* there were, *then* they would. . . .)

But we have paid an enormous price for the solution of our difficulty. It is difficult enough to count the votes of the present, and impossible in all but a few recorded cases of the past, and logically impossible with the future (i.e., to count it *now*); but what of the multitude of hypothetical cases—past, present, and future—of esthetically trained and sensitive persons who *would* enjoy it esthetically *if* they were repeatedly exposed to it? This includes persons who never existed and never will—it is enough that *if* they exist and grow up into trained and sensitive persons, *then* they will esthetically enjoy . . . and so on.

B. Non-naturalism

Many persons will wish to rebel against all these shiftings and re-formulations. What all subjectivistic theories forget (they would say) is the *object*, X, which is the cause of all the esthetic experiences in the first place. It is the object that we call beautiful; it is not our attitude toward it that makes it so. When we assert that something is beautiful, we mean that *that thing* is beautiful. If we apprehend its beauty, we have esthetic feelings, but when we say it is beautiful we are not talking about our feelings, but about the thing that evokes them. Common sense assumes that when we call X beautiful we are talking about X and not about ourselves; the man in the street would probably laugh at you if you said that a statement about something being beautiful (insofar as it was a statement at all and not a mere expression and/or evocation of feeling) was really a statement about yourself or about yourself plus others. It is the object that is beautiful, and it would be beautiful even if no human beings had esthetic experiences in its presence. So far the objectivists are correct; but they err in trying to identify beauty with non-esthetic properties. The truth is that the object has a property, beauty, which is uniquely esthetic and simply different from all other properties in the universe.

> The property in question is the property of being beautiful. This property is the differentiating property of esthetic objects. Beauty is directly apprehended by the mind in just the same way as shape is directly apprehended, and esthetic value is no more a characteristic of the apprehension of beauty or of the state of mind involved in such apprehension, than squareness is a characteristic of the apprehension of squareness or of the state of mind involved in such apprehension. Esthetic emotion is a mental process which accompanies the apprehension of beauty, as fear is a process which accompanies the apprehension of a tiger.[6]

An object may evoke in me an esthetic feeling, but my judgment is not about the feeling; it is not even about the object's power over me, but about a property of the *object that wields that power.*

> When I attribute beauty to an object the tribute seems to be wrung from me by the object, and if on reflection I conclude that I have misapprehended the object, I am unable to retain the attribution . . . I cannot at pleasure give it, withhold it, or change it. Under the influence of a mood beauty may lose its savor, but not its beauty; in a reflective person the judgment remains the same so long as the object does.[7]

[6] C. E. M. Joad, "The Limits of Psychology in Esthetics," in *Proceedings of the Aristotelian Society,* Supplementary Vol. XI, 1932, pp. 209–210.

[7] T. E. Jessop, "The Definition of Beauty," *Proceedings of the Aristotelian Society,* Vol. 33, 1932–3, pp. 161. 165.

It is in the esthetic *judgment* that I pronounce the object to be beautiful. Esthetic feelings may, and usually do, *precede* and *accompany* this judgment; but even this is not required. I can truly judge that X is beautiful without feeling any esthetic emotion. It would be less plausible, perhaps, to say that I can truly judge X to be beautiful even though *under no conditions* would I or anyone else have esthetic feelings toward it; that would cut off X's beauty from esthetic feeling entirely; but surely I can truly judge X to be beautiful even though at the moment I may not have any feeling at all toward X: I may be tired of it, at least temporarily, or I may be worried about something else (but still recognize it as the sort of object that would under *other* conditions arouse esthetic feelings), or I may be passing hastily through the museum and not take the time to enjoy the painting esthetically, yet recognize it as beautiful and judge it as such; or I may even admit that I have a "blind spot" esthetically and that others can experience its beauty, though I cannot because I cannot overcome certain unpleasant associations connected with it, though I can still perform the judgment. What the object must win from me is a *judgment* of its beauty; "whatever else it wins is largely a matter of accident, the accident of association, of mood, and of taste." [8]

What is the relation of the perceiving mind to beauty? The mind does not in any sense *create* an object's beauty; it *discovers* the beauty which is there. It would be there even if we did not find it: it is there in objects at the bottom of the ocean or in the starry heavens beyond the reach of telescopes. Indeed, it may be present in many objects around us, even though we have been too blind to see it. Mountains would be no less beautiful for the fact (if indeed it is a fact) that no one discovered their beauty until the eighteenth century. Perhaps there is beauty in objects we see every day to which none of us has yet been receptive.

Beauty, then, is an objective property of things; but it is not the kind of property which the objectivists of the naturalistic variety allege. They try to equate it with some natural property or group of such properties, and this simply cannot be done. Just as we said in the case of ethics (see page 458), no matter which such property or properties we select, we can still sensibly ask the question, "I admit that X has this property, but is X beautiful?" Beauty is a quality

[8] Jessop, *loc. cit.*

which is absolutely unique, and hence the word naming it is not definable in terms of any other properties. Indeed, it is not a property whose presence empirical investigation can discover.

Does not this very fact condemn it? Not unless one holds that empirically discoverable properties are the only ones there are. But there are unpleasant reminders of points we have discussed before. The existence of an objective property is being asserted; yet, since none of the tests of objectivity are fulfilled (see pages 342, 417), what is there to back up such a claim? Moreover, what is one to do in cases of disagreement? One person insists that X is beautiful and another denies it. How are we to decide? Unless we know what property of X to look for, how are we ever going to find it? Must our disagreement remain forever unresolved? There *is* genuine disagreement about beauty according to the present theory, and thus far it coincides with common sense; Smith says that X is beautiful and Jones says it isn't, and they are disagreeing about whether X possesses this unique property, beauty. The difficulty is not that the theory does away with disagreement, as some attitude theories do; rather it is that there is disagreement but no way in which to resolve it—and, it would seem to many, no way in which to resolve it because it is left a deep dark mystery *what* the property is which all the disagreement is about.

And so the present view, like the analogous one in ethics, leads directly into *intuitionism*. X has a property, but not an empirically discoverable property, namely its beauty; by what means are we then to discover its presence? Presumably by intuition: we simply intuit that the property is present in a particular case. And, however unavoidable this view may be, it is attended with all the usual difficulties (see pages 149–152).

The argument from uniformity. At this point an appeal is often made to an alleged empirical fact: the uniformity of esthetic judgments. "When people begin to enjoy objects of nature and works of art esthetically," it runs, "there is admittedly a great difference from person to person. One likes this, another likes that; and as a result they make snap judgments of the form 'X is beautiful' which disagree violently with each other. But as people's tastes mature, their judgments tend to converge toward one another. The person who didn't think much of Beethoven's music comes, on closer acquaintance, to share the judgment of the persons with whom he disagreed. It takes time, of course; but it does occur. Even with the most sensitive and trained individuals, of course, there is not complete unanimity; but this is only to say that none of us is perfect: seeing beauty with perfect accuracy is beyond human powers—but there is an increasing *convergence* of opinion, with increase in one's esthetic powers; and this convergence, if continued beyond the point of which we human beings are capable, *would* end in complete unanimity. We cannot of course expect so much; but there *is* progress, there is advance: people who enjoyed only James Whitcomb Riley before and now enjoy Shakespeare either admit that they were mistaken in their previous judgment, or admit that the former judgment was not even an esthetic one and that they mistakenly thought it was. Taste has its ups and downs, but when you examine the whole history of the arts through the past four thousand years, you are struck not so much by the disagreement as by the agreement among esthetic judgments: the same works of art, by and large, that have been considered the great masterpieces throughout the centuries (except sometimes in the age of their creation, a period when it is always dangerous to judge) are still considered so today. There is a uniformity in taste, accumulating throughout the ages, which shows that esthetic judgments in the long run are more stable and enduring than judgments in science, in politics, in morals, in perhaps anything else."

Thus runs the argument from uniformity. Some of the facts alleged in it could easily be contested: increased acquaintance with a work of art often leads to increased disagreement rather than a closer approach to agreement.[9] But the principal question about it that concerns us here is this: Can this argument be used in support of the theory we are now considering? And it seems quite plain that it cannot. *Suppose* that there were no uniformity of taste, or considerably less than there is now (considerably less, at any rate, than the proponents of the above argument allege that there is); would those who hold to the unique property theory take this as in any way damaging to their position? No—they would say precisely what they say now when there is disparity of taste between themselves and their opponents: namely, that the beauty is there all the same

---

[9] For a list of examples of this, see Bernard C. Heyl, *New Bearings in Esthetics and Art Criticism.* New Haven: Yale University Press, 1943. pp. 97–102.

but that most people are so esthetically blind that they cannot see it. The disparity of taste would be attributed to the stupidity or esthetic degeneracy of the opponents. But if the majority *can* be wrong, what guarantee is there that the majority view is right? If the absence of uniformity would not be interpreted as damaging to the theory, how could the presence of uniformity be interpreted as strengthening it?

The conclusion seems inevitable: the argument from uniformity has no bearing one way or the other upon our question. It cannot be used to support the esthetic non-naturalist's case. And the sensitive spot in his armor still remains: how are disagreements, whether many or few, to be resolved? In time, perhaps, with artistic criticism, education, persuasion, perhaps needling and bullying, disagreements may be reduced to a minimum; but even if they could be eliminated entirely and absolutely everyone agreed on what was beautiful, the question would still remain *how they knew*, and by what criterion they could tell. And this once again raises the familiar questions about the nature of intuiting and of the unique property whose presence is allegedly intuited.[10]

II. PROBLEMS OF ART

Esthetics is concerned with judgments of *esthetic value*. We have used the word "beauty" instead of "esthetic value" in order to have one simple word analogous to the word "good" in ethics; moreover, the word "good" is often used in esthetics to refer to esthetic value, and this would have complicated our account of esthetics with the same word we used in ethics. (We are just as likely, for example, to say "The sonata is *good*" as to say "The sonata is *beautiful*," but the word "good," as we saw in Chapter 7, has many usages, and in a sentence such as the above we are using it in an *esthetic* sense. "Is X (esthetically) good?" means "Is X esthetically valuable?") But the use of the word "beautiful" could easily be contested. For example, one might hold that X has esthetic value (is esthetically good) but *not* that X is beautiful. He might use the word "beauty" to stand for some particular *kind* of esthetic value, instead of for esthetic value in general. He might say that Picasso's "Guernica"

---

[10] For a clear and detailed analysis of theories of beauty, see Harold Osborne, *Theory of Beauty* (London: Routledge & Kegan Paul, 1952).

has esthetic value but is not beautiful. In the first section of this chapter we were concerned with arguments about esthetic value. This is the same as beauty in the *broad* sense of the term; in the *narrow* sense, the word "beauty" is reserved for some special type or species of esthetic value (*which* type, depends on the particular writer who is using the term)—and in this sense, of course, a work may have esthetic value even though that esthetic value is not of the special kind named by the word "beauty."

Continuing now to use "beauty" and "beautiful" in the broad sense, let us consider the question, What is the relation of beauty (esthetic value) to *art?* Is art the sole (or even the principal) locus of beauty, or is beauty to be found in nature as well? and if so, are the beauties of different kinds? And if beauty is found in art, is the sole function of art to produce beautiful objects, or has art other functions as well? Here we are concerned, strictly speaking, not with esthetics but with the *philosophy of art.*

The term "art." "Art" is a term of which definitions are almost inevitably persuasive (pages 71–73). The word "art" has a favorable emotive meaning—at least to those who practice the arts and talk about them—and thus anyone who has cherished ideals on the subject will want to use the word "art" to denote whatever kind of product he venerates most highly. Semantically, this makes the situation extremely confused though of course it is quite understandable. Thus, at one extreme, Tolstoy said that whatever works of art, so-called, did not express simple and profound emotions which could communicate themselves easily to all mankind and thus promote the brotherhood of man, were "false art"; and at the other extreme, Clive Bell has said that art has nothing to do with the life of humanity, that in approaching it one should leave all memories of life behind and view it as a realm of pure form, and that any work which fails to satisfy this approach is "not really art." Both of these, needless to say, are persuasive definitions of "art," "false art" being whatever does not live up to the writer's stipulative definition of the term "art."

As opposed to these persuasive definitions, there are fairly neutral ways in which the word "art" is used. (1) In its broadest descriptive sense, art is opposed to nature: a work of art is anything which exists as a result of human effort and contrivance (perhaps that of animals as well), as opposed to "nature as we find it." It may have no esthetic interest at all, yet it is a work of art in this broad sense. Bonfires, tractors, paintings, cities, and piles of garbage are all works of art in this sense.

(2) In a somewhat narrower sense, the arts are the "cultural subject-matters": thus, we speak of a Bachelor of Arts degree, and the arts here include all the natural sciences, history, philosophy, and all the subjects for which a candidate for the B. A. would ordinarily get credit. It excludes those subjects specifically designed for certain professions, such as stenography, medicine, engineering, and the like.

(3) In a narrower sense still, the arts include only works in those media which produce *esthetic* effects, for example, *every* painting is a work of art, regardless of its merit. (In a eulogistic or persuasive sense, only those paintings which fulfill certain criteria, whether Tolstoy's or Bell's or somebody else's, are works of art.)

Even here there is a distinction, albeit a vague one. There are the *fine* arts and the *practical* arts. The practical arts have some practical end in view, some function to fulfil in the business of daily life regardless of their esthetic value: for example, weaving, costume design, engraving, woodworking, glass making, and most architecture. Since each of these arts is capable of considerable esthetic effect, however, it is usual to call them "art" even in the esthetic sense we are now considering; while at the same time they are distinguished from the "fine arts," which fulfil no practical end but are cultivated primarily or entirely for purposes of esthetic appreciation: for example, music, literature, sculpture, painting.

The fine arts are usually classified according to their respective media: (1) Visual arts—or the arts of space. (2) Auditory art—music in its various forms. Here what is apprehended is not a group of simultaneously existing objects or colors and shapes in space, but a temporal succession of sounds. Many differences arise in the analysis of these arts because of a difference in their medium. (3) Symbolic arts: literature. The medium here is words and their meanings. The words alone are not sufficient: when uttered aloud, they are merely sounds (not even musical sounds), and when seen on paper, they are mere ink-marks, capable of esthetic contemplation as objects of graphic art (such as penmanship and typography) but hardly as literature. The beauty of the printed ink-marks makes no difference to the merit of the poem (although it may make the poem more enjoyable to read), but that of the marks on the canvas makes all the difference to the painting. (4) Arts of theatre. These employ no new medium but combine two or more of the other three. Drama combines the visual (stage design) with literature (the dialogue), opera combines all three, ballet combines the visual with music, and so on.

Many problems and distinctions arise when one begins to think and talk about the arts. Only a few of them can be listed here.

1. *Aspects of works of art.* Many writers employ a threefold division of the aspects of works of art: material (also called sensuous or surface), formal, and associational. Without attempting strict definitions, let us attempt very briefly to characterize them. (There are, of course, other possible divisions.)

(1) *The material aspect.* "When we find delight in the surface texture of an object, in hearing the sheer volume or the quality of a sound, or in noting the saturation or hue of some color," [11] we are responding to the material aspect. For example, a considerable part of our enjoyment from sculpture lies in the material—whether it be wood, stone, brass, marble, ivory, jade, or clay—from which the object is made. The esthetic enjoyment derived from jewels is chiefly of this kind. It is the most elementary and the most readily enjoyed of the types of esthetic value.

(2) *The formal aspect* is the one to which we respond in the contemplation of *relations* among the various elements in a work of art. Our enjoyment of a melody is principally the enjoyment of the relationships of tones to each other; single tones produce but little esthetic effect. Most paintings are highly complex structures of lines, colors, and masses, from whose mutual relations perhaps the chief esthetic satisfaction in visual art is to be drawn. This kind of esthetic value is not as easily appreciated as the others, but in the opinion of most of those who have studied the arts over a long period of time, it is the most enduring source of esthetic satisfaction once the appreciation of it has been developed.

(3) *The associational aspect* is different from both of the other kinds in that an appreciation of it is not an appreciation of something perceived in the work of art, but of something *conveyed by* it. Here we enjoy something that is not in the perceived object—

[11] Hunter Mead, *An Introduction to Esthetics* (New York: The Ronald Press, 1952), p. 84.

something read into the work rather than directly perceived in it. The recognition of a figure in a painting as a representation of Louis XIV, for example, is associational, unlike the esthetic effect to be derived from the relations of line and color. Whenever we say "The music is *triumphant,*" "The painting is religious in its feeling," "This play expresses the idea that man is a contemptible little animal," and the like, we are responding associationally.

The principal dispute in this region of the philosophy of art has to do with the comparative importance of these sources of esthetic response. Specifically, the dispute is between the formalists (who admit only the first two, with emphasis upon the second) and the associationists (who admit all three, with emphasis upon the third). The associationists hold that the chief esthetic value to be derived from works of art is the appreciation of the emotions expressed, the objects represented, and the ideas conveyed. The formalists hold that the enjoyment of these things is "not really esthetic" at all, and that the distinctively esthetic values are apprehended only when we derive our satisfaction from the intricate relationships of line and color, tones and harmonies, rhythms and cadences, in a work of art. Whereas the associationist might say of the first movement of Mozart's G Minor Symphony (No. 40) that it begins with a sprightly theme, gay and bouncing yet tinged with melancholy, as if the composer's joy were tempered with grief . . ., the formalist would find his satisfaction in the contemplation of the interweaving of the various themes and variations in the total structure of the movement:

I. *Exposition*	II. *Development*	III. *Recapitulation*
a1, a1	d1	a1, a1
a2	d2	a2 (extended)
bridge passage	d3	bridge passage
b1, b1	returning passage	b1, b1
b2		b2
bridge passage		bridge passage
c1, c1		c1, c1
c2		c2
c3		coda

The associationist would be interested primarily in the general mood evoked by a landscape painting, a hint of melancholy perhaps, a tinge of autumn in the air, the effect of the waning afternoon sun-

light on the reeds and water; the formalist meanwhile would derive
his principal enjoyment of the painting from viewing it as an inter-
play of forms—the curve of the hill here matching (but not exactly)
the curve of a cloud there, the rhythm of certain color-patterns
progressing from one end of the painting to another until stopped
by a massive form just at the edge, the total balance (satisfying
yet not perfectly symmetrical), the size and shape of the space here
between these two forms in relation to other sizes and shapes of
spaces between other forms in the painting, and so on.

To some it seems that these two sources of satisfaction necessarily
impede and conflict with each other [12]—that a tension is set up between them so great that if the one is there we cannot easily con-
centrate upon the other. To others it seems that the two are not in
opposition at all [13]—rather, that one must study them separately
for a time and then "fuse" them together, and that the ultimate in
esthetic experience occurs not in enjoying the formal aspect alone,
nor yet the associational aspect alone, but in the two together, so
closely related that in our response to the work of art we are not
aware of them as distinct entities at all: the two are transformed
as in a chemical compound rather than a mere mixture.

There are many controversies connected with this basic issue
into which we cannot enter here. Let us only stop to ask very briefly
a few typical questions:

First, do the two kinds of appreciation conflict? This seems surely
to be a question about what different observers of art feel—a question in descriptive psychology. Briefly, the answer would seem to
be something as unexciting as this: "Some people can enjoy the two
together and some can't."

Second, which source of esthetic satisfaction is more important?
Here again the question is not clear. Does it mean "Which affords
a more intense esthetic experience?" (and in this case, to whom does
it afford it?) or perhaps "Which is the more lasting in its esthetic
effects upon the observer?" Like so many questions, this one must
be made more specific before it can be answered intelligibly at all.

Third, is the controversy between formalists and associationists
a verbal one? The formalist says that the appreciation of the asso-

---

[12] See, for example, Roger Fry, *Transformations* (London: Chatto & Win-
dus, 1926).
[13] See, for example, L. A. Reid, *A Study in Esthetics* (New York: Macmillan, 1931).

ciational aspect of art is "not truly esthetic"; is he doing more than refusing to use the word "esthetic" to apply to something for which other people *do* use the word? Insofar as he is doing this, the controversy is surely a verbal one. But it is not therefore trivial; for by doing this he is calling attention to a source of satisfaction which is very likely to go unappreciated, one which, perhaps far more than most people are aware, is or can be so different from anything that the associative aspect of art can give that the two should not be put under the same heading by being given the same name. (See pages 21–22.)

2. *The function of art.* Some say that the function of art is to provide esthetic experiences (whether by means of all, or only some, of the sources just listed). Others say that the function of art is *not merely* to provide esthetic experiences but also (1) to evoke emotions (other than esthetic emotions),[14] or (2) to represent objects and situations from life, or (3) to wield a moral influence upon individuals or upon society, in favor of some particular code of ethics or some social or economic theory.

Many volumes have been written defending and attacking these different views of the function of art. We cannot go into the matter further here; let us only stop to ask ourselves, What kind of a dispute is this? If the function of a thing is what it actually does, then the answer seems to be that works of art do all of these things— some doing more of one and some more of another. But the dispute would usually be interpreted as being one about what works of art *ought* to do. Thus interpreted, the answer depends upon our answer to the general question about the meaning of judgments involving the word "ought"—and whether the word "ought" is here being used in a moral sense or in some other sense.

Or the issue may be represented as being one about the "purpose," or the "true purpose," of art. But, as we saw earlier (page 185), a purpose implies someone to have the purpose. In this case, the answer would have to be given in terms of what purpose the artist had in creating this particular work of art. Thus interpreted, there

---

[14] It is more usual to say *"express* emotions." But the word "express" is very misleading. More often than not the phrase "expression of emotions" stands for a process which takes place in the *artist,* not the audience. Here we are concerned, however, with the effect of works of art on the audience, and so for the sake of clarity we speak of *evoking* emotions. These emotions may or may not be of the same kind as those which the artist has expressed.

can hardly be a single answer to the question. Different artists have different purposes in mind, and some of them probably create as if by divine inspiration without any conscious purpose in mind at all.

3. Perhaps the most fruitful and challenging kind of enterprise in the philosophy of art lies in the detailed analysis of meaning— the meanings of terms used specifically in the arts, terms which are incessantly used in discussion but not often clarified. One such term, "beautiful," we have already considered in some detail. But there are others which, from the point of view of both the artist and the student of art, count at least as heavily: "style," "technique," "meaning," "form," "content," "expression," "classic," "romantic," "realistic," "naturalistic," and so forth. Many confusions and misapprehensions can result, even in a comparatively simple discussion of the arts, if such terms as these are not clarified. Consider, for example, the term "form": [15] people say "I don't care about the form, I only care about what it says," "If the subject-matter of a poem is not what makes it a good poem, it must be the form," and so on. But the term "form" is an elusive one. Sometimes by "form" we mean shape: we say that two pennies have the same form although they have different "matter." Sometimes we mean a species or class: thus, we speak of two compositions as both being in the sonata *form*. Sometimes we have reference to a mode of arrangement of things as opposed to the things that are so arranged: thus, three rhyming lines of poetry could be put in the orders ABC, ACB, BAC, BCA, CAB, or CBA, though the lines thus ordered are the same in each case. Sometimes we refer to the "how" as opposed to the "what": we take the underlying idea or theme of a work of art to be the content (the what), and the way in which it is expressed by the artist (the how) is called the form. Here is an example of how confusions can arise: a person is convinced that it is not the theme which an artist selects for treatment, but rather how he treats this theme, that determines the merit of a work of art: the how and not the what, the form and not the matter. He then feels himself committed to the view that only the form (in *another* sense of the word, though he is unaware of this) of a work of art is important (primarily the arrangement of its lines and colors) and that the other elements such as we have called the "associative" are of no

[15] See, for example, L. A. Reid, *A Study in Esthetics,* Chapter 7; Morris Weitz. *Philosophy of the Arts,* Chapter 3.

relevance at all. This conclusion, of course, is unwarranted; the mood the artist has created in his painting has just as much to do with his treatment of the theme as does the formal arrangement of its elements. But, through confusion in the use of the viciously ambiguous term "form," he may not know this.

We cannot enter here upon the analysis of these central terms in the philosophy of art. The analysis of them would be analogous to our analysis of terms like "cause," "vitalism," and others in previous chapters, but since their significance is only for the philosophy of art, books on these topics should be consulted for an extended treatment of them. They are surely of the very first importance: at least, if one's purpose is to think clearly about issues that arise when one studies the arts, that purpose can be most efficiently achieved by working diligently on such analyses. In spite of the large amount of literature in this field, most of the work remains to be done: the field of esthetics is one which is just beginning to be cultivated.

SELECTED READINGS FOR CHAPTER 8

Hunter Mead. *An Introduction to Esthetics*. New York: The Ronald Press, 1952.

E. F. Carritt. *What Is Beauty?* London: Oxford University Press, 1931.

W. T. Stace. *The Meaning of Beauty*. London: The Cayme Press, 1929.

Harold Osborne. *Theory of Beauty*. London: Routledge & Kegan Paul, 1952.

George Santayana. *The Sense of Beauty*. New York: Scribners, 1896.

John Dewey. *Art as Experience*. New York: Minton Balch & Co., 1934.

R. G. Collingwood. *The Principles of Art*. Oxford: Clarendon Press, 1938.

Eliseo Vivas and Murray Krieger. *The Problems of Esthetics*. New York: Rinehart & Co., 1953.

M. M. Rader (ed.). *A Modern Book of Esthetics*. 2nd ed. New York: Henry Holt & Co., 1952.

Ethel M. Bartlett. *Types of Esthetic Judgment*. London: Allen & Unwin, 1937.

John Hospers. *Meaning and Truth in the Arts*. Chapel Hill: University of North Carolina Press, 1946.

Louis A. Reid. *A Study in Esthetics*. New York: Macmillan, 1931.

Morris Weitz. *Philosophy of the Arts*. Cambridge: Harvard University Press, 1950.

W. Elton. *Essays in Esthetics and Language*. Oxford: Basil Blackwell, 1953.

EXERCISES

1. It is often not clear from the accounts of writers about beauty whether their theory concerns (1) what constitutes beauty (the "essence" of beauty, the "nature" of beauty, what beauty "is") or (2) what properties all or most beautiful objects possess (e.g. "All objects possessing beauty *also* possess. . . ."). Read some theories of beauty and try to decide which of these two kinds of theory is being propounded:

     a. The theory of significant form (in Clive Bell, *Art*).

     b. The theory of synaesthesis (in Ogden, Richards, and Wood, *Foundations of Esthetics*).

     c. The expression theory (held by Croce, but most succinctly stated by E. F. Carritt in *What Is Beauty?* Chapter 6).

     d. Other views described by Harold Osborne in *Theory of Beauty*, Chapters 3 and 4.

2. In the sentence, "X is interesting," "interesting" is a relational word (see pages 504–505), unlike the word "round" in "X is round." What about the following?

     a. X is difficult

     b. X is gorgeous

     c. X is weird

     d. X is important

3. Mention some respects in which the analysis of the term "beautiful" is analogous to that of "good" in ethics. Can you think of any respects in which the two may not be analogous?

4. Can you think of any more plausible subjectivistic theories than those we have considered in this chapter (pages 505–510)?

5. "In this chapter, much emphasis has been placed on what we *mean* by our esthetic terms. Actually, however, this is comparatively unimportant. If, for instance, there exists a uniquely esthetic property as one theory of beauty holds (pages 510–512), then this is the proper subject for our investigation, *not* whether people *mean* or *intend* to assert the existence of any such property when they utter esthetic statements. If such a property exists and they do not mean to refer to it when they use the word 'beautiful,' so much the worse for them." Discuss this criticism.

6. How, on each of the theories of beauty discussed in this chapter, would you go about discovering whether a given object is beautiful?

7. How do you conceive the relationship among these three concepts: (a) esthetic experience, (b) beauty, (c) art?

8. Analyze the following statements in an attempt to pin down precisely what they mean. In doing so, make use of whatever points you can from Chapter 1.

     a. Art is imagination.

     b. Art is the expression of emotions.

     c. True art must make us better men.

     d. Art is a revelation of reality.

e. All arts aspire to the condition of music.

f. Architecture is frozen music.

g. Music has no meaning.

9. Examine the following questions and try to indicate precisely (1) what they mean and (2) how you would go about answering them.

a. Where does *the* work of art exist? In the mind of the artist? But then after the artist dies the work of art no longer exists; all along we thought we were reading *Hamlet*, but according to this view *Hamlet* does not exist. On paper or on canvas? But the poem isn't merely the set of ink-marks on paper (or sounds uttered by you when you read the poem). Then there would be as many *Hamlets* as there are written copies; moreover, if all copies of it were destroyed, then the work of art would no longer exist. But surely it could still exist in the minds of those who had read it! Perhaps, then, the work of art exists as a state of mind or consciousness in observers or listeners; but this will not do either: every reader interprets *Hamlet* somewhat differently, and are there as many *Hamlets* as there are readers? If there were no readers, would *Hamlet* cease to exist? What are they reading, if not something distinct from their own state of mind?

b. How important is the title in a painting or in a work of program music? Should you be able to appreciate Debussy's "Reflets dans l'eau" ("Reflections in the Water") just as much if you didn't know the title? (The title, after all, is no part of the music itself.) What of Titian's painting "Sacred and Profane Love," which turned out not to have been given this title by the painter at all, but by an obscure commentator, a century later?

c. By what should the performer be guided in his interpretation of a work of music? By the declared intention of the composer (supposing that he has given this to us)? by the interpretation that produces the strongest esthetic response in the audience, either at once or "in the long run," even though this may be contrary to the intention or desire of the composer?

Index